Leading Contemporary Economists

T0304254

This book describes the important contributions of several contemporary economic figures including recent Nobel Laureates. Describing their work and putting it into an historical perspective, these chapters explain how their work constitutes a major contribution to the discipline of economics and how it has broadened economic science.

Co-editor of the *Review of Political Economy*, Steven Pressman has gathered together for the first time key chapters from the journal, discussing major figures such as Amartya Sen, Joseph Stiglitz, John Kenneth Galbraith, Thomas Schelling, Edmund Phelps and Robert Mundell. This volume is significant to the extent that it combines the study of the work of Nobel Laureates with the perspective of heterodox economists, including a comprehensive bibliography for the work of each economist covered.

This book will be useful to both students and professional economists who are interested in contemporary, cutting edge economics and how the economics profession has changed over the last couple of decades.

Steven Pressman is Professor of Economics and Finance at Monmouth University. He is the author of *Fifty Major Economists* (second edition 2006) and co-editor of *Women in the Age of Economic Transformation* (1994) and *A New Guide to Post-Keynesian Economics* (2001) all published by Routledge.

Routledge studies in the history of economics

Leading Contemporary Economists

Economics at the cutting edge

Edited by Steven Pressman

Routledge
Taylor & Francis Group

LONDON AND NEW YORK

First published 2009
by Routledge
2 Park Square, Milton Park, Abingdon, Oxfordshire OX14 4RN

Simultaneously published in the USA and Canada
by Routledge
711 Third Avenue, New York, NY 10017
First issued in paperback 2014

Routledge is an imprint of the Taylor and Francis Group, an informa business

Transferred to Digital Printing 2009

Typeset in Times by Wearset Ltd, Boldon, Tyne and Wear

British Library Cataloguing in Publication Data
A catalogue record for this book is available from the British Library

Library of Congress Cataloging in Publication Data
A catalog record for this book has been requested

ISBN 978-0-415-77501-4 (hbk)
ISBN 978-0-415-76220-5 (pbk)
ISBN 978-0-203-89309-8 (ebk)

To Jane, with love

Contents

Contributors

Morris Altman is Professor of Economics at the University of Saskatchewan and Editor of the *Journal of Socio-Economics*. He served as President of the Society for Advancement of Behavioral Economics from 2003 to 2006, and will serve as President of the Association for Social Economics in 2009. His publications include over seventy refereed papers and three books on behavioral economics, experimental economics, economic history and empirical macroeconomics.

Heather Boushey is Senior Economist at the Center for Economic and Policy Research. She is also a research affiliate with the National Poverty Center at the Gerald R. Ford School of Public Policy and on the editorial board of *Working USA* and the *Journal of Poverty* and on the *Voice* professional women advisory committee. Her (co-authored) books include *The State of Working America 2002–3* (Cornell University Press, 2003) and *Hardships in America: The Real Story of Working Families* (Economic Policy Institute, 2001).

Robert W. Dimand is a Professor of Economics at Brock University, St. Catharines, Ontario, Canada. He is the author of *The Origins of the Keynesian Revolution* (Stanford University Press, 1988) and co-author of *A History of Game Theory: From the Beginnings to 1945* (Routledge, 2002) editor or co-editor of ten books (including *A Biographical Dictionary of Women Economists* (Edward Elgar, 2000), and has published more than sixty journal articles.

Stephen P. Dunn is a Commonwealth Fund Harkness Fellow in Health Care Policy and is Deputy Director of Provider Development for NHS East of England. He has published numerous articles on Post Keynesian economics, health policy and the economics of the firm. In 2000 he received the K. William Kapp prize from the European Association for Evolutionary Political Economy.

James E. Hartley is a Professor of Economics at Mount Holyoke College. His publications include *The Representative Agent in Macroeconomics* (Routledge, 1997) and *Real Business Cycles: A Reader*, edited with Kevin Hoover and Kevin Salyer (Routledge, 1998).

Carolyn J. Heinrich is Professor and Regina Loughlin Scholar at the La Follette School of Public Affairs and the Associate Director of Research and Training at the Institute for Research on Poverty. She is co-author of several books on the empirical study of governance and public management, including *Improving Governance: A New Logic for Empirical Research* (Georgetown University Press, 2000) and *Governance and Performance: New Perspectives* (Georgetown University Press, 2002).

M. C. Howard is Professor of Economics at the University of Waterloo, Canada. He is the co-author (with John King) of *The Political Economy of Marx* (Longman, 1975) and *The Rise of Neoliberalism in Advanced Capitalist Economies: A Materialist Analysis* (Palgrave/Macmillan, 2008). Currently he is writing a book on *Economic Theory and Violent Conflict.*

J. E. King is Professor of Economics at La Trobe University, Melbourne. His research interests are in the history of heterodox economic thought. He is the author of *History of Post Keynesian Economics since 1936* (Edward Elgar, 2002) *The Elgar Companion to Post Keynesian Economics* (Edward Elgar, 2003) and editor of *A Biographical Dictionary of Australian and New Zealand Economists* (Edward Elgar, 2007).

Peter Hans Matthews is Professor of Economics at Middlebury College in Middlebury, Vermont. He has published numerous articles on macro-economics, game theory, labour economics and inequality in such journals as the *Review of Radical Poitical Economics, Metroeconomica, Theory and Decision* and the *Economic Journal.*

Paulette I. Olson is Professor of Economics at Wright State University. Her articles appear in such journals as the *Journal of Economic Issues*, the *Review of Social Economy*, and the *International Review of Applied Economics*. Her book *Engendering Economics: Conversations with Women Economists in the United States* (Routledge, 2002) melds her work on race, class and gender issues, the sociology of the profession, and economic methodology.

Dimitri B. Papadimitriou is President of The Levy Economics Institute and the Jerome Levy Professor of Economics at Bard College. He is author or editor of ten books, including *Profits, Deficits and Instability* (Palgrave/Macmillan, 1992); *Stability in the Financial System* (Palgrave/Macmillan, 1996); *Modernizing Financial Systems* (Palgrave/Macmillan, 1999); and *Government Spending on the Elderly* (Palgrave/Macmillan, 2007).

Robert E. Prasch is Associate Professor of Economics at Middlebury College. He has formerly taught at Vassar College, the University of Maine and San Francisco State University. He is the author of over eighty articles, book chapters, and reviews, and is the co-editor of two books – *Race, Liberalism and Economics* (University of Michigan Press, 2004), and *Thorstein Veblen and the Revival of Free Market Capitalism* (Edward Elgar, 2007).

Steven Pressman is Professor of Economics and Finance at Monmouth University in West Long Branch, NJ. He also serves as co-editor of the *Review of Political Economy*, and as Associate Editor and Book Review Editor of the *Eastern Economic Journal*. He has published more than 100 articles in refereed journals and as book chapters, and has authored or edited twelve books, including *A New Guide to Post Keynesian Economics* (Routledge, 2001) and *50 Major Economists*, 2nd ed. (Routledge, 2006).

S. Abu Turab Rizvi is Professor of Economics and Interim Dean of the Honors College at the University of Vermont. His research concerns general equilibrium and game theory and their history, as well as the study of poverty, well-being and preference. He is the co-author (with David P. Levine) of *Poverty, Wealth, and Freedom: Political Economy and the Moral Order* (Cambridge University Press, 2005).

J. Barkley Rosser, Jr. is Professor of Economics and Kirby L. Kramer, Jr. Professor of Business Administration at James Madison University. He also serves as editor of the *Journal of Economic Behavior and Organization*. He is the author of more than 100 published papers, and several books including *From Catastrophe to Chaos: A General Theory of Economic Discontinuities*, 2nd ed. (Springer, 2000) and (with David Colander and Richard Holt), *The Changing Face of Economics: Conversations with Cutting Edge Economists* (University of Michigan Press, 2004).

Gale Summerfield is Director of the Women and Gender in Global Perspectives Program and Associate Professor of Human and Community Development at the University of Illinois at Urbana-Champaign. Her co-edited books include *Women in the Age of Economic Transformation* (Routledge, 1994), *Women's Rights to House and Land: China, Laos, Vietnam* (Lynne Rienner, 1999) and *Women and Gender Equity in Development Theory and Practice: Institutions, Resources, and Mobilization* (Duke University Press, 2006).

Jeffrey B. Wenger is Assistant Professor of Public Policy at the University of Georgia's School of Public and International Affairs, Department of Public Administration and Policy. His research on unemployment insurance, health insurance and pension coverage has been published in the *Journal of Policy Analysis and Management, Journal of Aging and Social Policy, American Journal of Economics and Sociology* and the *Journal of Pension Economics and Finance*.

L. Randall Wray is a Professor of Economics and Research Director of the Center for Full Employment and Price Stability at the University of Missouri-Kansas City as well as Senior Scholar at the Levy Economics Institute of Bard College. He is the author of *Understanding Modern Money: The Key to Full Employment and Price Stability* (Edward Elgar, 1998) and *Money and Credit in Capitalist Economies* (Edward Elgar, 1990), and the editor of *Credit and State Theories of Money* (Edward Elgar, 2004).

1 Leading contemporary economists

An introduction to their cutting-edge work

Steven Pressman

Like any discipline, economics is dynamic and constantly changing. Moreover, as Colander, Holt & Rosser (2004a, 2004b), Davis (2006) and Garnett (2006) all point out, since the 1990s, economics has been changing for the better. It has become broader in its outlook, more pluralistic, and increasingly more tolerant of new ideas and new approaches to studying how the market economy works. In brief, economics today is not the economics of the 1970s, the 1980s and the early 1990s.

There are many ways economics has changed over the past decade or so. Economic analysis is no longer primarily about finding an equilibrium point, and then proving deductively that it is the one and only possible equilibrium. Economists are willing to accept the possibility of multiple equilibria, with the actual equilibrium point determined in part by where we start and how the economy moves through time. Economists are also focusing much more on economic growth and its causes rather than the allocation of scarce resources at a given point in time. Alternative techniques, such as computer simulations, agent-based modeling and actual experiments are recognized as legitimate ways of understanding how people behave and how real world economies operate. Likewise, complexity theory and nonlinear dynamics have been added to the tool kit of economists; formal deductive proofs are no longer the end all and be all of economic analysis.

Perhaps more important than these changes in technique are the new sorts of assumptions that economists are making about how people actually behave. Economic analysis no longer has to suppose that all economic actors are rational and selfish. The profession has become open to the possibility of altruistic motivations, or to multiple motives and even multiple selves. They are studying bounded rationality, norm-based rationality, habitual rationality and evolutionary rationality. In addition, the profession is more open to the insights from evolutionary game theory and from psychological theories that explain human behavioral dispositions. These alternative views have helped to broaden and redefine the notion of rationality, which forms the starting point for most economic analysis.

All these changes have been most pronounced for what Colander, Holt & Rosser (2004a, 2004b) call "the cutting edge of the profession." These are individuals doing new and creative work who teach at the top colleges and universities, publish in the top journals, and are frequently cited by other economists at top schools. Also, they are recent winners, or are likely to be winners in the near future, of the John Bates Clark award. This prize is given biennially by the American Economic Association to honor an American economist under the age of forty who is thought have made the most significant contribution to economic knowledge. Cutting-edge work shows where the discipline is moving. However, it takes most of us run-of-the-mill economists a lot longer to catch on and catch up with what is going on. The large and significant changes described above began, to a large extent, in the 1990s. So this process of change in economics is likely to continue and accelerate over the next decade or two, leading to an even greater transformation of economic analysis. What you see here is only the beginning.

There are several likely reasons for these recent changes. Some are intellectual in nature. Many economists became down-right bored with what was done in the past. After years of equilibrium modeling, most of the old problems were solved and new ones had to be found. This required stepping outside the equilibrium framework that dominated economics for several decades. At the same time, some economists came to realize that the profession reached the limits of what could be learned about the economy by using traditional techniques, while several distinguished economists identified some flaws or anomalies in standard economic analysis. All this opened the door for non-equilibrium methodologies, such as performing experiments, agent-based modeling, and complexity theory. Many different groups also thought that economics reached the limits of what could be learned by assuming that all agents are rational. This provided an opportunity to perform computer simulations that model some agents as perfectly rational but others as behaving in other ways.

There are also social reasons for the changes that are shaking up how economics is done. In most cases, new approaches are pioneered by the young, or those who are looking for ways to make their mark and establish a name for themselves. As Thomas Kuhn (1970) and Irme Lakatos (1978) have documented, the elders who dominate professional discourse in every discipline are reluctant to give up their methods, techniques and assumptions. These are the ideas that gained them recognition and fame, and that they struggled so hard to get accepted many years ago. Change begins with the rise of "Young Turks," rebelling against their elders, opening up new ways of understanding the economy, and developing new ways to gain insight into how the economy works. But they inevitably meet resistance from their elders. Over time, however, this resistance necessarily declines as a result of the inevitable aging process. Invoking a bit of black humor, Colander, Holt & Rosser (2004, p. 488) describe this phenomenon as a paradigm change in economics that takes place "funeral by funeral".

We can find considerable evidence of these changes, and their growing acceptance, in a number of places. Economists Amartya Sen and Thomas Schelling have both won the Nobel Prize, the most prestigious award that can be given to an economist, despite some of their objections to utility theory and equilibrium theorizing. Daniel Kahneman, whose background and publications are mainly in psychology, and whose work concerns how people actually behave, also received the Nobel Prize in Economics. Major changes can also be seen in the pages of the top professional journals, which now publish far fewer logical proofs and more papers that employ alternative techniques of analysis. Finally, we have some evidence that economics is changing from surveys of economists that have periodically been taken. These surveys found that economists at the beginning of the twenty-first century were more positive about their profession than economists surveyed during the early 1980s. In general, at the turn of the century economists felt that economics was more relevant compared to the results from 15–20 years earlier (see Colander & Klamer, 1987), and they felt less strongly that graduate education in economics needed to become less technical and more relevant (Colander, 2003).

The fourteen essays that follow were originally published in the *Review of Political Economy* during the past decade or so, just as the economics profession was changing and opening up. Some of these papers have been revised; others are reprinted as they appeared in print originally. Each paper identifies the major contributions of a key figure (or figures) in the economics profession. As such, the set of essays provide a guide to much of contemporary economics and a map that shows some of the many ways in which economics has been changing. Perhaps more important, the individual chapters provide insight into the ideas of major contemporary economists at the turn of the twenty-first century. The figures covered are all prominent economists. Many of them have won the Nobel Prize in Economic Science. Others have been on the fringe of the profession, awaiting greater acceptance of their ideas.

The essays themselves are organized chronologically, based upon their publication date in the *Review*. Besides an alphabetical ordering, which generates some sticky problems of its own for papers discussing two economists, I saw no other way to possibly organize this diverse material. Like the broad opening of the profession, the ideas of these key figures are eclectic and in many ways their contributions are not related in obvious ways. One common theme is how they pushed the boundaries of economics in new directions. But the boundaries have been pushed in so many different directions and so many different ways, that a chronological ordering seemed about the best that could be done under the circumstances.

The economic analysis of David Gordon has focused on identifying the factors that affect business investment and economic growth. Gordon's model of the social structure of accumulation (Gordon, 1978, 1980) looks at how different institutions affect economic growth and development. Gordon recognized that capital accumulation requires a stable political and economic environment. This includes a stable macroeconomic environment, where employment levels are high and people have secure jobs so they are willing to spend the money they make. It also includes a stable international environment where goods and services can easily be sold abroad. Finally, it includes stable labor relations. This means the absence of strikes that disrupt production and also requires that workers have sufficient income so that they can purchase the goods that they produce. With the right institutional structures, rapid capital accumulation will take place. This, in turn, will lead to sharp productivity growth and a prolonged economic boom. Conversely, an institutional setting that is not conducive to capital accumulation will result in less new investment; instead, more money will go to buying up existing capital assets. When businesses are reluctant to invest, productivity growth will stagnate and the economy will experience a recession or depression. A good deal of the work of David Gordon sought to show how different historical eras can be viewed through the lens of this framework, and how these different eras experienced different economic growth rates throughout the developed world. Finally, Gordon (1989, 1994) sought to compare his model of the social structure of accumulation empirically to both neoclassical growth models and other macroeconomic growth models.

Like John Maynard Keynes, Hyman Minsky believed that capitalist economies were unstable. But while Keynes saw this instability stemming from multiplier and accelerator relationships, for Minsky instability arises from the nature of financial institutions and human decision-making. Investment decisions depend on both the expected profits from investing now and the cost of new investment. According to Minsky's (1975) financial theory of investment, the cost of new investment depends on the cost of producing new capital assets and the cost of borrowing money to purchase these assets. Rather than taking the rate of interest as constant or given, for Minsky it was a function of the financial position of firms. During periods of prosperity, the decision makers running business firms become more optimistic and their profit expectations improve. Since greater investment generates greater profits, this reinforces previous expectations and firms become even more optimistic, taking even riskier financial positions. We can see evidence of this in the stock market bubble of the late 1990s and the US housing bubble of the middle 2000s. But as firms take on more debt, lenders will demand higher interest rates to compensate them for their greater risks. This paves the way for financial problems and an eventual economic downturn. It can even lead to another large stock market crash and depression (Minsky, 1963).

For Minsky (1986), preventing this requires having the right institutional structures in place to deal with potential problems. First, a large government is necessary so that its stable spending will counterbalance the unstable spending by business firms. Second, this spending should be focused on protecting the incomes of the lower and middle classes. In particular, Minsky wanted the government to serve as an employer of the last resort, using New Deal programs like the Works Progress Administration (WPA) as a model for job creation. Finally, Minsky wanted central banks to regulate financial markets more closely so that financial bubbles were less likely to develop.

The work of Amartya Sen, who was awarded the Nobel Prize in 1998, has covered a large number of areas. He has criticized the neoclassical view of rationality, noting that people do not actually behave according to the axioms laid down in the traditional economic notion of rationality, which requires that choices be both consistent and self-interested. In particular, Sen argues that people do not maximize their own self-interest or utility. One good example of this is that people vote, sometimes even risking their life to do so; yet the probability of any one vote determining the outcome of an election is effectively zero (Sen, 2000, p. 41). Rather than maximizing their own utility, people are concerned with how other people think about them and adjust their behavior accordingly. To take one of his favorite examples (Sen, 2000, p. 130), although I may want an apple badly, I may not take it if it is the last apple in the fruit bowl. Sen has also introduced the notion of capabilities into economic analysis. For Sen, the purpose of economics is not just to increase utility for individuals. Rather, it is to give people the abilities that enable them to be well-functioning human beings in society. Capabilities represent a person's opportunities to do things in society and to have the freedom and ability to be a certain sort of person (Sen, 1993, 1999). This has broadened the notion of well-being that economics seek to maximize. No longer is the only goal of economics to maximize the consumption of goods and services. Now part of the function of the economist is to figure out how to help develop human potential, or the opportunities for people to achieve their life goals.

Robert Mundell, who won the Nobel Prize in 1999, has written mainly about exchange rates. The famous Mundell–Fleming model (Mundell, 1960, 1961; Fleming, 1962) shows the impact of capital flows on the macroeconomy. The model demonstrates what can happen as a result of stimulative fiscal and monetary policies under different exchange rate regimes. For example, with the free flow of capital, any crowding out due to the effects of stimulative fiscal policy on the bond market will be mitigated because new government bonds to finance the debt can be sold abroad. But Mundell's major contribution was probably his persistent and persuasive arguments about fixed versus flexible exchange rates. These two different exchange rate regimes have very different benefits and costs. The main benefit of fixed rates is that they facilitate international trade; their main weakness, and the main benefit of flexible exchange rates, is that domestic economic policy is not constrained by the need to keep exchange rates fixed. Mundell argued that the benefits for continental Europe from a system of fixed rates exceeded the costs because of the extensive trade among the various European countries. His arguments had an important real world impact – they were instrumental in the adoption of the Euro in continental Europe beginning in 1999.

James Heckman and Daniel McFadden won the Nobel Prize in 2000. They were given the award mainly for their work on improving statistical methods in economics. In particular they developed econometric methods to deal with problems of sample bias and discrete variables. In empirical work that seeks to test a theory it is essential that a sample population be selected at random. However, in the real world this is rarely possible. For example, to perform tests on the welfare population versus people not collecting welfare it is usually assumed that everyone who is eligible for government benefits collects them. But some people may decide not to apply for public assistance, and this will bias the results of any study about the impact of changes in welfare benefits on the standard of living of those who are eligible for benefits. Heckman (1979) developed the procedures for dealing with these sample biases. His solution is to estimate the factors associated with people who tend to shun public assistance when they are eligible for it. Once known, these variables can be used to estimate the missing or incorrectly characterized parts of the sample and eliminate the biases in regression analysis that fail to control for "selective withdrawal." This work gives researchers a better understanding of the impact of public policy and much of Heckman's later work has used his statistical technique to do just this. For example, he has evaluated how civil rights policies impacted the economic condition of blacks and concluded that good government policies can improve the relative earnings of blacks (Donohue & Heckman, 1991).

McFadden has focused more on discrete and mutually exclusive choices. Should I drive to work or take the train? Should I live in the city or the suburbs? Should I have a(nother) child or not? These are not typical marginal choices, but either/or decisions that cannot be solved through some maximization process by having 0.2931 more children or by picking a spot halfway between the cultural and intellectual center of the city, which has one set of attractions, and the quaint and picturesque suburban town where I would like to live also. McFadden solved this problem by developing logit models to deal with decrete decision-making choices. He then applied this model to issues like the decisions about where to live (McFadden, 1978) as well as decisions about whether to buy alternative-fuel vehicles (McFadden & Train, 2000).

Joseph Stiglitz won the Nobel Prize in 2001 along with George Akerlof and Michael Spence. All three worked on the topic of asymmetric information. Akerlof (1970) laid the foundation for the asymmetric information revolution with his lemon model for used cars. He noted that car sellers know more about cars than buyers and this leads potential buyers to assume that any car for sale must be a lemon. When buyers believe that used cars are lemons, they reduce their demand for used cars. This lowers the price of used cars, which in turn drives high-quality used cars out of the market. The end result is a sort of self-fulfilling prophesy because when buyers assume that only lemons are offered for sale, the result is that only lemons get offered for sale. The used car market effectively becomes a market for lemons.

Spence (1974) has been concerned mainly with the question of signaling, and his work extends the framework of the lemon model. Just as selling a used car can signal that it is a lemon, low prices can signal low-quality goods and high prices can signal high-quality goods. Likewise, having more education signals to possible employers that someone will likely be a high-quality employee (Spence, 1973). Stiglitz has taken this idea one step further and drawn out its macroeconomic implications. He has shown that this makes it hard to separate supply and demand factors in market. In labor markets this can lead to "efficiency wages," where firms pay more than the equilibrium or market-clearing wage in order to get and keep better employees. Consequently, wages fail to clear labor markets and these efficiency wages lead to Keynesian unemployment. The solution to this problem is not reducing wages, but to employ stimulative macroeconomic policies to increase demand and stimulate employment (Stiglitz, 1984, 1995). Akerlof and Stiglitz have been leaders of the new Keynesian school of macroeconomics (see Mankiw & Romer, 1991), which retains assumptions about individual rationality and uses rational expectations arguments to refute the position of new classical macroeconomists that traditional Keynesian macroeconomic policy will be ineffective due to the behavior of rational agents.

Daniel Kahneman and Vernon Smith won the Nobel Prize jointly in 2002. They were recognized for contributing to the development of experimental economics. Both authors have also been concerned with whether or not individual behavior is rational, and both have approached this problem empirically rather than by assuming that all individuals are rational. But this is about as far as the similarities go between these two Nobel Laureates. Kahneman has used experiments to demonstrate that individual behavior deviates significantly from economic rationality and subjective utility theory. For example, he has shown that people generally prefer a small unpleasant experience after a very unpleasant one, even though this increases the total disutility of the whole experience (Kahneman, Schreiber & Redelmeier, 1993). Kahneman also finds that humans systematically make errors when they make decisions, and that they use heuristics that reduce the complex tasks of gathering information and making decisions. The complexity of the world and the limited capacity of the human mind is what keeps people from behaving as predicted by standard economic theory (Kahneman & Tversky, 1982). This is why framing is at least as important in decision making as economic rationality. Moreover, as I have argued elsewhere (Pressman, 2006b), there are good evolutionary reasons why people act based on frames and heurists rather than based on the economic notion of rationality – they have great survival value and so these dispositions have been passed down over many centuries and become part of our genetic and psychological make-up as human beings.

Smith, in contrast, has done experiments with students and other subjects in order to test economic hypotheses about the market process. For example, he carried out auctions to see if competitive markets move to market-clearing prices. Smith (1962, 1991) found that prices do in fact converge quickly to market-clearing equilibrium prices and that these results are robust in the sense that they occur under many different experimental designs. He has also examined whether people learn from the information they receive in markets, and found this to be the case. These results generally support the neoclassical position on the importance of incentives for economic behavior and on the neoclassical assumption regarding rationality in decision making. These differences between Kahneman and Smith also have important differences when it comes to policy. For Kahneman, government intervention may be necessary to correct persistent errors in decision making. For Smith, however, these errors are minor and tend to be self-correcting because, through experience, people learn about markets and how they operate. As a result, government intervention is not called for and is likely going to be inappropriate and make it more difficult for the market to work well.

Paul Sweezy is one of the most distinguished Marxist economists of the twentieth century. Like Galbraith (see p. 9), his ideas are more in tune with the eclectic sort of economics that was done right after World War II. And like Galbraith, Sweezy became increasingly ignored with the rise of free market neoclassical economics in the late 1960s and early 1970s. His first major work (Sweezy, 1938) examined competition and monopoly in the British coal industry over a period of three centuries. The insights gained from this historical analysis were then developed into a more general theory of the tendencies toward monopoly in modern economies and its consequences. This work (Sweezy, 1942; Baran & Sweezy, 1966) stressed the tendency for firms to become large oligopolies and monopolies and the consequences of this process of monopolization. First, the existence of large firms casts doubt on the traditional economic model of competitive pricing by firms. Large monopolies have a good deal of discretion regarding their pricing. They can set their prices very high and seek more in current profits, or they can price a bit lower in order to keep potential rivals away and to keep people from becoming so upset with high prices that they demand government price controls. Second, as a result of the lack of competition, monopolies are responsible for higher profits and lower wages. Lower wages, in turn, tend to reduce consumption and generate slow economic growth. One response to this problem is for the firm to spend more money on advertising and salesmanship. But this only contributes to the growth of wasteful consumption. It also results in low savings rates and high consumer indebtedness, which cannot be sustained in the long run. A third consequence of the rise of monopoly power is that firms exercise undue influence over the state. This leads to reduced regulation of large firms, and in the extreme, to fascism and imperialism as a result of the need for greater military spending to support the profits of large firms.

Clive Granger and Robert Engle jointly received the Nobel Prize in 2003. They worked together on cointegration (Engle & Granger, 1987), or the attempt to identify long-run relationships among a large set of variables that change over time. Granger has worked mainly in statistics and econometrics. He his best know for his causality tests (Granger, 1969), which are frequently used by economists to determine which of two related variables is leading to changes in the other variable. For example, money demand for new investment and money supply always increase together. But it is important that we know whether a greater demand for loans determine the money supply, making money endogenous, or if the central bank controls the money supply and interest rates, which then affects investment demand and loan demand. Granger (& Newbold, 1974) is also known for his Monte Carlo simulations to determine if correlations are spurious or likely the result of a real economic relationship. Spurious or nonsense correlations are likely to arise in time series data where many variables follow a similar trend line. The correlation between two variables may thus be due just to the fact that everything is growing together over time. To take one famous historical example, Jevons noticed a close correlation between sunspot activity and economic growth (but, to be fair to Jevons, he did have a theoretical explanation for this relationship; see Pressman, 2006a). After his pioneering paper with Granger, Engle (*et al.*, 1987) has moved on to study the area of finance, including such things as option pricing and properly measuring the value of risk.

In many ways, John Kenneth Galbraith is part of an earlier era in economics. The majority of his many contributions occurred during the 1950s, when economics was broader and more eclectic, before the dominance of free-market neoclassical ideas from the 1970s and 1980s. This is one reason why Galbraith has been ignored of late. It is also one reason that in some sense he was also ahead of his time because he was advocating ideas different from the economic mainstream. Galbraith dissented from the mainstream economics of the 1970s and 1980s in several ways. First, he saw the economic world as being characterized by affluence rather than scarcity. One reason for the affluence, according to Galbraith (1967), was the rise of large oligopolies with substantial economic power. These firms were very different from the small competitive firms assumed in neoclassical analysis. Because they made profits and could invest in new technology, oligopolies contributed to the rising standard of living and general affluence in the world. However, a world dominated by large firms is not without great difficulties and problems. One set of problems arises because firms control consumer demand rather than responding to the demand of consumers. Large corporations also influence public opinion and generate social problems, such as environmental degradation and pockets of poverty amid affluence, that stem from power imbalances in society. The only solution to these problems, according to Galbraith, is for the state to intervene in the public interest. This involves controlling the prices set by large oligopolies (Galbraith, 1952) as well as protecting the environment and aiding those without economic power (Galbraith, 1973).

In many ways, the chapter on Kydland and Prescott is much more closely associated with the economics of the 1970s and 1980s than the changes that have been taking place since. When the Nobel Prize committee announced that Kydland and Prescott had won the 2004 Nobel Prize, they cited real business cycle theory as their major achievement. According to Kydland & Prescott (1982), fluctuations in the economy do not result from economic policy decisions (because of rational expectations on the part of all agents); rather, they arise because of real forces affecting the economy. It is things such as oil shocks, climate changes that affect harvests, technological change and important scientific discoveries that cause recessions and protracted periods of rapid economic growth. Kydland & Prescott (1977) also showed that rational expectations about future policy decisions can give rise to a time consistency problem unless the policy maker is forced to follow some rule. For example, if the central bank lowers interest rates causing the economy to expand during a time of recession, it will also contribute to rising inflation. As a result, rational people will come to expect that whenever there is high unemployment the central bank will cut interest rates and thus create inflation. This leads to higher inflationary expectations, higher interest rates, and slower growth in the future. The policy consequence of this position is that central banks should follow some policy rule regarding the money supply or interest rates rather than being given discretion on these matters and deciding when the economy needs to be expanded or slowed down.

Thomas Schelling won the Nobel Prize in 2005 along with Bruce Aumann. Both were cited for their work in game theory, especially for their application of game theory to issues regarding nuclear war; however, Schelling and Aumann took different approaches to understanding the interactions that are modeled in game theory. Aumann used mathematics to model human interactions in repeated games, while Schelling took a more informal approach. Schelling also made important contributions to how economists view the individual. Consistent with a great deal of work in contemporary psychology, and with philosophical work that sees the mind as a computer programmed to perform many different functions (see Putnam, 1964), Schelling (1984) has argued that individuals are comprised of multiple selves. At times these different selves are in accord; but at other times they are at war with each other. I want to go on a diet now, so I throw out all the fattening food in the house. But then later I regret that decision and run to the grocery store to buy ice cream and cake. Coordination problems among individuals and strategic conflicts among nations are similar to the problems faced by one individual, and Shelling next moved on to examine these problems using informal game theory. In studying coordination problems, Schelling (1960) argued that there are natural focal points that could be used as a means of coordinating without communication. People who are trying to meet up in New York City will tend to select Grand Central Station as the place to look for others even though there was no agreement to meet anywhere and no logical reason why Grand Central Station should be chosen over the thousands of other possible meeting places. Schelling (1966) also used game theory to study nuclear deterrence and strategies during the Cold War. His work, along with that of Aumann (& Maschler, 1995), employed game theory to study war strategies. This work was instrumental in keeping the US and USSR from destroying each other in the decades following World War II. While Schelling's work on war strategies was non-mathematical, Aumann used formal mathematics to study long-run cooperation through repeated games where the same people play the same game over and over again. The work of Aumann on repeated games shows that over time cooperation among adversaries is a possible long-run outcome in prisoner's dilemma situations as well as in other conflict situations (such as nuclear rivalries).

The chapter on Barbara Bergmann emphasizes her role as a leader of feminist economics. Her path-breaking book *The Economic Emergence of Women* (Bergmann, 1986) examined the dual role of women as homemakers and labor force participants. Throughout her long career, Bergmann has argued that occupational segregation and discrimination against women in employment continue to exist, and is the main reason that women receive lower pay than men. In contrast, most neoclassical economists believe that lower relative pay for women results from their lower relative productivity, and that much of their lower productivity stems from decisions that women make about education and rearing children rather than gaining work experience. Consequently, for most neoclassical economists this outcome is the result of individual preferences and so is not a problem that needs to be addressed through policy measures. However, if overt discrimination and conscious decisions to keep women out of high-paying jobs is the main reason for gender wage differentials, then policy actions are needed. To deal with such problems, Bergmann advocates affirmative action as well as pay equity and child care policies that would allow women to spend more time in the labor force. Bergmann has not focused exclusively on feminist issues. Long before agent-based modeling became part of cutting-edge economics in the late 1990s, Bergmann (& Bennett, 1986) promoted using micro-simulations in order to model how people actually behave rather than assuming that everyone always behaves rationally. She also showed how this might be done, and argued that such an approach would have many benefits.

Edmund (Ned) Phelps won the Nobel Prize in 2006. Along with Milton Friedman (1968), Phelps (1967) was responsible for developing the notion of a long-run vertical Phillips Curve and the related notion of an equilibrium long-run natural rate of unemployment. The policy implication of this was simple and straightforward – attempts to reduce unemployment below its natural rate; by employing activist fiscal and monetary policies, would be worse than doing nothing. Unemployment would always return on its own to the natural rate; this means that trying to stimulate demand, aggregate policies would only increase inflation and inflationary expectations. This would, in turn, make it harder to return to full employment. But unlike Friedman and others, Phelps (1994) did not think of the natural rate as a constant; rather, it was variable and could change due to various structural factors. Phelps even accepted the possibility that government policies might help reduce the natural rate of unemployment through things like improving access to high quality education. Since it is well-known that more educated workers and better educated workers are less likely to be unemployed and are likely to be unemployed for shorter periods of time, improvements in education should lower the natural rate. Phelps (1972) was also instrumental in introducing the notion of hysteresis into macroeconomics. The basis idea is that a bout of unemployment may lead to the deterioration of work skills that then makes it harder for the worker to get a job. Unemployment can thus be prolonged by a bout of unemployment and this can increase the natural rate of unemployment.

The chapters that follow provide more details about these fascinating individuals who have helped to broaden economic analysis. Each chapter contains information about their lives and more details regarding their cutting-edge contributions to economics. These chapters should provide the reader with a greater appreciation of the contributions made by its major contemporary figures. They should also help the reader better understand contemporary economics and how it has been changing of late.

References

Akerlof, G. (1970) The market for lemons: quality uncertainty and the market mechanism, *Quarterly Journal of Economics*, 84, pp. 488–500.

Aumann, R. & Mascher, M. (1995) *Repeated Games with Incomplete Information* (Cambridge, MA: MIT Press).

Baran, P. & Sweezy, P. (1966) *Monopoly Capital* (New York: Monthly Review Press).

Bergmann, B. (1986) *The Economic Emergence of Women* (New York: Basic Books).

Bergmann, B. & Bennett, J. (1986) *A Microsimulated Transactions Model of the United States Economy* (Baltimore: Johns Hopkins University Press).

Colander, D. (2003) The aging of an economist, *Journal of the History of Economic Thought*, 25, pp. 157–176.

Colander, D. & Klamer, A. (1987) The making of an economist, *Journal of Economic Perspectives*, 1, pp. 95–111.

Colander, D., Holt, R. & Rosser, J.B. (2004a) *The Changing Face of Economics: Conversations with Cutting Edge Economists* (Ann Arbor: University of Michigan Press).

Colander, D., Holt, R. & Rosser, J.B. (2004b) The changing face of mainstream economics, *Review of Political Economy* 16, pp. 485–499.

Davis, J. (2006) The turn in economics: neoclassical dominance to mainstream pluralism?, *Journal of Institutional Economics*, 2, pp. 1–20.

Donohue, J. & Heckman, J. (1991) Continuous versus episodic change: the impact of civil rights policy on the economic status of blacks, *Journal of Economic Literature*, 29, pp. 1603–1643.

Engle, R. & Granger, C. (1987) Cointegration and error correction: representation, estimation and testing, *Econometrica*, 55, pp. 251–276.

Engle, R., Lilien, D. & Robins, R. (1987) Estimating time varying risk premia in the term structure: the ARCH-M model, *Econometrica*, 55, pp. 391–407.

Fleming, J. (1962) Domestic financial policies under fixed and floating exchange rates, *International Monetary Fund Staff Papers*, 9, 369–379.

Friedman, M. (1968) The role of monetary policy, *American Economic Review*, 58, pp. 1–17.

Galbraith, J.K. (1952) *A Theory of Price Control* (Cambridge, MA: Harvard University Press).

Galbraith, J.K. (1967) *The New Industrial State* (Boston: Houghton Mifflin).

Galbraith, J.K. (1973) *Economics and the Public Purpose* (New York: New American Library).

Garnett, R. (2006) Paradigms and pluralism in heterodox economics, *Review of Political Economy*, 18, pp. 521–546.

Gordon, D. (1978) Up and down the long roller coaster, in: Union for Radical Political Economy (Ed.) *U.S. Capitalism in Crisis* (New York: Union for Radical Political Economy), pp. 22–34.

Gordon, D. (1980) Stages of accumulation and long economic cycles: in: T. Hopkins & I. Wallerstein (Eds) *Processes of the World System* (London: Sage Publications), pp. 9–45.

Gordon, D. (1989) What makes epochs? a comparative analysis of technological and social explanations of long economic swings: in, M. DiMatteo, R.M. Goodwin & A.

Vercelli (Eds) *Lecture Notes in Economics and Mathematical Systems* (New York: Springer-Verlag), pp. 267–304.

Gordon, D. (1994) Putting heterodox macro to the test: comparing post-Keynesian, marxian, and social structuralist macroeconometric models of the post-war US economy, in: M.A. Glick (Ed.) *Competition, Technology and Money: Classical and Post Keynesian Perspectives* (Hants: Edward Elgar), pp. 143–185.

Granger, C. (1969) Investigating causal relations by econometric and cross-spectral methods, *Econometrica*, 37, pp. 424–438.

Granger, C. & Newbold, P. (1974) Spurious regressions in econometrics, *Journal of Econometrics*, 2, pp. 111–120.

Heckman, J. (1979) Sample selection bias as a specification error, *Econometrica*, 47, pp. 153–162.

Kahneman, D., Schreiber, C. & Redelmeier, D. (1993) When more pain is preferred to less, *Psychological Science*, 4, pp. 401–405.

Kahneman, D. & Tversky, A. (1982) Judgments of and by Representativeness, in: D. Kahneman, P. Slovic & A. Tversky (Eds) *Judgment under Uncertainty: Heuristics and Biases* (New York: Cambridge University Press), pp. 84–98.

Kuhn, T. (1970) *The Structure of Scientific Revolutions*, 2nd ed. (Chicago: University of Chicago Press).

Kydland, F. & Prescott, E. (1977) Rules rather than discretion: the inconsistency of optimal plans, *Journal of Political Economy*, 83, pp. 473–493.

Kydland, F. & Prescott, E. (1982) Time to build and aggregate fluctuations, *Econometrica*, 50, pp. 1345–1369.

Lakatos, I. (1978) *The Methodology of Scientific Research Programmes: Philosophical Papers*, Vol. 1 (Cambridge: Cambridge University Press).

Mankiw, G. & Romer, D. (Eds) *New Keynesian Economics*, 2 vols (Cambridge, MA: MIT Press).

McFadden, D. (1978) Modeling the choice of residential location, in: A. Karlquist *et al.* (Eds) *Spatial Interaction Theory and Planning Models* (Amsterdam: North Holland), pp. 75–96.

McFadden, D. & Train, K. (2000) Mixed multinomial logit models, *Journal of Applied Econometrics*, 15, pp. 447–470.

Minsky, H. (1963) Can "It" happen again?, in: D. Carson (Ed.) *Banking and Monetary Studies* (Homewood, IL: Irwin), pp. 101–111.

Minsky, H. (1975) *John Maynard Keynes* (New York: Columbia University Press).

Minsky, H. (1986) *Stabilizing an Unstable Economy* (New Haven, CT: Yale University Press).

Mundell, R. (1960) The monetary dynamics of international adjustment under fixed and flexible exchange rates, *Quarterly Journal of Economics*, 74, pp. 227–257.

Mundell, R. (1961) A theory of optimum currency areas, *American Economic Review*, 51, 657–665.

Phelps, E. (1967) Phillips Curves, expectations of inflation and optimal unemployment over time, *Econometrica*, 34, pp. 254–281.

Phelps, E. (1972) *Inflation Policy and Unemployment Theory: The Cost-Benefit Approach to Monetary Planning* (New York: W.W. Norton).

Phelps, E. (1994) *Structural Slumps: The Modern Equilibrium Theory of Unemployment, Interest, and Assets* (Cambridge, MA: Harvard University Press).

Pressman, S. (2006a) *Fifty Major Economists*, 2nd ed. (New York & London: Routledge).

Pressman, S. (2006b) Kahneman, Tversky and Institutional Economics, *Journal of Economic Issues*, 40, pp. 501–506.

Putnam, H. (1964) Minds and Machines, in: A. Anderson (Ed.) *Minds and Machines* (Englewood Cliffs, NJ: Prentice-Hall), pp. 72–97.

Schelling, T. (1960) *The Strategy of Conflict* (Cambridge, MA: Harvard University Press).

Schelling, T. (1966) *Arms and Influence* (New Haven: Yale University Press).

Schelling, T. (1984) Self-command in practice, in policy, and in a theory of rational choice, *American Economic Review*, 72, pp. 1–11.

Sen, A. (1993) Capability and well being, in: M. Nussbaum & A. Sen (Eds) *The Quality of Life* (Oxford: Oxford University Press), pp. 30–53.

Sen, A. (1999) *Development as Freedom* (New York: Alfred Knopf).

Sen, A. (2002) *Rationality and Freedom* (Cambridge, MA & London: Harvard University Press).

Smith, V. (1962) An experimental study of competitive market behavior, *Journal of Political Economy*, 70, pp. 111–137.

Smith, V. (1991) Rational choice: the contrast between economics and psychology, *Journal of Political Economy*, 99, pp. 877–897.

Spence, A.M. (1973) Job market signaling, *Quarterly Journal of Economics*, 87, pp. 355–374.

Spence, A.M. (1974) *Market Signaling: Informal Transfer in Hiring and Related Processes* (Cambridge, MA: Harvard University Press).

Stiglitz, J. (1984) Unemployment as a worker-discipline device, *American Economic Review*, 85, pp. 433–444.

Stiglitz, J. (1995) Labor market adjustments and the persistence of unemployment, *American Economic Review*, 85, pp. 219–225.

Sweezy, P. (1938) *Monopoly and Competition in the English Coal Trade, 1550–1850* (Cambridge, MA: Harvard University Press).

Sweezy, P. (1942) *The Theory of Capitalist Development* (Oxford: Oxford University Press).

2 The economic contributions of David M. Gordon

Heather Boushey and Steven Pressman

'The Economic Contributions of David M. Gordon' by Heather Boushey and Steven Pressman from *Review of Political Economy* (1997), Volume 9, Issue 2 (Taylor and Francis Ltd, http://www.informaworld.com), reprinted by permission of the publisher.

1 Introduction

It is rather surprising that throughout the long history of economics there have been so few prominent families of economists. During the early and middle years of the nineteenth century there were, of course, the Mills—first James and then John Stuart. They were shortly followed by John Neville and John Maynard Keynes. In the twentieth century, the most noted family of economists has been the Gordons.

Like the Mills and the Keyneses, the Gordon family spans only two genera-tions. But in contrast to the two Mills and the two Keyneses, the Gordons number four prominent economists. David's father, Robert Aaron Gordon, was a noted macroeconomist who studied US business cycles after World War II (R. A. Gordon, 1952) and who became President of the American Economic Association in 1975. He also edited a volume dealing with manpower policies as a cure for poverty (R. A. Gordon, 1967). David's mother, Margaret S. Gordon, made contributions to welfare and employment policy. Her edited volume *Poverty in America* (M. S. Gordon, 1965), published shortly after President Johnson declared a 'War on Poverty', contains interdisciplinary contributions concerning the causes of poverty and the possible policy solutions to deal with this persistent problem. David's older brother, Robert J. Gordon, is a leading New Keynesian macroeconomist who has studied price adjustment in macro-economic models (R. J. Gordon, 1981).

Based upon the interests of his parents, a reasonable conclusion to draw is that David grew up in a liberal household where the problems of unemploy-ment and poverty were a prominent topic of conversation, and where policy solutions to these problems were frequently presented and discussed. This must have made some impression on David and, one would guess, must have had some influence on his life and career decisions. Yet, surprisingly, David failed to acknowledge this influence when given the chance. To the contrary, he (Gordon, 1992a, p. 210) claims that he tried to 'avoid economics' at college.

It is thus likely that David was more influenced by the times he lived in than by his family background. Undoubtedly he was a child of the sixties. His interests were always politics and policy; and he was probably drawn to economics because of its political and policy side. He was committed to the cause of labor as an activist. At one point in class he mourned the fact that, given his career path, he was never able to be a unionist.

After receiving his bachelor's degree, magna cum laude, from Harvard University in 1965 David helped to found *The Southern Courier*. During the next three years he worked as both a reporter and fund raiser for this civil rights newspaper, which was published weekly in Alabama and Mississippi. This commitment to civil rights extended to his later years (from 1994 until his death), when he worked with the South Africa partnership.

In 1968 David returned to Harvard to pursue graduate study in Economics. He notes (Gordon, 1992a, p. 210) that the reason for his return to graduate school, was 'the problem of the draft and the Vietnam war', and that he chose to study Economics 'despite myself'. However, his experiences with the *Southern Courier,* combined with a long exposure to questions of poverty and race, probably made graduate study in economics a logical choice. Likewise, his experience as an activist probably made David realize the possibilities and the attractiveness of political economy.

In addition, as he began to assume his role as an economist, David took a decidedly different path than either his parents or his older brother—working in the heterodox tradition rather than in the mainstream. Helping to found the Union for Radical Political Economics (URPE) in the early 1970s as an organisation of leftist economists was also indicative of a leftist orientation as well as an activist approach to economics.

While working on his doctorate, David taught at Yale University during the 1969–70 academic year. Then he served for two years at the National Bureau of Economic Research. David completed his dissertation in 1971, a work entitled 'Class, productivity, and the ghetto: a study of labor market stratification'. Soon thereafter he married Diana R. Gordon, and in 1973 he began teaching at the New School for Social Research. At the New School he taught Economic History, Econometrics, Labor Economics, Political Economy, and Macroeconomics. In 1977 he was tenured and promoted to Associate Professor, in 1983 he was promoted to the rank of Professor. Then, in 1994, he became the Dorothy H. Hirshon Professor of Economics at the New School.

Besides the teaching, there was the endless dissertation advising. David, by far, carried the heaviest supervision burden among the New School faculty. One of the institutions at the New School were the long lines of graduate students waiting outside David's office. Students began to line up several hours before David arrived for office hours. And the lines at times could stretch across the entire length of the Economics Department, running considerably more than a dozen students. Here was someone who obviously attracted graduate students and was well worth waiting for.

There were many good reasons why graduate students queued up for hours just to get a few minutes with David—he cared about his students, and he got his students through the arduous task of doing a doctoral dissertation in a relatively short time period.

After the dissertation directing came other efforts for his students. Letters of reference from David were three, four or five pages (single spaced); and they demonstrated both a detailed knowledge of the individual student he was writing about and a great understanding of their work. Then came the telephone calls, reinforcing the points made in his letter, and again making the case for giving his student a job interview. There is no one who worked as hard as David to help his students get jobs.

David even supported his students after they finished their degrees and received academic teaching positions. His books and articles are filled with references to the work of his former students. Even when he did not completely agree with the results or the approach employed by one of his students, David would take their results seriously, reference their studies, and help to publicise them.

Economists, however, make their mark professionally not by helping and supporting students, but through writing and advancing economic knowledge. In this regard, David made a large mark. His scholarly contributions are notable for their magnitude as well as for their breadth. These contributions are the subject of the next section.

2 The work of David M. Gordon

Theory, it is frequently said, is when you know how something works but it doesn't. Practice, in contrast, is when things work, but you have no idea why they work and even suspect that things shouldn't work. This distinction between theory and practice has long haunted academics. Economists, in particular, have had a great deal of difficulty with it. On the one hand, they increasingly develop theoretical models that shed no light on real world economic practices or problems. On the other hand, they run regressions with no theoretical foundations. David Gordon was the rare individual who managed to bridge these sharp differences. He worked in both the theoretical world and the empirical world, and constantly tried to connect the two.

David was also able to transcend other important differences that tend to separate economists into opposing camps. He wrote for both orthodox and heterodox economists. He published in leftist journals like *Science and Society* (Bowles *et al.,* 1985), the *Monthly Review* (Gordon, 1972a, 1976a) and the *Review of Radical Political Economics* (Bowles *et al.,* 1986; Gordon, 1971), as well as in mainstream 'diamond' journals like the *American Economic Review* (Bowles *et al.,* 1983c; Gordon, 1972c, 1981b, 1988e, 1990, 1994a) and *Brookings Papers on Economic Activity* (Weisskopf *et al.,* 1983b).

Furthermore, David was not just an ivory tower intellectual. Besides writing for professional journals, he also tried to reach real people. With Bowles and Weisskopf (1983a, 1991) he wrote two books for the educated public. These works sought to explain the economic problems facing the United States economy and to develop a democratic policy alternative. Likewise, *Fat and Mean* (Gordon, 1996a), published shortly after David's death, was written to influence public opinion and public policy. It argues that bloated corporate bureaucracies and corporate ruthlessness are responsible for many problems facing the US economy at the end of the twentieth century; and it calls for a populist and democratic solution to these problems.

Seeking to explain his views to an even larger audience, David frequently appeared on radio talk shows, and his economic ideas appeared in newspapers as op-ed articles and through quotations. He wrote a regular column for the *Los Angeles Times,* and was a frequent guest on the MacNeill–Lehrer Newshour. He also contributed frequently to mainstream and radical popular presses including *The Nation* (Bowles *et al.,* 1983b, 1988a, 1992; Gordon, 1985, 1993b, 1996b), *The Atlantic* (Gordon, 1986, 1994d), the *New York Times* (Gordon, 1975c), and *Dollars and Sense* (Gordon, 1993c). From 1986 to 1989, he edited the *Progressive Agenda,* a newsletter which reported on the results of polls taken by various factions of the progressive movement. David hoped that by revealing the commonalities among these factions, progressives would be able to build a strong coalition that could better respond to the rise of the Right. In addition, David acted as an adviser to the 1988 Jesse Jackson Presidential campaign, drafting many of his economic and budget proposals.

David Gordon may not have been a man for all seasons, but he is certainly the closest the economics profession has come in this regard since John Maynard Keynes. From this breadth of vision, interest and approach, three things stand out as David's main contributions to political economy—the social structure of accumulation model, his prodigious work in labor economics, and his testing of various macroeconomic models. These contributions are summarised in the three sub-sections below.

2.1 Social structure of accumulation

Probably David's most important contribution to political economy was his development of the social structure of accumulation model. The model stems from a reconsideration and reconstruction of Marxist thought in general. This, in turn, stems from broad and serious readings outside economic theory. Throughout his life, David attempted to transcend disciplinary boundaries. At Harvard he majored in social science; and he always did a great deal of cross-disciplinary reading and writing. The social structure of accumulation model demonstrates this breadth. The model is also an outgrowth of his work in economic history on the transition from feudalism to capitalism. That body of work is not so much about transition as it is about the history of thought in the materialist tradition. David fell on the side of multiple determinations, and believed that the concrete was important to understanding and analysing capitalism in general.

The term 'social structure of accumulation' was coined by David Gordon in 1978 (see Gordon, 1978b) and then formalised by him (Gordon, 1980). The best, simple definition of this notion is 'the constellation of institutions which condition growth and accumulation in a given capitalist economy' (Gordon, 1994b). The basic idea behind this notion is that when the institutional setting is right, and is favourable to capital in general, there will be many opportunities to find profitable activities. Hence, rapid capital accumulation will take place; businesses will invest, productivity will rise, and the economy will prosper. Lacking this supportive institutional environment, capitalists will not expect a reasonable rate of return, and will be reluctant to invest. Instead of building new businesses and expanding old businesses, their money will go into financial assets. In this case, productivity growth and economic growth will stagnate.

The social structure of accumulation is based on the notion that accumulation does not occur in a vacuum; capitalists will only invest if environmental or institutional factors are conducive to accumulation. If this hypothesis is true, it is not possible to develop purely formal models of capitalist growth and instability because the political–economic environment must also be an important component of macrodynamics. The capitalist begins by investing funds for production, then organises the labor process and sells the product of labor, reconverting property back into money capital. These activities will not take place unless the capitalist thinks he can make money in the process. The social structure of accumulation consists of all institutions that impinge, both directly and indirectly, on the process of making profits. Among the most important institutions are those ensuring the availability of money and credit, those relating to state involvement in the economic process, and the nature of the class struggle.

The social structure of accumulation has both an inner and outer boundary. The inner boundary separates the institutional environment for capital accumulation from the process of accumulation itself. 'Capital accumulation is the microeconomic activity of profit-making and reinvestment' carried out by capitalists (Gordon *et al.*, 1994, p. 15); this is distinct from the institutional environment in which accumulation takes place. The outer boundary separates the institutional constraints on production and profitability from other social systems in society. The social system, and especially the political system, does set the ground rules according to which firms can produce, sell, and therefore make profits. But other aspects of the social system, for example family relationships and sports activities, lie outside the main social factors that impinge on profitability.[1] 'The social structure of accumulation, in short, is external to the decisions of individual capitalists, but it is internal to the macrodynamics of capitalist economies' (Gordon *et al.*, 1982, p. 26).

For any social structure of accumulation, profitability is closely tied to the power of the capitalist class relative to other classes. Three power relationships are especially important and directly affect the profit rate—the relationship that capitalists have with labor and their power over the labor process, the relationship capitalists have with the state, and the relationship between domestic capitalists on the one hand and foreign nations and capitalists on the other hand. Capitalists are thus engaged in a three-front war over the accumulation of capital.

The right institutions for accumulation and growth include a labor force that businesses can control, a stable macroeconomic environment, and a stable international environment. All of these require the support of the state. The state must help ensure access to wage-labor, final demand for goods, and access to foreign markets and foreign sources of raw materials. The state must also contribute to cultural and ideological perceptions that reinforce capitalism (Gordon *et al.*, 1982). For example, the postwar US economic boom grew out of numerous institutions that were developed by the state. The Wagner Act, the Taft–Hartley Act, the rise of Social Security for the elderly, and the Employment Act of 1946 all led to tranquil labor relations; at the same time they ensured that workers would have sufficient income to buy the goods produced by American business. Also, the Bretton Woods agreement fixed exchange rates among developed countries and helped to facilitate foreign trade. This, too, improved profit opportunities for American businesses. Finally, the state mitigated class conflict through wage–price guidelines and a hegemonic military posture that assured American businesses of cheap sources of raw material and stable overseas production facilities. With these supportive environmental factors, there were plentiful opportunities to make money in the postwar years. As a result, real investment rose and the economy boomed.

On the other hand, when the institutional setting is wrong, profitable opportunities will disappear for capitalists. In this case, investment and productivity will slacken, and problems like inflation, trade and budget deficits, and lower living standards will arise. For example, in the 1970s greater international competition, greater worker militancy, higher corporate taxes and more regulation of business activities all worsened the prospects for making profits. The previous social structure of accumulation could not be maintained. This, in turn, led to reduced investment and slower growth, and explains the demise of the US economy in the late twentieth century.

Clearly then, the social structure of accumulation approach can be used to explain the booms of capitalist economic development, as well as the inevitable contractions. Gordon *et al.* (1982, 1994) argue that changes in the social structure of accumulation can explain the major long-term (35 to 60 year) swings in the US economy from the late nineteenth century to the end of the twentieth century. They note five tendencies that dominate the trajectory of capitalist development:

> (1) Capitalist accumulation attempts to expand the boundaries of the capitalist system. (2) Capitalist accumulation persistently increases the size of large corporations and concentrates the control and ownership of capital in proportionately fewer hands. (3) The accumulation of capital spreads wage labor as the prevalent system of production, draws an increasing proportion

of the population into wage-labor status, and replenishes the reserve army of labor....(4) Capitalist accumulation continually changes the labor process through employers' introduction of improved technologies and new machines and through the imposition of increasingly intensive labor-management systems upon workers. (5) In order to defend themselves against the effects of capitalist accumulation, workers have responded with their own activities.

(Gordon *et al.,* 1994, p. 11f)

These five tendencies account for much of the concrete history of capitalist society. As processes (1) through (4) become predominant, businesses face a more favourable social structure of accumulation, with growing profit opportunities. Investment increases and the economy experiences a burst of economic activity. The persistence of existing institutions helps keep the upswing going for many years. But these structures or institutions contain fundamental contradictions, which become the seeds for destroying the good economic times. As capitalists gain more and more power, the economic condition of workers deteriorates, and at some point workers will resort to collective action to improve their situation. They will organise themselves and join unions, existing unions will become more militant, and they will rely more on the political process to pass laws to aid and protect them. When these defensive actions become more predominant, businesses face a less favourable social structure of accumulation. Profit opportunities now disappear, investment falls, and we enter the down phase of the long wave cycle.

Expansion is likely to occur within any social structure of accumulation as long as it is profitable. Economic crisis is defined as a period of instability that requires institutional reconstruction for renewed stability and growth. The resolution of a crisis is shaped by the relative power of capitalists, and by the respective objectives of the capitalists, workers, and other economic groups. Individual capitalists cannot resolve a crisis alone; they need some type of collective action to revive a favourable environment for investment. Because all groups must participate in ending the crisis, the rise of a new social structure of accumulation is dependent on the previous downswing, and more specifically on the concrete historical conditions that the downswing bequeaths to major economic groups.

Within this model, the capitalist class can be seen as either too weak or too strong, which alternatively can be seen as a distinction between a crisis in the realisation of surplus value and a crisis in the production of surplus value. Either way, the results are the same—decreased profits lead to decreased investment, which stalls accumulation, decreases demand and reduces output. In both cases, a resolution of the crisis requires finding the proper balance of power in society.

Recent US economic history can be viewed profitably through the lens of the social structure of accumulation model. As Bowles *et al.* (1983a, 1991) show, the success of the postwar social structure of accumulation was based on four specific institutions. However, each of these structures began to break down in the late 1960s and the early 1970s. In turn, this breakdown has led to the current economic problems plaguing the US economy.

First, after World War II, the capital–labor accord (among other things) allowed businesses to produce without worrying about militant labor unions, continual strikes, and demands for large wage hikes. Corporations were given control over production decisions and unions were recognised as legitimate representatives of the worker. In return, unions helped to maintain an orderly workforce, while unionised workers received higher pay, improved working conditions, and greater job security. But the capital–labor accord also led to increased labor market segmentation, especially along the lines of gender and race, and increased supervision of workers and therefore greater management costs. 'By the late 1960s, nearly twenty cents of every dollar of revenue paid to the private business sector covered the salaries of managerial and supervisory personnel' (Bowles *et al.*, 1991, p. 57).

Secondly, Pax Americana, or US military pre-eminence during the post-War years, opened the world economy to US capital. The Bretton Woods agreement made the US the dominant force in the World Bank and International Monetary Fund. This, combined with Marshall Plan aid to Europe, gave the US considerable economic leverage over Europe and resulted in lower tariffs and trade barriers for US goods. With favourable terms of trade and little competition, US exports surged. And whenever someone threatened US economic domination, US military might came to the rescue and protected US capital. For example, the CIA overthrew Iran's Prime Minister after he nationalised the Anglo-Iranian Oil Company, and Guatemala's President after he expropriated land owned by the United Fruit Company. But, in the early 1970s, US hegemony was challenged by the Third World, and by OPEC in particular. This decreased the leverage of US firms abroad, and reduced the profitability of US firms. Likewise, as Europe and Japan recovered economically and began to compete with the US, the costs of maintaining US military might resulted in a tax burden on American businesses that vastly exceeded the tax burden on foreign businesses.

Thirdly, the capital–citizen accord guaranteed workers a decent wage and provided economic security for all individuals through unemployment insurance and other provisions of the welfare state, and through government policies to reduce macroeconomic instability and maintain low unemployment rates. By the mid-1960s, with real wages high and rising, groups of citizens began campaigning to increase the regulation of business (affirmative action, occupational safety, environmental laws, etc.). This was in sharp contrast to the 1950s and early 1960s, when capital had nearly a free reign on these issues. In response to these demands for economic security, and for healthy work and living environments, new laws and regulations were passed. These increased the costs of production and began cutting into business profits. In addition, greater income security and plentiful employment opportunities reduced the ability of business firms to control labor. If workers were able to receive generous benefits from the government while they explored other employment opportunities, and if the economy was without serious unemployment or underemployment problems, firms had little leverage over their employees. As a result, turnover rates increased and labor could not be forced to work harder when the costs of job loss were so very small. This, too, reduced corporate profitability.

Fourthly, the Depression and World War II hurt smaller businesses and helped those larger firms that were the main beneficiaries of military expenditures. This increased the monopolistic powers of US business and moderated inter-capitalist rivalry or business competition. In addition, the lack of foreign rivals enabled American businesses to maintain their monopolistic positions. However, after the mid-1960s, the economic development of those nations previously devastated by World War II led to increased global competition, and reduced the monopoly power of US firms.

As noted above, David Gordon was never satisfied just developing theories; testing the theory was equally important to him. Toward this end, he (Gordon, 1991a) conducted empirical tests of the social structure of accumulation model. One main goal in performing these tests was to determine whether the driving force of long-run change was exogenous or endogenous. He began by distinguishing various explanations of economic upturns and downturns, from the arguments of Kondratieff that investments are bunched, to Schumpeterian and neo-Schumpeterian theories of the introduction and diffusion of technological innovations. Gordon (1991a, p. 227) noted that most theories of long-run swings posited endogenous forces as causes, and that this was especially true of economic downturns. The social structure of accumulation approach differs from these other approaches by arguing that 'both the upturns and the downturns are exogenously conditioned' (Gordon, 1991a, p. 281); that is, they are determined by forces outside the economic system and within the inner boundary of the social structure of accumulation.

Next, of course, came the tests of the respective theories. By developing a long-period model of economic swings, David was able to compare the explanatory power of social and technological factors. His finding was that the social factors were three times more important than the technological factors in explaining the rate of capital accumulation and ten times more important than technological factors in explaining the rate of productivity growth (Gordon, 1991a, p. 302). These results provide some empirical support for the social structure of accumulation model over the alternative hypothesis that technological factors are the prime determinants of profitability, investment, and the success of a capitalist economy.[2]

2.2 *Labor economics*

While the issues of productivity and profitability were important parts of the social structure of the accumulation model, they formed the heart and soul of David's work on the labor process and labor markets. His work on segmented labor markets (Gordon et al., 1982) was an extension of the labor-relations aspect of the social structure of accumulation model. This work was always based on the premise that there were interconnections between what is traditionally thought of as macro and micro issues and thus, his work on labor economics was grounded in history and institutions as well as the process of production itself.

Gordon *et al.* (1982) argue that relations between labor and capital changed following the advances in industrial organisation and technology after World War II. Management systems were designed in order to assert greater control over the workforce and to allow greater flexibility in production. In both union and non-union shops, new rules were instituted placing a tighter control over production activity by deterring social interaction among workers. This system of bureaucratic control was augmented by new technological developments. Technological designs reflected the desire of management for greater institutional control, and new technologies increasingly determined the direction of work tasks and the pace of work.

After World War II, a new management–labor accord also developed. Unions acquiesced to a restructuring of grievance procedures and to new arrangements of wage bargaining. Wage increases were tied to productivity, reflecting a compromise with capital. The development of these schemes was further encouraged by the economic prosperity of the 1950s and the early 1960s. The economic gains to both corporations and their workers minimised the attention that unions paid to the long-term effects of these concessions.

David argued that this process was instrumental in the development of dual labor markets. Large corporations became the core firms of the economy, dominating key industrial sectors, capturing rapidly expanding markets, and initiating innovative technological change. Profitability for these firms depended partly on their size, and hence their ability to institute the new system of control over their workforce, and partly on greater industrial concentration. Smaller firms resembled the entrepreneurial firms of the late nineteenth century and remained on the periphery. Following this dynamic, primary and secondary labor markets developed reflecting the larger divisions among firms (Gordon *et al.*, 1982, p. 193). In addition, secondary labor markets developed in order to service core firm needs; many of the administrative control functions required in large corporations drew labor from secondary markets.

Besides explaining the rise of dual labor markets historically and analytically, David also sought to asses the dual labor market hypothesis. This was actually the first of many attempts by David to compare the empirical consequences of different types of economic models. It was also a direct outgrowth of his doctoral dissertation. *Theories of Poverty and Underemployment* (Gordon, 1972d) examined three different views of the labor market—orthodox neoclassical theory, the dual labor market theory, and the radical paradigm which traces its roots to Marx. It attempted to put the best foot forward for each theory, explaining clearly and precisely how each viewed the operation of labor markets. It also provided a sympathetic treatment of how each paradigm explained the problems of poverty and underemployment. To aid the reader further, and to begin the move to the empirical side, David contrasted the various paradigms on various important theoretical issues (such as methodology, labor market imperfections, and technology). He then drew out the empirical consequences stemming from these different perspectives. This enabled him to test the empirical consequences of each view. One important finding was the existence of labor market segmentation and stratification. This provides evidence against orthodox, neoclassical labor market theories, which assumed that labor markets were competitive in nature and that competition would eliminate any segmentation. In addition, evidence that women and minorities do not gain from additional education and experience to the same degree as white males, also supports the radical and institutionalist (dual labor market) view of how labor markets actually work, and casts doubt on the neoclassical view of competitive labor markets.

Although he has done considerable work on the dual labor market hypothesis, David's most important work in the labor area concerned productivity and profitability. This work, too, followed from the social structure of accumulation model.

One of the main problems facing the US economy since the late 1960s or early 1970s has been the stagnation of incomes. Average wages have remained essentially the same in real terms over the past 25 to 30 years. Two explanations for stagnating wages are possible. First, as productivity or output per worker expands, average wage rates and living standards will rise. When productivity growth slows or stops, real wage growth must also come to an end. Secondly, there is the question of the distribution of income. If wages rise on average, but all the increase goes to those of the top of the income pyramid, most people gain nothing.

Few problems are more important or perplexing than this one. And few problems in labor economics occupied David more than this one. His work (Bowles *et al.,* 1983a, 1991; Weisskopf *et al.,* 1983) attempted to explain why productivity growth in the United States came to an abrupt halt in the late 1960s or early 1970s. His work also attempted to explain why the distribution of income in the United States became more unequal over the past quarter century. This work has appealed to both theory and econometric practice. It has relied on historical facts and trends, as well as economic institutions to provide a context or story for the empirical work. It has also been directed to both the mainstream of the profession and to the educated lay public. This work on the productivity slowdown points to one factor as an explanation for both the productivity problems and the distribution problems—the social structure of accumulation.

The theoretical insight driving this work comes from Marx and the Marxian analysis of labor power. When employers hire workers they are buying labor power, or the potential of people to work productively. Employers, though, must extract actual work from this labor power if they are to make money and remain profitable. Gordon (1981b) postulated that three factors were likely to affect the intensity of work effort—the size of a reserve pool of production workers, divisions within the work force, and the effectiveness of bureaucratic control over workers. Testing this Marxian hypothesis he finds both the size of the reserve labor pool and the level of bureaucratic control were statistically significant determinants of productivity growth (at the 0.01 level). In contrast, the traditional neoclassical variables (labor quality and the capital–labor ratio) were statistically insignificant. Moreover, Gordon found that the Marxian productivity equation does a better job than the neoclassical model of forecasting out-of-sample productivity changes.

The crux of the argument is that productivity problems in the United States have stemmed from a collapse of the accord between capital and labor. In the 1960s, problems arose when unemployment sank below 4% in the United States, and labor gained ascendancy. Consequently, labor was able to frustrate most attempts on the part of businesses to increase work intensity and introduce new innovations; as a result, productivity stagnated. In the 1970s capital began to plot its strategy for reasserting power and influence. Unemployment was allowed to rise, and economic theories were developed in right-wing think tanks arguing that labor was too powerful, employment was too high, welfare benefits were too high, and tax cuts were needed for the wealthy. In the 1980s the conservative strategy was put into effect. President Reagan fired the air traffic control (PATCO) workers, cut taxes for the very wealthy and for businesses, and allowed unemployment to rise to its so-called 'natural level' (6% during the Reagan years). The Great Repression had begun.

But, as pointed out in *Beyond the Wasteland* (Bowles *et al.,* 1983a), this strategy has severe limitations as a means of increasing living standards. Not only does it hurt those at the bottom of the income distribution, but productivity also suffers when economic power moves so rapidly, and so far, in favour of corporate interests. For example, in an attempt to squeeze more output from workers, the monitoring and supervision of workers must rise. But this has negative effects on productivity because of the increased number of supervisors hired and because more cooperative work environments are generally more productive work environments.

The strategy of increasing unemployment also had the side effect of reducing effective demand, capacity utilisation, and investment. Even the huge tax breaks given to businesses and the wealthy could not counteract this. The result was a continued decline in productivity growth.

With labor defeated at the end of the 1980s, and with the growth strategy of the Great Repression in shambles, one might have expected a shift in the pendulum toward labor or the development of a new capital–labor accord. These are the sorts of policy predictions and proposals were made by many liberal thinkers. For example, President Clinton's former Labor Secretary, Robert Reich, predicted a shift towards labor in the 1980s (Reich, 1983) and then advocated a new capital–labor accord based on the idea of developing human capital in the early 1990s (Reich, 1991). But the more radical David Gordon recognised that these two outcomes were unlikely because they were not consistent with the interests of the capitalist class. Productivity, profitability and distribution problems would thus continue, and would even intensify. In the 1990s, these pressures were released somewhat in the form of white collar layoffs, euphemistically called corporate downsizing, restructuring and reengineering.

Fat and Mean (Gordon, 1996a) addresses the labor problems left over from the Great Repression of the 1980s. It was put to press the day before David went into the hospital. The book describes the waste and inefficiency built into corporate America's bloated management ranks, and suggests several ways to restore productivity and income growth. David believed this to be his best work. In many ways, it is the synthesis of his long-standing interests in labor economics, macroeconomics and economic policy.

Fat and Mean argues that bloated corporate bureaucracies and corporate mistreatment of their workers are the main causes of slow productivity growth and stagnating wages. In short, since the early 1970s, US corporations have become both fat and mean. Moreover, fat and mean go together; the wage squeeze and bloated bureaucracies are both part of a corporate strategy that has relied on 'the stick' rather than 'the carrot' to improve profitability.

To support his case, David provides several measures of increasing corporate bureaucracy. Between the late 1940s and the early 1980s, non-production and supervisory employees increased from 12% of employment in the non-farm private sector to 19%. In contrast, administrative employment remained steady for most other developed countries. Administrative employment was also less prevalent in these nations. Japan, for example, produces goods with very little corporate bureaucracy; only 4% of Japanese employment consists of administrative or managerial help (Gordon, 1996a, p. 43).

Corporate obesity can also be measured in terms of the income going to supervisors. In 1973, 40% of national income went to private non-farm production workers and 16% went to supervisory employees. By 1993, supervisory employees increased their share to 24% of total income. Their gain came primarily at the expense of production workers, whose share of national income fell to 34.5% (Gordon, 1996, p. 82).

Corporate meanness refers to worsening labor–management relations. Since the 1970s, corporations have fought unions, pushed workers harder, and increasingly resorted to hiring disposable (contingent and part-time) workers. Corporations have also lobbied politicians for assistance with this strategy. The government has responded with reductions in the real minimum wage, reduced support for unions, and lower benefits for various social programmes. All of this has given business the upper hand in their dealings with labor.

Gordon blames corporate meanness for many economic problems plaguing the US. Worse labor–management relations reduce worker motivation and productivity growth. Living standards fall, and more family members must work just to make ends meet. From this follows other economic and social problems. Comparing those countries with adversarial labor–management relations to countries with cooperative labor–management relations, Gordon (1996a, ch. 6) finds that the adversarial countries had higher inflation rates, less investment relative to national income, and lower capital–labor ratios. On the other hand, countries with more cooperative labor–management relations had higher productivity growth and lower unemployment rates.

Gordon contends that the only way to reverse the problems plaguing the US is to reverse course and develop more cooperative labor–management relations.

In essence, what is needed is a new social structure of accumulation, where the power of business is reduced relative to other economic and social groups, most notably labor. This will require five main policy changes to improve the bargaining position of workers. First, the minimum wage must be increased (David suggests it should go up to $6.50 an hour) and indexed to inflation. Secondly, legislation is needed making it easier for workers to gain representation in the workplace. Thirdly, work needs to be made flexible rather than disposable. People need the option of working part-time or part-year; but businesses should not be able to force people into these situations. Fourthly, Gordon proposes a national investment bank to subsidise firms that have cooperative and democratic organisational structures. Finally, a national training and assistance agency is needed to help workers and managers acquire the skills necessary for cooperative labor relations.

2.3 Macroeconomic modelling

Macroeconomics was always a major concern of David Gordon, and macroeconomics permeated much of his other work. The social structure of accumulation model was distinctly macroeconomic in its orientation. It looked at the performance of the US economy over long periods of time and attempted to explain long-run macroeconomic trends based upon both economic and socio-institutional variables. Likewise, David's approach to labor economics was macro rather than micro oriented. Problems of low wages, unemployment and poor productivity were not the result of individual shortcomings, or individual decisions to maximise some utility function, but were the result of how capital and labor responded to global political and economic forces.

Later in his career, David (Gordon, 1989, 1994e) focused on macroeconomic questions more explicitly, and undertook the daunting task of comparing and evaluating several macroeconomic models. Although at times, David would focus on two or three heterodox models, in general his goal was to examine the standard neoclassical macro model relative to several heterodox macroeconomic models. At times, he perversely referred to this project as 'David's Folly'. Like his other major empirical projects, the task began by carefully setting forth the key characteristics of each model. This task was accomplished with the aid and consultation of other people who were close to these paradigms, thus making sure that he got all the models correct.

His first project along these lines (Gordon, 1989), compared technological and social explanations of long swings. While both approaches sought to explain long-run economic waves based on non-economic forces, each theory identified different forces and different mechanisms leading from changes in outside factors to long waves. The technological approach, which follows Schumpeter and has also received support from post-Keynesian economists, identifies technological development and innovation as the source of economic dynamics. Technological innovation then improves productivity growth. With a constant mark-up over costs, real wages and demand both rise, leading to further investment and growth. The social explanation, which stems from the social structure of accumulation model, identifies institutional factors affecting corporate profitability as the main source of long waves. If a set of stable institutions exist that promise healthy conditions for profitability, substantial investment will take place and the economy will prosper. On the other hand, when these institutional factors deteriorate, productivity growth slows, businesses are reluctant to invest, and stagnation quickly sets in.[3]

Then came the testing. This required a careful measurement of technological innovation. David developed several such measures, based upon factors like expenditures on research and development, patents issued, the number of new books published on technology, and the number of scientists and engineers employed in research and development. He then used factor analysis to combine them into a single index. Likewise, he developed several measures of capital–labor relations and other institutional factors that would affect profitability. Here, too, a single index was derived via factor analysis.

Always, David was sensitive to put the best foot forward for each theory, and was sensitive to the fact that we cannot do controlled experiments in macroeconomics. This made testing difficult, but not impossible. What was needed was an openmindedness and some creativity. Unfortunately, few economists and few individuals possess these traits. David did, and his work reflects this. He was probably too optimistic that others possessed these traits as well. Were this so, contemporary economics would be neither so narrow nor so narrow-minded, and the work of David Gordon would have received much greater attention and respect.

Empirical results from testing these respective models (Gordon, 1989) found the social explanation more promising as an account of the productivity decline because changes in technological innovation seemed to follow changes in institutional factors (but not vice versa), and changes in institutional factors affecting profitability tracked changes in productivity growth better than changes in technological factors. Also, technological innovation did not do a good job of explaining changes in investment (Gordon, 1989, p. 294ff.), especially relative to the institutional explanation.

Gordon (1994e) compared three heterodox macro models—a Marxian model, a post-Keynesian model, and a structuralist model stemming from the social structure of accumulation approach and the French regulationist school (see Aglietta 1979; Lipietz, 1986). Although sharing a number of similarities, David identified three main differences among these approaches. First, Marxian and structuralist models assume that investment increases with higher rates of profit, whereas post-Keynesian models assume that investment is primarily demand driven and that the profit rate has little effect on investment. Secondly, post-Keynesian and Marxian models both assume that profitability increases continuously with capacity utilisation, whereas structuralist models view the relationship between capacity utilisation and profitability as an upside-down U, with high levels of utilisation and employment creating a profit squeeze. Finally, each model picks up on different exogenous variables as determinants of the rate of profit. For post-Keynesians, monopoly power is the key exogenous variable, and the key factor determining the division of income between capital and labor, and thus the rate of profit. For Marxians, the key exogenous variable is the degree of competition, with greater competition reducing the profit rate. For structuralists, the key exogenous variable is capitalist power. As capitalist power increases, work intensity rises, as does productivity and profitability. After specifying the macroeconomic equations for each respective model, David estimated these equations for the US economy from 1955 to 1988 using quarterly data.

David frequently remarked that he always encountered great resistance when presenting the results of his macro heterodox model comparisons. The essence of the problem is a glaring human weakness—no one likes to be wrong or be only second best, yet whenever one compares several models some must perform better than others. Nonetheless, the results from David's comparisons are not that surprising if one thinks things about the different theories being compared and also has a relatively open mind about the strengths and weaknesses of different economic theories.

The post-Keynesian model that Gordon developed was primarily a short-run model; hence it is not surprising that such a model should be better at predicting short-run fluctuations. It is also a model that was designed to explain unemployment. Hence it is not surprising that the model would do a good job predicting this economic outcome. Conversely, the Marxian and structuralist models were designed to explain longer term trends and the rate of profit rather than the rate of unemployment. Consequently, it was not surprising that these models performed better in this regard. Finally, since the structuralist model was most concerned with productivity, and had the most detailed explanation for the determinants of wages, hours and productivity, it is not surprising that this model did the best job of forecasting these variables.

Going beyond an examination of just heterodox macro models, Gordon (1988a) attempted to test the social structure of accumulation model against the conservative, neoclassical theory that high taxes and income security programs reduce work incentives and productivity. Studying these relationships in greater detail, David found that there is a great variation across countries. In some countries (the US and the UK), there is a trade-off between tax rates and income security on the one hand, and productivity growth on the other hand. But for other nations (Germany and Sweden) tax rates and productivity growth are positively related, as are income security and productivity growth. He concludes that 'the character of the institutional regime' (Gordon, 1988a, p. 499) in different countries is responsible for this finding. This result has clear and distinct policy implications. Countries like the US and UK need to restructure their institutional class relations in such a way that greater income security and progressive taxes have a positive effect on productivity (through its effect on effective demand) rather than a negative effect (through its impact on worker behaviour).

3 Concluding remarks

In the pages above we were able to discuss only some of the many contributions that David Gordon made to economics. Yet another remarkable aspect of David's career was the breadth of his interests and the many, diverse areas of economics that he has written about. He has defended the ideals and the practicality of socialism, in the face of the collapse of the Soviet Union, at a time when many heterodox economists were proclaiming the victory of capitalism over socialism (Gordon, 1993d). This defence remained sensitive to the failures of the Soviet model. But, on the other hand, it took cognisance of the virtues of democratic socialism—its emphasis on community, on social equity, on individual security, on self-realisation, and on economic rationality (defined as the 'maximum possible reduction of waste in the allocation and utilisation of... natural, capital, and human resources'). Such a democratic socialism provided hope that economics could be reorganised to better satisfy human needs and desires (Gordon, 1993d, p. 476).

Early in his career, David produced a left-of-centre analysis of crime in the United States. This work argues that crimes are 'perfectly *rational* responses to the structure of institutions upon which capitalist societies are based' (Gordon, 1971, p. 379). Because capitalism depends on competition and inequality, it inevitably tempts people to get ahead by breaking the law. The prosecution of crimes serves primarily to neutralise opposition to the system by the poor and powerless. This leads to two different standards of justice—one for the poor, and one for the wealthy and powerful. Thus, individuals are prosecuted for stealing the property of others, but manufacturers are not prosecuted for making unsafe cars that kill and maim people.

David Gordon (1987a, 1988e) has also produced both theoretical and empirical arguments against the natural rate hypothesis. And he (Gordon, 1994c) has produced empirical evidence showing that while investment tends to increase savings (for demand and distributional reasons), greater savings do not have much effect on investment (as most neoclassical economists hold). As with his other empirical work, these assessments all relied on a careful specification of the relevant models, and a careful econometric testing of their relevant arguments using Granger causality test and vector autoregression (VAR) models.

One of David's primary concerns, although merely touched upon in Section 2 above, was methodology. He began his career stressing the central importance of power relationships, conflicts and institutional transformations (Gordon, 1972d). This concern with methodology permeated all of his work—from econometrics and model building, to labor economics, and to his concern with materialist/Marxian methods. It was part of David's meticulousness, but it also contributed to his reasonableness—he kept trying to demonstrate that if one accepts a method which fits the facts, then the solutions to pressing economic problems will become clear. Later in his career, Gordon (1994h) addressed more directly the issues of economic methodology and the sociology of economics. This work attempted to explain the narrowness of economic policy advice in the late twentieth century. It blames large economic think tanks, formalist training in graduate school, the simplifications of economics textbooks, and a large national job market where knowledge of regional economic issues and institutions does not matter.

Despite the breadth and variety of his many contributions to economics, the main intellectual legacy of David Gordon remains his attempt to develop a radical alternative to mainstream economics. Here, his main substantive contributions are two-fold—his argument that social structures and institutional factors are responsible for long-term economic growth; and his explanation of how labor market segmentation, socio-economic factors, and corporate policies have led to a decline in productivity growth and in living standards in the US during the last three decades of the twentieth century. Both of these theoretical contributions have given rise to considerable debate, testing, and refinement; and they have been employed by many other scholars to analyse twentieth century capitalism.[4]

Another part of David Gordon's legacy, and perhaps the part that will prove most enduring, is the many institutions that he helped to build during his lifetime. We have already mentioned David's role in starting up the *Southern Courier* and URPE. In addition, he helped to found the Institute of Labor Education and Research, an educational outreach institute, which later became the Centre for Democratic Alternatives. At the time of his death, David was the founding Director of the Centre for Economic Policy Analysis at the New School for Social Research.

Notes

The authors wish to thank Phil O'Hara for his comments on an earlier draft of this paper. The usual disclaimer applies.

1 O'Hara (1995) points out that family relationships are important social institutions that stabilize the market and contribute to long-term economic growth. Therefore, O'Hara argues, family relationships should be part of the social structure of accumulation. Similarly, a case could be made that sports activities are an important part of the social structure of accumulation. First, sports provides a diversion from work-related problems. Secondly, professional sports has become one of the most conspicuous examples of the winner-take-all society (see Frank, 1995) and, as such, has probably had a significant impact on worker motivation and productivity. But these points take us outside the main scope of this paper.

2 For an argument that these two factors are not really distinct, but actually mutually reinforcing and equally important, see Tylecote (1992).

3 Again, see Tylecote (1992) for an argument that the technological and social explanations are complimentary and overlapping rather than contradictory and oppositional.

4 On the productivity question see Moseley (1986) and Naples (1981, 1986). For further work on the social structure of accumulation model see Kotz (1987, 1990), Kotz *et al.* (1994), Harrison (1987), McDonough (1990), Norton (1988), O'Hara (1995) and Tylecote (1992).

References and a bibliography of the works of David M. Gordon

Aglietta, M. (1979) *A Theory of Capitalist Regulation: the U.S. experience* (London, New Left Books).

Bowles, S., Gordon, D. M. & Weisskopf, T. E. (1983a) *Beyond the Wasteland: A Democratic Alternative to Economic Decline* (Garden City, Anchor Press/Doubleday).

Bowles, S., Gordon, D. M. & Weisskopf, T. E. (1983b) Industrial policy—and now the bad news, *The Nation*, 239, 4 June, pp. 703–706 (a reply to responses appears in *The Nation*, 239, 8 September 1984, pp. 171–174).

Bowles, S., Gordon, D. M. & Weisskopf, T. E. (1983c) Long swings and the non-reproductive cycle, *American Economic Review*, 73, May, pp. 152–157.

Bowles, S., Gordon, D. M. & Weisskopf, T. E. (1984a) Long-term growth and the cyclical restoration of profitability, in: R. M. Goodwin, M. Kruger and A. Vercelli (Eds) *Non-Linear Models of Fluctuating Growth* (Berlin, Springer-Verlag).

Bowles, S., Gordon, D. M. & Weisskopf, T. E. (1984b) A social model for U.S. productivity growth, *Challenge*, 26, March/April, pp. 41–48.

Bowles, S., Gordon, D. M. & Weisskopf, T. E. (1985) Two views of capitalist stagnation: under-consumption and challenges to capitalist control, *Science and Society*, Fall, 49, pp. 259–286.

Bowles, S., Gordon, D. M. & Weisskopf, T. E. (1986) Power and profits: the social structure of accumulation and the profitability of the postwar U.S. economy, *Review of Radical Political Economics*, 18, pp. 132–167.

Bowles, S., Gordon, D. M. & Weisskopf, T. E. (1988a) Democratic economics: austerity vs. jobs and justice, *The Nation*, 246, 16 April, pp. 535–537.

Bowles, S., Gordon, D. M. & Weisskopf, T. E. (1988b) Power, accumulation and crisis: the rise and demise of the postwar social structure of accumulation, in: R. Cherry C. D'Onofrio, C. Kurdas, T. R. Michl, F. Moseley & M. Naples (Eds) *The Imperiled Economy, Vol. 1, Macroeconomics from a Left Perspective*, pp. 43–57 (New York, URPE).

Bowles, S., Gordon, D. M. & Weisskopf, T. E. (1989) Business ascendancy and economic impasse: a structural retrospective on conservative economics, 1979–87, *Journal of Economic Perspectives*, 3, pp. 107–134.

Bowles, S., Gordon, D. M. & Weisskopf, T. E. (1991) *After the Wasteland: A Democratic Economics for the Year 2000* (Armonk, NY: M. E. Sharpe).

Bowles, S., Gordon, D. M. & Weisskopf, T. E. (1992) An economic strategy for progressives, *The Nation*, 254, 10 February, pp. 145–149.

Frank, R. (1995) *The Winner-Take-All Society* (New York, Free Press).

Gordon, D. M. (1966a) Communities of despair and the civil rights movement, *Harvard Review*, pp. 49–68.

Gordon, D. M. (1966b) 'Rebellion' in context: a student's view of students, in: R. A. Morison (Ed.) *The Contemporary University* (Boston, Houghton-Mifflin), pp. 292–314.

Gordon, D. M. (1969) Income and welfare in New York City, *The Public Interest*, Number 16, pp. 64–88.

Gordon, D. M. (1971) Class and the economics of crime, *Review of Radical Political Economics*, 3, pp. 50–75. Reprinted in (1977) *Problems in Political Economy: An Urban Perspective*, 2nd edn, David M. Gordon (Ed.) (Lexington, D.C. Heath).

Gordon, D. M. (1972a) American poverty: functions, mechanisms, and contradictions, *Monthly Review*, 20, June, pp. 72–79.

Gordon, D. M. (1972b) From steam whistles to coffee breaks: notes on office and factory work, in *Dissent,* 19, Winter, pp. 197–210.

Gordon, D. M. (1972c) Taxation of the poor and the distribution of income, *American Economic Review,* 62, pp. 319–328. Reprinted in (1977) *Problems in Political Economy: An Urban Perspective,* 2nd edn, David M. Gordon (Ed.) (Lexington, D.C. Heath).

Gordon, D. M. (1972d) *Theories of Poverty and Underemployment* (Lexington, D.C. Heath).

Gordon, D. M. (1975a) Capital vs. labor: the current crisis in the sphere of production, in: Union for Radical Political Economics, *Radical Perspectives on the Economic Crisis* (New York, URPE).

Gordon, D. M. (1975b) Orthodox and radical economists: differences in perspectives on the economic crisis, Union for Radical Political Economics, *Radical Perspectives on the Economic Crisis* (New York, URPE).

Gordon, D. M. (1975c) Recession is capitalism as usual, *New York Times Magazine,* 18, 27 April, pp. 49–63.

Gordon, D. M. (1976a) Capitalist efficiency and socialist efficiency, *Monthly Review,* 24, July–August, pp. 19–39.

Gordon, D. M. (1976b) Economic dimensions of occupational segregation: comment, *Signs,* 1, Spring, pp. 238–244.

Gordon, D. M. (1977) Capitalism and the roots of urban crisis, in: R. Alcaly and D. Mermelstein (Eds) *The Fiscal Crisis of American Cities,* pp. 82–112 (New York, Random House).

Gordon, D. M. (1978a) Capitalist development and the history of American cities, in: W. Tabb and L. Sawers, (Eds.) *Marxism and the Metropolis,* pp. 25–63 (New York, Oxford University Press).

Gordon, D. M. (1978b) Up and down the long roller coaster, in *U.S. Capitalism in Crisis,* edited by Union for Radical Political Economics (New York Union for Radical Political Economies), pp. 22–34.

Gordon, D. M. (1979a) Social control and capitalist cities: a comment, *Social Science Quarterly* 60, April pp. 628–635.

Gordon, D. M. (1979b) *The Working Poor: Towards a State Agenda* (Washington, D.C. Council of State Planning Agencies). Reissued as (1983) *State Employment in Hard Times* (Durham, NC, Duke University Press).

Gordon, D. M. (1980) Stages of accumulation and long economic cycles, in: T. Hopkins & I. Wallerstein *Processes of the World-System,* pp. 9–45 (London, Sage Publications).

Gordon, D. M. (1981a) The best defense is a good defense: toward a Marxist theory of labor union structure and behavior, in: M. Carter & W. Leahy (Eds) *New Directions in Labor Economics,* pp. 167–214 (South Bend, Notre Dame University Press)

Gordon, D. M. (1981b) Capital–labor conflict and the productivity slowdown, *American Economic Review,* 71, pp. 30–35.

Gordon, D. M. (1982) *What is Wrong with the U.S. Economy?* (Boston, South End Press).

Gordon, D. M. (1985) Up from the ashes, *The Nation,* 26 January, 9 February and 23 February.

Gordon, D. M. (1986) Do we need to be no. 1? *The Atlantic,* April.

Gordon, D. M. (1987a) Six-percent unemployment ain't natural: demystifying the idea of a rising 'natural rate of unemployment', *Social Research,* 54, pp. 223–246.

Gordon, D. M. (1987b) Marxian theories of distribution: in *The New Palgrave: A Dictionary of Economics,* J. Eatwell, M. Milgate & P. Newman (Eds) pp. 878–883 (London, Macmillan).

Gordon, D. M. (1988a) Can we pay the piper? Linkages between the macroeconomy and the welfare state, *Politics and Society,* 16, pp. 487–502.

Gordon, D. M. (1988b) The global economy: new edifice or crumbling foundations?, *New Left Review,* No. 168, pp. 24–64.

Gordon, D. M. (1988c) Global transformation or decay?: alternative perspectives on recent transformations in the world economy, in: G. Magnum & P. Philips (Eds) *The Three Worlds of Labor Economics,* pp. 309–334 (Armonk, NY, M. E. Sharpe).

Gordon, D. M. (1988d) Left, right and center: an introduction to political economy, in: R. Cherry *et al.* (Ed.) *The Imperiled Economy, Vol. II, Through the Safety Net,* pp. 9–24 (New York, URPE).

Gordon, D. M. (1988e) The un-natural rate of unemployment: an econometric critique of the NAIRU hypothesis, *American Economic Review,* 78, pp. 117–123.

Gordon, D. M. (1989) What makes epochs? A comparative analysis of technological and social explanations of long economic swings, in: M. DiMatteo, R. M. Goodwin & A. Vercelli (Eds) *Lecture Notes in Economics and Mathematical Systems,* pp. 267–304 (New York, Springer-Verlag).

Gordon, D. M. (1990) Who bosses whom?: the intensity of supervision and the discipline of labor, *American Economic Review,* 80, pp. 28–32.

Gordon, D. M. (1991a) Inside and outside the long swing: the endogeneity/exogeneity debate and the social structures of accumulation approach, *Review,* XIV, pp. 263–312.

Gordon, D. M. (1991b) Comment: institutions for the transition to the 'free' market, in: A. B. Atkinson & R. Brunetta (Eds) *Economics for the New Europe,* pp. 196–205 (London, Macmillan).

Gordon, D. M. (1991c) Kaldor's macro system: too much cumulation, too few contradictions, in: E. J. Nell & W. Semmler (Eds) *Nicholas Kaldor and Mainstream Economics: confrontation or convergence?* pp. 518–48 (London, Macmillan).

Gordon, D. M. (1992a) David M. Gordon (born 1944), in: P. Arestis & M. Sawyer (Eds) *A Biographical Dictionary of Dissenting Economists,* pp. 210–214 (Hants, Edward Elgar).

Gordon, D. M. (1992b) The misreading of labor history: a spatial analysis, in: I. Marcus (ed.) *Major Issues in the Rise and Consolidation of U.S. Workers and the Labor Movement* (Pittsburgh, Edwin Mellen Press).

Gordon, D. M. (1993a) Clintonomics—a glass half empty, *Contention,* 3, pp. 109–134.

Gordon, D. M. (1993b) Clintonomics: the upsides and the downsides, *The Nation,* 256, 15 March, pp. 325, 329, 344.

Gordon, D. M. (1993c) Generating affluence: productive gains require worker support, *Dollars and Sense,* November, pp. 20–22.

Gordon, D. M. (1993d) Socialism: what's left after the collapse of the Soviet systems, *Social Research,* 60, pp. 471–492.

Gordon, D. M. (1994a) Bosses of different stripes: a cross-national perspective on monitoring and supervision, *American Economic Review,* 84, pp. 375–379.

Gordon, D. M. (1994b) Chickens home to roost: from prosperity to stagnation in the postwar U.S. economy, in: D. Adler & M. Bernstein (Eds) *The End of the American Century: the United States Economy since 1945,* pp. 34–76 (Cambridge, Cambridge University Press).

Gordon, D. M. (1994c) Must we save our way out of stagnation? The Investment/savings relation revisited. Paper presented at the Economic Policy Institute, November.

Gordon, D. M. (1994d) The pulse of capitalism, *The Atlantic Monthly,* September.

Gordon, D. M. (1994e) Putting heterodox macro to the test: comparing post-Keynesian, marxian, and social structuralist macroeconomometric models of the post-war US economy, in: M. A. Glich (Ed.) *Competition, Technology and Money: classical and post-Keynesian perspectives,* pp. 143–185 (Hants, Edward Elgar).

Gordon, D. M. (1994f) Reply, *Review,* XVII, pp. 9–11.

Gordon, D. M. (1994g) Right-wing economics in the U.S.: the anatomy of failure, in: M. A. Bernstein & D. Adler (Eds) *Understanding American Economic Decline,* pp. 243–275 (New York, Cambridge University Press).

Gordon, D. M. (1994h) Twixt the cut and the lip: mainstream economics and the formation of economic policy, *Social Research,* 61, pp. 1–33.

Gordon, D. M. (1995a) Growth, distribution, and the rules of the game: social structuralist macrofoundations for a democratic economic policy, in: G. Epstein & H. Gintis (Eds), *Macroeconomic Policy after the Conservative Era: studies in investment, savings and finance,* pp. 335–383 (New York, Cambridge University Press).

Gordon, D. M. (1995b) Politics and precision: pursuing economics outside the mainstream, in: M. Szenberg (Ed.) *Passion and Craft: How Economists Work* (Ann Arbor, University of Michigan Press).

Gordon, D. M. (1995c) Putting the horse (back) before the cart: disentangling the macro relationship between investment and savings, in: G. Epstein & H. Gintis (Eds), *Macroeconomic Policy after the Conservative Era: Studies in Investment, Savings and Finance,* pp. 57–108 (New York, Cambridge University Press).

Gordon, D. M. (1995d) Wageless recovery, wageless growth?: prospects for U.S. workers in the 1990s, in: J. Eatwell (Ed.) *Global Unemployment: Loss of Jobs in the 90s,* pp. 87–108 (Armonk, NY, M. E. Sharpe).

Gordon, D. M. (1996a) *Fat and Mean: The Corporate Squeeze of Working Americans and the Myth of Managerial 'Downsizing'* (New York, The Free Press).

Gordon, D. M. (1996b) Values that work, *The Nation,* 262(2), pp. 16–19.

Gordon, D. M., Doeringer, P. B. *et al.* (Eds) (1971) *Low-Income Labor Markets and Urban Management Programs: A Critical Assessment* (Washington, DC, U.S. Department of Labor).

Gordon, D. M., Edwards, R. & Reich, M. (1982) *Segmented Work, Divided Workers: The Historical Transformation of Labor in the United States* (Cambridge, Cambridge University Press).

Gordon, D. M., Edwards, R. & Reich, M. (1994) Long swings and stages of capitalism, in: D. M. Kotz, T. McDonough & M. Reich (Eds), *Social Structures of Accumulation: the political economy of growth and crisis,* pp. 11–28 (New York, Cambridge University Press).

Gordon, D. M., Weisskopf, T. E. & Bowles, S. (1987) Power, accumulation, and crisis: the rise and demise of the postwar social structure of accumulation, in: R. Cherry *et al.,* (Eds), *The Imperiled Economy,* Vol. 1, pp. 43–57. (New York, Union for Radical Political Economics).

Gordon, M. S. (1965) (ed.) *Poverty in America* (San Francisco, Chandler).

Gordon, R. A. (1952) *Business Fluctuations* (New York, Harper and Brothers).

Gordon, R. A. (ed.) (1967) *Toward a Manpower Policy* (New York, John Wiley).

Gordon, R. J. (1981) Output fluctuations and gradual price adjustments, *Journal of Economic Literature,* 19, pp. 493–530.

Harrison, B. (1987) Cold bath or restructuring? An explanation of the Weisskoft–Bowles–Gordon framework, *Science and Society,* 51, pp. 72–81.

Kotz, D. M. (1987) Long waves and the social structures of accumulation: a critique and reinterpretation, *Review of Radical Political Economics,* 19(4), pp. 16–38.

Kotz, D. M. (1990) A comparative analysis of the theory of regulation and the social structure of accumulation theory, *Science and Society,* 54(1), pp. 5–28.

Kotz, D. M., McDonough, T. & Reich, M. (Eds) (1994) *Social Structures of Accumulation: The Political Economy of Growth and Crisis* (New York, Cambridge University Press).

Lipietz, A. (1986) Behind the crisis: the exhaustion of a regime of accumulation: a 'regulation school' perspective on some French empirical works, *Review of Radical Political Economics,* 18 (1–2), pp. 13–32.

McDonough, T. (1990) The resolution of crises in American economic history: social structures of accumulation and stages of capitalism, *Research in Political Economy,* 13, pp. 129–183.

Moseley, F. (1986) The intensity of labor and the productivity slowdown, *Science and Society,* 50, pp. 210–218.

Naples, M. I. (1981) Industrial conflict and its implications for productivity growth, *American Economic Review,* 71(2), pp. 36–41.

Naples, M. I. (1986) Unraveling the union–capital truce and the U.S. industrial productivity crisis, *Review of Radical Political Economics,* 18, pp. 110–131.

Norton, B. (1988) The power axis: Bowles, Gordon, and Weisskopf's theory of postwar U.S. accumulation, *Rethinking Marxism,* 1(3), pp. 6–43.

O'Hara, P. A. (1995) Household labor, the family, and macroeconomic instability in the United States: 1940s–1990s, *Review of Social Economy,* 53, pp. 89–120.

Reich, R. (1983) *The Next American Frontier* (New York, Times Books).

Reich, R. (1991) *The Work of Nations* (New York, A. Knopf).

Tylecote, A. (1992) *The Long Wave in the World Economy: The Current Crisis in Historical Perspective* (London and New York, Routledge).

Weisskopf, T. E., Bowles, S. & Gordon, D. M. (1983) Heart and minds: a social model of U.S. productivity growth, *Brookings Papers on Economic Activity* (2), pp. 381–450.

Weisskopf, T. E., Bowles, S. & Gordon, D. M. (1992) We need handshakes and arm-twisting to mobilize our recovery, *Challenge,* 35(2), pp. 48–54.

3 The economic contributions of Hyman Minsky

Varieties of capitalism and institutional reform

Dimitri B. Papadimitriou and L. Randall Wray

'The Economic Contributions of Hyman Minsky: Varieties of Capitalism and Institutional Reform' by Dimitri B. Papadimitriou and L. Randall Wray from *Review of Political Economy* (1998), Volume 10, Issue 2 (Taylor and Francis Ltd, http://www.informaworld.com), reprinted by permission of the publisher.

1 Introduction

Hyman (Hy) Minsky was born in Chicago on 23 September 1919 and died in Rhinebeck, New York, after a year's battle with pancreatic cancer, on 24 October 1996. The influence of Oscar Lange, Paul Douglas, Jacob Viner, Frank Knight and Henry Simons, all members of the University of Chicago economics faculty in 1937 when Hyman Minsky was an undergraduate there, played a pivotal role in reinforcing his interest in studying economics, even though his BS degree was in mathematics. The courses and seminars taught by the 'Chicago greats', his friendship with Gerhard Meyer and Abba Lerner as well as the socio-economic environment of his youth contributed to Hy's decision to further his education in economics, which he did (after a number of years of involvement in the US Army serving in New York, Britain and Germany) at Harvard, where he earned his master's and doctoral degrees (Minsky, 1985). At Harvard, he asked Joseph Schumpeter to be his doctoral supervisor, which surprised Alvin Hansen, since Hy had been teaching assistant for the money and banking course that Hansen taught. As it turned out, however, Hy finished the thesis in 1954 under Wassily Leontief because of Schumpeter's untimely death. In his dissertation, and in later research, Hy explored the interrelationships among market structure, banking, the determinants of aggregate demand, and business cycle performance.

Many of his Chicago friends and other acquaintances had moved to the Harvard-MIT community, but Hy never considered Harvard as his intellectual home. To him, the intellectual powerhouse was the University of Chicago, which continued to influence him during the Harvard days. It was Chicago that he would visit every chance he had in order to renew his friendship with Carl Christ, Leonid Hurwicz and other remaining friends at the University and the Cowles Commission, and to meet new friends including Kenneth Arrow. The classes and seminars at Harvard were not challenging for they lacked the rigor and clarity of those at Chicago. The self-appointed American disciples of Keynes—Alvin Hansen leading them—were content with the conventional and almost mechanistic interpretation of countercyclical fiscal policy, ignoring the significance of uncertainty and the role that money and finance played in a complex capitalist system. Hy's refusal to accept this narrow and fundamentally incorrect interpretation of Keynes, which necessarily led to a simplistic belief that market behavior can be neutralized by interventions affecting aggregate demand, played a significant role in his later research and writings.

His first academic appointment was to the faculty of Brown University, where he was tenured and promoted to associate professor. He moved to the University of California at Berkeley in 1957. Two years earlier, he spent a sabbatical year there, and this turned into an offer for a permanent appointment. During his years at Berkeley, Hy developed his ideas about the importance of cash flows in contractual commitments. He said that current borrowing is obtained by committing future cash, a perspective not considered in the traditional flow of funds analysis (Minsky, 1963b). Hy felt pleased to be part of the economics program at Berkeley, which was distinctive in that it offered a broad spectrum of courses taught by a good group at the faculty. As the years went by, however, he became disillusioned with the changes that were tilting the economics program increasingly to emphasize mathematics. To be sure, he once confided, the years at Berkeley were very productive—his *John Maynard Keynes* book was conceived during that time. Also, while at Berkeley, he instituted a banking seminar sponsored by Bank of America, which helped sharpen his knowledge of institutional innovation in banking and the details of a bank's internal operations. This proved very valuable later when he joined the board of the Mark Twain Banks in St Louis. Moreover, the Berkeley years were rewarding in that a number of his honours students—Victoria Chick, Peter Gray, Robert Hall, Thomas Sargent—have distinguished themselves in the economics profession and beyond.[1] In the turbulent 1964–65 year of campus unrest at Berkeley, the decision to accept a permanent appointment at Washington University in St Louis seemed a good opportunity at least for the near term. As he admitted,

> I frankly went to Washington University with no intention of spending twenty-five years there. I thought I'd go there, get some things done and get out. But, I got involved with the banks [Mark Twain] and when the offer came through from the State University [New York], two or three years later, the bank made it worthwhile to stay. This happened a couple of times.
> (Quoted from Fazzari & Papadimitriou, 1992)

On his retirement in 1990 from Washington University, as an Emeritus Professor, he became a Distinguished Scholar at the Jerome Levy Economics Institute of Bard College, where he remained until his death.

Hy's work represents one of the most important links between Post Keynesians and Institutionalists. We begin, in this essay, with a brief summary of some of his earlier work, including his well-known 'financial instability hypothesis' and his policy proposals that were designed to reform the financial system, but pay more attention to his writings that explore other theoretical issues and policy proposals. These, for the most part, were developed in his later years, after the publication of *Stabilizing an Unstable Economy* (Minsky, 1986) and during his association with the Levy Institute.

Hy did not like to be labelled 'Post Keynesian'. This was probably for three reasons. First, he believed that a more accurate description of his approach was 'financial Keynesian', for this singled out his debt to Keynes while focusing on what he believed to be his clarification of, and extension to, the economics of Keynes—namely, the addition of complex financial relations, markets, and institutions. Second, he wanted to distance himself from a tendency in Post Keynesian economics to push institutions into the background in order to develop 'general theories'. He firmly believed that general theories are either plainly wrong, or are simply too general to be of any use. He would ask: what sort of economic theory can be applied equally well to a tribal society, a peasant economy, a small government capitalism, and a big government capitalism with complex financial arrangements? According to Hy, institutions must be brought into the analysis at the beginning; useful theory is institution-specific (Minsky, 1992d). All of his work emphasized that our economy operates within a modern capitalist system with a big government sector, with long-lived and privately owned capital, and with exceedingly complex financial arrangements.

Finally, as all who knew him would verify, even to his final days, Hy never gave up hope that communication with the profession is possible. While he was convinced that mainstream analysis is not only wrong-headed, but that it is also dangerous when it forms the basis of policy formation, he was also convinced that he could 'move the discipline'—at least a little. This conviction was amply evident in his work at the Jerome Levy Economics Institute, for otherwise there would have been no reason to attempt to influence policy and theory. To this point, we will return.

Hy had little use for pure exercises in 'history of thought', rather, he always argued that he stood 'on the shoulders of giants', like Keynes, Schumpeter and Simons. (His most famous book, *John Maynard Keynes,* is, of course, most assuredly *not* about Keynes.) Whether he got their theories 'right' was a matter of little consequence to him, for he used their contributions only as a springboard for his own analysis. Thus, it is with some trepidation that we attempt to do what Hy avoided and even disdained: to lay out the ideas of a giant—and surely Hy does qualify as a giant on whose shoulders we can stand. However, we note that he did enjoy being the topic of analysis and was always kind to authors even when they got Minsky 'wrong'. Thus, we have reason to believe that he would have enjoyed the following, even where it may be flawed. We only wish we could have his reply.

2 Becoming a Minskian

There has been some controversy over 'early' Minsky versus 'later' Minsky, with some arguing that Minsky's early work was essentially orthodox and that he really did not become a Post Keynesian until the 1970s.[2] Indeed, Minsky told one of the authors (Wray) that he only very gradually became a 'Minskian', with the transformation completed in his *John Maynard Keynes*. We do not, however, completely agree with this view, even if it *is* Minsky's view. As noted above, Minsky traced his intellectual heritage primarily to Chicago's Lange, Viner, Knight, and Simons (and to Harvard's Schumpeter), rather than to the Harvard 'Keynesians'. It might appear somewhat incongruous to claim that this heritage is less orthodox than the prevailing 'Keynesian' tradition, but it must be remembered that Chicago in the 1940s was not the post-Friedman Chicago of today. What Minsky took away from Chicago (and particularly from Simons) was the view 'that market structures matter in determining both efficiency and the efficacy of aggregate interventions', thus rejecting the Harvard notion that analysis could ignore market structure as it focused on control of the economy through aggregate interventions (Papadimitriou, 1992, pp. 18–19). This was Minsky's dissertation theme, which had explored the relations between market structure and aggregate demand, with a special emphasis on banking and investment decisions.

Minsky's first important publication (Minsky, 1957a) related institutional innovation to profit opportunities, demonstrating how innovation allows business activity to expand even in the absence of expansionary monetary policy. He showed how the development of the federal funds market allowed a given quantity of aggregate reserves to support a greater expansion of deposits, and how repurchase agreements allowed a given quantity of demand deposits to support a greater volume of loans. He also 'endogenized' innovation, making it a function of profit-seeking behavior. As the central bank tightens monetary policy, this raises interest rates and encourages new financial practices that 'stretch liquidity' as liquid balances are reduced. This means that tight monetary policy may not reduce the money supply (or even reduce the—more broadly defined—supply of credit) as higher interest rates encourage banks to seek new ways of providing finance. At the same time, these innovations increase the potential for instability because 'every institutional innovation which results in both new ways to finance business and new substitutes for cash assets decreases the liquidity of the economy' (Minsky, 1957a, p. 184). Minsky argued that early in an expansion, the supply curve of credit would be highly elastic so that rising demand for credit would not have much effect on interest rates (but would instead increase the supply of credit). However, later in the boom, as liquidity falls and the possibility of default increases, the supply curve becomes more inelastic so that rising demand raises interest rates. This, in turn, can induce further innovation, and further fragility.[3] This raises the possibility of a rapid deflation of the value of assets should some firms or households fail to meet contracted commitments. Ultimately, the monetary authorities might be called upon to halt a debt deflation process by intervening as a lender of last resort to increase the quantity of liquidity by accepting (at the discount window) illiquid assets (Minsky, 1957a, p. 185). Thus, even in his first important publication, we find many of the ideas that show up later in his work: endogenous money, innovation that stretches liquidity, behavioral changes induced by policy, lender of last resort activity, and instability-enhancing behavior over the course of the cycle. We return to these aspects of his analysis below.

Minsky also tried to extend the conventional multiplier–accelerator analysis to take account of monetary variables and financial institutions in his next two major publications. He bemoaned the fact that 'authors who have constructed these accelerator–multiplier models have paid little, if any, attention to the monetary pre-requisites and effects of the assumed processes' (Minsky 1957b, p. 859). He argued that Samuelson's multiplier-accelerator model could be applied only to 'small oscillations' which are neither great enough to disturb the accelerator or multiplier coefficients, nor great enough to lead to the imposition of new initial conditions; in other words, the model was valid only if cyclical growth of income and production were to occur without affecting behavior or inducing institutional innovation (Minsky, 1959). Thus, in Minsky (1957b), he 'endogenized' the coefficients, and in Minsky (1959), he allowed for changes of initial conditions.

He argued that '[t]he terms (interest rate) and the manner (type of liability) of financing investment are affected by the behavior of the monetary system. In turn, both money-market conditions and the balance-sheet structure of firms affect the response of firms to a change in income. This can be interpreted as making the accelerator coefficient an endogenous variable related to the monetary system' (Minsky 1957b, p. 869). He thus considered 'the following alternative monetary systems: (A) neither velocity nor quantity changes, (B) only velocity changes; (C) only quantity changes; (D) both velocity and quantity change'[4] (Minsky, 1957b, p. 863). He demonstrated that if an expansion takes place on the basis of an increase in the money supply, then the balance sheet positions of firms worsen. However, if both velocity and the money supply tend to rise over the course of an expansion, the 'rise in velocity tends to counteract the deterioration of firms' balance sheets in a business-cycle expansion financed by bank creation of money' (Minsky 1957b, p. 881). A decline in liquidity preference of the household sector can serve as an alternative to expansion of the money supply, in effect 'improving financing terms and...decreasing the dependence of business firms upon bank financing, rais[ing] the accelerator coefficient. A great stock-market boom, such as in the late 1920's, may be interpreted as reflecting a lowering of liquidity preferences; as a result business expansion could be financed with less reliance upon the banking system than otherwise'[5] (Minsky, 1957b, p. 881). On the other hand, rising liquidity preference during a downswing would cause a deterioration of firms' balance sheets, inducing a further fall of investment. Thus, liquidity preference, money supply conditions, and those factors that affect velocity all influence the financial position of firms, which in turn affects investment decisions and the accelerator process. He concluded that

> [g]overnment deficits financed by borrowing from banks result in an increase in the money supply without any corresponding increase in business debt....This is more conducive to steady growth....Therefore government deficit financing, even during a period of sustained growth and secularly rising prices, may be desirable in order to maintain the conditions for further growth.
>
> (Minsky, 1957b, p. 883)

We will return below to Minsky's later analysis of deficit spending.

Minsky (1959) reworked this theory, adding 'floors and ceilings' that imposed 'new initial conditions' on the model, interpreted as 'reflecting effective supply constraints' (Minsky, 1959, pp. 133–134). He showed that the time path of income generated by such a linear-accelerator model 'can generate either (a) steady growth, (b) cycles, (c) booms, or (d) long depressions' (Minsky, 1959, p. 134). He demonstrated that 'by feeding financial and money market developments into the formal model through the ratchet in the consumption function, booms and depressions of varying amplitude and length can be generated' (Minsky, 1959, p. 135). He used this model to explain the robust growth that followed WWII: forced wartime saving, highly liquid balance sheets (due in large part to wartime deficit spending), and exploitation of wartime technological change and accumulated productive capacity led to high autonomous consumption and high potential ('ceiling') output. He concluded that:

> Whenever income fell away from the ceiling—as in 1948 and 1954 in the United States—the financial ease, carried over from the war, resulted in a relatively high and nonfalling floor in income, so that recovery was quick. In order for more serious depressions to occur, it is necessary for the ratio of equilibrium income to ceiling income to decrease or for depreciation ratios to increase.... [T]his could occur if the downturn were accompanied by a financial crisis or if the preceding boom had been associated with a relatively small increase or even a decrease in the liquid asset position of households and firms.
>
> (Minsky, 1959, p. 144)

Thus, these early articles included financial positions as 'initial conditions' that would influence the path of the economy—whether that be tranquil or unstable—as well as the position Minsky would develop later that the US economy emerged from WWII with 'robust' balance sheets, full of government debt, that over time would become increasingly fragile, generating the conditions that might make 'It' (a debt deflation) happen again. Admittedly, these articles tend to rework and extend fairly conventional analysis; however, this was done in directions that would be developed over the next several decades until they became his *Stabilizing an Unstable Economy* (Minsky, 1986).

In the intervening years, three elements were added to the analysis: the 'financial theory of investment' presented in *John Maynard Keynes* (Minsky, 1975), the Kalecki–Levy view of profits, and the 'financial instability hypothesis' (FIH). In the remainder of this section, we will briefly discuss the first two elements, leaving the FIH for the next section.

Minsky's (1975)[6] *John Maynard Keynes* grew out of lectures he gave at Berkeley, discussions with Nicholas Kaldor, Frank Hahn, Donald Winch, Kenneth Arrow and Hollis Chenery (some taking place during their visits to Berkeley and during a seminar organized by Kaldor at Berkeley), a sabbatical at Cambridge (1969–70, where he was able to develop his views in discussion with

Donald Moggridge, Jan Kregel, Joan Robinson, and W.B. Reddaway), his work during the 1960s on the FIH, and his early work on multiplier–accelerator models. The main contribution made by this book is the 'financial theory of investment' which springs from the recognition that in any modern, capitalist society, there are 'two price levels'—one for 'current output' and another for 'capital assets'. In Minsky's view, the demand price for capital assets must exceed the supply price before investment can take place. The demand price for assets is related to the prospective returns from ownership of any asset; these prospective returns 'present views about the future, and therefore are prone to change as views about the future change' (Minsky, 1975, p. 95). The supply price of the capital asset depends on production (thus, on 'current output price' of investment goods) and finance costs. Minsky built Keynes's 'lender's risk' and 'borrower's risk' into the model, so that demand price is adjusted (downward) to account for the risk to the borrower of exceeding 'internal funds', while supply price is adjusted (upward) to take account of the increasing risk to the lender as the borrower takes on greater debt. These then provide a 'margin of security', which itself is subject to 'whirlwinds' of optimism and pessimism (the margins can decline in a boom, or rise in a bust). Because investment is the driving variable in the economy, Minsky labeled his approach 'a financial theory of investment and an investment theory of the cycle'. Thus, he was able to include the proposition that asset positions in a capitalist economy are 'financed' positions, and the view that financial positions affect behavior in ways that can be destabilizing (more on this below).

It is interesting that *John Maynard Keynes* contains no reference to Kalecki; when questioned, Minsky could not remember when he first adopted the Kaleckian view that investment *determines* profits, but surely, if he had been familiar with Kalecki's theory, it would have appeared in the book. Later, Minsky would make great use of the 'Kalecki–Levy' profit equation, which is derived from national identities and shows that aggregate profits are identically equal to the government's deficit, plus the trade surplus, plus investment, plus consumption out of profits, and less saving out of wages[7] (Minsky, 1992d). He would incorporate this view into his theory as the proposition that 'investment today is forthcoming only if investment is expected in the future' as aggregate profits will not exist unless investment occurs. He then argued that profits cannot be explained as a result of competition (since, in the aggregate, they are determined as in the Kalecki–Levy equation); this means that competition and innovation can only redistribute profits among firms.[8] Finally, if investment falls, then profits will fall, which will further discourage investment unless one of the other components of the profit equation should rise in compensation. The likely candidate, of course, is government deficit spending (Minsky, 1980). In this way, he came back to his earlier conclusion that government deficits can be stabilizing; here he added the notion that deficits *create* profits, and as it is the expectation of profit that *drives* the economy, countercyclical deficits can be stabilizing (Minsky, 1992d).

3 The financial instability hypothesis

During the 1960s, Minsky developed the financial instability hypothesis as he tried to answer the question 'can it happen again?'. As readers are no doubt familiar with Minsky's 'financial instability hypothesis' (FIH), we will only summarize it while emphasizing its institutional nature.[9] According to Minsky, a financial system naturally evolves from a robust structure to a fragile structure, or from a structure that is consistent with stability to one that is conducive to instability. Note that it is a bit misleading to use the word 'stability', for Minsky would emphasize that systems are continually evolving, generally toward fragility, so that a 'stable' position is ephemeral. Indeed, he continually argued that 'stability is destabilizing': 'The first theorem of the financial instability hypothesis is that the economy has financing regimes under which it is stable, and financing regimes in which it is unstable. The second theorem of the financial instability hypothesis is that over periods of prolonged prosperity, the economy transits from financial relations that make for a stable system to financial relations that make for an unstable system' (Minsky, 1992c, pp. 7–8).

It is important to emphasize that Minsky's financial instability hypothesis is institutionally-specific, applicable only to a capitalist economy with complex financing of long-lived capital assets. In the absence of long-term finance, undertaken on the basis of longer-term expectations, the Minskian transformation towards fragility would not occur (this does not mean that a simpler capitalism could not experience instability). According to Minsky, financial positions evolve from 'hedge' to 'speculative' and finally to 'Ponzi', first as expectations about future returns become increasingly optimistic, and later as expectations are disappointed or financial arrangements are disrupted.

> It can be shown that if hedge financing dominates, then the economy may well be an equilibrium seeking and containing system. In contrast, the greater the weight of speculative and Ponzi finance, the greater the likelihood that the economy is a deviation amplifying system.... [O]ver a protracted period of good times, capitalist economies tend to move from a financial structure dominated by hedge finance units to a structure in which there is large weight to units engaged in speculative and Ponzi finance.
>
> (Minsky, 1992c, pp. 7–8)

It is precisely the apparent 'stability' that generates changes of expectations that leads to adoption of financial positions that cannot be validated should events prove to be less favorable than expected—that is, the transformation from robust (hedge) arrangements to fragile (speculative) positions. These speculative positions then are pushed to Ponzi for a variety of reasons: the terms on which finance is available become less favorable (either because providers become concerned with their own positions or because the central bank adopts a tighter policy to head-off perceived inflationary pressures), some expectations are revised, income flows that had been expected are not forthcoming, and so on. In any case, the financial instability hypothesis depends critically on the institutional arrangements of the modern capitalist economy and on the evolution of behavior that is likely to take place given these arrangements.

According to Minsky, 'A capitalist, or if you wish a market, economy is a financial system' (Minsky, 1992b, p. 16). In contrast, 'The neoclassical way of doing economics, which rests upon splitting the financial system off from what is called the real economy, throws no appreciable light on the effect that a financial system has upon the functioning of the economy: the only relevant neoclassical position is that the financial structure makes no difference' (Minsky, 1992b, p. 15). It is precisely the absence of credible financial arrangements and institutional detail that renders neoclassical theory useless for analysing the capitalist system. By explicitly beginning with the financial system, and by analysing the transformation of the system from 'hedge' to 'speculative', Minsky's analysis is relevant to the real world capitalist economy. Analysis devoid of institutions 'throws no appreciable light' on real world economies.[10]

Second, from his earliest publications, Minsky realized the importance of explaining the new form(s) of capitalism with which he was concerned, and, in particular, with identifying the reasons why the forms of postwar capitalism were so different from those that existed before WWII. Again, the difference is institutional. Pre-war capitalism not only exhibited much greater amplitude in its business cycles, but financial crises regularly coincided with depressions. For Minsky, a defining characteristic of the Great Depression was the 'Fisher' debt deflation in conjunction with loss of real output. He frequently pointed out that while real output only fell by half (and unemployment rose to 'only' 25%), asset prices fell by 85%. Certainly he did not mean to minimize the suffering of the unemployed and underemployed, but in his view, the bigger problem for the capitalist system was the complete absence of aggregate profits (or, as he preferred, gross capital income). Further, during the Great Depression, balance sheets were 'simplified' as most financial debts and assets were wiped-out. This allowed the financial system to emerge from the Great Depression with 'simple', or robust, balance sheets with little leveraging and with most assets taking the form of equity positions. After the war, relatively stable, moderate growth occurred on the basis of hedge finance.

> Economic activity in the early postwar setting began with a cautious use of debt. But as the period over which the economy did well began to lengthen, margins of safety in indebtedness decreased and the system evolved toward a greater reliance on debt relative to internal finance, as well as toward the use of debt to acquire existing assets. As a result, the once robust financial system became increasingly fragile.
>
> (Minsky & Whalen, 1996, p. 4)

After 1966, 'the amplitude of the business cycle has increased and financial crises have become regular occurrences. Another Great Depression has been prevented, but the same actions that stabilize the economy also validate speculative financial practices' (Minsky & Whalen, 1996, pp. 4–5). Thus, even as business cycles have not been eliminated, neither depressions nor widespread balance sheet simplifications have occurred.[11] Something of fundamental importance seems to have occurred to prevent reoccurrence of a Fisher-type debt deflation. Minsky argued that 'ceilings and floors' were put into place during the 1930s and in the immediate postwar period to prevent (thus far) successfully another debt deflation.[12] These ceilings and floors take the form of a wide variety of institutional arrangements—some governmental, some private, some automatic, some discretionary; some intentional and some fortuitous. Minsky argued 'institutions and interventions thwart the instability breeding dynamics that are natural to market economies by interrupting the endogenous process and "starting" the economy again with non market determined values as "initial conditions"' (Minsky & Ferri, 1991, p. 4).

The two most important 'ceilings and floors' are the growth of big government that is capable of running large (relative to the size of the economy) countercyclical deficits and surpluses, and central bank intervention as the lender of last resort. Countercyclical deficits and surpluses allow the government to place ceilings and floors on aggregate demand and, thus, profits, which helps to maintain business income flows in bad times (through deficits) while dampening these flows in boom times (through fiscal surpluses). Similarly, the central bank places a floor on asset prices through its willingness to intervene and provide liquidity whenever pressure for 'firesales' of assets builds, and will likely cause prices to plummet. In this way, when private spending falls, a government deficit automatically is created that helps to maintain aggregate demand and business gross capital income, allowing firms to continue to service financial positions. Should some firms experience difficulty, central bank intervention can help to prevent problems from spreading. Of course, as Minsky continually emphasized (long before such problems came to pass), the problem is that if debt deflations are eliminated, increasingly fragile positions can be taken with no 'cleansing' (or balance sheet simplification) ever taking place. This is why other institutional arrangements have to be adopted to place a ceiling on expectations of asset prices. It should be emphasized that Minsky never argued that these constraints must come only from government; indeed, he argued that capitalists had long sought ways to protect asset values. In fact, capitalism without institutional constraints is impossible to imagine as the incentives to try to protect asset values are too great. The main point, however, is that possible constraints in a small-government capitalist economy are insufficient to prevent 'it' (a debt deflation) from happening.

This analysis led to what he called his 'anti-laissez-faire theorem', the proposition that 'in a world where the internal dynamics imply instability, a semblance of stability can be achieved or sustained by introducing conventions, constraints and interventions into the environment' (Minsky & Ferri, 1991, p. 20). Thus, 'Apt intervention and institutional structures are necessary for market economies to be successful' (Minsky & Ferri, 1991, p. 24). '[I]nstitutions can act as the equivalent of circuit breakers' (Minsky *et al.*, 1994, p. 2). 'To contain the evils that market systems can inflict, capitalist economies developed sets of institutions and authorities, which can be characterized as the equivalent of circuit breakers. These institutions in effect stop the economic processes that breed the incoherence, and restart the economy with new initial conditions and perhaps with new reaction coefficients' (Minsky *et al.*, 1994, p. 3). These institutions are *imposed,* and they *replace* the endogenously determined variables that generate incoherence; these interventions create new initial conditions from which the economy begins on a new path and 'the aptness of institutions and interventions will largely determine the extent to which the path of the economy through time is tranquil or turbulent: progressive, stagnant, or deteriorating' (Minsky *et al.*, 1994, p. 4). Thus, apt intervention is required for 'successful capitalism' (Minsky & Ferri, 1991, p. 24).

This provides the framework for Minsky's analysis of the modern capitalist economy. A special kind of instability results because of the primary features of this sort of economy; in particular, the longer lived and expensive capital assets in a modern private for-profit economy require complex and long-lived financial arrangements. Instability can be constrained through developing appropriate institutions that provide 'ceilings and floors'; however, 'stability' cannot be achieved because of the impact that 'tranquility' will have on expectations and thus behavior. Still, capitalism with ceilings and floors is preferable to capitalism without institutional constraints, and the constraints that are possible in a small-government capitalist economy are insufficient to prevent 'it' (a debt deflation) from happening. In contrast, the constraints that are possible with a big government form of capitalism have been sufficient. The problem is that the absence of 'it' has changed behavior in ways that are likely to increase the likelihood that 'it' *will* happen again. The question is what changes to these institutions can continue to forestall 'it', while at the same time promoting the values of a democratic society. We now turn to Minsky's policy analysis.

4 Stabilizing the unstable economy

In his 1986 book, *Stabilizing an Unstable Economy,* Minsky (1986) argued 'The policy problem is to devise institutional structures and measures that attenuate the thrust to inflation, unemployment, and slower improvements in the standard of living without increasing the likelihood of a deep depression' (Minsky, 1986, p. 295). His 'agenda for reform' addressed four areas—'Big Government (size, spending, and taxing), an employment strategy, financial reform, and market power' (Minsky, 1986, p. 295). We will very briefly summarize the reforms advocated.

4.1 Big government

According to Minsky, government must be large enough so that the swings of its budget are sufficient to offset swings of private investment; this dictates that government spending should be approximately 'the same order of magnitude as or larger than investment' (Minsky, 1986, p. 297). This means that at full employment, the budget should be balanced at about 20% of GDP; below full employment, spending would be somewhat more than this while tax revenues would be somewhat less; above full employment, revenues would exceed 20% of GDP while spending would be less. Minsky was quite concerned with maintaining the appearance of credit-worthiness, which necessitates 'a tax and spending regime in place that would yield a favorable cash flow (a surplus) under reasonable and attainable circumstances' (Minsky, 1986, p. 302). For this reason, he argued that the fiscal stance of the Reagan administration was out of line; while tax revenues were approximately the right size, spending was several percentage points of GDP too high—even at full employment a deficit would result. Spending cuts would be required.

Most importantly, Minsky wanted to reorder spending priorities toward employment programs, child allowances, and public infrastructure investment, and away from defence and non-Old Age, Survivors, Disability, and Hospital Insurance (OASDHI) transfers (Minsky, 1986, p. 308). He believed that an employment program could substitute for most transfers other than those aimed at the aged, which would allow substantial cuts in non-defence spending. Finally, he wanted to dispense with automatic cost-of-living adjustments so that inflation would move the government's budget toward balance (by increasing tax revenues through 'bracket creep' while avoiding increases of social spending). In some respects, Minsky's arguments appear to be very close to those recently discussed and in some cases implemented—i.e. President Clinton's proposal to 'end welfare as we know it'. However, as we will discuss below, Minsky's employment program would provide a greater safety net than do the new welfare 'reforms'.

Part of the reason Minsky wanted to reduce transfers is because he was convinced that these impart an inflationary bias to the economy (Minsky, 1986, p. 313). In his view, the level of aggregate demand determines the mark-up at the aggregate level over aggregate costs of production (primarily wages). As social spending generates income and adds to aggregate demand without contributing much to aggregate supply, the mark-up over costs is higher. If government spending could be shifted away from policies to raise aggregate demand without increasing production to those that would increase both aggregate demand as well as increase aggregate supply, then prices would be lower. In particular, public infrastructure development as well as workfare (rather than welfare) would be expected to reduce inflation.

With regard to taxes, Minsky believed that most taxes are inflationary because they add to costs; in particular, the portion of the Social Security tax paid by employers as well as the corporate income tax were believed to be a cost passed along in price (Minsky, 1986, p. 305). In addition, Minsky feared that the payroll tax encouraged substitution of capital for labor. He thus advocated elimination of the corporate income tax as well as the employer portion of the payroll tax. He supported, as will be discussed in greater detail below, a broad-based value-added tax as an alternative. He also supported greater use of excise taxes to influence behavior; in particular, he advocated a much larger tax on petroleum.

4.2 Employment

A key component of Minsky's reform strategy was to remove barriers to labor force participation and ensure that all who wanted a job would be able to obtain one (Minsky, 1986, p. 308). He argued that various transfer payment programs, in particular AFDC and Social Security, placed constraints on allowable wage income that provided significant barriers to work. His reforms would include the substitution of a universal children's allowance for AFDC, as well as elimination of wage income constraints for Social Security recipients, but with an extension of the retirement age for collecting Social Security benefits. More importantly, he advocated a true 'full employment' policy: the government would act as the employer of last resort, using a program modeled on the New Deal's Civilian Conservation Corps or Works Progress Administration (WPA). This would guarantee a public sector job to anyone unable to find a private sector job, at some established minimum wage.

> The policy problem is to develop a strategy for full employment that does not lead to instability, inflation, and unemployment. The main instrument of such a policy is the creation of an infinitely elastic demand for labor at a floor or minimum wage that does not depend upon long- and short-run profit expectations of business. Since only government can divorce the offering of employment from the profitability of hiring workers, the infinitely elastic demand for labor must be created by government.
>
> (Minsky, 1986, p. 308)

He argued that this program would allow full employment without generating inflationary pressures or, at least, that it would be no more inflationary than the current system. (Recall that he argued that transfer payments are inflationary because they generate aggregate demand without necessarily generating aggregate supply.) Since WPA-style jobs would pay less than those in the private sector and because they would generate at least some additional output, they would not place significant pressure on either private sector wages or prices.

Minsky argued that the current system actually sets a minimum wage at $0 because if one is unemployed, the wage is zero; in his scheme, a true minimum wage—one set by policy—would be in effect since all could work at the WPA-wage (Minsky, 1986, p. 310). Whereas in the current system, employment is subject to cyclical fluctuations, in Minsky's system fluctuations in private sector employment would be offset by variations in the proportion of workers in government-sponsored WPA jobs. Also in the current system, employers have to compete with government benefits that are given for not working; as such, wages must be set at a high enough level to induce those receiving transfers to accept employment. In Minsky's system, the alternative to private employment (and to public, non-WPA employment) is WPA employment. As long as the WPA wage is not adjusted upward very often, it could even dampen wage pressures and thus lead to less inflation than the current system.

4.3 Financial reform

As discussed above, Minsky believed that Fed willingness to intervene as the lender of last resort generates changes of behavior in financial markets; for this reason, the Fed must take greater responsibility for regulating financial markets to 'guide the evolution of financial institutions by favoring stability-enhancing and discourage instability-augmenting institutions and practices' (Minsky, 1986, p. 314). Foremost among his recommendations was greater reliance on prudential supervision of banks. He favored greater use of the discount window (and correspondingly less use of open market purchases) as the method through which reserves would be provided; this would allow the Fed to reward prudent bank practices with more favorable terms at the window. Further, he favored policies that would tie lending to specific assets—something like a 'real bills doctrine'—so that 'the payment commitments on the debts used can be closely related to the cash flows that these assets are expected to yield. The financial flow relations are analogous to those that characterize hedge financing' (Minsky, 1986, p. 315). Of course, this would not always be possible, but it can be encouraged by opening the discount window to a wide variety of types of financial institutions (he included sales finance companies, life insurance companies and even ordinary corporations) so long as they engage in 'to-the-asset financing' (Minsky, 1986, p. 322).

While the corporate form is necessary in an economy with extremely expensive capital assets, this sort of institutional arrangement 'facilitates the divorce of financing from the ownership and acquisition of particular assets....Consequently, the corporation, initially a device for extending hedge financing to long-lasting capital assets, can be a vehicle for speculative finance—and because it facilitates both capital intensive modes of production and speculative financing, a destabilizing influence' (Minsky, 1986, p. 316). He believed that policies could reduce the 'instability-enhancing power of corporations': Some of the policies he advanced were elimination of the corporate income tax, which leads to a bias in favor of debt-financing over equity financing, and policies that would favor employment of labor over investment in physical capital (such as elimination of the payroll tax on employers). Minsky also argued that governments should put less reliance on policies that favor 'bigness'—as discussed in the next section.

4.4 Market power

Countercyclical government deficits maintain profit flows, allowing firms to validate debt commitments even when private investment spending falls. Minsky saw no alternative to such behavior on an aggregate level (Minsky, 1986,

p. 332). However, it is essential that individual firms and banks are allowed to fail, otherwise there is no market discipline. In Minsky's view, the primary incentive to obtaining market power is the ability to set prices at a sufficient level to service debt. In the small government form of capitalism, collusion and government policy may be warranted to try to maintain prices in conditions of low demand. However, in big-government capitalism, where government deficits maintain profits, 'there is no need for policy to foster market power that protects profits' (Minsky, 1986, p. 318). Indeed, Minsky feared that conditions favoring large monopolies could be detrimental because they would lead to firms that are 'too big to fail'. Thus, he favored policies that would reduce the incentives to 'bigness'; in particular, he believed that policies that favored medium-sized banks would also favor medium sized firms, as bank size determines, to a large extent, the size of customers—big banks serve big customers, while medium-sized banks serve medium-sized customers. 'A decentralized banking system with many small and independent banks is conducive to an industrial structure made up of mainly small and medium-size firms' (Minsky, 1986, p. 319). Policies that would promote such a system include elimination of much of the segmentation of activities such as commercial banking and investment banking (at least for small-to-medium size banks so they could provide a wide range of services to their small-to-medium size customers), uniform and high capital-to-asset ratios (this would favor smaller banks as these typically have higher ratios), and freer entry.

Minsky also argued that 'industrial policy' could not only favor smaller firms, but could also favor employment over capital-intensive production techniques. Smaller firms tend to use more labor-intensive techniques merely because their ability to finance positions in long-lived and expensive capital assets is lower. He also favored regulation and government intervention into specific markets wherever these would promote competition. While he agreed with orthodoxy that 'competitive markets are devices to promote efficiency', he went on to note that 'The market is an adequate regulator of products and processes except when market power or externalities exist; once they exist— whether caused by the government or by market processes—regulation can be necessary to constrain the exercise of power' (Minsky, 1986, p. 329). Thus, 'An industrial policy that takes the form of promoting competitive industry, facilitating financing and aiding and abetting the development of a labor force that is trained and productive, is highly desirable' (Minsky, 1986, p. 329). Note, by the way, that he credited his teacher, Henry Simons, for this insight. He also saw industrial policy as a viable alternative to anti-trust prosecution, which he believed to be a failure precisely because it cannot create the conditions required to permit smaller firms to prosper.

Finally, Minsky admitted that these policies would have negative impacts on many mega-corps which would find that in the new environment they would be unable to service debt. He abhorred government bail-outs of Lockheed, Chrysler and some electric utilities; he would later criticize the Saving and Loan bail-out. Instead, he favored 'socialization of industries that require financial restructuring' through a 'government refinancing corporation', later, he would specifically advocate creation of such an organization to handle the savings and loan fiasco, modeled on the Reconstruction Finance Corporation (RFC) of the 1930s.

5 Minsky's work at the Jerome Levy Economics Institute

After taking his post at the Jerome Levy Economics Institute, Minsky continued, and indeed intensified, his efforts to formulate policy relevant for the institutions of modern capitalism. In particular, he emphasized that (a) capitalism is dynamic; (b) the 1930s reforms are no longer appropriate to the existing form of capitalism (dubbed 'money manager capitalism'); (c) the current conventional wisdom that 'free markets' promote stability is flawed and dangerous; and (d) new policies are required to reduce insecurity, promote stability, and encourage democracy. These concerns led to proposals regarding bank regulation, community development banking, tax reform, unemployment and poverty, and the introduction of institutions rather than markets to the formerly socialist states. We first examine his view that capitalism is dynamic. Then we address the policy reforms appropriate for the new forms of capitalism. Finally we examine the specific policies he advocated.

5.1 Varieties of capitalism

According to Minsky, capitalism comes in many forms: 'The Heinz Company... used to have a slogan "57 varieties" [and] I used to say that there are as many varieties of capitalism as Heinz has pickles...' (Minsky, 1991b, p. 10). To a great extent, these different forms of capitalism result from different financial arrangements. 'Capitalism is a dynamic, evolving system that comes in many forms. Nowhere is this dynamism more evident than in its financial structure...'. (Minsky & Whalen, 1996, pp. 2–3). 'There have been many different financial structures throughout history. These financial systems differ in how they affect economic efficiency and stability as well as the distribution of power in the economy' (Minsky, 1991b, p. 5).

After WWII, capitalism in the US took the form that Minsky labeled 'paternalistic capitalism' which could be characterized as a relatively high-consumption, big government, and big union form of capitalism that largely resulted from postwar reforms, institutions, and interventions that constrained instability in the financial system. Important interventions included countercyclical fiscal policy, 'low interest rates and interventions by the Federal Reserve', deposit insurance, 'establishment of a temporary, national investment bank (the Reconstruction Finance Corporation) to infuse government equity into transportation, industry and finance', and 'interventions by specialized organizations' (Minsky & Whalen, 1996, p. 3).

Relatively stable growth and the absence of debt deflation allowed the development of huge portfolios of financial instruments—representing accumulated pensions, distributed profits, personal financial wealth, and retained earnings. In addition, as discussed above, speculative finance increasingly replaced hedge finance—creating a demand for the accumulated financial wealth. As a result, a new form of capitalism emerged. 'Capitalism in the United States is now in a new stage, *money manager* capitalism, in which the proximate owners of a vast proportion of financial instruments are mutual and pension funds' (Minsky, 1996, p. 3). The values of portfolios are daily 'marked to market', forcing a 'short view' on managers, who have 'become increasingly sensitive to the stock market valuation of their firm', and thereby greatly increasing uncertainty (Minsky & Whalen, 1996, p. 5).

> When one considers the pressures due to both the rapidly evolving financial system and the economy's other structural changes, it is no surprise that economic insecurity is widespread. With the passing of the paternalistic financial structure, *corporate* paternalism has also faded. Workers at nearly all levels are insecure, as entire divisions are bought and sold and as corporate boards exhibit a chronic need to downsize overhead and to seek out the least expensive set of variable inputs.
>
> (Minsky & Whalen, 1996, pp. 5–6)

This new form of capitalism not only tends toward financial instability—as evidenced by increasingly frequent and severe financial crises—but has also eliminated the expectation and even the hope of rising living standards for most Americans.

5.2 Policy must be reformulated

'Sixty years ago capitalism was a failed economic order.... The capitalism that failed over 1929–33 was a small government, constrained central bank essentially laissez-faire economy. The capitalism that had a good run after the second world war was a big government interventionist economy with central banks that were less constrained than during the inter war years' (Minsky, 1993, pp. 2, 19). 'While the capitalisms of the United States and Western Europe were truly successful societies during the first two and a half decades after the second world war, their performance over the last decade and a half falls short...The successful capitalisms of the 1950s through the 1970s were not the same as the capitalisms that failed in the 1930s' (Minsky, 1993, pp. 2–3). 'If capitalisms are to be successful in the 21st century they are likely to be quite different from the models we are familiar with' (Minsky, 1993, p. 7).

Thus, 'Economies evolve, and so too must economic policy' (Minsky & Whalen, 1996, p. 8). Existing policies are no longer adequate to deal with the new form of capitalism—a conclusion reached even by orthodox economists. However, because orthodoxy ignores institutional detail, its policy recommendations are dangerous. In his view, much of the current debate over policy is driven by a misunderstanding of the way in which an economy with modern capitalist institutions functions. That is, most proposals are based on the belief that a market economy is basically stable, that 'markets *always* lead to the promotion of the public welfare', and that 'financial crises and deep depressions arise from one of the following: non-essential institutional flaws which prevent the market from working its wonders, the system of intervention contains openings which allow some dirty rotten scoundrels to operate, or external shocks dislodge the economy' (Minsky, 1991a, p. 5). In contrast, 'The Keynesian view leads to the proposition that the natural laws of development of capitalist economies leads to the emergence of conditions conducive to financial instability' (Minsky, 1991a, pp. 5–6). Minsky argued

> Over the past dozen or so years the 1933–1937 model has shown its age. Although it has not broken down as completely as the older laissez-faire model had over the 1929–33 period, quite clearly our current model of capitalism needs to be at least thoroughly overhauled if not replaced. Whether he realizes it or not, the historic task of President Clinton is to discover and put in place a new model capitalism.
>
> (Minsky, 1993, p. 1)

A number of problems with the new form of capitalism have been exposed. First, regulatory agencies have lost their power—partly due to the deregulation movement, but also due to private innovations that circumvent existing power. Second, the Social Security system was never adjusted for the enormous increase in life expectancy over the post-war period. Third, the existing welfare system locks poor families into a pattern of dependency. Fourth, employment security has eroded as the US abandoned its commitment to nearly full employment (Minsky, 1993).

While the reforms of the 1930s served the economy well for decades, institutional change and the evolution to a fragile system have made many of these outdated; what is needed 'is to put a financial structure in place which is conducive to doing the capital development well' (Minsky, 1991a, p. 27). Minsky argued 'Because some institutions, such as deposit insurance, the savings and loan industry, and a number of the great private banks, that served the economy well during the first two generations after the great depression, seem to have broken down, the need to reform and to reconstitute the financial structure is now on the legislative agenda' (Minsky, 1991a, p. 3). Quick 'policy fixes', however, such as a shift from government-insured bank deposits to private insurance will not do; these assume that market forces are inherently stabilizing, thus, all that is needed is to increase reliance on them. Rather, thorough-going reform is required, and no reform can be adopted and then left in place without continual revision that adapts to changing conditions.

5.3 *Promotion of stability, security and democracy*

Thus, while 'The New Deal restructuring of capitalism created institutions which contained uncertainty...[t]he evolution of the economy has decreased the effectiveness of the New Deal reforms and money manager capitalism has radically increased uncertainty. The creation of new economic institutions which constrain the impact of uncertainty is necessary' (Minsky, 1996, p. 4). 'The aim of policy is to assure that the economic prerequisites for sustaining the civil and civilized standards of an open liberal society exist. If amplified, uncertainty and extremes in income maldistribution and social inequalities attenuate the economic underpinnings of democracy, then the market behavior that creates these conditions has to be constrained' (Minsky, 1996, p. 15). He advocated a number of policies that he believed could reduce uncertainty while enhancing stability and democracy in the money manager form of capitalism—support for stronger trade unions; tax incentives to lead firms to offer family-friendly benefits and work arrangements; universal provision of high level health care and education services; full employment, which requires a larger and more innovative government sector; an enhanced minimum wage; an expanded Earned Income Tax Credit; portable pensions; institutional innovations to constrain money managers; a value added tax as a 'backdoor' tariff and export subsidy; and a network of community development banks (Minsky, 1996; Minsky & Whalen, 1996).

Minsky rejected the orthodox belief that government intervention designed to reduce insecurity must necessarily reduce efficiency by providing improper incentives. Indeed, he argued that policies to reduce insecurity can actually increase efficiency by creating the confidence necessary to engage in long-range planning. Similarly, he argued that workers can choose costly and long-term investments in self-improvement if there is a sufficient degree of secure employment at the end of the road. He believed that public–private partnerships are needed to promote science and technological advancement. Public infrastructure investment, aided by capital budgeting, is required not only to increase public and private 'efficiency' but also to increase the supply of public goods.

Minsky also proposed a number of reforms in the financial arena. These included additional Federal Reserve policies to encourage that credit be directed toward socially desirable activities; and a more secure and prosperous international finance system, including stable exchange rates and an international lender of last resort (Minsky, 1992a; Minsky & Whalen, 1996, p. 16). Minsky was always concerned with creating an environment to support financial institutions that would encourage the capital development of the economy in appropriate ways, including greater socialization of investment through such policies as using dedicated taxes for infrastructure development, capital budgeting, development banks, government holding companies, and greater reliance on government-operated fee-for-service infrastructure (Minsky, 1992b, pp. 24–25). He also argued 'Community banks are at the heart of a financial structure that will be biased towards resource creation' (Minsky, 1992b, p. 26). These would accept deposits and focus on mortgages and loans to local businesses, thereby encouraging local development (Minsky, 1992b, pp. 27–28).

Minsky also endorsed a version of 'narrow banking' that would separate 'the payments mechanism' from 'capital development'.[13] 'We are now in a position to realize the dual set-up of 100% money: financing the capital development of the economy by contingent-valued liabilities such as mutual funds, and a payments mechanism that is based upon a portfolio of government bonds that is held by the authority responsible for the payment system' (Minsky, 1994, p. 21). Deposit insurance would not be extended to the contingent-valued liabilities and would not be necessary for the payments mechanism backed by government bonds. This would reduce or eliminate the concern that federal deposit insurance encourages risk-taking by commercial banks. These would be free to finance commercial enterprise, but could not do so on the basis of government-insured liabilities. A 'safe and secure means of payments' would be provided while at the same time much of the functional segmentation of banking could be eliminated. Commercial banks would be permitted to engage in a wider range of activity, including activities that had been restricted to investment banking (although these restrictions are rapidly being removed). Banks would use the mutual funds financing technique to finance a variety of activities, with firewalls in place so that each 'mutual fund' issued by a bank would be linked to a particular activity that was financed. In this way, the returns to each fund would be related to a 'tranche' in the portfolio, varying by the degree of risk (Minsky, 1994, pp. 18–21).

Minsky helped to develop the Levy Institute's proposal to establish a nationwide system of community development banks. This was also linked to Minsky's belief that public policy should encourage creation of small-to-medium size firms. The Community Development Banks would finance small, local 'deals': 'Because it is in the public interest to foster the creation of new entrants into industry, trade, and finance, it is also in the public interest to have a set of strong, independent, profit-seeking banking institutions that specialize in financing smaller businesses' (Minsky *et al.,* 1993, p. 9). Further, as discussed, Minsky frequently advocated public equity investment; the Community Development Banks would be established with government capital infusions that would be gradually retired as they became profitable and accumulated private equity. Again, this followed the RFC model. The Community Development Banks would combine commercial banking, narrow banking, investment banking, and trust banking in a small, community-based bank that could offer a wide range of services to the community.

Minsky also turned his analysis of the sorts of financial institutions and arrangements that would be consistent with money manager capitalism toward an examination of alternatives facing the formerly socialist states. In his analysis of transitional economies (formerly socialist economies supposedly on the way to becoming market economies) Minsky (1991b, p. 1) argued 'The purported intent of achieving a market economy is not a clear directive. Because there are many varieties of market economies, the concept is not precise'. Further, 'It almost seems self-evident that the so-called planned economies were not in any sense planned' as they never considered 'interdependent relations in production and consumption' as well as the 'conditions of the labor force' or the 'environmental impact' of their decisions (Minsky, 1991b, p. 1). Minsky thus rejected both aspects of the conventional approach, as he denied that these states were moving away from a planned form and also denied they were moving toward a free market form.

Given the absence of private wealth and financial markets in these economies, both of which are essential to the functioning of modern capitalism, 'Questions of how to create legitimate titles need to be addressed in discussions of the transformation...' 'The lesson from history is that the privatization of the public domain should be done very carefully...' (Minsky, 1991b, p. 3). In the absence of private wealth and in the absence of a history of profits for the publicly held capital assets, privatization would be particularly difficult—even if the assets could be sold, there would be no basis on which to value them. Thus, Minsky advocated the creation of public holding companies which would temporarily hold assets until 'markets become thick enough to absorb them'. Initially the government would hold the shares and the holding company would direct the subsidiaries to operate 'for profit'; as private wealth is accumulated (in savings, pension funds, mutual funds), and as a record of profitability is generated, government ownership is replaced by private ownership. 'The public holding company is to be considered as a transitional device. The model is the previously mentioned Reconstruction Finance Corporation...' (Minsky, 1991b, p. 20). In Minsky's scheme. 'The pace of privatization is ruled by the rate at which enterprises begin to generate believable profit flows and the rate at which the market for equity assets grows...' (Minsky, 1991b, p. 21). The transition would be long, and can be contrasted with the market shock approach that was actually adopted in many countries without regard for the institutions that actually existed. Minsky's approach would have taken into account existing institutions, or lack thereof, and would thereby have avoided much of the pain caused by the market shock approach, which ignored institutions. Further, Minsky's proposal would have encouraged decentralization of power and widespread ownership. This stands in stark contrast to orthodox approaches, which forced premature sales, before prices could be established for capital assets, and before private wealth was generated. The end result was that a few players were able to buy assets at firesale prices. These are the people who will dominate these economies in the future.

6 Conclusions

Minsky always insisted that theory must be institution-specific. Because there are a variety of possible types of economies, and even '57 varieties' of capitalism, theory must be appropriate to the specific economy under analysis. His analysis concerned an evolving, developed, big-government capitalist economy with complex and long-lived financial arrangements. His policy recommendations were designed to promote a successful, democratic form of capitalism given these financial arrangements. These policies would have to constrain instability through creation of institutional ceilings and floors while at the same time they would have to address the behavioral changes induced by reduction of instability. The policies would also have to promote rising living standards, expansion of democratic principles, and enhancement of security for the average household. Thus, his proposals go far beyond the 'invisible handwaves' of free market idealogues, but also well beyond the macroeconomic tinkering normally associated with Keynesian Economics. Minksy also took into consideration the institutional change necessary to promote the sort of society he desired. In this sense, we think it is accurate to claim that Minsky successfully integrated 'Post' (or, better, 'financial') Keynesian theory with an institutionalist appreciation for the varieties of past, current, and feasible future economic arrangements.

Notes

1 Minsky seems to have produced relatively more students during his few years at Berkeley than he produced during his long tenure at Washington University. Perhaps this was somewhat intentional, for he later said that part of the reason he moved to St Louis was to obtain more time for his research in a relaxed atmosphere. One of the authors (Wray) notes that Minsky was very tough (at least on first year *graduate* students; he was notoriously soft-hearted when it came to undergraduates) at Washington University. Students could expect that their papers would be returned 'on the wing' as Minsky tossed the paper at the student while proclaiming that the paper was hopelessly confused and unacceptable. Many graduate students were said to be 'ABM' (all but Minsky), having completed all course work and exams (and even, in at least one case, having completed the dissertation!), but having failed to deliver an acceptable term paper to Minsky (his criterion was that the paper should be 'publishable'). Only a very few, particularly persistent, students would make it to the next stage, when Minsky would take them 'under his wing' and treat them almost like family members. In any case, Minsky was probably unusual in that most of those who would consider themselves to be students of Minsky in the intellectual sense were not students in the more formal sense; and, indeed, his influence on some of his formal students (for example, Hall and Sargent) is not readily apparent. (However, it should be noted that Minsky did claim these wayward students and always held out hope that some day their conversion would be complete. During his final weeks he was quite convinced that Sargent was undergoing such a transformation.)

2 See, for example, King (1996), who argues that Minsky only gradually became a Minskian; Lavoie (1985, 1992) argues that at least some of Minsky's work (including the financial instability hypothesis as well as his early work that concluded the credit supply curve is upward sloping with respect to the interest rate) borders on neoclassical loanable funds theory.

3 This was treated as a velocity-interest rate relation: as interest rates rise, velocity tends to rise; however, innovations can shift the curve out so that velocity can increase even without an increase of interest rates. For monetary policy to be effective in slowing an expansion, it would have to decrease reserves so much that it would compensate for the rising velocity that would result from the tight policy (both due to rising interest rates and due to innovations).

4 He noted, by the way, that 'Case D of course is similar to the existing monetary system' (Minsky, 1957b, p. 863).

5 He concluded, like Keynes, that '[t]here does not seem to be any endogenous factor which would lead to a fall in liquidity preference on a downswing. Changes in liquidity preference seem to be destabilizing' (Minsky, 1957b, p. 882).

6 Although published in 1975, this book was finished in 1972.

7 See, for example, Minsky (1980), which explicitly incorporates the Kalecki equation into his 'financial theory of investment', arguing that 'The fundamental vision in this argument is that private employment is determined by profit opportunities. The

aggregate profit opportunities in the economy are in the skeletal and essential analysis determined by investment and the government deficit' (Minsky, 1980 [1982], p. 40).

8 See, for example, Minsky (1995).

9 We will also abandon any attempt to present his development of the financial instability hypothesis in a chronological fashion, but will present the theory at a mature stage of development. Interested readers should look at some of the earlier pieces, including Minsky (1963a, 1972, 1978, 1980 [1982]).

10 We can see how the financial instability hypothesis continued his early analysis and rejected the Harvard Keynesian analysis. In contrast to the conventional multiplier-accelerator analysis, Minsky concluded that the free market system is subject to explosive oscillation because growth over the cycle changed behavioral parameters in a way that promotes instability. However, imposition of institutional floors and ceilings can maintain a semblance of stability.

11 Of course, balance sheet simplifications still occur, but 'simplification' at one institution is not normally allowed to spread to others. The Savings and Loan fiasco and bail-out is an example of a rather massive simplification of balance sheets as assets were written-down and liabilities written-off.

12 Note the connection to his earlier (1957b, 1959) articles.

13 See Phillips (1995) for a detailed examination of the narrow banking plan.

References

Fazzari, S. & Papadimitriou, D.B. (1992) *Financial Conditions and Macroeconomic Performance: Essays in Honor of Hyman P. Minsky* (Armonk, NY, M.E. Sharpe).

King, John E. (1996) Hyman Minsky: the making of a post Keynesian, in: S. Pressman (Ed.) *Interactions in Political Economy: Malvern After Ten Years,* pp. 61–73 (London and New York, Routledge).

Lavoie, M. (1985) Credit and money: the dynamic circuit, overdraft economics, and post Keynesian economics, in: M. Jarsulic (Ed.) *Money and Macro Policy,* p. 63 (Boston and Dordrecht, Kluwer-Nijhoff Publishing).

Lavoie, M. (1992) *Foundations of Post-Keynesian Analysis* (Aldershot, Edward Elgar).

Minsky, H.P. (1957a) Central banking and money market changes, *The Quarterly Journal of Economics,* 71, pp. 171–187.

Minsky, H.P. (1957b) Monetary systems and accelerator models, *American Economic Review,* 47, pp. 859–883.

Minsky, H.P. (1959) A linear model of cyclical growth, *Review of Economics and Statistics,* 41, pp. 133–145.

Minsky, H.P. (1963a) Can 'It' Happen Again?, in: D. Carson (Ed.) *Banking and Monetary Studies,* pp. 101–111 (Homewood, Illinois, R.D. Irwin).

Minsky, H.P. (1963b) Comment on Friedman and Schwartz's money and business cycles, *Review of Economics and Statistics,* 45 (supplement), pp. 64–72.

Minsky, H.P. (1972) Financial instability revisited: the economics of disaster, *Fundamental Reappraisal of the Federal Reserve Discount Mechanism,* Board of Governors, Federal Reserve System.

Minsky, H.P. (1975) *John Maynard Keynes* (New York, Columbia University Press).

Minsky, H.P. (1978) The financial instability hypothesis: a restatement, *Thames Papers in Political Economy,* North East London Polytechnic.

Minsky, H.P. (1980) Finance and profits: the changing nature of American business cycles, *The Business Cycle and Public Policy, 1929–1980,* Joint Economic Committee,

Congress of the United States, U.S. Government Printing Office, Washington, DC. [Reprinted in *Can It Happen Again?*, M.E. Sharpe, 1982.]

Minsky, H.P. (1986) *Stabilizing an Unstable Economy* (New Haven, Yale University Press).

Minsky, H.P. (1991a) Financial crises: systemic or idiosyncratic, Working Paper #51, The Jerome Levy Economics Institute of Bard College, April.

Minsky, H.P. (1991b) The transition to a market economy, Working Paper #66, The Jerome Levy Economics Institute of Bard College, November.

Minsky, H.P. (1992a) Reconstituting the United States' financial structure: some fundamental Issues. Working Paper #69, The Jerome Levy Economics Institute of Bard College, January.

Minsky, H.P. (1992b) The capital development of the economy and the structure of financial *institutions*, Working Paper #72, The Jerome Levy Economics Institute of Bard College, January.

Minsky, H.P. (1992c) The financial instability hypothesis, Working Paper #74, The Jerome Levy Economics Institute of Bard College, May.

Minsky, H.P. (1992d) Profits, deficits and instability: a policy discussion, in: D.B. Papadimitriou (Ed.) *Profits, Deficits and Instability* (New York, St Martin's Press).

Minsky, H.P. (1993) Finance and stability: the limits of capitalism. Working Paper #93, The Jerome Levy Economics Institute of Bard College, May.

Minsky, H.P. (1994) Financial instability and the decline (?) of banking: public policy implications. Working Paper #127, The Jerome Levy Economics Institute of Bard College, October.

Minsky, H.P. (1995) Financial factors in the economics of capitalism, *Journal of Financial Services Research*, 9, pp. 197–208.

Minsky, H.P. (1996) Uncertainty and the institutional structure of capitalist economies. Working Paper #155, The Jerome Levy Economics Institute of Bard College, April.

Minsky, H.P. & Ferri, P. (1991) Market processes and thwarting systems. Working Paper #64, The Jerome Levy Economics Institute of Bard College, November.

Minsky, H.P. & Whalen, C. (1996) Economic insecurity and the institutional prerequisites for successful capitalism. Working Paper #165, The Jerome Levy Economics Institute of Bard College, May.

Minsky, H.P., Delli Gatti, D. & Gallegati, M. (1994) Financial institutions, economic policy, and the dynamic behavior of the economy. Working Paper #126, The Jerome Levy Economics Institute of Bard College, October.

Minsky, H.P., Papadimitriou, D.B., Phillips, R.J. & Randall Wray, L. (1993) *Community Development Banking: A Proposal to Establish a Nationwide System of Community Development Banks* (Annandale-on-Hudson, NY, The Jerome Levy Economics Institute of Bard College). Public Policy Brief No. 3.

Papadimitriou, D.B. (1992) Minsky on himself, in: S. Fazzari & D.B. Papadimitriou (Eds) *Financial Conditions and Macroeconomic Performance: Essays in Honor of Hyman P. Minsky*, pp. 13–26 (Armonk, NY, M.E. Sharpe).

Phillips, R.J. (1995) *The Chicago Plan and New Deal Banking Reform* (Armonk, NY, M.E. Sharpe).

Appendix: some of Minsky's important publications

Books

(1975) *John Maynard Keynes* (New York, Columbia University Press). (Translated into Italian, Spanish, German, and Japanese.)

(1982) *Can 'It' Happen Again* (Armonk, New York, M.E. Sharpe). Published in Great Britain as *Inflation, Recession and Economic Policy* (Brighton, Sussex, Weatsheaf). (Translated into Italian and Japanese.)

(1986) *Stabilizing an Unstable Economy* (New Haven and London, Yale University Press).

(2005) *Induced Investment and Business Cycles* (Cheltenham, UK, Edward Elgar)

Edited book

(1965) *California Banking in a Growing Economy* (Berkeley, California, Institute of Business and Economic Research).

Academic articles

(1957) Central banking and money market changes, *Quarterly Journal of Economics* 71, pp. 171–187.

(1959) A linear model of cyclical growth, *Review of Economics and Statistics,* 61, pp. 135–145. (Reprinted in Gordon & Klein (Eds), *AEA Readings in Business Cycles,* 10, pp. 79–99 (Homewood, Illinois, R.D. Irwin).)

(1961) Employment growth and price levels: a review article, *Review of Economics and Statistics,* 42, pp. 1–12.

(1962) Financial constraints upon decisions, an aggregate view, *Proceedings of the American Statistical Association,* pp. 256–257.

(1963) Comment on Friedman and Schwartz, *Money and Business Cycles, Review of Economics and Statistics Supplement,* pp. 64–72.

(1963) Can 'It' Happen Again?, in: D. Carson (Ed.) *Banking and Monetary Studies,* pp. 101–111 (Homewood, Illinois, R.D. Irwin).

(1964) Longer waves in financial relations: financial factors in the more severe depressions, *American Economic Association Papers and Proceedings,* 54, pp. 324–332.

(1965) The integration of simple growth and cycle models, in: M.J. Brennan (Ed.) *Patterns of Market Behavior, Essays in Honor of Philip Taft,* pp. 175–192 (Providence, Rhode Island, Brown University Press).

(1965) The role of employment policy, in: M.S. Gordon (Ed.) *Poverty in America,* pp. 175–200 (San Francisco, Chandler Publishing).

(1969) Private sector asset management and the effectiveness of monetary policy: theory and practice, *Journal of Finance,* 24, pp. 223–238.

(1972) Financial instability revisited: the economics of disaster, *Fundamental Reappraisal of The Federal Reserve Discount Mechanism* (Washington, Board of Governors, Federal Reserve System).

(1972) An evaluation of recent monetary policy, *Nebraska Journal of Economics and Business,* 11, pp. 37–56.

(1973) The strategy of economic policy and income distribution, *Annals of the American Academy of Political and Social Science,* 409, pp. 92–101.

(1977) A theory of systemic fragility, in: E.D. Altman & A.W. Sametz (Eds), *Financial Crisis*, pp. 138–152.

(1977) How 'standard' is standard economics? *Society*, 14, pp. 24–29.

(1977) The financial instability hypothesis: an interpretation of Keynes and an alternative to 'standard' theory, *Nebraska Journal of Economics and Business*, 16, pp. 5–16. (Reprinted in *Challenge*, 20 (March/April).)

(1977) An 'economics of Keynes' perspective on money, in: S. Weintraub (Ed.) *Modern Economic Thought*, pp. 295–307 (Philadelphia, University of Pennsylvania Press).

(1978) Carter economics: a symposium, *Journal of Post Keynesian Economics*, 1, pp. 42–45.

(1978) The financial instability hypothesis: a restatement, *Thames Papers in Political Economy*, North East London Polytechnic. (Reprinted in P. Arestis & T. Skouras (Eds) (1985) *Post Keynesian Economic Theory* (Armonk, New York, M.E. Sharpe).)

(1979) Financial interrelations, the balance of payments and the dollar crisis, in: J.D. Aronson (Ed.) *Debt and the Less Developed Countries*, pp. 103–122 (Boulder, Colorado, West-view Press).

(1980) The federal reserve: between a rock and a hard place, *Challenge*, 23, pp. 30–36.

(1980) Finance and profits: the changing nature of American business cycles, *The Business Cycle and Public Policy 1929–80: a compendium of papers submitted to the Joint Economic Committee*. Congress of the United States, 96th Congress, 2nd Session, pp. 230–244 (Washington D.C., US Government Printing Office).

(1980) Capitalist financial processes and the instability of capitalism, *Journal of Economic Issues*, 14, pp. 505–522. (Translated as 'Los Procesos Financiers Capitalist as Y La Inestabilidad Del Capitalism', *Investigation Economics*, 167, enero marzo del, 1984, pp. 199–218.)

(1980) Money, financial markets and the coherence of a market economy, *Journal of Post-Keynesian Economics*, 3, pp. 21–31.

(1981) Financial markets and economic instability, 1965–1980, *Nebraska Journal of Economics and Business*, 20, pp. 5–16.

(1982) The financial-instability hypothesis: capitalist processes and the behavior of the economy, in: C.P. Kindleberger & J.-P. Laffargue (Eds) *Financial Crisis, Theory, History and Policy*, pp. 13–38 (New York, Cambridge University Press).

(1982) Can 'It' happen again? a reprise, *Challenge*, 25, pp. 5–13.

(1982) Debt deflation processes in today's institutional environment, *Banca Nazionale Del Lavoro Quarterly Review* (December), pp. 375–395.

(1983) Pitfalls due to financial fragility, in: S. Weintraub & M. Goldstein (Eds) *Reaganomics in the Stagflation Economy*, pp. 104–119 (Philadelphia, University of Pennsylvania Press).

(1983) The Legacy of Keynes, *Metroeconomica*, 35, pp. 87–103.

(1983) Institutional roots of American inflation, in: N. Schmokler & E. Marcus (Eds) *Inflation Through the Ages Economic, Social Psychological and Historical Aspects*, pp. 265–277 (New York, Social Science Monographs, Brooklyn College Press) (distributed by Columbia University Press).

(1984) Domestic monetary policy: if not monetarism, what?' *Journal of Economic Issues*, 18, pp. 101–116. (Reprinted in M. Tool (Ed.) *An Institutional Guide to Economics and Public Policy* (1984), pp. 101–106 (New York, M.E. Sharpe) (with S. Fazzari).)

(1984) Prices, employment and profits, *Journal of Post Keynesian Economics*, 6, pp. 489–498 (with P. Ferri).

(1984) Banking and industry between the two wars: the United States, *The Journal of European Economics History*, 13 (special issue), pp. 235–272.

(1985) Money and the lender of last resort, *Challenge,* 28, pp. 12–19.

(1985) Beginnings, *Banca Nazionale del Lavoro Quarterly Review* (September), pp. 211–221.

(1985) An introduction to post-Keynesian economics, *Economic Forum,* 15(2), pp. 1–13.

(1986) The evolution of financial institutions and the performance of the economy, *Journal of Economic Issues,* 20, pp. 345–353.

(1986) Money and crisis in Schumpeter and Keynes, in: H.S. Jagenmer & J.W. Drukker (Eds), *The Economic Law of Motion of Modern Society: a Marx-Keynes-Schumpeter centennial,* pp. 112–122 (Cambridge, Cambridge University Press).

(1986) Conflict and interdependence in a multipolar world', *Studies in Banking and Finance,* pp. 3–22 (Amsterdam, The Netherlands, North-Holland Publishing).

(1986) The crisis of 1983 and the prospects for advanced capitalist economics, in: W. Helburn & D.F. Bramhill (Eds) *Marx, Schumpeter and Keynes: a centenary celebration of dissent,* pp. 284–296 (Armonk, New York, and London, M.E. Sharpe).

(1989) The Macroeconomic safety net: does it need to be improved?, in: H.P. Gray (Ed.) *The Modern International Environment, Research in Business and Finance,* pp. 17–27 (Greenwich, Conn, JAI Press).

(1989) Financial structures: indebtedness and credit, in: A. Barrere (Ed.) *Money Credit and Prices in a Keynesian Perspective: Proceedings of a Conference held at the University of Paris I Pantheon Sorbonne,* pp. 49–70 (New York, St Martin's Press).

(1990) Sraffa and Keynes: effective demand in the long run, in: K. Bharadwaj & B. Schefold (Eds), *Essays on Piero Sraffa: critical perspectives on the revival of classical thinking,* pp. 362–371 (London, Routledge).

(1990) Schumpeter and Keynes, in: A. Heertje & M. Perlman (Eds) *Evolving Technology and Market Structures: Studies in Schumpeterian Economics,* pp. 51–74 (Ann Arbor, Michigan, The University of Michigan Press).

(1990) Money manager capitalism, fiscal independence and international monetary reconstruction, in: M. Szabo-Pelsoczi (Ed.) *The Future of the Global Economy and Monetary System,* pp. 209–218 (Budapest, International Szirak Foundation).

(1991) The financial instability hypothesis: a clarification, in: M. Feldstein, *The Risk Of Economic Crisis,* pp. 158–166 (Chicago and London, University of Chicago Press).

(1992) Market processes and thwarting systems, *Structural Change and Economic Dynamics,* 3, pp. 79–91 (with P. Ferri).

(1992) The transition to a market economy: financial options, in: M. Szabo-Pelsoczi (Ed.) *The Future of The Global Economic and Monetary Systems with Particular Emphasis on Eastern European Developments,* pp. 107–122 (Budapest, International Szirak Foundation).

(1993) Schumpeter and finance, in: S. Biasco, A. Roncaglia & M. Salvati (Eds), *Market and Institutions in Economic Development: Essays in Honor of Paolo Sylos Labini,* pp. 103–115 (New York, St Martins Press; London, Macmillan Press).

(1993) Community development banks: an idea in search of substance, *Challenge,* 36 (March–April), pp. 33–41.

(1994) Financial instability hypothesis, in: P. Arestis & M. Sawyer, *Radical Political Economy,* pp. 153–158 (Aldershot, Edward Elgar).

(1995) Longer waves in financial relations: financial factors in the more severe depressions II, *Journal of Economic Issues,* 29(1), pp. 83–96.

(1995) The creation of a capitalist financial system, in: M. Szabo-Pelsoczi (Ed.) *The Global Monetary System after the Fall of the Soviet Empire,* pp. 153–170 (Aldershot and Brookfield, Avebury).

(1996) The essential characteristics of post-Keynesian economics, in: G. Deleplace &

E. Nell (Eds), *Money in Motion: the Post-Keynesian Calculation Approaches*, pp. 70–88 (New York, St Martin's Press).

(1996) Uncertainty and the institutional structure of capitalist economies, *Journal of Economic Issues*, 30, pp. 357–368.

Reviews

(1974) Paul Davidson's *Money and the Real World:* a review article, *Quarterly Review of Economics and Business*, 14, pp. 7–17.

(1981) Review of N. Kaldor: *Essays on Economic Stability and Growth*, 2nd edn, *Journal of Economic Literature*, 19, pp. 1574–1577.

(1981) James Tobin's *Asset Accumulation and Economic Activity:* a review article, *Eastern Economic Journal*, 7, pp. 199–209.

(1982) Review of Axel Leijonhufved: *Information and Coordination*, *Economic Journal*, 92, pp. 976–977.

(1983) Review of Wallace C. Peterson: *Our Overloaded Economy*, *Journal of Economic Issues*, 17, pp. 228–232.

(1984) Frank Hahn's *Money and Inflation:* a review article, *Journal of Post Keynesian Economics*, 6, pp. 449–457.

(1985) Review of Michael J. Piore & Charles F. Sahel: *The Second Industrial Divide*, *Challenge*, 28, pp. 60–64.

(1985) Review of Christian Saint-Etienne: *The Great Depression 1929–1938: Lessons for the 1980's*, *Journal of Economic Literature*, 23, pp. 1226–1227.

(1986) Review of Lester G. Thurow: *The Zero Sum Solution: Building a World Class American Economy*, *Challenge*, 29, pp. 60–64.

(1987) Bashing bigness—but with blinders, a review of Walter Adams & James W. Birch: *The Bigness Complex*, *Challenge*, 30, pp. 29–31.

(1987) Review of Forest Capie & Geoffrey Wood (Eds) *Financial Crises and the World Banking System*, *Journal of Economic Literature*, 25, pp. 1341–1342.

(1988) A review of S. Strange: *Casino Capitalism*, *Journal of Economic Literature*, 25, pp. 1883–1885.

(1988) A review article: *Secrets of the Temple: How the Federal Reserve Runs the Country*, by William Greider, *Challenge*, 31.

(1990) Review of Robert Heilbroner & Peter Bernstein: *The Debt and the Deficit: False Alarms/Real Possibilities*, *Journal of Economic Literature*, XXVIII, pp. 1221–1222.

4 The economic contributions of Amartya Sen

Steven Pressman and Gale Summerfield

'The Economic Contributions of Amartya Sen' by Steven Pressman and Gale Summerfield from *Review of Political Economy* (2000), Volume 12, Issue 1 (Taylor and Francis Ltd, http://www.informaworld.com), reprinted by permission of the publisher.

1 Introduction

In October 1998 the Royal Swedish Academy of Science shocked many people when it awarded the Nobel Prize in Economic Science to Amartya Sen. The very next day an op-ed article in the *Wall Street Journal* complained that the award was given to an "establishment leftist" with "muddleheaded views" (Pollack, 1998). Further griping about the selection of Sen soon appeared elsewhere (Richman, 1998). Some commentators even hinted that Sen really did not deserve a Nobel Prize, but was chosen because the Swedish Academy was embarrassed by Myron Scholes and Robert Merton, its 1997 choices (Coy, 1998). (Scholes and Merton were the brains behind Long-Term Capital Management, a hedge fund that nearly brought down the US financial system in the Fall of 1998; see Lowenstein, 2000.) Selecting Sen, who has emphasized the inter-relationships between economics and ethics, it was argued, became a sort of Nobel penance for the evils perpetrated by Scholes and Merton.

The surprise surrounding the choice of Sen was almost as pronounced as the criticism. For several decades the Nobel Prize in Economics had gone primarily to Chicago economists. Political economists, especially those with leanings to the left of center, have been conspicuously passed over. John Kenneth Galbraith, Nicholas Kaldor, Joan Robinson and Piero Sraffa were all denied Nobel accolades in their lifetimes. And neither Barbara Bergmann nor Luigi Pasinetti (just two conspicuous oversights) has yet to receive the Nobel Prize.

With the shock and the surprise came feelings of hope. By selecting Sen the Swedish Academy made a bold statement about how economics might be opened up and made more relevant. Sen has broadened economists' notion of human "well-being" so that it encompasses not just additional consumption but also developing human potential. Sen has also studied how development policies at times adversely affect women and has argued that economists who study economic development need to focus more on developing opportunities for people and less on maximizing the production of goods and services. And Sen has spent his career studying important real world problems such as famines, poverty and discrimination.

After a brief biographical note, this paper examines the major economic contributions of Sen. These contributions fall into three main areas: a philosophical critique of traditional economic assumptions, an attempt to build a more realistic economic science based on the notion of entitlements and human capabilities, and a long series of practical contributions to welfare economics that follow from the capabilities approach – how to better measure poverty and inequality, how to understand famine and hunger, the importance of gender in economic development, and the differences between economic development and economic growth. The paper concludes with a brief assessment of Sen's significance.

2 Sen, the man

Sen was born in the village of Santinikeran, a small town outside Calcutta, in West Bengal, India on November 3, 1933. He was named "Amartya", which means "one who deserves immortality", by Bengali poet and Nobel laureate Rabindranath Tagore.

Sen was born into a family of academics. His maternal grandfather, K.M. Sen, was a distinguished philosopher who taught the philosophy of religion and Hinduism at Viswa Bharati University in Shantiniketan (Basu, 1998). His father was a professor of chemistry at Dhaka University, which is now in Bangladesh. Despite their academic pedigree, the Sens were not well off financially. Sen has described his family as lower middle class. He also noted that it was "committed" when it came to social matters (Gaertner & Pattanaik, 1988).

As a nine-year-old boy, Sen lived through the Great Bengal Famine of 1943. During this time he handed out tins of rice to starving victims of the famine. Close to three million people died, even though adequate grain was available at the time. The problem was that despite the efforts of Sen and others, the grain was not being distributed in sufficient quantities to those desperately in need. Greater government intervention was necessary. Sen claims (Klamer, 1989, p. 136) this event had a prolonged and lasting effect on him, and that it sparked his interest in economic development as well as his study of famines beginning in the 1970s (but not published until the 1980s).

In 1951 Sen enrolled at Presidency College in Calcutta. He planned to study physics, but wound up studying ethics, political philosophy, and economics. Sen cited his great interest in these subjects, as well as the excellent economics faculty at Presidency College, as being the main reason for his eventual choice of fields (Gaertner & Pattanaik, 1988). In 1953, Sen received a BA degree in Economics from Presidency College, and then went to Trinity College at Cambridge University to continue his education. At Cambridge, Sen studied economics with Maurice Dobb, Joan Robinson and Piero Sraffa. Robinson supervised his doctoral dissertation (Sen, 1960a) along with Amiya Dasgupta, and attempted to move his research away from "ethical rubbish" and toward abstract theory (Klamer, 1989, p. 139). Dasgupta was more supportive of his interests in ethics and the philosophical foundations of economic theory.

One important intellectual influence on Sen during his Cambridge days was the discovery of Kenneth Arrow's *Social Choice and Individual Values*, which his friend and classmate Sukhamoy Chakravaarty suggested he read (see Sen 1993m). Sen immediately became intrigued by the impossibility theorem, and sought out his Cambridge professors to discuss it. Robinson thought the impossibility theorem was a waste of time, and feared that Sen would become enthralled with a worthless analytical puzzle. Sraffa was similarly skeptical of the value of studying Arrow; but unlike Robinson, he thought little harm would come to Sen from pursuing this line of scholarship. Indeed, Sraffa thought that studying the impossibility theorem would be no worse than studying any neoclassical economic theory. It was Dobb, and Dobb alone, who encouraged Sen to pursue his interest in the work of Arrow, and Dobb who spent time with Sen talking about the implications of Arrow's theorem for questions about resource allocation and issues of social and economic policy. These questions and issues were to become central to Sen's economic research. In many ways, Sen has spent his career trying to overcome the limitations imposed by the impossibility theorem on economic theory and policy.

Sen received a BA degree (in 1955) and a Ph.D. (in 1959) from Trinity College. While working on his doctoral dissertation, Sen taught for two years (1956–58) at Jadavpur University in Calcutta, and became chairperson of the Economics Department there at age 23. After graduating from Cambridge, he taught briefly at MIT (from 1960 to 1961) and Stanford (in 1961). From 1963 to 1971 Sen taught at the University of Delhi, but took leaves of absence to pursue visiting positions in the US. During the 1964–65 academic year, he taught at the University of California at Berkeley and during the 1968–69 academic year at Harvard.

In 1971 Sen returned to England after accepting a teaching position at the London School of Economics. Then in 1977 he moved to Nuffield College of Oxford University. Three years later he became Drummond Professor of Political Economy at All Souls College (Oxford University), a position previously held by Edgeworth and by Hicks. In 1988 Sen accepted a permanent position in the US, becoming Lamont University Professor of Economics and Philosophy at Harvard. Sen returned to England from 1998 to 2003, this time to become Master of Trinity College (Cambridge University). He then returned to his Harvard position.

Over his distinguished career, Sen has received many academic awards and honors. He holds more than 50 honorary doctorates and serves on the editorial board of 15 different journals. His scholarly output, likewise, has been enormous. The attached bibliography includes more than 25 books and more than 300 published articles. Sen has also presided over several leading economic associations. From 1980 to 1982 he was President of the Development Studies Association. He was President of the Econometric Society in 1984. From 1986 to

1989 he served as President of the International Economic Association, and in 1989 he served as President of the Indian Economic Association. In 1994 Sen served as President of the American Economic Association.

3 A philosophical critique of traditional welfare economics

The main theme in the work of Sen is the importance of developing human potential. According to Sen, economics should be about developing the capabilities of people by increasing the options available to them. This contrasts rather sharply with traditional economic concerns, such as trying to produce more goods more efficiently, and thereby maximizing utility. For this reason, Sen has been highly critical of traditional welfare economics, which holds that free exchange will maximize the well-being of rational individuals.

Traditional welfare economics begins with the rationality assumption. The heart of the rationality assumption is the belief that individuals are rational utility maximizers. All people are thought to behave in a highly rational and rigorously logical fashion. They attempt to figure out the consequences of every possible action they might take and the utility they can expect to receive as a result of each different act. Traditional economic analysis then argues that allowing people to act freely, and to exchange goods at will, leads to a Pareto Optimal outcome – a situation in which no one can be made better off without making someone else worse off.

Since a long tradition in philosophy and economics holds that interpersonal comparisons of utility cannot be made, most economists maintain that Pareto Optimal economic outcomes are the best we can do to promote human well-being. We cannot increase overall welfare by redistributing goods from one person to another because we cannot measure "utils" and then compare the utility of the two individuals. Any redistribution might take something away from someone who values it highly and give it to someone else who gains little extra benefit from it. Since it is impossible to measure individual utility, it is impossible to know that any redistribution actually improves economic well-being. This approach holds that all we can know is that letting people freely exchange goods whenever it serves their own interests will maximize individual welfare; indeed, the fact that some trade takes place proves that the exchange enhances the welfare of both individual traders.

Sen has criticized this approach to understanding human welfare on a number of grounds.

First, he contends that utility maximization provides a bad description of how people actually behave. To take just one example, individuals should expect to receive no gain from voting in political elections. The chance that my vote will decide the outcome of any election is minuscule. In fact, the likelihood of my getting struck by lightning while waiting on line to vote is greater than the probability that my vote will decide an election. Nonetheless, I regularly vote; and so do large numbers of other people.

Sen (1970b, p. 195) has argued that the utility maximization approach misses the real reason people go to polling places and vote. People vote because of a sense of commitment – a desire to record their preferences, to participate in free elections, and to be part of a democratic process. These important human desires get ignored by traditional economic analysis, which focuses only on the utility derived from things chosen, but not on the actual process of choosing. In fact, many human motivations get ignored in traditional economic analysis. Economics ignores traditional social concerns, it ignores interest in the well-being of future generations, and most important of all, it pays no attention to ethical issues (see Sen, 1987d).

Pressman (2006) has identified the important political implication of this analysis. Pocock (1971, 1975, 1981), following Aristotle, argues that democratic government depends on civic virtues. Moreover, the rise of civic humanism in Renaissance Florence was part of a process of individual development toward self-fulfillment. This required partaking in political and social decisions rather than focusing on individual knowledge and contemplation. From this perspective, voting is rational from a human point of view because the act of voting is a social act like providing for public goods or not starting a nuclear war. It is done because we follow conventions, norms, and have a sense of our ethical duty. Indeed, Blais (2000, Chapter 5) finds, after interviewing over 100 individuals, that a sense of duty was the main reason that 73 percent of them went to the polls and voted.

Sen (1977e, p. 333f.) has drawn out some of the important policy implications that follow from adopting a broader view of human behavior. People work hardest at their jobs *not* when financial rewards and penalties are the greatest, but when they have a sense of commitment and a belief that some important goal is being pursued. Going even further, Sen (1997g) claims that people do not work because they perform some economic calculation and find the value of goods that can be bought with their pay is more than the value of their lost leisure. People face limited flexibility in the number of hours per week that they can work. Furthermore, employment yields many benefits besides economic goods and services; it provides social contacts, skills and psychological well-being or self-esteem. It is for this reason that the unemployed experience greater health problems, higher suicide and mortality rates, and intense psychological agony. It is also for this reason that unemployment weakens family relationships and contributes to higher divorce rates.

A second criticism of traditional welfare analysis concerns the consequences that *would* follow from obeying the dictates of rational utility maximization. Sen argues that if people did actually behave according to the rationality assumption they would become laughingstocks, since acting selfishly can lead to some rather absurd results. The Prisoner's Dilemma provides one example of this absurdity (Sen 1987e, pp. 80ff.). Another example is described by Sen in his famous paper "Rational Fools": " 'Where is the railway station?' he asks me. 'There', I say pointing at the post office, 'and would you please post this letter for me on the way?' 'Yes' he says, determined to open the envelope and check whether it contains something valuable" (Sen, 1977e, p. 332). Left out of this interaction is any concern for other people, any notion of personal integrity, and any idea about the sort of person one wants to be or the sort of society one wants to live in. In brief, rational economic man is a consummate social moron.

By making all choices akin to what brand of cereal should be bought at the supermarket, economics ignores the social and interpersonal aspects involved in choosing and making decisions. Non-trivial choices are menu-dependent or positional, and both consistency in preferences and utility maximization in choice require some context. In the real world, Sen (1997i) has noted, people do not maximize utility for a given set of choices. I do not grab the last piece of dessert sitting on the dinner table. This is not because I do not want the dessert, or because eating the dessert would not give me a great deal of happiness. Rather, I do not grab the last piece because I care about how others think of me. This example shows that it is not just outcomes that contribute to well-being. Processes and human relationships are as important as outcomes; and these things get ignored in traditional economic thinking. Sympathy for others, commitments, and other social interdependencies, which economists exclude from their analysis and treat as "externalities", are all important in understanding human behavior and all important determinants of human well-being. They are what Adam Smith called "the moral sentiments". Bringing these things back into economic analysis broadens economics, makes it more realistic and relevant, and gives it a firmer theoretical foundation.

A third problem with traditional welfare economics concerns the assumptions that get made about preferences. Due to conditions of poverty or illness or tyranny, due to one's upbringing, or due to the traditions one has been exposed to and the customs one has developed, people may be limited in terms of how they think about their options and what utility they will expect to receive from certain acts. For example, people who do not receive schooling early in life may come to mistrust schooling and reject all personal choices that involve more education. As a result of adjusting to their present situation, they may not feel deprived because they lack elementary reading and writing skills.

In a famous passage in *Utilitarianism*, John Stuart Mill addresses this issue. He argues that "It is better to be a human being dissatisfied than a pig satisfied. Better to be Socrates dissatisfied than a fool satisfied" (Mill, 1957, p. 14). Mill thought this was a clever and cogent defense of utilitarianism. Sen has recognized that this is not a defense of utilitarianism at all, but a powerful counterexample to it. An uneducated fool cannot compare current satisfactions with the satisfactions that would arise from having studied philosophy. Only a trained philosopher could do this. Thus, the utility maximization assumption requires things from people that they cannot do – become someone else (someone whom they might become) and then decide if it is worth doing certain things to become that person.

Going even further, Sen (1985a, 1993l) notes that most economists have gotten the relationship between preferences and actions backwards. Preferences do *not* determine human actions. People do *not* value illiteracy and then decide not to learn how to read. Rather, people who cannot read adapt their preferences and devalue literacy. On the standard utilitarian doctrine, because individual preferences are valued more than anything else, welfare is maximized when illiterate people are not encouraged to read. But for Sen, greater literacy would improve human welfare because it increases the opportunities available to people and enhances their capabilities.

Fourth, according to Sen, there are problems with the unit of analysis in standard welfare economics. Traditional theory assumes autonomous individuals and theorizes about how people behave. Yet, individuals willingly form themselves into families and households. The well-being of household members thus depends not just on aggregate household income, but also on how resources get divided up within the household. Outcomes may not be optimal whenever one family member controls most resources or controls the division of resources within the family (Sen, 1990c). In the real world such unequal power seems to be the rule rather than the exception.

Fifth, Sen (1985a) notes that many things provide utility and disutility that cannot be bought and sold in the market. A beautiful sunset, good friends, and a large family all yield utility; crime, pollution and social unrest all generate disutility. Traditional welfare economics fails to take any of these things into account. At best, they get called "externalities"; at worst, they get dismissed as unimportant. In either case, economic analysis ignores these important sources of human welfare. This limits the scope of economics and keeps welfare economics from dealing with human well-being writ large.

Traditional welfare economics goes wrong here because it has succumbed to a "fetishism of commodities." All that matters for traditional economic theory is the set of goods and services that can be consumed by an individual. But this omits what goods do for human beings. Some things (a quality education or a sustainable development plan) provide the ability to do things in the future, although they may provide little present utility. These goods have welfare and promote human well-being, but they get ignored by traditional welfare economics. "[W]hat people get out of goods depends on a variety of factors.... It seems reasonable to move away from a focus on goods as such to what goods do to human beings" (Sen, 1982a, p. 29f.).

Sixth, Sen (1985c, 1987e) has pointed out problems with using Pareto Optimality as a welfare criterion. He notes that outcomes can be Pareto Optimal, yet disastrous. For example, a case in which a few people are very rich and everyone else is starving would be Pareto Optimal, since the situation cannot be improved without taking income from the very wealthy and reducing their utility. However, the fact that many people are starving is obviously a highly undesirable outcome. Sen argues that making more resources available to individuals who are starving will improve overall well-being, even if some resources must be taken away from multi-millionaires and even if utilities cannot be directly compared. The fact that traditional welfare economics fails to arrive at this conclusion is both a major flaw and a severe limitation of this approach.

Seventh, Sen (1970c, 1976b) notes that utility maximization conflicts with traditional or classical liberalism – the belief that people should be able to do whatever they want so long as it does not keep others from doing what they want. If many people want pornography to be banned, utility maximization would require that pornography should be banned. Similarly, if a great many people prefer that everyone read pornographic novels, utility maximization demands that pornography be forced on people. Yet concern for liberty would allow each individual to make that decision.

It should be noted that Sen has not merely been a critic, taking pleasure in pointing out that the foundations of traditional welfare economics are shaky. His criticisms dovetail with his alternative view of economic welfare. And it is here that the Arrow impossibility theorem rears its ugly head and becomes a daunting challenge. Contrary to standard welfare economics, Sen has argued that economic and social policy can improve human well-being. The problem is that Arrow's results call into question any policy or strategy that might improve economic welfare by reducing economic and social inequalities. Any policy proposal or any approach could be easily dismissed as being arbitrary (a result of the order in which alternatives get presented for consideration) or dictatorial (the result of one person's preferences) by making reference to the impossibility theorem.

Sen has sought to counter this and to develop a positive and constructive set of rules for making social choices about important issues. He has argued for allowing interpersonal utility comparisons under certain circumstances, noting that we are all human and all make such comparisons regularly. He has also argued that partial comparisons can be made about what makes people better off and worse off without resorting to a comparison of mental states. And he has pointed to studies that use questionnaire data, spending patterns, and other informational inputs as a means of making such comparisons (Sen, 1994d, 1997f, 1999j). This literature attempts to provide empirical support to drawing conclusions about relative deprivation without resorting to the notion of individual utility. The heart of this positive approach to welfare economics has been the notion of capabilities.

4 Entitlements and capabilities

In his earliest attempts to move beyond utilitarian economics, Sen adopted the basic needs perspective. This approach, pioneered by development economist Paul Streeten (1979, 1981; Hicks & Streeten, 1979) in the late 1970s and early 1980s, draws attention to the sort of life people must live when their fundamental needs are not met. Without food, people will starve. Without health care and clean water, they will die young. Without adequate shelter and clothing, life will be brutish. The basic needs approach made it clear that per capita income is not useful because it ignores distributional issues, and just raising the incomes of poor people will not suffice to increase welfare. Rather, the issue was whether these incomes could (and would) be used to obtain basic necessities. Moreover, on the basic needs approach, it was important that *everyone* had access to the goods and services that satisfy their basic needs. This was regarded as a basic entitlement.

In the 1980s Sen sought to help develop and expand the basic needs approach. He started by distinguishing between production entitlements and exchange entitlements. Production entitlements stem from how a person produces goods and services. Small farmers have production entitlements to consume or sell what they grow; share croppers have rights to a proportion of whatever is produced; but regular laborers are only entitled to their wages and what they can purchase with it. In times of natural disaster, such as flood or drought, the wage earner is immediately vulnerable to a loss of income and will not be able to purchase many goods; however, the farmer and the share cropper typically both have direct access to food (Sen, 1981e; Drèze & Sen, 1989b).

Exchange entitlements are rights to control other commodities based on the ability to trade for them. Trading can be done either via barter or using the money received from helping to produce goods and services. Exchange entitlements expand the set of commodities that a person can have and consume. Under most circumstances the wage earner, who is paid money and must exchange that money for goods, is able to command more commodities than the share cropper or the farmer, who receives goods that must first be sold or bartered.

Institutional factors, in addition to economic factors, affect entitlements. Customs, traditions, laws, and welfare transfers, all augment or reduce entitlements (Sen, 1990c). Traditions of charity and customs of giving alms will keep the poor and unemployed from starving to death. These types of institutions acknowledge the right of people to have enough food and other goods to survive. They may even become embedded in national laws and social policies that provide assistance to the destitute.

By focusing on different types of entitlements Sen was able to address a broader set of issues than how to maximize output, the traditional concern of economists. This approach also opened the door for Sen to focus on distributional issues, relations of production, and the rights of people. But soon Sen recognized that this approach left many questions unanswered and was subject to a great deal of criticism that was similar to his case against traditional welfare economics. For example, what are basic needs? Are they the same for everyone at every time? Is consumption at or above some basic level all that we want for people? How do we justify entitlements and what determines these entitlements? If we favor greater equality, equality of what (Sen, 1980c)?

These questions led Sen to focus his attention more on people and less on goods. His answer to them was that equality of opportunity mattered most for well-being. What was important, Sen stressed, was what people were able to do with their lives rather than what people could buy with their income. In the late 1980s, and throughout the 1990s, Sen (1985a, 1985i, 1987j, 1992a, 1993a, 1996o) refined and expanded this view, and also defended it from various criticisms.

In attempting to answer these questions Sen came to focus on what is of intrinsic value in life, rather than on the goods that provide instrumental value or utility. In this manner, he came to the concept of capabilities. Capabilities comprise the freedom or real opportunities that a person has to actually do and achieve the things that are valued; "the ability to be well nourished, to avoid escapable morbidity or mortality, to read and write and communicate, to take part in the life of the community, to appear in public without shame" (Sen, 1990c, p. 126). Basic needs or a minimum standard of living constitute part of this, but capabilities are much broader.

According to this perspective, welfare is maximized when people are able to read, eat and vote. Literacy is important not because of the utility it yields, but because of the sort of person that one becomes when one can read. Eating is valued not because people love food, but because food is necessary for life and health. And people vote, not to increase their utility, but because they value a certain political system (democracy) and certain types of political activity (McPherson, 1992).

The number of options that people have, and their freedom to choose among options, also contribute to human well-being. When a slave gains independence, or a person gets divorced to end an intolerably oppressive marriage, he or she will experience greater well-being even if they have lower incomes and less security. Similarly, when a consumer buys some good but has no alternative, consumer well-being could be enhanced by giving the consumer greater choice, even if the consumer does not get more goods at the end (Sen, 1990c). While a utilitarian measure of human welfare would indicate that the person is worse off if their standard of living is lower, the capability approach can show that with greater freedom and greater choice individual welfare may have increased.

Since the early 1990s basic needs and downside risks have received more attention in Sen's work, and in the development field, through the concept of human security. Sen worked on the 1994 *Human Development Report*, which stimulated discussion of human security in contrast to national or military security. The *Report* defines human security as "safety from such chronic threats as hunger, disease and repression, and protection from sudden and hurtful disruptions in the patterns of daily life" (UNDP, 1994, p. 23). Sen also served on the UN Human Security Commission, which published a broader report on this issue (Commission on Human Security, 2003). Although human security stresses the importance of a set of core capabilities for every individual (including such things as income security, healthcare, housing, education, and environmental security), it is more than a reiteration of basic needs. Human security also emphasizes the sustainability of those needs and the participation of those involved as agents in developing their own capabilities (Alkire, 2003; Gasper, 2005). Human security, however, is narrower than the concept of human development. While human development is concerned with the expansion of a wide array of capabilities to augment the well-being and agency of the people involved, human security is focused on alleviating downside risks (Commission on Human Security, 2003).

Sen continues to work on human development and its related concepts, such as human rights and respect for difference. He discusses human security and human rights as having a good deal of overlap. Human rights include some aspects of human security – for example, the rights to core capabilities. However, human rights also include "process freedoms" that are beyond the focus of the capability approach (Sen, 2005d). The processes of going outside, for example, because of a personal desire to go out or because of an order by someone in authority that you must go out are clearly different. While in both cases people may want to go outside, and while in both cases people get the outcome that they desire, only in the first case to they have the freedom to choose the outcome they desire. Some of this difference is addressed by the concept of agency, but some aspects of process freedom need to be analyzed through the lens of rights.

For this reason, Sen (1999c, 1999d, 2001a, 2003c, 2005d) has increasingly centered his analysis of capabilities in the context of freedoms, responsibilities, and democracy since the late 1990s. These concerns are reflected in the 2007 Commonwealth Commission Report on Respect and Understanding, *Civil Paths to Peace*. Sen headed the commission that produced this report, and he noted that too much international effort on resolving violence and terrorism has focused on discussions of religious groups, without bringing in the crucial components of civil society – language, literature, education, social interactions, and political commitments. "The battle for people's minds cannot be won on the basis of a seriously incomplete understanding of the wealth of social differences that make individual human beings richly diverse in distinct ways."

5   Applications of the capabilities approach

The capabilities approach has numerous applications and leads to some important policy consequences. Many of these have been drawn out by Sen himself – beginning with his early attempts to measure poverty (Sen, 1976c, 1983g), and continuing through later work on the causes of hunger and famines (Drèze & Sen, 1989, 1990–91; Sen 1987c), work on inequality (Sen, 1997c, 1997g), and studies on the role of women in economic development (Sen, 1989d, 1990c).

First and foremost, the capabilities approach leads to fundamental changes within the field of economic development. It has helped change the development paradigm from promoting economic growth to promoting human well-being. Growth means producing more things regardless of what happens to the people producing and consuming these goods; human well-being involves "expanding the capabilities of people" (Sen, 1984c, p. 497). Economic growth raises per capita incomes and output. From the capabilities perspective development occurs when people can do more things not when they buy more things. Economic development means that more people vote, literacy rates rise, average years of schooling goes up, and life expectancy increases. The goal of economic development thus becomes expanding individual opportunities and providing more positive freedoms to people (Sen, 1984c, 1985a).

Second, Sen has established that gender issues are an integral part of the development process (see also Agarwal, Humphries & Robeyns, 2003; Aslanbeigui, Pressman & Summerfield, 1994). He has questioned the assumption that low levels of development affect men and women equally, and that development policy is gender neutral.

Sen (1990f) has shown how a parental preference for sons leads to discrimination against women in developing countries. All families must constantly make decisions about how to use the limited income at their disposal. As we have seen, one important decision concerns how to allocate income among family members. For more affluent families such decisions are usually not critical, but for poor families they can become life and death decisions. Family members who do not receive sufficient food will become ill and may die; likewise family members who fail to receive adequate medical care when they are sick may die.

Sen (1993d) has shown that, within families, women and men do not have the same access to health care and nutritious food. During famines in India, for example, women had to be sicker before they were taken to the hospital and they were more likely to die after being taken to the hospital. Women were also less likely to be given adequate supplies of food (Sen, 1984c: Chapter 15).

Sen (1990f, 1992d, 1993d) has documented in stark and concrete terms the consequences of this unequal treatment. In more developed countries there are around 105 women for every 100 men. Even in sub-Saharan Africa there are around 102 women for every 100 men. In countries like China and India, however, there are only 94 to 96 women for every 100 men. If men and women were treated equally in these countries, the sex ratio should also be around 100–105 women for every 100 men. To put this another way, if women were treated by their families in the same way that men were treated there would be another 100 million women alive today.

Drèze & Sen (1989) argue that there are fewer missing females in countries and areas where women enjoy greater independence. Likewise, there are fewer missing women in places where women have more control over resources (such as land) and better access to jobs. In general, women are more likely to survive whenever and wherever their capabilities are expanded.

Several policy conclusions follow from this analysis. Development projects become more effective when they are focused on helping women. In India, for example, direct feeding programs have been more successful in improving the nutrition of girls than general food disbursements that families consume at home. Programs that encourage women to work outside the house enhance the status of women within the family; this enables them to bargain for and receive more of the family's economic resources. As many empirical studies have documented (see Sen 1990c; Drèze & Sen, 1990–91), one result of women earning their own income is vastly improved well-being for both women and children.

Third, Sen's work on famines and hunger has helped economists to understand the causes of these important real world problems. It has also changed the way that many international agencies approach famine prevention and relief.

Prior to the work of Sen, development economists stressed that famines were primarily due to insufficient food production. Sen pointed out that distribution issues were separate from the question of food supply. Famines could result from insufficient production; but they could also arise from poor or unequal distribution mechanisms. Sen has argued that distributional problems are in fact the major cause of famines, and his empirical work has documented that famines generally stem from distributional problems rather that from supply problems (Sen, 1981e; Drèze & Sen, 1989, 1990–91).

This work has drawn on his experiences and research on the 1943 Bengal famine. As Sen (1981c, p. 49) notes, during the Great Bengal Famine "people ... died in front of well-stocked food shops protected by the state". The problem was not a lack of food; rather, the problem was that floods deprived poor wage earners of a source of income. Without income they could not buy food, and the food supply did not move to where it was needed most. Worker entitlements collapsed as they lost the ability to feed themselves and their families. Many people died because poor rural workers could not obtain food without adequate wages. Similarly, during the Bangladesh famine in the 1970s the food supply was at record levels but wage workers lost their jobs because of the floods and therefore their entitlements to food.

Sen (1981c; Drèze & Sen, 1989) shows how traditional concerns about economic incentives can greatly worsen the famine problem. In the Irish famines of the 1840s, and the Wollo famine in Ethiopia in 1973, food actually moved out of famine areas because income and demand were too low there.

Sen & Drèze (1989; Sen, 1981e) point out that famines do not occur in democracies or in countries with a fairly free press. They (Drèze & Sen, 1996) show that although China has generally done a better job than India of eliminating hunger, India has had no famines since it gained independence, while China had a disastrous famine (with 15–30 million people dying) from 1958 to 1961. Sen (1981e, 1994n; Drèze & Sen, 1989, 1990–91) notes that more authoritarian forms of government, such as military regimes in sub-Sahara Africa, have also been less sensitive to the plight of famine victims and have experienced more famines. The absence of famines has less to do with the higher output that results from democratic forms of government and more to do with the fact that democratic governments must respond to political pressure from the electorate. Similarly, countries with a free press are less likely to experience famines. When the media spreads information far and wide about citizens dying of starvation, the government must respond to the critical needs of its people.

A fourth consequence of the capabilities approach concerns how poverty gets measured. Here, too, Sen's work has shifted the focus of economists from income and utility to capabilities. Traditionally, economists have sought to define poverty by finding the level of income necessary to sustain families of different sizes and types (see Ruggles, 1990). Larger families, urban families, and families with relatively more adults (and relatively fewer children) obviously will require more income and have higher poverty lines than small families, rural families, and families with relatively fewer adults. Poor families are defined as those that do not reach the poverty line based on its size and type; poverty rates are measured as the percentage of all families that fall below their poverty line.

Sen has identified numerous problems with this standard attempt to measure poverty. For starters, it equates more income with greater well-being. As Sen has stressed continuously, there are many things besides income that create utility or well-being. An individual in poor health with a large income that must be spent on health care would not be regarded as poor using the traditional approach. According to the capabilities approach deprivation means a lack of certain capabilities, and so the "wealthy but not healthy" may be counted as poor.

Another problem with the traditional measure of poverty arises from the use of equivalence scales in determining family well-being. As Sen has noted many times, if households consist of one primary income earner, that earner has considerable power over other family members in the distribution of family resources. Other members may not get equal or equivalent shares, and may not partake in "average household welfare". Only on the assumption that the head of household is purely benevolent (which contradicts other economic assumptions) does it make sense to measure household welfare using equivalence scales and assume similar welfare levels for all household members. Most households are not fully cooperative, but sometimes work together and sometimes struggle over allocations. Sen (1990c) terms this "the family as cooperative-conflict". In addition, there are differences in household needs due to environmental diversity (living in storm-prone areas), social climate (higher crime rates), and customary consumption patterns (Foster & Sen, 1997; Sen, 1983g, 1992a). One poverty line cannot fit all families, even those families with the same demographic composition.

Finally, and most important, as poverty rates are now calculated, if the government took money from a very poor family and gave it to another family just below its poverty line, the poverty rate would fall. For Sen, such a transfer should not be considered poverty-reducing or welfare-enhancing since the lives of the very poor will be made much worse. Some other measure of poverty was called for.

In the 1970s, Sen (1976c) developed such a measure. It took into account not only the fraction of families that were poor but also how far below the poverty line each poor family fell. The greatest weight was given to the poorest of the poor – those who fall below the poverty line by the greatest amount. This poverty measure thus puts the greatest weight on the most serious part of the poverty problem. It also has some important policy implications. Evaluated by the Sen poverty index, governments will not succeed in reducing poverty by focusing anti-poverty efforts on those just below the poverty line. Rather, reducing poverty means spending to help those at the very bottom of the economic ladder and most in need of assistance.

Sen (1973d, 1973e) has also developed a measure of inequality similar to his poverty measure. Unlike the Gini coefficient or the coefficient of variation, which tends to treat all parts of the income distribution equally, Sen's inequality measure gives the greatest weight to those at the bottom of the distributional structure. Redistributions that favor the poorest of the poor thus contribute the most to greater measured income equality on the Sen index.

More recently, Sen (1993a, 1994p, 2000c, 2005d) has focused more on capabilities, rejecting the use of income to measure and compare human welfare. As we have seen, for Sen income is not an end in itself, but a means to an end. The end is to increase the functionings and capabilities of people. An adequate measure of welfare would have to measure these capabilities. Sen worked for many years constructing a simple summary index that would capture the extent that basic opportunities were available to people in a country. Such an index, he noted, would provide a more meaningful measure of human well-being. It would also allow more insightful inter-country and inter-temporal comparisons of development.

Despite his work on an index to compare basic opportunities within and between countries, Sen has long been critical of the tendency to rely on simple aggregate measures of development. Mahbub ul Haq, however, convinced him to be a consultant to the United Nations in its effort to construct indices that would provide easily available alternatives to the GDP growth rates emphasized by the World Bank's *World Development Report* (Fukuda-Parr, 2003). These reports and the ranking of countries based on the Human Development Index (HDI) have drawn heavily on the conceptual framework of the capability approach since they were first published in 1990. The HDI is a weighted average of income adjusted for distribution and purchasing power, life expectancy, and literacy and education. It is expressed in terms of what is potentially achievable, so the highest possible HDI value would be 1 and the lowest 0. Related indices have been developed for gender disparities (the GDI or gender development index) and empowerment (the GEM or gender empowerment measure). These two measures have appeared in each annual *Human Development Report* beginning with 1995. The Human Development Index and its sister indices are the first scholarly attempt to measure success and failure in development based upon key capabilities in different countries.

Using the HDI to evaluate development changes the rankings and our perceptions of how well different countries are performing. It also alters many of the conclusions about development that are usually drawn as a consequence of the neoliberal growth-centered paradigm. In the *Human Development Report 2006*, for example, Luxembourg ranks first in GDP per capita but only 12th on the HDI (data are given for 2004, the most recent year available). Norway has a per capita GDP of just US$38,454 (using purchasing power parity) in contrast to Luxembourg's US$69,961; but Norway ranks first in both HDI and GDI. Costa Rica is 61st by GDP per capita and 48th by HDI and 42nd by GDI. Similarly, Chile, Tanzania, Egypt, and the Czech Republic all move up when the HDI rankings are contrasted with GDP per capita rankings. In contrast, Bahrain, Angola, Namibia, and the United Arab Emirates move down. Social policies to improve income equality and access to education and health care for women and men can offset lower levels of per capita income to expand capabilities within a country. Still, aggregate measures can hide wide disparities within countries. In 2006, the *Human Development Report* calculated within-country HDI's for a subset of countries. These calculations indicate that Burkina Faso, Madagascar, and Zambia have high HDI scores for the richest fifth of the population and that these scores are twice those of the poorest quintile. In contrast, in high-income countries the HDI differences are smaller "partly because income differentials translate less emphatically into life expectancy differences and basic education outcome. Even so, the United States displays significant HDI disparities by income group" (UNDP, 2006, p. 270). Technical difficulties make these more disaggregated HDI measures less applicable to cross-country comparisons.

These HDI rankings also have important real world consequences. When countries focus only on income and income growth, policies tend to get employed that promote only economic growth. Distributional issues become irrelevant; education is likely to get short changed; the environment is likely to be ignored; and long-run growth may be sacrificed. By drawing attention to other factors that promote human well-being, the HDI leads governments to direct their policy efforts toward different ends – providing health and education for its citizens, and supporting a sustainable environment and a sustainable living standard.

6 Summary and conclusions

Although Sen has criticized the most basic assumptions of neoclassical economics, he has been more than just a critic. He has attempted to build a better economic theory based upon a set of more realistic and plausible assumptions. For Sen, social relationships are important, human potential is important, and things have value that cannot be bought and sold in the market. This all gets lost in traditional welfare economics, which starts with rational economic man and ends by justifying the results of free exchange because it cannot compare individual utilities and it claims to abhor making any value judgments.

The unifying theme in Sen's work has been a focus on creating human potential and showing how this leads to greater well-being in society and within the household. He has seen the development of human capabilities as the real end of economic growth and the real goal of economics.

Such a perspective, by its nature, forces a broadening of economic analysis. Sen has pressed economists to take a different view of human economic agents. He has made a strong case that people are shaped by their environments and have some intrinsic worth; they are not just rational utility maximizers. He has pointed out that the goal of a well-performing economic system is not just providing more goods and services, but improving the lives of people – for women as well as men.

Out of this broader approach comes a broader and a more humane economics. It is an economics which, as Vivian Walsh (2000) points out, harkens back to Adam Smith and classical political economy. Economics again seeks to understand and solve important real world problems. Economics again cares about ethical issues. Likewise, the role of the professional economist changes for the better. No longer the narrow technocrat or the socially inept fool, once economists adopt the capabilities perspective they again become worldly philosophers.

References

Agarwal, B., Humphries, J. & Ingrid Robeyns, I. (Guest Eds) (2003) Special issue on Amarty Sen's work and ideas, *Feminist Economics*, 9 (2–3).

Alkire, S. (2003) A conceptual framework for human security, Centre for Research on Inequality, University of Oxford.

Aslanbeigui, N., Pressman, S. & Summerfield, G. (1994) *Women in the Age of Economic Transformation* (London & New York: Routledge).

Basu, K. (1998) Amartya Sen, Economics Nobel Laureate, *Challenge*, 42, pp. 41–51.

Blais, A. (2000) *To Vote or Not to Vote?* (Pittsburgh: University of Pittsburgh Press).

Commission on Human Security (2003) *Human Security Now* www.humansecuritychs.org/finalreport/English/FinalReport.pdf.

Coy, P. (1998) The Mother Teresa of economics, *Business Week*, 3601, p. 44.

Fukuda-Parr, S. (2003) The human development paradigm: operationalizing Sen's ideas on capabilities, *Feminist Economics*, 9, pp. 301–317.

Gaertner, W. & Pattanaik, P.K. (1988) An interview with Amartya Sen, *Social Choice and Welfare*, 5(1), pp. 69–79.

Gasper, D. (2005) Securing humanity: situating "human security" as concept and discourse, *Journal of Human Development*, 6, pp. 221–245.

Hicks, N. & Streeten, P. (1979) Indicators of development: the search for a basic needs yardstick, *World Development*, 7, pp. 568–580.

Klamer, A. (1989) A conversation with Amartya Sen, *Journal of Economic Perspectives*, 3(1), pp. 135–150.

Lowenstein, R. (2000) *When Genius Failed: The Rise and Fall of Long-Term Capital Management* (New York: Random House).

McPherson, M. (1992) Amartya Sen, in: W. Samuels (Ed.) *New Horizons in Economic Thought: Appraisals of Leading Economists* (Hants, UK: Edward Elgar), pp. 294–309.

Mill, J.S. (1957) *Utilitarianism* (Indianapolis: Bobbs-Merrill).

Pocock, J.G.A. (1971) Civic humanism and its role in Anglo-American thought, in: J.G.A. Pocock (Ed.) *Politics, Language and Truth* (London: Methuen), pp. 80–103.

Pocock, J.G.A. (1975) *The Machiavellian Moment* (Princeton: Princeton University Press).

Pocock, J.G.A. (1981) Virtues, rights, and manners, *Political Theory*, 9, pp. 353–368.

Pollack, R. (1998) The wrong economics won, *Wall Street Journal*, 232(75), p. A22.

Pressman, S. (2006) Clap happy: applause and the voting paradox, *Journal of Economic Methodology*, 13, pp. 241–256.

Richman, S. (1998) Nobel Prize committee got its economics wrong, *Human Events*, 54(46), p. 10.

Ruggles, P. (1990) *Drawing the Line* (Washington, D.C.: Urban Institute).

Streeten, P. (1979) From growth to basic needs, *Finance and Development*, 16(3), pp. 28–31.

Streeten, P. (1981) *First Things First* (New York: Oxford University Press).

United Nations Development Programme (UNDP) (1994) *Human Development Report 1994* (New York: Oxford University Press).

United Nations Development Programme (UNDP) (2006) *Human Development Report 2006* (New York: Oxford University Press).

Walsh, V. (2000) Smith after Sen, *Review of Political Economy*, 12(1), pp. 5–25.

Works of Amartya Sen

Ahmad, E., Drèze, J.P., Hills, J. & Sen, A.K. (Eds) (1991) *Social Security in Developing Countries* (Oxford: Oxford University Press).

Anand, S., Fabienne, P. & Sen, A. (Eds) (2004) *Public Health, Ethics, and Equity* (Oxford & New York: Oxford University Press).

Anand, S. & Sen, A.K. (1997) Concepts of human development and poverty: a multidimensional perspective, *Human Development Papers 1997* (New York: UNDP).

Anand, S. & Sen, A.K. (2000a) Human development and economic sustainability, *World Development*, 28, pp. 2029–2049.

Anand, S. & Sen, A.K. (2000b) The income component of the human development index, *Journal of Human Development*, 1, pp. 83–106.

Anand, S. & Sen, A.K. (2003a) Concepts of human development and poverty: a multidimensional perspective, in: S. Fukuda-Parr & A.K.S. Kumar (Eds) *Readings in Human Development and Poverty: A Multidimensional Perspective* (New Delhi: Oxford University Press), pp. 228–244.

Anand, S. & Sen, A.K. (2003b) Gender inequality in human development: theories and measurement, in: S. Fukuda-Parr & A.K.S. Kumar (Eds) *Readings in Human Development and Poverty: A Multidimensional Perspective* (New Delhi: Oxford University Press), pp. 210–227.

Anand, S. & Sen, A.K. (2003c) Human Development Index: methodology and measurement, in: S. Fukuda-Parr & A.K. Shiva Kumar (Eds) *Readings in Human Development* (New Delhi: Oxford University Press), pp. 138–151.

Arrow, K.J., Sen, A.K. & Suzumura, K. (Eds) (1997) *Social Choice Re-examined*, 2 vols. (New York: St. Martin's Press).

Chaudhuri, M.D. & Sen, A.K. (1970) Durgapur fertilizer project: an economic evaluation, *Indian Economic Review*, 5, pp. 41–70.

Colland, D.A., Helm, D.R., Scott, M.F.G. & Sen, A.K. (Eds) (1984) *Economic Theory and Hicksian Themes* (Oxford: Oxford University Press).

Dasgupta, P. Marglin, S.A. & Sen, A.K. (1972) *Guidelines for Project Evaluation* (New York: United Nations).

Dasgupta, P., Sen, A.K. & Starret, D. (1973) Notes on the measurement of inequality, *Journal of Economic Theory*, 6(2), pp. 180–187.

Drèze, J. & Sen, A.K. (1989) *Hunger and Public Action* (Oxford: Clarendon Press).

Drèze, J. & Sen, A.K. (Eds) (1990–91) *The Political Economy of Hunger*, 3 vols. (Oxford: Clarendon Press).

Drèze, J. & Sen, A.K. (1991) Public action for social security, in: E. Ahmad, J. Drèze, J. Hills & A.K. Sen (Eds) *Social Security in Developing Countries* (Oxford: Oxford University Press).

Drèze, J. & Sen, A.K. (1995a) Basic education as a political issue, *Journal of Educational Planning and Administration*, 9, pp. 27–43.

Drèze, J. & Sen, A.K. (1995b) *India: Economic Development and Social Opportunity* (Oxford: Clarendon Press).

Drèze, J. & Sen, A.K. (Eds) (1996) *Indian Development: Selected Regional Perspectives* (Oxford & Delhi: Oxford University Press).

Drèze, J. & Sen, A.K. (2002) *India: Development and Participation* (New Delhi: Oxford University Press).

Grusky, D., Kanbur, S.M.R. & Sen, A.K. (Eds) (2006) *Poverty and Inequality* (Stanford, CA: Stanford University Press).

Kane, J. & Sen, A.K. (1996) Justice, impartiality and equality: why the concept of justice does not presume equality, *Political Theory*, 24(3), pp. 375–406.

Kynch, J. & Sen, A.K. (1993) Indian women: well-being and survival, *Cambridge Journal of Economics*, 7, pp. 363–380.

Majumdar, M. & Sen, A.K. (1976) A note on representing partial orderings, *Review of Economic Studies*, 43(3), pp. 543–545.

Nussbaum, M. & Sen, A.K. (1989) Internal criticism and Indian rationalist traditions, in: M. Krauss (Ed.) *Relativism, Interpretation and Confrontation* (Notre Dame: University of Notre Dame Press), pp. 229–325.

Nussbaum, M. & Sen, A.K. (Eds) (1993) *The Quality of Life* (Oxford: Clarendon Press).

Osmani, S. & Sen, A.K. (2003) The hidden penalties of gender inequality: fetal origins of ill-health, *Economics and Human Biology*, 1, pp. 105–121.

Raj, K.N. & Sen, A.K. (1961) Alternative patterns of growth under conditions of stagnant export earnings, *Oxford Economic Papers*, 13, pp. 43–52.

Raj, K.N. & Sen, A.K. (1962) Alternative patterns of growth: a reply, *Oxford Economic Papers*, 14, pp. 200–204.

Rothschild, E. & Sen, A.K. (2001) Adam Smith's economics, in: K. Haakonssen (Ed.) *The Cambridge Companion to Adam Smith* (Cambridge: Cambridge University Press), pp. 319–365.

Runciman, W.G. & Sen, A.K. (1965) Games, justice and the general will, *Mind*, 74, pp. 554–563.

Runciman, W.G. & Sen, A.K. (1974) Prisoner's dilemma and social justice: a Reply, *Mind*, 83, p. 83.

Scazzieri, R., Sen, A.K. & Zamagni, S. (Eds) (2008) *Markets, Money and Capital* (Cambridge: Cambridge University Press).

Sen, A.K. (1957a) A note on foreign exchange requirements of development plans, *Economica Internazionale*, 10, pp. 248–254.

Sen, A.K. (1957b) A note on Tinbergen on the optimum rate of saving, *Economic Journal*, 67, pp. 745–748.

Sen, A.K. (1957c) Some notes on the choice of capital-intensity in development planning, *Quarterly Journal of Economics*, 71, pp. 561–584.

Sen, A.K. (1957d) Unemployment, relative prices and the savings potential, *Indian Economic Review*, 56–63.

Sen, A.K. (1958) A note on the Mahalanobis model of sectoral planning, *Arthaniti*, 1, pp. 26–33.

Sen, A.K. (1959a) The choice of agricultural techniques in underdeveloped countries, *Economic Development and Cultural Change*, 7, pp. 279–285.

Sen, A.K. (1959b) Choice of capital-intensity further considered, *Quarterly Journal of Economics*, 73, pp. 466–484.

Sen, A.K. (1959c) Determinism and historical predictions, *Enquiry*, 2, pp. 99–115.

Sen, A.K. (1960a) *Choice of Techniques* (Oxford: Basil Blackwell).

Sen, A.K. (Ed.) (1960b) *Growth Economics* (Harmondsworth: Penguin Books).

Sen, A.K. (1961) On optimizing the rate of saving, *Economic Journal*, 71, pp. 479–496.

Sen, A.K. (1962a) An aspect of Indian agriculture, *Economic Weekly*, Annual Number, 16.

Sen, A.K. (1962b) Neo-classical and neo-Keynesian theories of distribution, *Economic Record*, 39, pp. 53–64.

Sen, A.K. (1962c) On the usefulness of used machines, *Review of Economics and Statistics*, 44, pp. 346–362.

Sen, A.K. (1963a) Distribution, transitivity and Little's welfare criterion, *Economic Journal*, 73, pp. 771–778.

Sen, A.K. (1963b) The money rate of interest in the pure theory of growth, in: F. Hahn & F. Brechling (Eds) *Theories of the Rate of Interest* (London: Macmillan), pp. 267–280.

Sen, A.K. (1964a) The efficiency of indirect taxes, in: *Problems of Economic Dynamics and Planning: Essays in Honour of M. Kalecki* (New York & Oxford: Pergamon Press), pp. 365–372.

Sen, A.K. (1964b) A planning model for the educational requirements of economic development: comments, in: *The Residual Factor and Economic Growth* (Paris: OECD), pp. 188–197.

Sen, A.K. (1964c) Preferences, votes and the transitivity of majority decisions, *Review of Economic Studies*, 31, pp. 163–165.

Sen, A.K. (1964d) Size of holdings and productivity, *Economic Weekly*, Annual Number, 16, pp. 323–326.

Sen, A.K. (1964e) Surplus labour and the degree of mechanization, in: K. Berrill (Ed.) *Economic Development with Special Reference to East Asia* (London: Macmillan), pp. 386–398.

Sen, A.K. (1964f) Working capital in the Indian economy, in: P.N. Rosenstein-Rodan (Ed.) *Pricing and Fiscal Policies* (London: Allen & Unwin), pp. 125–164.

Sen, A.K. (1965a) The commodity pattern of British enterprise in early Indian industrialization 1854–1914, in: *Proceedings of the Second International Conference of Economic History* (Paris), pp. 781–816.

Sen, A.K. (1965b) Mishan, Little and welfare: a reply, *Economic Journal*, 75, p. 442.

Sen, A.K. (1966a) Economic approaches to education and manpower planning, *Indian Economic Review*, New Series, 1, pp. 1–21.

Sen, A.K. (1966b) Education, vintage and learning by doing, *Journal of Human Resources*, 1, pp. 3–21.

Sen, A.K. (1966c) Hume's Law and Hare's Rule, Philosophy, 155, pp. 75–79.

Sen, A.K. (1966d) Labour allocation in a cooperative enterprise, *Review of Economic Studies*, 33, pp. 361–71.

Sen, A.K. (1966e) Peasants and dualism with or without surplus labor, *Journal of Political Economy*, 74, pp. 425–450.

Sen, A.K. (1966f) A possibility theorem on majority decisions, *Econometrica*, 34(2), pp. 49–109.

Sen, A.K. (1967a) Isolation, assurance and the social rate of discount, *Quarterly Journal of Economics*, 81, pp. 112–124.

Sen, A.K. (1967b) The nature and classes of prescriptive judgements, *Philosophical Quarterly*, 17, pp. 46–62.

Sen, A.K. (1967c) The pattern of British enterprise in early Indian industrialization, 1854–1914, in: B. Singh & V.B. Singh (Eds) *Social and Economic Change* (Bombay: Allied Publishers), pp. 409–429.

Sen, A.K. (1967d) Surplus labour in India: a critique of Schultz's statistical test, *Economic Journal*, 77, pp. 154–161.

Sen, A.K. (1967e) Terminal capital and optimum savings, in: C. Feinstein (Ed.) *Socialism, Capitalism and Economic Growth* (London: Cambridge University Press), pp. 40–53.

Sen, A.K. (1968) General criteria of industrial project evaluation, in: *Evaluation of Industrial Projects* (New York: UN Industrial Development Organization).

Sen, A.K. (1969a) Choice functions and revealed preference, *Review of Economic Studies*, 36(1), pp. 381–393.

Sen, A.K. (1969b) Choice of techniques: a critical survey of a class of debates, in: *Planning for Advanced Skills and Technologies* (New York: United Nations), pp. 45–57.

Sen, A.K. (1969c) A game-theoretic analysis of theories of collectivism in allocation, in: T. Majumdar (Ed.) *Growth and Choice* (London: Oxford University Press), pp. 1–17.

Sen, A.K. (1969d) Planner's preferences: optimality, distribution and social welfare, in: J. Margolis & H. Guitton (Ed.) *Public Economics* (London: Macmillan), pp. 201–221.

Sen, A.K. (1969e) Quasi-transitivity, rational choice and collective decision, *Review of Economic Studies*, 36(1), pp. 381–393.

Sen, A.K. (1969f) The role of policy-makers in project formulation and evaluation, *Industrialization and Productivity*, Bulletin 13 (New York: United Nations).

Sen, A.K. (1970a) Aspects of Indian education, in: S.C. Malik (Ed.) *Management and Organization of Indian Universities* (Simla: Institute of Advanced Study), pp. 245–274.

Sen, A.K. (1970b) *Collective Choice and Social Welfare* (San Francisco: Holden Day).

Sen, A.K. (1970c) The impossibility of a Paretian liberal, *Journal of Political Economy*, 78(1), pp. 152–157.

Sen, A.K. (1970d) Interpersonal aggregation and partial comparability, *Econometrica*, 38(3), pp. 393–409.

Sen, A.K. (1970e) Interrelations between project, sectoral and aggregate planning, *Economic Bulletin for Asia and the Far East*, 21, pp. 66–75.

Sen, A.K. (1970f) A quantitative study of the flow of trained personnel from the developing countries to the United States of America, *Journal of Development*, Planning, 3, pp. 105–139.

Sen, A.K. (1970g) Strategies of economic development: feasibility constraints and planning, in: E.A.G. Robinson & M. Kidron (Eds) *Economic Development in South Asia* (London: Macmillan), pp. 369–378.

Sen, A.K. (1971a) Choice functions and revealed preference, *Review of Economic Studies*, 38(115), pp. 304–317.

Sen, A.K. (1971b) The impossibility of a Paretian liberal: a reply, *Journal of Political Economy*, 79, pp. 1406–1407.

Sen, A.K. (1971c) A quantitative study of brain drain from the developing countries to the United States, *Journal of Development Planning*, 3, pp. 105–139.

Sen, A.K. (1972a) Aspects of Indian education, in: P. Chaudhuri (Ed.) *Aspects of Indian Economic Development* (London: Allen & Unwin), pp. 144–159.

Sen, A.K. (1972b) Control areas and accounting prices: an approach to economic evaluation, *Economic Journal*, 82(325), pp. 486–501.

Sen, A.K. (1972c) Interpersonal comparison and partial comparability: a correction, *Econometrica*, 40(5), p. 959.

Sen, A.K. (1972d) *Objectivity and Position* (Kansas: University of Kansas Press).

Sen, A.K. (1973a) Behaviour and the concept of preference, *Economica*, 40, pp. 241–259.

Sen, A.K. (1973b) Brain drain: causes and effects, in: B.R. Williams (Ed.) *Science and Technology in Economic Growth* (London: Macmillan), pp. 385–404.

Sen, A.K. (1973c) *Dimensions of Unemployment in India* (Calcutta: Indian Statistical Institute).

Sen, A.K. (1973d) *On Economic Inequality* (Oxford: Clarendon Press).

Sen, A.K. (1973e) On ignorance and equal distribution, *American Economic Review*, 63(5), pp. 1022–1024.

Sen, A.K. (1973f) On the development of basic income indicators to supplement the GNP measure, *United Nations Economic Bulletin for Asia and the Far East*, 24(2–3), pp. 1–11.

Sen, A.K. (1973g) Poverty, inequality and unemployment: some conceptual issues in measurement, *Economic and Political Weekly*, 8, pp. 1457–1464.

Sen, A.K. (1974a) Choice, orderings and morality, in: S. Korner (Ed.) *Practical Reason* (Oxford: Blackwell), pp. 54–67.

Sen, A.K. (1974b) Informational bases of alternative welfare approaches: aggregation and income distribution, *Journal of Public Economics*, 3(4), pp. 387–403.

Sen, A.K. (1974c) On some debates in capital theory, *Economica*, 41(163), pp. 328–335.

Sen, A.K. (1974d) Poverty, inequality and unemployment: some conceptual issues in measurement, *Sankhya: The Indian Journal of Statistics*, 36, pp. 67–82.

Sen, A.K. (1974e) Rawls versus Bentham: an axiomatic examination of the pure distribution problem, *Theory and Decision*, 4, pp. 283–292.

Sen, A.K. (1975a) The concept of efficiency, in: M. Parkin & A.R. Nobay (Eds) *Contemporary Issues in Economics* (Manchester: Manchester University Press), pp. 196–210.

Sen, A.K. (1975b) Employment, institutions and technology: some policy issues, *International Labour Review*, 112(1), pp. 45–73.

Sen, A.K. (1975c) *Employment, Technology & Development* (Oxford: Clarendon Press).

Sen, A.K. (1975d) Is a Paretian liberal really impossible?: a reply, *Public Choice*, 21(21), pp. 111–113.

Sen, A.K. (1975e) Minimal conditions for monotonicity of capital value, *Journal of Economic Theory*, 11(3), pp. 340–355.

Sen, A.K. (1976a) Famines as failures of exchange entitlements, *Economic and Political Weekly*, 11, pp. 1273–1280.

Sen, A.K. (1976b) Liberty, unanimity and rights, *Economica*, 43(171), pp. 217–245.

Sen, A.K. (1976c) Poverty: an ordinal approach to measurement, *Econometrica*, 44(2), pp. 219–231.

Sen, A.K. (1976d) *Poverty and Economic Development* (Ahmedabad: Vikram A. Sarabhai AMA Memorial Trust).

Sen, A.K. (1976e) Real national income, *Review of Economic Studies*, 43(1), pp. 19–39.

Sen, A.K. (1976f) Social choice theory: a re-examination, *Econometrica*, 45(1), pp. 53–89.

Sen, A.K. (1976g) Welfare inequalities and Rawlsian axiomatics, *Theory and Decision*, 7, pp. 243–262.

Sen, A.K. (1977a) Non linear social welfare functions, in: R. Butts & J. Hintikka (Eds) *Logic, Methodology and the Philosophy of Science* (Dordrecht: Reidel), pp. 297–302.

Sen, A.K. (1977b) On the approach to planning against hunger, *CERES: FAO Review on Agriculture and Development*, 58, pp. 14–17.

Sen, A.K. (1977c) On weights and measures: informational constraints in social welfare analysis, *Econometrica*, 45(7), pp. 1539–1572.

Sen, A.K. (1977d) Poverty and welfarism, *Intermountain Economic Review*, 8, pp. 1–13.

Sen, A.K. (1977e) Rational fools: a critique of the behavioral foundations of economic theory, *Philosophy and Public Affairs*, 6(4), pp. 317–344.

Sen, A.K. (1977f) Social choice theory: a re-examination, *Econometrica*, 45(1), pp. 53–89.

Sen, A.K. (1977g) Starvation and exchange entitlements: a general approach and its application to the Great Bengal Famine, *Cambridge Journal of Economics*, 1(1), pp. 33–59.

Sen, A.K. (1977h) The statistical chickens, *CERES*, 10(4), pp. 14–17.

Sen, A.K. (1978a) Ethical measurement of inequality: some difficulties, in: W. Krelle &

A.F. Sharrocks (Eds) *Personal Income Distribution* (Amsterdam: North-Holland), pp. 81–94.

Sen, A.K. (1978b) On the labour theory of value: some methodological issues, *Cambridge Journal of Economics*, 2, pp. 175–190.

Sen, A.K. (1978c) Welfare theory, in: Beckmann, Menges & Selten (Eds) *Encyclopedic Handbook of Mathematical Economic Sciences* (Gabler).

Sen, A.K. (1979a) Informational analysis of moral principles, in: R. Harrison (Ed.) *Rational Action* (Cambridge: Cambridge University Press), pp. 115–132.

Sen, A.K. (1979b) Interpersonal comparisons of welfare, in: M. Boskin (Ed.) *Economics and Human Welfare* (New York: Academic Press), pp. 183–201.

Sen, A.K. (1979c) Issues in the measurement of poverty, *Scandinavian Journal of Economics*, 81, pp. 285–307.

Sen, A.K. (1979d) Personal utilities and public judgements: or what's wrong with welfare economics, *Economic Journal*, 89(355), pp. 537–558.

Sen, A.K. (1979e) Strategies and revelation: informational constraints in public decisions, in: J.J. Laffont (Ed.) *Aggregation and Revelation of Preferences* (Amsterdam: North-Holland), pp. 13–28.

Sen, A.K. (1979f) Utilitarianism and welfarism, *Journal of Philosophy*, 76, pp. 463–488.

Sen, A.K. (1979g) The welfare basis of real income comparisons: a survey, *Journal of Economics Literature*, 17(1), pp. 1–45.

Sen, A.K. (1980a) Description as choice, *Oxford Economic Papers*, 32, pp. 353–369.

Sen, A.K. (1980b) Economic development: objectives and obstacles, in: R.F. Dernberger (Ed.) *China's Development Experience in Comparative Perspective* (Cambridge, MA: Harvard University Press), pp. 19–37.

Sen, A.K. (1980c) Equality of what?, in: S. McMurrin (Ed.), *Tanner Lectures on Human Values*, Vol. 1 (Cambridge: Cambridge University Press), pp. 197–220.

Sen, A.K. (1980d) Famine mortality: a study of the Bengal Famine of 1943, in: E.J. Hobsbawm, A. Mitra, K.N. Raj, I. Sachs, & A. Thorner (Eds) *Peasants in History: Essays in Memory of Daniel Thorner* (Calcutta: Oxford University Press), pp. 194–220.

Sen, A.K. (1980e) Famines, *World Development*, 8, pp. 613–621.

Sen, A.K. (1980f) Labour and technology, in: J. Cody, H. Hughes & D. Walls (Eds) *Policies for Industrial Progress in Development Countries* (New York: Oxford University Press), pp. 121–158.

Sen, A.K. (1980g) The welfare basis of real income comparisons: a reply, *Journal of Economic Literature*, 18, pp. 1547–1552.

Sen, A.K. (1980–81) Plural utility, *Proceedings of the Aristotelian Society*, 80, pp. 193–215.

Sen, A.K. (1981a) Economic development: objectives and obstacles, in: R.F. Demberger (Ed.) *China's Development Experience in Comparative Perspective* (Cambridge, MA: Harvard University Press), pp. 19–37.

Sen, A.K. (1981b) Ethical issues in income distribution: national and international, in: S. Grassman & E. Lundberg (Eds) *The World Economic Order: Past and Prospects* (London: Macmillan), pp. 464–494.

Sen, A.K. (1981c) Ingredients of famine analysis: availability and entitlements, *Quarterly Journal of Economics*, 95, pp. 433–464.

Sen, A.K. (1981d) A positive concept of negative freedom, in: E. Morscher & R. Stranzinger (Eds) *Ethics: Foundations, Problems and Applications: Proceedings of the 5th International Wittgenstein Symposium* (Vienna: Holder-Pichler-Tempsky), pp. 43–56.

Sen, A.K. (1981e) *Poverty and Famines: An Essay on Entitlement and Depression* (Oxford: Oxford University Press).

Sen, A.K. (1981f) Public action and the quality of life in developing countries, *Oxford Bulletin of Economics and Statistics*, 43, pp. 287–319.

Sen, A.K. (1981g) A reply to welfarism: a defense against Sen's Attack, *Economic Journal*, 91, pp. 531–535.

Sen, A.K. (1982a) *Choice, Welfare and Measurement* (Oxford: Basil Blackwell).

Sen, A.K. (1982b) The food problem: theory and policy, *Third World Quarterly*, 4, pp. 447–459.

Sen, A.K. (1982c) How is India doing?, *New York Review of Books*, 29, pp. 41–45.

Sen, A.K. (1982d) Liberty as control: an appraisal, *Midwest Studies in Philosophy*, 7, pp. 207–221.

Sen, A.K. (1982e) Approaches to the choice of discount rates for social cost benefit analysis, in: R. Lind (Ed.) *Discounting for Time and Risk in Energy Policy* (Washington, DC: Resources for the Future), pp. 325–353.

Sen, A.K. (1982f) The right not to be hungry, in: G. Floistad (Ed.) *Contemporary Philosophy: A New Survey*, Vol. 2 (The Hague: Martinus Nijhoff), pp. 343–360.

Sen, A.K. (1982g) Rights and agency, *Philosophy and Public Affairs*, 11(2), pp. 113–132.

Sen, A.K. (1983a) Accounts, actions and values: objectivity of social science, in: C. Lloyd (Ed.) *Social Theory and Political Practice* (Oxford: Clarendon Press), pp. 87–107.

Sen, A.K. (1983b) Carrots, sticks and economics: perception problems in economics, *Indian Economic Review*, 18, pp. 1–16.

Sen, A.K. (1983c) Development: which way now?, *Economic Journal*, 93, pp. 745–762.

Sen, A.K. (1983d) Economics and the family, *Asian Development Review*, 1, pp. 14–16.

Sen, A.K. (1983e) Evaluator relativity and consequential evaluation, *Philosophy and Public Affairs*, 12(2), pp. 113–132.

Sen, A.K. (1983f) Liberty and social choice, *Journal of Philosophy*, 80(1), pp. 5–28.

Sen, A.K. (1983g) Poor, relatively speaking, *Oxford Economic Papers*, 35(2), pp. 153–169.

Sen, A.K. (1983h) The profit motive, *Lloyds Bank Review*, 147, pp. 1–20.

Sen, A.K. (1984a) Food battles: conflicts in access to food, *Food and Nutrition*, 10, pp. 81–89.

Sen, A.K. (1984b) The living standard, *Oxford Economic Papers*, 36, pp. 74–90.

Sen, A.K. (1984c) *Resources, Values and Development* (Oxford: Blackwell & Cambridge, MA: Harvard University Press).

Sen, A.K. (1985a) *Commodities and Capabilities* (Amsterdam: North-Holland).

Sen, A.K. (1985b) Goals, commitment, and identity, *Journal of Law, Economics and Organization*, 1(2), pp. 341–355.

Sen, A.K. (1985c) The moral standing of the market, in: E.F. Paul, F.D. Miller, Jr. & J. Paul (Eds) *Ethics and Economics* (Oxford: Basil Blackwell), pp. 1–19.

Sen, A.K. (1985d) Rationality and uncertainty, *Theory and Decision*, 18, pp. 109–127.

Sen, A.K. (1985e) A reply to Professor Townsend, *Oxford Economic Papers*, 37, pp. 669–676.

Sen, A.K. (1985f) Rights and capabilities, in: T. Honderich (Ed.) *Morality and Objectivity* (London: Routledge), pp. 130–148.

Sen, A.K. (1985g) Rights as goals, in: S. Guest & A. Milne (Eds) *Equality and Discrimination: Essays in Freedom and Justice* (Stuttgart: Franz Steiner), pp. 11–25.

Sen, A.K. (1985h) Social choice and justice: a review article, *Journal of Economic Literature*, 23, pp. 1764–1776.

Sen, A.K. (1985i) Well-being, agency and freedom: the Dewey Lectures 1984, *Journal of Philosophy*, 82, pp. 169–221.

Sen, A.K. (1985j) Women, technology and sexual divisions, *Trade and Development* (UNCTAD), 6, pp. 195–223.

Sen, A.K. (1986a) Adam Smith's prudence theory and reality in development, in: S. Lall & F. Stewart (Eds) *Essays in Honour of Paul Streeten* (New York: St. Martin's Press), pp. 28–37.

Sen, A.K. (1986b) The causes of famine: a reply, *Food Policy*, 11, pp. 125–132.

Sen, A.K. (1986c) The concept of well-being, in: S. Guhan & M. Shroff (Eds) *Essays on Economic Progress and Welfare: In Honour of I.G. Patel* (Oxford: Oxford University Press), pp. 174–192.

Sen, A.K. (1986d) Economic distance and the living standard, in: K. Ahooja-Patel, A.G. Drabek & M. Nerfin (Eds) *World Economy in Transition: Essays Presented to Surendre Patel on his Sixtieth Birthday* (Oxford & New York: Pergamon Press), pp. 63–74.

Sen, A.K. (1986e) Food, economics and entitlements, *Lloyds Bank Review*, 160, pp. 3–20.

Sen, A.K. (1986f) Foundations of social choice theory: an epilogue, in: J. Elster & A. Hylland (Eds) *Foundations of Social Choice Theory* (New York: Cambridge University Press), pp. 213–248.

Sen, A.K. (1986g) Information and invariance in normative choice, in: W.P. Heller, R.M. Starr, & D.A. Starret (Eds) *Essays in Honor of Kenneth J. Arrow*, Vol. 1 (Cambridge: Cambridge University Press), pp. 29–55.

Sen, A.K. (1986h) Planning and the judgement of economic Progress, *Review of Indian Planning Processes: Proceedings of the Golden Jubilee Celebrations of the Indian Statistical Institute* (Calcutta: I.S.I.).

Sen, A.K. (1986i) Prediction and economic theory, in: J. Mason, P. Mathias & J.H. Westcott (Eds) *Predictability in Science and Society* (London: The Royal Society & The British Academy), pp. 3–22.

Sen, A.K. (1986j) Rationality, interest and identity, in: A. Foxley, M. McPherson & G. O'Donnell (Eds) *Development, Democracy, and the Art of Trespassing* (Notre Dame: University of Notre Dame Press), pp. 343–353.

Sen, A.K. (1986k) The right to take personal risks in: D. MacLean (Ed.) *Values at Risk* (Totowa, NJ: Rowman & Allanheld), pp. 155–169.

Sen, A.K. (1986l) Social choice theory in: K.J. Arrow & M. Intriligator (Eds) *Handbook of Mathematical Economics*, Vol. III (Amsterdam: North-Holland), pp. 1073–1081.

Sen, A.K. (1986m) *Welfare Economics and the Real World* (Memphis: P.K. Seidman Foundation).

Sen, A.K. (1987a) Defense spending as a priority: comment, in: C. Schmidt & F. Blackaby (Eds) *Peace, Defense and Economic Analysis* (New York: St. Martin's Press), pp. 45–49.

Sen, A.K. (1987b) Goods and people, in: V.L. Urguidi (Ed.) *Structural Change, Economic Interdependence and World Development*, Vol. 1 (New York: St. Martin's Press), pp. 153–177.

Sen, A.K. (1987c) *Hunger and Entitlements* (Helsinki: WIDER).

Sen, A.K. (1987d) Justice, in: J. Eatwell, M. Milgate & P. Newman (Eds) *The New Palgrave: A Dictionary of Economics*, Vol. 2 (London: Macmillan), pp. 1039–1043.

Sen, A.K. (1987e) *On Ethics and Economics* (Oxford & New York: Basil Blackwell).

Sen, A.K. (1987f) Maurice Herbert Dobb, in: J. Eatwell, M. Milgate & P. Newman (Eds) *The New Palgrave: A Dictionary of Economics*, Vol. 1 (London: Macmillan), pp. 910–912.

Sen, A.K. (1987g) Rational behaviour, in: J. Eatwell, M. Milgate & P. Newman (Eds)

The New Palgrave: A Dictionary of Economics, Vol. 4 (London: Macmillan), pp. 68–76.

Sen, A.K. (1987h) Reply: famines and Mr. Bowbrick, *Food Policy*, 12, pp. 10–14.

Sen, A.K. (1987i) Social choice, in: J. Eatwell, M. Milgate & P. Newman (Eds) *The New Palgrave: A Dictionary of Economics*, Vol. 4 (London: Macmillan), pp. 382–393.

Sen, A.K. (1987j) *The Standard of Living*, Tanner Lectures with discussion by J. Muellbauer and others (Cambridge: Cambridge University Press).

Sen, A.K. (1988a) Africa and India: what do we have to learn from each other?, in: K.J. Arrow (Ed.) *The Balance between Industry and Agriculture in Economic Development*, Vol. 1 (London: Macmillan), pp. 105–137.

Sen, A.K. (1988b) The concept of development, in: H.B. Chenery & T.N. Srinivasan (Eds) *Handbook of Development Economics*, Vol. 1 (Amsterdam: North-Holland), pp. 9–26.

Sen, A.K. (1988c) Family and food: sex bias in poverty, in: T.N. Srinivasan & P.K. Bardhan (Eds) *Rural Poverty in South Asia* (New York: Columbia University Press), pp. 453–472.

Sen, A.K. (1988d) Freedom of choice: concept and content, *European Economic Review*, 32, pp. 269–294.

Sen, A.K. (1988e) Property and hunger, *Economic Philosophy*, 4, pp. 57–68.

Sen, A.K. (1988f) Sri Lanka's achievements: how and when, in: T.N. Srinivasan & P.K. Bardhan, P.K. (Eds) *Rural Poverty in South Asia* (New York: Columbia University Press), pp. 549–556.

Sen, A.K. (1989a) Economic methodology: heterogeneity and relevance, *Social Research*, 56, pp. 299–329.

Sen, A.K. (1989b) Food and freedom, *World Development*, 17(6), pp. 769–781.

Sen, A.K. (1989c) Indian development: lessons and non-lessons, *Daedalus*, 118, pp. 369–392.

Sen, A.K. (1989d) Women's survival as a development problem, *Bulletin of the American Academy of Arts and Sciences*, 43, pp. 14–29.

Sen, A.K. (1990a) Entitlements and the Chinese Famine, *Food Policy*, 15, pp. 261–263.

Sen, A.K. (1990b) Food entitlement and economic chains, in: L.F. Newman (Ed.) *Hunger in History* (Oxford: Blackwell), pp. 374–386.

Sen, A.K. (1990c) Gender and cooperative conflict in: I. Tinker (Ed.) *Persistent Inequalities* (New York: Oxford University Press), pp. 123–149.

Sen, A.K. (1990d) Individual freedom as a social commitment, *New York Review of Books*, 37(10), pp. 49–54.

Sen, A.K. (1990e) Justice: means versus freedoms, *Philosophy and Public Affairs*, 19, pp. 111–121.

Sen, A.K. (1990f) More than 100 million women are missing, *New York Review of Books*, 37(20), pp. 61–66.

Sen, A.K. (1990g) Public action for social security, in: E. Ahmed *et al.* (Eds) *Social Security in Developing Countries* (Oxford: Clarendon Press), pp. 1–40.

Sen, A.K. (1990h) *Public Action to Remedy Hunger* (New York: The Hunger Project).

Sen, A.K. (1990i) Welfare, freedom and social choice: a reply, *Recherches économiques de Louvain*, 56, pp. 451–485.

Sen, A.K. (1991a) The nature of inequality, in: K.J. Arrow (Ed.) *Markets and Welfare* (London: Macmillan), pp. 3–21.

Sen, A.K. (1991b) Utility: ideas and terminology, *Economics and Philosophy*, 7, pp. 277–283.

Sen, A.K. (1991c) Welfare, preference and freedom, *Journal of Econometrics*, 50, pp. 15–29.

Sen, A.K. (1991d) What did you learn in the world today?, *American Behavioral Scientist*, 34, pp. 530–548.

Sen, A.K. (1992a) *Inequality Re-examined* (Oxford: Clarendon Press & Cambridge, MA: Harvard University Press).

Sen, A.K. (1992b) Life and death in China: a reply, *World Development*, 20, pp. 1305–1312.

Sen, A.K. (1992c) Minimal liberty, *Economica*, 59(234), pp. 139–160.

Sen, A.K. (1992d) Missing women, *British Medical Journal*, 304(6827), pp. 587–588.

Sen, A.K. (1993a) Capability and well-being, in: M. Nussbaum & A.K. Sen (Eds) *The Quality of Life* (Oxford: Oxford University Press), pp. 30–53.

Sen, A.K. (1993b) The causation and prevention of famines: a reply, *Journal of Peasant Studies*, 21, pp. 29–40.

Sen, A.K. (1993c) Does business ethics make economic sense?, *Journal of Business Ethics Quarterly*, 3, pp. 45–54.

Sen, A.K. (1993d) The economics of life and death, *Scientific American*, 268(5), pp. 40–47.

Sen, A.K. (1993e) India and the West, *New Republic*, 208(23), pp. 27–34.

Sen, A.K. (1993f) Indian pluralism, *India International Centre Quarterly*, pp. 37–46.

Sen, A.K. (1993g) Internal consistency of choice, *Econometrica*, 61, pp. 495–521.

Sen, A.K. (1993h) The labour-capital partnership: reconciling insider power with full employment: comment, in: A.B. Atkinson (Ed.) *Alternatives to Capitalism: The Economics of Partnership* (New York: St. Martin's Press & London: Macmillan), pp. 78–80.

Sen, A.K. (1993i) Life expectancy and inequality: some conceptual Issues, in: P. Bardhan *et al.* (Eds) *Development and Change* (Oxford: Oxford University Press), pp. 3–11.

Sen, A.K. (1993j) Markets and freedoms, *Oxford Economic Papers*, 45, pp. 519–551.

Sen, A.K. (1993k) On the Darwinian view of progress, *Population and Development Review*, 19(1), pp. 123–137.

Sen, A.K. (1993l) Positional objectivity, *Philosophy and Public Affairs*, 22, pp. 126–145.

Sen, A.K. (1993m) Sukhamoy Chakravarty: An Appreciation, in: K. Basu & M. Majumdar (Eds) *Sukhamoy Chakravarty* (Delhi: Oxford University Press), pp. xi–xx.

Sen, A.K. (1993n) The third way: inside the firm or out in the economy?, in: A.B. Atkinson (Ed.) *Alternatives to Capitalism: The Economics of Partnership* (New York: St. Martin's Press & London: Macmillan), pp. 278–282.

Sen, A.K. (1993o) The threats to secular India, *New York Review of Books*, 40(7), pp. 26–32.

Sen, A.K. (1994a) Amiya Kumar Dasgupta (1903–1992), *Economic Journal*, 104(426), pp. 1147–1154.

Sen, A.K. (1994b) The Darwinian view of progress: reply to Guha, *Population & Development Review*, 20, pp. 866–870.

Sen, A.K. (1994c) *Economic Wealth and Moral Sentiments* (Zurich: Bank Hoffman).

Sen, A.K. (1994d) The formulation of rational choice, *American Economic Review*, 84(2), pp. 385–390.

Sen, A.K. (1994e) Freedoms and needs, *New Republic*, 210(2–3), pp. 31–38.

Sen, A.K. (1994f) Growth economics: what and why?, in: L. Pasinetti & R. Solow (Eds) *Economic Growth and the Structure of Long-Term Development* (London: Macmillan), pp. 363–368.

Sen, A.K. (1994g) Liberty and poverty, *Current*, 362, pp. 22–28.

Sen, A.K. (1994h) Markets and the freedom to choose, in: H. Siebert (Ed.) *The Ethical Foundations of the Market Economy* (Tubingen: J.C.B. Mohr), pp. 123–138.

Sen, A.K. (1994i) Non-binary choice and preference: a tribute to Stig Kanger, in: D. Prawitz *et al.* (Eds) *Logic, Methodology and Philosophy of Science*, IX (Amsterdam: Elsevier Science), pp. 913–924.

Sen, A.K. (1994j) Objectivity and position: assessment of health and well-being, in: L. Chen & A. Kleinman (Eds) *Health and Social Change in International Perspective* (Cambridge, MA: Harvard University Press), pp. 115–128.

Sen, A.K. (1994k) The Darwinian view of progress: reply to Guha, *Population and Development Review*, 20, pp. 866–870.

Sen, A.K. (1994l) The political economy of hunger, in: I. Serageldin & P. Landell-Mills (Eds) *Overcoming Global Hunger* (Washington, D.C.: World Bank), pp. 85–90.

Sen, A.K. (1994m) Population: delusion and reality, *New York Review of Books*, 41(15), pp. 62–71.

Sen, A.K. (1994n) Population and reasoned agency, in: K. Lindahl-Kiessling & H. Landberg (Eds) *Population, Economics Development, and the Environment* (Oxford: Oxford University Press), pp. 51–78.

Sen, A.K. (1994o) Poverty and famines, *Economic Development and Cultural Change*, 32, pp. 881–886.

Sen, A.K. (1994p) Well-being, capability and public policy, *Giornale Degli Economisti e Annali di Economica*, 53(79), pp. 333–347.

Sen, A.K. (1994q) Why does poverty persist in rich countries?, in: P. Guidicini & G. Pieretti (Eds) *Urban Poverty and Human Dignity* (Milan: Franco Angeli), pp. 97–106.

Sen, A.K. (1995a) Agency and well-being: the development agenda, in: N. Heyzer, S. Kapoor & J. Sandler (Eds) *A Commitment to the World's Women* (New York: UNIFEM), pp. 103–112.

Sen, A.K. (1995b) Demography and welfare economics, *Empirica*, 22(1), pp. 1–21.

Sen, A.K. (1995c) *Economic Development and Social Change: India and China in Comparative Perspectives* (London: Development Economics Research Programme).

Sen, A.K. (1995d) Economic regress: concepts and features, *Proceedings of the World Bank Annual Conference on Development Economics, 1993* (Washington, DC: World Bank), pp. 315–333.

Sen, A.K. (1995e) Environmental evaluation and social choice: contingent valuation and the market analogy, *Japanese Economic Review*, 46(1), pp. 23–37.

Sen, A.K. (1995f) Environmental Values and Economic Reasoning, *Nexus*, 13, pp. 51–73 [in Dutch].

Sen, A.K. (1995g) Gender inequality and theories of justice, in: M. Nussbaum & J. Glover (Eds) *Women, Culture and Development* (Oxford: Clarendon Press), pp. 259–273.

Sen, A.K. (1995h) How to judge voting schemes, *Journal of Economic Perspectives*, 9, pp. 91–98.

Sen, A.K. (1995i) Moral codes and economic success, in: S. Brittan & A. Hamlin (Eds) *Market Capitalism and Moral Values* (Aldershot: Edward Elgar), pp. 23–24.

Sen, A.K. (1995j) Nobody need starve, *Granta*, 52, pp. 213–220.

Sen, A.K. (1995k) The political economy of targeting in: D. Vande Walle & K. Nead (Eds) *Public Spending and the Poor: Theory and Evidence* (Baltimore: Johns Hopkins University Press), pp. 11–24.

Sen, A.K. (1995l) Rationality and social choice, *American Economic Review*, 85, pp. 1–24.

Sen, A.K. (1995m) Varieties of deprivation: comments, in: E. Kuiper & J. Sap (Eds) *Out of the Margin: Feminist Perspectives on Economics* (London & New York: Routledge), pp. 51–58.

Sen, A.K. (1995n) World economy, *Nieman Reports*, 49(3), pp. 32–34.

Sen, A.K. (1996a) The concept of wealth, in: R.H. Mayers (Ed.) *The Wealth of Nations in the Twentieth Century* (Stanford: Hoover Institution Press), pp. 3–21.

Sen, A.K. (1996b) Economic interdependence and the world food summit, *Development*, 4, pp. 5–10.

Sen, A.K. (1996c) Employment, institutions and technology: some policy issues, *International Labour Review*, 135(3–4), pp. 445–471 [reprint of 1975 publication].

Sen, A.K. (1996d) Famine as alienation, in: *State, Market and Development: Essays in Honour of Rehman Sobhan* (Dhaka: University Press Limited), pp. 15–32.

Sen, A.K. (1996e) Family fortunes of bronze age mint, *Times Higher Education Supplement*, 1230, pp. 20–25.

Sen, A.K. (1996f) Fertility and coercion, *University of Chicago Law Review*, 63(3), pp. 1035–1061.

Sen, A.K. (1996g) Freedom, capabilities and public action: a response, *Notizie di Politeia* 12(43–44), pp. 105–125.

Sen, A.K. (1996h) Freedom favors development, *New Perspectives Quarterly*, 13(4), pp. 23–27.

Sen, A.K. (1996i) Is the idea of purely internal consistency of choice bizarre?, in: J.E.J. Altham & T.R. Harrison (Eds) *Language, World and Reality* (Cambridge: Cambridge University Press), pp. 19–31.

Sen, A.K. (1996j) Legal rights and moral rights: old questions and new problems, *Ratio Juris*, 9, pp. 153–167.

Sen, A.K. (1996k) A matter of choice, *UNESCO Courier*, 49(8), pp. 10–13.

Sen. A.K. (1996l) On the status of equality, *Political Theory*, 24(3), pp. 394–400.

Sen, A.K. (1996m) On the foundations of welfare economics: utility, capability and practical reason, in: F. Farina, F. Hahn & S. Vannucci (Eds) *Ethics, Rationality and Economic Behaviour* (Oxford: Clarendon Press), pp. 50–65.

Sen, A.K. (1996n) Our culture, their culture, *New Republic*, 214(14), pp. 27–34.

Sen, A.K. (1996o) Population policy: authoritarianism versus cooperation, *Social Change*.

Sen, A.K (1996p) Rationality, joy and freedom, *Critical Review*, 10, pp. 481–494.

Sen, A.K. (1996q) Rights: formulation and consequences, *Analyse and Kritik*, 18, pp. 53–70.

Sen, A.K. (1996r) Secularism and its discontents, in: K. Basu & S. Subramamyam (Eds) *Unraveling the Nation: Sectarian Conflict and India's Secular Identity* (Penguin Books), pp. 11–43.

Sen, A.K. (1996s) Social commitment and democracy: the demands of equity and financial conservatism, in: P. Barker (Ed.) *Living as Equals* (Oxford: Oxford University Press), pp. 9–32.

Sen, A.K. (1996t) Social commitment and financial conservatism, *Il Mulino*, 364, pp. 199–216.

Sen, A.K. (1996u) Welfare economics and two approaches to rights, in: J.C. Pardo, & F. Schneider (Eds) *Current Issues in Public Choice* (Cheltenham, UK & Brookfield, VT: Edward Elgar), pp. 21–39.

Sen, A.K. (1997a) Economics, business principles and moral sentiments, *Business Ethics Quarterly*, 7, pp. 5–15.

Sen, A.K. (1997b) Editorial: human capital and human capability, *World Development*, 25(12), pp. 1959–1961.

Sen, A.K. (1997c) From income inequality to economic inequality, *Southern Economic Journal*, 64(2), pp. 384–401.

Sen, A.K. (1997d) Human rights and Asian values, *New Republic*, 217(2/3), pp. 33–40, 48.

Sen, A.K. (1997e) Indian traditions and the Western imagination, *Daedalus*, 126(2), pp. 1–26.

Sen, A.K. (1997f) Individual preference as the basis of social choice, in: K.J. Arrow, A.K. Sen & K. Suzumura (Eds) *Social Choice Re-examined*, Vol. 2 (New York: St. Martin's Press), pp. 15–37.

Sen, A.K. (1997g) Inequality, unemployment and contemporary Europe, *International Labour Review*, 136(2), pp. 155–172.

Sen, A.K. (1997h) *La liberta individuale come impegno sociale* (Rome & Bari: Editori Laterza).

Sen, A.K. (1997i) Maximization and the act of choice, *Econometrica*, 65(4), pp. 745–779.

Sen, A.K. (1997j) Quality of life and economic evaluation, *Academia Economic Papers*, 25, pp. 269–316.

Sen, A.K. (1997k) Radical needs and moderate reforms, in J. Drèze & A.K. Sen (Eds) *Indian Development: Selected Regional Perspectives* (Oxford & Delhi: Oxford University Press), pp. 1–32.

Sen, A.K. (1997l) The subject of human rights has ended up being a veritable battleground, *Chronicle of Higher Education*, 43(40), pp. B11-B14.

Sen, A.K. (1997m) Tagore and his India, *New York Review of Books*, 44(11), pp. 55–63, 69.

Sen, A.K. (1997n) The vision that worked, *Times Literary Supplement*, 4923, pp. 3–4.

Sen, A.K. (1997o) What's the point of a development strategy?, in: E. Malinvaud *et al.* (Eds) *Development Strategy and the Management of the Market Economy* (Oxford: Clarendon Press), pp. 35–60.

Sen, A.K. (1998a) Human development and financial conservatism, *World Development*, 26, pp. 733–742.

Sen, A.K. (1998b) India: what prospects?, *Indian Horizons*, 45, pp. 19–46.

Sen, A.K. (1998c) Morality as an indicator of economic success and failure, *Economic Journal*, 108(446), pp. 1–25.

Sen, A.K. (1998d) Universal truths, *Harvard International Review*, 20(3), pp. 40–43.

Sen, A.K. (1999a) *Beyond the Crisis: Development Strategies in Asia* (Singapore: Institute of Southeast Asian Studies).

Sen, A.K. (1999b) The value of democracy, *World Bank Development Outlook*, 1, pp. 4–9.

Sen, A.K. (1999c) Democracy as a universal value, *Journal of Democracy*, 10, pp. 3–17.

Sen, A.K. (1999d) *Development as Freedom* (New York: Knopf).

Sen, A.K. (1999e) Economic policy and equity: an overview, in: V. Tanzi (Ed.) *Economic Policy and Equality* (Washington, DC: International Monetary Fund), pp. 28–43.

Sen, A.K. (1999f) Economics and health, *The Lancet*, 354, p. S20.

Sen, A.K. (1999g) Economics and the value of freedom, *Civilization*, 6(3), pp. 83–84.

Sen, A.K. (1999h) Galbraith and the art of description, in: H. Sasson (Ed.) *Between Friends: Perspectives on John Kenneth Galbraith* (New York: Houghton Mifflin), pp. 139–145.

Sen, A.K. (1999i) Health in development, *Bulletin of the World Health Organization*, 77, pp. 619–623.

Sen, A.K. (1999j) The possibility of social choice, *American Economic Review*, 89, pp. 349–378.

Sen, A.K. (1999k) *Reason Before Identity* (Oxford: Oxford University Press).

Sen, A.K. (1999l) Things to come, in S. Griffiths (Ed.) *Predictions* (Oxford: Oxford University Press), pp. 213–226.

Sen, A.K. (1999m) The universal value of democracy, *Journal of Democracy*, 10, pp. 3–17.

Sen, A.K. (2000a) Business ethics and economic success, *Politeia*, 16, pp. 3–13.

Sen, A.K. (2000b) Consequentialist evaluation and practical reason, *Journal of Philosophy*, 97, pp. 477–502.

Sen, A.K. (2000c) A decade of human development, *Journal of Human Development*, 1, pp. 17–23.

Sen, A.K. (2000d) Democracy: the only way out of poverty, *New Perspectives Quarterly*, 17, pp. 28–30.

Sen, A.K. (2000e) The discipline of cost-benefit analysis, *Journal of Legal Studies*, 29, pp. 931–952.

Sen, A.K. (2000f) East and west: the reach of reason, *New York Review of Books*, 47, pp. 33–38.

Sen, A.K. (2000g) Economic progress and health, in: D.A. Leon & G. Walt (Eds) *Poverty, Inquality and Health* (Oxford: Oxford University Press), pp. 333–345.

Sen, A.K. (2000h) Global doubts, *Harvard Magazine*, 103, pp. 68–70, 106.

Sen, A.K. (2000i) India and the bomb, *The New Republic*, September 25, 32–38.

Sen, A.K. (2000j) India through its calendars, *The Little Magazine*, 1, pp. 4–12.

Sen, A.K. (2000k) Merit and justice, in: K. Arrow, S. Bowles & D. Durlaf (Eds) *Meritocracy and Economic Inequality* (Princeton: Princeton University Press), pp. 5–16.

Sen, A.K. (2000l) The play's the thing, *The Little Magazine*, 1, pp. 4–9.

Sen, A.K. (2000m) Population and gender equity, *The Nation*, July 24, pp. 16–18.

Sen, A.K. (2000n) *Social Exclusion: Concept, Application and Scrutiny, Social Development Papers, No. 1* (Manila: Asian Development Bank).

Sen, A.K. (2000o) Social justice and the distribution of income, in: A.B. Atkinson & F. Bourguignon (Eds) *Handbook of Income Distribution*, Vol. 1 (Amsterdam: Elsevier), pp. 9–26.

Sen, A.K. (2000p) Why health equity, *Health Economics*, 11, pp. 659–666.

Sen, A.K. (2000q) Work and rights, *International Labour Review*, 139(2), p. 119.

Sen, A.K. (2001a) The fear of freedom, in: T. Pelagidis, L.T. Katseli & J. Milios (Eds) *Welfare State and Democracy in Crisis: Reforming the European Model* (Aldershot, UK & Burlington, VT: Ashgate), pp. 17–25.

Sen, A.K. (2001b) Global inequality and persistent conflicts, in: War and Peace in the 20th Century and Beyond: Proceeding of the Nobel Centennial Symposium (London: World Scientific), pp. 101–120.

Sen, A.K. (2001c) Globalization: value and ethics, *Journal of Legal Hermeneutics*, pp. 15–28.

Sen, A.K. (2001d) History and the enterprise of knowledge, *Social Scientist*, 29, pp. 3–15.

Sen, A.K. (2001e) Hunger: old torments and new blunders, *The Little Magazine*, 2, pp. 9–13.

Sen, A.K. (2001f) The individual and the world, in E. Wilson (Ed.) *Equality and the Modern World* (London: Macmillan).

Sen, A.K. (2001g) The many faces of gender inequality, *The New Republic*, 225, pp. 35–40.

Sen, A.K. (2001h) Other people, *Proceedings of the British Academy*, 111, pp. 319–335.

Sen, A.K. (2001i) Ten truths about globalization, *The International Herald Tribune*, July 14.

Sen, A.K. (2002a) Democracy and its global roots, *The New Republic*, October 6, pp. 28–35.

Sen, A.K. (2002b) Globalization, inequality and global protest, *Development*, 45, pp. 11–16.

Sen, A.K. (2002c) How to judge globalism, *The American Prospect*, 13, pp. 1–14.

Sen, A.K. (2002d) *Rationality and Freedom* (Cambridge, MA: Harvard University Press).

Sen, A.K. (2002e) The right to one's identity, *Frontline*, 19, pp. 63–64.

Sen, A.K. (2003a) Continuing the conversation, *Feminist Economics*, 9, pp. 319–332.

Sen, A.K. (2003b) Democracy and its global roots, *The New Republic*, 229, pp. 28–35.

Sen, A.K. (2003c) Development as capability, in: S. Fukuda-Parr & A.K.S. Kumar (Eds) *Readings in Human Development* (New Delhi & New York: Oxford University Press), pp. 3–16.

Sen, A.K. (2003d) Gender inequality and population growth, in: S. Gaughen (Ed.) *Women's Rights* (San Diego, CA: Greenhaven Press), pp. 131–136.

Sen, A.K. (2003e) Missing women revisited, *British Medical Journal*, 327, pp. 1297–1298.

Sen, A.K. (2003f) The role of early childhood investment in development, in: R. Moran (Ed.) *Escaping the Poverty Trap: Investing in Children in Latin America* (Washington, DC: Inter-American Development Bank), pp. 75–80.

Sen, A.K. (2003g) Social choice theory and justice, in: H. Pauer-Studer (Ed.) *Constructions of Practical Reason: Interviews on Moral and Political Philosophy* (Stanford, CA: Stanford University Press), pp. 148–178.

Sen, A.K. (2003h) The social demands of human rights, *New Perspectives Quarterly*, 20(4), pp. 83–84.

Sen, A.K. (2003i) Sraffa, Wittgenstein, and Gramsci, *Journal of Economic Literature*, 41, pp. 1240–1255.

Sen, A.K. (2004a) Capabilities, lists and public reason: continuing the conversation, *Feminist Economics*, 10(3), pp. 77–80.

Sen, A.K. (2004b) Democracy and secularism in India, in: K. Basu (Ed.) *India's Emerging Economy: Performance and Prospects in the 1990s and Beyond* (Cambridge & London: MIT Press), pp. 35–47.

Sen, A.K. (2004c) Elements of a theory of human rights, *Philosophy & Public Affairs*, 32, pp. 315–356.

Sen, A.K. (2004d) Freedom as progress, *Finance & Development*, 41, pp. 36–39.

Sen, A.K. (2004e) Health achievement and equity: external and internal dimensions, in: S. Anand, P. Fabienne & A. Sen (Eds) *Public Health, Ethics, and Equity* (Oxford & New York: Oxford University Press), pp. 263–268.

Sen, A.K. (2004f) How does culture matter?, in: V. Rao & M. Walton (Eds) *Culture and Public Action* (Stanford, CA: Stanford University Press), pp. 37–58.

Sen, A.K. (2004g) Incompleteness and reasoned choice, *Synthese*, 140, pp. 43–59.

Sen, A.K. (2004h) Passage to China, *New York Review of Books*, 51(19), pp. 61–65.

Sen, A.K. (2004i) Social identity, *Revue de Philosophie Economique*, 9, pp. 7–27.

Sen, A.K. (2004j) What's the point of democracy?, *American Academy of Arts and Sciences Bulletin*, 57, pp. 8–11.

Sen, A.K. (2004k) Why we should preserve the spotted owl, *London Review of Books*, 26, pp. 10–11.

Sen, A.K. (2005a) Argument and history, *The New Republic*, 233, pp. 25–32.

Sen, A.K. (2005b) *The Argumentative Indian: Writings on Indian History, Culture and Identity* (London: Penguin).

Sen, A.K. (2005c) How does development happen?, *Cato Journal*, 25, pp. 455–459.

Sen, A.K. (2005d) Human rights and capabilities, *Journal of Human Development*, 6, pp. 151–166.

Sen, A.K. (2005e) Indian traditions and the Western imagination, *Daedalus*, 134, pp. 168–185.

Sen, A.K. (2005f) Jim Wolfensohn's contribution to the development agenda: development as construction, in: R. Kagia (Ed.) *Balancing the Development Agenda: The Transformation of the World Bank under James D. Wolfsohn, 1995–2005* (Washington, DC: World Bank), pp. 148–149.

Sen, A.K. (2005g) Mary, Mary, quite contrary, *Feminist Economics*, 11, pp. 1–9.

Sen, A.K. (2005h) Realizing rights as enforceable claims, in: A. Kuper (Ed.) *Global Responsibilities: Who Must Deliver on Human Rights?* (New York: Routledge), pp. 53–76.

Sen, A.K. (2005i) The three r's of reform, *Economic and Political Weekly*, May 7.

Sen, A.K. (2005j) Walsh on Sen after Putnam, *Review of Political Economy*, 17, pp. 107–113.

Sen, A.K. (2005k) Why exactly is commitment important for rationality?, *Economics and Philosophy*, 21, pp. 5–14.

Sen, A.K. (2006a) Central banks and the challenge of development, in: *The Challenges of Development* (Basel: Bank for International Settlements), pp. 19–26.

Sen, A.K. (2006b) Chili and liberty, *The New Republic*, 234(7), pp. 25–30.

Sen, A.K. (2006c) Conceptualizing and measuring poverty, in: D. Grusky, S.M.R. Kanbur & A.K. Sen (Eds) *Poverty and Inequality* (Stanford, CA: Stanford University Press), pp. 30–46.

Sen, A.K. (2006d) Human rights and the limits of the law, *Cardozo Law Review*, 27, pp. 2913–2927.

Sen, A.K. (2006e) *Identity and Violence: The Illusion of Destiny* (New York: W.W. Norton).

Sen, A.K. (2006f) The man without a plan: can foreign aid work?, *Foreign Affairs*, 85, pp. 171–177.

Sen, A.K. (2006g) Normative evaluation and legal analogues, in: J.N. Drobak (Ed.) *Norms and the Law* (Cambridge: Cambridge University Press), pp. 80–96.

Sen, A.K. (2006h) Reason, freedom and well-being, *Utilitas*, 18, pp. 80–96

Sen, A.K. (2006i) What do we want from a theory of justice?, *Journal of Philosophy*, 103, pp. 215–238.

Sen, A.K. (2007a) Population and reasoned agency: population growth and food security, *Development*, 50, pp. 98–102.

Sen, A.K. (2007b) Turkey: not about Islamic vs. Western values, *New Perspectives Quarterly*, 24, p. 24.

Sen, A.K. & Pattanaik, P. (1969) Necessary and sufficient conditions for rational choice under majority decision, *Journal of Economic Theory*, 1(2), pp. 178–202.

Sen, A.K. & Sengupta, S. (1983) Malnutrition of rural children and the sex bias, *Economic and Political Weekly*, 19.

Sen, A.K. & Williams, B. (Eds) (1992) *Utilitarianism and Beyond* (New York: Cambridge University Press).

5 The economic contributions of Robert A. Mundell

Robert E. Prasch

'The Economic Contributions of Robert A. Mundell' by Robert E. Prasch from *Review of Political Economy* (2001), Volume 13, Issue 1 (Taylor and Francis Ltd, http://www.informaworld.com), reprinted by permission of the publisher.

1 Introduction

Robert Mundell, the McVicker Professor of Political Economy at Columbia University, was recognized by the Royal Swedish Academy of Sciences with the 1999 Nobel Memorial Prize in Economics. Congratulations are certainly due, for he has had a long and distinguished career. Mundell received his doctorate from the Massachusetts Institute of Technology in 1956. Since then he has held numerous faculty appointments including positions at the University of British Columbia, Stanford University, the University of Chicago, the University of Waterloo and, from 1974, Columbia University. In addition, he has served on the staff of, or as an advisor to, numerous international organizations and governments, including the International Monetary Fund, the United Nations, the World Bank, the Federal Reserve Board, the US Treasury and the Canadian government.

His academic writings have contributed to several important fields of economics, including the theory of the monetary and fiscal policy mix, the monetary approach to the balance of payments, supply-side economics, and the theory of optimal currency areas. Because Mundell's list of publications is too long for a detailed overview, this essay will focus instead on some of the more prominent themes in his work.

2 The method of Mundell's economics

To my knowledge, Professor Mundell has not written on the rhetoric or method of economics. Yet, viewed from a methodological perspective, Mundell's work stands apart from several important trends within contemporary economics. Specifically, his writings, especially those of the past 20 years, are intended to both instruct and persuade his readers that his particular position on the genesis, character, and solution to a particular problem is correct. With persuasion as his goal, Professor Mundell does not share the profession's implicit (and too-often explicit) disdain for economic history or the history of economic ideas. If only intuitively, Mundell understands that theory without content or context is a barren exercise, and that a narrative without a structure has no point. To achieve a sense of context and relevance, Mundell often begins his articles on policy matters with extensive and detailed discussions of the history of a problem. This, sad to say, almost unique style is most evident in his articles on the choice of foreign exchange regimes (1989a, b, 1993, 1995a, b).

Any meaningful history of the events of a period, and of the policies that were pursued, must include a discussion of the goals and motivations behind these policies. Hence a good history must demonstrate a command of the ideas of the era in question. To apply this rule to economics, it is evident that the history of economic thought is a necessary element of any serious presentation of economic history. It follows that a command of the history of economic thought is required if one is to give a meaningful argument for or against any particular economic policy. Among the more striking and compelling aspects of so many of Mundell's articles on exchange rate regimes or European monetary integration are his reflections on the policy proposals and analyses of some of the great economists of the past. Working within such a broad context also allows Mundell to make arguments that draw on deductive, inductive, comparative and historical lessons and sources. In short, he can make formidable arguments for his chosen policies.

Nothing stated thus far should leave the reader with the impression that Mundell neglects the use of mathematical models. Indeed, during the first decade of his career, he was clearly on the forefront of this particular art. But the modeling that Mundell engaged in then, and now, remains closely tied to the practicalities of the problem at hand. While his models typically assume 'rational behavior', 'optimizing agents' and 'profit maximization', these models are rarely asked to bear a disproportionate burden of the proof for or against any particular policy. Moreover, with a few lapses excepted, Mundell avoids sweeping or overdrawn conclusions. He readily acknowledges that economic policies, even policies that he strongly supports, will involve costs, and often substantial costs.

In short, Mundell's style makes him an accomplished practitioner of what John Neville Keynes (1917) referred to as the 'art' of economic policy. His essays are not designed to make him a divo of the modern seminar room. He does not try to dazzle his readers with the latest in mathematical or statistical technique. To paraphrase a distinguished economist of an earlier era, Mundell's goal is not to theorize about the world, but rather to change it. Mundell's speech to the Swedish Academy confirms that he always meant to change things, and insofar as the world pays any attention to the economists in its midst, he seems to have enjoyed a measure of success.

3 International capital flows and the Mundell–Fleming model

For more than a generation of economists, Robert Mundell's name has been most closely associated with what has come to be known as the Mundell–Fleming model. For a long time, and to a certain extent even today, this model served as the benchmark account of the influence that capital flows have on a country's macroeconomic policies (Mundell, 1960, 1961b, 1962, 1963; Fleming, 1962, 1963). While the development of this model was a contribution to economic theory, it most certainly was not a mere exercise in abstract logic. The model could be adapted to a variety of scenarios, including fixed versus floating exchange rates, monetary and fiscal policy, and perfect or imperfect substitutability between domestic and foreign assets. Since this theory was consistent with a variety of starting assumptions, it was readily applicable to a host of policy problems. What made the model a staple of textbook and academic presentations was its tractability. Another of its merits, although this may not have been as important to its author, was that the theory fit nicely into the textbook presentations of the neo-Keynesian IS–LM models that came to dominate the textbooks of the 1970s and 1980s (e.g. Dornbusch & Fischer, 1978, chs 18–19; Branson, 1972, ch. 15).

The Mundell–Fleming model examines the possibilities that can emerge when a country pursues fiscal or monetary policies under several varying initial conditions, namely fixed or floating exchange rates, in a world that features reasonably prompt capital flows. The model demonstrated that under a regime of fixed exchange rates, capital flows would enhance the effectiveness of fiscal policy, while monetary policy would be ineffective. On the other hand, under a regime of floating exchange rates, capital flows would render fiscal policy ineffective, while the effects of monetary policy would be amplified (Mundell, 1962; Fleming, 1962).

These results followed because, depending on a policy's effect on the domestic interest rate, capital flows would either support or offset the government's initiatives. Take as an example the case of expansionary fiscal policy under fixed exchange rates. Capital flows would weaken the liquidity constraint that causes interest rates to rise in an expansion: crowding-out is offset. In the case of expansionary monetary policy under fixed exchange rates, capital flows could offset the scheduled expansion as investors move away from lower interest rates, *ceteris paribus*.

Floating rates induce a different set of results. In this case, capital flows amplify the effect of monetary policy. To see the logic, suppose a country were to increase its supply of money with the goal of lowering the short-term rate of interest and stimulating economic activity. Given a stable demand for money, the increase in the money supply should result in an excess supply of money relative to the domestic demand for real balances. The result would be a fall in the interest rate and consequently the exchange rate. This lower exchange rate will induce an increase in exports and a decrease in imports, thereby amplifying the short-term stimulus that is afforded by the increase in the money supply. A decrease in the money supply would have the opposite effect: with a stable demand for money, it should increase the interest rate and the exchange rate, thereby inducing a fall in the balance of payments.[1]

Despite its several qualities, the Mundell–Fleming model no longer enjoys the dominance that it once had. The most important reason for this is that the mainstream of macroeconomic theorizing has been drawn to intertemporal models that claim to be long term in orientation, and based on 'rigorous micro-foundations'. When translated, the latter term means a problematic summation of the activities of a set of identical hyper-rational economic agents with infinite time horizons. In such models, the flows of capital into a country represent the rational 'choice' of the residents of that country to consume more goods today relative to tomorrow. It follows that a balance of payments deficit is *prima facie* evidence that a country is 'choosing' to live beyond its means.[2] Under some circumstances, such models can be made consistent with the Mundell–Fleming model if the latter is held to be descriptive of the 'short term', but the two approaches can also diverge in important instances. While many theoretical economists, and some textbooks, are beginning to downplay the Mundell–Fleming model, it still enjoys wide use in economic policy discussions—particularly when short- or medium-run phenomena are being explored.

For economists who never shared the mainstream of the profession's largely aesthetic and pre-analytic preference for models featuring rational expectations, market efficiency and general equilibrium, the movement away from Mundell–Fleming toward the newer intertemporal models is poorly motivated. But, independently of these trends, both varieties of models share several limitations. The most important concern the characterization of capital flows. These models depict capital movements as motivated by, and adapting to, changes in 'economic fundamentals' (Blecker, 1999, pp. 66–83). Post-Keynesians (hereafter referred to as Keynesians), have located the primary cause of international capital flows, and the consequent exchange rate volatility, in the peculiar manner in which expectations and conventions are formed among investors:

> [I]n the event that the market is actually dominated by the speculators, then *the link between asset prices and careful analyses of the issuer's future viability is broken.* Now the game is to guess what everyone else is guessing.... This effect is made greater by the environment of uncertainty in which agents must operate. The end result is higher turnover, greater volatility, and prices that may be driven more by whim than reason. Efficient allocation of resources as defined in the neoclassical model is still *possible,* but cannot be expected.
>
> (Harvey, 1999, pp. 204–205; italics in original text)

To Keynesians, models based on 'fundamentals' ignore the possibility that the foreign exchange market, like other asset markets, could be an independent, and relatively autonomous, source of instability (Kindleberger, 1996; Minsky,

1986). Following directly in the line of Keynes's thoughts on these matters, Keynesian economists have long harbored doubts about the underlying stability of markets built around interdependent expectations (Dequech, 2000). In the Keynesian theory the larger, more competitive, and more 'perfect' an asset market becomes, the more likely it is that it will constitute a source of instability with damaging repercussions for the economy. This lesson is readily applied to the market for foreign exchange which has grown in both size and volatility over these past several decades (Blecker, 1999, pp. 66–83; Harvey, 1999; Davidson, 1997, 1999; Prasch, 1998).

A second critique of models based on 'fundamentals', including the Mundell–Fleming model, concerns their failure to distinguish between real and portfolio investment, and whether or not a country's foreign debt is denominated mainly in foreign or domestic currency. Simply put, models based on fundamentals tend to treat all capital flows as perfect substitutes. For this reason, these models fail to stress any issues related to the structure and stability of a country's indebtedness. While this problem is not apparent when international capital markets are operating in an orderly fashion, it is a fatal flaw when such models are applied during crisis periods. At the level of policy, the difference in these approaches is evident in Keynesian analyses of the recent financial turmoil in East Asia (Arestis & Demetriades, 1999; Felix, 1998; Wade & Veneroso, 1998).

To his credit, Mundell is too familiar with economic history to suggest, as many economists have, that speculation is necessarily a stabilizing force. Indeed, the need to rein in speculation is one of his arguments against floating exchange rates (Mundell, 1973b, p. 147). When all is said and done, Mundell's position is that incorrect fundamentals, and the uncertainty that flawed government policies can induce, are the ultimate causes of speculation and financial instability.

4 Monetary history and policy

4.1 A concern for inflation

To understand Mundell's approach to the international economy, one must appreciate that his take on political economy is firmly grounded in the 'Chicago tradition'. In this 'vision' of the economic process the real economy, employment, and output are overwhelmingly determined by supply-side factors. Inflation, by contrast, is caused by an excess supply of money and the central banks of this world are responsible for it. To Mundell, it follows that with the proper incentives, room for independent operation, and the application of correct and credible policies, the world's central banks can eradicate inflation if they choose to do so. In keeping with the political economy of his monetarist colleagues, Mundell is skeptical about the resolve of central bankers to suppress inflation, especially in the face of democratic political processes that impose a relatively short time horizon on political leaders. Moreover, modern society's bias toward inflation will be exacerbated if the country in question is trying to mask mistaken macroeconomic policies such as an over-ambitious welfare state.

Like many monetarists, Mundell views inflation as neither benign nor inconsequential. He views inflation, even a fairly modest inflation, as a tempting policy choice that can be very costly to an economy for three interrelated reasons.[3] First, it is disruptive to the formation of expectations of savers. Second, inflation disrupts the formation of expectations on the part of investors and entrepreneurs: 'Entrepreneurial capitalism involves the allocation of resources guided by profit incentives. The profit-motive cannot be mobilized without a stable currency' (Mundell, 1993, p. 72). Third, in a progressive tax system, inflation pushes people into higher tax brackets, thereby diminishing the rate of return on investments and, consequently, lowering the rate of economic growth. Moreover, Mundell believes that the rate of inflation does not have to be very high for any of the above effects to occur.[4]

4.2 Fixed exchange rates and the control of inflation

Given his preoccupation with the control of inflation, and his belief that it is caused by excessive growth in a country's money supply, Mundell concludes that the case for a regime of fixed exchange rates is overwhelming: 'Exchange rate stability is associated with monetary discipline; instability with indiscipline. Monetary instability leads to inflation and unemployment' (1995a, p. 34). He believes that monetary discipline is at its strongest when fixed rates are joined to credible commitments on the part of central banks to abide by automatic mechanisms in the event of any disequilibria in the nation's balance of payments. This distinctive approach to the control of inflation led Mundell to break with some of his monetarist colleagues. For example, Milton Friedman (1953), in a widely cited paper, argues that exchange rates are just another price, and that floating exchange rates would be more market oriented and efficient. Mundell counters that:

> Under a fixed exchange rate system, the responsibility for inflation rests with the country or the mechanism determining the level of international reserves. The movement to flexible exchange rates shifted the responsibility for solving the inflation problem back to individual countries, outside the framework of an international monetary system. The moot question was whether national self-discipline would be better than global discipline.
>
> (1995b, p. 464)

In keeping with these themes, Mundell's support for a common European currency is grounded in its potential for controlling inflation. He is very much in favor of any regime that controls the ability of central banks to engage in discretionary monetary policy, and suggests that he would even favor a global currency if it had the correct safeguards built into its operating rules (Mundell, 1995a, pp. 33–35).

Mundell's support for the euro is not based solely on the fact that a single currency is the ultimate fixed-rate system. He also argues that in a regime with either credibly fixed rates or a common currency, money is more effective in its roles as unit of account and store of value (Mundell, 1995b, p. 477). Besides reducing transactions costs, a single currency would mean that fewer resources would be devoted to hedging against exchange rate changes, to the pursuit of speculation, and to the holding of adequate international reserves to counter this speculation (Mundell, 1968b, pp. 182–184). Contrary to what the proponents of floating exchange rates once claimed, Mundell points out that 'The need for an international unit of account for purposes of international trade and finance was just as great as ever [after the introduction of flexible exchange rates], and the increased uncertainty associated with flexible exchange rates increased, rather than eliminated, the need for international reserve assets' (1995b, p. 465).

Mundell's support for fixed exchange rates has nothing to do with the Keynesian aim of constructing an international structure that would be more conducive to activist fiscal policies. Rather, he wishes to promote a structure that will check discretionary monetary policies, including monetary expansions that occur in support of fiscal policies:

> A truly fixed exchange rate system even with separate national currencies leaves little scope for independent national monetary policies. Confidence in the exchange rate parity requires affirmation of a commitment to a mechanism for adjusting the balance of payments. Countries must allow their money supplies to increase or decrease according to whether they have a surplus or a deficit in the balance of payments.
>
> (Mundell, 1993, p. 80)

We should note the provision at the end of this quotation. Mundell is arguing that the world's central banks should operate under clear, and ideally binding, 'rules of the game' as these rules were once termed under the gold standard. These rules will discourage or prohibit central banks from 'sterilizing' monetary flows by managing the level of domestic bank reserves.[5]

Knowing that this is a rather tall order, Mundell would settle for several large currency areas, each equipped with its own independent central bank that is subject to a clear mandate to control inflation. Naturally, those persons or regions finding themselves subject to disproportionate adjustment pressures will object to such restrictive monetary policies, but Mundell has never claimed that a firm anti-inflation policy would be a populist measure.

4.3 The gold standard

Mundell has remarked that 'From the standpoint of long run price stability gold-based money was perhaps the most stable monetary system of all time' (1989b, p. 354). His history of the rise and fall of the gold standard is instructive because it reveals some of the qualities that he would like to see retained by any modern fixed exchange rate system. Specifically, he praises the performance of the pre-World War I gold standard as an example of a largely automatic adjustment system that presented an international bulwark against inflation (Mundell, 1968b, p. 217):

> The international gold standard at the beginning of the twentieth century operated smoothly to facilitate trade, payments, and capital movements. Balance of payments were kept in equilibrium at fixed exchange rates by an adjustment mechanism that had a high degree of automaticity. The world price level may have been subject to long-term trends but annual inflation or deflation rates were low, tended to cancel out, and preserve the value of money in the long run. The system gave the world a high degree of monetary integration and stability.
>
> (Mundell, 2000, p. 328)[6]

Mundell's policy proposals, including his qualified endorsement of the euro, are all derivative of his interest in replicating the automatic checks that the gold standard placed on central bank behavior. At the same time, he wishes to avoid some of the problems that eventually led to the demise of the gold standard. These included the concentration of gold in a few countries, and the degree of discretion that this allowed to a few central banks, specifically the Federal Reserve, that eventually undermined this system.

As the last paragraph implies, Mundell does not present the gold standard period as one without its own problems, and for this reason he does not propose bringing it back.[7] In keeping with Cassel's analysis, he acknowledges that pegging the world's supply of money to an arbitrary constraint such as the supply of gold had its drawbacks. Specifically:

> The long run stability of gold was a great benefit from the standpoint of the long term capital market. But against this long run stability must be set the inconvenience and perhaps injustice of the troublesome swings. These movements created disturbing shifts in the distribution of income between creditors and debtors that led to resentment by the losers and political controversy over the nature of the standard itself.
>
> (Mundell, 1989b, p. 355)

In his analysis of this episode Mundell argues, with John Maynard Keynes and other authorities, that Britain's decision to return to gold on pre-war parities was a clear mistake (Keynes, 1925; Mundell, 1989b, pp. 366–372, 1995a, pp. 11–15). What he does not allow is that this episode undermined the *principle* of a gold standard, only its practice during the interwar period.

The blunder, according to Mundell, was the fact that the *de facto* numeraire currency, in this case the dollar, was overvalued by about 30% in light of the increase in the demand for gold that was a direct result of so many central banks needing reserves after adopting the gold standard over such a short period of time. 'The focus of attention on the overvaluation of the pound distracted attention from the vastly more important problem of the overvaluation of all currencies against gold' (Mundell, 1989b, p. 369). The effects of this overvaluation were particularly acute since so much of the world's gold had accumulated in the US over the course of World War I. Finally, the tendency on the part of the newly operational Federal Reserve System to sterilize gold inflows, thereby offsetting inflationary pressures in the US, meant that the automatic mechanism that could have restored some of the gold supply to Europe did not function properly, turning the worldwide gold shortage into an even more severe crisis.

Of course, the option always existed to re-adopt the gold standard at more sustainable par values, but a concern for credibility meant that this possibility was never seriously contemplated at the highest levels. National pride and an overzealous concern for the fortunes of creditors also precluded this option.

4.4 Fixed exchange rates, Bretton Woods and a new European currency

Like the Keynesians, Mundell has a strong appreciation for the financial order that emerged under the Bretton Woods agreements. To Mundell, this emergent world order, while not exactly planned by anyone, could have been a lasting success. It certainly did embody the idea of fixed exchange rates across a wide variety of currencies. However, the use of the dollar as the world's primary reserve currency had one flaw that proved to be important: essentially, the world's inflation rate would now be equivalent to the inflation rate of the US. To Mundell, this meant that the world's inflation rate would be determined by the Federal Reserve's policies.

The Bretton Woods agreement did have one key clause that, had it been binding, could have offset this problem. This was the anchoring of the dollar to gold at $35 per ounce. While individuals were precluded from trading their dollars at this price, the world's central banks were not, and many of them did just that as their supply of dollars outstripped their need for reserves. Throughout the 1950s the steady outflow of gold from the US was not seen to be much of a problem, and was even welcomed as an opportunity to redistribute the world's stock of reserve gold. But this trend was unsustainable, particularly since the Federal Reserve was not about to allow the stock of dollars to decline, and the domestic interest rate to rise, as gold flowed out. The result was a continually overvalued dollar and a continuous outflow of gold that was unchecked by any automatic mechanism, such as a rise in the US price level, that would correct the balance of payments and stem the outflow of gold.

Mundell concludes that the Federal Reserve could have kept the Bretton Woods system going by depreciating the dollar in terms of gold, or ending its policy of sterilization. Either choice could have preserved the world's fixed exchange rate arrangements and, in Mundell's view, avoided the disastrous inflation of the 1970s. Mundell considers this inflationary environment to be the root cause of several of the economic problems that characterized those years, including reduced economic growth, the Third World debt crisis, and even the severity of the dislocations that followed from the oil price shocks.[8]

Most Keynesians would concur with Mundell's view that the adoption of floating exchange rates undermined the institutional conditions that contributed to the Golden Age of post-war capitalism. But they might also remark on his neglect of the role that the widespread use of capital controls played during this period. To Keynesians, the limits placed on speculative capital movements, and the consequent limits on deflationary pressures, were what accounted for the successes of the Bretton Woods era (Davidson, 1997, 1999; Palley, 1998, ch. 10).

It is interesting that, in light of the recent financial crises in East Asia, one is beginning to see, at least among economists who are not employed by the Clinton administration, or by its clients among the larger financial institutions, a renewed awareness of the stability that judicious capital controls can bring to the financial sector (Cooper, 1999; Williamson, 1999; Bhagwati, 1998). This is a most welcome development after the largely unreflective embrace of globalism that has been so characteristic of the American economics profession over these past 20 years.

Finally, and perhaps most important, Keynesian economists believe that the world's economic arrangements embody a strong bias toward deflation (Arestis & Sawyer, 1999; Davidson, 1997, 1999). This position builds directly upon several of the insights that John Maynard Keynes originally brought to the Bretton Woods meetings. The concern is that the major international organizations have placed the burden of balance-of-payments adjustments on deficit countries. To meet the conditionality requirements on IMF and World Bank loans, deficit nations are obliged to pursue austerity programs that typically feature a combination of lower government spending, higher interest rates and, ultimately, lower incomes in their effort to import less and export more. In such a deflationary environment many otherwise viable business ventures are forced into bankruptcy, and unemployment becomes unnecessarily severe (Wade & Veneroso, 1998; Arestis & Demetriades, 1999).

Similar dynamics are evident in the requirements that European countries are obliged to meet in order to align their currencies with the euro. Lower debt/GDP ratios, along with lower deficits, and penalties for running a deficit higher than 3% of GDP, are part of the agreement. These policies, in addition to a mandate to converge on low inflation rates, all imply slower growth rates. Philip Arestis & Malcolm Sawyer (1999) claim that the Maastricht Treaty has exacerbated Europe's unemployment problem and, because it fails to include levels of employment in its convergence criteria, is likely to impose a long-lasting deflationary structure on Europe.

4.5 Is Europe an 'optimal currency area'?

Early in his career, Mundell began to work on what was to become one of his most important papers (1961a). Along with an important follow-up paper

(1973a), it explored the qualities that would be conducive to the formation of what he called an 'Optimal Currency Area'. In the original paper, Mundell considered the implications for economic adjustment if two formerly disparate regions or countries were to share a single currency. In other words, what were the economic, as opposed to the political or national, conditions for a single currency area? Mundell suggests that an optimal currency area would be one in which either (a) wages and prices were relatively flexible, or (b) the movement of factors between regions was relatively rapid and costless. In either case, a single currency could be successful since the economic adjustments that would be required to offset any disequilibria in the balance of payments between the various regions or countries could be made without changing the value of the currency unit. It followed that if the productive factors of a region or country were immobile, and wages and prices were inflexible, then that region or country would be a poor candidate for joining a currency area.

Mundell considers Europe to be an excellent candidate for a currency area (Mundell, 1993). But his optimism, while clearly shared by many of Europe's most prominent political leaders, has not drawn the same level of assent from economists. For example, Ronald McKinnon (1994) claims that the best long-term arrangement for Europe would be a 'common monetary standard', with separate currencies that may fluctuate within narrow boundaries. In essence, McKinnon believes that countries need to retain their own currencies and their own central banks in order to manage their sovereign debts. McKinnon also thinks that countries need to retain the option to devalue their currencies in the event that serious misalignments emerge over time.

A greater concern emerges when one drops the assumption that the marginal products of capital and labor are diminishing functions of the amounts of those factors employed. In this case, the argument for a common currency area is seriously weakened because uneven growth rates between regions will bring about chronic disequilibria in the balance of payments that are unlikely to be offset by capital flows. For example, take a large free market with a common currency. Now suppose that many firms use technologies that feature increasing returns to scale, and add in, for good measure, external economies. With such conditions, we can anticipate highly uneven growth rates across the several regions of this common currency area (Arthur, 1994, chs 4, 6, 7). Moreover, capital flows will be likely to exacerbate, rather than mitigate, such trends. With uneven growth we can expect that regions growing more slowly will experience capital outflows and chronic balance-of-payments difficulties. These problems will just get worse if they cannot be at least partially offset by periodic devaluations or fiscal policies that enact inter-regional transfers (Kaldor, 1970; McCombie, 1999; Arestis & Sawyer, 1999).

5 Supply-side economics

Robert Mundell was the most prominent academic economist associated with the supply-side economics of the Reagan administration. But his commitment was not the result of a sudden conversion or a passing enthusiasm, rather it evolved from ideas on which he had been working for some time (Mundell, 1990b, pp. 116–123, 1996, 1998, 2000, pp. 335–337; Laffer, 1999). In recognition of this, one of President Reagan's closest economic advisors, Martin Anderson (1988, p. 146), identifies Mundell as 'the godfather of modern supply-side economics'.

It is difficult, even after 20 years, to separate out the facts from the myths of supply-side economics, in large part because a number of prominent conservative journalists were responsible for many exaggerated claims on its behalf. (It would be unfair, for example, to saddle Mundell with the claim that cuts in high-end marginal tax rates would have the happy effect of diminishing prostitution, pornography and abortions.) But it is the case that substantial claims were made by responsible members of the Reagan administration. Specifically, a budget surplus was predicted for 1984, although some former Reagan officials claim that this promise was premised on draconian cuts in the Federal budget that were never enacted (Stockman, 1986). But for the true believers, budget cuts were besides the point; the main point was that cuts in the higher marginal tax brackets would so tremendously increase economic activity and national income that any loss of tax revenues to the Treasury from lower marginal tax rates would soon be restored by an increase in aggregate economic activity. Some years later, Martin Anderson (1988, ch. 4) argued that the economists comprising Reagan's inner circle never held such a naive view and merely claimed that the cuts would be partially, but not fully, restored.

Anderson also argues, correctly, that the core supply-side concepts have a long heritage in the history of economic ideas. Nevertheless supply-side economics reflected a specific policy agenda that became prominent at a specific time in economic history. Mundell recalls the essence of the policy proposals as follows:

> Supply-side economics began as a policy system alternative to short-run Keynesian and monetarist demand-side models. It was based on a policy mix that delivered price stability through monetary discipline, and economic stimulation and growth through the tax and regulatory systems.... [C]uts in marginal tax rates were needed to create output incentives to spur the economy, and tight money would produce price stability.
>
> (Mundell, 2000, pp. 335–336)

What set the theory behind the supply-side tax policies apart from the Keynesian perspective on fiscal policy was the idea that it would be better to target a tax cut toward the wealthy because of, and not despite, the fact that they have a lower marginal propensity to consume. While Keynesian fiscal policies are designed to increase the level of aggregate demand, the supply-siders presumed on the basis of a rearticulation of Say's Law that the level of aggregate demand would automatically adjust to the level of aggregate supply, and turned their attention to increasing the rate and magnitude of savings. Since supply-side models presumed an underlying loanable funds model, this additional saving would automatically be converted into investment, either from increased purchases of stock and bonds, or through the banking system. It followed that these reductions in the upper end of marginal tax rates would lead to increased investment, increased productivity growth, and an increased rate of growth in the economy. Again, since a loanable funds theory was presumed, increases in savings would soon induce lower real rates of interest, and thereby higher rates of investment. Moreover, as classical economists, supply-siders were unconcerned that their fiscal policy would be offset or diminished by the simultaneous pursuit of a tight money policy. Presumably, any momentary increase in short-term interest rates that might appear would soon give way to lower long-term interest rates as 'rational' investors revised their inflationary expectations. Such was the idea.

Much has been written both for and against this policy, and this is not the place for a lengthy recounting of these debates (e.g. Anderson, 1988; Greider, 1982; Stockman, 1986). Keynesians take the view that the loanable funds theory, which is a crucial underpinning to the theory, was debunked some time ago (Chick, 1983, chs 9–11; Keynes, 1936, chs 13–14). Say's Law, the proposition that 'supply creates its own demand', was another important premise of the supply-side school and, once again, Keynesians took the position that this idea has also been definitively critiqued (Chick, 1983, chs 6–8; Keynes, 1936, chs 2–3).

Supply-side enthusiasts were never much interested in addressing these theoretical challenges to their theory. But they could not ignore the statistics which showed neither a surge nor even an increase in the rates of aggregate savings and investment over the course of the 1980s. A comparison of the average annual levels of investment and consumption during the 4 years of the Carter administration, and the second term of the Reagan administration indicates that the predicted structural changes never occurred.[9] Measured in constant 1987 dollars, the annual average of both net private domestic investment and net fixed non-residential investment fell in *absolute terms* between these two periods. The fall in percentage terms is even more striking. Net private domestic investment was 7.0% of GDP during the Carter years, and 5.7% of GDP during Reagan's second term. The average of net fixed non-residential investment fell from 3.5% of GDP to 2.8% (Council of Economic Advisors, 1992, table B-15; author's calculations). With this decline in investment, we might expect to see a rise in consumption between these two periods, and we do. Consumption during Carter's 4 years averaged 64.7% of GDP, and it rose to 67.2% of GDP during Reagan's second term (Council of Economic Advisors, 1992, table B-2; author's calculations). Since we know that the median wage also fell between these two periods, it follows that this rise in the rate of consumption was mainly the result of increased consumption by the wealthy. This last fact is particularly troubling for the claims of supply-siders since the point of Reagan's massive tax cuts was to induce the wealthy to increase their levels of savings and investment. We did indeed see what the *Wall Street Journal* editorial writer Robert Bartley described as 'Seven Fat Years', but the fat had to do with a redistribution toward the upper income brackets, and with the consequent rise in conspicuous consumption on the part of America's elites. In the end, investment fell, savings fell, and no higher social purpose was served by these policies. We can only conclude that supply-side economics failed to deliver on its promises.

In 1990, Mundell attributed the failure of savings rates to respond to the supply-side tax cuts to the relatively small number of individuals who were then in the high-savings brackets of 40–60 years old (Mundell, 1990b, p. 121). But 10 years later this is not a particularly satisfying explanation since the 'baby-boomers' are now well into this age bracket, and yet the savings rate shows no signs of recovery. In view of the fact that the supply-side tax structure has remained in place through the Reagan, Bush, and Clinton administrations, it is indeed ironic that the primary engine of growth since the mid-1980s has been debt-financed consumption (Godley, 1999). The predicted surge in the rates of savings and investment has been most conspicuous for its absence. Given the supply-siders' uncritical confidence in the predictions they made in the early 1980s, and the conceptual problems that plagued the theory, one is tempted to conclude that the supply-siders were just wrong.

That said, Reagan's supply-side experiment induced an important realignment in American economic policy. The Reagan tax cuts, in conjunction with the military buildup, resulted in a surge in the budget deficit that, for a variety of short-term political expedients, the Democratic Party adopted as a core political issue. As a result, when the Democratic Party returned to power in the early 1990s, it was pre-committed to a new posture as the party of 'fiscal responsibility'. When the Clinton administration took office, high and stable prices for long-term bonds constituted its highest priority, crowding out any interest in social spending or industrial policies (Woodward, 1994; Reich, 1997, pp. 59–65). This realignment in the priorities of the Democratic Party, rather than the specifics of Mundell's or Reagan's tax policies, represents the legacy of the supply-siders to the political economy of the US.

6 Conclusion: Mundell and the spirit of contemporary economic policy

Just as Richard Nixon once proclaimed that 'we are all Keynesians now', so we might now proclaim, in concert with Bill Clinton, Tony Blair and Gerhard Schroeder, that 'we are all supply-siders now'. Across the formerly left-leaning parties of North America and Europe, time-honored conservative nostrums about tight money and fiscal surpluses are combined with more palatable, but nonetheless supply-oriented, calls for increased 'education', 'training' and 'public–private partnerships' intended to remedy an alleged erosion of 'skills' among the workforce.[10] In the American election cycle that just ended, the debate over fiscal policy was reduced to an argument about whether to retire more debt (Gore) or to enact more supply-side tax cuts (Bush). Monetary policy that targets anything other than the inflation rate and the 'confidence' of the financial sector is simply out of the question. Similar policies are now enshrined in the culture of international organizations such as the IMF and the World Bank. To the extent that they are responsible for these trends, Professor Mundell and his allies in the economics profession can claim to have had a substantial, if indirect, impact on what the world takes to be the new consensus of all right-thinking people on economic policy. The rest of us will have a long way to go to repair the damage.

Notes

The author would like to thank Falguni Sheth for her assistance with this paper.
1 This last insight is an important element of another of Mundell's areas of research that is now known as the Monetary Approach to the Balance of Payments. In Mundell's words, 'The balance of payments is a monetary phenomenon and its correction implies monetary policies. There are, broadly speaking, only two monetary means of bringing about equilibrium. One is to change the price of money—the flexible exchange rate solution; the other is to change the quantity of money—the flexible money solution. The debate is on whether it is better to fix the stock of money (or its rate of change) and let the price of one money vary in terms of others; or to fix the price of money and let the quantity vary' (Mundell, 1973b, p. 145).
2 We should note that Mundell is anything but resistant to this 'short-term' and 'long-term' dichotomy in economic theorizing. Some of his articles on savings and national debt reflect the same underlying structure of these newer models (Mundell, 1990a, b).
3 In some of his early work on pure theory Mundell demonstrates that the 'Classical Dichotomy' between real and monetary phenomena does not strictly hold, and that a modest inflation can increase the rate of economic growth. This would be the case even if the increase in the supply of money were to be fully anticipated (Mundell, 1971, chs 2–6). Since he concludes that increases in the supply of 'outside' money are not strictly neutral over the long term, it would be inaccurate to think of his monetary theory as 'monetarist' in the sense that this term is conventionally used. Indeed, by today's taxonomy, such a position would place Mundell in the New Keynesian camp. But this says more about trends in contemporary academic economics than it does about Mundell. Since Mundell maintains the related propositions that (a) inflation has its origin in the quantity of outside money, (b) the demand for money is relatively stable, and (c) that central banks have the ability to control this supply of outside money, it would appropriate to think of him as working within the Quantity Theory or Monetarist tradition that characterized the University of Chicago Economics Department of the 1950s, 1960s and 1970s.
4 While everyone would agree that a hyperinflation is disastrous, recent econometric evidence fails to support the view that low levels of inflation are detrimental to an economy's growth prospects (Bruno & Easterly, 1998).
5 Sterilization occurs when a country's central bank uses open market operations to offset international monetary flows. For example, take a country operating under a gold standard that enjoys a positive balance of trade and a consequent gold inflow. This gold inflow should cause an increase in the domestic money supply, and an increase in the domestic price level, thereby partially offsetting the attractiveness of the country's exports. But if the central bank were to sell treasury bills to banks, thereby lowering the banks' excess reserves, the domestic money supply and prices could remain stable, and the country could continue to run its balance of trade surplus.
6 Unfortunately, Mundell's appreciation for the 'automatic' qualities of the pre-World War I gold standard is undermined by, among others, one of his favorite authorities

on its operation, Gustav Cassel. To fully appreciate the different perspective, it will be worthwhile to quote from Cassel at some length:

> The automatic functioning of the gold standard was looked upon as its principal strength, the exclusion of all sorts of political influences upon the monetary system being held to be of primary importance.
>
> However, in reality the system never—not even in the pre-War period of its existence—functioned in such a simple way. For the sake of security central banks had to keep larger gold reserves than those legally required and were therefore in a position both to export and to import gold without letting these gold movements necessarily influence the country's volume of means of payment or its internal price-level. The gold supply of a country exercised such an influence only via the policy of the central bank and its regulation of the market by means of its rate of discount and its open market operations. Thus the currency necessarily became a 'managed currency,' whose value depended entirely on the policy of the central bank. (Cassel, 1936, pp. 2–3)

7 For example, Mundell is critical of Jude Wanniski and Wayne Angell's proposal for a Russian gold standard because, among other reasons, 'the ruble exchange rate would fluctuate with the vicissitudes of the gold market, arbitrarily destabilizing the domestic economy' (Mundell, 1993, p. 74). When discussing the then-proposed European currency, he always expresses a strong desire to see this currency 'anchored' (Mundell, 1970b). In the case of the proposed European currency, he thought that gold should play a role as an anchor:

> A more interesting proposal would be to create a basket currency not only of the national currencies, as the ECU is, but also of gold. The assets of the ECB [European Central Bank] could include gold, dollars and national currencies, and the ECU or Europa could, in principle, be convertible into the basket of assets the ECB holds. The inclusion of gold in the basket would partly compensate for the absence of an all-Europe government backing the currency.
>
> (Mundell, 1993, p. 86)

> None of these suggestions adds up to a return to the nineteenth-century gold standard.

8 Obviously each of these problems can be attributed to sources other than the adoption of a floating exchange rate regime, but it would take us rather far afield to address them here.

9 In choosing to compare an average of the Carter years (1977–80) with an average of the second Reagan term (1985–88), I am deliberately biasing the analysis in favor of the supply-siders' arguments. For example, these periods include the recession of Carter's last year and exclude the even steeper recession of Reagan's first term. Presumably, the effects of the supply-side policies were in full bloom by Reagan's second term, so their failure to change the performance of certain important aggregates by this time casts serious doubts on the claims of supply-side economists.

10 David Howell (1996), Thomas Palley (1998, pp. 70–73), and David Gordon (1996, pp. 175–187) have each written detailed refutations of the conventional belief that the reason for the declining fortunes of so many workers in the US is a lack of skills.

References

Anderson, M. (1988) *Revolution* (New York, Harcourt Brace Jovanovich).

Arestis, P. & Demetriades, P. (1999) Financial liberalization: the experience of developing countries, *Eastern Economic Journal*, 25, pp. 441–457.

Arestis, P. & Sawyer, M. (1999) Prospects for the single European currency and some proposals for a New Maastricht, in: P. Davidson & J. Kregel (Eds) *Full Employment and Price Stability in a Global Economy* (Northampton, Edward Elgar).

Arthur, B. (1994) *Increasing Returns and Path Dependence in the Economy* (Ann Arbor, University of Michigan Press).

Bhagwati, J. (1998) The capital myth: the difference between trade in widgets and dollars, *Foreign Affairs,* 77, pp. 7–12.

Blecker, R.A. (1999) *Taming Global Finance: A Better Architecture for Growth and Equity* (Washington, DC, Economic Policy Institute).

Branson, W. (1972) *Macroeconomic Theory and Policy* (New York, Harper & Row).

Bruno, M. & Easterly, W. (1998) Inflation crises and long-run growth, *Journal of Monetary Economics,* 41, pp. 3–36.

Cassel, G. (1936) *The Downfall of the Gold Standard* (Oxford, Oxford University Press).

Chick, V. (1983) *Macroeconomics after Keynes: A Reconsideration of the General Theory* (Cambridge, MA, MIT Press).

Cooper, R.N. (1999) Should capital controls be banished?, *Brookings Papers on Economic Activity,* 1, pp. 89–125.

Council of Economic Advisors (1992) *Economic Report of the President* (Washington DC, US Government Printing Office).

Davidson, P. (1997) Are grains of sand in the wheels of international finance sufficient to do the job when boulders are often required?, *Economic Journal,* 107, pp. 671–686.

Davidson, P. (1999) Global employment and open economy macroeconomics, in: J. Deprez & J. Harvey (Eds) *Foundations of International Economics: Post Keynesian Perspectives* (New York, Routledge).

Dequech, D. (2000) Asset choice, liquidity preference, and rationality under uncertainty, *Journal of Economic Issues,* 34, pp. 159–176.

Dornbusch, R. & Fischer, S. (1978) *Macroeconomics* (New York, McGraw-Hill).

Felix, D. (1998). Asia and the crisis of financial globalization, in: D. Baker, G. Epstein & R. Pollin (Eds) *Globalism and Progressive Economic Policy* (New York, Cambridge University Press).

Fleming, J. (1962) Domestic financial policies under fixed and under floating exchange rates, *International Monetary Fund Staff Papers,* 9, pp. 369–379.

Fleming, J. (1963) Developments in the international payments system, *International Monetary Fund Staff Papers,* 10, pp. 461–482.

Friedman, M. (1953) The case for flexible exchange rates, in: *Essays in Positive Economics* (Chicago, University of Chicago Press).

Godley, W. (1999) *Seven Unsustainable Processes: Medium-Term Prospects and Policies for the United States and the World* (Jerome Levy Institute Special Report).

Gordon, D. (1996) *Fat and Mean: The Corporate Squeeze of Working Americans and the Myth of Managerial Downsizing* (New York, The Free Press).

Greider, W. (1982) *The Education of David Stockman and Other Americans* (New York, Dutton).

Harvey, J.T. (1999) Exchange rates: volatility and misalignment in the post-Bretton Woods era, in: J. Deprez & J. Harvey (Eds) *Foundations of International Economics: Post Keynesian Perspectives* (New York, Routledge).

Howell, D.R. (1996) Institutional failure and the American worker, Public Policy Brief, No. 29 (Annandale-on-Hudson, Jerome Levy Institute).

Kaldor, N. (1970) The case for regional policies, in: *Further Essays on Economic Theory* (New York, Holmes & Meier, 1978).

Keynes, J.N. (1917) *The Scope and Method of Political Economy* (Clifton, NJ, Augustus M. Kelley, 1973).

Keynes, J.M. (1925) The economic consequences of Mr. Churchill, in: *Essays in Persuasion* (New York, W.W. Norton, 1963).

Keynes, J.M. (1936) *The General Theory of Employment, Interest and Money* (London, Macmillan).

Kindleberger, C. (1996) *Manias, Panics, and Crashes: A History of Financial Crises,* 3rd edition (New York, John Wiley & Sons).

Laffer, A. (1999) Economist of the century, *Wall Street Journal* (15 October), p. A16.

McCombie, J.S.L. (1999) Economic integration, the EMU and European regional growth, in: P. Davidson & J. Kregel (Eds) *Full Employment and Price Stability in a Global Economy* (Northampton, Edward Elgar).

McKinnon, R. (1994) A common monetary standard or a common currency?, in: M. Baldassarri, M. Di Matteo & R. Mundell (Eds) *International Problems of Economic Interdependence* (New York, St. Martin's Press).

Minsky, H. (1986) *Stabilizing an Unstable Economy* (New Haven, Yale University Press).

Palley, T. (1998) *Plenty of Nothing* (Princeton, Princeton University Press).

Prasch, R. (1998) In defense of a tax on foreign exchange, *Journal of Economic Issues,* 32, pp. 325–331.

Reich, R. (1997) *Locked in the Cabinet* (New York, Alfred A. Knopf).

Stockman, D. (1986) *The Triumph of Politics: The Inside Story of the Reagan Revolution* (New York, Avon).

Wade, R. & Veneroso, F. (1998) The Asian crisis: the high debt model versus the Wall Street–Treasury–IMF complex, *New Left Review,* 228, pp. 3–23.

Williamson, J. (1999) Comment on Cooper, *Brookings Papers on Economic Activity,* 1, pp. 130–135.

Woodward, B. (1994) *The Agenda: inside the Clinton White House* (New York, Simon & Schuster).

Works by Robert Mundell cited in this paper

Mundell, R.A. (1960) The monetary dynamics of international adjustment under fixed and flexible exchange rates, *Quarterly Journal of Economics,* 74, pp. 227–257.

Mundell, R.A. (1961a) A theory of optimum currency areas, *American Economic Review,* 51, pp. 657–665.

Mundell, R.A. (1961b) Flexible exchange rates and employment policy, *Canadian Journal of Economics and Political Science,* 27, pp. 509–517.

Mundell, R.A. (1962) The appropriate use of monetary and fiscal policy for internal and external balance, *International Monetary Fund Staff Papers,* 9, pp. 70–79.

Mundell, R.A. (1963) Capital mobility and stabilization policies under fixed and flexible exchange rates, *Canadian Journal of Economics and Political Science,* 29, pp. 475–485.

Mundell, R.A. (1968a) *Man and Economics* (New York, McGraw-Hill).

Mundell, R.A. (1968b) *International Economics* (New York, Macmillan).

Mundell, R.A. (1971) *Monetary Theory: Inflation, Interest and Growth in the World Economy* (Pacific Palisades, Goodyear).

Mundell, R.A. (1973a) Uncommon arguments for common currencies, in: H.G. Johnson & A.K. Swoboda (Eds) *The Economics of Common Currencies* (Cambridge, MA, Harvard University Press).

Mundell, R.A. (1973b) A plan for a European currency, in: H.G. Johnson & A.K. Swoboda (Eds) *The Economics of Common Currencies* (Cambridge, MA, Harvard University Press).

Mundell, R.A. (1989a) Trade balance patterns as global general equilibrium: the seventeenth approach to the balance of payments, *Rivista di Politica Economica,* 79(6), pp. 9–60.

Mundell, R.A. (1989b) The global adjustment system, *Rivista di Politica Economica,* 79(12), pp. 351–464.

Mundell, R.A. (1990a) The international distribution of saving: past and future, *Rivista di Politica Economica,* 80(10), pp. 5–56.

Mundell, R.A. (1990b) Debts and deficits in alternative economic models, *Rivista di Politica Economica,* 80(7–8), pp. 5–129.

Mundell, R.A. (1993) Monetary policies for the New Europe, in: M. Baldassarri & R. Mundell (Eds) *Building the New Europe,* Vol. 1: *The Single Market and Monetary Unification* (New York, St. Martin's Press).

Mundell, R.A. (1995a) Exchange rate systems and economic growth, *Rivista di Politica Economica,* 83(6): pp. 3–36.

Mundell, R.A. (1995b) The future of the exchange rate system, *Economic Notes,* 24, pp. 453–478.

Mundell, R.A. (1996) Unemployment, competitiveness and the welfare state, in: M. Baldassarri, L. Paganetto & E.S. Phelps (Eds) *Equity, Efficiency and Growth: The Future of the Welfare State* (New York, St. Martin's Press).

Mundell, R.A. (1998) A progrowth fiscal system, in: J. Jasinowski (Ed.) *The Rising Tide* (New York, John Wiley).

Mundell, R.A. (2000) A reconsideration of the twentieth century, *American Economic Review,* 90, pp. 327–340.

6 The 'rocket science' of economics

The 2000 Nobel Prize winners – James J. Heckman and Daniel L. McFadden

Carolyn J. Heinrich and Jeffrey B. Wenger

'The Economic Contributions of James J. Heckman and Daniel L. McFadden' by Carolyn J. Heinrich and Jeffrey B. Wenger from *Review of Political Economy* (2002), Volume 14, Issue 1 (Taylor and Francis Ltd, http://www.informaworld.com), reprinted by permission of the publisher.

1 Introduction

In October 2000, the Royal Swedish Academy of Sciences awarded the Nobel Prize in Economic Science to James J. Heckman and Daniel L. McFadden for their development of theory and methods analyzing selective samples and discrete-choice methodologies. In honoring McFadden and Heckman, the Nobel committee builds on a tradition of recognizing economists who have pioneered new methods of economic analysis. Other prize winners who have advanced methodologies are Ragnar Frisch and Jan Tinbergen, both honored in 1969 (the first time a Nobel in economics was awarded), Wassily Leontief (1974), Richard Stone (1984), and Trygve Haavelmo (1989).

Heckman and McFadden's econometric research has been described as the 'rocket science' of economics (Cohen, 2000, p. 45). Although theoretical and technical sophistication characterize their research, they have nevertheless seen their methodologies and applications extend across academic disciplines. In the Nobel committee's words, their techniques have become 'standard tools, not only among economists, but also among other social scientists', such as sociologists, political scientists, and policy analysts. Together, McFadden and Heckman's research traverses a broad range of policy applications – from business, employment and training, education, transportation, housing, utilities, and the environment to public assistance and other social programs – and has made important contributions to resolving the information problems that daily confront researchers and policy makers.

2 James J. Heckman

2.1 Academic history

James J. Heckman was born in Chicago, where his academic career has since flourished. He earned a BA in mathematics from Colorado College in 1965 and a MA (1968) and PhD (1971) in economics from Princeton University. His dissertation, 'Three Essays on Household Labor Supply and the Demand for Market Goods', was the foundation for his early, influential research on female labor supply.

Heckman's first academic appointment was at Columbia University, where in three short years he became an associate professor. That same year (1973) he came home to Chicago, joining the Department of Economics at the University of Chicago as an associate professor with tenure. Heckman, like McFadden, was recognized early as a bright star in his field, receiving the John Bates Clark medal (Heckman in 1983 at the age of 39, and McFadden in 1975 at the age of 38). In the late 1980s, Heckman joined the economics department at Yale University as the A. Whitney Griswold Professor of Economics, but he returned to the University of Chicago economics department in 1990. At that time, he also accepted a joint appointment at the Irving B. Harris Graduate School of Public Policy at Chicago, where he has played an integral role in developing programs. Heckman founded (in 1991) and continues to direct the Center for Evaluation of Social Programs. In addition to his appointment as the Henry Schultz Distinguished Service Professor in Economics, he is currently a Senior Research Fellow of the American Bar Foundation and the National Bureau of Economic Research, and a member of the National Academy of Sciences, and continues to serve his field in many other professional capacities.

In his Nobel lecture, Heckman described 'two conceptually distinct policy evaluation questions' that have motivated his research: (1) 'What is the effect of a program in place on participants and nonparticipants compared to no program at all or some alternative program?' and (2) 'What is the likely effect of a new program or an old program applied to a new environment?' His econometric work has explored the limitations of using statistical methodologies to answer these questions and the conditions and assumptions required to answer them with imperfect data. Throughout his academic career, his contributions to the advance of statistical methodologies have been made in the context of his application of theory to crucial public policy and social welfare issues, including labor force participation, human capital accumulation, and racial inequalities. This review of his work will thus highlight the importance of his microeconomic research for both methodology and applications.

2.2 Early labor supply research and selective samples

In the early 1970s, female labor supply increased, and a growing number of women entered paid employment. The analysis of female labor force participation relies on observing employment outcomes for women. For a woman who chooses not to work, earnings data are non-existent. In the absence of these data, it is difficult to assess who among women is more likely to enter the workforce, as well as the implications of the choice on their families. In effect, data on the forgone market opportunity cannot be observed by researchers or used to analyze labor force participation.

Heckman's microeconomic research on labor supply in the early 1970s confronted this thorny econometric issue of observed and unobserved factors influencing preferences for work, constraints on female labor force participation, and the problem of missing data on wages. In one of his most highly regarded and frequently cited papers in *Econometrica* (Heckman, 1974b), he developed a model that allowed for separate yet interrelated analyses of preferences for work, the reservation wage or 'shadow price' of time, and constraints on labor force participation. This model (the likelihood function shown in equation (1)) extended the Tobit estimator and was applied by Heckman to data on married women in the National Longitudinal Survey to simultaneously estimate the probability of a woman working, the determinants of labor force participation (e.g., number of children, education, husband's wage), and annual hours worked.

In the model below, where K of T married women work, $n[h_i, l(W_i)]$ is a multivariate normal density, with h measuring hours worked and $l(W_i)$ a linear function measuring determinants of the observed wage rate, W. The cumulative normal density function $pr[(W_i < W_i^*)_{h=0}]$ is the probability that a woman does not work (shown for the $K + 1$ to T women that do not work), where W_i^* is the reservation wage or shadow price of time. (See Heckman, 1974b for the derivation and proof of this model.)

$$L = \prod_{i=1}^{K} n[h_i, l(W_i)] \prod_{i=K+1}^{T} pr[(W_i < W_i^*)_{h=0}] \tag{1}$$

An important caveat is that when $K < T$ – which in reality will always be the case – this maximum likelihood estimation will not have the desired properties for parameter identification, if any parameter exists that affects both the multivariate normal density for hours of work and wages and the probability of a woman working. This problem was a motivator for a prolific body of work that followed this paper.

One of the early policy applications of this model was in the study of work (child care) subsidy programs initiated by the US presidential administration of Richard Nixon. In his analysis of these policies, Heckman (1974a) considered the labor force participation implications of a provision that required a minimum number of work hours to qualify for tax deductions for work-related child care expenses. He employed this method in estimating workers' preferences for income and nonmarket time, reservation wages and the value of non-working women's time, labor force participation and hours of work functions, and welfare losses associated with income taxes. By separating preferences from constraints, he showed that the administration's tax-rebate policy might actually have the unintended effect of making these programs differentially more attractive to higher-wage females than to female welfare recipients. In the same analysis, Heckman also raised questions about the effects of these policies on parents' choices of the mode of child care (formal, informal, custodial, etc.). His insights continue to inform child care policy discussions.

In addition to the substantive contributions of this particular work to the analysis of household consumption and labor supply decisions, this model was a precursor for the index-function model of potential outcomes that Heckman developed through the integration of simultaneous-equations theory and models of discrete choice. As shown in his labor supply analyses, we observe wages only if the offered wage is greater than or equal to the reservation wage or shadow price of time (W), producing a 'selective sample' of potential outcomes. If no unobservable variables influenced labor force participation, then unbiased, consistent outcome estimates could be obtained for those who do not work using information on those who do work. This is rarely the case in applied microeconomic research, however, where observable variables typically explain a small proportion of the variance in outcomes. Moreover, as Heckman's research demonstrates, accounting for selective sampling on unobservables becomes imperative for estimating structural relationships.

2.3 The selection bias problem

Selection bias presents a common identification problem that applies to any area of statistical research: How do researchers estimate population parameters when selection rules distort or bias the observed sample? These distortions may arise as a result of self-selection by individuals into samples and/or by the sample selection decisions of analysts. Although Heckman's research on the selection bias problem originated in his study of labor force participation (the decision to go to work) and the distribution of market wages, the potential applications of his research are far reaching: on decisions to join unions, to enter college or training programs (human capital accumulation), to apply for public assistance, and so on.

Heckman's 1979 paper 'Sample Selection Bias as a Specification Error' is likely the single most widely read essay beyond the disciplinary boundaries of economics to appear in *Econometrica*. Immediately following its publication, Heckman received thousands of requests for the software program used in estimating the model introduced in the paper. In this work, Heckman developed what is now known as the two-stage Heckman selection model (or 'Heckit' estimator), advancing conventional approaches to the analysis of omitted variables or specification error.

The two-stage Heckman selection model addresses a fundamental problem that occurs in applied statistical research when the sample-selection rule violates the assumption (based on a random sampling scheme) that the expected value of the error term in a simple regression function is zero. The regression function for the sample of data produced by the selection rule is:

$E(Y_{ji} \mid X_{ji}, \text{sample selection rule}) = X_{ji}\beta + E(U_{ji} \mid \text{sample selection rule})$ (2)

The bias that results from estimating equation (2) under the incorrect assumption that $E(U_{ji}) = 0$ is fundamentally a problem of omitted variables. The implications of leaving out theoretically important variables that are non-random are, of course, serious, resulting not only in bias among remaining estimators (β) but also inaccurate causal inferences. For example, in studies of the comparative effectiveness of public versus private schools, understanding and measuring the factors that influence individuals' choices between public and private schools (selection into the public or private sample) are critical to unbiased estimates of the relative effectiveness of the schools (typically measured by student test scores or future earnings). If students entering private schools are inherently different from those attending public schools in ways that affect schooling outcomes but are not measured and included in the outcome model, then the estimates of schooling effectiveness will be biased, and we may draw inappropriate inferences about the relative effects of public and private schools on student outcomes.

The logic of the two-stage Heckman selection model in solving this problem is straightforward and elegant: One estimates the parameters which when omitted from the regression give rise to specification error and uses the estimated values from this first-stage model as regressors in a second-stage least squares model of the outcome, Y. In his 1979 *Econometrica* paper, Heckman derives the result that knowing Z_i, a standard normal (instrumental) variable that determines sample selection but not the outcome (Y_i), allows one to estimate λ_i, the probability that an observation is selected into the sample. λ_i, the inverse of Mill's ratio, is a monotone decreasing function of the ratio of the density φ of a standard normal variable (Z_i) and its distribution function Φ:

$$\lambda_i = \frac{\varphi(Z_i)}{1-\Phi(Z_i)}$$ (3)

Two key requirements for choosing the standard normal (instrumental) variable are: (1) Z_i must be a determinant of sample selection, and (2) it must also be mean-independent of the error terms in the second-stage outcome model. An example of an instrumental variable used in the school-effectiveness literature is the distance to a student's school from his home. A probit function with Z_i estimated on the entire sample of observations is used to obtain an estimate of l_i for each observation, and the estimated values of l_i are then used as a regressor in the least squares equation on the selected sample. Heckman presents detailed proofs in this paper showing the relationship between the disturbances, l_i, and other model parameters. In addition, Heckman develops a correction procedure for computing standard errors, which are understated in the presence of selection bias.

A significant contribution of this research is Heckman's treatment of stochastic disturbance terms as an integral part of model specification. This work has fundamentally influenced the way microeconomic researchers (and others) analyze and interpret data, and its contributions to policy evaluation research have been inestimable. Numerous publications by Heckman and his colleagues followed, which explicated the econometric properties of the selection model and advanced its application in the estimation of labor supply functions and minimum wage, schooling, and training policies (Heckman, 1983; Heckman & MaCurdy, 1981; Heckman & Sedlacek, 1981, 1985).

An example of an important application of this model is found in Heckman's analysis of racial disparities in employment and earnings and the impact of public policies aimed at improving the economic status of African Americans. These analyses of black labor force participation identify and adjust for the 'selective withdrawal' of low-wage black workers from employment during the 1940–80 period, showing how selective samples of wages have biased upward estimates of black male economic progress relative to that of whites. With Donohue, Heckman evaluated the impact of civil rights policies on the economic progress of African Americans (Donohue & Heckman, 1991). They showed how the sources of improvements in relative earnings for blacks – migration, improvements in schooling quality, and policies to eliminate discrimination – varied across decades, controlling for black labor force participation. And they concluded that the government can play an important role in improving black economic status.

In his work with Sedlacek, Heckman also showed how selective withdrawals and re-entry into the labor force by low-wage workers in response to cyclical economic conditions – along with employment transitions across sectors – offset measures of wage variability and caused the economic consequences of cyclical changes for low-wage workers to be understated (Heckman & Sedlacek, 1985). If policy makers gain a better understanding of the separate effects of general social change, cyclical economic changes, and government actions, they will be able to address more effectively the labor market participation problems of minority and low-wage workers.

As with the Tobit estimator and other two-step structural estimation procedures, however, data problems still may limit applications of the selection model. Sampling rules frequently exclude observations for particular values of X and Y that make it necessary to invoke additional assumptions to determine the population distribution of X and Y at those values. Two important publications by Heckman & Robb (1985, 1986) assess alternative sampling plans and methods for addressing the selection bias problem, describing the assumptions they make, the data to which they may be applied (e.g., panel, repeated cross-section), and the econometric approaches researchers may use in applying them to policy evaluation problems.

Another common data problem is the challenge of finding a valid exclusion restriction, that is, identifying at least one variable included in Z that is not among the X that determine Y (outcomes). For example, if selection occurs on unobservables in the outcome equation or on variables that are stochastically dependent on changes in these unobservable variables, Z will determine Y and will not be a valid instrument, and the model will not be identified. Non-identification is a problem for researchers because a number of alternative structural models may be consistent with the data, unless restrictions are imposed. A large body of literature has developed on the identification issues associated with finding appropriate instrumental variables, and Heckman's more recent work continues to advance our knowledge in this area and the econometric models applied in policy evaluation research.

Heckman (1997) shows the importance of identifying variation in responses to treatment or program interventions, given that conventional applications of the instrumental variables method assume that the treatment has the same effect on all persons with given values of the regressors in X. In this paper, Heckman describes the identifying assumptions required to apply the method of instrumental variables in estimating parameters such as 'the mean effect of treatment on the treated' when individual responses to treatment vary, and he demonstrates the sensitivity of estimation results to alternative assumptions about how people select into programs. As he points out, the application of instrumental variables methods to cases with varying responses to treatment requires behavioral assumptions about selection that are typically not statistically verifiable.

Heckman's extensive contributions to the econometric literature concerning selective samples, unobserved heterogeneity, and related identification problems have been widely applied to the evaluation of public policies. His work on developing econometric frameworks for the analysis of the 'evaluation problem' ignited academic and policy debates on the use of non-experimental versus experimental methodologies to evaluate policy interventions (Heckman, Hotz & Dabos, 1987), and his papers, including those with Robb (Heckman & Robb, 1985, 1986), have become essential reading for any researcher engaged in policy evaluation research.

2.4 Treatment effects and policy evaluation

An early policy motivation for Heckman's evaluation research was the widely varying, non-experimental estimates of the impact of the Comprehensive Employment and Training Act (CETA) program (the federal job-training program of the 1970s), even when researchers were using the same data and econometric methods. The sensitivity of these non-experimental evaluation estimates to choices about model specifications for estimation led the US federal government to commission the National Job Training Partnership Act (JTPA) Study (an experimental evaluation of CETA's successor) in the mid-1980s. Heckman and his colleagues became involved in the non-experimental component of the JTPA study, and their subsequent research on non-experimental methods for identifying treatment effects has skillfully demonstrated both the limits and potential of econometric methods in estimating the impact of policy interventions.

In a plethora of essays, Heckman and his colleagues have challenged conventional approaches to estimating mean program effects and advanced non-experimental techniques for investigating a broader range of interesting evaluation questions and for recovering different treatment parameters. As Heckman & Smith (2000, p. 332) note, researchers using experimental data do not have to select among non-experimental evaluation methods, but 'they must still make many choices regarding how to construct, report, and interpret their estimates'. Heckman and Smith found in re-analyses of the JTPA study data that a number of decisions about the choice of job-training centers included in the experiment, the treatment of outliers, missing data, and dropouts by analysts, and different methods for constructing and interpreting earnings variables contributed to divergent estimates of the program's experimental earnings effects. These findings are particularly important in light of the US federal government's action in response to the experimental impact findings: authorizing substantial cuts in funding for the JTPA program, in particular the youth component.

Today, we still frequently read of studies commissioned by policy makers to find out 'what works, and what doesn't work' among public programs and policies. Welfare reform policies, school-to-work transition programs, public school initiatives to improve student performance, adult education and training programs, and the like are subject to experimental and non-experimental evaluations to determine their relative or approximate effectiveness. Heckman's model of the evaluation problem (described briefly below) is becoming a classic in this area of study and research.

As Heckman and a colleague's work illustrates (Heckman & Smith, 1996), the evaluation model focuses on a narrower subset of questions than those addressed with structural equation models and is not useful in evaluating universal interventions and general-equilibrium consequences. In this model (Heckman & Smith, 1995), two potential outcomes or states of the world are considered (Y_0, Y_1), where Y_1 is the outcome obtained given participation in the program and Y_0 is the outcome in the counterfactual or benchmark state of non-participation. If (Y_0, Y_1) could be observed for all, no evaluation problem would exist. However, we typically observe only Y_1 for program participants (where $D = 1$ if a person participates, and $D = 0$ otherwise) and Y_0 for nonparticipants. With these limited data, we are unable to construct the counterfactual conditional distributions, $F_0(Y_0 \mid D = 1)$, that is, outcomes for participants in the absence of program participation, and $F_1(Y_1 \mid D = 0)$, that is, outcomes for nonparticipants had they participated.

Additionally, Heckman (1996) and Heckman, Smith, & Clements (1997) show that even if data from randomized treatment and control groups are available to estimate mean program impacts, $E(Y_1Y_0 \mid D = 1)$, there are a variety of means that answer different questions and other interesting questions about the distribution of program effects that cannot be answered without making additional assumptions. In the presence of selection (sorting into treatment) on unobservables, the treatment effects defined depend on the conditioning sets used to identify them.

One of the more common treatment effects estimated in the literature and in practice is the effect of treatment on the treated (TT), $E(Y_1 - Y_0 \mid X = x, D = 1) = TT(x)$. Heckman, Smith, & Clements (1997) establish that if participants select into a program on the basis of their expectations about Y_0, estimates of the effect of treatment on the treated will be biased, where the term below in brackets is selection bias:

$$\underbrace{E(Y_i - Y_0 \mid X = x, D = 1)}_{TT(x)} + \underbrace{E(Y_0 \mid X = x, D = 1) - E(Y_0 \mid X = x, D = 0}_{\text{selection bias}} \qquad (4)$$

Selection bias arises because we do not directly measure the counterfactual state, $E(Y_0 \mid D = 1)$. If there were no unobservables, or if conditioning on X eliminated mean differences in unobservables, the selection bias term would be zero.

Methods of matching that have been widely used in non-experimental evaluations make either one of these assumptions (i.e., that there are no unobservables or conditioning on X eliminates mean differences in unobservables), albeit not always in a convincing manner. Matching methods identify pairs of treated and untreated cases with similar observed attributes and construct estimates of treatment effects on the basis of differences in outcomes between the paired cases. Using data from the JTPA study, Heckman, Ichimura, & Todd (1997) show that different approaches to matching vary widely in their ability to approximate actual effects. They also investigate 'what features of the data and matching method are essential to reducing bias in non-experimental estimates'. They consider the extent to which treatment and comparison group members have the same distributions of unobserved and observed characteristics, whether the same questionnaire is used for both groups in data collection, and whether or not the two groups have a common economic environment. Contrary to previous studies, they find that eliminating differences in unobservables contributes less to reducing bias than matching pairs on observable characteristics and using data from the same questionnaires and individuals from the same economic environment. This result is confirmed in a subsequent study of propensity score matching methods by Smith and Todd (2005), using data from the National Supported Work experiment in Canada. Smith and Todd conclude that the 'differences-in-differences' matching estimator performs best, most likely because it eliminates time-invariant sources of bias, such as geographical mismatches or differences in questionnaires.

In other recent research, Heckman & Vytlacil (2000) further advance the treatment effects and policy evaluation literature with their elaboration of the Marginal Treatment Effect (*MTE*), which they relate to the structural approach and a range of policy evaluation questions. The *MTE* is the mean effect of a program for those at the 'margin of participation', for given values of observables and with conditioning on unobservables in the program participation equation. The *MTE* is an exceptionally useful measure because it generates local estimates of the effects of a program on those most likely to change states in response to the intervention. Heckman and Vytlacil demonstrate that all the conventional treatment parameters may be represented as weighted averages of the *MTE*.

Having recognized the limits of econometric methods in evaluating the general-equilibrium effects of programs such as education vouchers (for which national adoption is presently being proposed in the US), Heckman and his colleagues are also developing new approaches that combine micro and macro data and use estimates from partial-equilibrium (non-experimental) analyses to determine parameters in a dynamic, general-equilibrium model. For example, Heckman, Lochner, & Taber (1998a, 1998b) elucidate this approach in their studies of rising wage inequality in the US and of how tuition reductions affect college enrollment. Although there are empirical challenges to overcome in this line of research, Heckman and his collaborators will undoubtedly triumph in advancing the study of the general-equilibrium effects of policy interventions and produce many important findings as they apply their research to pressing policy questions.

2.5 Human capital and the economics of cognitive and noncognitive skill formation

Most recently, Heckman has initiated a major research program that focuses on the economics of human development. He is building on his past work that has included the economic analysis of skills development and training as conventionally measured and is expanding this line of research by integrating theory and methods from pyschology, neuroscience and biology and demography to address a broader set of research questions on human development. His motivation for this research stems in part from his study of growing inequality in America and its relationship to the slowdown in the growth of the quality of the US labor force. With Pedro Carneiro (2003), he investigates the widening wage differentials between skilled and unskilled workers and the uneven response from various socioeconomic groups to the increasing returns to schooling. They describe the meager returns to low-cost public policies that attempt to offer remediation or training to unskilled adults or to implement quick fixes for improving the quality of secondary schools. They also point to the generally feeble evidence on the effectiveness of alternative policies to foster human capital accumulation and skill formation.

Heckman's basic arguments in this research are that human capital accumulation is a dynamic process, and that the knowledge and skills acquired in one stage of the life cycle will importantly influence both the 'initial conditions and technology of learning' at the next stage (Carneiro & Heckman, 2003: 88). Drawing on studies in neuroscience and child development, he makes the case that opportunities missed to form different types of abilities at one stage may permanently limit skill formation, given the prohibitively high costs and absence of effective policies for full remediation. A second focal argument is that families contribute critically to the human capital development process and play a key role in fostering early investments in the development of both cognitive and noncognitive abilities (Carneiro & Heckman, 2003; Cunha, Heckman, Lochner, & Masterov, 2006). Furthermore, Heckman and colleagues find that differences in these abilities are persistent, with gaps among income and racial groups beginning early and influencing both social and economic success.

Building on this general thesis, Heckman's research program is expanding in several important directions. He is accumulating a substantial body of work on the measurement and effects of cognitive and noncognitive skills on earnings and other economic and social outcomes. In a paper with Urzua & Stixrud (2006), they draw on the psychometrics literature to develop measures of noncognitive ability, in addition to more common cognitive skills measures, and specify an original approach to estimation that allows latent skills to determine measured skills and schooling choices, and for schooling to determine measured skills. Importantly, they show that a few low-dimensional latent traits contribute to explaining a wide variety of human behaviors. In this and related work (Hansen & Mullen, 2004), Heckman and his colleagues also advance this literature by addressing problems of measurement error, imperfect proxies, and reverse causality that have limited previous studies. In Heckman, Urzua, & Stixrud (2006), they find that for a variety of behavioral dimensions as well as labor market outcomes, a change in noncognitive skills (from the lowest to the highest level) has an effect on behavior comparable to or greater than a corresponding change in cognitive skills.

In an important extension of this work, Heckman and colleagues are challenging traditional conceptions in psychology and economics that view cognitive and noncognitive traits as stable or invariant. In recent papers (Cunha & Heckman, 2007; Borghan et al., 2007), he and his colleagues are developing new frameworks that allow for the dynamic evolution of latent skills and nonlinear skill formation technologies and that facilitate the analysis of alternative policies for human capital development, including early childhood interventions, later youth investments and remediation. Using these theoretical frameworks to interpret the evidence from a large and diverse empirical literature, Cunha & Heckman (2006) suggest that because parental investments are central in shaping individual abilities (i.e., in contributing to genetic endowments and to the environments that interact to determine abilities, behaviors, and skills), policies that add to family resources and compensate for adverse environments early in children's lives are likely to be most effective in addressing problems of societal inequality. They also note that to achieve long-term success, supplements provided in early developmental stages should be balanced with later investments to promote ongoing human capital accumulation and skills formation.

To advance the empirical component of this new research agenda, Heckman has formed and is chairing the new Pritzker Consortium on Early Childhood Development (based at the University of Chicago). The Consortium, which has brought together leading experts on childhood development from a range of disciplines, is assembling data from studies conducted across the globe to facilitate analyses that will inform public policymakers and practitioners in the non-profit and business communities of the value of public investment in early childhood programs. The studies include those that generated most of the major experimental data sets with a long-term follow-up period and that provide information for analyzing new outcomes that have previously not been explored.

2.6 Other contributions

The above discussion suggests that although Heckman's academic home is a university known for its highly intellectual milieu and zealous research productivity, he is not an ivory tower economist. He has testified on Capitol Hill and presented his ideas and research findings in countless public forums. For example, in an essay for *The Public Interest* (1999), he addressed current public policies regarding education and job training and identified blind spots in policy discussions. Asking whether the decline in labor market activity among low-skilled workers might be reversed by a tuition policy or other subsidy to promote skill formation, he drew upon his research with Cameron to show that, controlling for scholastic ability, 'long-run family factors ... are the driving force behind school attainment, and not short-term credit constraints' (Cameron & Heckman, 1998, p. 97). He also pointed to the significant expenses of government-funded adult training programs (e.g., with training costs about ten times higher than the average earnings increases they produce) in arguing that these programs are a poor investment of public dollars. These findings were the early seeds of his now expanding research agenda on policies to improve the environments of children and to intervene early in fostering change in the home environment and generating lasting effects on children's economic and social well-being.

A front-page *Wall Street Journal* article (2001) described how advisors to US President George W. Bush used Heckman's research on job-training programs to make decisions about funding priorities for workforce development programs. Few scholars can claim such widespread influence in both academic and policy domains.

3 The economic contributions of Daniel L. McFadden

3.1 McFadden, academic history

Daniel L. McFadden received his BS and PhD from the University of Minnesota. As an undergraduate, he studied physics, but thereafter switched to economics (behavioral science). His dissertation, 'Factor Substitution in the Economic Analysis of Production', was published with a similar title in the *Review of Economic Studies*. McFadden's first job was at the University of Pittsburgh. A year later, he moved to the University of California, Berkeley, which he would intermittently call home for the next 27 years. Three years after arriving at Berkeley, he received tenure, and two years later he was promoted to full professor. In 1978, he left Berkeley for the Massachusetts Institute of Technology, where he was integrally involved with the statistics center and worked on many of the problems that would eventually lead to his Nobel award. In 1990, he returned to Berkeley as the E. Morris Cox Professor of Economics.

McFadden has garnered professional awards and honors throughout his career. Apart from the John Bates Clark medal (1975), he has also been awarded the Frisch medal by the Econometrics Society (1986) and the Nemmers Prize in Economics (2000). He has also been honored by MIT as an outstanding teacher (1981). Since winning the Nobel Prize, McFadden has written papers on a number of health and health policy related issues such as Medicare prescription drug coverage and enrollment, and the relationship between health and socioeconomic status. He has also continued to make theoretical contributions to the field. In 2005 at the quinquennial Frisch Lecture McFadden presented 'The New Science of Pleasure', in which he argues that the 'modern behavioral revaluation of the consumer will lead to profound changes in the way economics is done' (McFadden, 2005 p. 1). McFadden's sees these changes as a challenge and an opportunity, and finds the standard assumption of maximizing individual utility is insufficient in fully explaining economic behavior. Indeed he claims that social networks, reciprocity and altruism enter human behavior and can no longer be ignored by economists.

3.2 Theory

Decision-making in economics starts with the premise that individuals choose from a set of possible and mutually exclusive alternatives. Researchers analyze these choices either by assuming that individuals maximize utility based on their preferences, or that people make decisions based on budgets and choice rules. In the second case the choice is the object of analysis and the preference relation is circumvented. (Mas-Collel, Whinston & Green, 1995). Using choice structures to model individual behavior allows us to make assumptions about things that are directly observable (objects of choice) rather than things that cannot be seen – preferences. These types of choices may involve discrete goods or services – lumpy goods that come bundled with a whole set of attributes and involve choices conditioned on prior decisions. The tools we have at our disposal to analyze these choices must be considerably different from the differential calculus and ordinary least squares regression we use to analyze continuous choices of commodities. Everyday life is filled with examples of mutually exclusive choices. For example:

1   Labor market decisions: exit the labor force, search for work, accept a job.
2   Transit decisions: bus, car, train.
3   Residential choice: city, suburb, country.

In each of these cases, the choice of outcome precludes choosing another outcome[1]. Although we can own both butter and guns, we cannot simultaneously be employed and not in the labor force. Therefore we must utilize different modeling techniques to examine these choices. Moreover, in these examples, choices are not dichotomous; we have multiple distinct outcomes from which to choose. One key assumption in estimating these types of models is that the choice sets of feasible alternatives (bus, car, train) contain finite numbers of choices that are mutually exclusive and exhaustive. Additionally, the alternatives must be distinctive, and choices must be characterized by their observable attributes. McFadden's fundamental contribution to economics has been to use existing theory to develop empirical strategies for modeling these choices.

McFadden has coupled the existing theoretical framework of choice behavior with an empirical strategy that provides insights about the factors contributing to individual decisions. First, he describes how various option-specific attributes enter into the decision framework; it is through this theoretical development that he addresses unobserved heterogeneity. Second, he deals with the behavioral and econometric implications of how different choice sets affect the probability of making a particular choice. One key assumption of his early work on discrete-choice modeling was that choice probabilities are independent of the number of choices being offered. This is known as the 'assumption of independence from irrelevant alternatives', or IIA.

McFadden regularly comments on the integration of theory and empirical estimation. In his Nobel lecture he stated:

> The reason my formulation of the MNL [multinomial logit] model received more attention than others that were developed independently during the same decade seems to be the direct connection that I provided to consumer theory, linking unobserved preference heterogeneity to a fully consistent description of the distribution of demands.
>
> (McFadden, 2001, p. 354)

In fact, we can see that McFadden is very attentive to the theoretical underpinnings of the multinomial logit model. According to Maddala (1983), the multinomial logit model is algebraically equivalent to McFadden's 'conditional logit model'. The major difference between these models are theoretical underpinnings that determine the explanatory variables.

McFadden's model explicitly includes attributes of the outcome under consideration to be modeled in the empirical estimation. Consider an individual choosing among three outcomes:

$$Y_1^* = \beta_1 X_{1i} + \gamma_1 Z_i + \varepsilon_{1i} \tag{5}$$

$$Y_2^* = \beta_2 X_{2i} + \gamma_2 Z_i + \varepsilon_{2i} \tag{6}$$

$$Y_3^* = \beta_3 X_{3i} + \gamma_3 Z_i + \varepsilon_{3i} \tag{7}$$

In this case, the latent variable Y^* represents the indirect utility associated with each choice. The $\beta_j X_{ji}$ allow for the attributes of the option under consideration to influence the outcome Y_j^*. Note that X_{ji} is double indexed. The i allows the observation to change based on the attributes and can be thought of as proxies for individual preferences, the choice outcome is indexed by j (in this example j takes values 1–3). Additionally, the $\gamma_j Z_i$ consist of a set of variables that take into consideration individual attributes that may systematically affect tastes and consequent choice outcomes. The errors are assumed to be drawn from an extreme value type I distribution (Gumbel distribution[2]) and are assumed to be independent and identically distributed.

3.2.1 Unobserved heterogeneity

By linking unobserved preference heterogeneity and choice-specific demand, McFadden demonstrates how behavioral assumptions underlie the econometric techniques he develops. He begins by adopting the basic precepts of the 'random utility model' developed by Thurstone (1927). In this model, the individual is assumed to be a utility maximizer, but two sets of factors limit the researcher's ability to analyze the decision. First, the researcher cannot observe the full set of factors that contribute to the decision. Second, the optimization is imperfect due to limits on information and perception. Thus there exists a component of unobserved heterogeneity in the preferences of the individual. We may think of this unobserved heterogeneity as different tastes, experiences, and information sets for the individual that are known only to the person making the decision. Succinctly, we (the researchers) cannot know what they (the subjects) know.

Unobserved heterogeneity is a problem that emerges when we are trying to discern the relationships between choices and the attributes of the options under consideration. If we assume that a choice was determined by some particular interaction of tastes and option attributes, then we can say that attributes affected choice. This assumes that tastes and perceptions are adequately described by the observed characteristics of the choice under consideration. If, however, the unobserved tastes do not vary continuously with the observed attributes of the option, or the attributes do not adequately describe the choice being made, then correlations between choice outcomes and attributes may prove spurious. In this case, including choice attributes in the model will not adequately control for unobserved heterogeneity.

Consider choosing one of three candy bars: milk chocolate, milk chocolate with nuts, or nougat. Researchers assume that the options under consideration are adequately described by their observable attributes and that these attributes map to a set of preferences held by the individual consumer. In this case, we can say that the option attributes – chocolate, chocolate with nuts, and nougat – provide an adequate map of an individual's tastes. If the candy bars differed only by their wrappers, there would be no way to map their attributes to an individual's preferences. In this case, the observed outcome contains all the information about the choice.

A special case of the issues surrounding unobserved heterogeneity occurs when unobserved tastes are a function of current economic variables, such as income. One fundamental underpinning of the discrete-choice model formulated by McFadden (1974) is the assumption that current economic conditions affect the feasibility of the choice through the budget constraint but not the preferences of an individual. Thus the consumption of 'snob' or prestige goods violates this assumption and is difficult to model with these techniques.

Econometrically, McFadden builds on the model laid out in equations (5)–(7) by allowing the latent variables to have the form $Y_1^* = V_1 + \mu_1$. In this case, V_1 is the indirect utility associated with choosing option 1, and μ_1 is the error in optimization. The individual utility-maximization problem is thought to be complex and imperfect. Errors in judgment and limited information are thought to lead to suboptimal outcomes. This type of optimization is a fairly radical departure from the standard neoclassical model of perfect information and error-free homo economicus. This implies that the regression error is derived from a substantively different mechanism. Choice errors, not just measurement errors, are the primary component of μ. It is because of this that understanding the regression error is so important for the development of these models.

3.2.2 Independence of irrelevant alternatives: red bus–blue bus

Although it is important that tastes and attributes represent a systematic mapping, it is equally important that attributes provide a basis for meaningful distinctions among the choices. Thus, one of the most serious limitations of multinomial choice models is the assumption that irrelevant alternatives do not influence decisions. In the candy bar example, suppose you always choose chocolate and prefer it with nuts. In this case, removing the nougat option should have no effect on the probability of choosing chocolate with nuts. If the addition and subtraction of alternate irrelevant (not chosen) options affects the probability of choosing an observed outcome, we say that the independence of irrelevant alternatives is violated.

The assumption of the independence of irrelevant alternatives requires that decision probabilities be unaffected by irrelevant information. The red bus–blue bus problem is the most commonly cited example; we follow the discussion of Train (1986). Consider a person making a choice about how to get to work. This worker may choose a blue bus or a car. The ratio of probabilities for the blue bus and car is:

$$\frac{P_{bb}}{P_c} = \frac{e^{V_{bb}}/\Sigma_{j\epsilon j_n} e^{V_{jn}}}{e^{V_c}/\Sigma_{j\epsilon j_n} e^{V_{jn}}} \tag{8}$$

where V is the indirect utility associated with each option. It needs to be noted that the ratio of probabilities depends only on the car and blue bus options. Suppose that a person were indifferent to taking a car or riding a bus to work. Then the $P_c = P_{bb} = \frac{1}{2}$ and the ratio of probabilities equals 1. Now suppose that another option, a red bus, is introduced into the choice problem. Now the traveler sees the red bus and blue bus as perfect substitutes and is indifferent to the choice of bus. In the logit model, the probability ratios are the same regardless of the existence of another option; therefore $P_{bb}/P_c = 1$ and $P_{bb}/P_{rb} = 1$. This implies that $P_{bb} = P_{rb} = P_c$ and the only solution is that the probabilities equal $\frac{1}{3}$. A reasonable person may complain that the true probabilities are really $P_c = \frac{1}{2}$, $P_{bb} = \frac{1}{4}$ and $P_{rb} = \frac{1}{4}$. In other words, the traveler is half as likely to take a particular bus when there are two nearly identical buses, and the introduction of a new bus has no effect on the likelihood of taking a car.

Debreu (1960, p. 188) probably first laid out the IIA problem in comments on Luce's work. He wrote: 'To meet this [IIA] difficulty, one might say that the alternatives have not been properly defined. But how far can one go in the direction of redefining the alternatives?' Redefining the alternatives is a centrally important question; it is at the heart of how we model discrete-choice decisions.

Researchers interested in modeling discrete-choice outcomes have developed econometric tools to restructure the choice problem when faced with new options. A considerable amount of McFadden's later research can be thought of as dealing with this problem. Rather than redefine the alternatives, he has sought to restructure the choice problem by addressing it with three alternate empirical models: the nested logit, the generalized extreme value, and the mixed multinomial logit.

3.3 Empirical strategy

Although the theoretical foundations for the multinomial logit model laid out by McFadden are quite complex, the empirical estimation of these models has become increasingly simple. McFadden has argued that 'the conditional logit model and its nested cousins are now sufficiently standardized so they can be estimated more or less mindlessly as options in many statistical packages'. Yet these models are far from ubiquitous. Part of the difficulty with them is not their estimation but rather their interpretation. The likelihood function for the multinomial logit can be compactly written

$$L_c (i; x) = e^{xi\beta} / \sum_{j \in J} e^{x_j \beta} \tag{9}$$

where c is the choice set, of which j is an element. Because McFadden's model explicitly allows for the possibility of including the attributes of the choice, we can be more clear about the choice probability. In this case, we have an X_{it} that captures the influence of the attributes on the decision to choose option t. Thus the probability of individual i choosing option t from a set of c options is expressed as:

$$P_{i,t} = \frac{e^{\beta X_{it} + \gamma Z_i}}{\sum_{k=1}^{c} e^{\beta X_{ik} + \gamma Z_i}} \tag{10}$$

X_{it} is a vector of the values of the tth option as perceived by individual i; the Z_i are individual-specific variables. First, the importance of the theory in equation (10) must be noted. In this case, we are allowing a specific form of the individual's taste and value perceptions to enter into the model. If, as McFadden assumes, the mapping between perceived value and attributes is consistent, then this model limits the spurious effects of unobserved heterogeneity.

Estimating this model produces $k - 1$ sets of coefficients, making interpretation problematic. Additionally, due to the scaling and multiple outcomes, neither the sign nor the magnitude of the variables is intuitively obvious. For example, suppose we have a three-outcome model, in which two sets of coefficients are produced. For both outcomes 1 and 2, the parameter estimate of interest is positive: $\beta^{(2)} > \beta^{(1)} > 0$. You may reason that marginal changes in this variable lead to higher probabilities of the associated outcomes. Most of the time, this will be correct. Occasionally, however, a marginal increase in this variable will lead to a lower probability of observing the outcome. This may occur when $\beta^{(2)} > \beta^{(1)} > 0$; the large effect of $\beta^{(2)}$ on outcome 2 may lower the probability of observing outcome 1.

Although the structure of these models copes well with unobserved heterogeneity, the models are suspect when they violate the independence of irrelevant alternatives. McFadden, Train, & Tye (1978), Hausman (1978), Hausman & McFadden (1984), & McFadden (1987) have developed specification tests that allow researchers to determine if their results violate IIA. These tests essentially involve estimating the model with different categories excluded (this essentailly eliminates options). The coefficient estimates from the various models (each with a different excluded choice option) are then compared. If the differences in the parameter estimates are statistically significant, this implies that eliminating different choices from the feasible set affects the choice probabilities. If this is true, then the IIA assumption is presumed to have been violated.

3.3.1 Nested logit models and generalized extreme value

The dependence on the IIA assumption to provide consistent results has motivated researchers to develop other empirical tools that are consistent with the random utility model but do not require this assumption. Three types of models have been developed by McFadden to address these issues. Each model uses information about the interaction of choice probabilities to limit reliance on the IIA assumption.

The nested multinomial alters the structure of the problem to allow a sequential decision process. By separating the decisions and using the conditional probability information in estimating the other branches of the decision tree, we limit the effect of irrelevant alternatives. In essence, the nested multinomial logit models isolate the source of interrelated alternatives via the inclusive value (see below). The generalized extreme value distribution explicitly models the extent to which the alternatives are correlated.

The nested multinomial logit model was developed by McFadden (1978) on the basis of Tversky's elimination-by-aspects model (Tversky, 1972a, 1972b). In this model, the discrete-choice decision is modeled by a sequence of choices. This modeling strategy gives rise to a tree structure in decision making. This

Figure 1

entire tree can be estimated with information moving up the tree in terms of inclusive values. These inclusive values provide information about the effective probabilities on each branch of the tree. They can be thought of as probability weights that differ from 1. For example:

The decision to drive a car is conditional on the decision to take private transportation. In this case, the probability that we are interested in is $P_{private,car} = P_{car/private,public} \cdot P_{private}$. These models are very effective at eliminating violation of the IIA assumption. McFadden (1978) uses a nested multinomial logit to model decisions about residential housing location.

The generalized extreme value models developed by McFadden (1978) allow for a relationship between the choice parameters. In this case, the standard multinomial logit model is modified to incorporate a generalized extreme value distribution. The standard multinomial logit used an extreme value type I error and assumed that the errors were independent and identically distributed. In the generalized extreme value models, we allow for a potential error correlation to occur between choices. By accounting for this error correlation, the 'irrelevant' effects on estimated parameters are eliminated. In this case, the choice probability of outcome 1 in a three-outcome model is:

$$P = \frac{e^{\beta X_{1},\gamma Y/(1-\sigma)}}{e^{\beta X_{1},\gamma Y/(1-\sigma)} + e^{\beta X_{2},\gamma Y/(1-\sigma)} + e^{\beta X_{3},\gamma Y/(1-\sigma)}} \tag{11}$$

If σ is zero, the model reduces to the multinomial logit. As σ increases, the effect of the correlation between the choices becomes more important. This error structure is flexible, allowing for cases in which only two of the outcomes are correlated. Maddala (1983) provides an overview of these options.

3.4 Policy applications and contributions

We need only look at the types of practical policies to which this theory and empirical strategy have been applied to appreciate their real world value and contributions. McFadden has analyzed residential choice decisions (1978a) transportation decisions, road building, travel demand forecasting, and choice of transportation type. (McFadden, 1974, 1975, 1978b; McFadden and Train, 1978, and McFadden et al. 1977). Recent research has focused on environmental and health related outcomes for the elderly. In particular, McFadden has done research on the housing decisions of the elderly (McFadden & Feinstein, 1989; McFadden & Hoynes, 1997). Recent research on the environment has investigated issues about how best to value non-market goods (Hurd, McFadden, & Merrill 1999; Train, McFadden & Johnson, 2000).

McFadden is perhaps best known for his applied work on transportation modeling. Recent extensions of this research have explored the environmental and technology issues of adopting alternative-fuel vehicles in California. The adoption of a new technology is an excellent example of the application of the random utility model. Errors in judgment are likely to be important because the technology is new. Additionally, researchers and policy makers (not to mention manufacturers) are interested in the factors that influence consumer decisions about these new vehicles. In McFadden & Train (2000), the researchers are concerned with modeling the factors that lead to different consumer decisions. In particular, they show that estimates of the effects on the decision to choose an alternative-fuel vehicle are sensitive to the types of choices available, and that the choices are interrelated. Nevertheless, the findings provide clear avenues for policy makers to pursue. For example, McFadden and Train find that the choice of an alternative-fuel vehicle is based not only on the vehicle's attributes (purchase price, size, operating cost, and luggage space) but also of the type of fuel system. People were less inclined to choose electric-powered vehicles (negative effect). Yet further analysis of the data indicated that commuting distance and education levels were important factors that interacted with the choice of an electric vehicle. In particular, those with short commutes and college degrees were favorably disposed toward electric cars. Thus, McFadden and Train's research may help auto manufacturers target the population willing to purchase these vehicles and may also help the public sector target information campaigns and public incentives toward drivers most likely to use these vehicles.

In more recent research McFadden has continued to focus on methodological issues. One continued area of interest is how to incorporate both stated and revealed preference data into behavioral models. Research with Morikawa & Ben-Akiva (2002) develops a set of empirical methods that allows researchers to incorporate psychometric data (e.g., stated preferences and subjective ratings of service) into economic travel demand models. Similarly, McFadden and his colleagues have sought to bridge the gap between discrete choice models and behavioral theory by including additional information about decision-making directly into the model. Often this information takes the form of accounting for attitudes and perceptions which may be closely aligned with stated (rather than revealed) preferences. Other times McFadden (1999) has argued that 'choice behavior can be characterized by a *decision process*, which is informed by perceptions and beliefs based on available information, and influenced by affect, attitudes, motives, and preferences'. Under these conditions the gap between discrete choice models and behavioral theory has prompted attempts to explicitly model the components of the 'black-box' of decision making.

This emphasis on decision making has naturally led McFadden into issues of survey design and testing. In his 2004 Gorman lecture, presented at University College, London, McFadden argues that economists have neglected survey design issues. Furthermore, this neglect may not be benign; it can result in the mis-reporting of economic facts, can arise in nearly any stage of the response process, and can dramatically alter the difficulty of modeling choice behavior. The survey design itself can influence errors, problematically from a modeling standpoint, at various stages of the response process. Integrated into this theoretical/behavioral framework McFadden has sought to employ his methods by combining information from a variety of sources into models of decision making. For example, his work with Adams, *et al.* (2003) focuses on unravelling the relationship between socio-economic status (SES) and health outcomes. McFadden and his co-authors focus on testing direct causal links between SES and find that the evidence supports that there is no direct causal link from SES to mortality. However they do find some evidence of a link between SES and the gradual onset of poor health (e.g., mental health conditions, and some degenerative and chronic conditions). Most importantly for our discussion the authors cannot determine if these links are causal or are linked to persistent unobserved behavioral or genetic factors. In two papers on Medicare Part D enrollment (the US prescription drug benefit for seniors) McFadden and his co-authors use survey data to examine intentions to enroll and enrollment in the program (Heiss *et al.* 2006). In general, they find that customers have stated preferences that closely match their revealed preferences (intended to sign up for the program and ultimately enrolled) however, a lack of acuity among vulnerable populations, and procrastination may lead to suboptimal choices for a substantial minority. The authors follow-up assessment was that concerns about large numbers of seniors would fail to be covered has not been borne out.

Finally, in McFadden's 2005 Frisch Lecture we see how many of the important themes of McFadden's career have come together. In the paper he discusses why he believes that the 'neoclassical model of the consume is largely a finished subject' and goes on to assert that the 'modern behavioral revaluation of the consumer will lead to profound changes in the way economics is done'. He discusses how perception and choice, the sociality of choice and the biology of sensation will have important roles to play in these new behavioral models. McFadden is interested in a theory of the consume that expands our understanding of the psychology, sociology and biology of the consumer. He is not calling for a newfangled socio-biology of choice but to expand our repetoire of social science theories and integrate them into a more congruent whole.

4 Concluding comment

Our previous discussion has focused on the substantial theoretical and empirical contributions made by James Heckman and Daniel McFadden. Yet perhaps the most remarkable aspect of their work has been its ubiquity and usefulness. While complex, each man's contribution to economics is also fundamental. In James Heckman's case researchers who begin to see the world through the lens of sample selection understand some of the limits of economic research. This understanding is likely to make us more cautious about our policy prescriptions. Realizing our statistical information about people may be systematically biased makes generalizing our result difficult at best. The crux of James Heckman's research is that the people about whom we have information are likely to be fundamentally different from those we cannot observe. Such is the case for women, African Americans, the elderly, and others who reveal labor market information only under certain circumstances. In these cases research questions hinge on labor market information about people we do not observe.

Daniel McFadden's contribution is equally fundamental. Economic choices are increasingly made between discrete outcomes. In particular, monopolistic competition has structured choices so that they are perceived by consumers as discrete. Millions of dollars are spent to advertise everything from candy bars to soap powder in an effort to 'inform' consumers about different choices. Daniel McFadden has provided researchers with econometric tools to analyze the factors influencing consumer decisions. Whereas economics used to be primarily concerned with 'quantity' and 'price', it is now equally concerned with 'outcome'. Employment decisions, residential location decisions, and travel mode decisions have all been analyzed with tools that Daniel McFadden helped develop. Prior to the advent of these tools, such outcomes could not be econometrically modeled.

These tools should not be wielded carelessly, however. Heckman's sample selection model is sensitive to the specification of the variables included in the 'selection' equation. In particular, Mroz (1987) has demonstrated how assumptions about the exogeneity of labor market experience and 'tastes for work' result in different estimates of selectivity bias. The inexact application of McFadden's empirical tools is equally perilous. In the case of the multinomial logit estimation, structuring the choice decision is very important. The multinomial logit makes strong assumptions about the degree of similarity between choices. In cases where choices are not distinct, these models may provide spurious estimates.

Daniel McFadden and James Heckman have seen their empirical tools extend well beyond economics. Political scientists use selection models to determine if voting reflects the popular will or just the will of those who vote. Multinomial logit models can be used to determine whether a third-party candidate made a difference in an election outcome, as third-party candidates did in the 2000 and 1992 presidential elections. Sociologists deal with both selective samples and discrete outcomes when they analyze occupational choice. In international comparative research, where data are only available for more developed countries, there may be systematic differences between less developed and more developed countries. But perhaps it is in the evaluation of public policy that selection models have their greatest impact. Participants are likely to be considerably different from non-participants in public and private programs such as welfare, unemployment insurance, education, and training. Controlling for differences between participants and non-participants may mean the difference between evaluating a program as a failure or as a success. Growing demands for more objective analysis and accountability in public policy will continue to make sample selectivity a cornerstone of public policy analysis.

The most interesting econometric applications of Daniel McFadden and James Heckman's research are still to come. Our rapidly increasing capacity to process and analyze large amounts of information provides many new venues for applying these tools. Already, data analysis corporations analyze large stores of consumer data to investigate questions of brand switching, brand choice modeling, and consumer segmentation. These applications are far from the academic roots of the selection bias and discrete outcomes, let alone unobserved heterogeneity, but demonstrate the ubiquity of the advanced econometric frameworks that drive these analyses.

Too often we find that the old ordinary least squares regression results are robust to many specification errors, making up-to-date tools extraneous. Not so with the discrete-choice and selection-correction models of Daniel McFadden and James Heckman. McFadden and Heckman have enabled researchers to investigate economic decisions that were previously impossible to analyze correctly. In an era awash in data and high-powered statistical programs, where marginal computing costs are nearly zero, these tools will become ever more useful for converting data into information.

Notes

1 The decisions presented here are asserted to be mutually exclusive, although in some cases this may not be true. E.g., we may combine bus and rail transit methods, as I do each day. In this case, we have more than three options, and the model would have to incorporate all the observed choices.
2 The Gumbel distribution is one distribution in a family of 'extreme value type' distributions. These extreme value distributions are used in modeling errors that have extreme values – mimima and maxima. The Gumbel distribution is a distribution of random variables that are the minima of a series of random variables. To the extent that utility maximizers seek to minimize their errors associated with choices the Gumbel distibution corresponds well to this behavioral assumption.

References

Adams, P., Hurd, M., McFadden, D. L., Merrill, A. & Ribeiro, T. (2003) Healthy, wealthy, and wise? tests for direct causal paths between health and socioeconomic status, *Journal of Econometrics*, 112(1), pp. 3–56.

Ben-Akiva, M., McFadden, D. L., Train, K., Walker, J., Bhat, C., Bierlaire, M., Bolduc, D., Boersch-Supan, A., Brownstone, D., Bunch, D., Daly, A., de Palma, A., Gopinath, D., Karlstrom, A. & Munizaga, M. (2002) Hybrid choice models: progress and challenges, *Marketing Letters* 13(3), pp. 163–175.

Cameron, S. & Heckman, J. J. (1998) Life cycle schooling and educational selectivity: models and choice, *Journal of Political Economy*, 106(2), pp. 262–333.

Carneiro, P. & Heckman, J. J. (2003) Human capital policy, in: J. Heckman & A. Krueger (Eds) *Inequality in America: What Role for Human Capital Policy?* (Cambridge, MA: MIT Press), pp. 77–240.

Cohen, H. (2000) The Nobel that counts, *The Industry Standard Magazine*, 6, pp. 45–48.

Cunha, F. & Heckman, J. J. (2006) Investing in our young people, Working Paper, University of Chicago.

Cunha, F. & Heckman, J. J. (2007) The technology of skill formation, *American Economic Review*, 97(2), pp. 31–47.

Debreu, G. (1960) Review of R. Luce, *Individual Choice Behavior, American Economic Review*, 50, pp. 186–188.

Donohue, J. & Heckman, J. J. (1991) Continuous versus episodic change: the impact of civil rights policy on the economic status of blacks, *Journal of Economic Literature*, 29, pp. 1603–1643.

Hausman, J. (1978) Specification tests in econometrics, *Econometrica*, 46, pp. 1251–1271.

Hausman, J. & McFadden, D. L. (1984) Specification tests for the multinomial logit model, *Econometrica*, 52, pp. 1219–1240.

Heckman, J. J. (1974a) Effects of child-care programs on women's work effort, *Journal of Political Economy*, 82, pp. S136–S163.

Heckman, J. J. (1974b) Shadow prices, market wages and labor supply, *Econometrica*, 42, pp. 679–94.

Heckman, J. J. (1979) Sample selection bias as a specification error, *Econometrica*, 47, pp. 153–162.

Heckman, J. J. (1983) A life cycle model of family labor supply, in: B. Weisbrod & H. Hughes (Eds) *Structural Analysis of Discrete Data with Econometric Applications* (Cambridge, MA: MIT Press), pp. 179–183.

Heckman, J. J. (1996) Randomization as an instrumental variable, *Review of Economics and Statistics*, 78, pp. 336–341.

Heckman, J. J. (1997) Instrumental variables: a study of implicit behavioral assumptions used in making program evaluations, *Journal of Human Resources*, 32, pp. 441–462.

Heckman, J. J. (1999) Doing it right: job training and education, *The Public Interest*, 135, pp. 86–108.

Heckman, J., Borghans, L., Duckworth, A. & ter Weel, B. (2007) The economics and psychology of personality and motivation, *Journal of Human Resources* (forthcoming).

Heckman, J. J., Cunha, F., Lochner, L. & Masterov, D. (2006) Interpreting the evidence on life cycle skill formation, in: E. Hanushek & F. Welch (Eds) *Handbook of the Economics of Education* (Amsterdam: North-Holland), pp. 697–812.

Heckman, J. J., Hansen, K. & Mullen, K. (2004) The effect of schooling and ability on achievement test scores, *Journal of Econometrics*, 121, pp. 39–98.

Heckman, J. J., Hotz, J. & Dabos, M. (1987) Are classical experiments necessary for evaluating the impact of manpower training programs?: a critical assessment, *Industrial Relations Research Association: Proceedings of the Annual Meeting*, 40, pp. 291–302.

Heckman, J. J., Ichimura, H. & Todd, P. (1997) Matching as an econometric evaluation estimator: evidence from evaluating a job training programme, *Review of Economic Studies*, 64, pp. 605–654.

Heckman, J. J., Lochner, L. & Taber, C. (1998a) General equilibrium treatment effects: a study of tuition policy, *American Economic Review*, 88, pp. 381–387.

Heckman, J. J., Lochner, L. & Taber, C. (1998b) Tax policy and human capital formation, *American Economic Review*, 88, pp. 293–298.

Heckman, J. J. & MaCurdy, T. (1981) New methods for estimating labor supply functions: a Survey, *Research in Labor Economics*, 4, pp. 65–102.

Heckman, J. J. & Robb, R. (1985) Alternative methods for estimating the impact of interventions, in: J. Heckman & B. Singer (Eds) *Longitudinal Analysis of Labor Market Data* (New York: Wiley), pp. 156–245.

Heckman, J. J. & Robb, R. (1986) Alternative methods for solving the problem of selection bias in evaluating the impact of treatments on outcomes, in: H. Wainer (Ed.) *Drawing Inferences from Self-Selected Samples* (Berlin: Springer Verlag), pp. 63–107.

Heckman, J. J. & Sedlacek, G. (1981) The impact of the minimum wage on the employment and earnings of workers in South Carolina, in: *Report of the Minimum Wage Study Commission, US*, Vol. 5 (Washington, DC: Government Printing Office), pp. 225–272.

Heckman, J. J. & Sedlacek, G. (1985) Heterogeneity, aggregation and market wage functions: an empirical model of self-selection in the labor market, *Journal of Political Economy*, 93, pp. 1077–1125.

Heckman, J. J. & Smith, J. (1995) Evaluating the case for randomized social experiments, *Journal of Economic Perspectives*, 9, pp. 85–100.

Heckman, J. J. & Smith, J. (1996) Experimental and non-experimental evaluation, in: G. Schmidt, J. Reilly, & K. Schomann (Eds) *International Handbook of Labor Market Policy and Evaluation* (Cheltenham, UK: Edward Elgar), pp. 37–88.

Heckman, J. J. & Smith, J. (2000) The sensitivity of experimental impact estimates: evidence from the national JTPA study, in: D. Blanchflower & R. Freeman, (Eds) *Youth Employment and Joblessness in Advanced Countries* (Chicago: University of Chicago Press), pp. 331–356.

Heckman, J. J., Smith, J. & Clements, N. (1997) Making the most out of social experiments: the intrinsic uncertainty in evidence from randomized trials with an application to the national JTPA experiment, *Review of Economic Studies*, 64, pp. 487–535.

Heckman, J. J., Stixrud, J. & Urzua, S. (2006) The effects of cognitive and noncognitive abilities on labor market outcomes and social behavior, *Journal of Labor Economics*, 24, pp. 411–482.

Heckman, J. J. & Vytlacil, E. (2000) The relationship between treatment parameters with a latent variable framework, *Economics Letters*, 66, pp. 33–39.

Heiss, F., McFadden, D. L. & Winter, J. (2006) Who failed to enroll in Medicare Part D, and why? early results, *Health Affairs*, 25, pp. w344–w354.

Hurd, M., McFadden, D. L. & Merrill, A. (1999) Predictors of mortality among the elderly, in: D. Wise (Ed.) *Themes in the Economics of Aging* (Chicago: University of Chicago Press), pp. 171–200.

Maddala, G. (1983) *Limited-Dependent and Qualitative Variable in Econometrics* (Cambridge: Cambridge University Press).

Mas-Collel, A., Whinston, M. & Green, J. (1995) *Microeconomic Theory* (New York: Oxford University Press).

McFadden, D. L. (1973) Conditional logit analysis of qualitative choice behavior, in: P. Zarembka (Ed.) *Frontiers in Econometrics* (New York: Academic Press), pp. 105–142.

McFadden, D. L. (1974) The measurement of urban travel demand, *Journal of Public Economics*, 3, pp. 303–328.

McFadden, D. L. (1978a) Modeling the choice of residential location, in: A. Karlquist, *et al.* (Eds) *Spatial Interaction Theory and Residential Location* (Amsterdam: North-Holland), pp. 75–96.

McFadden, D. (1978b) Quantitative methods for analyzing travel behaviour of individuals: some recent developments, in: Hensher, D. & Stopher, P. (Eds) *Behavioural Travel Modelling* (London: Croom Helm), pp. 279–318.

McFadden, D. L. (1981) Econometric models of probabilistic choice, in: C. Manski & D. McFadden (Eds) *Structural Analysis of Discrete Data: With Econometric Applications* (Cambridge, MA: MIT Press), pp. 198–269.

McFadden, D. L. (1987) Regression based specification tests for the multinomial logit model, *Journal of Econometrics*, 34, pp. 63–82.

McFadden, D. L. (1989) Econometric modeling of locational behavior, *Annals of Operations Research: Facility Location Analysis: Theory and Applications*, 18(1), pp. 1–15.

McFadden, D. L. (1997) Modeling the choice of residential location, in: A. Karlqvist, L. Lundqvist, F. Snickars, & J. Weibull (Eds) *Spatial Interaction Theory and Planning Models* (Amsterdam: North-Holland), pp. 75–96.

McFadden, D. L. (1999) Rationality for economists, *Journal of Risk and Uncertainty*, 19(1/3), pp. 73–105.

McFadden, D. L. (2002) Disaggregate behavioral travel demand's RUM side: a 30-year retrospective, in: D. Heshner & J. King (Eds) *The Leading Edge of Travel Behavior Research* (Oxford: Pergamon Press), pp. 17–64.

McFadden, D. L. (2005) The new science of pleasure: consumer behavior and the measurement of well-being, Frisch Lecture. Accessed from the web at http://www.econ.berkeley.edu/wp/mcfadden0105/ScienceofPleasure.pdf.

McFadden, D. L., Cosslett, S., Duguay, G. & Jung, W. (1977) Demographic data and policy analysis, in: *Urban Travel Demand Forecasting Project, Final Report*, Vol. VIII (Berkeley, CA: Institute of Transportation Studies, University of California).

McFadden, D. L. & Feinstein, D. (1989) The dynamics of housing demand by the elderly: wealth, cash flow, and demographic effects, in: D. Wise (Ed.) *The Economics of Aging* (Chicago: University of Chicago Press), pp. 55–91.

McFadden, D. L. & Hoynes, H. (1997) The impact of demographics on housing and non-housing wealth in the United States, in: M. Hurd & N. Yashiro (Eds) *The Economic Effects of Aging in the United States and Japan* (Chicago: University of Chicago Press), pp. 153–194.

McFadden, D. L. & Reid, F. (1975) Aggregate travel demand forecasting from disaggregated behavioral models, *Transportation Research Record: Travel Behavior and Values*, 534, pp. 24–37.

McFadden, D. L. & Train, K. (1978) The goods/leisure tradeoff and disaggregate work trip mode choice models, *Transportation Research*, 12, pp. 349–353.

McFadden, D. L. & Train, K. (2000) Mixed multinomial logit models, *Journal of Applied Econometrics*, 15, pp. 447–470.

McFadden, D. L, Train, K. & Tye, W. (1978) An application of diagnostic tests for the independence from irrelevant alternatives property of the multinomial logit model, *Transportation Research Record*, 637, pp. 39–46.

Morikawa, T., Ben-Akiva, M. & McFadden, D. L. (2002) Discrete choice models incorporating revealed preferences and psychometric data, in: P. Franses & A. Montgomery (Eds) *Econometric Models in Marketing* (Greenwich, CT: JAI Press), pp. 153–194.

Smith, J. & Todd, P. (2005) Does matching overcome LaLonde's critique of non-experimental estimators?, *Journal of Econometrics*, 125, pp. 305–353.

Train, K. (1986) *Qualitative Choice Analysis* (Cambridge, MA: MIT Press).

Train, K., McFadden, D. L. & Johnson, R. (2000) Comment on discussion of Morey and Waldman's measurement error in recreation demand models, *Journal of Environmental Economics and Management*, 40, pp. 76–81.

Tversky, A. (1972a) Choice by elimination, *Journal of Mathematical Psychology*, 9, pp. 341–367.

Tversky, A. (1972b) Elimination by aspects: a theory of choice, *Psychological Review*, 79, pp. 281–299.

Winter, J., Balza, R., Caro, F., Heiss, F., Jun, B., Matzkin, R. & McFadden, D. L. (2006) Medicare prescription drug coverage: consumer information and preferences, *Proceedings of the National Academy of Sciences*, 103, pp. 7929–7934.

7 A Nobel Prize for asymmetric information

The economic contributions of George Akerlof, Michael Spence and Joseph Stiglitz

J. Barkley Rosser, Jr.

'A Nobel Prize for Asymmetric Information: The Economic Contributions of George Akerlof, Michael Spence and Joseph Stiglitz' by J. Barkley Rosser, Jr. *from* Review of Political Economy (2003), Volume 15, Issue 1 (Taylor and Francis Ltd, http://www.informaworld.com), reprinted by permission of the publisher.

1 Introduction

The 2001 Bank of Sweden Prize in Economic Sciences in Memory of Alfred Nobel was awarded to George A. Akerlof, A. Michael Spence, and Joseph E. Stiglitz for their work on the economic implications of asymmetric information during the 1970s. The press release and the presentation speech by Jörgen Weibull noted specific key papers for each recipient—Akerlof (1970) on the market for lemons, Spence (1973) on signaling in labor markets through education, and Stiglitz (& Rothschild, 1976) on self-screening in insurance markets.

It is a sign of how important the economics of information has become, and also the key role of asymmetric information in the economics of information, that a Nobel Prize was given largely for work on asymmetric information to William Vickrey (1961) and James Mirrlees (1971) only five years earlier.[1] At that time, the Nobel committee signaled that the work of Vickrey and Mirrless had important consequences and cited the later work of Akerlof as evidence of this fact. By awarding a Nobel Prize in 2001 to Akerlof, Spence and Stiglitz, whose work comprises the hard core of what is now known as the 'information economics revolution,' the Nobel committee has acknowledged that understanding how information is obtained and disseminated is critical for understanding how economies function.

The careers of these economists have had numerous parallels, especially those of Akerlof and Stiglitz. All three economists began as theoretical economists whose work was quickly recognized as innovative and of high quality. However, all three were interested in real-world economic problems and would come to deal with practical policy problems, although Spence did so more through work in court cases and consulting than through holding policy-making positions. Another difference is that while Spence largely abandoned economic research after 1980, when he moved into academic administration positions where he has had a distinguished career, Akerlof and Stiglitz both continue to produce research in a wide variety of areas within economics. Stiglitz, in particular, has generated one of the most prolific output records of any economist ever.

Spence's research has focused almost entirely on microeconomics, while both Akerlof and Stiglitz have ranged across both microeconomics and macroeconomics, with Akerlof especially motivated by macroeconomic issues even when he has been writing more specifically on microeconomics, as in his paper on the market for lemons that was cited by the Nobel Prize committee. Akerlof and Stiglitz are among the chief developers and expositors of *New Keynesian macroeconomics,* which seeks to use rational expectations arguments to refute the policy ineffectiveness arguments put forth by the New Classical School during the 1970s.

The next section of the paper will examine the careers of the three 2001 Nobel Prize winners. The section after will discuss the evolution of the idea of asymmetric information, focusing especially on the work of Vickrey and Mirrlees and their predecessors. The section after that presents the main arguments of Akerlof, Spence, and Stiglitz about asymmetric information. This will be followed by a section on extensions and applications with subsections dealing respectively with industrial organization and microeconomic dynamics, New Keynesian theories of unemployment, New Keynesian theories of credit market rationing, and models of economic development and global financial stability. The final section discusses the degree to which the New Keynesian approach of Akerlof and Stiglitz can be viewed as genuinely Keynesian.

2 The men and their careers

2.1 George A. Akerlof

George Akerlof was born in 1940 in New Haven, Connecticut, where his parents, Swedish immigrant Gustav, and German–Jewish-descended Rosalie, were both graduate students in chemistry. His father, a research chemist, was involved in the Manhattan Project, as was his maternal uncle, Joseph Hershfelder, a famous physical chemist. This family emphasis on chemistry and physical science led George to feel inferior as a youth to his older brother, Carl, who would become a physicist. Akerlof was somewhat sickly when young, and admits to having been in a circle of friends 'who in today's terminology would be called nerds.' He remembers first thinking of economics at the age of 11 when he independently discovered the principle of the multiplier while contemplating the possible unemployment of his father, an early signal of his lifelong interest in the problem of unemployment.

Akerlof received his B.A. and his Ph.D. from Yale University in 1962 and 1966 respectively, following in the footsteps of his parents and his brother. From that time forward he has been located at the University of California-Berkeley where he has been Professor of Economics since 1980. While maintaining his base at Berkeley, Akerlof has enjoyed visiting positions at numerous institutions, including the Indian Statistical Institute, Harvard University, the staff of the Council of Economic Advisers, the Special Studies Section of the Board of Governors of the US Federal Reserve System (where he met his current wife, Janet Yellen), the London School of Economics, and the Brookings Institution. He has served as Vice President of the American Economic Association, was its Ely Lecturer in 1990, and was Director of the National Bureau of Economic Research.

He has been co-editor of *Economics and Politics,* and an associate editor of the *American Economic Review, Quarterly Journal of Economics,* and *Journal of Economic Behavior and Organization,* where he is now an honorary editor. He has also been a Fellow of the Econometric Society, the American Academy of Arts and Sciences, the Institute for Policy Reform, and the American Academy of Political Science, an Associate of the Canadian Institute for Advanced Research and the MacArthur Initiative on Economics, Group Values and Norms, and a Member of the Russell Sage Foundation Roundtable on Behavioral Economics.

Besides his famous work on asymmetric information, Akerlof has published many papers on macroeconomics whose major focus has been on explaining involuntary unemployment. He has been a crucial pioneer in bringing insights from psychology and sociology into economic analysis, and in recent years has focused on broader social issues of identity and social class formation. Besides great breadth and innovativeness, Akerlof's work has also long been noted for its wit. This is demonstrated in the titles he has chosen for his articles and books—for example, 'The economics of caste and of the rat race and other woeful tales' (Akerlof 1976).

Among his many co-authors, one of the most important has been his wife, Janet Yellen, who has also served in important policy positions in Washington as a member of the Board of Governors of the Federal Reserve System and as Chair of the Council of Economic Advisers during the Clinton presidency.

2.2 A. Michael Spence

Born in 1943 in Montclair, New Jersey, Michael Spence received a B.A. in philosophy from Princeton University in 1966, a B.S.-M.A. from Oxford University following a Rhodes Scholarship, and a Ph.D. from Harvard University in 1972. His article on education and signaling, the one singled out by the Nobel Prize committee, derived from his Ph.D. dissertation, which was published by Harvard University Press as *Market Signaling: informational transfer in hiring and related processes* (Spence 1974a). He followed this initial work by applying the notion of signaling to the field of industrial organization, an area in which Spence would become a leading figure (Caves *et al.,* 1980; Hayes *et al.,* 1983). Spence (2002) summarizes his recent views on signalling. He has also published in such areas as growth theory and natural resource economics.

Spence was Associate Professor of Economics at Stanford University from 1973–75 and then was jointly Professor of Economics and Business Administration at Harvard University until 1990 when he returned to Stanford, from where he retired in 2000 to Emeritus status. Named George Gund Professor in 1983, he served as Chairman of the Business Economics Program from 1981–83, as Chairman of the Economics Department in 1983–84, and as Dean of Faculty, 1984–90. He was also Dean at Stanford from 1990–99.

Spence has been a Fellow of the Econometric Society and the American Academy of Arts and Sciences as well as serving on various corporate boards of directors. He received the John Kenneth Galbraith Prize for Excellence in Teaching in 1978 and the John Bates Clark Award in 1981. In recent years he has been involved in numerous antitrust cases, many of them involving high technology industrial enterprises.

Although his work in academic administration kept him from being involved in economic research after 1980, Spence's administrative academic career must be noted for its exceptional quality. The Dean of Faculty at Harvard is arguably the most powerful academic officer of that premier academic institution, as is the equivalent position at Stanford. He has been described by observers as having been 'incredibly smart and hard-working' in those positions and as having been likely to become President of Harvard except for having 'gotten athwart of his long-serving boss, Derek Bok.'

Despite his 'earnestness' in these positions, he is described as having retained 'a Puckish delight in extreme sports and similar activities.' One weekend during the 1980s he escaped to a family retreat in Maine where he went skinny-dipping by moonlight in a local pond. An attack by a group of beavers drove him to shore and required him to receive rabies shots. But then nothing compares to the attacks deans receive from irate faculty members.

Alfred Kahn, long time Dean at Cornell, once remarked that 'a dean is to a faculty what a fire hydrant is to a pack of dogs.'

2.3 Joseph E. Stiglitz

Joseph Stiglitz was born in 1943 in Gary, Indiana, the hometown of Paul Samuelson whose *Collected Papers* Stiglitz would edit. He received his B.A. from Amherst College in 1964 and his Ph.D. from MIT in 1967. Stiglitz was a Fulbright Scholar and Tapp Junior Research Fellow at Cambridge University in 1970. Appointed Professor of Economics at Yale University in 1969, he moved to Princeton University in 1979, where he remained until 1988. Then he went to Stanford University. From 1993–97 he served on the Council of Economic Advisers, eventually becoming its Chair. During 1997–2000 he was Senior Vice President for Development Economics and Chief Economist at the World Bank. He left there after a widely publicized dispute with then Treasury Secretary, Lawrence Summers, about the management of global economic policy. He currently holds a joint appointment in the Economics Department, the School for International Affairs, and the Graduate School of Business at Columbia

University. Since departing the World Bank he has become a very public critic of the policies of the 'Washington Consensus' on international economics.

He is a Fellow of the National Academy of Sciences, the American Academy of Arts and Sciences, the Econometric Society, and the American Philosophical Society. He has also been elected to various honorary societies in Britain, Italy, France, and Germany, and has received numerous honorary doctorates. He received the John Bates Clark Award in 1979. He has served on the editorial boards of many journals and was the Founding Editor of the *Journal of Economic Perspectives*.

Stiglitz is one of the most prolific living economists. His list of publications extends to 30 pages, in small font, and includes textbooks in various fields and at different levels as well as monographs, position papers, and articles. The breadth of his interests was indicated in the statement from the American Economic Association when he was awarded the John Bates Clark Award in 1979, well before a majority of his published research. It is stated that he was beyond compare among younger economists for the range and variety of his theoretical work, and also for its vigor and liveiness. Among the areas cited to which he had contributed were growth and capital theory, the economics of discrimination, public and corporate finance, the economics of information and incentives, competitive equilibria with exhaustible resources, and monoglistic competition with product diversity. And this is now a very incomplete list.

Stiglitz has long been reported to have a tendency towards absent-mindedness and mild eccentricity, characteristics associated with academic brilliance but thought not to travel well into the arena of public policy making. At Stanford, one secretary was assigned solely to him, partly because of his immense productivity, but also to keep an eye on him to make sure that he did not tie his shoelaces together or engage in other similar acts. When he became President Clinton's Chair of the Council of Economic Advisers he attended cabinet meetings. At an early one, prior to Clinton's arrival, Stiglitz was sitting with his tie wrapped around the outside of his collar. Treasury Secretary Lloyd Bentsen, known to be a fashionable dresser, walked over and rearranged his tie for him.

As with many academic economists who become policy makers, Stiglitz constantly confronted conflicts between the ideals of economic theory and the compromises of practical political economy, a problem he discussed in a distinguished lecture to the Society of Government Economists (Stiglitz, 1998). An anecdote not included in that lecture brings home this conflict. During an episode of high oil prices that would lead President Clinton to decide to release oil from the Strategic Petroleum Reserve into the market, Stiglitz met with Clinton and Chief of Staff Leon Panetta to discuss the matter. Stiglitz advised against releasing the oil on the grounds that doing so would have no effect on the market and that the price of oil would come down on its own fairly soon anyway. Panetta responded to this argument by declaring that Clinton should therefore go ahead and release the oil anyway because 'it won't cause any harm and we'll get the credit for the drop in the price of oil.' Panetta's argument carried the day.

3 Development of the economics of asymmetric information

As noted earlier, by previously awarding a Nobel Prize for the economics of asymmetric information to Vickrey and Mirrlees, the problem of the economics of information and the special issue of asymmetries of information had been under discussion for some time prior to the crucial breakthroughs by Akerlof, Spence, and Stiglitz in the 1970s. According to Stiglitz (1987, 2000a, 2002a) early economists who evinced some awareness of information issues included Adam Smith (1776), Simonde de Sismondi (1814), John Stuart Mill (1848), Alfred Marshall (1890), and Max Weber (1925). Smith observed that, as interest rates rise, the best borrowers drop out of the market. Marshall observed that workers are not always paid on the basis of tasks performed because of the difficulty of observing exactly what they do, and argued that information imperfections would 'greatly complicate' economic analysis. However, Stiglitz argues that none of these individuals pursued the logical implications of their arguments and viewed these problems as essentially secondary issues.

Léon Walras (1874), who wrestled with the problem of achieving a general equilibrium, failed to make Stiglitz' list. Although it has not been widely noted, the problem of *tâtonnement* is at least partly an information processing problem. The auctioneer gathers the various responses to the proposed price vectors in order to adjust the price vector toward the general equilibrium, all prior to any market trading taking place. In the earlier editions of his work, Walras was clearer that this was an artificial mechanism and that the problem in real markets was very serious, although he tended to downplay this in the more widely read later editions (Walker, 1996). This later attitude was predominant when Arrow & Debreu (1954) formulated their now standard version of general equilibrium theory, and essentially assumed perfect information without even discussing the matter.[2]

Also on Stiglitz' list is Friedrich Hayek (1945), a previous Nobel Prize winner. Stiglitz argues that Hayek did not really appreciate the issue of asymmetric information, being concerned more with prices serving as efficient information signals regarding relative scarcities. But this misses an important aspect of Hayek's work. His work on dispersed and tacit information grew out of his involvement in the socialist planning controversy. The controversy concerned whether or not socialist planners could play the role of the Walrasian auctioneer and gather sufficient information in a centralized way to achieve an efficient general equilibrium. Hayek argued that socialist central planners would never be able to plan efficiently. This argument ultimately drew on an asymmetric information concept, although he did not use this terminology. For Hayek, the central planner would never be able to learn the information that is dispersed throughout the economy in a tacit way, and therefore could never play the role of the Walrasian auctioneer. Ironically, Stiglitz himself would come to emphasize such information issues when he came to discuss economic transition problems in his book, *Whither Socialism?* (Stiglitz, 1994).

Although Arrow & Debreu essentially ignored the possibility of imperfect information, another Nobel Laureate, Herbert Simon (1955, 1957), emphasized it forcefully when arguing for the inevitability of bounded rationality. Simon was concerned more with problems of computability, in particular the sheer scale and complexity of information, rather than with asymmetric information in specific transactions. However, Akerlof (2002) argues in his Nobel address that asymmetric information ultimately leads us to behavioral economics, and many see Simon's work as fundamental for this whole approach.

Berle & Means (1933) were among the first specifically to identify asymmetric information as a problem for firm management. What they labeled the 'problem of the separation of ownership and control' we now recognize as a canonical version of the principal–agent problem, a classic problem of asymmetric information. This problem would be put into its modern formulation by Ross (1973) and Townsend (1979). It is not surprising that standard graduate texts in micro theory tend to discuss these issues either in the same chapter (Varian, 1992, ch. 26) or in adjacent chapters (Mas-Colell *et al.*, 1995, chs 13 and 14).

In addition to the seminal work of Vickrey and Mirrlees, a number of economists dealt with problems of information during the 1960s. It was understood that, because gathering information is costly, it is optimal to be less than fully informed. Stigler (1961, 1967) argued that this was not a problem and that these were just general transactions costs that are no different from any other costs and that markets can be expected to be efficient anyway. However, Radner (1968) and Arrow (1974) both noted that imperfect information can lead to incomplete contracts with resulting inefficiencies. Williamson (1979), a student of both Simon and Arrow, identified transactions costs as a source of incomplete contracts, and Hirshleifer (1971) argued that excess incentives to search for information might arise.

Although much of this literature, to the present, identifies equilibria in which transactions costs are accounted for, a more fundamental problem was raised by Raiffa (1968) that remains unresolved. This is how to optimize the discovery of transactions costs or the degree of imperfect information. Ultimately, this involves an infinite regress of economizing on economizing on economizing. Binmore (1987), Lipman (1991), and Koppl & Rosser (2002) have studied this problem, and Conlisk (1996) identifies it as a fundamental source of bounded rationality in economic decision making.

4 The core arguments

The key paper in the economics of asymmetric information is Akerlof's (1970) study of the market for lemons, one of the most frequently cited papers in the last half of the 20th century. The 'lemons' in question are used cars. Akerlof began by noting that the owner of a car knows more about it than any potential buyer. Therefore, the used car market inevitably involves asymmetric information. Akerlof (2002) claims that he first became interested in the used car market from his interest in macro fluctuations, and from the fact that the new car market exhibits large fluctuations that contribute significantly to macro fluctuations. But he soon realized that applications of his discovery went well beyond both the used car market and basic macroeconomics.

Akerlof showed that awareness of their relative ignorance would lead potential buyers to assume that any used car would have a high probability of being low quality, a 'lemon.' This would cause them to bid down the price of used cars in general, and this would drive most high quality used cars out of the market. Indeed, in his original theoretical model, Akerlof showed that, in principle, *only* lemons would be offered for sale.

However, Akerlof observed that, in the real world, some people would be forced by circumstance to offer a high quality car for sale, using the example of someone transferred abroad. The inefficiency arising from asymmetric information would essentially be borne by these individuals, who would be unable to receive a sufficient price for their car because it was likely to be viewed as just another lemon. Although there are markets where repeat sales and reputation may resolve the problem, Akerlof observed that in many markets these problems are not easily resolved, including in insurance, labor, and credit. His finding of lemons driving out good cars from the market is known as *adverse selection.*

Just as Akerlof noted that reputation may resolve the problem, Spence (1973) pursued this particular solution in his study of *signaling* in labor markets. He found that it does not always work to remove inefficiency. In his example, the asymmetry is between an employer and a potential employee. Because the employer is unable to discern accurately the skills of the potential employee, she relies upon signals. The most prominent signal is the costly attainment of certain educational levels by the potential employee. It is believed that only employees who are sufficiently skilled will bear the costs of getting educated and thus sending the signal. Spence notes that the signal will only signify something real if there is a negative correlation between signaling costs and productive capability. This means (for the case of education as a signal) that grades in schools (and the availability of scholarships) must be positively correlated with productive work capability.

Spence identifies the possibility of an infinite set of signaling equilibria, with each equilibrium associated with a cutoff level of education (or amount of the signal), which will be based on the conditional probabilities believed in by the employers. Potential employees will be sorted as being either above or below this level and, in theory, people will either invest in the signal up to that level and no further or will not invest in the signal at all. As the level of the signal rises, the higher group will be worse off due to higher signaling costs. Although the lower group is not hurt by an increase in the signal level, it is worse off than a no-signal equilibrium in which everybody gets paid their unconditional expected marginal product.

Although it is possible to construct cases where some groups gain from signaling, very often all groups would be better off with no signaling, a clear case of a Pareto inferior outcome. A crucial part of the argument is that the cost of generating the signals lowers net aggregate product, although Spence recognizes that education may have external benefits that overcome this factor. He further notes the possibility of signaling becoming entangled in various kinds of unfair discrimination in labor markets (Spence 1974a, 1974b, 1976a).

Rothschild & Stiglitz (1976) extend the analysis by introducing the concept of *screening*. They apply this to insurance markets which, as noted above, are rife with asymmetric information problems leading to both adverse selection and moral hazard. The screening mechanism is aimed to offer a variety of contracts that encourage agents to reveal accurate information about their riskiness through a process of self-selection. Thus, lower risk agents will tend to select contracts that charge lower premiums but higher deductibles. However, there is an inherent conflict between the two functions of transmitting information and redistributing risk.

Stiglitz (1975) applies this argument to the education example studied by Spence and comes up with results that are partly similar and partly dissimilar. He also identifies multiple equilibria that can be Pareto ranked and notes various costs of screening. However, he argues that the Pareto optimal solution would be a full screening that properly identifies each agent's true capabilities. However, this outcome is not sustainable as a market equilibrium.

5 Extensions and applications

5.1 Industrial organization and microeconomic dynamics

In response to Rothschild & Stiglitz (1976), Spence (1976a) argues that there is no meaningful distinction between signaling and screening. Both are self-selection mechanisms. What matters are two things—whether buyers or sellers do the self-selecting, and the details of the information cost structures. This has shifted the discussion in the direction of questions more closely related to industrial organization and micro market dynamics.

Spence (1976b) argued that competition in signaling can reduce the inefficiencies associated with signaling, thereby initiating a line of argument that has resonated in many areas of economics. He distinguishes between *passive response signals* and *active response* signals. The former involve receivers of signals simply reading them in the light of past market experiences. These cases lead to inefficiency as there tends to be over-investment in the signals. With active response signals, the receivers anticipate the effect of their own responses on the patterns of investment in the signal and attempt to compete in this dimension. This allows for the possibility of improved efficiency.

Besides the kinds of multiple contract offerings suggested for insurance companies by Rothschild & Stiglitz (1976), Spence (1977) notes that product guarantees are another way to achieve such a goal by using competitive signaling. In addition, product differentiation, which is associated with monopolistic competition, reduces information problems by expanding the availability of options (Spence 1976c). This argument was followed up on by Dixit & Stiglitz (1977), whose work has been widely cited as a fountainhead of both the 'new inter-national trade' and the 'new economic geography.' In these papers, one could say that the degree of product heterogeneity is limited by the scale of the market.

Given his emphasis upon signaling and information transmission, it is not surprising that Spence (1980) came to study the role of advertising. He argues that advertising as well as R&D are fixed costs that create barriers to entry. He also argues that the inability of one firm to observe the behavior of another firm reduces the ability tacitly to collude (Spence 1978). But, Scitovsky (1950) argued that even a small amount of imperfect information can lead to monopoly power. Dixit & Stiglitz (1977) and Salop & Stiglitz (1977) further pursue some of these themes. One outcome of this work is that dispersions of information will lead to dispersions of price as well as of product quality and advertising. Stiglitz (1979) also provides an information-based argument for kinked demand curves in monopolistic competition. In a world of search costs, if a firm raises its price, its customers may search for lower priced competitors; however, if it lowers its price, too few other customers will learn about it to make it worthwhile.

This strand of research culminated in the argument (Stiglitz, 1987) that if price becomes a signal of quality, then 'quality can depend on price.' Besides the possibility of overly thin markets due to adverse selection (as in the lemons market), Stiglitz noted that this can lead to difficulties in separating supply effects from demand effects as changes in supply characteristics can shift demand curves. Also, Stiglitz notes the possibility of upward-sloping demand curves. He applies this to the efficiency wage theory (which we shall discuss in the next section) and also to stock market informational paradoxes (Grossman & Stiglitz, 1976, 1980). These paradoxes have been thought to underlie dynamics in financial markets due to learning among heterogeneous agents as strategies become more or less profitable as fewer or more people are using them, leading to complex dynamics as agents oscillate back and forth among different strategies (Brock & Hommes, 1998).

5.2 New Keynesian theories of unemployment

Akerlof was motivated to study the used car market in order to understand macroeconomic fluctuations. Although his lemons paper (Akerlof, 1970) was written prior to the emergence of the New Classical revolution in macro-economics based on the assumption of rational expectations (Lucas, 1972), the models of asymmetric information that have followed from his lemons paper underpin the New Keynesian counterattack against the New Classical revolution. In essence, rational expectations in the face of asymmetric information can be shown to result in sticky wages that are above market clearing levels and thus can explain the existence of 'involuntary unemployment.'[3]

Probably the most important such argument is the *efficiency wage hypothesis.* Akerlof (2002) argues that the New Classical view that unemployment was solely voluntary implies that quits should rise with unemployment. But as the

Old Keynesian James Tobin (1972) pointed out, this is the opposite of what happens empirically. The efficiency wage hypothesis—drawing partly on the difficulty potential employers face in learning the qualities of potential employees and the associated difficulties unemployed potential employees face in obtaining a job—implies that quits will fall as unemployment rises. Workers, or at least some workers, will be paid more than their unconditionally expected marginal product in order to induce greater productivity out of them. Fear of being laid off, and the associated difficulty of getting rehired, bring this about. This argument was developed from the mid-1970s to the mid-1980s (Stiglitz, 1976; Salop, 1979; Solow, 1979; Shapiro & Stiglitz, 1984; Akerlof, 1984; Yellen, 1984; Bowles, 1985).

Akerlof, in turn (Akerlof, 1976, 1980, 1982, 1984; Akerlof & Yellen, 1990), has used the asymmetric information argument to pursue more sociologically and psychologically based theories of unemployment. This has led to his more recent interest in sociological and psychological models (Akerlof, 1991; Akerlof & Kranton, 2000). The emphasis is on interactions among workers themselves more than any interactions between bosses and workers as in the efficiency wage hypothesis. Concerns about equity and fairness and group dynamics come to the fore. Akerlof has emphasized a study by Donald Roy (1952) regarding the behavior of workers in an Illinois machine shop. In effect, workers have a great deal of control over their own and each other's productivity and effectively work together to keep out workers who would lower the going wage. In a (Akerlof) 1980 paper such behavior leads to social customs that include unemployment, and in a (Akerlof) 1982 paper, labor and management engage in partial gift exchanges of higher productivity for efficiency wages.

Akerlof has provided two further elements to this strand of argument. His widely cited Ely Lecture (Akerlof, 1991) has been seen as encouraging concern for psychological elements and also for highlighting the strength of both fairness motives and the endowment effect in leading to downward stickiness of wages (Rabin, 1998). The endowment effect depends on people measuring their utility relative to some level to which they are adapted and to demand much greater compensation for a given loss than they would be willing to pay for an equal gain. This deeply rooted downward stickiness of wages implies that it is non-optimal to have zero inflation because there will be a failure of labor markets to adjust relative wages sufficiently rapidly (Akerlof *et al.*, 1996, 2000).

A more general result derived from asymmetric information, which has broad microeconomics and macroeconomics implications—is the theory of *near rationality* (Akerlof & Yellen, 1985a, 1985b). The existence of asymmetric information implies that there are some small deviations from optimal behavior. In contrast to the arguments of Marshall and Stigler, as well as Arrow and Debreu, these small deviations from rationality can have large economic implications. For example, a small amount of wage-price inertia can induce large aggregate demand fluctuations. Stiglitz (2000a) cites this general result as one of the most important emerging from the entire asymmetric information literature—small changes in information conditions can generate large changes in final outcomes.

5.3 New Keynesian credit market rationing

Stiglitz (2000a) points out that the idea of credit rationing was first noted by Adam Smith. But since Smith's time, economists have failed to give clear explanations as to why it occurs (Jaffee, 1971; Jaffee & Russell, 1976; Keeton, 1979). Stiglitz & Weiss (1981, 1983) brought the discussion within the framework of asymmetric information that had developed by this time, with banks being the less-informed principals dealing with the better-informed borrower agents regarding their own risk. In such an environment, two interest rate equilibria can arise and the interest rate can serve as a screening device. In a high interest rate environment, good borrowers will be driven away, just as Adam Smith observed and just as people with good used cars cannot sell them for a decent price in the lemons market. Credit is arbitrarily restricted by banks, implying different channels for monetary policy to work than in Old Keynesian or Monetarist models.

One particular result of these models is that an arbitrarily volatile fluctuation of credit can arise, with obvious implications for macroeconomic (in)stability. It also suggests a violation of standard financial theory, developed by Miller & Modigliani (1958, 1961), because there is now a major difference between debt and equity financing due to this behavior by the banks.

The implications of these arguments for macroeconomic stability are laid out in Greenwald & Stiglitz (1987, 1988); Stiglitz & Weiss (1992), and Stiglitz (1992, 1999a). These papers combine the New Keynesian labor market results discussed above with the credit rationing model. As Stiglitz (1999a, p. 80) puts it, 'I have argued that asymmetries are particularly pronounced between those markets (like assets) where auction processes prevail and those in which firms engage in price setting. It is relative rigidities, not absolute ones, that matter.' It is worth noting that these final remarks were made near the end of Stiglitz's tenure at the World Bank when he was in deep disagreement with the Washington Consensus (and Treasury Secretary Lawrence Summers and the IMF) over their handling of the East Asian financial crisis of 1997, and he concludes this paper by specifically applying the remarks to that particular situation.

5.4 Economic development and global stability

Both Akerlof and Stiglitz exhibited great interest in problems of economic development quite early in their careers (Akerlof, 1969; Stiglitz, 1974).[4] Stiglitz (1974) was arguably one of the first places in which he postulated a version of the efficiency wage model. The argument was expanded and applied to compare sharecropping and fixed wage payments in rural agriculture in less developed economies, with the landlord now in the position of the principal and the peasant in the position of the agent (Braverman & Stiglitz, 1982). Indeed, this paper dates from the same period that Stiglitz & Weiss (1982) were developing their credit rationing argument, and it would later be noted that the restrictions on credit by a landlord in this situation resemble those by a bank in a financially advanced economy (Hoff *et al.*, 1993).

Unsurprisingly, after Stiglitz became Chief Economist of the World Bank during a period of erupting international financial crises, his attention turned to the problems of global financial stability. He carried his analysis of asymmetric information in credit and financial markets from less developed countries to the global level, arguing for an extreme fragility and volatility due to the problems in the financial sectors of these countries. Stiglitz applied this analysis to East Asia after the 1997 crisis in what would become his very public critique of the policies of the Washington Consensus as embodied in the IMF and Lawrence Summers (Furman & Stiglitz, 1998; Stiglitz, 1999b, 2000b). To him, the policies recommended by the IMF of monetary and fiscal austerity simply exacerbated the underlying problems. He has since blamed such policies for the more recent crisis in Argentina (Stiglitz, 2002b).

In his Nobel address, Akerlof (2002) also addresses the problem of financial volatility at some length, tying it to the deeper psychological and sociological factors that he has come to see as the more profound extensions of asymmetric information. He particularly praises the work of Robert Shiller (1999) in this regard and sees this as one of six fundamental problems that behavioral macro-economics may be able to help us understand.[5] When one contemplates Akerlof's discussion on myopia and procrastination dating from his 1991 Ely Lecture, it is tempting to say that he has shifted the ground of asymmetric information from being between two parties in exchange to being within a single party, experiencing conflict between the self at one point in time and the self at another point in time. Thus, the time inconsistency associated with hyperbolic discounting (Strotz, 1956; Laibson *et al.*, 1998) can be seen as an internal species of asymmetric information and the problem of the market for lemons.

6 But is it Keynesian?

Although Spence has mostly worked in the area of microeconomics and avoided the battles over labels and identities that have plagued macroeconomics, both Akerlof and Stiglitz have plunged wholeheartedly into macroeconomic debates. They have both been self-styled and strong advocates of New Keynesian macro-economics, basing it on the asymmetric information models discussed above. They have argued that while Keynes (1936) was wrong in various particulars (about the nature of bond markets, about the causes of the persistence of unem-ployment, about the channels of monetary policy, and various other items) some of his important views have been essentially correct—that there can be persistent involuntary unemployment, that fluctuations of aggregate demand can trigger fluc-tuations in that unemployment, that savings may be disconnected from investment, and that fiscal policy may be useful to overcome these problems in managing aggregate demand (Greenwald & Stiglitz, 1987; Akerlof, 2002).[6]

Akerlof and Stiglitz argue that they have provided the key to turning back the tide of New Classical macroeconomics based on rational expectations; asymmetric information implies very different outcomes and policy approaches even when rational expectations hold. There is no doubt that this argument is correct and that they have played a major role in reviving the respectability of Keynes in the economics profession in recent years. But this does not mean that they have the final word.

Their models, especially their labor market models, still rely on the idea that unemployment fundamentally arises from wages in some sense being 'too high.' Much of their approach has sought to explain the various rigidities that in a neo-Keynesian framework lead to persistent involuntary unemployment. But a New Classical can respond to this that these are not true equilibria, that the workers are still choosing to be unemployed when they allow themselves to get into contractual arrangements where wages are 'too high' in some sense, even if they are 'efficiently' so.

Post Keynesians, such as Davidson (1994), argue that Keynes (1936) himself did not rely on wage and price stickiness for his arguments regarding persistent involuntary unemployment, although one can find discussions of the downward stickiness of wages in the *General Theory,* something that even many New Classicals accept is a stylized fact of most labor markets. Keynes saw the problem as inherent in the nature of money and in the failure of animal spirits that can generate a profound collapse of investment and output. The Post Walrasian emphasis on nonlinearities and self-fulfilling sunspot equilibria and multiple equilibria with coordination failures is relevant here (Woodford, 1990). However, it appears that Akerlof at least has become more open to the idea of the role of animal spirits in financial markets, given his more recent remarks about the work of Shiller.

Finally, there is a broader arena of dynamic analysis involving models of learning that are receiving attention from Keynesian macroeconomists of various stripes as well as many New Classical economists (Brock & Hommes, 1998; Sargent, 1993, 1998). The older asymmetric information models of Akerlof, Spence, and Stiglitz had a certain degree of certitude about them, with known probabilities of being able to observe outcomes. These were the elements that saved this variety of the economics of information from the horrible paradoxes of infinite regress and trying to economize on how to economize first suggested by Raiffa (1968). In a world of deeper Keynesian uncertainty, the processes by which agents learn these probabilities, and whether they can even do so, have moved to the fore, especially in a world increasingly haunted by the specter of complex nonlinear dynamics.[7]

7 Conclusions

Our subjects must be given their due. They have enormously increased our understanding of models about knowledge and what they can imply and what they can lead to, especially when that knowledge is distributed asymmetrically among interacting agents. Their influence has been vast and deserved, as is their receipt of the Bank of Sweden prize in Economic Sciences in Memory of Alfred

Nobel in 2001. Both microeconomics and macroeconomics have been profoundly transformed by their efforts.

Notes

The author wishes to acknowledge comments and useful provision of materials by George Akerlof, Michael Spence, and Joseph Stiglitz, as well as comments by Steven Pressman and several informants who have requested anonymity. The usual caveat applies.

1 Although Mirrlees's paper appeared after Akerlof's, it was written considerably earlier and had circulated widely in mimeo form. Stiglitz (2000a, p. 1450) notes that this was true of several important early papers in this area, as many of them were hard to get published due to their unconventional content.

2 Although Arrow ignored information issues in his work with Debreu, he would later become one of the most important students of the problem, inventing the concept of moral hazard (Arrow, 1971) and independently publishing a paper on educational signaling in the same year (1973) as Spence. This work arose from his studies of risk bearing (Arrow, 1964).

3 Rosser (1990) distinguishes 'weak New Keynesian' from 'Strong New Keynesian' economics. The former is the variety being discussed here that ultimately relies on (near) rational expectations models of wage or price stickiness or credit rationing to arrive at 'Keynesian' conclusions. 'Strong New Keynesian' economies can hold with perfect information and involve nonlinearities to generate complex dynamics, multiple equilibria, and coordination failures (Grandmont, 1985; Cooper & John, 1988). Colander (1996) calls such models 'Post Walrasian,' although Stiglitz (1993) has used this term in a different context. Rosser (1998) argues that the strong New Keynesian view is more easily reconciled with certain varieties of Post Keynesian approaches. What is now called 'Old Keynesian' economics is what has also been called 'neo-Keynesian' and is associated with use of the IS-LM model in the neoclassical synthesis.

4 Although they collaborated on only one paper quite early in their careers (Akerlof & Stiglitz, 1969), it did not contribute much to the development of the New Keynesian apparatus based on asymmetric information that both of them have played such large roles in developing, despite providing some hints of what was to come. Later in their careers they would also both write about problems of economic transition (Akerlof *et al.*, 1991; Stiglitz, 1994). However, neither of them has ever co-authored with Spence.

5 The other five are the existence of involuntary unemployment, the impact of monetary policy on output and employment, the failure of deflation to accelerate when unemployment is high, the prevalence of undersaving for retirement, and the stubborn persistence of a self-destructive underclass.

6 Akerlof is more strongly complimentary of Keynes than is Stiglitz, seeing in him a forerunner of the sort of psychological analysis and approach that Akerlof himself currently favors, although he believes that Keynes' psychological arguments were not too sophisticated.

7 However, Stiglitz (2000a) has recently cited work out of the Santa Fe Institute and Akerlof supported the work of various complexity economists while at the Brookings Institution.

References

Arrow, K. J. (1964) The role of securities in the optimal allocation of risk bearing, *Review of Economic Studies*, 31, pp. 91–96.

Arrow, K. J. (1971) *Essays in the Theory of Risk Bearing* (Chicago, H. Markham).

Arrow, K. J. (1974) Limited knowledge and economic analysis, *American Economic Review*, 44, pp. 1–10.

Arrow, K. J. & Debreu, G. (1954) Existence of an equilibrium for a competitive economy, *Econometrica*, 22, pp. 265–290.

Berle, A. A. & Means, G. C. (1933) *The Modern Corporation and Private Property* (New York, Macmillan).

Binmore, K. (1987) Modeling rational players I, *Economics and Philosophy*, 3, pp. 9–55.

Bowles, S. (1985) The production process in a competitive economy: Walrasian, neo-Hobbesian, and Marxian models, *American Economic Review*, 75, pp. 16–36.

Brock, W. A. & Hommes, C. H. (1998) Heterogeneous beliefs and routes to chaos in a simple asset pricing model, *Journal of Economic Dynamics and Control*, 22, pp. 1235–1274.

Colander, D. (Ed) (1996) *Beyond Microfoundations: Post Walrasian Macroeconomics* (Cambridge, Cambridge University Press).

Conlisk, J. (1996) Why bounded rationality? *Journal of Economic Literature*, 34, pp. 669–700.

Cooper, R. & John, A. (1988) Coordinating coordination failures, *Quarterly Journal of Economics*, 103, pp. 441–465.

Davidson, P. (1994) *Post Keynesian Macroeconomic Theory* (Aldershot, Edward Elgar).

Grandmont, J.-M. (1985) On endogenous competitive business cycles, *Econometrica*, 53, pp. 995–1054.

Hayek, F. A. (1945) The use of knowledge in society, *American Economic Review*, 35, pp. 519–530.

Hirshleifer, J. (1971) The private and social value of information and the reward to inventive activity, *American Economic Review*, 61, pp. 561–574.

Jaffee, D. (1971) *Credit Rationing and the Commercial Loan Market* (New York, Wiley).

Jaffee, D. & Russell, T. (1976) Imperfect information and credit rationing, *Quarterly Journal of Economics*, 90, pp. 651–666.

Keeton, W. (1979) *Equilibrium Credit Rationing* (New York, Garland).

Keynes, J. M. (1936) *The General Theory of Employment, Interest and Money* (London, Macmillan).

Koppl, R. & Rosser, J. B., Jr. (2002) All that I have to say has already crossed your mind, *Metroeconomica*, 53, pp.339–60.

Laibson, D. I., Repetto, A. & Tobacman, J. (1998) Self-control and saving for retirement, *Brookings Papers on Economic Activity*, (1), pp. 91–172.

Lipman, B. L. (1991) How to decide how to decide how to…: modeling limited rationality, *Econometrica*, 59, pp. 1105–1125.

Lucas, R. E., Jr. (1972) Expectations and the neutrality of money, *Journal of Economic Theory*, 4, pp. 103–124.

Marshall, A. (1890) *Principles of Economics* (London, Macmillan).

Mas-Colell, A., Whinston, M. D. & Green, J. R. (1995) *Microeconomic Theory* (New York, Oxford University Press).

Mill, J. S. (1848) *Principles of Political Economy* (London, J.P. Parker).

Miller, M. & Modigliani, F. (1958) The cost of capital, corporate finance and the theory of investment, *American Economic Review*, 48, pp. 261–297.

Miller, M. & Modigliani, F. (1961) Dividend policy, growth, and the valuation of shares, *Journal of Business*, 34, pp. 411–433.

Mirrlees, J. (1971) An exploration in the theory of optimal income taxation, *Review of Economic Studies*, 41, pp. 261–278.

Rabin, M. (1998) Psychology and economics, *Journal of Economic Literature,* 36, pp. 11–46.

Radner, R. (1968) Competitive equilibrium under uncertainty, *Econometrica,* 36, pp. 31–58.

Raiffa, H. (1968) *Decision Analysis: Introductory Lectures on Choices under Uncertainty* (Reading, Addison-Wesley).

Ross, S. A. (1973) The economic theory of agency: the principal's problem, *American Economic Review,* 63, pp. 134–139.

Rosser, J. B., Jr. (1990) Chaos theory and the new Keynesian economics, *The Manchester School of Economic and Social Studies,* 58, pp. 265–291.

Rosser, J. B., Jr. (1998) Complex dynamics in new Keynesian and post Keynesian economics, in: R. Rotheim (Ed.) *New Keynesian Economics/Post Keynesian Alternatives* (London, Routledge).

Roy, D. (1952) Quota restriction and gold bricking in a machine shop, *American Journal of Sociology,* 57, pp. 427–442.

Salop, S. (1979) A model of the natural rate of unemployment, *American Economic Review,* 69, pp. 117–125.

Sargent, T. J. (1993) *Bounded Rationality in Macroeconomics* (Oxford, Clarendon Press).

Sargent, T. J. (1998) *The Conquest of American Inflation* (Princeton, Princeton University Press).

Scitovsky, T. (1950) Ignorance as a source of oligopoly power, *American Economic Review,* 40, pp. 48–53.

Shiller, R. J. (1999) *Irrational Exuberance* (Princeton, Princeton University Press).

Simon, H. A. (1955) A behavioral model of rational choice, *Quarterly Journal of Economics,* 69, pp. 99–118.

Simon, H. A. (1957) *Models of Man* (New York, Wiley).

Sismondi, S. de (1814) *Political Economy* (New York, Kelley, 1966).

Smith, A. (1776) *An Inquiry into the Nature and Causes of the Wealth of Nations* (London, Strahan & Cadell).

Solow, R. M. (1979) Another possible source of wage stickiness, *Journal of Macroeconomics,* 1, pp. 79–82.

Stigler, G. J. (1961) The economics of information, *Journal of Political Economy,* 69, pp. 213–225.

Stigler, G. J. (1967) Imperfections in the capital market, *Journal of Political Economy,* 75, pp. 287–292.

Strotz, R. H. (1956) Myopia and inconsistency in dynamic utility maximization, *Review of Economic Studies,* 23, pp. 165–180.

Tobin, J. (1972) Inflation and unemployment, *American Economic Review,* 62, pp. 1–18.

Townsend, R. (1979) Optimal contracts and competitive markets with costly state verification, *Journal of Economic Theory,* 21, pp. 265–293.

Varian, H. R. (1992) *Microeconomic Analysis,* 3rd edn (New York, Norton).

Vickrey, W. (1961) Counterspeculation, auctions, and competitive sealed tenders, *Journal of Finance,* 16, pp. 8–37.

Walker, D. A. (1996) *Walras' Market Models* (Cambridge, Cambridge University Press).

Walras, L. (1874) *Élemens d'Économie Politique Pure* (Lausanne, F. Rouge).

Weber, M. (1925) *The Protestant Ethic and the Spirit of Capitalism* (New York, Scribner).

Williamson, O. E. (1979) Transactions-cost economics: the governance of contractual relations, *Journal of Law and Economics,* 22, pp. 233–261.

Woodford, M. (1990) Learning to believe in sunspots, *Econometrica,* 58, pp. 277–307.
Yellen, J. L. (1984) Efficiency wage models of unemployment, *American Economic Review, Papers and Proceedings,* 74, pp. 200–205.

Works by George A. Akerlof cited in this paper

Akerlof, G. A. (1969) Centre-state fiscal relations in India, *Indian Economic Review,* 4 (New Series), 99–121.
Akerlof, G. A. (1970) The market for lemons: quality uncertainty and the market mechanism, *Quarterly Journal of Economics,* 84, pp. 488–500.
Akerlof, G. A. (1976) The economics of caste and of the rat race and other woeful tales, *Quarterly Journal of Economics,* 90, pp. 599–617.
Akerlof, G. A. (1980) A theory of social custom, of which unemployment may be one consequence, *Quarterly Journal of Economics,* 94, pp. 749–775.
Akerlof, G. A. (1982) Labor contracts as partial gift exchange, *Quarterly Journal of Economics,* 97, pp. 543–569.
Akerlof, G. A. (1984) Gift exchange and efficiency wage theory: four views, *American Economic Review, Papers and Proceedings,* 74, pp. 79–83.
Akerlof, G. A. (1991) Procrastination and obedience, *American Economic Review, Papers and Proceedings,* 81, pp. 1–19.
Akerlof, G. A. (2002) Behavioral macroeconomics and macroeconomic behavior, *American Economic Review,* 92, pp. 411–433.
Akerlof, G. A. & Kranton, R. E. (2000) Economics and identity, *Quarterly Journal of Economics,* 115, pp. 715–753.
Akerlof, G. A. & Stiglitz, J. E. (1969) Capital, wages and structural unemployment, *Economic Journal,* 79, pp. 269–281.
Akerlof, G. A. & Yellen, J. L. (1985a) A near rational model of the business cycle, with wage and price inertia, *Quarterly Journal of Economics,* 100, pp. 823–838.
Akerlof, G. A. & Yellen, J. L. (1985b) Can small deviations from rationality make significant differences to economic equilibria? *American Economic Review,* 75, pp. 708–720.
Akerlof, G. A. & Yellen, J. L. (1990) The fair wage hypothesis and unemployment, *Quarterly Journal of Economics,* 105, pp. 255–283.
Akerlof, G. A., Rose, A., Yellen, J. L. & Hessenius, H. (1991) Eastern Germany in from the cold: the economic aftermath of currency union, *Brookings Papers on Economic Activity,* (1), pp. 1–87.
Akerlof, G. A., Dickens, W. T. & Perry, G. L. (1996) The macroeconomics of low inflation, *Brookings Papers on Economic Activity,* (1), pp. 1–59.
Akerlof, G. A., Dickens, W. T. & Perry, G. L. (2000), Near rational wage and price setting and the long-run Phillips curve, *Brookings Papers on Economic Activity,* (1), pp. 1–44.

Works by A. Michael Spence cited in this paper

Caves, R. E., Porter, M. E. & Spence, A. M. (1980) *Industrial Organization in an Open Economy* (Cambridge, Harvard University Press).
Hayes, S., Marks, D. & Spence, A. M. (1983) *Competitive Structure in Investment Banking* (Cambridge, Harvard University Press).
Spence, A. M. (1973) Job market signaling, *Quarterly Journal of Economics,* 87, pp. 355–374.

Spence, A. M. (1974a) *Market Signaling: Informational Transfer in Hiring and Related Processes* (Cambridge, Harvard University Press).

Spence, A. M. (1974b) Competitive and optimal responses to signals: an analysis of efficiency and distribution, *Journal of Economic Theory,* 7, pp. 296–332.

Spence, A. M. (1976a) Competition in salaries, credentials, and signaling prerequisites for jobs, *Quarterly Journal of Economics,* 90, pp. 51–74.

Spence, A. M. (1976b) Informational aspects of market structure: an introduction, *Quarterly Journal of Economics,* 90, pp. 591–597.

Spence, A. M. (1976c) Product selection, fixed costs, and monopolistic competition, *Review of Economic Studies,* 43, pp. 217–235.

Spence, A. M. (1977) Consumer misperceptions, product failure and producer liability, *Review of Economic Studies,* 44, pp. 561–572.

Spence, A. M. (1978) Tacit co-ordination and imperfect information, *Canadian Journal of Economics,* 11, pp. 490–505.

Spence, A. M. (1980) Notes on advertising, economies of scale, and entry barriers, *Quarterly Journal of Economics,* 95, pp. 493–507.

Spence, A. M. (2002) Signaling in retrospect and the informational structure of markets, *American Economic Review,* 92, pp. 434–459.

Works by Joseph E. Stiglitz cited in this paper

Akerlof, G. A. & Stiglitz, J. E. (1969) Capital, wages and structural unemployment, *Economic Journal,* 79, pp. 269–281.

Braverman, A. & Stiglitz, J. E. (1982) Sharecropping and the interlinking of agrarian markets, *American Economic Review,* 72, pp. 695–715.

Dixit, A. & Stiglitz, J. E. (1977) Monopolistic competition and optimal product diversity, *American Economic Review,* 67, pp. 297–308.

Furman, J. & Stiglitz, J. E. (1998) Economic crises: evidence and insights from east Asia, *Brookings Papers on Economic Activity,* (2), pp. 1–114.

Greenwald, B. & Stiglitz, J. E. (1987) Keynesian, new Keynesian, and new classical economics, *Oxford Economic Papers,* 39, pp. 119–133.

Greenwald, B. & Stiglitz, J. E. (1988) Examining alternative macroeconomic theories, *Brookings Papers on Economic Activity,* (1), pp. 207–270.

Grossman, S. J. & Stiglitz, J. E. (1976) Information and competitive price systems, *American Economic Review,* 66, pp. 246–253.

Grossman, S. J. & Stiglitz, J. E. (1980) On the impossibility of informationally efficient markets, *American Economic Review,* 70, pp. 393–408.

Hoff, K., Braverman, A. & Stiglitz, J. E. (Eds) (1993) *The Economics of Rural Organization: Theory, Practice, and Policy* (New York, Oxford University Press for the World Bank).

Salop, S. & Stiglitz, J. E. (1977) Bargains and ripoffs: a model of monopolistically competitive price dispersions, *Review of Economic Studies,* 44, pp. 493–510.

Shapiro, C. & Stiglitz, J. E. (1984) Equilibrium unemployment as a worker discipline device, *American Economic Review,* 74, pp. 433–444.

Stiglitz, J. E. (1974) Incentives and risk sharing in sharecropping, *Review of Economic Studies,* 41, pp. 219–255.

Stiglitz, J. E. (1975) The theory of screening, education and the distribution of income, *American Economic Review,* 65, pp. 283–300.

Stiglitz, J. E. (1976) The efficiency wage hypothesis, surplus labor and the distribution of income in l.d.c.'s, *Oxford Economic Papers,* 28, pp. 185–207.

Stiglitz, J. E. (1979) Equilibrium in product markets with imperfect information, *American Economic Review, Papers and Proceedings*, 69, pp. 339–345.

Stiglitz, J. E. (1987) The causes and consequences of the dependence of quality on price, *Journal of Economic Literature*, 25, pp. 1–48.

Stiglitz, J. E. (1992) Capital markets and economic fluctuations in capitalist economies, *European Economic Review*, 36, pp. 269–306.

Stiglitz, J. E. (1993) Post Walrasian and post Marxian economics, *Journal of Economic Perspectives*, 7(1), pp. 109–114.

Stiglitz, J. E. (1994) *Whither Socialism?* (Cambridge, MIT Press).

Stiglitz, J. E. (1998) The private uses of public interests: incentives and institutions, *Journal of Economic Perspectives*, 12(2), pp. 3–22.

Stiglitz, J. E. (1999a) Toward a general theory of wage and price rigidities and economic fluctuations, *American Economic Review, Papers and Proceedings*, 89, pp. 75–80.

Stiglitz, J. E. (1999b) Responding to economic crises: policy alternatives for equitable recovery and development, *The Manchester School*, 67, pp. 409–427.

Stiglitz, J. E. (2000a) The contributions of the economics of information to twentieth century economics, *Quarterly Journal of Economics*, 115, pp. 1441–1478.

Stiglitz, J. E. (2000b) Capital market liberalization, economic growth, and instability, *World Development*, 28, pp. 1075–1086.

Stiglitz, J. E. (2002a) Information and the change in the paradigm in economics, *American Economic Review*, 92, pp. 460–501.

Stiglitz, J. E. (2002b) Argentina shortchanged, *Washington Post*, May 12, p. B1.

Stiglitz, J. E. & Rothschild, M. E. (1976) Equilibrium in competitive insurance markets, *Quarterly Journal of Economics*, 90, pp. 629–649.

Stiglitz, J. E. & Weiss, A. (1981) Credit rationing in markets with imperfect information, *American Economic Review*, 71, pp. 393–410.

Stiglitz, J. E. & Weiss, A. (1983) Alternative approaches to the analysis of markets with asymmetric information, *American Economic Review*, 73, pp. 246–249.

Stiglitz, J. E. & Weiss, A. (1992) Asymmetric information in credit markets and its implications for macroeconomics, *Oxford Economic Papers*, 44, pp. 694–724.

8 The Nobel Prize in behavioral and experimental economics

A contextual and critical appraisal of the contributions of Daniel Kahneman and Vernon Smith

Morris Altman

'The Nobel Prize in Behavioral and Experimental Economics: A Contextual and Critical Appraisal of the Contributions of Daniel Kahneman and Vernon Smith' by Morris Altman from *Review of Political Economy* (2004), Volume 16, Issue 1 (Taylor and Francis Ltd, http://www.informaworld.com), reprinted by permission of the publisher.

1 Introduction

The Nobel Prize in Economics for 2002 was jointly awarded to Daniel Kahneman, a psychologist, and Vernon Smith, an economist. As Kahneman points out, his award is very much for collaborative work with the late Amos Tversky, also a psychologist. The Royal Swedish Academy of Sciences recognized the important insights and contributions from psychology that Kahneman brought to the development of economics. In giving the Nobel Prize to Smith, the Academy recognized the role of human laboratory experiments for testing economic theory and for evaluating the potential impact of public policy on economic efficiency.

The work of Kahneman challenges the assumption that individuals behave in a manner consistent with conventional economic theory, largely as a result of the complexity of real world decision-making processes and the limited cognitive capacity of the human mind. It thus follows in the tradition of Herbert Simon, who was awarded the Nobel Prize in Economics in 1978. The press release issued when announcing the 2002 winners noted that (Nobel E-Museum, 2003): 'Kahneman's main findings concern decision-making under uncertainty, where he has demonstrated how human decisions may systematically depart from those predicted by standard economic theory. Together with Amos Tversky, he has formulated prospect theory as an alternative, that better accounts for observed behavior. Kahneman has also discovered how human judgment may take heuristic shortcuts that systematically depart from basic principles of probability.'

Finding that individual behavior tends to deviate from the norms established by conventional economic theory, Kahneman and Tversky maintain that individuals tend to be systematically error prone and possibly irrational. This raises important questions for economic theory and policy. How can error prone individuals provide the microfoundations for an efficient economy? How can such individuals make decisions that are in their own best interest or the interest of the larger society? Can individuals learn to become 'rational'? Should the decisions of individuals be replaced by decisions made by some external body, such as a government, to maximize individual and social welfare?

Smith developed controlled experiments and experimental environments to test neoclassical hypotheses as well hypotheses stemming from the work of Kahneman and Tversky. Smith also developed experimental methods to test the implications of different public policies, especially related to deregulation. The 2002 Nobel Prize press release (Nobel E-Museum, 2003) noted that: 'Vernon Smith has laid the foundation for the field of experimental economics. He has developed an array of experimental methods, setting standards for what constitutes a reliable laboratory experiment in economics. In his own experimental work, he has demonstrated the importance of alternative market institutions – e.g., how the revenue expected by a seller depends on the choice of auction method'. Smith also developed 'wind-tunnel tests' or laboratory trials of new market designs and new policies (e.g. deregulating electricity markets and auctioning off radio frequencies) before they are implemented, in an attempt to identify their real world impacts. Smith finds that simulated economies in the laboratory tend to be efficient, and that economic agents tend to be rational in the sense of behaving (making choices) as predicted by standard economic theory. However, he also finds that those markets usually thought to be the most efficient (the stock market) are actually the least efficient.

In many ways the work of Kahneman and Smith complement each other. Both are committed to getting the facts straight about human decision-making. However, they often differ on what are the relevant facts and what are the implications of these facts. This article places their different views and contributions in the context of current methodological and public policy debates in economics.

2 Some background

Since 1993, Kahneman has been the Eugene Higgins Professor of Psychology and professor of public affairs in the Woodrow Wilson School of Public and International Affairs at Princeton University. Born in Tel Aviv, Israel in 1934, Kahneman earned a bachelor's degree in psychology and mathematics from Hebrew University. In 1961 he was awarded his PhD from the University of California-Berkeley. From 1961 to 1978 Kahneman taught at the Hebrew University in Jerusalem, from 1978 to 1986 at the University of British Columbia in Canada, and from 1986 to 1993 he taught at the University of California-Berkeley. Tversky, Kahneman's long-time collaborator and close friend, was born in Haifa, Israel in 1937, earning his BA from Hebrew University in 1961, and his doctorate in 1965 from the University of Michigan. After a brief stint teaching at Michigan and Harvard, Tversky returned to Hebrew University where he remained until 1978, when he joined the Psychology Department at Stanford University. Both Kahneman and Tversky spent their formative years in Israel. They began collaborating at the Hebrew University where Tversky raised critical questions about decision-making under uncertainty, which sparked their dynamic long-term research program. In particular, Tversky suggested further research in the area of mathematical psychology and, related to this, on expected utility theory and the foundational work of eighteenth century Swiss mathematician Daniel Bernoulli. This research ultimately led Kahneman and Tversky to develop prospect theory as an alternative to expected utility theory. Tversky's life was cut short by metastatic melanoma when he passed away on June 2, 1966 at the age of 59.

Since 2001, Smith has been at George Mason University where he is Director of the Interdisciplinary Center for Experimental Science (ICES). He came to George Mason from the Economic Science Laboratory, which he had established at the University of Arizona, and brought with him six Arizona colleagues to engage in his new venture. They were all interested in the emphasis on free market economics at George Mason.

Smith was born in Wichita, Kansas in 1927, just prior to the Great Depression. He initially had a strong socialist orientation, which inspired him to think about testing for the inefficiency of the market economy in its various dimensions. But his laboratory findings convinced him that the market could function more efficiently than its critics maintained, and it could do so under much more reasonable and realistic assumptions than its champions thought possible and which standard economic theory presumed. Smith thus evolved into an advocate of the Hayekian view of the efficacy of the market and of free individual choice as its underlying motivating force.

Smith's first university degree was in electrical engineering at the California Institute of Technology in 1949. But he was attracted to economics, and in 1952 he earned a Masters in Economics from the University of Kansas and then, in 1955, a PhD from Harvard University. For much of the 1955–67 period, Smith was a professor of Economics at Purdue, where he developed many of his core ideas in experimental economics. This work was regarded as being outside mainstream boundaries of what constituted important and proper research. Yet Smith persisted in spite of the odds, and perhaps chose a research agenda that he might not have chosen had he behaved as if he were to maximize his expected utility in terms of states of wealth. From 1968 to 1975 Smith was at the University of Massachusetts in Amherst, and from 1975 to 2001, at the University of Arizona, which he built into one of world's leading, if not the foremost, center for experimental economics.

3 The Methodological context—assumptions and rationality

The work of Kahneman and Smith raises key questions about the importance of empirically based behavioral assumptions in constructing economic theory, whether the behavior of economic agents is typically rational, whether the context or frame within which individual behavior takes place is an important determinant of human action, and whether the context or frame affects the predictions of economic theory. The last question speaks to the broader issue of whether institutions matter in the construction of economic theory.

The conventional view of empirically based behavioral assumptions in building economic theory stems from the methodological perspective put forth by Milton Friedman in the early 1950s. For Freidman (1953, pp. 4–6), economic theory has little to do with the accuracy of the behavioral assumptions, and less still with understanding why individuals behave as they do. Instead, economic theory is about generating predictions that flow from a specified change in circumstances; and the scientific worth of a theory is determined by how well the predictions conform to experience. The better the prediction, the better the theory. If prediction fails, it should raise questions about the theory, or at least components of the theory; and weak theories will need to be revised to yield more precise predictions (Friedman, 1953, p. 12).

But testing economic theory does not involving testing its assumptions. Testing an assumption's realism 'is fundamentally wrong and productive of much mischief. . . . [I]t only confuses the issue, promotes misunderstanding about the significance of empirical evidence for economic theory, produces a misdirection of much intellectual effort'. Rather, 'the relevant question to ask about the "assumptions" of theory is not whether they are descriptively "realistic," for they never are, but whether they are sufficiently good approximations for the purpose at hand' (Friedman, 1953, pp. 14–15).

This methodological approach amounts to using correlation analysis rather than causal analysis in order to test for the scientific legitimacy of a theory. It allows us to construct an array of theories built upon behavioral assumptions ranging from the wildly unrealistic to ones that capture the essence of economic behavior. If the prediction is good, one can simply assume that the individual behaves as if he or she followed the dictums of the theory's behavioral assumptions.

Although individuals don't actually behave in this fashion, Friedman argues that these unrealistic assumptions yield strong predictions regarding the type of economic performance necessary for the survival of the firm in the market place. Moreover, he argues that individual survival will force individuals to behave 'as if' they were following the script contained in even wildly unrealistic behavioral assumptions. Friedman (1953, p. 21) writes: 'firms behave as if they were seeking rationally to maximize their expected returns...and had full knowledge of the data needed to succeed in this attempt; as if, that is, they knew the relevant cost and demand functions, calculated marginal cost and marginal revenue from all actions open to them, and pushed each line of action to the point at which the relevant marginal cost and marginal revenue were equal.' Any other behavior (non-maximizing) would be inconsistent with the survival of the firm in the marketplace.

As Melvin Reder (1982) points out, the survival principle remains important to contemporary economic reasoning. Friedman's methodological position assumes that a certain set of behaviors (optimizing or efficient economic behavior) must prevail. But this methodological approach remains vague and ephemeral as to the specifics of such behaviors apart from it having to be cost minimizing and wealth maximizing. The content of optimal or efficient behavior is not deemed to be important, although it must be from a normative and public policy perspective since it is assumed that economic agents behave in accordance with the optimal norms specified by the theory. This approach also raises questions as to what efficient and optimal economic behavior means, and whether there are alternative behaviors consistent with economic efficiency and optimality.

Herbert Simon (1955, 1956, 1959, 1978, 1987) questioned this methodological perspective, arguing that it is important to understand how economic agents behave in order to understand better the workings of the economy and to improve the accuracy of predictions generated by economic theory. Thus, contrary to Friedman, assumptions matter to economic theory from causal, normative, and public policy perspectives; one cannot simply assume that assumptions do not matter. For Simon, behavioral economics is concerned with determining the empirical validity of neoclassical assumptions and documenting as accurately as possible the behavior of individual economic agents. Wildly inaccurate behavioral assumptions that yield strong predictions are not good enough for scientific purposes. Moreover, Simon argues that economic agents typically deviate from neoclassical assumptions. This raises the question of what specifically constitutes efficient and optimal economic behavior. Moreover, behavioralists must address the Friedmanite challenge of how can economic agents who operate in a market environment survive if they perform suboptimally or inefficiently relative to the neoclassical, albeit poorly defined, norms. Or, are the neoclassical definitions and norms with respect to efficiency and optimality misspecified?

Simon (1955) coined the term 'bounded rationality' to refer to rational choices given the physiological cognitive limitations on the individual decision maker in terms of acquiring and processing of information. These limitations translate into costly decision-making processes, and Simon argues that decision makers take into consideration decision-making costs and the limited capacity of the human mind. Thus, the bounds or constraints on rational decision-making are set by the natural limitations of the human mind. Individuals do not behave in the manner assumed by neoclassical theory; rather they adopt heuristic shortcuts in making decisions. This is particularly important when decision-making processes become increasing complex. A boundedly rational decision is not irrational or even sub-optimal. Rather, it is rational and optimal *given* the constraints faced by the decision maker. To do otherwise—to follow the neoclassical norms for best practice behavior—would be too costly given the cognitive limitations of the human mind. Individuals do not engage in neoclassical optimizing because of their mental setup; but they do the best they can, engaging in what Simon (1956) refers to as 'satisficing'. There may be various best practice satisficing decisions depending on the context, as opposed to one unique optimal decision as per neoclassical theory—a multi as opposed to a unique equilibrium solution to a decision making problem.

Kahneman and Tversky have sought to demonstrate numerous deviations of individual behavior (as expressed in survey and human laboratory experiments) from neoclassical norms, including subjective expected utility theory, Baysian updating, and knowledge of future consequences of current choice behavior. At times, individuals make choices that are inconsistent or lack coherence, and that contradict the neoclassical descriptive and normative theory of rationality. Moreover, Kahneman and Tversky developed an alternative substantive theory (prospect theory) to better describe and predict human choice behavior. But they present no alternative normative theory. Rather, their normative point of reference for rational or optimal behavior remains neoclassical norms. Deviations from these norms are considered to be errors and biases and indicative of irrationality (Tversky & Kahneman 1992, p. 323; Kahneman, 1994).

These errors and biases are a product of the heuristics that individuals use given the cognitive limitations of the human mind. Tversky & Kahneman (1974, p. 1124, 1131) argue that 'people rely on a limited number of heuristic principles which reduce the complex tasks of assessing probabilities and predicting values to simpler judgemental operations. In general, these heuristics are quite useful, but sometimes they lead to severe and systematic errors....A better understanding of these heuristics and of the biases to which they lead could improve judgments and decisions in situations of uncertainty.' Moreover, public policy should be oriented towards correcting human choice behavior where possible or, where this is not possible, towards employing the state or related decision making bodies to make the 'correct' choices on behalf of individuals whose cognitive limitations preclude them from getting it right by themselves.

The notion that deviations from neoclassical norms imply errors or biases or irrationality has been subject to considerable debate. There is another school in behavioral economics that views human choice as highly rational or intelligent and argues that the neoclassical norms are not appropriate to evaluate choice behavior (Gigerenzer, 2000; Gigerenzer & Selten, 2001; Todd & Gigerenzer, 2003). What appears to be an error may thus not be so when decision-making is structured in a manner more consistent with how individuals typically face real-world decisions. From this perspective, bounded rationality is

> not simply a discrepancy between human reasoning and the laws of probability or some form of optimization. Bounded rationality dispenses with the notion of optimization and, usually, with probabilities and utilities as well. It provides an alternative to current norms, not an account that accepts current norms and studies when humans deviate from these norms. Bounding rationality means rethinking the norms as well as studying the actual behavior of minds and institutions...bounded rationality is not an inferior form of rationality; it is not a deviation from norms that do not reflect the structure and representation of information and environments. Theories of bounded rationality should not be confused with theories of irrational decision making.
>
> (Gigerenzer & Selten, 2001, p. 6)

Smith is not concerned with identifying errors and biases relative to neoclassical norms, and he also questions whether some of Kahneman's and Tversky's findings are evidence of errors and biases. In addition, Smith is critical of traditional approaches to economics where theory reigns supreme and evidence, especially evidence garnered from laboratory experiments, does not seem to be important. He (Smith, 1991a, p. 4) maintains: 'Experimentation in economics owes much of its development to the challenge to reexamine continually everything we do—our procedures, our empirical interpretation of theories, the replicability and robustness of results, and the implications of experiment for new and better theory.' Theory should be modified to account for new or contrary stylized facts; so should assumptions. As with the behavioralists, the empirical side of economics is important for Smith.

Smith argues (1991b, p. 878; 2000, p. 3) that both economic theorists and cognitive psychologists, such as Kahneman, have a flawed understanding of the underlying assumptions of their analytical approaches. Both groups agree, argues Smith, that rationality in the economic and social context is derived from the rationality of individuals. Thus, irrational behavior by isolated individuals translates into irrationality in group behavior and in the marketplace. Neoclassical theorists tend to deny individual irrationality. Both groups also agree that individual rationality is a cognitive process, and that if people get things right (as predicted by the neoclassical theory) it is because they thought through and understood the cognitive process. It follows that both groups agree that one can test for the economic rationality of individuals, and thereby the market, by assessing the behavior of individuals isolated from one another and extracted from social economic institutions or contexts that they would actually face in the real world of choice behavior. Smith argues that it is most appropriate to examine individual behavior, either in a survey or laboratory setting, where the institutional environment or context wherein real world decision-making is replicated.

Smith accepts the findings of cognitive psychology suggesting that choice is often not a self-aware cognitive process. He also notes that the findings of cognitive psychologists do well in describing and explaining individuals' initial thinking and that this thinking is often at odds with what economic theory predicts rational individuals should think. Thus, a standard assumption of neoclassical theory does not hold. But, contrary to Kahneman and other cognitive psychologists, as well as some behavioral economists, Smith (2000, p. 4) argues that experimental research strongly suggests that: 'efficiency and convergence to competitive equilibria occur ubiquitously in experimental markets without subjects having the remotest awareness and understanding of the unconscious ends they have achieved'. More often than not, neoclassical predictions hold in the long run. Therefore, traditional models of the economic agent need to be modified to reconcile the discrepancy between individual views about their decision-making and how they actually behave. In particular, these models must incorporate the cognitive limitation of the human mind in their modeling of the economic agent. We must garner a better understanding of the process by which neoclassical predictions are often realized. Cognitive psychologists need to place their experiments and surveys in the context of the incentive environment in which real decisions takes place. For Smith, human decision-making is not error prone relative to the predictions of neoclassical theory, especially relative to long run results, nor is the traditional neoclassical standard the ideal measure of appropriate expressed decision making behavior.

Assumptions thus matter for both Kahneman and Smith. But this concern for assumptions and empirics carries with it different implications for understanding individual decision-making, and different implications of decision making for market efficiency and rationality. Kahneman regards his evidence as demonstrating that the heuristics adopted by economic agents often yield systematic errors and biases in decision-making, contrary to the presumptions and predictions of neoclassical theory. Although Kahneman argues that this does not necessarily imply that individuals are irrational, he thinks that human decision makers are cognitively unable to avoid significant and systematic errors, which many scholars and public policy experts take to imply irrationality or systematic deviations from intelligence in the decision-making process. Moreover, Kahneman is clear that individuals are irrational from a neoclassical normative perspective, which he accepts as a benchmark for determining whether there exist systematic errors and biases in decision-making.

Smith, on the other hand, finds human decision-making to be consistent with rational behavior, where rationality is related to the end results of the decision-making process with regards to market efficiency, most often referring to market clearing at competitive equilibria. When individuals mess up in their decisions, such errors are wont to be corrected over time through learning.

These distinct views of human agency have important implications for public policy. Kahneman advocates government or other forms of exogenous intervention to correct for persistent decision-making errors. Such intervention is not a product of market failure or institutional failures wherein individual decision makers can be quite rational individually, but where the global, group or multi-individual outcome is inefficient or sub-optimal. Smith, on the other hand, is a libertarian who views the individual in the context of the 'free' market and continuous social interaction of decision makers as the best determinant of global decision making. Government intervention would be rarely recommended to correct the persistent errors and biases of individual decision makers, which Smith, unlike Kahneman, does not believe to be a significant problem. When errors in decision-making do occur, they are largely a product of lack of knowledge or experience. This is rectified through learning and experience.

Hammond (2000) distinguishes two fundamental types of metatheories of decision-making—coherence theories and correspondence theories. This distinction can help us understand the different approaches of Kahneman and Smith.

Coherence is often identified with rationality. Coherence theorists are concerned with determining whether individuals meet the test of consistency relative to some model. Lack of consistency is thought be a product of irrational or error-prone heuristics. Correspondence theorists view decision making as an adaptive or functional mechanism. It is concerned with how well a decision maker's choices function to realize a particular objective irrespective of the coherence of the choices made. Correspondence theory does not prescribe a particular choice set which must be adopted for correspondence to occur. Competence is largely a function of the task conditions faced by the decision makers. Thus, the correspondence need not take place instantaneously, especially in highly complex and uncertain environments; but correspondence is expected to occur with time.

Mainstream economic theory is concerned primarily with coherence; it focuses upon logical, mathematical, and statistical consistency. Mainstream theory also assumes that human decision-making corresponds to particular and unique norms of coherence, a view of how the mind ought to work that is rejected by Simon and Smith.

Hammond (2000, pp. 59–60) takes Kahneman's and Tversky's research as part of the contemporary coherence approach, whose negative conclusions about decision makers' lack of coherence have resulted in a now widely held belief in the incompetence of human decision making. Smith, however, does not take the findings of the coherence theorists as evidence of irrationality, but rather as evidence of flaws in the neoclassical approach to decision-making, as evidence of flaws in the methodology used by coherence theorists in deriving their results, or as evidence of the momentary short-term perspective of the decision maker not yet mediated by learning or market processes.

This view of adaptive decision-making encapsulates quite nicely the methodological perspective of Smith who is concerned much less with coherence than with the end results of the decision making process. And like correspondence theorists, Smith not only expects, he also finds that correspondence more often than not takes place, at least in terms of the realization competitive market equilibria.

Smith's worldview fits much better than Kahneman's with the behavioral economics enterprise, and the understanding of rationality, as articulated by Simon and James Marsh. Simon and March do not use neoclassical norms as benchmarks for rational or intelligent behavior, and they are interested in the actual process by which objectives are achieved. Simon rejects neoclassical theory as a normative theory to use as a benchmark from which to determine the rationality of decision-making. He focuses instead on the process by which correspondence occurs, or on process rationality. Decision-making that deviates from neoclassical rationality does not imply irrationality or even errors or biases. Indeed, given the complexity of the decision-making process and the limited computational capacity of the human mind, it would be irrational for decision makers to adopt neoclassical norms, where the latter assumes a simple world with no substantive limitations upon the computational capacity of the economic agent.

Simon argues that social scientists tend to use broader definitions of rationality than is traditionally found in economics, which focus upon coherence and optimization. The broader definition of human decision-making is built upon intelligent and sensible behavior that is 'agreeable to reason, not absurd, preposterous, extravagant, foolish, fanciful' (Simon, 1978, p.2). Marsh (1978, p. 589) speaks to this same point:

> Modern students of human choice behavior frequently assume, at least implicitly, that actual human choice behavior in some way or other is likely to make sense. It can be understood as being the behavior of an intelligent being or group of intelligent beings. Much theoretical work searches for intelligence in apparently anomalous human behavior. This process of discovering sense in human behavior is conservative with respect to the concept of rational man and to behavioral change. It preserves the idea of rationality; and it preserves the idea that human behavior is intelligent, even when it is not obviously so. But it is not conservative with respect to prescriptive models of choice. For if there is sense in the choice behavior of individuals acting contrary to standard engineering procedures of rationality, then it seems reasonable to suspect that there may be something inadequate about our normative theory of choice or the procedures by which it is implemented.

Economic theory, therefore, must be modified to incorporate behavior that deviates from mainstream norms where that behavior is found to be intelligent and reasoned.

A critical point of departure for Simon and March is how individuals actually behave to achieve particular ends. From such behaviors one builds theories of rational decision-making with both analytical-substantive and normative dimensions. Their analytical starting point is quite different from that of Kahneman. Kahneman (Kahneman & Tversky, 2000; Kahneman *et al.*, 1982) presents evidence suggesting that decision makers consistently deviate from mainstream 'rational' norms. This supports the Simon hypothesis that neoclassical norms tend to be incorrect. Smith, on the other hand, is concerned with the process by which, and the institutional setting (laboratory context) within which, decision-making takes place. Neoclassical behavioral norms are not, for Smith, of analytical significance. And, as discussed above, for Smith rationality relates to the outcome of the decision-making process, where neoclassical results such as rapid market clearing, is a measure of rationality. Irrational markets can be a product of incorrect decision-making procedures or the context in which decisions take place, but these problems can be corrected. Although this perspective is consistent with that of Simon, Simon and the early behavioralists do not define rationality in terms of rational expectations and market clearing. Irrationality here does not refer to the absence of intelligence. Errors and mistakes in decision-making do not translate into lack of intelligence, as it does for Kahneman.

Von Mises (1949, pp. 16–17) clearly articulates the view that errors and biases in decision making are not irrational. He argues that all purposeful acts are rational. He further stipulates (Von Mises, 1949, p. 20): 'It is a fact that human reason is not infallible and that man very often errs in selecting and applying means. An action unsuited to the end sought falls short of expectation. It is contrary to purpose, but it is rational, i.e. the outcome of a reasonable—although faulty—deliberation and attempt—although an ineffectual attempt—to attain a definite goal.' Moreover, one cannot deem a particular decision as irrational simply because some external set of desires (goals or objectives) differs from those adhered to by the individual (Von Mises, 1949, pp. 21–22). Von Mises, by defining sub-optimal behaviors or outcomes as a mistake as opposed to irrational, is able to present a clear distinction between intelligent purposeful behavior that is effective from that which is ineffective. In this framework, neither Kahneman's error-prone behavior nor Smith's inefficient macroeconomic results need be irrational, which is suggestive of a lack intelligence in decision making, although they might be indicative of procedural problems with the intelligent behavior of decision makers.

4 Kahneman's economic contributions

The Nobel Prize committee noted the following core contributions of Kahneman (and Tversky)—rules of thumb which yield errors and biases in decision making (Gilovich et al., 2002; Kahneman & Tversky, 2000; Kahneman et al., 1982; Tversky & Kahneman, 1974), an analysis of decision making under uncertainty, and the concept of framing.

A critical contribution of Kahneman's research is that human decision-making is far removed from economic rationality. Kahneman and Tversky demonstrate that there are many instances where human decision-making deviates from standard neoclassical norms. 'Real-world decision-makers frequently appear not to evaluate uncertain events according to the laws of probability; nor do they seem to make decisions according to the theory of expected-utility maximization' (Nobel E-Museum, 2003). Instead, individuals use heuristics shortcuts to arrive at decisions, especially when circumstances are complex and outcomes are uncertain. Kahneman and Tversky refer to these deviations from neoclassical economic rationality as 'errors and biases'. There are several such errors and biases.

First, Kahneman and Tversky (1982c, 1984) found that most people display insensitivity to sample size. Experimental subjects typically pay undue attention to the law of large numbers in probability theory, assigning similar probabilities to large and small samples. Yet a higher probability should be assigned to the larger sample since the variance about the mean declines significantly with increasing sample size. This can result in serious decision errors as expressed in an example provided by the Nobel Prize committee statement: 'an investor who recognizes that a fund manager beats the index two years in a row may conclude that the manager is systematically more competent than the average investor, whereas the true statistical implication is much weaker' (Nobel E-Museum, 2003). One requires a larger run (sample size) to get a better idea of whether the fund manager is really good.

Second, Kahneman and Tversky (Tversky and Kahneman 1981) found that individuals are insensitive to the probability of outcomes, or they suffer from 'base rate neglect'. This occurs when we evaluate probabilities by representativeness rather than considering the base rate frequency or prior probabilities of outcomes. People tend to make decisions based on the extent to which they believe someone has characteristics of a certain individual (e.g. lawyer, engineer, politician), ignoring their true distribution in the population. For example, if an individual fits the description of a lawyer, people tend to identify the individual as a lawyer even if the probability of being a lawyer is quite low in the population as a whole.

Other types of cognitive errors concern 'misconceptions of chance' (Tversky & Kahneman 1974, 1982). Thus, people tend to think that three runs of heads with a fair coin should be followed by three tails. People also tend to base their predictions on the subjective representativeness of information, such as predicting above average profitability for a firm based on partial information on firm performance. Related to this is the so-called 'illusion of validity', where individuals tend to have a high degree of confidence in predictions based upon imperfect inputs. Individuals also tend to gain confidence in their prediction when new but redundant information is added. We also have the 'misconception of regression', where individuals tend not to expect regression towards the mean where it should occur or ascribe causation to spurious correlation. For example, individuals tend *not* to expect IQ scores or other test performances (either above or below average) to regress towards some mean and therefore expect a particular score to be the representative one. Thus, it is argued that if an individual scores high on one exam of a particular type one should expect this individual to score low on the next exam. On average there should be a regression towards a mean performance. However, there is no discussion of the context in which one might expect mean performances to change over real time or the conditions under which this happens, or the timing of an expected regression to some fixed mean.

Another important set of 'cognitive illusions' is called 'adjustment and anchoring'. This occurs when decisions are based upon initial values or marginal adjustments in initial values where the latter are not sufficient to reflect 'true' values. Thus one would arrive at different decisions depending upon initial values; ones' decisions are anchored upon initial values. If individuals are given particular values, which are way off the mark (true values), decisions will be highly inaccurate (Kahneman 1992, Tversky & Kahneman 1974, 1992). If a non-American is asked to estimate the population of the United States and is exposed to a random set of relatively high numbers, that individual will tend to low-ball the population of the United States. If the same individual is exposed to a random set of relatively high numbers, that individual will tend to high-ball the population of the United States. The individual is anchoring her or his decision upon recent or convenient information which, in turn, produces errors in decision making. However, is this heuristic a poor one (error-prone or biased) if the individual knows very little about the United States? Or, is such a heuristic an intelligent one for such an individual in a world of incomplete and costly information?

It should be noted that these examples are not universally accepted as errors and biases (see Gigerenzer, 1996, 2000; Gigerenzer & Selten, 2001; Smith, 1990a). One frequent criticism is that the error-prone behavior in Kahneman and Tversky's experiments is a product of one-shot games or experiments, and that these errors are often corrected through learning (or repeat experiments). It is also argued that behavior described as error-prone is actually optimal behavior given the complexity of the problem presented, the limited information given to subjects, and the imperfect computational capacities of people. If so, improvements in information, knowledge, and computational capacity would improve decisions much like technical change would improve output from what it was under the old technology. Kahneman and Tversky, however, do demonstrate how decision-making deviates from narrow neoclassical norms.

Prior to discussing decision-making under uncertainty and framing it, we should mention two additional ideas that Kahneman and Tversky developed, but which were given little note in the Nobel Prize announcement—fairness and the endowment effect. Neoclassical theory assumes that fairness has no effect in the market economy, especially where competitive markets hold sway. However, Kahneman *et al.* (1986a, 1986b) suggest that fairness can affect pricing policy (at least in the short run), and provide as evidence surveys of potential consumers. If consumers behaved as their survey responses indicate, markets would fail to clear in the short run because suppliers would be reluctant to charge market-clearing prices that consumers might judge to be unfair. This violates neoclassical norms of rational behavior and what many economists deem to be intelligent behavior. (However, some economists, such as Gary Becker (1996, p. 197) would not view fairness considerations to be inconsistent with (utility) maximizing behavior (Altman, 2004)).

Thaler (1980) coined the term 'endowment effect,' building upon the work of Kahneman & Tversky (1984; also see Knetch, 1989). Simply put, the endowment effect stipulates that an item is worth more to you once you gain possession over it than when you initially purchase it. For example, if you pay $5.00 for an item, once you gain possession over it, you would be willing to sell the same item only for a greater (usually much greater) price, resulting in the buying price ($5.00) exceeding the selling price. This asymmetry, or preference for what one currently possesses, is referred to as 'status quo bias', 'loss aversion' and 'the endowment effect'. Once one possesses an item, the loss associated with giving up a good exceeds the gains from receiving the item. The endowment effect suggests that the revealed preference for a product in terms of the market price underestimates the utility of the product to the buyer. The endowment effect also suggests the indifference between two products changes into a preference for one once one purchases it. Initially A = B, but after one acquires A, A > B, and so the indifference curves effectively cross.

The endowment effect is said to challenge the neoclassical assumption that buying and selling prices should coincide net of transaction costs and the assumption of reversible indifference curves, although Kahneman & Tversky (1984) admit that the endowment effect is probably of little consequence to actual market exchanges. Also, Smith (2000, p. 4) argues that the evidence suggests that endowment effects exist in the short run, but that differences between buying and selling prices dissipate over time in experimental market.

Becker (1996, p. 128) argues it is wrong to hold that individuals are irrational if their economic behavior is influenced by non-economic variables such as the possession of a good (the endowment effect). Utility maximization should incorporate such a non-economic variable where relevant to economic discourse. Thus, once a good is possessed it is no longer the same thing as a good never possessed or experienced by the individual. In this scenario, indifference curve irreversibility does not take place as a consequence of the endowment effect. Endowment effect research suggests revisions may be needed to economic theory, but these might be of little consequence for understanding the market process of commodities actually traded on the market.

Providing an alternative to subjective expected utility theory (SEU) may be Kahneman's (and Tversky's) most important contribution, for it challenges a long-standing literature that holds SEU theory is the best descriptor of human decision-making under uncertainty (see Kahneman & Tversky, 1979b, 1982c, 1984; Tversky & Kahneman, 1981). SEU theory stipulates that rational agents should choose the alternative prospect that maximizes expected utility as opposed to expected value. Rational agents are expected to accept a gamble with an expected utility greater than the utility generated by the agent's initial state of wealth. Utility is a function of the state of wealth where there is assumed to be diminishing returns to wealth. Thus, for example, the utility assigned to $20 in addition to $100 would be greater than the utility accorded to $20 in addition to $200. This yields a concave utility function across states of wealth and characterizes behavior as risk adverse (Fig. 1). Risk adverse behavior refers to a situation where a certain outcome (particular state of wealth) is preferred over a gamble (uncertain outcome) with an equal or greater monetary expected value. For example, if the sure thing is $700 and the expected value of the gamble is $0.90 \times \$1000 + 0.10 \times \$0$ or $900, the risk adverse individual chooses the sure thing even though it yields a lower monetary value. The utility of the sure thing (no gamble) exceeds the utility of the uncertain but higher monetary value. To accept a gamble requires an even higher return to offset the disutility of engaging in the risky prospect. In contrast, risk-seeking behavior refers to a situation where a certain outcome is rejected in favor of a gamble yielding an equal or lower monetary expected value.

Rational individuals are expected to be risk adverse and to be characterized by diminished utility returns to wealth, always choosing prospects that maximize expected utility. One should also note that the utility and disutility associated with an equal gain or loss are equal and offsetting. Expected utility is given by:

$$EU = P_0 U(W_0 + G_0 + P_1 U(W_0 + G_1),$$ \hfill (1)

where *EU* is the expected utility of the prospect, P_0 and P_1 are the probabilities of the gamble which sum to 100, W_0 is the state of wealth, G_0 and G_1 are values of the pre-probabilistic values of the gamble (in the above $1000 and $0 respectively, and *U* is the utility weight.

Kahneman and Tversky argue that individuals tend to behave contrary to expected utility theory, making decisions independent of ones' state of wealth and treating gains and losses asymmetrically in terms of their effect upon utility and disutility respectively. They argue that these assumptions reflect typical decision-making behavior although they do not do not speak about optimal behavior. They simply represent a simplified description of common behavior under uncertainty. These assumptions do not yield a normative theory of behavior under uncertainty as do the assumptions underlying SEU theory. These basic assumptions yield a value function such as presented in Fig. 2. As compared to SEU theory, the value function has both positive and negative domains and is drawn to reflect changes in states of wealth from some neutral starting point— decision makers do not factor into their decision-making process their original state of wealth as in SEU theory. The value function is concave in the positive domain (as it is in SEU theory) and convex in the negative domain, yielding an S-shaped value function. Thus, the value retains the SEU theory assumption of diminishing returns to wealth. Moreover, the slopes of the two components of the value function are drawn such that the disutility from losing some value is always greater than the utility from gaining an identical value. Finally, the

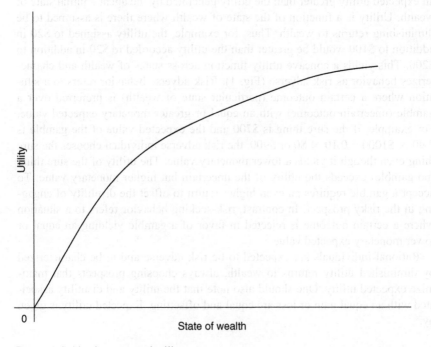

Figure 1 Subjective expected utility

S-shaped function assumes that the utility of the uncertain outcome is weighted by a decision weight as opposed to a probability weight as in SEU theory, where the decision weight is a monotonic function of the probability. Impossible events are given a zero weight, low probabilities are over-weighted and moderate and high probabilities are underweighted.

One distinctive characteristic of the value function is that individuals are risk adverse in gains and risk seeking in losses. Another is that because of the two domains for the value function and the greater slope in the negative domain, a monetary gain exceeding a monetary loss might still yield a net loss in utility leading an individual to reject such a prospect where it would not be rejected in SEU theory.

Although Kahneman and Tversky view their model as contravening the norms of rational choice, Smith (1989) maintains that economists have assumed that utility theory applies to different amounts of wealth, that this is an appropriate modification of SEU theory, and that it is consistent with rational choice. Smith also argues that modifying SEU theory by introducing riskadverse behavior in the positive domain of the S-shaped value function and risk-seeking behavior in the negative domain is consistent with expected utility theory. As long as prospects are preference ordered, decision-making in terms of state of wealth or changes in states of wealth are consistent with expected utility theory and rational choice. Thus, Smith argues that Kahneman's and Tversky's value function represents a necessary modification to SEU theory, but one that does not challenge the fundamental assumptions of rational choice and utility maximization.

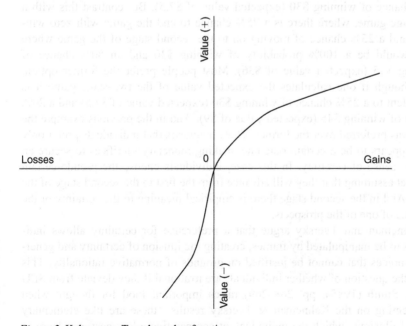

Figure 2 Kahneman–Tversky value function

Kahneman and Tversky argue that certain results contravene SEU theory relating to how choices get framed. In one instance, Tversky & Kahneman (1981, p. 457) asked individuals what would they do if they lost a $10 bill prior to going to the theater to purchase a $10 ticket. Would they buy another? Most respondents (88%) replied in the affirmative. But when asked if they would purchase a $10 replacement ticket if they lost a $10 ticket on the way to the theater, only 54% of the respondents replied affirmatively. Kahneman and Tversky argue that ticket purchases are set up in a separate mental account and are categorized as losses, thus the reluctance of many to purchase a replacement ticket. Of course, this reluctance can also be related to the costs incurred in purchasing the ticket (or the imagined costs on the part of the respondents) and this reluctance might dissipate in a real world situation depending upon the actual situation faced by the theatre fan. In another example, most survey respondents express their willingness to make an extra trip to save $5 on a $15 calculator, but only a minority is willing to do the same to save $5 on a $115 calculator. Thus, it appears that many individuals evaluate gains and losses from a relative perspective. The same amount of money takes on a different utility depending on its context or frame.

Another result, referred to as 'the certainty effect' and 'the pseudocertainty effect', concerns individual preferences for certain outcomes or the appearance of certainty in outcomes. Tversky & Kahneman (1981, p. 455) found that a sure win (100% probability) of $30 is preferred over an 80% chance of winning $45 (expected value of $36); but if one reduces the above probabilities, preferences reverse and a 20% chance to win $45 (expected value of $9) is preferred to a 25% chance of winning $30 (expected value of $7.5). But contrast this with a two-stage game, where there is a 75% chance to end the game with zero winnings and a 25% chance of moving on to the second stage of the game where there would be a 100% probability of winning $30 and an 80% chance of winning $45 (expected value of $36). Most people prefer the former option, even though if one calculates the expected value of the two-stage game it is equivalent to a 25% chance of winning $30 (expected value of $7.5) and a 20% chance of winning $45 (expected value of $9). And in the previous example the latter was preferred over the former. Thus, it appears that individuals prefer only what appears to be a certain outcome, making monetary sacrifices to secure an illusory sense of certainty. In this case, individuals choose the pseudo-certain prospect assuming that they will advance from the first to the second stage of the game. And in the second stage there is empirical meaning to the certainty of the outcome of one of the prospects.

Kahneman and Tversky argue that a preference for certainty allows individuals to be manipulated by frames, creating the illusion of certainty and generating choices that cannot be justified on grounds of normative rationality. This raises the question of whether individuals are irrational if they deviate from SEU norms. Smith (1985a, pp. 268–269) raises important food for thought when commenting on the Kahneman & Tversky results: 'these are like elementary optimal illusions, which the individual, at comparatively low cost, can learn to recognize as such.... We all learn that when the sun is low, the pond in the highway ahead is just a reflection, and we do not risk a near-end collision by jamming on the breaks. In saying this, I do not mean to suggest that the study of framing effects is of no interest. On the contrary, these examples show how bad we can be at intuitive problem solving, and why it is important to examine a decision from alternative perspectives.' Smith argues that these illusions will be resolved when it is worth it to the decision maker in terms of transaction costs (the cost of thinking, calculating, deciding and acting). Thus, illusions might only be transitory short-term phenomena.

5 Smith's economic contributions

The Nobel Prize award statement (Nobel E-Museum, 2003) identified three core contributions of Smith (1991a, 2000). First, he developed experiments to test the hypothesis that competitive markets generate equilibrium (market-clearing) prices that approximate their theoretical values. Second, he was able to test the price and revenue outcomes of different types of auctions. In an English auction, buyers announce their bids in increasing order until no higher bid is submitted; in a Dutch auction, a high initial bid is gradually lowered until a buyer is found; in a sealed-price first-price auction, the highest bidder pays his own bid to the seller; and in a sealed-bid second-price auction, the highest bidder pays the second highest bid. The third key contribution of Smith identified by the Nobel Prize statement is his effort to design laboratory experiments that reflect real-world incentive structures. He developed the induced-value method as one device to help close the gap between real world and laboratory incentive structures and to construct more controlled laboratory experiments.

Smith first designed and executed experiments in the late 1950s at Purdue University, from a perspective that was skeptical of the efficacy of the market process. His goal was to confirm the results of Edward Chamberlin's informal classroom experiments at Harvard University, where neither prices nor quantities approached their expected equilibrium values. From these experiments, Chamberlin argued that supply and demand analysis could not explain the most basic of all market processes—price formation and resource allocation. Using the double oral market (where there are bids by buyers, offers by sellers, and acceptances by both) employed by stock and commodity exchanges, Smith tested the proposition that competitive markets move towards market-clearing prices. He ran a number of experiments (not trusting his initial results which contravened Chamberlin's informal findings) employing both symmetrical and asymmetrical demand and supply curves. His findings (Smith, 1962b) were robust to different experimental designs. They were published in the *Journal of Political Economy* when the editor, Harry Johnson, overruled the recommendations of his referees. (Apparently, evidence supporting Chicago School type propositions were not necessary if deductive proofs of markets efficiency existed.)

Over the past four decades Smith and his colleagues have refined and repeated these types of experiments, adding further substance and reconfirming the basic findings on the efficiency of the private market economy and the rationality of markets. Smith (1991a, p. 1957) comments on the significance of these results: 'I have shown that with remarkably little learning, strict privacy, and a modest number, inexperienced traders converge rapidly to a competitive equilibrium under the double oral auction mechanism. The market works under much weaker conditions than had traditionally been thought to be necessary. You didn't have large numbers. Economic agents do not have perfect knowledge of supply and demand. You do not need price-taking behavior—everyone in the double-oral auction is as much of a price maker as price taker.'

Smith (1991b, pp. 879–880) argues that Kahneman, Tversky and other researchers and economic theorists have assumed that individual rationality is a 'consciously cognitive phenomenon'. Moreover, economic theorists assume complete information on payoffs and that economic agents have knowledge of a general equilibrium model of the economy. Smith writes (1991b, p. 880): 'it has been hard for either the theorist or the psychologist to imagine optimal market outcomes being achieved by other than conscious cognition; it cannot occur by "magic" so to speak. The reason is that neither has traditionally modeled markets as a learning process, capable of converging to a rational equilibrium [market clearing] outcome.' But decades of experiments have shown that rational equilibrium outcomes are obtained when all information on the economic environment is private, agents only know their own circumstances, and experimental markets are decentralized. Under these circumstances: 'prices and allocations converge quickly to the neighborhood of the predicted rational expectations competitive equilibrium and...these results generalize to a wide variety of post-price, sealed-bid, and other institutions of exchange, although convergence rates tend to vary.' Smith (1991b, p. 881) concludes that bidding, auctioning, and price-posting experiments, 'show the predictive power of non-cooperative equilibrium concepts (competitive or Nash) without any requirement that knowledge is complete or common. In these cases, economic theory works under weaker conditions than expected, and no support is provided for the interpretation that the equilibrating process is consciously cognitive. The verbal behavior of subjects strongly contradicts what their actual behavior achieves.'

Even if surveys and experiments reveal behavior that seems irrational or appears unintelligent, what is more important is how people actually behave in real world environments containing real world incentives. Following from his finding of the oft-found discrepancy between expressed and actual behavior, Smith (1991b, p. 881) argues that the most important implication of experimental economics research is the need to understand better the process by which individual behavior is transformed into system-wide behavior. For Smith (1991b, p. 894) 'an important part of the answer resides in the properties of exchange institutions and in how privately informed, but globally poorly informed, decision making is mediated by institutions.' The research of Smith and others suggest that the rules (institutions) within which experiments take place affect outcomes. Smith (1991a, p. 802) argues: 'rules determine incentives, and incentives determine the performance of markets by encouraging desirable behavior and discouraging undesirable behavior in a way that is self-regulating.' Since experimental markets typically yield globally efficient (market clearing) results, and this is strongly suggestive of the efficiency of real world private markets, Smith (1991b, p. 894) concludes that 'the structure and rules we observe have survived because of their merit in coaxing Pareto-efficient behavior out of agents who do not know what that means.' This implies that institutions must always be efficient in the long run in a market economy since markets (at least product markets) appear to be efficient given the results from experimental markets.

An important footnote to this discussion is the finding of Smith and others that laboratory stock market experiments generate price bubbles relative to fundamental values that persist over many trading periods, although equilibrium is eventually restored when the bubble bursts. Bubbles arise from expectations of capital gains in environments with common knowledge of the probabilistic dividend value in each trading period. Bubbles are particularly common in markets with many first time or inexperienced traders. Smith argues that bubbles occur in asset markets as opposed to other experimental markets due to the complete common information characterizing asset markets, uncertain expectations about others, and the lack of common expectations. This results in myopic behavior. Only experience generates the common expectations required to return prices to their fundamental values (Smith, 1991a, p. 886; Porter & Smith, 1995; Smith, 2000, pp. 409–413). Markets are rational, but it can take some time for them to become rational.

Smith's research on experimental markets, and his interpretation of his findings, challenge both the assumptions of standard economic theory and the substantive importance of errors and biases found in the research of Kahneman and Tversky. For Smith, the standard assumption that rationality is necessarily a cognitive process does not hold; nor is it required for markets to be rational. Moreover, markets work better with imperfect information than with perfect information. To the extent that markets are efficient and that the actual behavior of economic agents yield rational (efficient, market-clearing) results, discoveries of non-neoclassical behavior as expressed by individuals through surveys and other instruments are not proof of economic inefficiency or even of irrational economic behavior. Of course, this challenge requires accepting Smith's experimental markets as representative of real-world markets, and taking as reasonable his adjustment procedure yielding equilibria in experimental markets through learning over time. One must also accept Smith's definition of 'rational' or 'efficient markets', which focuses upon market clearing and price formation. The former two assumptions of representativeness and reasonableness have been challenged (see Lowenstein, 1999), but this challenge also applies to the work of Kahneman and Tversky.

Smith's appreciation of the importance of the environment where experiments takes place has been critical to the development of experimental economics as well as to critiques of laboratory experiments critical of the rationality of markets and of the rational behavior of individual decision makers.

Important aspects of this incentive-based experimental design research was inspired by the work of Sid Siegel (1961). Siegel challenged a long-standing view in the psychology literature that decision makers are irrational if they fail to maximize. He pointed out that maximization takes place in particular incentive environments with specific incentives, and that individuals will fail to maximize when there is nothing of value worth maximizing. Therefore, monetary values need to be incorporated into an experimental design to understand the extent to which maximization takes place; in short, incentives matter for maximization. Moreover, maximization takes place in terms of utility when one recognizes that utility is a function of both monetary and non-monetary variables. This view, consistent with that of Simon, recognizes that decision-making is a costly process and that a rational decision maker cannot be expected to devote cognitive resources to a decision problem when the consequences are expected to be of little value. This perspective was developed in greater detail by Smith at a later date (Walker & Smith, 1993b, 1993c).

Smith (1991a, p. 5) writes that induced value theory was developed to: 'provide some structured guidelines for designing and interpreting the results of experiments.' It assumes that given a costless choice between identical alternatives, that prospect will be chosen which yields the greatest monetary reward. Induced value theory facilitates designed controlled experiments (Smith, 1976c, p. 275): 'Control is the essence of experimental methodology, and in experimental exchange studies it is important that one be able to state that, as between two experiments, individual values (e.g., demand or supply) either do or do not differ in a specified way.' Experiments must be designed to take into account the types of incentives that characterize the real world if one wishes to test the validity of either the assumptions or predictions of theory. Proper experimental design also controls for institutional factors such as the language and rules under which trades can take place. In addition, there must be controls for the cultural and social setting in which an experiment takes place. Smith is critical of much of the Kahneman and Tversky type research for not properly controlling for incentive and institutional effects on the decision-making process. If experimental results cannot be shown to have parallels in the real word in terms of the overall environmental context within which the experiment takes place, such results cannot be substantively significant.

This fundamental caution with regards to the construction of experiments and the interpretations of their results is highlighted in Smith's work and analyses of ultimatum and dictator games (Smith *et al.*, 1994b; Hoffman *et al.*, 1995, 1996a, 1996b, 1997, 1998, 1999, 2000; Smith *et al.*, 1996; Smith, 2000, pp. 79–89). The results of the conventional ultimatum and dictator games are believed to challenge core behavioral assumptions of narrow neoclassical theory, especially the notion that individuals tend to be selfish materially-oriented maximizers. In the ultimatum game, the proposer offers a split of a prize and the responder decides whether or not to accept the offer. Only if the offer is accepted do the two players receive a share of the prize; if rejected, both players receive nothing. Materially selfish maximizing behavior predicts that the respondent should accept minimal offers above zero. However, the results of ultimatum games demonstrate that modal offers and acceptances tend towards a fifty-fifty split (Güth *et al.,* 1982; Güth, 1995). In a dictator game, the respondent cannot punish the proposer for making what are deemed to be unfair offers. Although modal offers are now much below the fifty-fifty split of so many ultimatum games, they are greater than one would expect from a materially-oriented maximizer proposer. Smith does not deny the results of these games. Rather, he argues that these contrary results are a product of the context out which the players come to the game and the specific rules and rewards specified for the game. History (context), rules and incentives matter substantively to the type of results generated. Neoclassical-like results are generated when players believe that unequal splits are fair or just or when there is complete anonymity between players and players and experimenter—when players are removed from social context. In terms of the relevance of such experiments for understanding actual human behavior, one must determine which experimental settings have real–world parallels and under what real-world circumstances will decision makers choose or be forced to accept more or less equitable splits of the pie.

6 Beyond Kahneman and Smith

Kahneman has tried to build a case that human decision makers do not behave in a manner consistent with neoclassical norms. He has (with Tversky) used survey techniques and experimental instruments to explain how individuals might behave under an array of choice environments, and he has developed prospect theory and the S-shaped value function to describe real-world decision-making behavior. Kahneman and Tversky argue that much behavior is error prone, biased and possibly irrational. Sometimes such behavior can be corrected through learning, but not always. The conclusion of this work—that individual choice is frequently laden with persistent errors and biases—has important policy implications. It opens the door to public policy, which substitutes more intelligent decision makers for the individual decision maker, imposing intelligent choice behavior upon those deemed incapable of making rational choices on their own volition—a controversial proposition with a long history which raises serious questions of governance and of the determinants of norms that define intelligent behavior (Berlin, 1969).

Smith has challenged traditional economic assumptions about the conditions necessary to achieve market equilibrium, has challenged the view that markets are inefficient in terms of market clearing and price formation, and has developed an analytical framework and experimental design to address these and other questions. He also has also challenged the conventional view that intelligent behavior must adhere to neoclassical norms and that 'anomalous' behavior should result in economic inefficiencies. For Smith, human decision-making is not error-prone or biased, but intelligent and subject to improvements through learning, analogous to the notion of adaptive expectations. Yet Smith defines economic efficiency narrowly and thus does not address issues of efficiency that stand outside of the price formation and market clearing framework. Nonetheless, his positive findings regarding efficiency and other critical questions related to socio-economic wellbeing force us to study the behavioral, social and institutional assumptions about human choices that all too often fail to achieve efficiencies in terms of productivity, in terms of Amartya Sen's capabilities such as low mortality rates and high life expectation levels (Altman & Lamontagne, 2004; Pressman & Summerfield, 2000), and in terms of environmental sustainability. Smith provides an analytical toolbox to tackle these and other important questions.

The research of both Kahneman and Smith faces the challenge of those who argue that their results are a product of artificial environments with limited applicability to real-world scenarios. However, as Smith readily admits, the applicability of survey or laboratory research critically depends on how these tools are designed and whether their incentive structure reflects what would be faced in particular real-world scenarios. Research instruments must be carefully designed so that they have parallels in the real world, and research results from such instruments must be carefully assessed for their external validity. When this is done, survey methods and laboratory instruments can enrich our understanding of human decision-making, and market forces and processes, and can help us determine which assumptions best serve our models in terms of causality and predictability.

The research programs and findings of Kahneman and Smith are central for understanding important market and decision-making processes that affect socio-economic wellbeing. Behavioral and experimental methodologies can help address other important issues, such as broader questions of efficiency that go beyond Smith's focus on prices and market equilibria, and the manner which intelligent decision-making can impact economic efficiency and socio-economic wellbeing.

One example should help to illustrate this point. Harvey Leibenstein (1966, 1979), a pioneer in behavioral economics, made the case that economic efficiency might not exist even when markets clear and price and output equilibria are realized. He recognized the reality of effort discretion as a behavioral assumption of decision makers within the firm and how effort discretion impacts upon the capacity of firms to maximize the quantity and quality of output—neoclassical theory assumes that effort is fixed at some maximum. It can be shown that effort levels are affected by variables such as industrial relations, bargaining power, and cultural and social context (Altman 1996, 1999, 2001, 2002, 2004). In a world where decision makers are characterized by different and often incompatible objective functions, rational decision makers maximize their utility by making choices that yield inefficient levels of effort. Even in a highly competitive market economy with limited government intervention (the ideal type of economy for Vernon Smith), product markets clear but at multiple potential levels of efficiency, only one of which would be consistent with maximizing society's material well being. Each level of efficiency would be consistent with the product market equilibrium in the sense that equilibrium prices are consistent with the long run survival of the firm in a competitive market place.

This scenario is illustrated by equation (2):

$$AC = \frac{w}{\dfrac{Q}{L}}, \tag{2}$$

where AC is average costs, w is rate of labor compensation, L is labor input, and Q is output. For simplicity we assume one factor input, and Q/L is a positive function of e/t (effort inputs per unit of time) which, in turn, is a positive function of w, which is a proxy for the overall work environment. *Ceteris paribus*, Q/L is maximized when e/t is maximized. In this case, average cost would be minimized. The conventional model, of course, assumes that e/t is always at a maximum. But in a world of x-inefficiency, where e/t is not maximized, average or unit costs are greater than they need be. X-inefficient firms remain cost competitive if low levels of x-efficiency are related to low rates of labor compensation, and high wage firms remain competitive by becoming relatively x-efficient. In other words, x-efficient and x-inefficient firms can both survive if they both produce at the same average cost and if they both function at offsetting differential levels of x-efficiency. It would be possible for there to exist in competitive equilibrium an array of firms characterized by different wage rates and levels of working conditions producing at an identical unit cost if these differentials are compensated for by differentials in the level of x-efficiency.

In this scenario, product markets are rational in the sense discussed by Vernon Smith, but they can also be inefficient from a productivity perspective. Moreover, there is no incentive for profit-maximizing managers or owners to make their firms more x-efficient if this has no impact on unit costs. They will be indifferent between x-efficient and x-inefficient forms of production since there is no material advantage to be gained from producing x-efficiently. Thus, free market rules of the game need not generate overall market efficiency and market forces need not generate efficient rules of the game since the cost of being inefficient does not force decision-makers to change from an inefficient to an efficient path of decision-making (Altman 2000). Efficiency thus becomes a function of political, social, and institutional variables (the rules of the game) as well of basic market forces. As elaborated upon by the noted free market oriented scholar F.A. Hayek (1944), it is the rules of game which set the context for how decision makers behave and thus for the economic outcomes affected by market forces in a competitive market economy. The research tools developed, and the decision-making issues addressed by Kahneman and Smith, can help tackle complex issues such as these.

Acknowledgements

The author acknowledges the helpful suggestions and comments of Louise Lamontagne, Steve Pressman, and the research assistance of Rokon Bhuiyan, Catherine Mudola Bulogosi and Jason Straus. The author also appreciates the assistance provided to him on the Smith bibliography by Geoffrey S. Underwood, Managing Director, Interdisciplinary Center for Economic Science, George Mason University.

References

Altman, M. (1996) *Human Agency and Material Welfare: Revisions in Microeconomics and their Implications for Public Policy* (Boston, Dordrecht & London: Kluwer).

Altman, M. (1998) High path to economic growth and development, *Challenge,* 41, pp. 91–104.

Altman, M. (1999) The methodology of economics and the survivor principle revisited and revised: some welfare and public policy implications of modeling the economic agent, *Review of Social Economy,* 57, pp. 427–429.

Altman, M. (2000) A behavioral model of path dependency: the economics of profitable inefficiency and market failure, *Journal of Socio-Economics,* 29, pp. 127–145.

Altman, M. (2001) *Worker Satisfaction and Economic Performance* (Armonk, NY: M.E. Sharpe).

Altman, M. (2002) Economic theory, public policy and the challenge of innovative work practices, *Economic and Industrial Democracy: An International Journal,* 23, pp. 271–290.

Altman, M. (2004) Reconciling altruistic, moralistic, and ethical behavior with the rational economic agent and competitive markets, *Journal of Economic Psychology,* forthcoming.

Altman, M. & Lamontagne, L. (2004) Gender, human capabilities and culture within the household economy: different path to socio-economic well-being?, *International Journal of Social Economics,* 31, pp. 325–364.

Becker, G. S. (1996) *Accounting for Tastes* (Cambridge, MA: Harvard University Press).

Berlin, I. (1969) *Four Essays on Liberty* (Oxford, New York & London: Oxford University Press).

Friedman, M. (1953) The methodology of positive economics, in: M. Friedman, *Essays in Positive Economics,* pp. 3–43 (Chicago, IL: University of Chicago Press).

Gigerenzer, G. (1996) On narrow norms and vague heuristics: a reply to Kahneman and Tversky, *Psychological Review,* 103, pp. 592–596.

Gigerenzer, G. (2000) *Adaptive Thinking: Rationality in the Real World* (Oxford: Oxford University Press).

Gigerenzer, G. & Selten, R. (2001) *Bounded Rationality: The Adaptive Toolbox* (Cambridge, MA: MIT Press).

Güth, W., Schmittberger, R. & Schwarze, B. (1982) An experimental analysis of ultimatum bargaining, *Journal of Economic Behavior and Organization,* 3, pp. 367–388

Güth, W. (1995) On ultimatum bargaining experiments—a personal review, *Journal of Economic Behavior and Organization,* 27, pp. 329–344.

Hammond, K. R. (2000) Coherence and correspondence theories in judgement and decision making, in: T. Connoly, H. R. Arkes & K. R. Hammond (Eds) *Judgement and*

Decision Making: An Interdispliplinary Reader, 2nd edn, pp. 53–65 (Cambridge: Cambridge University Press).

Hayek, F. A. (1944) *The Road to Serfdom* (Chicago, IL: University of Chicago Press).

Knetch, J. (1989) The endowment effect and evidence of nonreversible curves, *American Economic Review,* 79, pp. 1277–1284.

Leibenstein, H. (1966) Allocative efficiency vs. 'x-efficiency', *American Economic Review,* 56, pp. 392–415.

Leibenstein, H. (1979) A branch of economics is missing: micro-micro theory, *Journal of Economic Literature,* 17, pp. 477–502.

Lowenstein, G. (1999) Experimental economics from the vantage point of behavioural economics, *The Economic Journal,* 109, pp. 25–34.

Maital, S. & Maital, S. L. (Eds) (1993) *Economics and Psychology* (Aldershot: Edward Elgar).

Marsh, J. G. (1978) Bounded rationality, ambiguity, and the engineering of choice, *Bell Journal of Economics,* 9, pp. 587–608.

Nobel E-Museum (2003) The Bank of Sweden Prize in Economic Sciences in Memory of Alfred Nobel 2002 (http://www.nobel.se/economics/laureates/).

Nobel Prize 2002 Interviews (2003) The Kahneman–Smith Nobel Prize Interviews (http://www.nobel.se/economics/laureates/2002/kahneman-interview.html).

Pressman, S. & Sumerfield, G. (2000) The economic contributions of Amartya Sen, *Review of Political Economy,* 12, pp. 89–113.

Reder, M. W. (1982) Chicago economics: permanence and change, *Journal of Economic Literature,* 20, pp. 1–38.

Siegel, S. (1961) Decision making and learning under varying conditions of reinforcement, *Annals of the New York Academy of Science,* 89, pp. 766–783.

Simon, H. A. (1955) A behavioral model of rational choice, *Quarterly Journal of Economics,* 69, pp. 99–118.

Simon, H. A. (1956) Rational choice and the structure of the environment, *Psychological Review,* 63, pp. 129–138.

Simon, H. A. (1959) Theories of decision making in economics and behavioral science, *American Economic Review,* 49, pp. 252–283.

Simon, H. A. (1978) Rationality as a process and as a product of thought, *American Economic Review,* 70, pp. 1–16.

Simon, H. A. (1987) Behavioral economics, in: J. Eatwell, M. Millgate & P. Newman (Eds) *The New Palgrave: A Dictionary of Economics,* pp. 221–225 (London: Macmillan).

Thaler, R. H. (1980) Toward a positive theory of consumer choice, *Journal of Economic Behavior and Organization,* 1, pp. 39–60.

Todd, P. M. & Gigerenzer, G. (2003) Bounded rationality in the real world, *Journal of Economic Psychology,* 24, pp. 143–165.

Von Mises, L. (1949) *Human Action: A Treatise on Economics,* 3rd edn. (Chicago: Contemporary Books).

Bibliography and references to the work of Daniel Kahneman

Ariely, D., Kahneman, D. & Loewenstein, G. (2000) Joint comment on 'When does duration matter in judgment and decision making', *Journal of Experimental Psychology: General,* 129, pp. 524–529.

Beatty, J. & Kahneman, D. (1966) Pupillary changes in two memory tasks, *Psychonomic Science,* 5, pp. 371–372.

Flom, M. C., Weynouth, F. W. & Kahneman, D. (1963) Visual resolution and contour interaction, *Journal of the Optical Society of America,* 53, pp. 1026–1032.

Fox, C. & Kahneman, D. (1992) Correlation, causation and inference in surveys of life satisfaction, *Social Indicators,* 27, pp. 221–234.

Fredrickson, B. L. & Kahneman, D. (1993) Duration neglect in retrospective evaluations of affective episodes, *Journal of Personality and Social Psychology,* 65, pp. 45–55.

Gilovich, T., Griffin, D. & Kahneman, D. (Eds) (2002) *Heuristics and Biases: The Psychology of Intuitive Judgment* (New York: Cambridge University Press).

Gilovich, T., Medvec, V. H. & Kahneman, D. (1998) Varieties of regret: a debate and partial resolution, *Psychological Review,* 105, pp. 602–605.

Green, D., Jacowitz, K., Kahneman, D. & McFadden, D. (1998) Referendum contingent valuation, anchoring and willingness to pay for public goods, *Resource and Energy Economics,* 20, pp. 85–116.

Green, D., Kahneman, D. & Kunreuther, H. (1994) How the method and scope of public funding affects willingness to pay for public goods, *Public Opinion Quarterly,* 58, pp. 48–67.

Jacowitz, K. E. & Kahneman, D. (1995) Measures of anchoring in estimation tasks, *Personality and Social Psychology Bulletin,* 21, pp. 1161–1166.

Kafry, D. & Kahneman, D. (1977) Capacity sharing and refractoriness in successive reactions, *Perceptual and Motor Skills,* 44, pp. 327–335.

Kahn, B. E., Ratner, R. & Kahneman, D. (1997) Patterns of hedonic consumption over time, *Marketing Letters,* 8, pp. 85–96.

Kahneman, D. (1961) An analytical model of the semantic differential, PhD Thesis, University of Michigan.

Kahneman, D. (1963) The semantic differential and the structure of inferences among attributes, *American Journal of Psychology,* 76, pp. 554–567.

Kahneman, D. (1964) Temporal summation in acuity tasks at different energy levels: a study of the determinants of summation, *Vision Research,* 4, pp. 557–566.

Kahneman, D. (1965a) Control of spurious association and the reliability of the controlled variable, *Psychological Bulletin,* 64, pp. 326–329.

Kahneman, D. (1965b) Exposure duration and effective figure–ground contras, *Quarterly Journal of Experimental Psychology,* 17, pp. 308–314.

Kahneman, D. (1966a) Time–intensity reciprocity in acuity as a function of luminance and figure-ground contrast, *Vision Research,* 6, pp. 207–215.

Kahneman, D. (1966b) Time-intensity reciprocity under various conditions of adaptation and backward masking, *Journal of Experimental Psychology,* 71, pp. 543–549.

Kahneman, D. (1967a) An onset-onset law for one case of apparent motion and metacontrast, *Perception and Psychophysics,* 2, pp. 577–584.

Kahneman, D. (1967b) Temporal effects in the perception of light and form, in: W. Wathen-Dunn (Ed.) *Models for the Perception of Speech and Visual Form,* pp. 157–170 (Cambridge, MA: MIT Press).

Kahneman, D. (1968a) Effects of verbalization and incentive on the pupillary response to mental activity, *Canadian Journal of Psychology,* 22, pp. 186–196.

Kahneman, D. (1968b) Methods, findings and theory in studies of visual masking, *Psychological Bulletin,* 70, pp. 404–425.

Kahneman, D. (1970a) Changes in pupil size and visual discrimination during mental effort, in: J. Pierce (Ed.) *Visual Science,* pp. 295–304 (Bloomington: University of Indiana Press).

Kahneman, D. (1970b) Remarks on attention control, in: A. F. Sanders (Ed.) *Attention and Performance, III,* pp. 118–131 (Amsterdam: North–Holland).

Kahneman, D. (1973) *Attention and Effort* (Englewood Cliffs, NJ: Prentice–Hall).

Kahneman, D. (1974) Cognitive limitations and public decision making, in: Science and Absolute Values, *Proceedings of the Third International Conference on the Unity of the Sciences* (London: International Cultural Foundation).

Kahneman, D. (1975) Effort, recognition and recall in auditory attention, in: P. M. A. Rabbitt & S. Dornic (Eds) *Attention and Performance IV,* pp. 65–80 (New York: Academic Press).

Kahneman, D. (1979) Mechanisms that produce critical durations, *The Behavioral and Brain Sciences,* 2, pp. 265–266.

Kahneman, D. (1980a) Human engineering of decisions, in: M. Kranzberg (Ed.) *Ethics in an Age of Pervasive Technology,* pp. 190–192 (Boulder, CO: Westview Press).

Kahneman, D. (1980b) A review of M. Posner's 'An experimental study of consciousness', *Contemporary Psychology,* 25, pp. 3–5.

Kahneman, D. (1986) Comment, in: R. G. Cummings, D. S. Brookshire, & W. D. Schultze (Eds) *Valuing Environmental Goods,* pp. 185–193 (Totowa, NJ: Rowman & Allenheld).

Kahneman, D. (1987) Experimental economics: a psychological perspective, in: R. Tietz, W. Albers & R. Selten (Eds) *Modeling Bounded Rationality,* pp. 11–20 (New York: Springer-Verlag).

Kahneman, D. (1991) Judgment and decision making: a personal view, *Psychological Science,* 2, pp. 142–145.

Kahneman, D. (1992) Reference points, anchors, norms, and mixed feelings, *Organizational Behavior and Human Decision Processes,* 51, pp. 296–312.

Kahneman, D. (1994) New challenges to the rationality assumption, *Journal of Institutional and Theoretical Economics,* 150, pp. 18–36.

Kahneman, D. (1995) Varieties of counterfactual thinking, in: N. J. Roese & J. M. Olson (Eds) *What Might Have Been: The Social Psychology of Counterfactual Thinking,* pp. 375–396 (Hillsdale, NJ: Erlbaum).

Kahneman, D. (1997) New challenges to the rationality assumption, *Legal Theory,* 3, pp. 105–124.

Kahneman, D. (1999a) Comments on Fetherstonehaugh and Ross, in: H. Aaron (Ed.) *Behavioral Dimensions of Retirement Economics,* pp. 210–214 (Washington, DC: Brookings Institution & Russell Sage Foundation).

Kahneman, D. (1999b) Objective happiness, in: D. Kahneman, E. Diener & N. Schwarz (Eds) *Well-Being: Foundations of Hedonic Psychology,* pp. 3–27 (New York: Russell Sage Foundation).

Kahneman, D. (2000a) Evaluation by moments: past and future, in: D. Kahneman & A. Tversky (Eds) *Choices, Values and Frames,* pp. 693–703 (New York: Cambridge University Press & Russell Sage Foundation).

Kahneman, D. (2000b) Experienced utility and objective happiness: a moment-based approach, in: D. Kahneman & A. Tversky (Eds) *Choices, Values and Frames,* pp. 673–692 (New York: Cambridge University Press & Russell Sage Foundation).

Kahneman, D. (2000c) New challenges to the rationality assumption, in: D. Kahneman, & A. Tversky (Eds) *Choices, Values and Frames,* pp. 758–774 (New York: Cambridge University Press & Russell Sage Foundation).

Kahneman, D. (2000d) A psychological point of view: violations of rational rules as a diagnostic of mental processes (Commentary on Stanovich and West), *Behavioral and Brain Sciences*, 23, pp. 681–683.

Kahneman, D. & Beatty, J. (1966) Pupil diameter and load on memory, *Science*, 154, pp. 1583–1585.

Kahneman, D. & Beatty, J. (1967) Pupillary responses in a pitch-discrimination task, *Perception and Psychophysics*, 2, pp. 101–105.

Kahneman, D. & Chajczyk, D. (1983) Tests of the automaticity of reading: dilution of Stroop effects by color–irrelevant stimuli, *Journal of Experimental Psychology: Human Perception and Performance*, 9, pp. 497–509.

Kahneman, D. & Frederick, S. (2002) Representativeness revisited: attribute substitution in intuitive judgment, in: T. Gilovich, D. Griffin & D. Kahneman (Eds) *Heuristics and Biases: The Psychology of Intuitive Judgment*, pp. 49–81 (New York: Cambridge University Press).

Kahneman, D. & Ghiselli, E. E. (1962) Validity and nonlinear heteroscedastic models, *Personnel Psychology*, 15, pp. 1–12.

Kahneman, D. & Henik, A. (1976) Effects of visual grouping on immediate recall and selective attention, in: S. Dornic (Ed.) *Attention and Performance V*, pp. 307–332 (New York: Academic Press).

Kahneman, D. & Henik, A. (1981) Perceptual organization and attention, in: M. Kubovy & J. Pomerantz (Eds) *Perceptual Organization*, pp. 181–211 (Hillsdale, NJ: Erlbaum).

Kahneman, D. & Knetsch, J. (1992a) Contingent valuation and the value of public goods: reply, *Journal of Environmental Economics and Management*, 22, pp. 90–94.

Kahneman, D. & Knetsch, J. (1992b) Valuing public goods: the purchase of moral satisfaction, *Journal of Environmental Economics and Management*, 22, pp. 57–70.

Kahneman, D. & Lovallo, D. (1993) Timid choices and bold forecasts: a cognitive perspective on risk taking, *Management Science*, 39, pp. 17–31.

Kahneman, D. & Miller, D. T. (1986) Norm theory: comparing reality to its alternatives, *Psychological Review*, 93, pp. 136–153.

Kahneman, D. & Norman, J. (1964) The time–intensity relation in visual perception as a function of observer's task, *Journal of Experimental Psychology*, 68, pp. 215–220.

Kahneman, D. & Peavler, W. S. (1969) Incentive effects and pupillary changes in association learning, *Journal of Experimental Psychology*, 79, pp. 312–318.

Kahneman, D. & Riepe, M. (1998) Aspects of investor psychology, *Journal of Portfolio Management*, 24, pp. 52–65.

Kahneman, D. & Ritov, I. (1994) Determinants of stated willingness to pay for public goods: a study in the headline method, *Journal of Risk and Uncertainty*, 9, pp. 5–38.

Kahneman, D. & Schild, E. O. (1966) Training agents of social change in Israel: definitions of objectives and a training approach, *Human Organization*, 25, pp. 323–327.

Kahneman, D. & Snell, J. (1990) Predicting utility, in: R. M. Hogarth (Ed.) *Insights in Decision Making*, pp. 295–310 (Chicago, IL: University of Chicago Press).

Kahneman, D. & Snell, J. (1992) Predicting a changing taste, *Journal of Behavioral Decision Making*, 5, pp. 187–200.

Kahneman, D. & Thaler, R. (1991) Economic analysis and the psychology of utility: applications to compensation policy, *American Economic Review*, 81, pp. 341–352.

Kahneman, D. & Treisman, A. (1984) Changing views of attention and automaticity, in: R. Parasuraman, D. R. Davies & J. Beatty (Eds) *Variants of Attention*, pp. 29–61 (New York: Academic Press).

Kahneman, D. & Tversky, A. (1972) Subjective probability: a judgment of representativeness, *Cognitive Psychology*, 3, pp. 430–454.

Kahneman, D. & Tversky, A. (1973) On the psychology of prediction, *Psychological Review*, 80, pp. 237–251.

Kahneman, D. & Tversky, A. (1979a) Intuitive prediction: biases and corrective procedures, *Management Science*, 12, pp. 313–327.

Kahneman, D. & Tversky, A. (1979b) Prospect theory: an analysis of decisions under risk, *Econometrica*, 47, pp. 313–327.

Kahneman, D. & Tversky, A. (1982a) Judgment of and by representativeness, in: D. Kahneman, P. Slovic & A. Tversky (Eds) *Judgment under Uncertainty: Heuristics and Biases*, pp. 84–100 (New York: Cambridge University Press).

Kahneman, D. & Tversky, A. (1982b) On the study of statistical intuitions, *Cognition*, 11, pp. 123–141.

Kahneman, D. & Tversky, A. (1982c) The psychology of preferences, *Scientific American*, 246, pp. 160–173.

Kahneman, D. & Tversky, A. (1982d) The simulation heuristic, in: D. Kahneman, P. Slovic & A. Tversky (Eds) *Judgment under Uncertainty: Heuristics and Biases*, pp. 201–210 (New York: Cambridge University Press).

Kahneman, D. & Tversky, A. (1982e) Variants of uncertainty, *Cognition*, 11, pp. 143–157.

Kahneman, D. & Tversky, A. (1984) Choices, values and frames, *American Psychologist*, 39, pp. 341–350.

Kahneman, D. & Tversky, A. (1995) Conflict resolution: a cognitive perspective, in: K. Arrow *et al.* (Eds) *Barriers to Conflict Resolution*, pp. 44–61 (New York: W. W. Norton).

Kahneman, D. & Tversky, A. (1996) On the reality of cognitive illusions: a reply to Gigerenzer's critique, *Psychological Review*, 103, pp. 582–591.

Kahneman, D. & Tversky, A. (Eds) (2000) *Choices, Values and Frames* (New York: Cambridge University Press & Russell Sage Foundation).

Kahneman, D. & Varey, C. A. (1990) Propensities and counterfactuals: the loser that almost won, *Journal of Personality and Social Psychology*, 59, pp. 1101–1110.

Kahneman, D. & Varey, C. (1991) Notes on the psychology of utility, in: J. Roemer & J. Elster (Eds) *Interpersonal Comparisons of Well-Being*, pp. 127–163 (New York: Cambridge University Press).

Kahneman, D. & Wolman, R. (1970) Stroboscopic motion: effects of duration and interval, *Perception and Psychophysics*, 8, pp. 161–164.

Kahneman, D. & Wright, P. (1971) Changes in pupil size and rehearsal strategies in a short–term memory task, *Quarterly Journal of Experimental Psychology*, 23, pp. 187–196.

Kahneman, D., Beatty, J. & Pollack, I. (1967a) Perceptual deficit during a mental task, *Science*, 157, pp. 218–219.

Kahneman, D., Norman, J. & Kubovy, M. (1967b) Critical duration for the resolution of form: centrally or peripherally determined?, *Journal of Experimental Psychology*, 73, pp. 323–327.

Kahneman, D., Onuska, L. & Wolman, R. (1968) Effects of grouping on the pupillary response in a short-term memory task, *Quarterly Journal of Experimental Psychology*, 20, pp. 309–311.

Kahneman, D., Tursky, B., Shapiro, D. & Crider, A. (1969) Pupillary heart rate and skin resistance changes during a mental task, *Journal of Experimental Psychology*, 79, pp. 164–167.

Kahneman, D., Ben-Ishai, R. & Lotan, M. (1973) Relation of a test of attention to road accidents, *Journal of Applied Psychology,* 58, pp. 113–115.

Kahneman, D., Slovic, P. & Tversky, A. (Eds) (1982) *Judgment under Uncertainty: Heuristics and Biases* (New York: Cambridge University Press).

Kahneman, D., Treisman, A. & Burkell, J. (1983) The cost of visual filtering, *Journal of Experimental Psychology: Human Perception and Performance,* 9, pp. 510–522.

Kahneman, D., Knetsch, J. & Thaler, R. (1986a) Fairness and the assumptions of economics, *Journal of Business,* 59, pp. S285–S300.

Kahneman, D., Knetsch, J. & Thaler, R. (1986b) Fairness as a constraint on profit seeking: entitlements in the market, *American Economic Review,* 76, pp. 728–741.

Kahneman, D., Knetsch, J. & Thaler, R. (1990) Experimental tests of the endowment effect and the Coase theorem, *Journal of Political Economy,* 98, pp. 1325–1348.

Kahneman, D., Knetsch, J. & Thaler, R. (1991) The endowment effect, loss aversion, and status quo bias, *Journal of Economic Perspectives 5, pp.* 193–206.

Kahneman, D., Treisman, A. & Gibbs, B. J. (1992) The reviewing of object files: object-specific integration of information, *Cognitive Psychology,* 24, pp. 175–219.

Kahneman, D., Fredrickson, D. L., Schreiber, C. A. & Redelemeier, D. A. (1993a) When more pain is preferred to less: adding a better end, *Psychological Science,* 4, pp. 401–405.

Kahneman, D., Ritov, I., Jacowitz, K. E. & Grant, P. (1993b) Stated willingness to pay for public goods: a psychological analysis, *Psychological Science,* 4, pp. 310–315.

Kahneman, D., Wakker, P. P. & Sarin, R. (1997) Back to Bentham? Explorations of experienced utility, *Quarterly Journal of Economics,* 112, pp. 375–405.

Kahneman, D., Schkade, D. & Sunstein, C. (1998) Shared outrage and erratic awards: the psychology of punitive damages, *Journal of Risk and Uncertainty,* 16, pp. 49–86.

Kahneman, D., Diener, E. & Schwarz, N. (Eds) (1999a) *Well-Being: Foundations of Hedonic Psychology* (New York: Russell Sage Foundation).

Kahneman, D., Ritov, I. & Schkade, D. (1999b) Economic preferences or attitude expressions? An analysis of dollar responses to public issues, *Journal of Risk and Uncertainty,* 19, pp. 220–242.

Keinan, G., Friedland, N., Kahneman, D. & Roth, D. (1999) The effect of stress on the suppression of erroneous competing responses, *Anxiety, Stress and Coping,* 12, pp. 455–476.

Lovallo, D. & Kahneman, D. (2000) Living with uncertainty: attractiveness and resolution timing, *Journal of Behavioral Decision Making,* 13, pp. 179–190.

McCaffery E. J., Kahneman, D. & Spitzer, M. L. (1995) Framing the jury: cognitive perspectives on pain and suffering awards, *Virginia Law Review,* 81, pp. 1341–1420.

Mellers, A., Hertwig, R. & Kahneman, D. (2001) Do frequency representations eliminate conjunction effects? An exercise in adversarial collaboration, *Psychological Science,* 12, pp. 269–275.

Ninio, A. & Kahneman, D. (1974) Reaction time in focused and in divided attention, *Journal of Experimental Psychology,* 103, pp. 393–399.

Ratner, R. K., Kahn, B. E. & Kahneman, D. (1999) Choosing less-preferred experiences for the sake of variety, *Journal of Consumer Research,* 26, pp. 1–15.

Redelmeier, D. & Kahneman, D. (1996) Patients' memories of painful medical treatments: real-time and retrospective evaluations of two minimally invasive procedures, *Pain,* 66, pp. 3–8.

Redelmeier, D. A., Rozin, P. & Kahneman, D. (1993) Understanding patients' decisions: cognitive and emotional perspectives, *Journal of the American Medical Association,* 270, pp. 72–76.

Ritov, I. & Kahneman, D. (1997) How people value the environment: attitudes vs economic values, in: M. Bazerman, D. Messick, A. Tembrunsel & K. Wade-Benzoni (Eds) *Psychological Approaches to Environmental and Ethical Issues in Management*, pp. 33–51 (San Francisco, CA: New Lexington Press).

Schkade, D. & Kahneman, D. (1998) Does living in California make people happy? A focusing illusion in judgments of life satisfaction, *Psychological Science*, 9, pp. 340–346.

Schkade, D., Sunstein, C. & Kahneman, D. (2000) Deliberating about dollars: the severity shift, *Columbia Law Review*, 100, pp. 1139–1175.

Schreiber, C. A. & Kahneman, D. (2000) Determinants of the remembered utility of aversive sounds, *Journal of Experimental Psychology: General*, 129, pp. 27–42.

Sunstein, C., Kahneman, D. & Schkade, D. (1998) Assessing punitive damages, *Yale Law Journal*, 107, pp. 2071–2153.

Sunstein, C., Schkade, D. & Kahneman, D. (2000) Do people want optimal deterrence?, *Journal of Legal Studies*, 29, pp. 237–254.

Thaler, R., Tversky, A., Kahneman, D. & Schwartz, A. (1997) The effect of myopia and loss aversion on risk taking: an experimental test, *Quarterly Journal of Economics*, 112, pp. 647–661.

Treisman, A., Kahneman, D. & Burkell, J. (1983) Perceptual objects and the cost of filtering, *Perception and Psychophysics*, 33, pp. 527–532.

Tversky, A. & Kahneman, D. (1971) Belief in the law of small numbers, *Psychological Bulletin*, 76, pp. 105–110.

Tversky, A. & Kahneman, D. (1973) Availability: a heuristic for judging frequency and probability, *Cognitive Psychology*, 5, pp. 207–232.

Tversky, A. & Kahneman, D. (1974) Judgment under uncertainty: heuristics and biases, *Science*, 185, pp. 1124–1131.

Tversky, A. & Kahneman, D. (1977) Causal thinking in judgment under uncertainty, in: R. Butts & J. Hintikka (Eds) *Basic Problems in Methodology and Linguistics*, pp. 167–190 (Dordrecht: D. Reidel).

Tversky, A. & Kahneman, D. (1980) Causal schemata in judgments under uncertainty, in: M. Fishbein (Ed.) *Progress in Social Psychology*, pp. 49–72 (Hillsdale: NJ, Erlbaum).

Tversky, A. & Kahneman, D. (1981) The framing of decisions and the psychology of choice, *Science*, 211, pp. 453–458.

Tversky, A. & Kahneman, D. (1982) Evidential impact of base rates, in: D. Kahneman, P. Slovic & A. Tversky (Eds) *Judgment under Uncertainty: Heuristics and Biases*, pp. 153–162 (New York: Cambridge University Press).

Tversky, A. & Kahneman, D. (1983) Extensional vs. intuitive reasoning: the conjunction fallacy in probability judgment, *Psychological Review*, 90, pp. 293–315.

Tversky, A. & Kahneman, D. (1986) Rational choice and the framing of decisions, *Journal of Business*, 59, pp. S251–S278.

Tversky, A. & Kahneman, D. (1991) Loss aversion in riskless choice: a reference-dependent model, *Quarterly Journal of Economics*, pp. 1039–1061.

Tversky, A. & Kahneman, D. (1992) Advances in prospect theory: cumulative representation of uncertainty, *Journal of Risk and Uncertainty*, 5, pp. 297–323.

Tversky, A., Slovic, P. & Kahneman, D. (1990) The causes of preference reversal, *American Economic Review*, 80, pp. 204–217.

Varey, C. & Kahneman, D. (1992) Experiences extended across time: evaluation of moments and episodes, *Journal of Behavioral Decision Making*, 5, pp. 169–186.

Wright, P. & Kahneman, D. (1971) Evidence of alternative strategies of sentence retention, *Quarterly Journal of Experimental Psychology*, 23, pp. 197–213.

Bibliography and references to the work of Vernon Smith

Anderson, T., Simmons, E. & Smith, V. L. (1999) Privatized federal land would yield better environmental quality, *Policy Analysis,* Cato Institute Report #36.

Backerman, S., Michael, D., Smith, V. L. & Rassenti, S. (2001) Market power in a deregulated electrical Industry, *Journal of Decision Support Systems,* 30, pp. 357–381.

Boening, M. V., Wellford, C. & Smith, V. L. (2000) Dividend timing and behavior in laboratory asset markets, *Economic Theory,* 16, pp. 567–583.

Bronfman, C., McCabe, K., Porter, D., Rassenti S. & Smith, V. L. (1996) An experimental examination of the Walrasian tatonnement mechanism, *Rand Journal of Economics,* 27, pp. 681–699.

Buccola, S. & Smith, V. F. (1987) Uncertainty and partial adjustment in double auction markets, *Journal of Economic Behavior and Organization,* 8, pp. 587–60.

Caginalp, G., Ilieva, V., Porter, D. & Smith, V. L. (2002) Do speculative stocks lower prices and increase volatility of value stocks?, *The Journal of Psychology and Financial Markets,* 3, pp. 118–132.

Caginalp, G., Porter, D. & Smith, V. L. (1998) Initial cash/stock ratio and stock prices: an experimental study, *Proceedings of the National Academy of Sciences,* 95, pp. 756–761.

Caginalp, G., Porter, D. & Smith, V. L. (1999) Experimental asset markets, in: P. Earl & S. Kemp (Eds) *The Elgar Companion to Consumer Research and Economic Psychology,* pp. 215–222 (Cheltenham, UK: Edward Elgar).

Caginalp, G., Porter, D. & Smith, V. L. (2000) Momentum and overreaction in experimental asset markets, *International Journal of Industrial Organization,* 18, pp. 187–204.

Coppinger, V., Titus, T. & Smith, V. L. (1980) Incentives and behavior in English, Dutch, and sealed-bid auctions, *Economic Inquiry,* 18, pp. 1–22.

Coursey, D. & Smith, V. L. (1982) Price control in posted-offer markets, *American Economic Review,* 73, pp. 218–221.

Coursey, D., Isaac R. M., Luke, M. & Smith, V. L. (1984) Market contestability in the present of sunk costs, *Rand Journal of Economics,* 15, pp. 69–84.

Cox, J., Smith, V. L. & Walker, J. (1983) Tests of a heterogeneous bidders theory of first price auctions, *Economic Letters,* 12, pp. 207–212.

Cox, J., Roberson, B. & Smith, V. L. (1991) Theory and behavior of single object auctions, in: V. Smith (Ed.) *Research in Experimental Economics,* pp. 537–579 (Greenwich: JAI Press).

Dinar, A., Howitt, R., Rassenti S. & Smith, V. L. (1998) Development of water markets using experimental Economics, in: K. W. Easter, M. Rosegrant & A. Dinar (Eds) *Markets for Water Potential and Performance,* pp. 259–275 (Boston: Kluwer).

Dinar, A., Howitt, R. E., Murphy, J. J., Rassenti, S. J. & Smith, V. L. (2000) The design of 'smart' water market institutions using laboratory experiments, *Environmental and Resource Economics* 17, pp. 375–394.

Durham, Y., Rassenti, S., Boening, M. V., Wilcox, N. & Smith, V. L. (1996) Can core allocations be achieved in avoidable fixed cost environments using two-part pricing competition?, *Annals of Operations Research, Special Issue on Computational Economics,* 68, pp. 61–88.

Durham, Y., Hirshleifer, J. & Smith, V. L. (1998) Do the richer get richer and the poor poorer? experimental tests of a model of power, *American Economic Review,* 88, pp. 970–983.

Franciosi, R., Kujal, P., Michelitsch, R., Deng, G. & Smith, V. L. (1995) Fairness: effect on temporary and equilibrium prices in posted offer markets, *Economic Journal*, 431, pp. 938–950.

Franciosi, R., Kujal, P., Michelitsch, R., Deng, G. & Smith, V. L. (1996) Experimental tests of the endowment effect, *Journal of Economic Behavior and Organization*, 30, pp. 213–227.

Gillis, F. E. & Smith, V. L. (1958) An economic analysis of contributions under the income tax laws, *Journal of Political Economy*, 66, pp. 432–439.

Gunnthorsdottir, A., McCabe, K. & Smith, V. L. (2002) Using the Machiavellianism instrument to predict trustworthiness in a bargaining game, *Journal of Psychology and Economics*, 23, pp. 49–66.

Hoffman, E., McCabe, K. & Smith, V. L. (1995) Ultimatum and dictator games, *Journal of Economic Perspectives*, 9(4), pp. 236–239.

Hoffman, E., McCabe, K. & Smith, V. L. (1996a) On expectations and monetary stakes in ultimatum games, *International Journal of Game Theory*, 25, pp. 289–301.

Hoffman, E., McCabe, K. & Smith, V. L. (1996b) Social distance and other regarding behavior in dictator games, *American Economic Review*, 86, pp. 653–660.

Hoffman, E., McCabe, K., & Smith, V. L. (1997) Reciprocity: the behavioral foundations of socio-economic games, in: W. Albers *et al.* (Eds) *Understanding Strategic Interaction—Essays in Honor of Reinhard Selten*, pp. 328–344 (Berlin: Springer-Verlag).

Hoffman, E., McCabe, K., & Smith, V. L. (1998) Behavioral foundations of reciprocity: experimental economics and evolutionary psychology, *Economic Inquiry*, 36, pp. 335–352.

Hoffman, E., McCabe, K. & Smith, V. L. (1999) Social distance and other-regarding behavior in dictator games: Reply, *American Economic Review*, 89, pp. 340–341.

Hoffman, E., McCabe, K. & Smith, V. L. (2000) The impact of exchange context on the activation of equity in ultimatum games, *Experimental Economics*, 3, pp. 5–9.

Houser, D., McCabe, K., Ryan, L., Trouard, T. & Smith, V. L. (2001) A functioning imaging study of 'Theory of Mind' in two person reciprocal exchange, *Proceedings of the National Academy of Sciences*, 98, pp. 11832–11835.

Isaac, M. R. & Smith V. L. (1985) In search of predatory pricing, *Journal of Political Economy*, 93, pp. 320–345.

Ketcham, J., Smith V. L. & Williams, A. W. (1984) A comparison of posted offer and double auction pricing institutions, *Review of Economic Studies*, 51, pp. 595–614.

Kruse, J. B., Rassenti S., Reynolds, S. S. & Smith, V. L. (1994) Bertrand–Edgeworth competition in experimental markets, *Econometrica*, 62, pp. 343–371.

Kurzban, R., McCabe, K., Wilson, B. & Smith, V. L. (2001) Incremental commitment and reciprocity in a real time public good game, *Personality and Social Psychology*, 27, pp. 1662–1673.

Manes, R. & Smith, V. L. (1965) Economic joint cost theory and accounting practice, *Accounting Review*, 40, pp. 31–35.

McCabe, K. & Smith, V. L. (1998) Experimental economics, in: D. Jacobs, E. Kalai & M. Kamien (Eds) *Frontiers of Research in Economic Theory*, pp. 104–122 (Cambridge: Cambridge University Press).

McCabe, K. & Smith, V. L. (1999) Who do you trust?, *Boston Review*, 23.

McCabe, K. & Smith, V. L. (2000) A Comparison of naïve and sophisticated subject behavior with game theoretic predictions, *Proceedings of the National Academy of Sciences*, 97, pp. 3777–3781.

McCabe, K. & Smith, V. L. (2001) Goodwill accounting in economic exchange, in: G.

Gigerenzer & R. Selten (Eds) *Bounded Rationality: The Adaptive Toolbox,* pp. 319–340 (Cambridge, MA: MIT Press).

McCabe, K., Burnham, T. & Smith, V. L. (2000a) Friend-or-foe intentionality priming in an extensive form trust game, *Journal of Economic Behavior and Organization*, 93, pp. 57–73.

McCabe, K., LePore, M. & Smith, V. L. (2000b) Intentionality detection and 'Mindreading': why does game form matter?, in: *Proceedings of the National Academy of Sciences,* 97, pp. 4404–4409.

McCabe, K., Rigdon, M. & Smith, V. L. (2002) Cooperation in single play, two-person extensive form games between anonymously matched players, in: R. Zwick & A. Rapoport (Eds) *Experimental Business Research,* pp. 49–67 (Boston: Kluwer).

McCabe, K., Rigdon, M. & Smith, V. L. (2003) Positive reciprocity and intentions in trust games, *Journal of Economic Behavior and Organization,* 52, pp 267–275.

Miller, R. M., Plott C. R. & Smith, V. L. (1977) Intertemporal competitive equilibrium: an empirical study of speculation, *Quarterly Journal of Economics,* 91, pp. 599–624.

Porter, D. & Smith, V. L. (1994) Stock market bubbles in the laboratory, *Applied Mathematical Finance,* 1, pp. 111–127.

Porter, D. & Smith, V. L. (1995) Futures contracting and dividend uncertainty in experimental asset markets, *Journal of Business,* 68, pp. 509–541.

Rassenti, S. & Smith, V. L. (1986) Electric utility deregulation, in: J. Fischer & J. Robert (Eds) *Pricing Electric, Gas and Telecommunication Services,* pp. 53–74 (Washington, DC: Institute for the Study of Regulation).

Rassenti, S., Smith, V. L. & Bulfin. R. (1982) A combinatorial auction mechanism for airport time slot allocation, *Bell Journal of Economics,* 13, pp. 402–417.

Smith, V. L. (1957a) Economic equipment policies: an evaluation, *Management Science,* 4, pp. 20–37.

Smith, V. L. (1957b) On the use of engineering data and statistical techniques in the analysis of production and technological change: fuel requirements in the trucking industry, *Econometrica,* 25, pp. 281–301.

Smith, V. L. (1958) An Econometric Study of Aircraft Malfunction Behavior (The Rand Corporation), P–1424.

Smith, V. L. (1959) The theory of investment and production, *Quarterly Journal of Economics,* 73, pp. 61–87.

Smith, V. L. (1960) Problems in production-investment planning over time, *International Economic Review,* 1, pp. 198–216.

Smith, V. L. (1961a) *Investment and Production* (Cambridge, MA: Harvard University Press).

Smith, V. L. (1961b) Time preference and risk in investment theory, *American Economic Review,* 51, pp. 121–130.

Smith, V. L. (1962a) *Economics: An Analytical Approach,* 2nd edn (Homewood, Ill: Richard D. Irwin).

Smith, V. L. (1962b) An experimental study of competitive market behavior, *Journal of Political Economy,* 70, pp. 111–137.

Smith, V. L. (1962c) Models of production and investment: a reply, *International Economic Review,* 3, pp. 366–372.

Smith, V. L. (1962d) The theory of capital, *American Economic Review,* 52, pp. 481–491.

Smith, V. L. (1963a) Depreciation, market valuations, and investment theory, *Management Science,* 9, pp. 690–696.

Smith, V. L. (1963b) Minimization of economic rent in spatial price equilibrium, *Review of Economic Studies*, 30, pp. 24–31.

Smith, V. L. (1963c) Review of R.F. Lundy 'The economics of loyalty–incentives rates in the railroad Industry', *American Economic Review*, 53, pp. 815–816.

Smith, V. L. (1963d) Tax depreciation policy and investment theory, *International Economic Review*, 4, pp. 80–91.

Smith, V. L. (1964a) Effect of market organization on competitive equilibrium, *Quarterly Journal of Economics*, 78, pp. 181–201.

Smith, V. L. (1964b) The measurement of capital, in: *Measuring the Nation's Wealth*, pp. 329–353 (Washington, DC: Wealth Inventory Planning Study, Subcommittee on Economic Statistics of the Joint Economic Committee, Congress of the United States).

Smith, V. L. (1964c) Review of A. Manne & H. Markowitz 'Studies in process analysis,' *Journal of the American Statistical Association*, 59, pp. 387–393.

Smith, V. L. (1965a) Comment on M. Peck & J. Meyer 'The determination of a fair return on investment for regulated industries', in: *Transportation Economics; a Conference of the Universities–National Bureau Committee for Economic Research*, pp. 199–241 (New York: Columbia University Press).

Smith, V. L. (1965b) Experimental auction markets and the Walrasian hypothesis, *Journal of Political Economy*, 73, pp. 387–393.

Smith, V. L. (1966a) Does price discrimination increase bill prices?, *Review of Economics and Statistics*, 48, pp. 141–146.

Smith, V. L. (1966b) Review of F. Christy & A. Scott 'The common wealth in ocean fisheries', *American Economic Review*, 56, pp. 1341–1343.

Smith, V. L. (1967) Experimental studies of discrimination versus competition in sealed bid auction markets, *Journal of Business*, 40, pp. 56–84.

Smith, V. L. (1968a) Economics of production from natural resources, *American Economic Review*, 58, pp. 409–431.

Smith, V. L. (1968b) Optimal insurance coverage, *Journal of Political Economy*, 76, pp. 68–77.

Smith, V. L. (1968c) Review of R. Cassady 'Auctions and auctioneering', *American Economic Review*, 58, pp. 959–963.

Smith, V. L. (1968d) The theory of production, *International Encyclopedia of the Social Sciences*, 12, pp. 511–519.

Smith, V. L. (1969a) Measuring non-monetary utilities, *Quarterly Journal of Economics*, 83, pp. 324–329.

Smith, V. L. (1969b) On models of commercial fishing, *Journal of Political Economy*, 77, pp. 181–198.

Smith, V. L. (1969c) Taxes and share valuation in competitive markets, *Review of Economics and Statistics*, 51, pp. 96–99.

Smith, V. L. (1970a) Corporate financial theory under uncertainty, *Quarterly Journal of Economics*, 84, pp. 451–471.

Smith, V. L. (1970b) Investment behavior: discussion, *American Economic Review*, 60, pp. 28–31.

Smith, V. L. (1971a) The borrower–lender contact under uncertainty, *Western Economic Journal*, 9, pp. 52–56.

Smith, V. L. (1971b) Economic theory of wage markets, *Western Economic Journal*, 9, pp. 242–255.

Smith, V. L. (1971c) Economics of production from natural resources: a reply, *American Economic Review*, 71, pp. 488–491.

Smith, V. L. (1971d) Investment decision, uncertainty and the incorporated firm, in: A. Zarley (Ed.) *Papers in Quantitative Economics 2*, pp. 121–145 (Lawrence: University of Kansas Press).

Smith, V. L. (1972a) Default risk, scale and the homemade leverage theorem, *American Economic Review*, 62, pp. 66–76.

Smith, V. L. (1972b) Dynamics of waste accumulation: disposal versus recycling, *Quarterly Journal of Economics*, 86, pp. 600–616.

Smith, V. L. (1972c) On models of commercial fishing: the traditional literature needs no defenders, *Journal of Political Economy*, 80, pp. 776–778.

Smith, V. L. (1972d) The theory of credit rationing—some generalizations, *American Economic Review*, 63, pp. 477–483.

Smith, V. L. (1974a) Economic theory and its discontents, *American Economic Review*, 64, pp. 320–322.

Smith, V. L. (1974b) Optimal costly firm entry in general equilibrium, *Journal of Economic Theory*, 9, pp. 397–417.

Smith, V. L. (1974c) An optimistic theory of exhaustible resources, *Journal of Economic Theory* 9, pp. 384–396.

Smith, V. L. (1975a) Economics of the primitive hunter culture with applications to pleistocene extinction and the rise of agriculture, *Journal of Political Economy*, 83, pp. 727–756.

Smith, V. L. (1975b) General equilibrium with a replenishable resource, *Review of Economic Studies*, 41, pp. 105–115.

Smith, V. L. (1976a) Bidding and auctioning institutions: experimental results, in: Y. Amihud (Ed.) *Bidding and Auctioning for Procurement and Allocation*, pp. 43–64 (New York: New York University).

Smith, V. L. (1976b) Economics of wilderness resources, *Intermountain Economic Review*, 7, pp. 1–14.

Smith, V. L. (1976c) Experimental economics: induced value theory, *American Economic Review*, 66, pp. 274–279.

Smith, V. L. (1977a) Control theory applied to natural and environmental resources: an exposition, *Journal of Environmental Economics and Management*, 4, p 1.

Smith, V. L. (1977b) *Economics of Natural and Environmental Resources* (New York: Gordon & Breach).

Smith, V. L. (1977c) Experimental mechanisms for public choice, in: P. Ordeshook (Ed.) *Game Theory and Political Science*, pp. 323–355 (New York: New York University Press).

Smith, V. L. (1977d) The principle of unanimity and voluntary consent in social choice, *Journal of Political Economy*, 85, pp. 1125–1140.

Smith, V. L. (1977e) Water deeds: a proposed solution to the water valuation problem, *Arizona Review*, 26, pp. 7–10.

Smith, V. L. (1978) Economics, psychology and protective behavior: discussion, *American Economic Review*, 68, pp. 64–69.

Smith, V. L. (1979) An experimental comparison of three public good decision mechanisms, *Scandinavian Journal of Economics*, 2, pp. 198–215.

Smith, V. L. (1980a) Experiments with a decentralized mechanism for public good decision, *American Economic Review*, 70, pp. 584–599.

Smith, V. L. (1980b) Relevance of laboratory experiments to testing resource allocation theory, in: J. Kmenta & J. B. Ramsey (Ed.) *Evaluation of Econometric Models*, pp. 345–377 (New York: Academic Press).

Smith, V. L. (1981a) An empirical study of decentralized institutions of monopoly restraint, in: G. Horwich & J. P. Quirk (Eds) *Economic Essays in Honor of E. R. Weiler*, pp. 83–106 (West Lafayette, IN: Purdue University Press).

Smith, V. L. (1981b) Experimental economics at Purdue, in: G. Horwich & J. P. Quirk (Eds) *Economic Essays in Honor of E. T Weiler*, pp. 154–156 (West Lafayette, IN: Purdue University Press).

Smith, V. L. (1982a) Reflections on some experimental market mechanisms for classical environments, in: L. McAlister (Ed.) *Proceedings Conference on Choice Theory*, pp. 206–239 (Greenwich: JAI Press).

Smith, V. L. (1982b) Markets as economizers of information: experimental examination of the Hayek Hypothesis, *Economic Inquiry*, 20, pp. 165–179.

Smith, V. L. (1982c) Microeconomic systems as an experimental science, *American Economic Review*, 72, pp. 923–955.

Smith, V. L. (1982d) On divestiture and the creation of property rights in public lands, *Cato Journal*, 2, pp. 563–629.

Smith, V. L. (1984a) Experimental tests of an allocation mechanism for private, public or externality goods, *Scandinavian Journal of Economics*, 86, pp. 468–484.

Smith, V. L. (1984b) Property rights—from ancient origins and spontaneous invention to conscious design?, in: A. Scott (Ed.) *Progress in Natural Resource Economics*, pp. 3–13 (New York: Oxford University Press).

Smith, V. L. (1985a) Experimental Economics (Reply to R. Heiner), *American Economic Review*, 75, pp. 265–272.

Smith, V. L. (1986b) Experimental methods in the political economy of exchange, *Science*, 234, pp. 167–173.

Smith, V. L. (1987a) Auctions, in: J. Eatwell, M. Milgate & P. Newman (Eds) *The New Palgrave: a Dictionary of Economics*, pp. 138–144 (New York: Macmillan).

Smith, V. L. (1987b) Experimental methods in economics, in: J. Eatwell, M. Milgate & P. Newman (Eds) *The New Palgrave: a Dictionary of Economics*, pp. 241–249 (New York: Macmillan).

Smith, V. L. (1987c) Hunting and gathering economies, in: J. Eatwell, M. Milgate & P. Newman (Eds) *The New Palgrave: a Dictionary of Economics*, pp. 695–699 (New York: Macmillan).

Smith, V. L. (1988a) Electric power deregulation: background and prospects, *Contemporary Policy Issues*, 6, pp. 14–22.

Smith, V. L. (1988b) New directions in economics, *Journal of Business Administration*, 18, pp. 41–52.

Smith, V. L. (1989) Theory, experiment and economics, *Journal of Economic Perspectives*, 3, pp. 151–169.

Smith, V. L. (1990a) Experimental economics: behavioral lessons for microeconomic theory and policy, Nancy L. Schwartz Memorial Lecture (Evanston: J.L. Kellogg Graduate School of Management, Northwestern University).

Smith, V. L. (1990b) Man as an ecological factor within nature, in: J. Baden & D. Leal (Eds) *The Yellowstone Primer*, pp. 187–195 (San Francisco, CA: Pacific Research Institute for Public Policy).

Smith, V. L. (1990c) *Schools of Economic Thought: Experimental Economics* (Aldershot, Hampshire: Edward Elgar).

Smith, V. L. (1991a) *Papers in Experimental Economics* (New York: Cambridge University Press).

Smith, V. L. (1991b) Rational choice: the contrast between economics and psychology, *Journal of Political Economy*, 99, pp. 877–897.

Smith, V. L. (1992) Game theory and experimental economics: beginnings and early influences, in: E. R. Weintraub (Ed.) *Toward a History of Game Theory, History of Political Economy, Annual Supplement*, 24, pp. 241–282.

Smith, V. L. (1993a) Can electric power—a natural monopoly—be deregulated?, in: H. H. Landsberg (Ed.) *Making National Energy Policy*, pp. 131–151 (Washington, DC: Resources for the Future).

Smith, V. L. (1993b) Humankind in prehistory: economy, ecology and institutions, in: T. Anderson & R. Simmons (Eds) *The Political Economy of Customs and Culture*, pp. 157–184 (London: Rowman & Littlefield).

Smith, V. L. (1994) Economics in the laboratory, *Journal of Economic Perspectives*, 8, pp. 113–131.

Smith, V. L. (1995) Regulatory reform in the electric power industry, *Regulation*, 1, 1996, pp. 33–46.

Smith, V. L. (1996) Puzzle solving: reciprocity, reasoning and behavior, in: S. Medema & W. Samuels (Eds) *Exploring the Foundations of Economics: How Should Economists Do Economics?*, pp. 216–226 (Cheltenham, UK: Edward Elgar).

Smith, V. L. (1997) Experimental price bubbles, in: D. Glasner (Ed.) *Business Cycles and Depressions*, pp. 207–209 (New York: Garland Publishing).

Smith, V. L. (1998a) Economy, Ecology and Institutions in the emergence of humankind, in: L. Barrington (Ed.) *The Other Side of the Frontier: Economic Explorations into Native American History*, pp. 57–86 (Boulder, CO: Westview Press).

Smith, V. L. (1998b) The law of unintended consequences in the experimental laboratory, *National Conference on Innovative Applications of the Laffer Curve, Papers and Proceedings*, pp. 115–133 (Hartford: Association of Private Enterprise Education).

Smith, V. L. (1998c) Property rights as a natural order: reciprocity, evolutionary and experimental considerations, in: P. J. Hill & R. Meiners (Eds) *Who Owns the Environment?*, pp. 55–85 (New York: Rowman & Littlefield).

Smith, V. L. (1998d) The two faces of Adam Smith, *Southern Economic Journal*, 65, pp. 1–19.

Smith, V. L. (1999) Human action after fifty years, *Cato Journal*, 19, pp. 195–209.

Smith, V. L. (2000) *Bargaining and Market Behavior, Essays in Experimental Economics* (New York: Cambridge University Press).

Smith, V. L. (2001) Experimental Economics, in: N. J. Smelser & P. B. Baltes (Eds) *International Encyclopedia of the Social and Behavioral Sciences*, pp. 5100–5108, (Amsterdam: Elsevier).

Smith, V. L. & Day, R. (Eds) (1993) *Experiments in Decision, Organization and Exchange* (Amsterdam: Elsevier).

Smith, V. L. & Knez, M. (1987) Hypothetical valuations and preference reversals in the context of asset trading, in: A. Roth (Ed.) *Laboratory Experiments in Economics—Six Points of View*, pp. 131–154 (New York: Cambridge University Press).

Smith, V. L. & Plott, C. (1978) An experimental examination of two exchange institutions, *Review of Economic Studies*, 45, pp. 133–153.

Smith, V. L. & Plott, C. (1979) Further comments on the application of laboratory experimental methods to political choice, in: C. S. Russel (Ed.) *Collective Decision Making*, pp. 167–169 (Baltimore: John Hopkins University Press).

Smith, V. L. & Quirk, J. (1970) Dynamic economic models of fishing, in: A. D. Scott (Ed.) *Economic of Fisheries Management*, pp. 3–32 (Vancouver: University of British Columbia).

Smith, V. L. & Rassenti, J. S. (1999) Turning on the lights: deregulating the market for electricity, *National Center for Policy Analysis*, Report #228.

Smith, V. L. & Rice, D. (1964) Nature, the experimental laboratory, and the credibility of hypotheses, *Behavioral Science,* 9, pp. 239–246.

Smith, V. L. & Saposnik, R. (1959) Allocation of a scarce resource to alternative probabilistic demands: transport equipment pool assignments, *Naval Research Logistics Quarterly,* 6, pp. 193–207.

Smith, V. L. & Williams, A. W. (1981) On nonbinding price controls in a competitive market, *American Economic Review,* 71, pp. 467–474.

Smith, V. L., Davidson, K. & Wiley, J. (1958) *Economics: An Analytical Approach,* 1st edn (Homewood, IL: Richard D. Irwin).

Smith, V. L., Cox, J. & Walker, J. (1982a) Auction market theory of heterogeneous bidders, *Economic Letters,* 9, pp. 319–325.

Smith, V. L., Williams, A. W., Bratton, K. W. & Vannoi, M. G. (1982c) Competitive market institutions: double auctions versus sealed bid offer auctions, *American Economic Review,* 72, pp. 58–77.

Smith, V. L., Cox, J. & Isaac, M. (1983a) OCS leasing and auctions: incentives and the performance of alternative bidding institutions, *Supreme Court Economic Review,* 2, pp. 43–87.

Smith, V. L., Cox, J. & Walker, J. (1983b) A test that discriminates between two models of the Dutch-first auction nonisomorphism, *Journal of Economic Behavior and Organization,* 4, pp. 205–219.

Smith, V. L., Coursey, D. & Isaac, M. J. (1984a) Natural monopoly and the contestable markets hypothesis: some preliminary results from laboratory experiments, *Journal of Law and Economics,* 27, pp. 91–113.

Smith, V. L., Cox, J. & Walker, J. (1984b) Expected revenue in discriminative and uniform price sealed–bid auctions, in: C. Plott (Ed.) *Research in Experimental Economics,* 3, pp. 183–323 (Greenwich, Connecticut: JAI Press).

Smith, V. L., Cox, J. & Walker, J. (1984c) Theory and behavior of multiple unit discriminative auctions, *Journal of Finance,* 39, pp. 983–1010.

Smith, V. L., Cox, J. & Walker, J. (1985a) Experimental development of sealed–bid auction theory: calibrating controls for risk aversion, *American Economic Review,* 75, pp. 160–165.

Smith, V. L., Cox, J. & Walker, J. (1985b) Individual rationality, market rationality, and value estimation, *American Economic Review,* 75, pp. 160–165.

Smith, V. L., Cox, J. & Walker, J. (1987) Bidding behavior in first price auctions: use of computerized Nash competitors, *Economic Letters,* 23, pp. 239–244.

Smith, V. L., Cox, J. & Walker, J. (1988) Theory and individual behavior in first price auctions, *Journal of Risk and Uncertainty,* 1, pp. 61–99.

Smith, V. L., McCabe, K. A. & Rassenti, J. R. (1989) Designing 'smart' computer assisted-markets: an experimental auction for gas networks, *European Journal of Political Economy,* 5, pp. 259–283.

Smith, V. L., Cox, J. & Walker, J. (1990a) Inducing risk neutral preferences: an examination in a controlled market environment, *Journal of Risk and Uncertainty,* 3, pp. 5–24.

Smith, V. L., McCabe, K. A. & Rassenti, J. S. (1990b) Auction design for composite goods: the natural gas industry, *Journal of Economic Behavior and Organization,* 14, pp. 127–149.

Smith, V. L., McCabe, K. A., Rassenti, J. S. & Reynolds, S. (1990c) Auction institutional design: theory and behavior of simultaneous multiple unit generalizations of the Dutch and English auctions, *American Economic Review,* 80, pp. 1276–1283.

Smith, V. L., Campbell, J., LaMaster, S. & Boening, M. V. (1991a) Off–floor trading,

Disintegration and the bid-ask spread in experimental markets, *Journal of Business*, 64, pp. 495–522.

Smith, V. L., McCabe, K. A. & Rassenti, J. S. (1991b) Experimental research on deregulated markets for natural gas pipeline and electric power transmission networks, *Research in Law and Economics*, 13, pp. 161–189.

Smith, V. L., McCabe, K.A. & Rassenti, J. S. (1991c) Lakatos and experimental economics, in: N. de Marchi & M. Blaug (Eds) *Appraising Economic Theories*, pp. 197–226 (Aldershot, UK: Edward Elgar).

Smith, V. L., McCabe, K. A., & Rassenti, J. S. (1991d) Smart computer-assisted markets, *Science*, 254, pp. 534–538.

Smith, V. L., McCabe, K. A. & Rassenti, J. S. (1991e) Testing Vickrey's and other simultaneous multiple unit versions of the English auction, *Research in Experimental Economics*, 4, pp. 45–69.

Smith, V. L., Cox, J. & Walker, J. (1992a) Theory and behavior of first price auctions: comments, *American Economic Review*, 83, pp. 1392–1412.

Smith, V. L., McCabe, K. A., & Rassenti, J. S. (1992b) Designing call auction institutions: is double Dutch the best?, *Economic Journal*, 102, pp. 9–23.

Smith, V. L., King, R., Williams. A. W. & Boening, M. V. (1993a) The robustness of bubbles and crashes in experimental stock markets, in: R. Day & P. Chen (Eds) *Non Linear Dynamics and Evolutionary Economics*, pp. 183–200 (Oxford: Oxford University Press).

Smith, V. L., McCabe, K. A. & Rassenti, J. S. (1993b) Designing a uniform price double auction: an experimental evaluation, in: D. Friedman & J. Rust (Eds) *The Double Auction Market: Institutions, Theories and Evidence*, pp. 307–332 (Reading, MA: Addison-Wesley).

Smith, V. L., Rassenti, S. J. & Reynolds, S. S. (1993c) Cotenancy and competition in an experimental auction market for natural gas pipeline networks, *Economic Theory*, 4, pp. 41–65.

Smith, V. L., Durham, Y. & Rassenti, S. (1994a) Experimental design of computer coordinated markets for network industries, in: E. Hillebrand & J. Stender (Eds) *Many Agent Simulation and Artificial Life*, pp. 149–168 (Washington, DC: IOS Press).

Smith, V. L., Hoffman, E., McCabe, K. & Shachat, K. (1994b) Preferences, property rights and anonymity in bargaining games, *Games and Economic Behavior*, 7, pp. 346–380.

Smith, V. L., McCabe, K. A. & Rassenti, J. S. (1994c) Designing a real time computer assisted auction for natural gas networks, in: W. Cooper & A. Whinston (Eds) *New Directions in Computational Economics*, pp. 41–54 (Amsterdam: Kluwer).

Smith, V. L., McCabe, K. A. & Rassenti, J. S. (1994d) Institutional design for electronic trading, in: R. Schwartz & I. Walter (Eds) *Structure and Integration in Securities Markets*, pp. 121–156 (New York: Irwin).

Smith, V. L., McCabe, K. A. & Rassenti, J. S. (1996) Game theory and reciprocity in some extensive form experimental games, *Proceedings National Academy of Science*, 93, pp. 13421–13428.

Smith, V. L., McCabe, K. A. & Rassenti, J. S. (1998a) Reciprocity, trust and payoff privacy in extensive form bargaining, *Games and Economic Behavior*, 24, pp. 10–24.

Smith, V. L., Rassenti, S. J. & Boening, M. V. (1998b) Numerical computation of equilibrium bid functions in a first price auction with heterogeneous risk attitudes, *Experimental Economics*, 1, pp. 147–159.

Smith, V. L., Suchanek, G. L. & Williams, A. W. (1988c) Bubbles, crashes and endogenous expectations in experimental spot asset markets, *Econometrica*, 56, pp. 1119–1151.

Smith, V. L., McCabe, K. A. & Rassenti, J. S. (1999) Designing auction institutions for exchange, *IIE Transactions*, 31, pp. 803–811.

Smith, V. L., Rassenti, S. & Backerman, S. (2000a) Efficiency and income shares in high demand energy network: who receives the congestion rents when a line is constrained?, *Pacific Economic Review*, 5, pp. 331–347.

Smith, V. L., Rassenti, S., Reynolds, S. & Szidarovszky, F. (2000b) Adaptation and convergence of behavior in repeated experimental Cournot games, *Journal of Economic Behavior and Organization*, 41, pp. 117–146.

Smith, V. L., Rassenti, S. & Wilson, B. (2001) Turning off the lights, *Regulation*, 24(3), pp. 70–76.

Smith, V. L., Rassenti, S. & Wilson, B. (2002a) Demand side bidding will reduce the level and volatility of electricity prices, *The Independent Review*, 60, pp. 441–445.

Smith, V. L., Rassenti, S. & Wilson, B. (2002b) Using experiments to inform the privatization/deregulation movement in electricity, *Cato Journal*, 21, pp. 514–544.

Smith, V. L., Banks, J., Rassenti, S., Olson, M. & Porter, D. (2003a) An experimental analysis of the Federal Communications Commission's eligibility rules for spectrum auctions, *Journal of Economic Behavior and Organization*, 51, pp. 303–350.

Smith, V. L., Banks, J., Rassenti, S. & Olson, M. & Porter, D. (2003b) Theory, experiment and the FCC spectrum auctions, *Journal of Economic Behavior and Organization*, 51, pp. 303–350.

Smith, V. L., Williams, A., Ledyard, J. & Gjestad, S. (2000) Concurrent trading in two experimental markets with demand interdependence, *Economic Theory*, 16, pp. 511–528.

Walker, J. & Smith, V. L. (1993a) Experimental methods in economics, Inaugural lecture at the Laboratori d'Economia Experimental (LeeX), Universitat Pompeu Fabra, Barcelona, Spain.

Walker, J. & Smith, V. L. (1993b) Monetary rewards and decision cost in experimental economics, *Economic Inquiry*, 31, pp. 245–261.

Walker, J. & Smith, V. L. (1993c) Rewards, experience and decision costs in first price auctions), *Economic Inquiry*, 31, pp. 237–244.

Weg, E. & Smith, V. L. (1993) On the failure to induce meager offers in ultimatum games, *Journal of Economic Psychology*, 14, pp. 17–32.

Williams, A. & Smith, V. L. (1982a) Effect of rent asymmetries in experimental auction markets, *Journal of Economic Behavior and Organization*, pp. 99–116

Williams, A. & Smith, V. L. (1982b) An experimental comparison of alternative rules for competitive market exchange, in: M. Shubik (Ed.) *Auctioning and Bidding*, pp. 307–337 (New York: New York University Press).

Williams, A. & Smith, V. L. (1984) An experimental study of speculation in cyclical markets, *Journal of Business*, 57, pp. 1–33.

Williams, A. & Smith, V. L. (1992) Experimental market economics, *Scientific American*, 267, pp. 116–121.

9　The economic contributions of Paul Sweezy

M. C. Howard and J. E. King

'The Economic Contributions of Paul Sweezy' by M. C. Howard and J. E. King from *Review of Political Economy* (2004), Volume 16, Issue 4 (Taylor and Francis Ltd, http://www.informaworld.com), reprinted by permission of the publisher.

1 Introduction

Perhaps not surprisingly, no Marxist has ever won a Nobel Prize in economics but, of all the Marxian economists in the West who survived into the Nobel era, Paul Sweezy had the strongest grounds for complaint against the Swedish academy. His *Theory of Capitalist Development* (1942) is probably the best book on Marxian economic theory to have appeared since the death of Marx himself; it is lucid, scholarly and, as will be seen, also highly original. Sweezy's second great book, *Monopoly Capital,* written with Paul Baran, is a masterly popularisation of Marxian theory that has been more influential than any other work in radical political economy since it was published in 1966. Do not let the very high quality of his prose deceive you: Paul Sweezy asked deep and disturbing questions on issues that mainstream economists normally shy away from, above all on the connections between micro and macro analysis and the dangerously irrational social consequences of rational individual behaviour in a capitalist society. Had it been awarded, his Nobel Prize would have been very richly deserved.

2 A fortunate life

Paul Marlor Sweezy was born in New York City on 10 April 1910, and died in Larchmont, New York, on 27 February 2004. The son of a Wall Street banker, Sweezy was educated at Philips Exeter Academy and at Harvard University, where he graduated in 1931. 'I was introduced to economics in the late 1920s. I took Ec A in my sophomore year, 1928–1929, and Taussig's advanced theory course (Ec 7 I think it was called) in the following year. What we learned was basically Marshallian theory with a little Austrian capital theory mixed in' (1995b, p. 1). Despite the severity of the Great Depression, none of his teachers made any reference to Marx, or Marxism: 'I do not recall Marx's name, let alone his ideas, ever being mentioned in any of the courses I took as an undergraduate' (1981a, p. 11). He spent the academic year 1932–33 as a graduate student at the London School of Economics, where the faculty, led by Friedrich von Hayek and Lionel Robbins, were even more conservative than their Harvard colleagues. They taught 'a sort of Austrian–Swedish mixture, more distinctive but basically a variant of the bourgeois orthodoxy I had grown up with' (1981a, p. 12). But Sweezy was greatly influenced by Harold Laski, a politics professor and dedicated socialist, and by his fellow graduate students from all social sciences. 'By the time I got back to Cambridge [MA] in '33–'34, I considered myself to be a Marxist' (1999, p. 35).

In the United States, Sweezy found a radically changed political environment. There was now greater interest in Marxism, even at Harvard, where 'discussion groups proliferated, and even a few formal course offerings made their appearance' (1981a, p. 13). Before long Sweezy was teaching a course on socialism with Edward S. Mason and writing his PhD dissertation under the supervision of J. A. Schumpeter, who had joined the Economics department in 1932 and somehow managed to combine ultra-conservatism in politics with great respect for Marx and Marxist ideas (for a discussion of the PhD thesis, see Section 3 below). Schumpeter played an important role in the young Sweezy's academic career. Equally significant was Sweezy's involvement between 1934 and 1942 with Roosevelt's New Deal administration. During several summer vacations he worked for federal government agencies in Washington, including the Temporary National Economic Committee and the Natural Resources Planning Board. Then, on the outbreak of war, Sweezy joined the Research and Analysis Branch of the Office of Strategic Services, the forerunner of the CIA, where Herbert Marcuse was one of his colleagues. Here he had a purely backroom function: 'We did strictly office stuff. The OSS was really the Oh So Social Group' (Lifschultz, 1974, p. 54).

By the end of the war the political pendulum had already swung back a long way to the right, and Sweezy sensed that he was unlikely to be granted tenure at Harvard. He resigned his job and moved to the family farm in New Hampshire, deciding to earn his living as an independent scholar and radical journalist. He obtained a scholarship from the Social Science Research Council and started work on the book that was finally published as *Socialism* (1949a). Sweezy's support for Henry Wallace's 1948 presidential campaign eventually got him into deep water with the powerful McCarthyite forces in his home state. He was subpoenaed by the New Hampshire Attorney-General in 1954 but refused to testify. Three groups had been summonsed, Sweezy said. They were Communists, McCarthyites and, 'Third, those who are not Communists and do not believe they are in danger of being prosecuted, but who yet deeply disapprove of the purposes and methods of these investigations....I belong to this third group' (1954b[2000], p. 38). He declined to take the Fifth Amendment because it would be misinterpreted. Sweezy did agree to answer questions on himself and his ideas on force and violence. 'But I shall respectfully decline to answer questions concerning ideas, beliefs and associations... on the grounds that it [the New Hampshire Subversive Activities Act] violates the First Amendment'. Imprisoned for contempt, Sweezy was released on bail and finally acquitted on appeal, after his case had gone all the way to the Supreme Court (Simon, 2000).

Meanwhile, Sweezy and his friend Leo Huberman had established *Monthly Review,* the independent socialist monthly that he edited from its first issue in May 1949 until his effective retirement in March 1997, when Ellen Meiskins Wood took over as editor. The original finance for the journal came from the literary critic F. O. Matthiessen, and Albert Einstein was the first of a long series of famous contributors that included Aneurin Bevan, Martin Bronfenbrenner, G.D.H. Cole, Basil Davidson, Maurice Dobb, Oskar Lange, Joan Robinson, C.P. Snow, Paolo Sylos Labini and R.H. Tawney. In its early decades, *Monthly Review* was run by 'a sort of informal collective' (1994a, p. 3) that included Paul Baran, before his death in 1964, and Harry Braverman, who died in 1978. In more formal terms, Sweezy's co-editors included Huberman, until his death in 1968, and Harry Magdoff, who also retired in 1997. Initially Huberman handled the business side of the operation and was also responsible for the clarity of the contributors' prose, while Sweezy dealt with editorial correspondence and wrote most of the (jointly-authored) 'Reviews of the Month' (1993b). In 1951, Monthly Review Press was established to provide an outlet for radical writers whose work was being rejected by mainstream publishing houses. Sweezy wrote tirelessly for the journal for almost half a century; appropriately, his final contribution was a sesquicentennial appreciation of the *Communist Manifesto* (1998). The Press published—or in the case of *Theory of Capitalist Development,* republished—all of Sweezy's books, together with many collections of his *Monthly Review* articles.

Although, after his departure from Harvard, Sweezy never again held a full-time university position, he was in constant demand as a guest lecturer. (It was a speech at the University of New Hampshire that incurred the odium of the state authorities there.) He held visiting appointments at Cornell, Stanford and Yale, and in 1971 delivered the prestigious Marshall lectures at the University of Cambridge (they were subsequently published as 1972j). Sweezy's overseas travels also took him to the Soviet Union and Yugoslavia in 1957 and to Cuba in 1960, where, with Leo Huberman, he met Che Guevara and other revolutionary leaders (1993b). In 1974 he visited China, where he spent a month but never managed to meet Mao Tse-Tung (1999, p. 51).

Among the many honours conferred on Sweezy are the Italian Omegna Award in 1966 (1967f), the National Emergency Civil Liberties Committee Tom Paine Award in 1995 (1995a) and the Veblen-Commons Award of the Association for Evolutionary Economics in 1999 (Foster, 1999). Sweezy's last public appearance was in 1998, when he spoke on the *Communist Manifesto* at the Socialist Scholars' Conference. Subsequently, he lived in seclusion at his New Hampshire home, until his death in February 2004. In its April 2000 issue, *Monthly Review* published 90th birthday tributes to Sweezy from Noam

Chomsky, John Kenneth Galbraith and Pete Seeger, among many others (Symposium, 2000).

3 Before Marx

Sweezy often claimed to have returned from England, in late 1934, as a Marxist. There is, however, very little evidence of it in his earliest writings. His first publication was a lengthy review of A. C. Pigou's *Theory of Unemployment,* in which he corrects Pigou's algebra at some length and endorses his argument that unemployment is the result of wage-earners demanding real wages above their equilibrium level (1934, p. 807). This is a quintessentially neoclassical—or, as Keynes would soon christen it, 'classical'—analysis of unemployment. But Sweezy soon changed his mind on this issue, and by 1938 he was a convinced Keynesian. As he later recalled, the *second* depression, in 1937–38, came as an even greater surprise to economists than the 'Great' Depression of 1929–33: 'no-one had expected it, and no-one had a plausible explanation' (1995a, p. 2). Young economists at Harvard and Tufts held a series of informal meetings to discuss alternative policy responses. The result was a tract entitled *An Economic Program for American Democracy* (1938), which was published under the names of Sweezy and six others and proved to be a best-seller, at least in Washington (May 1981, pp. 146–149). Sweezy and his co-authors called for a sustained increase in federal government expenditure, continuing budget deficits, and public ownership of utilities and railroads. Their arguments represent an ambitious application to the United States economy of Keynes's policy proposals in the *General Theory,* and were not in any sense Marxist. However, as Sweezy subsequently noted, 'It was hard to draw the line in those days between the left New Dealers and the beginnings of the Marxist movement' (1999, p. 38), and there was broad support at the time for collaboration between the two groups.

Sweezy was by now deeply dissatisfied with neoclassical theory, and he was especially critical of his own 1934 position on unemployment. At the December 1937 meeting of the American Economic Association in Atlantic City he spoke at a round-table discussion on 'Wage policies', making the first recorded public presentation of the kinked demand curve model of price stability under oligopoly. (This was implicit in Richard Kahn's 1929 dissertation on the economics of the short-period, which was published 60 years later, and Kahn had actually drawn the diagram in 1933 (Kahn, 1933, 1989).) If each oligopolist expects competitors to match a price cut, but to ignore a price increase, the expected elasticity of demand will be much greater upwards than downwards from the existing price. This, Sweezy demonstrates, introduces a kink into the demand, or average revenue, curve. More important, it gives rise to a vertical discontinuity in the firm's marginal revenue function and hence a discontinuity also in its marginal revenue product of labour curve, although Sweezy does not use the term. In these circumstances, a wage cut 'will be accompanied by no increase in employment at all, or, in so far as the employers are more prone to saving than the workers, the effect will tend to be adverse' (1938d, p. 156). Changes in employment, Sweezy concludes, come from shifts in demand curves, not from shifts in cost curves. This fundamentally Keynesian position was supported from the platform by Lorie Tarshis and from the floor by his old friend from the LSE, Abba Lerner.

There are no diagrams in the (very short) 1938 article, but Sweezy provided one, and developed his argument in greater depth, in a celebrated paper in the *Journal of Political Economy* in the following year. Here he attributes the notion of an 'imagined demand curve' to another of his LSE friends, Nicholas Kaldor. Sweezy's conclusions are even more forthright than before: 'a successful strike for higher wages may be without influence on either price or output. Trade-unionists who believe that the only effect of higher wages is lower profits may have more truth on their side than economists have been willing to grant' (1939c, p. 570). For several decades the kinked demand curve was a staple of mainstream microeconomic textbooks (although normally without any endorsement of militant trade unionism). As Sweezy conceded at the time, his analysis had nothing to contribute on the question of how the oligopolist's stable price is arrived at in the first place. His article was savaged by the Chicago theorist George Stigler (1947), who was particularly critical of Sweezy's conclusion that the conventional concept of equilibrium had little or no meaning in oligopoly (1939, pp. 572–573). Sweezy himself eventually concluded that collusive models offer a more realistic solution to the problem of oligopoly pricing than his non-collusive interpretation, rather contentiously attributing this point to Stigler. 'I think the criticism was quite justified', he wrote, some 40 years later, 'and Baran and I took it into account (without mentioning either the kinked curve or Stigler) in the section on pricing in *Monopoly Capital* (pp. 57–64) where we concluded that in general oligopoly would lead to an approximation of the "true" monopoly price' (Paul M. Sweezy to Frederic S. Lee, 11 June 1980).

In 1938, Harvard University Press published Sweezy's doctoral dissertation, *Monopoly and Competition in the English Coal Trade, 1550–1850* (1938a), which we discuss in Section 6 below. In the following year the Natural Resources Committee published his long, descriptive account of interest groups in the American economy (1939b). The Committee was 'a characteristically New Deal agency which would be unthinkable in the Washington of today' (1953a, p. 158), and Sweezy's paper documents the interlocking directorships that united leading American capitalists into eight large and extremely powerful groups, themselves interconnected through minority shareholdings and shared directorships. He concludes that the evidence clearly demonstrates 'the degree of concentration of economic leadership in the hands of a few' (1939b [1953a], p. 188). It was a theme that was central to his first major published work, three years later.

4 The theory of capitalist development

As Sweezy acknowledged in his preface to the 1956 reprint of *The Theory of Capitalist Development*, he owed the title of the book (and much more) to

Joseph Schumpeter, with whom he had taught a course on socialist economics at Harvard before the war. The book is divided into four parts, three of them dedicated to exposition of the ideas of Marx and some of his followers, and the fourth containing Sweezy's own original analysis of what he terms 'Imperialism' (that is, the monopoly stage of capitalist development). Part I, 'Value and Surplus Value', begins with a very clear account of Marx's method, concentrating on his use of abstraction and the historical character of his thought (Chapter I), while Chapters II and III deal respectively with the 'Qualitative-Value Problem' and the 'Quantitative-Value Problem'. Here Sweezy draws on an important but obscure work by a little-known Austrian Marxist, Franz Petry (1916), who emphasised the significance of Marx's distinction between these two problems. The qualitative problem, Sweezy explains, concerns the relations between producers, while the quantitative problems concern the relations between their products. The distinction, he notes, is often difficult to grasp for those brought up in the neoclassical tradition (1942a, p. 15). As we shall see in Section 7, it also poses serious difficulties for Marxians.

The chapter on the qualitative problem sets out with great lucidity the issues examined by Marx in the notoriously abstruse early sections of Volume I of *Capital,* including the concepts of abstract labour and the fetishism of commodities. The chapter on the quantitative problem isolates several important issues relevant to the determination of relative exchange values, including the role of competition and demand and the precise meaning of 'the law of value'. Part I concludes with a brief elaboration of Marx's theory of surplus value, profit and the rate of profit (Chapter IV).

Part II (Chapters V–VII) has the title, 'The Accumulation Process'. It deals with Marx's analysis of simple and expanded reproduction, concentrating on the formation and constant replenishment of a 'reserve army' of the unemployed (Chapter V); the tendency for the rate of profit to decline (Chapter VI); and the transformation of values into prices of production (Chapter VII). Sweezy strongly endorses Marx's analysis of the reserve army but is highly critical of the falling rate of profit theory, which he describes as 'not very convincing' (p. 104), since Marx does not satisfactorily explain why the organic composition of capital will normally increase more rapidly than the rate of exploitation. Quite apart from the 'counteracting tendencies' that Marx himself identified, Sweezy points (pp. 107–108) to four other factors tending to increase the rate of profit (employers' organisations, export of capital, formation of monopolies, and state action designed to benefit capital). These are partially offset by two tendencies working in the opposite direction (trade unions and state action designed to benefit labour).

If competitive forces establish a strong tendency for the rate of profit to be equal in every industry, the resulting 'prices of production' will differ systematically from labour values. The resulting 'transformation problem' is the subject of Chapter VII. Sweezy presents the solution offered by Marx in Volume III of *Capital,* but concludes that it is 'logically unsatisfactory' because it violates the conditions for simple reproduction. He provides an alternative solution based on the work of Ladislaus von Bortkiewicz (1907), which is not subject to this criticism; we shall return to Bortkiewicz in Section 6 below, but simply note here that this was the first time that this important article had been summarised in English. At the end of Chapter VII Sweezy raises a question that remains contentious today: 'The real world is one of price calculations; why not deal in price terms from the outset?' (1942a, p. 128). His answer begins provocatively: 'A Marxist can safely concede something to this point of view' since, for purely quantitative purposes, 'value calculation is of little assistance'. However, this does not dispose of the qualitative problem: 'value calculation makes it possible to look beneath the surface phenomena of money and commodities to the underlying relations between people and classes', while price calculation 'mystifies the underlying social relations of capitalist production' (p. 129). Thus, Sweezy concludes, 'there is no way of dispensing with value calculation and the labour theory of value on which it is based' (p. 131). In the 1960s and 1970s, however, some of Sweezy's Marxian critics would accuse him of doing precisely that.

The third part of the book (Chapters VIII–XII) deals with 'Crises and Depressions'. Sweezy begins by outlining Marx's position that Say's Law is logically false in any commodity-producing (money-using) economy, and dangerously false in capitalism. This leads him to distinguish two types of crisis. The first assumes that Say's Law does apply, so that all commodities sell at their values (or at their prices of production; the transformation problem is not relevant to this issue); crises occur as a result of the tendency for the rate of profit to fall. The second type of crisis occurs when capitalists are not able, in aggregate, to 'realise' in the form of money profits all the surplus value contained in their commodities, so that Say's Law does not prevail. Sweezy discusses the first type of crisis in the very short Chapter IX. He finds it rather uninteresting. To drop the assumption of Say's Law, on the other hand, 'is to open up a new range of possibilities' in which—to use contemporary terms—economic crises are the effect and not the cause of a shortage of effective demand (p. 155). In Chapter X, Sweezy identifies two categories of these 'realisation crises', those due to disproportionality between the different branches of production, as emphasised by M. I. Tugan-Baranovsky, and those resulting from underconsumption. Disproportionality crises are entirely possible, Sweezy concedes, but like Marx he regards them as being of 'secondary importance' (p. 161). The bulk of the chapter is thus devoted to crises arising from underconsumption. In Marx's words, 'The last cause of all real crises always remains the poverty and restricted consumption of the masses as compared to the tendency of capitalist production to develop the productive forces in such a way that only the absolute power of consumption of the entire society would be their limit' (p. 177).

This was to be the *leitmotiv* of Sweezy's entire analysis, in *The Theory of Capitalist Development*, in *Monopoly Capital*, and in everything that followed. In Chapter X he develops the argument by means of a detailed analysis of Marx's reproduction models, as found in Volume II of *Capital* (supplemented by an Appendix written by Shigeto Tsuru). Sweezy concludes the chapter by setting out a mathematical model of underconsumption derived from the work of the Austro-Marxist Otto Bauer (1942a, pp. 187–189; cf. Bauer, 1936). Chapter XI consists of a blow-by-blow account of the 'Breakdown Controversy' in post-1883 Marxian political economy, from Eduard Bernstein to Henryk Grossmann (see Section 6 below). Chapter XII has the stark title, 'Chronic Depression?'. Given the tendency towards underconsumption that is inherent in capitalism, Sweezy asks, what might offset it? 'Generally speaking', he responds,

> the counteracting forces may be grouped together into two main categories: those which have the effect of raising the rate of growth of consumption relative to the rate of growth of means of production, and those which deprive a disproportionate growth in means of production of its economically disruptive consequences. In the latter category fall (1) new industries, and (2) faulty investment; in the former, (3) population growth, (4) unproductive consumption, and (5) state expenditures.
>
> (1942a, pp. 217–18)

The first three have been weakening, he suggests, while the fourth and fifth have been growing stronger. Must underconsumption triumph? Before this question can be answered, Sweezy maintains, a less abstract model must be constructed, which complements Marx's analysis of the accumulation process with a detailed and historically specific study of the state, monopoly, and the world economy.

This task is undertaken in Part IV (Chapters XIII–XIX), which has the slightly misleading heading of 'Imperialism'; here Sweezy follows Lenin in using the term to denote the 'highest', that is the most recent, stage of capitalism, which is characterised by the growth of monopoly, the export of capital and the increasing influence of the nation-state. He begins (Chapter XIII) with the state, asserting as a general principle that 'the state comes into action in the economic sphere in order to solve problems which are posed by the development of capitalism' (p. 249). In the early twentieth century these problems emanated from the increasing concentration and centralisation of capital, the rise of the large corporation, and the growth of cartels, trusts and mergers; in short, from 'The Development of Monopoly Capital' (chapter XIV).

How, then, does monopoly affect the laws of motion of capital? Sweezy identifies several important changes. First, there are consequences for the law of value, since '[u]nder conditions of monopoly, exchange ratios do not conform to labor-time ratios, nor do they stand in a theoretically demonstrable relation to labor-time ratios as is the case with prices of production' (p. 270). Second, while there can be no *general* theory of monopoly price, it is true that the higher profit rates obtained by monopolists come at the expense of competitive capitalists, so long as trade unions are able to protect real wages and prevent monopolists from benefiting at the expense of the working class (pp. 272–273). Third, monopoly tends to reduce the rate of capital accumulation 'in two ways: because output is restricted in the interest of maintaining the maximum possible overall profit rate; and because the rate of introduction of technological innovations is consciously regulated in such a way as to minimize the need for new capital' (p. 277). Fourth, if monopolists are in fact able to reduce real wages, the underlying tendency towards underconsumption is strengthened. Finally, monopoly is associated with a huge increase in selling costs, by comparison with competitive capitalism. There is an 'enormous development of the arts of salesmanship and advertising' (p. 282), which increases consumption out of the wages of unproductive workers and therefore constitutes 'a powerful counteracting force to the tendency for underconsumption' (p, 283). This process, Sweezy observes, involves the growth of 'socially unnecessary and hence wasteful' activities (p. 286).

In Chapter XVI, 'The World Economy', he brings the state back into the picture. With the rise of monopoly capital there has come 'a complete transformation of the character of economic policy', with free trade giving way to protection and a new aggressive colonial policy 'designed to corner valuable sources of raw materials, extend the scope of protected markets, and guarantee profitable investment outlets for exported capital' (p. 306). Sweezy's discussion of imperialism proper (Chapter XVII) emphasises its political consequences, which include growing nationalism, militarism and racism; intensified class conflict; greatly increased state intervention in the economy; and periodic world wars of imperial redivision. The limits of imperialism are again political. They are imposed by mounting opposition from the working class in the metropolitan capitalist countries and from national resistance movements in the colonies. Here Sweezy follows Lenin (1917) very closely, and even cites Stalin approvingly at one point (1942a, 325n).

His analysis of Fascism (Chapter XVIII) treats it as 'one form which imperialism assumes in the age of wars of redivision' (p. 329). It is neither a form of state capitalism, as Sweezy himself had once mistakenly suggested (see 1941a) nor does it represent one version of 'managerial society', as claimed by James Burnham (1941). Fascism is simply a new variant of capitalism, in which '[t]he expanding functions of the state and the centralization of capital meet in what might be described as a formal marriage between the state and monopoly capital' (p. 370). This unlikely union is not, however, able to overcome the economic contradictions of capitalism.

Although he is sceptical of the possibility of liberal capitalist reform, Sweezy ends the book by taking issue with Stalin on the crucial question of an 'inevitable clash' between the rival socialist and imperialist systems. He ends on an optimistic note. It is at least possible that socialist ideas will win over the great mass of the population in the advanced capitalist countries, rendering the old order impotent, so that 'democracy may at long last be able to fulfil the promises which have so far remained unhonored amid the frustrations of a self-contradictory economic system' (p. 362).

Sweezy's taxonomy of capitalist crises was a major contribution, informing much subsequent work in this important area. The crucial distinction between difficulties arising in the production of surplus value and those associated with its realisation had never been made as clearly as this. Slightly amended,

Sweezy's categorisation of crises formed the basis (for example) of Weisskopf's seminal analysis of fluctuations in the profitability of US capital in the three decades after 1945, where underconsumption (realisation problems), increasing organic composition of capital and falling rate of exploitation (production problems) are distinguished (Weisskopf, 1979). Sweezy's followers continue to employ his taxonomy, sometimes rather mischievously describing the opponents of realisation theories of crisis as 'supply-side Marxists' (Foster, 1986, pp. 11–16).

On the 50th anniversary of publication Sweezy noted that *The Theory of Capitalist Development* had been 'translated into many languages (German, French, Italian, Spanish, Polish, Serbo-Croat, Japanese, Chinese, among others)…[and] the Monthly Review Press edition still has a steady sale, mostly for classroom use' (1992c, p. 14). Many of those who paid tribute to Sweezy on his 90th birthday, eight years later, made special reference to it, including Samir Amin, Doug Dowd, Richard du Boff, Martha Giminez, Edward Herman (who described it as 'the clearest and most compelling exposition of Marxist thought I had ever read'—Symposium, 2000, p. 53), Lukin Robinson, William Tabb ('after more than half a century, it remains the best introduction to Marxism'— p. 58) and Shigeto Tsuru. Sweezy was never tempted to produce a revised second edition. 'In that respect I sort of agree with Schumpeter, who once said that books are like children, and when they leave home you cannot fool with them any more. They have a life of their own' (1999, p. 39; cf. 1942a [1956], p. ix). But the book did have a much younger half-brother, as we shall see in Section 7.

5 Sweezy on socialism

Down to about 1960 Sweezy could best be described as an independent Stalinist, in the sense that he was a firm supporter of the Soviet Union but never a member of the US Communist Party, which always repelled him with its 'extreme dogmatism in an intellectual sense. I knew that was death to your independent thinking' (1999, p. 37). As the title suggests, *The Theory of Capitalist Development* is about capitalism. His second book, written for McGraw-Hill's 'Economics Handbooks' series, has a one-word title: *Socialism* (1949a). Its analysis of the Soviet Union (Chapter 2) and Poland (Chapter 4) is entirely uncritical, and Sweezy draws upon the pro-Soviet writings of Sidney and Beatrice Webb to assert 'the capacity of socialism to invoke an enthusiastic response from the mass of the workers and the relative unimportance of the profit motive under modern conditions of large-scale industry' (p. 219). He defends the rationality of economic planning against 'the Viennese school of Anti-Socialism' (Chapter 11), and concludes that socialism is entirely consistent both with the maintenance of existing civil liberties and with the development of new freedoms (Chapter 12).

It is, to repeat, Stalin's non-market, planned economy version of socialism that Sweezy is defending. He is much less enthusiastic about contemporary

Fabian and market socialist ideas. Reviewing the jubilee edition of *Fabian Essays,* he objects that 'while Marxists have always been fully aware that socialism must be a centrally planned society, British socialist thought, following in the footsteps of the Fabians (and somewhat later of the Guild Socialists, who in this aspect showed a close affinity to the Fabians), has always been vague and obscure on this crucially important question' (1949f [1953a], p. 329). Although he welcomes Oskar Lange's critique of the Mises–Hayek–Robbins position, that efficient resource allocation is in principle impossible under socialism, Sweezy is much less happy with Lange's positive proposals. 'The truth is', he objects, 'that Lange's Board is not a *planning* agency at all but rather a *price-fixing* agency; in his model production decisions are left to a myriad of essentially independent units, just as they are under capitalism'. And this is unsatisfactory. 'Such a system is certainly conceivable, but most socialists will probably feel that it reproduces some of the worst features of capitalism and fails to take advantage of the constructive possibilities of economic planning' (1949a, p. 233, original stress; cf. 1938e, where Sweezy reviews Lange but manages to evade this question altogether).

Sweezy later expressed considerable dissatisfaction with *Socialism,* which 'took a very simplistic view of the problems of socialism and socialist planning' (1999, p. 40), and he refused to allow it to be reprinted. This seems to reflect literary more than political self-criticism, for he continued for many years to defend the Stalinist model of socialism against its social democratic and market socialist challengers. He was always sceptical of the supposed advantages of Yugoslav self-management, which he believed 'to defy the logic of modern technological and managerial methods' (1958d, p. 369). But in the late 1950s he did at least show some sympathy for what the Tito regime was trying to achieve. Self-management might be more appropriate to a more highly-developed country, Sweezy concluded. 'The Yugoslavs may have introduced their system too early to realize its full benefits' (p. 374). Ten years later, Sweezy took a very much harder line against the Prague Spring. While opposing the Soviet invasion of Czechoslovakia, he was convinced that the country had been moving in the direction of capitalism. 'The very term "market socialism" is self-contradictory', he suggested, just like the phenomenon itself. 'And it is precisely this inner contradiction which impels the market socialist societies towards capitalism' (1968g, pp. 7–8n). Neither in Czechoslovakia nor in Yugoslavia was this the reformers' intention. But 'whoever acts to strengthen the market instead of struggling against it is, regardless of intentions, promoting capitalism and not socialism' (p. 11).

By this time the breach between China and the Soviet Union had provoked a profound shift in Sweezy's thinking. He took the Maoist side in the schism, and was forced to reconsider his attitude to the entire Soviet experience. In 1967, looking back on the first half-century of the Soviet Union with Leo Huberman, he described it as 'a stratified society, with a deep chasm between the ruling stratum of political bureaucrats and economic managers on the one side and the mass of working people on the other, and an impressive spectrum of income and status differentials on both sides of the chasm' (1967e [1980a], p. 20). It was a stagnant society, showing clear signs of impending crisis (1968g, pp. 12–16). Sweezy is now prepared to criticise Stalin himself, whom he faults for giving too many privileges to the bureaucracy, placing insufficient faith in the masses, and allowing far too little inner-party democracy (1967e[1980a], p. 31). He notes that the inequalities in Soviet society are continually increasing, so that there is the very real prospect that the ruling 'stratum' will congeal into a genuine ruling class (p. 27).

By 1977 Sweezy was convinced that this had occurred and declared, in a broadly favourable review of the French Maoist Charles Bettelheim's work on class struggle in post-revolutionary Russia, that 'the Soviet Union today is a society with a new ruling class ("state bourgeoisie")' (1977g [1980a], p. 111). But Sweezy continued to reject both the Trotskyist position, that there can be no class society without private ownership of the means of production, and the official Chinese line, that the Soviet Union represented a form of state capitalism. Sweezy's own conclusion is now that 'proletarian revolution can give rise to a new form of society, neither capitalist nor socialist' but no less divided on class lines (1980a, p. 138). Hence he puts the term 'state bourgeoisie' in inverted commas, and repudiates the very notion of 'state capitalism' as a source of potential confusion. Soviet Russia was a class society, but not a capitalist one. The rulers' power came not from ownership of wealth but from control over the state apparatus, 'and hence over total social capital'. The USSR 'had none of the economic laws of motion comparable to those of capitalism' (1999, p. 53).

This is an entirely defensible position, though it leaves some important questions unanswered. First, how can socialism result from revolutions that are clearly *non*-proletarian in nature, as in China and then in Cuba? Second, what were the prospects for the new class societies of the Soviet Union and Eastern Europe, assuming that the working class had been so repressed and demoralised that a genuinely socialist revolution was no longer to be hoped for? Sweezy never really confronted the first question, always remaining a loyal supporter of Mao and interpreting the Cultural Revolution as 'a struggle between the capitalist roaders and the socialist roaders, and the capitalist roaders won the battle. I don't think there's anything else to it, really' (1999, p. 50). But the new capitalist development in China was very unstable, rendering the country 'vulnerable to internal crises and external shocks. Marx's "absolute general law of capitalist accumulation" seems to be operating at full throttle' (1994b, p. 18).

By 1990, Sweezy's enthusiasm for the Cuban revolution had also faded, and he attacked the island's political system as 'a variant of *caudillismo*' (1990f, p. 19), by which he meant that it was not democratic, and not moving that way, despite the many improvements in social conditions that the Castro regime could claim credit for. Whether there were objective, structural reasons for the degeneration of the Cuban revolution Sweezy does not say (see 1967 [1980a], pp. 27–30, for his views on the relative importance of voluntarism and determinism in post-revolutionary societies).

As for the second question, Sweezy claimed with some justice to have pre-dicted the eventual disintegration of the Soviet Union (1991c, p. xx), having concluded his 1980 book on *Post-Revolutionary Society* with the following prognosis:

> It would perhaps be too much to say that post-revolutionary society, as represented by its oldest and most advanced exemplar, has reached a dead end. But at least one can say that it seems to have entered a period of stag-nation, different from the stagflation of the advanced capitalist world but showing no more visible signs of a way out.
>
> (1980a, pp. 150–151)

There was a material basis for this stagnation, but it was also the consequence of mistaken political decisions. The economic crisis of the Soviet Union was the result of 'the exhaustion of the model of *extensive* industrialization adopted by Stalin in the late 1920s', which relied too heavily on increased labour power and raw materials and made increasingly inefficient use of them (1991c, p. 3; ori-ginal stress). Gorbachov's reforms simply threw the economy into great confu-sion (on Sweezy's reactions to *perestroika,* see 1990a, 1990b).

There is just a hint, in Sweezy's final writings on socialism, of a historical materialist critique of the entire Stalinist experience and even of Marx's claim that a socialist economy without markets is both necessary and feasible. Thus he now acknowledged that markets are necessary in socialism (though they need to be controlled), and accepted that democracy is also essential. On the other hand he continued to find Stalin an attractive historical figure; asked about an editorial in *Monthly Review* describing him as 'one of the greatest men in history', Sweezy replied: "Well, in some ways he was, but he had his underside, too' (1999, p. 51). Thus, Sweezy failed fully to come to terms with the collapse of 'actually existing socialism'. But in this, of course, he was by no means alone.

6 Historian of events and ideas

Sweezy's first important contribution to economic history was made in his doc-toral dissertation, 'The Limitation of the Vend', which was published in 1938 as *Monopoly and Competition in the English Coal Trade 1550–1850*. ('The Vend' was the name given to the cartel of coal producers in the Durham and Northum-berland coalfield). In addition to a very scholarly history of attempts to fix coal prices over three centuries, Sweezy assesses the implications of this episode in economic history for both the theory of price competition and for what he describes as 'the larger problem of the relation of monopoly and competition to capitalist development as a whole' (1938a, p. 146). His conclusion foreshadows not only the immediate course of world history, but also his own life's work:

> Fostering of monopoly at home and the autarchic [*sic*] policies which necessarily accompany preparations for expansion abroad serve further to

contract markets and outlets for investment. More monopoly, more autarchy, more imperialist expansion follow each other in an endless chain, interrupted by an occasional extraneous link which misleads only the unwary. A new world war, which it is difficult to imagine that the capitalist system will survive, is the only conclusion to which one can logically look forward.

(pp. 149–150)

Sweezy's next contribution came on the much broader question of the transition from feudalism to capitalism in Western Europe. Here Sweezy emphasised the importance of the expanded world market that resulted from the discovery and colonisation of the Americas. It was the growth of demand, he argued, that loosened the barriers that feudal economic relations imposed upon the development of the productive forces and stimulated the development of capitalist relations in their place (1950f, 1953g). Maurice Dobb rejected this interpretation, pointing out that, in other circumstances, the growth of the market could have quite different consequences. In Eastern Europe, for example, a rising demand for grain in the early modern period led to an intensification of feudal exploitation in what is sometimes referred to as the 'second feudalism'. Like Marx, Dobb maintained that the effects of expanding markets differed, depending on the nature of the social relations of production in the regions affected by it; production, not consumption, played the dominant role. The debate between Sweezy and Dobb attracted a considerable amount of attention in the early 1950s, and again in the 1970s when Robert Brenner attacked both theorists, but especially Sweezy, for exaggerating the importance of the market in the emergence of the capitalist mode of production (the contributions of Sweezy and Dobb are reprinted, with critical commentaries, in Hilton, 1976; see also Brenner, 1977). Sweezy's position on this issue was the furthest removed from that of Marx, and perhaps also the furthest from the truth. But the discussion that his work provoked was a very fruitful one.

Sweezy also took a distinctive position on the historical development of capitalism after 1890 in the United States and—by implication—in the world as a whole. He was strongly critical of the Hilferding–Lenin periodisation, according to which the latest stage of capitalism was marked by the dominance of financial capital Hilferding (1910) referred to this as the era of 'finance capital', while Lenin (1916) used the term 'imperialism' to mean much the same thing. For Sweezy it is the growth of monopoly that is critical, not the increased power of financiers, who were never as influential in the United States (or much of Western Europe) as the Hilferding–Lenin conception implied. The rise of monopoly capital, Sweezy claims, led to fundamental changes in the laws of motion of US capitalism, with underconsumption taking over from the falling rate of profit as the basic contradiction of the system. The latter, he suggests, was historically specific to the early nineteenth-century transition from 'manufacture' to 'modern industry', in which mechanisation and the factory system replaced handicraft production located in small workshops and the organic composition of capital really did increase rapidly while competition prevented profit margins from rising. Once the giant corporation began to supplant the small competitive firm, Marx's Volume III analysis of the profit rate lost much of its explanatory power, to be replaced (as we shall see in Section 7) by a new 'law of the rising surplus'. The tendency for the rate of profit to fall, Sweezy concludes, is historically specific to the transition from manufacture to modern industry, and had thus largely worked itself out by the end of the nineteenth century (1966a, Chapter 8; 1981a, pp. 51–52; 1994b, p. 17).

This historical analysis of the evolution of US capitalism proved very influential, both in North America and elsewhere. The French regulation school interpreted the history of twentieth-century European capitalism in a very similar way (Aglietta, 1979), and the 'social structure of accumulation' theorists in the United States also made extensive use of Sweezy's arguments (Bowles *et al.,* 1984). The emergence of monopoly capital was central to the efforts of labour process theorists in explaining long-run changes in the nature of work, the structure of the working class and the nature (and relative absence) of class conflict after 1890 (Edwards, 1979). Somewhat ironically, Sweezy's arguments led him to exactly the same conclusions that Hilferding and (especially) Lenin had reached by a quite different route: capitalism is decadent, prone to stagnation, and dangerously militaristic. His historical periodisation is, like theirs, rather suspect; at the very least, it is open to the objection that 'monopoly capital' itself has a finite life span, which was effectively ended with the second era of globalisation, and ferocious international competition, that began around 1970 (see Sections 7 and 8 below). As a theory of economic history, though, it was undeniably important in its day.

Although he is not generally thought of as an historian of economic thought, Sweezy had the history of ideas 'in his bones', to paraphrase Joan Robinson (1953, p. 20). That is to say, his automatic reaction when discussing a theoretical issue was to go back to the original sources. This is particularly obvious in his writings on Marx, but goes far beyond them. Sweezy was, in fact, a major historian of post-1883 Marxian political economy. *The Theory of Capitalist Development* is easily the most authoritative text of its kind in English, even today, and it was especially valuable when it first appeared, given that most of the German-language literature on value, distribution, accumulation and crises was unknown in Britain and the United States. Sweezy's erudition is most apparent in Chapter XI, on the 'Breakdown controversy', but it pervades the entire book, from the repeated references to Mikhail Tugan-Baranovsky on the nature of capitalist crisis through to the discussion of the transformation of values into prices of production (e.g. 1942a, 158–173, 115–125). His own analysis of the laws of motion of monopoly capital is deduced from his sympathetic critique of many Marxian predecessors, while his formal model of underconsumption is a modification of that first set out by Otto Bauer (1936). None of Sweezy's contemporaries knew as much, or cared as much, about these writers. Maurice Dobb, for example, who was a scholar of great learning and breadth of vision, barely hints at their work in his own influential *Political Economy and Capitalism* (Dobb, 1937).

Among Sweezy's most important contributions was his edition of classic texts on the transformation problem, which brought together translations of Böhm–Bawerk, Hilferding and the (then) little-known Ladislaus von Bortkiewicz, whose critique of Marx was to dominate scholarly controversy on the labour theory of value for the next three decades (1949a; Howard & King, 1992, Chapter 12). Sweezy was also an enthusiast for the ideas of Rosa Luxemburg at a time when her brand of Marxian underconsumption theory was deeply unfashionable (1951f), and wrote a detailed and careful account of the failure of Marxian economic theory to take root in the United States (1952a). He was less interested in the history of bourgeois economic thought (contrasting with Dobb in this respect also). But he did write at some length, and with considerable sympathy, on those few non-Marxian theorists whom he believed to have anticipated his own approach to the theory of monopoly capital. They included Thorstein Veblen, towards whom Sweezy was more favourable in his later assessments than he had been earlier on (compare 1946b and 1958e); John Maynard Keynes, for Sweezy a quintessentially honest but short-sighted bourgeois economist (1946h, 1963a, 1981e, 1983a); and his old teacher, Joseph Schumpeter (1946a, 1951a). He never showed any interest in the institutionalists (apart from Veblen), in the emergence of a neoclassical-Keynesian synthesis, or in the rise of neo-Schumpeterian evolutionary economics. A more serious deficiency, perhaps, is Sweezy's lack of interest in developments in Marxian economics (other than his own) after 1939. This allowed him to maintain a sensible distance from the sectarian infighting that often disfigured such debates, but it also meant that he wrote little or nothing by way of criticism of Marxian crisis theories other than his own. And, apart from a few critical asides in the 1970s (1970d, 19711), he also largely ignored developments in mainstream economic theory in the second half of the twentieth century.

7 Monopoly capital

Sweezy's *Theory of Capitalist Development* was published at the height of the Second World War, and while it was described in the *American Economic Review* as 'a work of outstanding merit' (Bober, 1943, p. 386) it had little immediate impact. He himself left full-time academic life in 1946, never to return. His mathematical model of underconsumption, however, did receive critical attention from Evsey Domar (1948) and from Y. Yoshida, whose criticisms Sweezy very largely accepted (1950c[1953a], pp. 352–360). A decade later the model was dissected by N. Georgescu-Roegen (1960), in a rare example of a Marxian theme gracing the austere columns of *Econometrica*.

After 1945, Sweezy wrote on some important broader issues relevant to the book, highlighting the role of armaments expenditure in preventing a postwar recession and—in the longer term—staving off the forces of stagnation (1953a, pp. 364–369). He returned to this question in a review of Josef Steindl's *Maturity and Stagnation in American Capitalism* (Steindl, 1952). Steindl approached the question from a Marxian (or, more precisely, a Kaleckian) viewpoint, focusing exclusively on the growth of monopoly as the cause of a chronic tendency towards over-saving, relative to investment, in the United States after 1850. Sweezy objects that this is a mistake, not least because it leads Steindl to overlook the exogenous factors that had stimulated growth in the previous century, above all the First World War and the construction of railways. Similar historical accidents, Sweezy concludes, are now most unlikely: 'Can one even conceive of a single new industry having a similar *relative* importance as an outlet for investment today?" (1954f, p. 532n). Nonetheless, he showed considerable sympathy for the underlying analysis. Now Steindl was a disciple of Michal Kalecki, who came to New York in 1946 to work for the United Nations and was a regular visitor to the *Monthly Review* offices in the early 1950s, even though, as an international public servant, he was unable to publish in the journal. Kalecki was another important postwar influence on Sweezy, not least because his probing but rather pragmatic approach to political economy allowed him to merge Marx and Keynes without any hint of Hegel or any direct reference to the labour theory of value.

By far the most important of Sweezy's collaborators, however, was Paul Baran, an émigré Russian Marxist who came to the United States in 1939 via Moscow and Frankfurt. Sweezy first met Baran in the same year at Harvard, where he arrived with a letter of recommendation from Oskar Lange (1999, p. 45). After 1949, Baran was part of the 'informal editorial collective' that ran *Monthly Review,* even though he was now based 3000 miles from New York, at Stanford University. Monthly Review Press published his *Political Economy of Growth* (Baran, 1957), and a handful of his articles appeared in the journal prior to the blockbuster pieces in their joint names that announced the impending arrival of *Monopoly Capital.*

It would be quite wrong to see Sweezy as the pupil and Baran the teacher; indeed, to some extent the reverse was the case. But Baran did bring something of his own to the project. First and foremost, the concept of the economic surplus was his, not Sweezy's. Broader and more flexible than the orthodox Marxian notion of surplus value, the surplus was defined as 'the difference between what a society produces and the costs of producing it' (1966a [1968], p. 23). This permitted a distinction to be drawn between the actual and the potential surplus, the latter reflecting the reality of a wasteful capitalist economy in which more could be produced, at lower cost—and would be, under socialism (Baran 1957 [1973], pp. 133–134). This *critical* element in Baran's economic analysis came from his time with the Frankfurt School (Jacoby, 1982), which also encouraged him to place a much greater emphasis on the ideological and cultural dimensions of the capitalist mode of production than Sweezy had ever done. This was Baran's second vital contribution. The final 80 pages of *Monopoly Capital,* dealing with alienation, the joylessness of leisure, and the decay of education, religious belief and family life (1964a, Chapters 10–11), are testimony to this profoundly non-economistic aspect of Baran's thought.

Third, and again perhaps linked to his background in German critical theory, Baran had a focus on the Third World that was much sharper than anything to be found in *The Theory of Capitalist Development*. The backward areas of the world had become so, he argued in *The Political Economy of Growth*, as a result of the systematic extraction of their economic surplus by the advanced, metropolitan capitalist core. This explained both the passivity of the working class in the United States, who had been bought off by a small share in the proceeds of imperialism, and the revolutionary potential of the proletarian and (especially) the peasant masses in the colonial and ex-colonial territories, who really did have 'nothing to lose but their chains'. It also gave the world as a whole a revolutionary subject, which was palpably lacking in Sweezy's earlier work. Finally, Baran had a more fully developed analysis of the capitalist state than Sweezy had been able to produce. His long article on 'National Economic Planning' (Baran, 1952) foreshadows many of the arguments which were to be central to *Monopoly Capital*.

Paul Baran died suddenly in March 1964, with the manuscript substantially complete but the authors still attempting to resolve disagreements over two chapters (on the labour process, and the market for labour power; neither was included in the published version). It appeared early in 1966, with only the briefest of references to the role of unions in wage determination (1966a, pp. 84–86). In addition to Baran's specific contributions, noted above, there are other evident influences on *Monopoly Capital*. One is American institutionalism, most notably the classic work of Berle & Means (1932) on the giant corporation, which is largely immune from competitive pressures, administering its own prices rather than bowing to the dictates of the product market and securing a considerable degree of independence from banks and financial markets through its use of internal finance ('retained earnings') for its investment projects. This is the subject of Chapter 2 of *Monopoly Capital*. In Chapter 3, the influence of imperfect competition theory is prominent, as Baran and Sweezy infer from the literature on pricing under oligopoly that the most plausible generalisation is a prohibition on price-cutting combined with a decision to maximise the joint profits of the (few) corporations that make up the industry. 'The abandonment of price competition', however, 'does not mean the end of all competition: it takes new forms and rages on with ever-increasing intensity' (p. 76). Continuing technical change is an important part of this process, and it reduces costs of production. With prices fixed, this entails a widening of profit margins for the individual corporation and a tendency for the surplus to rise, as a proportion of total output, for the economy as a whole. Here two further influences can be seen: the tradition of Marxian underconsumptionism that Sweezy had reviewed in *The Theory of Capitalist Development*, and the Kalecki–Steindl model of oligopoly that predicts rising mark-ups as the degree of monopoly increases over time. In the monopoly stage of capitalist evolution, Baran and Sweezy maintain, the law of the rising surplus replaces the law of the falling rate of profit (p. 80).

How is this rising surplus to be absorbed? This question defines the core of *Monopoly Capital*, in which Baran and Sweezy assess the possibility that absorption might occur through rising consumption and investment expenditure by capitalists (Chapter 4); through increasing advertising and other marketing expenses (Chapter 5, on 'the sales effort'); via growth in civilian government expenditure (Chapter 6); and by means of militarism and imperialism (Chapter 7). To the extent that none of these outlets proves sufficient, there is a constant danger of economic stagnation in monopoly capital. One final influence emerges at this point, in the form of the 'stagnation thesis' advanced in the late 1930s by the mainstream American Keynesian, Alvin Hansen. Apparently unknown to Baran and Sweezy—or for that matter to Hansen—a very similar argument had been set out by an obscure British Marxist, D. H. Stott, writing under the pseudonym Frederick Allen (1953a, pp. 267–273; Hansen, 1939; Allen, 1938; cf. King, 2004).

There is thus an implicit macroeconomic model in *Monopoly Capital,* which is in this respect entirely Kaleckian (see Kalecki, 1942). Workers spend what they receive, so that consumption out of wages is (roughly) equal to the total wage bill. Aggregate profits are then equal to the sum of capitalist consumption, investment, the government deficit and the trade surplus; increases in any or all of these magnitudes are good for corporate health. In familiar notation, the equality of income and expenditure requires that

$$W+P+T+M=Cw+Cc+I+G+X \tag{1}$$

Recognising that $W = Cw,$ and rearranging terms, it follows that

$$P=Cc+I+(G-T)+(X-M) \tag{2}$$

Baran and Sweezy deal with the first two terms on the right-hand side of equation (2) in Chapter 4 of *Monopoly Capital,* and discuss the second two terms in Chapters 6–7. The 'sales effort', which is the subject of Chapter 5, keeps $Cw = W$ and also tends to increase Cc as a proportion of P. They argue that neither I nor Cc can be expected to grow rapidly enough to maintain profitability, while capitalists themselves have strong political objections to the expansion of civilian government expenditure (cf. Kalecki, 1943). Only military spending, which is used to support imperialist aggression in the interests of the corporations, is free from these constraints, so that it is only by means of 'military Keynesianism' that stagnation can be avoided.

In *The Theory of Capitalist Development,* Sweezy had devoted very little space to the economics of militarism (1942a, pp. 308–310, 343), but after 1945 he acknowledged the economic effects of military spending much more clearly (1949g; 1953a, pp. 363–369). Even here, however, economic and political factors do limit the surplus-absorbing power of the state, leading Baran and Sweezy to conclude that militarism and imperialism cannot offer a permanent cure for stagnation (1966a, pp. 211–214). Their arguments are not entirely convincing, any more than is their blunt rejection of any state capitalist, social democratic or welfare state alternatives to stagnation, even though in the mid-1960s these could be observed, and seemed to be operating quite successfully, in much of northern and western Europe.

Baran and Sweezy are on much firmer ground in condemning the irrationality of a system that relies so heavily upon waste, and in demonstrating the dependence of monopoly capital on racism, alienation and the fetishism of commodities (Chapters 9–11). 'This state of affairs cannot be changed by wishing or incantation' they conclude, but only by a conscious decision to confront 'the emptiness, the degradation, and the suffering which poison human existence in this society' (pp. 348–349). They no longer share the faith of orthodox Marxists in the revolutionary potential of the proletariat, which in the United States has 'to a large extent been integrated into the system as consumers and ideologically conditioned members of the society' (p. 349). What hope there is comes from the 'revolutionary peoples' of Vietnam, China, Korea, Cuba and Algeria; in short, from world revolution.

Monopoly Capital was an enormous popular success, being translated into many languages and selling hundreds of thousands of copies on all five continents. It was widely reviewed, in all the best journals. Orthodox Marxists objected to Baran's and Sweezy's apparent abandonment of the labour theory of value, and were unimpressed by their replacement of Marx's concept of surplus value by the much vaguer notion of the 'economic surplus'. Less dogmatic critics were concerned by the definition and measurement of the surplus, and by the rejection in *Monopoly Capital* of the possibility that military or civilian government spending might offer a permanent solution to the problem of effective demand. (See Meek, 1966; O'Connor, 1966; Sherman, 1966; Symposium, 1966, for a range of criticisms from generally sympathetic reviewers.) The book was especially influential in Latin America and in Asia, but reviewers on the eastern shores of the Atlantic complained that Baran and Sweezy had ignored the distinctive features of European capitalism, above all the much greater tolerance of Old World capitalists for economic intervention by the state. As James O'Connor (1966, p. 50) wrote, in *New Left Review:* 'The question still to be resolved is, does the US show Gaullist France the future, or is it the other way round?'.

That question is no easier to answer in 2008 than it was in 1966. Looking back on *Monopoly Capital* 25 years after its publication, Sweezy himself concluded that 'it holds up pretty well' in the light of subsequent developments (1991b, p. 52), and continued to affirm the validity of the law of rising surplus (e.g. 1994b, p. 17). He took some comfort from the recession of the early 1990s, which he interpreted as the return of stagnation: 'the explanation of our present predicament can be summed up by saying that we are back in the 1930s' (1993a, p. 8), the big difference being that capitalism was once 'confronted by a powerful [Soviet] enemy, while today it is virtually unopposed' (1994a, p. 6).

8 After Baran

On one important question, Sweezy did become more self-critical. As he admitted in 1991, *Monopoly Capital* failed to predict the growth of the financial sector. Chapter 2 assumes the independence of corporate management from financial market pressures, whereas in fact takeovers, and threats of takeovers, exercise a profound influence on the behaviour of even the largest corporations, as management is forced 'to take on the coloration of speculative finance. To the extent that this occurs, it calls into question the corporate paradigm Baran and I had treated as a built-in feature of monopoly capitalism' (1991e, p. 55). Why, Sweezy asks, did *Monopoly Capital* miss this important development? 'Basically, I think the answer is that its concentration on the capital accumulation process is one-sided and incomplete' (p. 56). Accumulation is not just about goods, but also about the stock of financial assets. Hence there is a need for a better theory of accumulation, one that places 'special emphasis on the interaction of its real and financial aspects' (p. 57).

Sweezy began to take finance seriously quite soon after the publication of *Monopoly Capital* (see, for example, 1971p). It was a constant theme in his final writings, and led him to take a more favourable view of Keynes once again, since speculation plays such a prominent role in the *General Theory* (1994b, p. 1). Financial capital, Sweezy argues, has been cut loose from its original role as 'a modest helper of a real economy to meet human needs' and has become 'speculative capital geared solely to its own self-expansion. In earlier times no one ever dreamed that speculative capital, a phenomenon as old as capitalism itself, could grow to dominate a national economy, let alone the whole world. But it has'. Thus capital accumulation 'has ceased to be on the whole a positive and benign force and itself has turned into a terribly destructive one' (1994b, p. 2). In the late nineteenth century, 'on the whole finance was subordinate to production', despite the growth of monopoly capital (1994b, p. 5). The two decades after 1975, however, have seen the development of a 'relatively independent... financial superstructure sitting on top of the world economy and most of its national units' (1994b, p.7). Investment in financial rather than real assets was the result of the growth of surplus 'as the economy sank once again into stagnation in the 1970s' (1994b, p. 9). In consequence there has been a shift in the locus of economic and political power from corporate boardrooms to financial markets. 'It looks as though Adam Smith's invisible hand is staging a comeback in a new form and with increased muscle' (1994b, p. 10). And financial markets increasingly control political decisions, too. Thus, by the end of the 1980s, 'the old structure of the economy, consisting of a production system served by a modest financial adjunct, had given way to a new structure in which a greatly expanded financial sector had achieved a high degree of independence and sat on top of the underlying production system. That, in essence, is what we have now' (1995a, pp. 8–9).

Sweezy concludes that 'the financialization of the capital accumulation process' is one of the three main changes in recent capitalist history, the others being the slowdown in the growth rate since the mid-1970s, and the growth of monopoly and oligopoly (1997b, p. 3).

This analysis is not without its problems. Sweezy's use of the base-superstructure metaphor in this context is confusing, and his account of the growth of the financial sector is more than a little ambiguous. If it is merely a consequence of the law of rising surplus, perhaps it amounts to nothing more than one additional way in which the surplus can be absorbed. In this vein Magdoff and Sweezy claim that 'the financial explosion' has been 'a force counteracting stagnation' by opening up profitable investment opportunities in real estate and construction and by stimulating luxury consumption financed by interest income. On this reading, the growth of finance is costless, since without it there would simply be more excess capacity (1985g, p. 8). But they also maintain that it is potentially dangerous, since the increasing fragility of the financial system raises the prospect of 'a bust of classic dimensions'. 'What would be the long-run implications' they ask rhetorically, 'of government's undertaking to guarantee the financial system against the kind of collapse and generalized deflation that was the prelude to the Great Depression of the 1930s?' (p. 10). They leave the question unanswered.

Sweezy's refusal to engage with other streams of heterodox macroeconomic thought is especially regrettable in this context. An investigation of Hyman Minsky's 'financial instability hypothesis', for example, would have added some rigour to what is a rather informal and discursive treatment of some very important issues (Minsky, 1986). Sweezy might also have reflected back on his dismissal of Rudolf Hilferding's *Finance Capital,* and on the revisionist debates of the 1890s where Eduard Bernstein and his orthodox Marxian critics were divided on precisely this issue: did the increasing role of credit tend to stabilise the capitalist system or to destabilise it? (Tudor & Tudor, 1988). Finally, Sweezy's 'back to the 1930s' slogan is not very convincing. He never really confronts the possibility that a new, competitive, neoliberal stage of capitalist development might have begun in the 1970s, with the increased global power of financial capital fundamentally altering the behaviour of the giant corporation, undermining its monopoly position and thereby also undermining the law of the rising surplus. On this interpretation, *Monopoly Capital* is the theory of a bygone age.

One criticism that Sweezy did take seriously was the role of the labour theory of value in—or rather its absence from—the 1966 book. This became a problem for him with the revival of Marxian political economy in the United States in the late 1960s, a phenomenon that (ironically) owed much to Baran and Sweezy themselves. In Section 4 we noted Sweezy's ambivalence on the question of value in *The Theory of Capitalist Development.* There is no such uncertainty in *Monopoly Capital,* where the surplus is defined and measured in terms of market prices. Is Sweezy, then, as more doctrinaire Marxists sometimes alleged, nothing more than a vulgar economist in disguise? Not at all, on his account of the matter. The labour theory of value is not rejected in *Monopoly Capital,* but taken for granted. Implicit in the analysis is a *dual* transformation, first from labour values to competitive prices of production, and then from competitive prices to monopoly prices. This could and should, Sweezy acknowledges, have been made explicit in the book itself (1974e, 1979g).

This is a deeply unsatisfactory argument, which avoids all the difficulties with the labour theory of value identified by Sraffian critics of Marx (Steedman,

1977) and also contradicts Sweezy's own earlier recognition that there can be *no* general theory of monopoly price (1942a, pp. 270–271). It raises the spectre of Paul Samuelson's (1971, p. 400) sardonic 'erase and replace' algorithm: write down the wrong set of relative prices, rub them out, and replace them with the correct set. But Sweezy would have to use the eraser twice. He did not need the quantitative labour theory of value to establish the law of the rising surplus—a defence of the falling rate of profit theory would have been a different matter—and he would have been better advised to follow Kalecki and Steindl and permit it to die a silent death.

One important question not discussed in *Monopoly Capital* is that of the natural limits to the accumulation of capital, and the related issue of the environmental damage that capitalism inflicts upon our planet. In an article on 'Cars and cities' (1973f), Sweezy describes the destruction of the inner city and the uncontrollable suburban sprawl caused by the automobile. The old dividing line between city and country has disappeared, and the resulting traffic congestion, pollution and wasted commuting time have imposed huge human and environmental costs. Nothing less than a fundamental change in the social order can reverse the process, Sweezy maintains, with public ownership of the land, a huge expansion of public transport and the socialisation of the entire investment process being required.

Significantly, this was the paper that he chose to reprint in the issue of *Monthly Review* dedicated to a celebration of his 90th birthday (2000). In his final years, Sweezy showed considerable sympathy for 'green Marxism', arguing that capitalists' inability to enforce property rights over the sun posed an almost insuperable obstacle to the development of solar energy in place of fossil fuels (1997a) and observing, in his 150th anniversary reflections on the *Communist Manifesto,* that Marx and Engels had identified 'the common ruin of the contending classes' as one possible outcome of the class struggle (1998, p. 10). The looming environmental crisis, Sweezy concludes, is the responsibility of capitalism, and it requires non-capitalist solutions.

9 Conclusion

It would be surprising if Sweezy's confidence in a socialist future had not been shaken by the events of the 1980s and 1990s. Quite apart from any impending ecological disaster, he never ceased to warn of the dangers of imperialist war. Inter-imperialist rivalry between the United States, the European Union and Japan was a constant threat to world peace, he suggested, and George Bush Senior's assertion of US global supremacy was 'just a dream' (1991a, p. 4; cf. 1991d, p. 16). The popular notion of a unipolar system was totally unrealistic: 'The idea of a globalized and centralized imperialism makes no more sense than it did a hundred years ago' (1994b, pp. 16–17). Despite everything, Sweezy continued to 'hope for the best' (1994a, p. 7). In 1995 he returned, in effect, to the reformist position that he had taken in the mid-1930s. The long-run answer to the world's problems is still socialism, but this is simply not on the agenda now, 'and won't be any time soon' (1995b, p. 10). Instead, he proposes two short-run solutions: 'First, there must be a relatively large sector of the economy—of the order of 20 to 25 per cent of the total—that is publicly financed and controlled', to do for surplus absorption what the military-industrial establishment did in the Cold War, but is unlikely to do any more. And no one can deny the social imperative for a big increase in civilian government spending on housing, urban development and environmental regeneration. 'The second indispensable change needed to make the private enterprise economy work better is a redistribution of wealth and income towards greater equality' (p. 10). After half a century of sustained opposition to reformism, Sweezy ended his life as a left social democrat.

Paul Sweezy's life's work encapsulates many of the problems facing Marxists—especially North American Marxists—in the twentieth century. Most obviously, he was denied an academic career. In a sense this was to his advantage: Paul Baran would probably have written more, and died older, if he had not been systematically overworked at Stanford (1965d, pp. 57, 60–61). Sweezy was unusually fortunate, however, in being able to support himself and his work without a 'proper' job. Second, he lacked a convincing revolutionary project. Unable to accept Marx's predictions of an insurgent proletariat, Sweezy might have become a lifelong reformist, dedicated to piecemeal improvements through an admittedly grossly imperfect political system. For most of his life, though, he found this position unacceptable. Or he might have followed Herbert Marcuse in finding insurgent potential within the United States in students, Afro-Americans and the urban underclass (Marcuse, 1969). Even in the later 1960s, Sweezy never regarded this as at all plausible. Instead, he took the Third World proletariat, and above all its peasantry, as his revolutionary subject. This was a heretical position (although Marx himself flirted with it in his later writings on the Russian peasant commune). It could be defended, as Rosa Luxemburg might have done, on the grounds that the proletariat must be defined globally, and the North American (and Western European) working class represents only a very large labour aristocracy. Sweezy never quite faced up to the full implications of this stance, which include the possibility that the interests of metropolitan and peripheral workers might be quite fundamentally opposed (Emmanuel, 1972). But it is implicit in much of his work, and in particular in his support for Mao against the Soviet bureaucracy.

This points to a third problem, the lack of a 'revolutionary home'. Until the late 1950s, Sweezy identified with the Soviet Union, and then with Communist China until the victory of the 'capitalist roaders' after the death of Mao (and with Castro's Cuba until much later). But he was never an uncritical Stalinist, and unlike the functionaries of the US Communist Party he never contemplated the importation of the Soviet system into the United States. In this respect, Sweezy was closer to dissident Marxists (Trotskyists, Council Communists and others) than he himself perhaps realised.

Finally, Sweezy's very distinguished intellectual career highlights some of the intellectual dilemmas that faced twentieth-century Marxian political economy. What was the principal cause of economic crises: the production of surplus value or its realisation? Did the capitalist system face vigorous but unstable cyclical growth, or stagnation? Should it be analysed in terms of labour values or market prices? Could central planning completely replace the market under socialism? Was the capitalist state a class adversary or a potential agent of social reform? Over more than 60 years Sweezy confronted all these questions, and as we have seen he was not always consistent in his answers to them. Only dogmatists *were* consistent, and many of them ended in bitter disillusion with 'The God That failed', lurching drastically to the right in the process (James Burnham in the 1940s, David Horowitz in the 1980s, Christopher Hitchens in the 2000s). Paul Sweezy kept the faith, even if it was a rather battered faith for much of the time. He will be remembered, above all for *The Theory of Capitalist Development* and *Monopoly Capital,* long after his more dogmatic Marxian opponents have been completely forgotten.

Bibliography

Works by Paul Sweezy

A very large proportion of Sweezy's articles appeared in *Monthly Review.* We have not included in this bibliography the majority of the 'Review of the Month' editorials that he co-authored with Leo Huberman for the journal between 1949 and late 1968. Many of these discuss topical political events of relatively little enduring interest, and a large number of them—especially those from the 1950s—consist of three or four brief and unconnected pieces. We have, however, included short notes and reviews appearing under Sweezy's name where these have some lasting economic or political significance. *Monthly Review* sets some traps for the unwary scholar. One peculiar feature is the use of the inside front and back cardboard covers for the editors' comments on the progress of the journal and related issues, including personalities; these are sometimes missing from photographic reproductions, and are occasionally removed from library copies during the bookbinding process. We have not included any references to these comments, but they do constitute an important source of material on the history of *Monthly Review.* Two important and potentially confusing changes were made in May 1965, with the first issue of volume 17: since this date, each individual issue has been paginated separately, and the July-August combined issue (a feature of *Monthly Review* since the very beginning) has been numbered '3' instead of '3–4', subsequent issues from September to April being numbered '4 to 11' instead of '5 to 12'. We have made use of the extensive (but error-ridden) bibliography by D. Hillard, 'Harry Magdoff and Paul Sweezy: selected bibliographies', in S. A. Resnick & R.D. Wolff (eds), *Rethinking Marxism: Essays for Harry Magdoff and Paul Sweezy,* Brooklyn, NY: Autonomedia/Prager, 1985, pp. 405–421.

1934. Professor Pigou's theory of unemployment, *Journal of Political Economy*, 42(4), December, pp. 800–811.

1937a. On the definition of monopoly, *Quarterly Journal of Economics*, 51(2), February, pp. 362–363.

1937b. Review of L. von Mises, *Socialism, Science & Society*, 2, pp. 265–269.

1938a. *Monopoly and Competition in the English Coal Trade, 1550–1850* (Cambridge, MA: Harvard University Press). Reprinted Westport, CT: Greenwood Press, 1972, and as volume 2 of M. Casson (ed.), seven-book set on *Entrepreneurship and the Industrial Revolution* (London: Thoemmes Press, 1996).

1938b. (with R.V. Gilbert *et al.*) *An Economic Programme for American Democracy* (New York: Vanguard Press).

1938c. Review of A. C. Pigou, *Socialism Versus Capitalism, The Nation* 5 February, and *Plan Age*, March. (Reprinted as 'Pigou and the case for socialism' in 1953a, pp. 263–236).

1938d. Contribution to discussion of 'Wage policies', *American Economic Review*, 28(1), March, pp. 156–157.

1938e. Review of F. M. Taylor & O. Lange, *On the Economic Theory of Socialism, The Nation*, 25 June. (Reprinted as 'Strategy for socialism' in 1953a, pp. 338–340).

1938f. Review of A. H. Hansen, *Full Recovery or Stagnation?, The Nation*, 19 November. (Reprinted in 1953a, pp. 267–270).

1938g. The thinness of the stock market, *American Economic Review*, 28(4), December, pp. 747–748.

1939a. Power of the purse, *New Republic*, 98, 8 February, pp. 7–8.

1939b. Interest groups in the American economy, in U.S. Natural Resources Committee, *The Structure of the American Economy, Part I* (Washington: U.S. Government Printing Office), Appendix 13. (Reprinted in 1953a, pp. 158–188.)

1939c. Demand under conditions of oligopoly, *Journal of Political Economy*, 47(3), August, pp. 568–573.

1939d. Marx on the significance of the corporation, *Science & Society*, 3, pp. 238–241.

1940. A Marxist on American history, *New Republic*, 103, 21 October, pp. 564–566. (Reprinted as 'The heyday of the investment banker' in 1953a, pp. 153–157.)

1941a. The decline of the investment banker, *Antioch Review*, 1(1), Spring, pp. 63–68. (Reprinted in 1953a, pp. 189–196.)

1941b. Review of A. H. Hansen, *Fiscal Policy and Business Cycles, The Nation*, 27 September. (Reprinted in 1953a, pp. 270–273.)

1942a. *The Theory of Capitalist Development: Principles of Marxian Political Economy* (New York: Oxford University Press). Reprinted New York: Monthly Review Press, 1956. (Chapter 1 is reprinted as 'The theory of capitalist development, chapter one: Marx's method', *Monthly Review*, 44(7), December, pp. 14–27, and as 'Appendix. Paul M. Sweezy, "Marx's method" ', in E. Fischer (ed.), *How to Read Karl Marx*, New York: Monthly Review Press 1996, pp. 159–169. Unpaginated extracts are reprinted as 'The state' in D. Horowitz (ed.), *Radical Sociology: An Introduction*, San Francisco: Canfield Press, 1971, pp. 60–68).

1942b. Review of F. Neumann, *Behemoth, Science and Society* 6, pp. 281–285. (Reprinted as ''National socialism' in 1953a, pp. 233–241.)

1942c. The illusion of the managerial revolution, *Science & Society*, 6, pp. 1–23. (Reprinted in 1953a, pp. 39–66.)

1943. Rationing and the war economy, *Science & Society*, 7, pp. 64–71.

1944. [Pseud.]. Review of F. A. von Hayek, *The Road to Serfdom, Left News*, September. (Reprinted as 'Hayek's road to serfdom' in 1953a, pp. 283–290.)

1946a. Professor Schumpeter's theory of innovation, *Review of Economic Statistics,* 25(1), February, pp. 93–96. (Reprinted in 1953a, pp. 274–282.)

1946b. Review of T. Veblen, *The Nature of Peace, New Republic,* 114, 25 February, pp. 287–288. (Reprinted as 'Thorstein Veblen: strengths and weaknesses' in 1953a, pp. 295–301).

1946c. Review of N. S. Timasheff, *The Great Retreat, New Republic,* 114, 18 March, pp. 287–288.

1946d. Unions now, *New Republic,* 114, 1 April, pp. 452–453.

1946e. Review of S. Padover, *Experiment in Germany,* and J. Bach, Jr. *An Account of the Occupation, New Republic,* 22 April. (Reprinted 1953a, pp. 244–250.)

1946f. Review of A. Baykov, *The Development of the Soviet Economic System, New Republic,* 114, 1 July, pp. 937–938.

1946g. Review of C. Brinton, *The United States and Britain, New Republic,* 115, July, pp. 53–54.

1946h. John Maynard Keynes, *Science and Society,* 10, pp. 398–405. (Reprinted in 1953a, pp. 253–62; as part of 1963a; and, as 'Keynes the economist (3)', in S. E. Harris (ed.), *The New Economics: Keynes' Influence on Theory and Public Policy,* London: Dobson, 1947, pp. 102–109.)

1946i. Signs of the times, *The Nation,* 163, 19 October, pp. 440–444. (Reprinted as 'Toynbee's universal history' in 1953a, pp. 30–38.)

1946j. (with L. S. Feuer) Has colonialism a future?, *New Republic,* 115, 25 November, pp. 687–688.

1947a. Marxian and orthodox economics, *Science & Society,* 11, pp. 225–233. (Reprinted in 1953a, pp. 305–316.)

1947b. Review of A. Gray, *The Socialist Tradition, Journal of Political Economy,* 55(5), October, pp. 465–466.

1947c. Review of C. Madison, *Critics and Crusaders, American Economic Review,* 37(5), December, pp. 1951–1952. (Reprinted as 'Critics and crusaders' in 1953a, pp. 197–201.)

1947d. Review of A. Baykov, *Soviet Foreign Trade,* and M. V. Condoide, *Russian–American Trade, Science and Society,* 11, pp. 372–376.

1948a. Origins of present day socialism, *Science & Society,* 12, pp. 65–81. (Reprinted in S. Bernstein (ed.), *Centenary of Marxism,* New York: Science and Society, pp. 65–81.)

1948b. Review of S. Lurie, *Controlled Investment in a Private Economy, Journal of Political Economy,* 56(2), April, pp. 175–6. (Reprinted in 1953a, pp. 242–243.)

1948c. Review of *Writings and Speeches of Eugene V. Debs,* edited A. M. Schlesinger, Jr., *Journal of Political Economy,* 56(6), December, pp. 541–542. (Reprinted as 'socialist humanitarianism' in 1953a, pp. 202–204.)

1948d. Review of L. Huberman, *We, the People, Science & Society,* 12, pp. 450–452.

1949a. *Socialism* (New York: McGraw-Hill).

1949b. (editor), *Karl Marx and the Close of His System* (NY: Kelley. Reprinted London: Merlin Press, 1975).

1949c. (with L. Huberman), 'Where we stand', *Monthly Review,* 1(1), May, pp. 1–2.

1949d. 'Recent developments in American capitalism', *Monthly Review,* 1(1), May, pp. 16–21. (Reprinted in 1953a, pp. 111–119).

1949e. The German problem, *Monthly Review,* 1(2), June, pp. pp. 37–43. (Reprinted in 1953a, pp. 223–232.)

1949f. Review of M. M. Bober, *Karl Marx's Interpretation of History, Journal of Political Economy,* 57(3), June, pp. 255–256.

1949g. Is the Marshall Plan an instrument of peace?, *Monthly Review,* 1(3), July, pp.

80–84. (Reprinted as 'The Marshall Plan and the crisis of Western Europe' in 1953a, pp. 67–73.)

1949h. (with L. Huberman), The Communist Manifesto after 100 years, *Monthly Review,* 1(4), August, pp. 102–120. (Reprinted in 1953a, pp. 3–29 and in 1968b, pp. 87–113.)

1949i. The devaluation of the pound, *Monthly Review,* 1(6), November, pp. 198–206.

1949j. Review of Labor Research Association, *Trends in American Capitalism, Journal of Political Economy* 57(6), December, pp. 547–548.

1950a. (Edited, with L. Huberman), *F. O. Matthiessen, 1902–1950. A Collective Portrait* (New York: Monthly Review Press). (Reprint of the October 1950 issue of *Monthly Review.*)

1950b. (with L. Huberman), Cooperation on the left, *Monthly Review,* 1(11), March, pp. 334–344.

1950c. A reply to critics [of 1942a], *Economic Review* [of Hitotsubashi University, Tokyo], April. (Reprinted in 1953a, pp. 352–362.)

1950d. The Varga controversy: comment, *American Economic Review,* 40(3), June, pp. 405–406.

1950e. Capitalism and race relations, *Monthly Review,* 2(2), June, pp. 40–49. (Reprinted in 1953a, pp. 139–152.)

1950f. The transition from feudalism to capitalism, *Science & Society,* 14, pp. 134–157.

1950g. (with L. Huberman), Korea, *Monthly Review,* 2(4), August, pp. 105–118. (Reprinted in B. S. Ortiz (ed.), *History As It Happened: Selected Articles From Monthly Review 1949–1989,* New York: Monthly Review Press, 1990, pp. 23–35.)

1950h. Labor and political activities [of F. O. Matthiessen], *Monthly Review,* 2(6), October, pp. 229–243. (Reprinted in 1950a, pp. 61–75.)

1950i. The American economy and the threat of war, *Monthly Review,* 2(7), November, p. 336–344.

1950j. The Varga controversy: a reply to Professor Domar, *American Economic Review,* 40(5), December, pp. 898–899.

1950k. An economic program for America, in National University Extension Association, *Welfare State.* (Reprinted as part of *Socialism is the Only Answer,* New York: Monthly Review Pamphlet, 1951; in 1953a, pp. 205–20; and in 1968a, pp. 103–114.)

1951a. Introduction, to J. A. Schumpeter, *Imperialism and Social Classes* (NY: Kelley, pp. vii–xxv). (Reprinted as 'Schumpeter on "Imperialism and Social Classes", in S. E. Harris (ed.), *Schumpeter: Social Scientist,* Cambridge, MA: Harvard University Press, 1951, pp. 119–124.)

1951b. Untitled contribution to R. McKeon (ed.), *Democracy in a World of Tensions* (Chicago: Chicago University Press), pp. 391–405; with C. J. Ducasse, 'Comments on Dr. Sweezy's answers', pp. 406–409; Sweezy, 'Reply to Professor Ducasse', pp. 409–412; C. G. Field, 'Comments on Dr. Sweezy's answers', pp. 412–418; and Sweezy, 'Reply to Professor Field', pp. 418–424; this volume reprinted New York: Greenwood Press, 1968. (Sweezy's contribution, but not the related discussion, reprinted as 'Science, Marxism and democracy', in 1953a, pp. 330–337.)

1951c. Duesenberry on economic development, *Explorations in Economic History,* 3(1), February, pp. 182–184.

1951d. The American ruling class—part I, *Monthly Review,* 3(1), May, pp. 10–17. (Reprinted in 1953a, pp. 120–9; excerpts reprinted in R. Gillam (ed.), *Power in Postwar America,* Boston: Beacon Press, 1971, pp. 42–49.)

1951e. The American ruling class—part II, *Monthly Review,* 3(2), June, pp. 58–64. (Reprinted in 1953a, pp. 129–38; excerpts reprinted in R. Gillam (ed.), *Power in Postwar America,* Boston: Little Brown, 1971, pp. 42–49.)

1951f. Review of R. Luxemburg, *The Accumulation of Capital,* edited by J. Robinson, *New Statesman and Nation,* 2 June. (Reprinted as 'Rosa Luxemburg and the theory of capitalism' in 1953a, pp. 291–294.)

1951g. Certain aspects of American capitalism, *Monthly Review,* 3(7), November, pp. 220–227.

1952a. The influence of Marxian economics on American thought and practice, in D. D. Egbert & S. Perssons (eds), *Socialism and American Life, Volume I* (Princeton: Princeton University Press), pp. 453–486.

1952b. (Editor and translator), *Principles of Communism,* by Friedrich Engels (New York: Monthly Review Press).

1952c. Review of A. Ulam, *Philosophical Foundations of English Socialism, Journal of Political Economy,* 60(1), February, p. 79.

1952d. Review of B. Schwartz, *Chinese Communism and the Rise of Mao, Journal of Political Economy,* 60(2), April, pp. 181–182. (Reprinted as 'Marxism in the East: decomposition or enrichment' in 1953a, pp. 74–76).

1952e. (with others), How shall we vote?, *Monthly Review,* 4(6), November, pp. 231–232.

1953a. *The Present as History* (New York: Monthly Review Press).

1953b. A crucial difference between capitalism and socialism, in 1953a, pp. 341–351.

1953c. Peace and prosperity, in 1953a, pp. 363–369.

1953d. A Marxist view of imperialism, *Monthly Review,* 5(11), March, pp. 414–424. (Reprinted in 1953a, pp. 79–92.)

1953e. Three works on imperialism, *Journal of Economic History,* 13(2), Spring, pp. 195–201. (Reprinted in 1953a, pp. 93–107.)

1953f. Review of R.H.S. Crossman *et al., New Fabian Essays, Journal of Political Economy,* 61(3), June, pp. 271–272. (Expanded version reprinted as 'Fabian political economy' in 1953a, pp. 317–329.)

1953g. Comments on Professor H. K. Takahashi's 'Transition from feudalism to capitalism', *Science & Society,* 17, pp. 155–164.

1953h. (with L. Huberman), Class justice, *Monthly Review,* 5(4), August, pp. 145–157. (Reprinted in B. S. Ortiz (ed.), *History As It Happened: Selected Articles From Monthly Review 1949–1989,* New York: Monthly Review Press, 1990, pp. 41–44.)

1953i. Reflections on Japanese–American relations, *Monthly Review,* 5(6), October, pp. 245–250.

1954a. (and others), *The Transition from Feudalism to Capitalism,* with Introduction by Rodney Hilton (New York: Science and Society). (Reprinted London: New Left Books, 1976.)

1954b. Statement to the New Hampshire Attorney-General, *Monthly Review,* 51(11), April 2000, pp. 37–41. (Reprinted as 'Sweezy vs. the state of New Hampshire', in: P. Warren, *Public Papers of Chief Justice Earl Warren,* ed. H. Christman, New York: Greenwood Press, pp. 175–190.)

1954c. Review of A. T. Peacock *et al.* (eds), *International Economic Papers, No. 2, Econometrica,* 22(2), April, pp. 257–258.

1954d. Labor and socialism: a revealing incident, *Monthly Review,* 6(1), May, pp. 7–11.

1954e. (with L. Huberman), The road to another war, *Monthly Review,* 6(1), May, pp. 1–6. (Reprinted in B. S. Ortiz (ed.), *History As It Happened: Selected Articles From Monthly Review 1949–1989,* New York: Monthly Review Press 1990, pp. 45–49.)

1954f. Review of J. Steindl, *Maturity and Stagnation in American Capitalism, Econometrica,* 22(4), October, pp. 531–533.

1956a. From Paris to Peking to New York, *Monthly Review,* 7(10), March, pp. 455–460.

(See also J. R. Starobin, 'Reply to Sweezy', *Monthly Review,* 8(2), June 1956, pp. 50–56.)

1956b. (with Leo Huberman), After the Twentieth Congress, *Monthly Review,* 8(3–4), July–August, pp. 65–83.

1956c. Power elite or ruling class?, *Monthly Review,* 8(5), September, pp. 138–150. (Reprinted in 1972c, pp. 92–109.)

1956d. (with L. Huberman), We'll vote socialist, *The Nation,* 183, 20 October, pp. 322–333.

1956e. (with L. Huberman), What every American should know about the Suez crisis, *Monthly Review,* 8(6), October, pp. 177–195. (Also published as a monograph, New York: Monthly Review Press, 1956.)

1956f. Marxian socialism, *Monthly Review,* 8(7), November, pp. 227–241. (Reprinted in 1968a, pp. 83–94.)

1956g. (with L. Huberman), In affectionate memory of Henry Pratt Fairchild, *Monthly Review,* 8(7), November, pp. 242–243.

1957a. (with L. Huberman), Thorstein Bunde Veblen, 1857–1957, *Monthly Review,* 9(3–4), July–August, pp. 65–75.

1957b. The theory of business enterprise and absentee ownership, *Monthly Review,* 9(3–4), July–August, pp. 105–112.

1957c. Review of G. D. H. Cole, *The History of Socialist Thought* (three volumes), *American Economic Review,* 50(5), December, pp. 984–985.

1958a. What is socialism?, in H. Alfred (ed.), *Towards a Socialist America,* pp. 94–105 (New York: Peace Publishers).

1958b. Poland a year after, *Monthly Review,* 9(9), January, pp. 289–294.

1958c. Socialism in Europe, east and west, *Monthly Review,* 9(10), February, pp. 328–339.

1958d. The Yugoslav experiment, *Monthly Review,* 9(11), March, pp. 362–374.

1958e. Veblen's critique of the American economy, *American Economic Review,* 48(2), Papers and Proceedings, May, pp. 21–29. (Reprinted as 'Veblen on American capitalism', in: D. F. Dowd (ed.), *Thorstein Veblen: a Critical Appraisal,* Ithaca, NY: Cornell University Press, 1958, pp. 177–197.)

1958f. The condition of the working class, *Monthly Review,* 10(3–4), July–August, pp. 118–126.

1958g. Marxism: a talk to students, *Monthly Review,* 10(6), October, pp. 219–223.

1959a. The dilemma of inflation, *The Nation,* 188, March, pp. 200–204.

1959b. Power blocks to a peace economy, *The Nation,* 188, 28 March, pp. 275–278.

1959c. Theories of the new capitalism, *Monthly Review,* 11(3–4), July–August, pp. 65–75. (Reprinted in 1972c, pp. 64–78.)

1960a. (with L. Huberman), *Cuba: Anatomy of a Revolution* (New York: Monthly Review Press). (Also published as *Monthly Review,* 12(3–4), July–August 1960, pp. 1–176; entire issue.)

1960b. Review of G. D. H. Cole, *The History of Socialist Thought, volume 4, American Economic Review,* 50(1), March, pp. 218–220.

1960c. Economic planning, *Monthly Review,* 12(1), May, pp. 7–17.

1960d. (with L. Huberman), The theory of U.S. foreign policy—I, *Monthly Review,* 12(4), September, pp. 273–279.

1960e. (with L. Huberman), The theory of U. S. foreign policy—II, *Monthly Review,* 12(6), October, pp. 321–333.

1960f. (with L. Huberman), The theory of U. S. foreign policy—III, *Monthly Review,* 12(7), November, pp. 353–362.

1960g. (with L. Huberman), 'Cuba revisited', *Monthly Review,* 12(8), December, pp. 401–432.

1961a. Has capitalism changed?, in: S. Tsuru (ed.), *Has Capitalism Changed?,* pp. 83–91 (Tokyo: Iwanami Shoten).

1961b. (with L. Huberman), The economics of insanity, *Monthly Review,* 12(9), January, pp. 449–458.

1961c. (with L. Huberman), A new New Deal?, *Monthly Review,* 12(10), February, pp. 497–505.

1961d. A contribution to the critique of American society [review of P. Goodman, *Growing Up Absurd*], *Monthly Review,* 12(11), March, pp. 573–576.

1961e. The resumption of testing, *Monthly Review,* 13(5), October, pp. 241–247.

1962a. The common market, *Monthly Review,* 13(9), January, pp. 385–396

1962b. (with L. Huberman), Stagnation and steel, *Monthly Review,* 14(1), May, pp. 1–10.

1962c. The 22nd Congress and international socialism, *Monthly Review,* 14(1), May, pp. 45–53.

1962d. A great American, *Monthly Review,* 14(2), June, pp. 74–81. (Reprinted in *Monthly Review,* 40(11), April 1989, pp. 37–44.)

1962e. (with P. Baran), Monopoly capital: two chapters on the American economic and social order, *Monthly Review,* 14(3), July–August, entire issue, pp. 131–224. [Introduction, pp. 131–134; The giant corporation, pp. 135–166; On the quality of monopoly capital society, pp. 167–224].

1962f. (with L. Huberman), U.S. capitalism at an impasse, *Monthly Review,* 14(5), September, pp. 225–235.

1963a. John Maynard Keynes [1946] and The first quarter century, in: R. Lekachman (ed.), *Keynes' General Theory: Reports of Three Decades,* pp. 297–305 and 305–314 (New York: St. Martin's Press, 1963). (A reprint of 1946h, with a 1963 commentary; the latter is reprinted in 1972b, pp. 79–91.)

1963b. (with L. Huberman), Notes on Latin America, *Monthly Review,* 14(11), March, pp. 593–612.

1963c. (with P. A. Baran), Rejoinder, *Monthly Review,* 14(11), April, pp. 669–678. [Reply to Anatoly Butenko, 'The great debate: a reply to Baran and Sweezy' [1962a], *ibid.,* pp. 663–669.]

1963d. (with L. Huberman), The split in the capitalist world, *Monthly Review,* 14(12), April, pp. 641–655.

1963e. (with L. Huberman), The split in the socialist world, *Monthly Review,* 15(1), May, pp. 1–20.

1963f. Communism as an ideal, *Monthly Review,* 15(6), October, pp. 329–340.

1963g. (with L. Huberman), Economic fluctuations and trends, *Monthly Review,* 15(7), November, pp. 363–363.

1963h. (with L. Huberman), Imperialism and national independence, *Monthly Review,* 15(8), December, pp. 418–431.

1964a. Kennedy: the man and the President, *Monthly Review,* 15(8), January, pp. 511–515.

1964b. (with P. Baran), Theses on advertising, *Science and Society,* 20(1), Spring, pp. 20–30.

1964c. (with L. Huberman), Cuba's economic future, *Monthly Review,* 15(12), April, pp. 633–650.

1964d. Economics of two worlds, in: *On Political Economy and Econometrics: Essays in Honor of Oskar Lange,* pp. 15–29 (Warsaw: PKN Polish Scientific Publishers). (Reprinted in *Monthly Review,* 18(10), March 1967, pp. 1–22.)

1964e. (with P. Baran), Notes on the theory of imperialism, in *Problems of Economic Dynamics and Planning: Essays in Honor of Michal Kalecki,* pp. 13–25 (Warsaw: PWN–Polish Scientific Publishers). (Reprinted in *Monthly Review,* 17(10), March 1966, pp. 15–31.

1965a. (Edited, with L. Huberman), *Paul Baran, 1910–1964: a Collective Portrait* (New York: Monthly Review Press). (Also published as *Monthly Review,* 16(11), March 1965, entire issue, pp. 1–135.)

1965b. (with L. Huberman), Foreword, in: 1965a, pp. vi–viii.

1965c. (with L. Huberman), Foreign investment, *Monthly Review,* 16(9), January, pp. 529–540. (Reprinted in 1972a, pp. 31–42.)

1965d. (with L. Huberman), The Kennedy–Johnson boom, *Monthly Review,* 16(10), February, pp. 577–587.

1965e. Paul A. Baran: a personal memoir, *Monthly Review,* 16(11), March, pp. 28–62. (Reprinted in 1965a, pp. 28–62.)

1965f. Gert [Gertrude Huberman] and *MR, Monthly Review,* 17(6), November, pp. 54–58.

1966a. (with Paul Baran), *Monopoly Capital* (New York: Monthly Review Press). (Reprinted Harmondsworth: Penguin, 1968.)

1966b. (with L. Huberman), The boom continues, *Monthly Review,* 17(9), February, pp. 1–9.

1966c. (with P. Baran), Notes on the theory of imperialism, *Monthly Review,* 17(10), March, pp. 15–31. (Reprint of 1964e.)

1966d. (with L. Huberman), Why Vietnam?, *Monthly Review,* 18(6), November, pp. 1–9.

1966e. (with L. Huberman), The Omegna award, *Monthly Review,* 18(6), November, p. 59. (See also 1967f.)

1966f. (with L. Huberman), Weak reeds and class enemies, *Monthly Review,* 18(7), December, pp. 1–10. (Shorter version reprinted as 'Dollars and gold' in 1972a, pp. 149–157.)

1967a. (with L. Huberman), Lessons of Soviet experience, in: L. Huberman (ed.), *50 Years of Soviet Power,* pp. 9–21 (New York: Monthly Review Press). (Reprinted in *Monthly Review,* 19(6), November 1967, pp. 9–21; in 1968a, pp. 115–27; and in 1980a, pp. 19–31.)

1967b. (with L. Huberman), The Kennedy–Johnson boom, in: M. Gentleman & D. Mermelstein (eds), *The Great Society Reader,* pp. 97–112 (New York: Random House).

1967c. Obstacles to economic development, in: C. H. Feinstein (ed.), *Socialism, Capitalism and Economic Growth: Essays in Honour of Maurice Dobb,* pp. 191–197 (Cambridge: Cambridge University Press).

1967d. (with L. Huberman), The Cultural Revolution in China, *Monthly Review,* 17(8), January, pp. 1–17. (Reprinted in B. S. Ortiz (ed.), *History As It Happened: Selected Articles From Monthly Review 1949–1989,* New York: Monthly Review Press 1990, pp. 90–103.)

1967d. (with P. Baran), Economics of two worlds, *Monthly Review,* 18(10), March, pp. 1–27. (Reprint of 1964d.)

1967e. (with L. Huberman), End of the boom, *Monthly Review,* 18(11), April, pp. 1–9.

1967f. Untitled article, *Monthly Review,* 19(1), May, pp. 43–47. [Part of a symposium on the award of the Omegna prize to *Monthly Review;* also includes articles by A. Boldini, *ibid.,* pp. 36–38, and L. Huberman, pp. 38–42; and 'judges' statement', pp. 47.]

1967g. Rosa Luxemburg's *The Accumulation of Capital, Science and Society,* 31(4), pp. 474–485.

1967h. The Israeli–Arab conflict: Israel and imperialism, *Monthly Review,* 19(5), October, pp. 1–8.

1967i. Marx and the proletariat, *Monthly Review,* 19(6), December, pp. 25–42. (Reprinted in 1972b, pp. 166–184.)

1967j. (with L. Huberman), Notes on the centennial of *Das Kapital, Monthly Review,* 19(7), December, pp. 1–16. (Reprinted in 1972b, pp. 110–124.)

1968a. (with L. Huberman), *Introduction to Socialism* (New York: Monthly Review Press).

1968b. *The Communist Manifesto* (co-editor Leo Huberman) (New York: Modern Reader Paperbacks). [Includes Huberman & Sweezy, 'The *Communist Manifesto* after 100 years', *Monthly Review,* 1(4), August 1949, pp. 102–120.]

1968c. (edited, with L. Huberman), *Regis Debray and the Latin American Revolution: A Collection of Essays* (New York: Monthly Review Press).

1968d. Karl Marx and the industrial revolution, in: R. V. Eagly (ed.), *Events, Ideology and Economic Theory,* pp. 107–119, 124–126 (Detroit: Wayne State University Press). (Reprinted in 1972b, pp. 127–146.)

1968e. Gold, dollars, and empire, *Monthly Review,* 19(9) February, pp. 1–9. (Reprinted in 1972a, pp. 158–166.)

1968f. (with L. Huberman), Debray: the strengths and the weakness, *Monthly Review,* 20(3), July–August, pp. 1–11.

1968g. Czechoslovakia, capitalism, and socialism, *Monthly Review,* 20(5), October, pp. 5–16.

1969a. (with L. Huberman), *Socialism in Cuba* (New York: Monthly Review Press).

1969b. The future of capitalism, in: D. Cooper (ed.), *To a Free Generation,* pp. 99–108 (New York: Macmillan).

1969c. Preface, in: P. A. Baran, *The Longer View: Essays Towards a Critique of Political Economy,* (edited by J. O'Neill), pp. xi–xii (New York: Monthly Review Press).

1969d. Reply [to C. Bettelheim, 'On the transition between capitalism and socialism'], *Monthly Review,* 20(10), March, pp. 10–19.

1969e. (with L. Huberman), The merger movement: a study in power, *Monthly Review,* 22(2), June, pp. 1–19. (Reprinted in 1972a, pp. 68–87.)

1969f. Reply [to F. L. Schuman, 'Definitions of socialism'], *Monthly Review,* 21(2), June, pp. 63–64.

1969g. Where are we going?, *Monthly Review,* 21(4), September, pp. 43–50.

1969h. (with H. Magdoff), Notes on the multinational corporation—part one, *Monthly Review,* 21(5), October, pp. 1–13. (Reprinted in 1972a, pp. 88–100.)

1969i. (with H. Magdoff), Notes on the multinational corporation—part two, *Monthly Review,* 21(6), November, pp. 1–13. (Reprinted in 1972a, pp. 100–112).

1970a. (edited, with H. Magdoff), *Lenin Today: Eight Essays on the Hundredth Anniversary of Lenin's Birth* (New York: Monthly Review Press). (Also published as *Monthly Review,* 22(11), April 1970, pp. 1–125; entire issue. Includes H. Magdoff & P. Sweezy, Foreword, pp. 6–7.)

1970b. (edited, with L. Huberman & H. Magdoff), *Vietnam: the Endless War* (New York: Monthly Review Press).

1970c. Introduction, to P. Baran, *The Longer View,* pp. xi–xii (New York: Monthly Review Press).

1970d. Toward a critique of economics, *Monthly Review,* 21(8), January, pp. 1–9. (Reprinted in *Review of Radical Political Economics,* 2, Spring, pp. 1–8, and in 1972b, pp. 53–63.)

1970e. (with H. Magdoff), Notes on inflation and the dollar, *Monthly Review,* 21(10), March, pp. 1–13. (Reprinted in 1972a, pp. 167–179.)

1970f. (with H. Magdoff), The war spreads, *Monthly Review,* 22(1), May, pp. 1–10.

1970g. The teaching of economics: discussion, *American Economic Review,* 60(2), Papers and Proceedings, May, p. 376.

1970h. (with H. Magdoff), War and crisis, *Monthly Review,* 22(2), June, pp. 1–12.

1970i. (with H. Magdoff), Foreword [to A. El Kodsy, 'Nationalism and class struggles in the Arab world'], *Monthly Review,* 22(3), July–August, pp. iii–viii.

1970j. (with H. Magdoff), The long-run decline in liquidity, *Monthly Review,* 22(4), September, pp. 1–17. (Reprinted in 1972a, pp. 180–196.)

1970k. (with H. Magdoff), The economics of stagnation and the stagnation of economics, *Monthly Review,* 22(7), December, pp. 1–11.

1970l. Reply [to C. Bettelheim, 'More on the society of transition'], *Monthly Review,* 22(7), December, pp. 14–21.

1971a. (with C. Bettelheim), *On the Transition to Socialism* (New York: Monthly Review Press).

1971b. The American ruling class, in: R. Gillam (ed.), *Power in Postwar America,* pp. 42–49 (Boston: Little Brown) (reprint of excerpts from 1951d and 1951e).

1971c. Excerpts from 1966a (with Paul Baran), in: R. Romano & M. Leiman (eds), *Views on Capitalism,* pp. 376–420 (Beverly Hills: Glencoe Press).

1971d. The state, in: D. Horowitz (ed.), *Radical Sociology: An Introduction,* pp. 60–68 (San Francisco: Canfield Press). (Excerpts, unpaginated, from 1942a.)

1971e. (with H. Magdoff), Peaceful transition to socialism, *Monthly Review,* 22(8), January, pp. 1–18. (Reprinted in 1974a, pp. 32–49.)

1971f. (with H. Magdoff), Lessons of Poland, *Monthly Review,* 22(9), February, pp. 1–14. (Reprinted in 1980a, pp. 32–45.)

1971g. The future of socialism, *Monthly Review,* 22(10), March, pp. 9–17.

1971h. (with H. Magdoff), Economic stagnation and the stagnation of economics, *Monthly Review,* 22(11), April, pp. 1–11. (Reprinted in 1972a, pp. 43–53.)

1971i. On the teaching of Marxian economics, *Monthly Review,* 22(11), April, pp. 31–33.

1971j. The transition to socialism, *Monthly Review,* 23(1), May, pp. 1–16. (Reprinted in 1980a, pp. 46–54.)

1971k. Modern capitalism, *Monthly Review,* 23(2), June, pp. 1–10. (Reprinted in 1972b, pp. 3–14.)

1971l. Towards a critique of economics (II), *Review of Radical Political Economics,* 3, July, pp. 59–66.

1971m. (with H. Magdoff), Vietnam, China, and the coming crisis, *Monthly Review,* 23(4), September, pp. 1–10.

1971n. (with H. Magdoff), The end of U.S. hegemony, *Monthly Review,* 23(5), October 1971, pp. 1–16. (Reprinted in 1972a, pp. 197–212.)

1971o. The resurgence of financial control: fact or fancy?, *Monthly Review,* 23(6), November, pp. 1–33. (Reprinted in 1972a, pp. 113–145.)

1972a. (with H. Magdoff), *The Dynamics of US Capitalism: Corporate Structure, Inflation, Credit, Gold, and the Dollar* (New York: Monthly Review Press).

1972b. *Modern Capitalism and Other Essays* (New York: Monthly Review Press).

1972c. Capitalism and persistent poverty, in: H. Ginsburg (ed.), *Poverty, Economics, and Society,* pp. 164–166 (New York: Little, Brown.)

1972d. Socialism: an advocacy position, in: K. G. Elzinga (ed.), *Economics: A Reader* (New York: Harper), pp. 307–314.

1972e. (with P. Baran), Militarism and imperialism, in: A. F. Davis & H.D. Woodman (eds), *Conflict and Consensus in American History,* pp. 356–369 (New York: Heath).

1972f. Chile: advance or retreat?, *Monthly Review,* 23(8), January, pp. 1–15. (Reprinted in 1974a, pp. 79–83.)

1972g. Towards a program of studies of the transition to socialism, *Monthly Review,* 23(9), February, pp. 1–13.

1972h. (with H. Magdoff), Imperialism in the seventies: problems and perspectives, *Monthly Review,* 23(10), March, pp. 1–8.

1972i. Paul Sweezy replies [to A. Zimbalist, 'Sweezy on Chile'], *Monthly Review,* 23(10), March, pp. 53–54. (Reprinted in 1974a, pp. 100–102.)

1972j. On the theory of monopoly capitalism, *Monthly Review,* 23(11), April, pp. 1–23. (Reprinted in 1972b, pp. 25–52.)

1972k. Socio-cultural transformation in developing countries, *Intermountain Economic Review,* 3, Spring, pp. 1–6. (Reprinted in 1972b, pp. 15–24.)

1972l. Paul Sweezy comments [on A. Zimbalist, 'Reply to Sweezy'], *Monthly Review,* 24(1), May, p. 83.

1972m. (with H. Magdoff), The mind of the ruling class, *Monthly Review,* 24(2), June, pp. 1–15.

1972n. Introduction [to 'Some contradictions of capitalism: a supplement'], *Monthly Review,* 24(2), June, pp. 49–50.

1972o. (with H. Magdoff), Vietnam, Nixon, and the McGovern candidacy, *Monthly Review,* 24(4), August, pp. 1–11.

1972p. Some notes on a radical's view of the development process in the Third World, *Intermountain Economic Review,* 3, Fall, pp. 73–76.

1972q. On the irrelevance of bourgeois economics, *Monthly Review,* 24(5), October, pp. 1–14.

1972r. (with H. Magdoff), Terrorism and Marxism, *Monthly Review,* 24(6), November, pp. 1–6.

1972s. The economics of the New Left: comment, *Quarterly Journal of Economics,* 86(4), November, pp. 658–664.

1973a. Notes on the US situation at the end of 1972, *Monthly Review,* 24(8), January, pp. 1–11.

1973b. (with H. Magdoff), Vietnam: the options narrow, *Monthly Review,* 24(9), February, pp. 5–14.

1973c. (with H. Magdoff), The importance of calling a defeat a defeat, *Monthly Review,* 24(10), March, pp. 1–9.

1973d. On discovering Marxism, *Monthly Review,* 24(10), March, pp. 54–56.

1973f. Cars and cities, *Monthly Review,* 23(11), April, pp. 1–18. (Reprinted in *Monthly Review* 51(11), April 2000, pp. 19–34.)

1973g. (with H. Magdoff), The dollar crisis: what next?, *Monthly Review,* 25(1), May, pp. 1–14.

1973h. Op-Ed liberalism, *Monthly Review,* 25(1), May, pp. 44–49.

1973i. (with H. Magdoff), Watergate and Indochina, *Monthly Review,* 25(2), June, pp. 1–11.

1973j. (with H. Magdoff), Introduction, to A. Lichauco, 'The Lichauco papers', *Monthly Review,* 35(3), July–August, pp. vii–xv. (Reprinted in A. Lichauco, *The Lichauco Papers: Imperialism in the Philippines,* pp. vii–xv, New York: Monthly Review Press.)

1973k. Fifteenth and twentieth anniversaries for Cuba, *Monthly Review,* 22(4), September, pp. 23–27.

1973l. Utopian reformism, *Monthly Review,* 25(6), November, pp. 1–11.

1973m. Galbraith's utopia, *New York Review of Books,* 20, November, pp. 1–6.

1973n. Chile: the question of power, *Monthly Review,* 25(7), December, pp. 1–11. (Reprinted in 1974a, pp. 11–21, and in B. S. Ortiz (ed.), *History As It Happened: Selected Articles From Monthly Review 1949–1989,* New York: Monthly Review Press 1990, pp. 162–170.)

1974a. (edited, with H. Magdoff), *Revolution and Counter-Revolution in Chile* (New York: Monthly Review Press).

1974b. Watergate and the war (with H. Magdoff), in: S. Weissman (ed.), *Big Brother and the Holding Company: the World Behind Watergate* (Palo Alto: Ramparts Press), pp. 173–183.

1974c. Foreword, to: H. Braverman, *Labor and Monopoly Capital,* pp. ix–xiii (New York: Monthly Review Press). New edition 1996 with new Introduction by J. B. Foster (also contains Sweezy's original Foreword).

1974d. Monopoly capital and the theory of value, *Monthly Review,* 25(8), January, pp. 31–33.

1974e. Capitalism, for worse, *Monthly Review,* 25(9), February, pp. 1–7. (Reprinted in L. Silk (ed.), *Capitalism: the Moving Target,* New York: Quadrangle, pp. 121–128.)

1974f. (with H. Magdoff), Keynesian chickens come home to roost, *Monthly Review,* 25(11), April, pp. 1–12.

1974g. Growing wealth, declining power, *Monthly Review,* 25(10), March, pp. 1–10.

1974h. (with H. Magdoff), Notes on Watergate one year later, *Monthly Review,* 26(1), May, pp. 1–11.

1974i. Some problems in the theory of capital accumulation, *Monthly Review,* 26(1), May, pp. 38–55.

1974j. (with H. Magdoff), Twenty-five eventful years, *Monthly Review,* 26(2), June, pp. 1–13.

1974k. Review of M. H. Dobb, *Theories of Value and Distribution Since Adam Smith, Journal of Economic Literature,* 12(2), June, pp. 481–483. (Reprinted as 1976b.)

1974l. The end of Keynesianism, *Business and Society Review,* 10, Summer, p. 7.

1974m. The nature of Soviet society, *Monthly Review,* 26(6), November, pp. 1–16. (Reprinted in 1980a, pp. 55–70.)

1974n. Baran and the danger of inflation, *Monthly Review,* 26(7), December, pp. 11–14.

1975a. The nature of Soviet society—part II, *Monthly Review,* 26(8), January, pp. 1–15. (Reprinted in 1980a, pp. 71–84.)

1975b. (with H. Magdoff), Banks: skating on thin ice, *Monthly Review,* 26(9), February, pp. 1–21.

1975c. (with H. Magdoff), The economic crisis in historical perspective, *Monthly Review,* 26(10), March, pp. 1–8.

1975d. (with H. Magdoff), The economic crisis in perspective—part II, *Monthly Review,* 26(11), April, pp. 1–13.

1975e. (with H. Magdoff), The historic victory in Indochina, *Monthly Review,* 27(1), May, pp. 1–13.

1975f. No economic crisis in China, *New China Magazine,* Spring, pp. 43–46.

1975g. The road to socialism: Chile, *Social Policy,* 6(1), May–June, pp. 53–54. (Reprinted in *Monthly Review,* 27(6), November 1975, pp. 33–35.)

1975h. (with H. Magdoff), Capitalism and unemployment, *Monthly Review,* 27(2), June, pp. 1–14.

1975i. China: contrasts with capitalism, *Monthly Review,* 27(3), July–August, pp. 1–11.

1975j. Class struggles in Portugal, *Monthly Review,* 27(4), September, pp. 1–26.

1975k. Class struggles in Portugal—part 2, *Monthly Review,* 27(5), October, pp. 1–15.

1975l. Savings, consumption, and investment, *Monthly Review,* 27(7), November, pp. 1–7. [An interview with Sweezy by the editors of Salvat Editores of Barcelona.]

1976a. Foreword to: Helen B. Lamb, *Studies on India and Vietnam,* pp. 7–12 (New York: Monthly Review Press).

1976b. Dobb on ideology and economic theory, *Monthly Review,* 27(9), February, pp. 51–55. (Review of M. H. Dobb, *Theories of Value and Distribution Since Adam Smith;* first published as 1974k.)

1976c. More on the nature of Soviet society, *Monthly Review,* 27(10), March, pp. 15–24.

1976d. (with H. Magdoff), Capital shortage: fact and fancy, *Monthly Review,* 27(11), April, pp. 1–19.

1976e. (with H. Magdoff), The new reformism, *Monthly Review,* 28(2), June, pp. 1–11.

1976f. (with H. Magdoff), Third World debt problems: the wave of new defaults (a comment), *Monthly Review,* 28(4), August, pp. 19–22.

1976g. (with H. Magdoff), The editors comment, *Monthly Review,* 28(4), September, pp. 19–22. [Comment on C. Payer, Third World debt problems, *ibid.,* pp. 1–19.]

1976g. Socialism in poor countries, *Monthly Review,* 28(5), October, pp. 1–13.

1976h. (with H. Magdoff), The editors comment [on: 'The new reformism'], *Monthly Review,* 28(6), November, pp. 5–13.

1976i. Contributions to a bicentennial program, *Monthly Review,* 28(7), December, pp. 60–62.

1976j. Marxian economics, *Monthly Review,* 28(7), December, pp. 1–6.

1977a. (with H. Magdoff), *The End of Prosperity: The American Economy in the 1970s* (New York: Monthly Review Press).

1977b. (with H. Magdoff), Creeping stagnation, *Monthly Review,* 28(8), January, pp. 1–14.

1977c. Theory and practice in the Mao period, *Monthly Review,* 28(9), February, pp. 1–12. (Reprinted in 1980a, pp. 85–95.)

1977d. (with H. Magdoff), Keynesianism: illusions and delusions, *Monthly Review,* 28(11), April, pp. 1–12. (Reprinted in B. S. Ortiz (ed.), *History As It Happened: Selected Articles From Monthly Review 1949–1989,* New York: Monthly Review Press 1990, pp. 178–188.)

1977e. Paul Sweezy replies [to: B. Chavance, 'On the relations of production in the USSR'], *Monthly Review,* 29(1), May, pp. 13–19.

1977f. (with H. Magdoff), The editors reply [to: C. Marzani and M. Gordon, 'In defense of the Italian CP'], *Monthly Review,* 29(2), June, pp. 15–24.

1977g. (with H. Magdoff), Mao on Soviet economics and other subjects, *Monthly Review,* 29(4), September, pp. 1–20.

1977h. (with H. Magdoff), Bettelheim on revolution from above: the USSR in the 1920s, *Monthly Review,* 29(5), October, pp. 1–18. (Reprinted in 1980a, pp. 96–112.)

1977i. (with H. Magdoff), Steel and stagnation, *Monthly Review,* 29(6), November, pp. 1–9. (Reprinted in 1981b, pp. 23–30.)

1977j. (with H. Magdoff), Comment by the editors [on: J. Frieden, 'The Trilateral Commission'], *Monthly Review,* 29(7), December, pp. 19–22.

1978a. (with H. Magdoff), Multinational corporations and banks, *Monthly Review,* 29(8), January, pp. 1–9. (Reprinted in 1981b, pp. 31–39.)

1978b. Paul Sweezy replies [to: B. Pollitt, 'War and Soviet development strategy'], *Monthly Review,* 29(8), January, p. 63.

1978c. (with H. Magdoff), Emerging currency and trade wars, *Monthly Review,* 29(9), February, pp. 1–7. (Reprinted in 1981b, pp. 40–46.)

1978d. The present stage of the global crisis of capitalism, *Monthly Review,* 29(11), April, pp. 1–11. (Reprinted in 1981b, pp. 47–58.)

1978e. (with H. Magdoff), Debt and the business cycle, *Monthly Review,* 30(2), June, pp. 1–11. (Reprinted in 1981b, pp. 70–80.)

1978f. Paul Sweezy comments [on: H. Blumenfeld, 'Urban planning in the Soviet Union and China'], *Monthly Review,* 30(2), June, pp. 62–64.

1978g. Harry Braverman's achievement, *Monthly Review,* 30(4), September, pp. 30–35.

1978h. Is there a ruling class in the USSR?, *Monthly Review,* 30(5), October, pp. 1–17. (Reprinted in 1980a, pp. 113–133.)

1978i. Corporations, the state, and imperialism, *Monthly Review,* 30(6), November, pp. 1–10. (Reprinted in 1981b, pp. 81–89.)

1978j. Crisis within the crisis, *Monthly Review,* 20(7), December, pp. 7–10. (Reprinted in 1981b, pp. 90–93.)

1979a. (with H. Magdoff), Iran: the new crisis of American hegemony, *Monthly Review,* 30(9), February, pp. 1–24.

1979b. Varieties of inflation, *Monthly Review,* 30(10), March, pp. 44–49.

1979c. On the new global disorder, *Monthly Review,* 30(11), April, pp. 1–9. (Reprinted in 1981b, pp. 107–114.)

1979d. (with H. Magdoff), China: new theories for old, *Monthly Review,* 31(1), May, pp. 1–19.

1979e. (with H. Magdoff), Productivity slowdown: a false alarm, *Monthly Review,* 31(2), June, pp. 1–12. (Reprinted in 1981b, pp. 115–126.)

1979f. A crisis in Marxian theory, *Monthly Review,* 31(2), June, pp. 20–24.

1979g. Marxian value theory and crises, *Monthly Review,* 31(3), July–August, pp. 1–17. (Reprinted in I. Steedman *et al., The Value Controversy,* London: New Left Books, 1981, pp. 20–35.)

1979h. Paul Sweezy replies to Ernest Mandel, *Monthly Review,* 31(3), July–August, pp. 76–86.

1979i. (with H. Magdoff), Inflation without end?, *Monthly Review,* 31(6), November, pp. 1–10. (Reprinted in 1918b, pp. 127–136.)

1979j. (with H. Magdoff), Whither U.S. capitalism?, *Monthly Review,* 31(7), December, pp. 1–12. (Reprinted in 1981b, pp. 137–148.)

1980a. *Post–Revolutionary Society* (New York: Monthly Review Press).

1980b. Post–revolutionary society, in: 1980a, pp. 139–151.

1980c. (with H. Magdoff), Gold mania—capitalism's fever chart, *Monthly Review,* 31(8), January, pp. 1–8. (Reprinted in 1981b, pp. 149–156.)

1980d. Japan in perspective, *Monthly Review,* 31(9), February, pp. 1–14.

1980e. (with H. Magdoff), Cold war, inflation, and controls, *Monthly Review,* 31(10), March, pp. 1–9.

1980f. (with H. Magdoff), U.S. foreign policy in the 1980s, *Monthly Review,* 31(11), April, pp. 1–12. (Reprinted in 1981b, pp. 157–168.)

1980g. (with H. Magdoff), Wage-price controls and the working class, *Monthly Review,* 32(1), May, pp. 1–8.

1980h. (with H. Magdoff), The uses and abuses of measuring productivity, *Monthly Review,* 32(2), June, pp. 1–9. (Reprinted in 1981b, pp. 169–177.)

1980i. Capitalism and democracy, *Monthly Review,* 32(2), June, pp. 27–32.

1980j. The crisis of American capitalism, *Monthly Review,* 32(5), October, pp. 1–13. (Reprinted in 1981b, pp. 178–190.)

1980k. (with H. Magdoff), Are low savings ruining the U.S. economy?, *Monthly Review,* 32(7), December, pp. 1–12. (Reprinted in 1981b, pp. 191–202.)

1980l. (with H. Magdoff), Revolution and counter–revolution in Chile, *Journal of Latin American Studies,* 12(4), November, pp. 445–452.

1981a. *Four Lectures on Marxism* (New York: Monthly Review Press).

1981b. (with H. Magdoff), *The Deepening Crisis of US Capitalism* (New York: Monthly Review Press).

1981c. (with H. Magdoff), Reagan and the nemesis of inflation, *Monthly Review,* 32(8), January, pp. 1–10. (Reprinted in 1981b, pp. 203–212.)

1981d. (with H. Magdoff), Supply-side economics, *Monthly Review,* 32(10), March, pp. 1–7. (Reprinted in 1981b, pp. 213–219.)

1981e. Keynes as critic of capitalism, *Monthly Review,* 32(11), April, pp. 33–36.

1981f. Competition and monopoly, *Monthly Review* 33(1), May, pp. 1–16.

1981g. Paul Sweezy replies [to: C.L.R. James], *Monthly Review,* 33(1), May, pp. 55–56.

1981h. (with H. Magdoff), The deepening crisis of U.S. capitalism, *Monthly Review,* 33(5), October, pp. 1–16.

1981i. The economic crisis in the United States, *Monthly Review,* 33(7), December, pp. 1–10.

1982a. (with H. Magdoff), A new New Deal?, *Monthly Review,* 33(9), February, pp. 1–10.

1982b. Investment banking revisited, *Monthly Review,* 33(10), March, pp. 1–14.

1982c. Why stagnation?, *Monthly Review,* 34(2), June, pp. 1–10. (Reprinted 1987a, pp. 29–38.)

1982d. (with H. Magdoff) Nuclear chicken, *Monthly Review,* 34(4), September, pp. 1–11.

1982e. (with H. Magdoff), Financial instability: where will it all end?, *Monthly Review,* 34(6), November, pp. 18–23.

1982f. (with H. Magdoff), The responsibility of the left, *Monthly Review,* 34(7), December, pp. 1–9.

1983a. (with H. Magdoff), Listen Keynesians!, *Monthly Review,* 34(8), January, pp. 1–11. (Reprinted 1987a, pp. 39–49.).

1983b. The suppression of the Polish workers' movement, *Monthly Review,* 34(8), January, pp. 27–30.

1983c. (with H. Magdoff), The struggle to save social security, *Monthly Review,* 34(9), February, pp. 13–16.

1983d. Marxism and revolution 100 years after Marx, *Monthly Review* 34(10), March, pp. 1–11.

1983e. (with H. Magdoff), Supply-side theory and capital investment, *Monthly Review,* 34(11), April, pp. 1–9. (Reprinted in 1987a, pp. 50–58.)

1983f. (with H. Magdoff), Production and finance, *Monthly Review,* 35(1), May, pp. 1–13. (Reprinted in 1987a, pp. 93–105.)

1983g. (with H. Magdoff), Unemployment: the failure of private enterprise, *Monthly Review,* 35(2), June, pp. 1–9. (Reprinted in 1987a, pp. 59–67.)

1983h. (with H. Magdoff), Full recovery or stagnation, *Monthly Review,* 35(4), September, pp. 1–12.

1983i. (with H. Magdoff), International finance and national power, *Monthly Review,* 35(5), October, pp. 1–13. (Reprinted in 1987a, pp. 163–175.)

1983j. The Great Depression, *Monthly Review,* 35(4), September, pp. 51–56.

1983k. On socialism, *Monthly Review,* 35(5), October, pp. 35–39.

1983l. (with H. Magdoff), Where are we going?, *Monthly Review* 35(7), December, pp. 1–13.

1984a. (with H. Magdoff), The two faces of Third World debt, *Monthly Review,* 35(8), January, pp. 1–10. (Reprinted in 1987a, pp. 176–185.)

1984b. (with H. Magdoff), The left and the 1984 elections, *Monthly Review,* 35(9), February, pp. 1–6.

1984c. (with H. Magdoff), The federal deficit: the real issues, *Monthly Review,* 35(11), April, pp. 1–12. (Reprinted in 1987a, pp. 106–117.)

1984d. What's wrong with the American economy?, *Monthly Review,* 36(1), May, pp. 1–10. (Reprinted in B. S. Ortiz (ed.), *History As It Happened: Selected Articles From Monthly Review 1949–1989,* New York: Monthly Review Press 1990, pp. 211–218.)

1984e. Preface [to: C. West, 'Religion and the Left'], *Monthly Review,* 36(3), July–August, pp. 1–8.

1984f. (with H. Magdoff), A lesson from history, *Monthly Review,* 36(4), September, pp. 1–12.

1984g. (with H. Magdoff), The need for tax reform, *Monthly Review,* 36(6), November, pp. 1–9.

1984h. (with H. Magdoff), Money out of control, *Monthly Review,* 36(7), December, pp. 1–12. (Reprinted in 1987a, pp. 118–129.)

1985a. (with H. Magdoff), Four more years—of what?, *Monthly Review,* 36(8), January, pp. 1–12.

1985b. (with H. Magdoff), What is Marxism?, *Monthly Review,* 36(10), March, pp. 1–6.

1985c. (with H. Magdoff), The deficit, the debt, and the real world, *Monthly Review,* 37(1), May, pp. 1–11. (Reprinted in 1987a, pp. 130–140.)

1985d. (with H. Magdoff), Lessons of Vietnam, *Monthly Review,* 37(2), June, pp. 1–13.

1985e. After capitalism—what?, *Monthly Review,* 37(3), July–August, pp. 98–111.

1985f. (with H. Magdoff), The strange recovery of 1983–1984, *Monthly Review,* 37(5), October, pp. 1–11. (Reprinted in 1987a, pp. 68–78.)

1985g. (with H. Magdoff), The financial explosion, *Monthly Review,* 37(7), December, pp. 1–10. (Reprinted in 1987a, pp. 141–150.)

1986a. The regime of capital, *Monthly Review,* 38(8), January, pp. 1–11. (Reprinted in 1987a, pp. 163–175.)

1986b. (with H. Magdoff), Questions for the peace movement, *Monthly Review,* 37(10), March, pp. 1–13. (Reprinted in 1987a, pp. 196–208.)

1986c. (with H. Magdoff), The stakes in South Africa, *Monthly Review,* 37(11), April, pp. 1–6.

1986d. (with H. Magdoff), The alternative to stagnation, *Monthly Review,* 38(2), June, pp. 1–12. (Reprinted in 1987a, pp. 79–90.)

1986e. (with H. Magdoff), The logic of stagnation, *Monthly Review,* 38(5), October, pp. 1–19.

1986f. (with H. Magdoff), All eyes on SDI, *Monthly Review,* 38(7), December, pp. 1–9.

1986g. A final word [on: C. Bettelheim, 'More on the nature of the Soviet system'], *Monthly Review,* 38(7), December, pp. 38–41.

1987a. *Stagnation and the Financial Explosion* (with Harry Magdoff) (New York: Monthly Review Press).

1987b. Baran, Paul Alexander (1910–1964), in: J. Eatwell, M. Milgate & P. Newman (eds), *The New Palgrave: A Dictionary of Economics,* Volume I, pp. 188–189 (London: Macmillan).

1987c. Monopoly capitalism, in: J. Eatwell, M. Milgate & P. Newman (eds), *The New Palgrave: A Dictionary of Economics,* Volume III, pp. 541–544 (London: Macmillan).

1987d. (with H. Magdoff), Vietnam and Nicaragua, *Monthly Review,* 38(10), March, pp. 1–6.

1987e. Interview with Paul M. Sweezy [by: E. A. Tonak & S. Sauran], *Monthly Review,* 38(11), April, pp. 1–28.

1987f. (with H. Magdoff), The coming crisis and the responsibility of the Left, *Monthly Review,* 39(2), June, pp. 1–5.

1987g. (with H. Magdoff), Capitalism and the distribution of income and wealth, *Monthly Review,* 39(5), October, pp. 1–16. (Reprinted in 1988a, pp. 27–42.)

1987h. (with H. Magdoff), International cooperation—a way out?, *Monthly Review,* 39(6), November, pp. 1–19.

1988a. *The Irreversible Crisis* (with Harry Magdoff) (New York: Monthly Review Press).

1988b. (with H. Magdoff), The stock market crash and its aftermath, *Monthly Review,* 39(10), March, pp. 1–13. (Reprinted in 1988a, pp. 43–56.)

1988c. (with H. Magdoff), The great malaise, *Monthly Review,* 39(11), April, pp. 1–8. (Reprinted in 1988a, pp. 57–64.)

1988d. (with H. Magdoff), Historic moments, *Monthly Review,* 40(1), May, pp. 1–8.

1988e. (with H. Magdoff), The uprising in Palestine, *Monthly Review,* 40(5), October, pp. 1–17. (Reprinted in B. S. Ortiz (ed.), *History As It Happened: Selected Articles From Monthly Review 1949–1989,* New York: Monthly Review Press 1990, pp. 259–272.)

1988f. (with H. Magdoff), Anniversary of the crash, *Monthly Review,* 40(6), November, pp. 1–12. (Reprinted in 1988a, pp. 65–76, and in B. S. Ortiz (ed.), *History As It Happened: Selected Articles From Monthly Review 1949–1989,* New York: Monthly Review Press 1990, pp. 273–281.)

1989a. (with H. Magdoff), Lessons of the 1988 elections, *Monthly Review,* 40(9), February, pp. 1–9.

1989b. A great American, *Monthly Review,* 40(11), April, pp. 37–44 (first published in *Monthly Review,* 14(2), June 1962, pp. 74–80).

1989c. (with H. Magdoff), A new stage of capitalism ahead?, *Monthly Review,* 41(1), May, pp. 1–15.

1989d. (with H. Magdoff), Capitalism and the environment (with Harry Magdoff), *Monthly Review,* 41(2), June, pp. 1–10.

1989e. (with H. Magdoff), Socialism and ecology, *Monthly Review,* 41(4), September, pp. 1–8.

1989f. US imperialism in the 1990s, *Monthly Review,* 41(5), October, pp. 1–17.

1990a. (with H. Magdoff), *Perestroika* and the future of socialism—Part 1, *Monthly Review,* 41(10), March, pp. 1–13.

1990b. (with H. Magdoff), *Perestroika* and the future of socialism—Part Two, *Monthly Review,* 41(11), April, pp. 1–17.

1990c. Nineteen eighty-nine, *Monthly Review,* 41(11), April, pp. 18–21.

1990d. (with H. Magdoff), Investment for what?, *Monthly Review,* 42(2), June, pp. 1–10.

1990e. Preface for a new edition of *Post-Revolutionary Society, Monthly Review,* 42(3), July–August, pp. 5–9.

1990f. Cuba: a left US view, *Monthly Review,* 42(4), September, pp. 17–21.

1990g. Marxist views: an interview with Paul M. Sweezy, [by: Y. Watanabe & Y. Wakima], *Monthly Review,* 42(5), October, pp. 1–15.

1990h. (with H. Magdoff), Dangers of democracy, *Monthly Review,* 42(7), December, pp. 1–7.

1991a. (with H. Magdoff), Where are we going?, *Monthly Review,* 42(10), March, pp. 1–15.

1991b. What's new in the new world order?, *Monthly Review*, 43(2), June, pp. 1–4.

1991c. (with H. Magdoff), Pox Americana, *Monthly Review*, 43(3), July–August, pp. 1–13.

1991d. Class societies: the Soviet Union and the United States. Two interviews with Paul Sweezy [interviewed by K. Okonogi & R. Weissman], *Monthly Review*, 43(7), December, pp. 1–17.

1991e. *Monopoly Capital* after twenty-five years, *Monthly Review*, 43(7), December, pp. 52–57.

1992a. (with H. Magdoff), Globalization—to what end? Part I, *Monthly Review*, 43(9), February, pp. 1–18.

1992b. (with H. Magdoff), Globalization—to what end? Part II, *Monthly Review*, 43(10), March, pp. 10–19.

1992c. The theory of capitalist development, chapter one: Marx's method, *Monthly Review*, 44(7), December, pp. 14–27. (Reprinted from 1942a, chapter 1.)

1993a. Socialism: legacy and renewal, *Monthly Review*, 44(8), January, pp. 1–9.

1993b. Leo Huberman and *Monthly Review*, *Monthly Review*, 45(6), November, pp. 49–54.

1994a. *Monthly Review* in historical perspective, *Monthly Review*, 45(8), January, pp. 1–7.

1994b. A brief interview for *Contropiano*, *Monthly Review*, 45(9), February, pp. 16–18.

1994c. The triumph of financial capital, *Monthly Review*, 46(2), June, pp. 1–11.

1995a. Remarks on receiving the National Emergency Civil Liberties Committee Tom Paine award, *Monthly Review*, 46(9), February, pp. 37–38.

1995b. Economic reminiscences, *Monthly Review*, 47(1), May, pp. 1–11.

1996. D. Colander & H. Landreth (eds), *The Coming of Keynesianism to America*, chapter IV (Elgar) [an interview with Sweezy].

1997a. Review of D. Berman and J. O'Connor, *Who Owns the Sun?*, *Monthly Review*, 49(2), July, pp. 60–61.

1997b. More (or less) on globalization, *Monthly Review*, 49(4), September, pp. 1–4.

1998. The *Communist* Manifesto today, *Monthly Review*, 50(1), May, pp. 8–10. (Reprinted as 'Foreword' in: K. Marx & F. Engels, *The Communist Manifesto*, edited by E. Meiskins Wood, New York: Monthly Review Press, 1998, pp. ix–xi.)

1999. An interview with Paul M. Sweezy, *Monthly Review*, 51(1), May, pp. 31–53 [interview with C. Phelps. This interview is a composite from three sessions conducted by Christopher Phelps in tape-recorded telephone conversations in 1997 and 1999, and seven sessions conducted by Andros Skotnes for the Columbia Oral History Project in 1986 and 1987].

2000a. Cars and cities, *Monthly Review*, 51(11), April, pp. 19–34 (first published in *Monthly Review*, 23(11), April 1973, pp. 1–18).

2000b. Statement to the New Hampshire Attorney General, *Monthly Review*, 51(11), April, pp. 37–41 [written in 1954].

Other references

Note that Sweezy's middle name is occasionally incorrectly spelt 'Malor'.

Aglietta, M. (1979) *A Theory of Capitalist Regulation* (London: New Left Books).

Allen, F. (1938) *Can Capitalism Last?* (London: Left Book Club).

Baran, P. A. (1952) National economic planning, in: B. F. Haley (ed.), *A Survey of Contemporary Economics, Volume II*, pp. 355–403 (Homewood, IL: Irwin).

Baran, P. A. (1957) [1973] *The Political Economy of Growth* (New York: Monthly Review Press). (Reprinted Harmondsworth: Penguin.)

Bauer, O. (1936) *Zwischen Zwei Weltkriegen?* (Bratislava: Eugen Prager Verlag).

Berle, A. A., Jr. & Means, G. C. (1932) *The Modern Corporation and Private Property* (New York: Macmillan).

Bober, M. M. (1943) Review of P. M. Sweezy, *The Theory of Capitalist Development, American Economic Review* 43(2), pp. 380–386.

Bortkiewicz, L. von. (1907) On the correction of Marx's fundamental theoretical construction in the third volume of *Capital, Jahrbuch für Nationalökonomie und Statistik.*

Bowles, S., Gordon, D. M. & Weisskopf, T. E. (1984). *Beyond the Wasteland: A Democratic Alternative to Economic Decline* (London: Verso).

Brenner, R. (1977) The origins of capitalist development: a critique of neo-Smithian Marxism, *New Left Review,* 104, pp. 25–92.

Burkitt, P. (1991) From equilibrium to Marxian crisis theory: expectations in the work of Paul Sweezy, *Economie Appliquee,* 44(3), pp. 59–80.

Burnham, J. (1941) *The Managerial Revolution* (New York: John Day).

Davis, J. B. (Ed.) (1992) *The Economic Surplus in Advanced Economies* (Aldershot: Edward Elgar).

Dobb, M. H. (1937) *Political Economy and Capitalism: Some Essays in Economic Tradition* (London: Routledge & Kegan Paul).

Domar, E. S. (1948) The problem of capital accumulation, *American Economic Review* 38(5), pp. 777–794.

Edwards, R. C. (1979) *Contested Terrain: The Transformation of the Workplace in the Twentieth Century* (London: Heinemann).

Emmanuel, A. (1972) *Unequal Exchange: A Study of the Imperialism of Trade* (New York: Monthly Review Press).

Foster, J. B. (1986) *The Theory of Monopoly Capitalism* (New York: Monthly Review Press).

Foster, J. B. (1987) Sweezy, Paul Malor (born 1910), in J. Eatwell, M. Milgate & P. Newman (Eds), *The New Palgrave: A Dictionary of Economics,* Volume IV, pp. 580–582 (London: Macmillan).

Foster, J. B. (1999) Remarks on Paul Sweezy on the occasion of his receipt of the Veblen-Commons award, *Journal of Economic Issues,* 33(2), June, pp. 223–228. [Same issue includes brief valedictory address by P. Burkett, pp. 219–221; Foster's piece reprinted in *Monthly Review,* 51(4), September, pp. 39–44].

Foster, J. B. (2000) *Monopoly Capital* at the turn of the millennium, *Monthly Review,* 51(11), pp. 1–18.

Foster, J. B. (2002a) Paul Sweezy and the monopoly capital school, in: D. Dowd (ed.), *Understanding Capitalism,* pp. 132–150 (London & Sydney: Pluto).

Foster, J. B. (2002b) Paul Marlor Sweezy (born 1910), in: P. Arestis & M. Sawyer (Eds), *A Biographical Dictionary of Dissenting Economists,* 2nd edn, pp. 642–651 (Cheltenham, UK & Northampton, MA: Edward Elgar).

Foster, J. B. & Szlajfer, H. (Eds) (1984) *The Faltering Economy* (New York: Monthly Review Press).

Georgescu-Roegen, N. (1960) Mathematical proofs of the breakdown of capitalism, *Econometrica,* 28(2), pp. 225–243.

Hansen, A. H. (1939) Economic progress and declining population growth, *American Economic Review,* 29(1), pp. 1–15.

Hilferding, R. [1910] (1980) *Finance Capital* (London: Routledge & Kegan Paul).

Hilton, R. (ed.) (1976) *The Transition from Feudalism to Capitalism* (London: New Left Books).

Howard, M. C. & King, J. E. (1992) *A History of Marxian Economics: Volume II, 1929–1990* (Princeton: Princeton University Press & London: Macmillan).

Jacoby, R. (1982) *Dialectics of Defeat: Contours of Western Marxism* (Cambridge: Cambridge University Press).

Kahn, R. F. (1933) Letter to Joan Robinson, 24 February 1933: Richard Kahn Papers, King's College Modern Archive Centre, Cambridge, RFK/13/90/1/151, p. 5.

Kahn, R. F. (1989) *The Economics of the Short Period* (London: Macmillan).

Kalecki, M. (1942) A theory of profits, *Economic Journal* 52(206–7), pp. 258–267.

Kalecki, M. (1943) Political aspects of full employment, *Political Quarterly, pp.* 322–331.

King, J. E. (1988) *Economic Exiles* (London: Macmillan).

King, J. E. (2004) Frederick Allen and the Future of Capitalism, *History of Economic Ideas,* 12 (2), pp. 1–18.

Lebowitz, M. (1990) Paul M. Sweezy, in: M. Berg (ed.), *Political Economy in the Twentieth Century* (Hemel Hempstead, UK: Phillip Allan), pp. 131–161.

Lenin, V. J. [1917] (1968) *Imperialism, the Highest Stage of Capitalism* (Moscow: Progress Publishers).

Lifschultz, L. F. (1974) Could Karl Marx teach economics in America?, *Ramparts,* 12, pp. 27–30.

Marcuse, H. (1969) *An Essay on Liberation* (Boston: Beacon Press).

May, D. L. (1981) *From New Deal to New Economics: The American Liberal Response to the Recession of 1937* (New York: Greenwood Press).

Meek, R. L. (1966) Review of P. Baran & P. Sweezy, *Monopoly Capital, Economic Journal,* 77(305), pp. 114–116.

Minsky, H. P. (1986) *Stabilizing an Unstable Economy* (New Haven: Yale University Press).

O'Connor, J. (1966) Review of P. Baran & P. Sweezy, *Monopoly Capital, New Left Review,* 40, pp. 38–50.

Petry, F. (1916) *Der Soziale Gehalt der Marzschen Werttheorie* (Jena: Gustav Fischer).

Resnick, S. A. & R. D. Wolff (Eds) (1985) *Rethinking Marxism: Essays for Harry Magdoff and Paul Sweezy* (Brooklyn, NY: Autonomedia/Prager). [Includes comprehensive bibliography by David Hillard, up to April 1984.]

Robinson, J. (1953) An open letter from a Keynesian to a Marxist, in: J. Robinson, *On Re-Reading Marx* (Cambridge: Students' Bookshops Ltd), pp. 19–23.

Samuelson, P. A. (1971) Understanding the Marxian notion of exploitation: a summary of the so-called transformation problem between Marxian values and competitive prices, *Journal of Economic Literature,* 9(2), pp. 399–431.

Sherman, H. J. (1966) Review of P. Baran & P. Sweezy, *Monopoly Capital, American Economic Review,* 56(5), pp. 919–921.

Simon, J. J. (2000) *Sweezy versus New Hampshire:* the radicalism of principle, *Monthly Review,* 51(11), April, pp. 35–37.

Stanfield, J. R. (1973) *The Economic Surplus and Neo-Marxism* (Lexington, MA: D.C. Heath).

Steedman, I. (1977) *Marx After Sraffa* (London: NLB).

Steindl, J. (1952) *Maturity and Stagnation in American Capitalism* (Oxford: Blackwell).

Stigler, G. J. (1947) The kinky oligopoly demand curve and rigid prices, *Journal of Political Economy,* 55(4), pp. 432–459.

Symposium (1966) *Monopoly Capital:* a symposium, *Science & Society,* 30(4), pp. 461–496. (Contributions from M. E. Sharpe, pp. 461–470; M. Dobb, pp. 470–445; J. M. Gillman, pp. 475–481; T. Prager, pp. 481–487; and O. Nathan, pp. 487–496).

Symposium (2000) Happy birthday, Paul!, *Monthly Review,* 51(11), April, pp. 42–64.

Tudor, H. & Tudor, J. M. (Eds) (1988) *Marxism and Social Democracy: The Revisionist Debate 1896–1898* (Cambridge: Cambridge University Press).

Weisskopf, T. E. (1979) Marxian crisis theory and the rate of profit in the postwar U.S. economy, *Cambridge Journal of Economics,* 3(3), pp. 341–378.

10 Paradise lost and found?

The econometric contributions of Clive W. J. Granger and Robert F. Engle

Peter Hans Matthews

'Paradise Lost and Found? The Econometric Contributions of Clive W. J. Granger and Robert F. Engle' by Peter Hans Matthews from *Review of Political Economy* (2005), Volume 17, Issue 1 (Taylor and Francis Ltd, http://www. informaworld.com), reprinted by permission of the publisher.

1 Introduction

The 2003 Bank of Sweden Nobel Prize in Economic Science was awarded to Clive W. J. Granger, Professor Emeritus of Economics at the University of California at San Diego, and Robert F. Engle, the Michael Armelinno Professor of Finance at the Stern School at New York University, for their contributions to time series econometrics. In its official announcement, the Royal Swedish Academy of Sciences cited Granger's work on 'common trends' or *cointegration* and Engle's on 'time-varying volatility', but this understates their influence, both on the broader profession and, in this particular case, on each other.

Much of the research that the Royal Academy cited, not least their co-authored papers on cointegration (Engle & Granger, 1987) and 'long memory processes (Ding *et al.*, 1993), has been published over the last two decades, but even before then, both laureates were well known for their other contributions to econometrics. Granger's (1969) eponymous *causality test* and the results of his Monte Carlo studies with Paul Newbold on *spurious regression* (Granger & Newbold, 1974) were already (and still are) part of most economists' tool kits, Engle's (1974a) research on urban economics was familiar to specialists, and both (Granger & Hatanaka, 1964; Engle, 1973) were pioneers in the application of *spectral methods* to economic data. And both have pursued other, related, research avenues since then: Granger continues to build on his earlier research on nonlinear models (Granger & Anderson, 1978), forecasting (Granger & Bates, 1969) and long memory models (Granger & Joyeux, 1980), and in addition to his seminal paper on the concept of exogeneity (Engle *et al.*, 1983), Engle has become the pre-eminent practitioner of the 'new financial econometrics' and its practical applications, like *value at risk* (Engle & Manganelli, 2001) and options pricing (Engle & Rosenberg, 1995).

For more than two decades from the mid-1970s until the late 1990s, Engle and Granger were colleagues at the University of California at San Diego, during which time its Economics Department joined LSE and Yale as the most productive centers of econometric research in the world. The paths that took them to UCSD were quite different, however. Clive Granger was born in Swansea, Wales, in 1934, and completed both his undergraduate (BA, 1955) and graduate (PhD, 1959) degrees in statistics at the University of Nottingham, UK, where he remained to research and teach, as a member of the Mathematics Department, until 1973. In an interview with Peter C. B. Phillips (1997, p. 257), he recalls that when he first started to teach, 'I knew all about Borel sets...but I did not know how to form a variance from data...so I had to learn real statistics as I went along.' But as someone who was from the start interested in the application of statistical methods, he benefitted from his position as the lone 'official statistician' on campus:

> Faculty from all kinds of areas would come to me with their statistical problems. I would have people from the History Department, the English Department, Chemistry, Psychology, and it was terrific training for a young statistician to be given data from all kinds of different places and be asked to help analyze it. I learned a lot, just from being forced to read things and think about...diverse types of problems with different kinds of data sets. I think that now people, on the whole, do not get that kind of training.
>
> (Phillips, 1997, p. 258)

Some of his earliest publications reveal this breadth: in addition to his first papers in economics, there are papers on (real) sunspots (Granger, 1957), tidal river floods (Granger, 1959) and personality disorders (Granger *et al.,* 1964)! By the time Granger had moved to southern California, in 1974, his reputation as an innovative econometrician with a preference for 'empirical relevance' over 'mathematical niceties' (Phillips, 1997, p. 254) was well-established.

Robert Engle was born almost a decade later, in 1942, in Syracuse, New York, and received a BSc from Williams in physics in 1964. He continued these studies at a superconductivity lab at Cornell but switched to economics after one year, earning his PhD in 1969. In a recent interview with Francis Diebold (2003), he reflected briefly on this transformation. When Diebold (2003, p. 1161) observes that Engle is one of several prominent econometricians – he mentions John Cochrane, Joel Horowitz, Glenn Rudebusch, James Stock and another Nobel laureate, Daniel McFadden – with a physics background, Engle responds that 'physicists are continually worried about integrating theory and data, and that's why...physicists tend to make good econometricians [since] that's what econometricians do.' So far, so good. But when he later recounts his job interviews at Yale and MIT, he speculates that 'one of things that impressed them was that I knew things from my physics background that had been useful in analyzing this time aggregation problem, like contour integrals and stuff like that, and they thought "Oh, anyone who can do that can probably do something else!"' (Diebold, 2003, p. 1164). To be fair, and as this remark hints, his dissertation, written under the supervision of T. C. Liu, tackled an important econometric problem, namely the relationship between the frequency of economic data and model specification, and led to his first professional publication (Engle & Liu, 1972). Furthermore, a number of the tools and ideas would later become relevant for his research on cointegration. After six years at MIT, where he found a climate that was 'inhospitable in an intellectual sense for the time-series people' (Diebold, 2003, p. 1166) – one immediate consequence of which was an impressive series of papers (Engle, 1974a, 1974b, 1976, and Engle *et al.,* 1977, for example) in urban economics – he moved to UCSD in 1974.

The new econometricians at UCSD – another theorist, Halbert White, was hired soon after, for example – found themselves in a world where the presumptions of classical statistics – stationary (constant mean and finite variance) random variables with 'thin-tailed' (normal, for example) distributions – were often implausible *and* the usual remedies had become suspect. In short, paradise lost.

As the next section describes, the development of *autoregressive conditional heteroscedastic* (ARCH) models, and the extensions it soon inspired – GARCH, ARCH-M, IGARCH, EGARCH, FIGARCH and TARCH, to mention just a few! – allowed researchers to model the otherwise unexplained variability of some time series in a more systematic fashion and, in the process, to represent (at least) two common properties of numerous series, *clustered volatility* and the *leptokurtosis* (or fat tailedness) of unconditional distributions. The third section considers Granger's radical reformulation of the old *nonsense correlation* problem, a consequence of the unreflective use of non-stationary data, and his new solution of such data – paradise found? – based on the concept of *cointegration.* Because Granger's name will (also) be forever linked to the problem of causality – even if this was not the reason he was awarded the Prize – the fourth section provides a brief but critical review of this literature, as well as some of the laureates' other contributions. The fifth section then provides the rationale for the question mark in the title: it reflects on several practical and methodological criticisms of the 'revolution' in time series econometrics, with an emphasis on the particular concerns of heterodox economists.

2 Paradise lost and found, part I

Consider the annual rate of return on the American stock market from 1871 to 2002, as reported in Shiller (2003). As the histogram in Figure 1 reveals, the distribution of returns is fatter tailed than the (superimposed) normal distribution or, as Mandelbrot (1963) was one of the first to appreciate, 'extreme values' are more common in economics than in nature. (Inasmuch as Mandelbrot and his intellectual heirs have been most interested in financial market data, this seems an appropriate point of departure.) The plot of the *squares* of these returns in Figure 2 also hints, however, that if one were to model these returns as independent draws from some leptokurtic distribution, important information

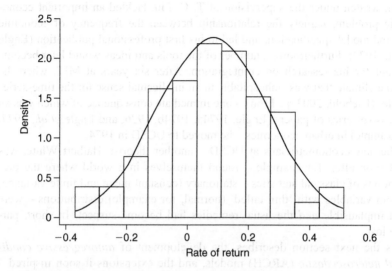

Figure 1 Rates of return in the stock market, 1871–2002

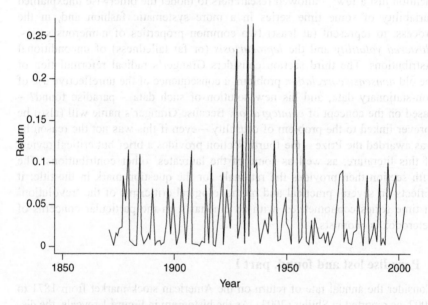

Figure 2 Squared returns in the stock market, 1871–2002

would be lost. In particular, it seems that extreme returns were more common when returns in the previous period(s) were also extreme, a phenomenon known as *volatility clustering*. One reason for the immediate success of ARCH models, first introduced in Engle (1982), was their consistency with both features.

To illustrate, consider another sort of time series, an important but understud-

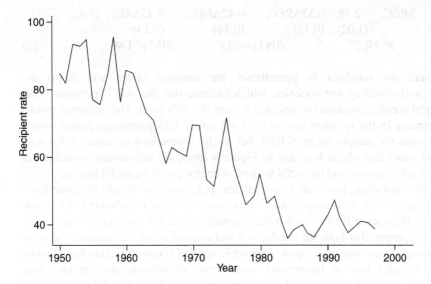

Figure 3 The UI recipient rate in the United States

ied element of labor market behavior, the *recipient rate* for unemployment insurance (UI) in the United States between 1950 and 1997, as depicted in Figure 3. The recipient rate, the ratio of insured to total unemployment, is an imperfect measure of UI utilization: while the collection rate and fraction of insured unemployment (Blank & Card, 1991) are perhaps more intuitive measures, both are more difficult to measure.[1]

As Figure 3 shows, this rate peaked, at close to 100%, in the early 1950s, but has fallen, more or less steadily, ever since, with two sharp declines in the mid 1960s and early 1980s. At the end of the sample period, it stood at 39%, close to its nadir of 36% in 1984.

The simplest dynamic model of the recipient rate would perhaps assume that its difference from one year to the next, ΔREC_t, was equal to:

$$\Delta REC_t = \beta_0 + \sum_{j=1}^{p} \beta_j \Delta REC_{t-j} + u_t \qquad (1)$$

where u_t is some mean zero, constant variance error or 'innovation'. Under this specification, the expected annual change in the recipient rate will be $\beta_0/(1 - \sum_{j=1}^{p} \beta_j)$ over the long run, but the expected change in any one year, *conditional on the history of past changes,* can be higher or lower than this. The standard specification tests reveal $p = 3$ to be a reasonable choice, and least squares estimation of equation (1) produces:

$$\Delta REC_t = -2.38 - 0.33\Delta REC_{t-1} - 0.42\Delta REC_{t-2} - 0.35\Delta REC_{t-3} + \hat{u}_t$$
$$\quad\;\;(1.02)\quad(0.15)\qquad\quad(0.14)\qquad\quad(0.13)$$
$$R^2 = 0.27\qquad\qquad BP(1) = 0.58\qquad BP(2) = 1.80 \qquad\qquad (2)$$

where the numbers in parentheses are standard errors and $BP(x)$ are Breusch–Godfrey test statistics, which indicate that the null hypothesis of no serial correlation cannot be rejected at even the 10% level. The estimated annual decrease in the recipient rate in the long run is 1.13 percentage points, which exceeds the sample mean of 0.98, but as the comparison of actual differences and (one) step ahead forecasts in Figure 4 hints, the information contained in past differences could be useful to those who, for example, set UI premia.

It is not clear, however, how confident policy-makers should be about these forecasts, *even if the simple model that produced them is believed to be 'sensible'*. The reason for this is that the standard confidence intervals for such forecasts assume that both the conditional and unconditional variances of the error term u_t are constant and equal. And while applied econometricians have known for decades how to incorporate some forms of *heteroscedasticty* into their models, none of the proposed variations systematically captured the intuition of most policy-makers that (a) some periods are more *turbulent* than others and (b) in such periods, forecast confidence is diminished.

To see whether UI claim behavior exhibits such turbulence, consider the behavior of the squared residuals $\hat{u}_t^2$ from this model over time, as depicted in Figure 5. If clusters were present, these squared residuals should persistently exceed their sample mean, the horizontal line in the same diagram, for sustained periods of time. With the exception of a run of three years in the late 1950s – which comes as a surprise inasmuch as this has never been considered a turbu-

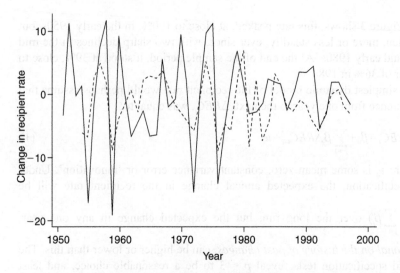

Figure 4 Actual and predicted changes in the recipient rate, simple univariate model

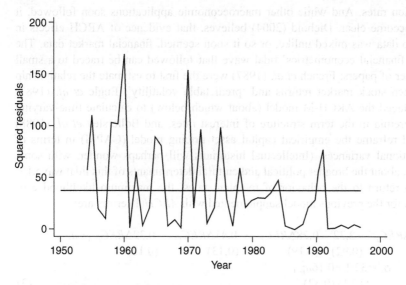

Figure 5 Squared residuals from the simple model

lent period from the perspective of the UI program – there is little evidence of this.

A more formal test of whether or not the introduction of ARCH effects is warranted was first proposed in Engle (1982): in an auxiliary regression of the squared residuals on a constant and q lags of themselves, the product of the sample size T and R^2 will be distributed $\chi^2(q)$ under the null hypothesis of no ARCH effects. Consistent with Figure 5, the null cannot be rejected at the 10% level – or for that matter, the 50% level – in this model.

In this context, it is still useful to understand how such effects *could* be incorporated into the model. In the spirit of Engle (1982), suppose the error term u_t is equal to $v_t \sqrt{\delta_0 + \delta_1 u_{t-1}^2}$, where v_t is an independent and identically distributed (i.i.d.) random variable with mean 0 and variance 1, and the parameters are restricted such that $\delta_0 > 0$ and $0 \le \delta_1 < 1$. It is not difficult to show that the unconditional variance of u_t will be constant and equal to $\delta_0/(1 - \delta_1)$ – the reason for the restrictions on δ_0 and δ_1 – but that, conditional on u_{t-1}^2, the variance of $u_t + k$, $k = 0, 1,\ldots$, is $\delta_0(1 + \delta_1 + \delta_1^2 + \cdots + \delta_1^{k-2}) + \delta_1^{k-1} u_{t-1}^2$. Furthermore, the kurtosis of the (unconditional) distribution of innovations is $3(1 - \delta_1^2)/(1 - 3\delta_1^2)$ which exceeds that of the normal (which is 3) if $\delta_1 \ge 0$, and is therefore consistent with 'fat tails'. This is the *ARCH*(1) model but in most applications with high(er) frequency data, a natural extension of this model, *ARCH*(p), is needed, in which $u_t = v_t \sqrt{\delta_0 + \delta_1 u_{t-1}^2 + \delta_2 u_{t-2}^2 + \cdots + \delta_p u_{t-p}^2}$.

In his first illustration of the concept, for example, Engle (1982) fit an *ARCH*(4) to a similar (autoregressive, that is) model of quarterly inflation rates in the UK and soon after, Engle & Kraft (1983) would conclude that an *ARCH*(8) model was needed to represent clustered volaility in quarterly US inflation rates. And while other macroeconomic applications soon followed, it had become clear, Diebold (2004) believes, that evidence of ARCH effects in macro data was mixed unlike, or so it soon seemed, financial market data. The 'new financial econometrics' tidal wave that followed can be traced to a small number of papers: French et al. (1987) were the first to estimate the relationship between stock market returns and 'predictable volatility', Engle et al. (1987) introduced the ARCH-M model (about which below) to calculate time-varying risk premia in the term structure of interest rates, and Bollerslev et al. (1988) would reframe the empirical capital asset pricing model (CAPM) in terms of conditional variances. (Intellectual historians will perhaps wonder, with some cause, about the broader political and cultural determinants of this tidal wave.)

To return to the behavior of recipient rates, the maximum likelihood estimates for the previous model supplemented with $ARCH(1)$ errors are:

$$\Delta REC_t = -2.32 - 0.28\Delta REC_{t-1} - 0.41\Delta REC_{t-2} - 0.32\Delta REC_{t-3} + \hat{u}_t$$
$$\quad\quad (0.92)\quad (0.19)\quad\quad\quad (0.13)\quad\quad\quad (0.12)$$
$$\sigma_t^2 = 32.1 + 0.16u_{t-1}^2$$
$$\quad (12.1)\ (0.32) \tag{3}$$

where σ_t^2 is the conditional variance of u_t. Given the results of the Engle (1982) test, it comes as no surprise that this has little effect: the estimated coefficients on the ΔREC_{t-k} variables, and their standard errors, are almost the same as in equation (2), and the coefficient on u_{t-1}^2, which drives the ARCH effect, is statistically insignificant. The size of the last coefficient calls for comment, however: if significant, it would mean that a squared residual of 100 in one year, which is substantial but not implausible in this context, would push the conditional variance in the next year to 48.1, or 25% above the unconditional variance of 38.2 and, as a result, diminish forecast confidence.

Two of ARCH's numerous descendants also deserve mention in this context. *Generalized ARCH*, or GARCH, models, the brainchild of Tim Bollerslev (1986), a student and later collaborator of Engle's, have become even more common than their ancestor. A *GARCH(q, r)* specification, for example, assumes that the conditional variance of the error in period t, σ_t^2, is $\delta_0 + \delta_1 u_{t-1}^2 + \delta_2 u_{t-2}^2 + \cdots + \delta_q u_{t-q}^2 + \tau_1 \sigma_{t-r}^2 + \cdots + \tau_r \sigma_{t-r}^2$, but this is more parsimonious than first seems: in practice, *GARCH(1, 1)* or *GARCH(2, 1)* is often sufficient.

If heterodox economists should be interested in GARCH models for practical reasons, the *ARCH in mean* or ARCH-M specification, first proposed in Engle et al. (1987), is important for substantive reasons. In the UI example, it *could* have been the case that the recipient rate was itself a function of labor market turbulence or, to be more precise, conditional variance both past and present:

$$\Delta REC_t = \beta_0 + \sum_{j=1}^{p} \beta_j \Delta REC_{t-j} + \sum_{k=0}^{w} \beta_k \sigma_{t-k}^2 + u_t$$

where the conditional variance of u_t is modelled as an ARCH or GARCH process. In a similar vein, the determination of wages, or even the 'division of the working day', could reflect not just relative bargaining power, however measured, but also the conditional turbulence of this process. (As alluded to earlier, it was not Marx that inspired Engle *et al.* (1987), however, but William Sharpe, one of the founders of modern finance!)

It should be noted, however, that in small samples like this one – and sometimes in much more substantial ones – the algorithms that econometric software programs use to calculate the maxima of likelihood functions often fail to converge. (Over some of its domain, the likelihood function is so 'flat' that local maxima are difficult to find.) Indeed, in this particular case, where the evidence of ARCH effects is far from decisive, it would not surprise experienced practitioners that neither *GARCH*(1, 1) nor *ARCH-M*(1) converged reliably.

Finally, the development of ARCH owes at least little to the influence of David Hendry and the 'LSE approach' to econometrics: in his interview with Diebold (2003), Engle recalls that the first ARCH paper (Engle, 1982) was started, and then finished, while on leave at LSE, and that Hendry's influence even extended to the choice of name and memorable acronym. Because cointegration is also consistent with, perhaps even a hallmark of, this approach, a more detailed discussion will be postponed until the fifth section.

3 Paradise lost and found, part II

Cointegration theory is perhaps best understood as a new approach to *the identification of long-run (equilibrium) relationships in data with stochastic trends.* Few recent contributions to economics have influenced its actual practice more: a keyword search of EconLit shows almost three and a half thousand papers on 'cointegration', most of them published since 1990, a number that is more than four fifths that for 'Keynes' or more than double that for 'Marx'. The two most common sorts of application have been the reconsideration of traditional (that is, orthodox) macroeconomic relationships – the list of canonical examples includes the consumption function (Banarjee & Hendry, 1992), the demand for money (Dickey *et al.,* 1992) and purchasing power parity (Taylor, 1995) – and the behavior of asset prices (Campbell & Shiller, 1987).

Interest in cointegration has not been limited to the mainstream, however. Zacharias' (2001) re-evaluation of the evidence for profit rate equalization in the United States, for example, has a distinct classical, even Marxian, flavor, and Loranger (2001) specifies a 'regulationist' model of the Canadian economy in these terms. And despite the concerns of Davidson (1991) about reliance on probabilistic methods in an *uncertain* world, a substantial number of post Keynesians have used these methods: in a series of papers, Atesoglu (2000, 2002) finds support for what he calls the Keynes–Weintraub–Davidson (!) model of employment, while Lopez & Cruz (2000) discern the operation of Thirlwall's Law in several Latin American economies. Cliometricians have sometimes adopted this framework as well: Rappoport & White (1993), for example, conclude that it reaffirms the once traditional view that a 'bubble' inflated the pre-Depression stock market.

To understand better both its appeal and possible limitations, consider the data on recipient rates once more. The simple and self-referential model of the previous section cannot meet the expectations of those heterodox (and other) economists interested in *structure:* it is almost silent on the possible causes of claim behavior.

In contrast, Blank & Card (1991) conclude that much of the decline in the recipient rate over the last five decades can be attributed to a decrease in collection rates, which prompts the question why so many *eligible* workers do not, or are somehow unable to, claim UI benefits. To answer it, Blank & Card (1991) exploit the substantial interstate variation in recipient rates, and find that a combination of economic and social factors – from the *replacement rate,* the ratio of benefits to wages, and the mean duration of jobless spells to the shares of non-white, female and unionized workers – can explain a substantial fraction of this variation, consistent with Matthews *et al.* (2002) who also discern evidence of a 'political culture' effect.

For purposes of exposition, the influence of a 'consolidated' explanatory variable, denoted Z, is considered first. A scatter plot of *REC* and Z, depicted in Figure 6, holds considerable promise, and the results of a simple bivariate regression seems to confirm this:

$$REC = 102.8 - 0.51Z + \hat{u}_t$$
$$(2.68)\quad(0.29)$$
$$\bar{R}^2 = 0.86\qquad DW = 1.09 \tag{4}$$

Under the usual (if unfortunate) rhetorical conventions, this streamlined model 'explains' 86% of the variation in recipient rates over time, and the influence of Z is statistically significant at the 1% (0.1%, in fact) level. More impres-

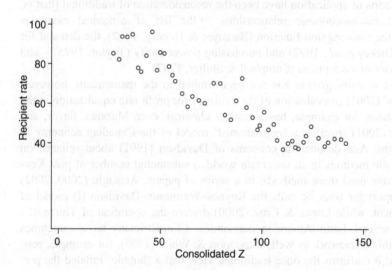

Figure 6 The recipient rate and consolidated variable Z

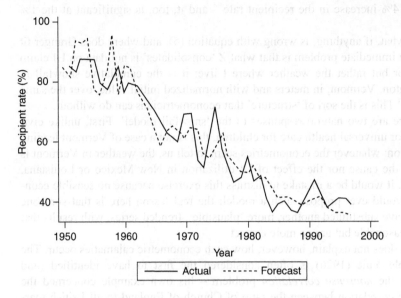

Figure 7 Actual and forecast recipient rates, basic regression model

sive, it passes a battery of diagnostic checks, including the so-called RESET test for omitted variables and/or misspecified functional form, the CUSUM test for structural change and Breusch-Pagan test for non-spherical (heteroscedastic) errors.[2]

The one obvious cause for concern, in fact, is the smallish Durbin–Watson statistic, consistent with the presence of serial correlation. The usual (first order) correction appears to solve the problem, however – the Durbin–Watson statistic of the transformed model increases, to 1.81 – and has almost no effect on the estimated coefficients and some, but not much, effect on their standard errors, so is not reported here. The step ahead forecasts based on this pattern of serial correlation seem to track actual recipient rates well, as shown in Figure 7.

As a final check, a narrow(er) variable, the replacement rate, REP_t, was added to the model. After correction for serial correlation, the results are:

$$REC = -30.0 - 0.53Z + 3.85REP + \hat{u}_t$$
$$(33.9) \quad (0.09) \quad (0.97)$$
$$\bar{R}^2 = 0.65 \qquad DW = 1.67 \qquad \rho = 0.76 \tag{5}$$

The importance of the consolidated variable Z seems to be confirmed: its estimated coefficient is close to its previous value and remains significant at the 1% level. On the other hand, consistent with the borderline results for the RESET test, it appears that Z does not capture the effects of the replacement rate on claim behavior. Both the sign and size of the REP coefficient are plausible – a 1% increase in the (relative) value of UI benefits is associated with an almost 4% increase in the recipient rate – and it, too, is significant at the 1% level.

So what, if anything, is wrong with equation (5), and where does Granger fit in? The immediate problem is that what Z 'consolidates' is not data on UI claim behavior but rather the weather where I live: it is the cumulative snowfall in Burlington, Vermont, in meters and with normalized initial value, over the same period![3] This is the sort of 'structure' that econometricians can do without.

There are two natural responses to the 'snowfall model'. First, unlike civil unions or universal health care for children, this is not a case of Vermont leading the nation: whatever the econometrics seem to tell us, the weather in Vermont is neither the cause nor the effect of UI utilization in New Mexico or Louisiana. Second, it would be a mistake to dismiss this exercise because no sensible economist would ever propose such a model: the real lesson here is that someone could have substituted another, more 'plausible', trended series, with results that seem reasonable but are no more correct.

This does not explain, however, how such econometric calamaties occur. The venerable Yule (1926) is often considered the first to have identified (and named) the *nonsense correlation* problem – his own example concerned the positive correlation between the ratio of Church of England to all British marriages and the mortality rates – but Frain (1995) quotes the lesser known Hooker (1901), who observed that:

> The application of the theory of correlation to economic phenomena frequently presents many difficulties, more especially where the element of time is involved; and it by no means follows as a matter of course that a high correlation coefficient is a proof of a causal connection between any two variables, or that a low coefficient is to be interpreted as demonstrating the absence of such a connection.
>
> (Frain 1995: 13)

(As Hendry [2004], reminds us, it was the 'Yule critique' that Keynes [1940], would later invoke in his assessment of Jan Tinbergen's work and, in broader terms, macroeconometrics.) Hooker's (1901) intuition, later formalized in Granger & Newbold's (1974) seminal paper on *spurious regression,* is that the use of non-stationary data – in particular, 'trended' time series – undermines classical inference: there is no reason to suppose, for example, that the distribution of the t statistic will be the familiar one, so that one cannot conclude, on the basis of equation (4), that Z/snowfall matters. (It was not until much later, however, that the critical t values could be calculated.) In heuristic terms, when two random variables rise or fall over time, correlation is inevitable, whether or not there is a relationship between them.

The obvious solution to the nonsense correlation problem is first to detrend the data and to then (re)estimate the model with deviations from trend, but there are two problems with this. First, it is seldom obvious *how,* or even if, a particular time series should be detrended. And second, information about possible relationships between *levels* is lost in the process, and economists are often more interested in these. In the UI example, the secular relationship between the recipient and replacement rates is no less important than the short(er) run effects of fluctuations in one on the other. Or, to use a more conventional example, data on the deviations from trend in consumption and disposable income cannot tell us much about autonomous consumption or its level.

To consider the first problem in more detail, it should first be noted that, for decades, econometricians who were sensitive to the 'Yule critique' allowed for *deterministic* trends. In practice, this meant that trend deviations were calculated as the residuals of a regression of the relevant series on some simple polynomial in time. For the UI data, the recipient rate and cumulative snowfall were each regressed on a quadratic time function and when the deviations from trend in the former, denoted $REC_t - TRENDREC_t$, are then regressed on deviations from trend in the latter, $Z_t - TRENDZ_t$, the results are:

$$REC - TRENDREC = 0.35 + 0.05(Z - TRENDZ) + \hat{u}$$
$$(1.35)\ (0.82)$$
$$R^2 = -0.02 \quad DW = 1.83 \qquad\qquad \rho = 0.35 \quad (6)$$

after correction for first order serial correlation. And with these results comes a small, and perhaps premature, sense of relief: someone with the presence of mind to detrend the data would have *decisively* rejected the hypothesis that snowfall is a determinant of UI recipient rates. Better, perhaps, if the detrended replacement rate is added to the model, the results are:

$$REC - TRENDREC = -0.10 - 0.97(Z - TRENDZ) + 3.76(REP - TRENDREP)$$
$$(1.29)\ (0.79) \qquad\qquad\qquad (1.04)$$
$$\overline{R}^2 = 0.19 \qquad DW = 1.48 \qquad \rho = 0.40$$

Snowfall still does not matter – even if the rejection is much less emphatic than it was in equation (6) – but replacement rates do.

To situate Granger & Newbold's (1974) contribution, reconsider the fundamental premise of this exercise, that all of the variables are stationary around some deterministic trend or, as this property is sometimes called, *trend stationary*. This means that each time series X_t can be decomposed into the sum of (at least) two parts, $TREND_t + CYCLE_t$ where $TREND_t$ is some non-random function, more often than not of time, and $CYCLE_t$ is an autocorrelated series with mean zero and finite and constant variance. In the case of cumulative snowfall, for example, $TREND_t$ was estimated to be $25.7 + 2.55t - 0.002t^2$ for $t = YEAR - 1950$. As a consequence, the best forecast of X_{t+k} in period t tends to $TREND_{t+k}$, its trend value, as k increases. In other words, the effects of $CYCLE_t$ are *assumed* to wear out over time, a formulation that reinforces the (too) sharp distinction between the short and long runs that is characteristic of much empirical research.

But as some Vermonters would put it, no one but a 'flatlander' would model cumulative snowfall as a trend stationary process: last winter's substantial snows have increased forecasts of *cumulative* snowfall one, five, ten or even 50 years from now the same amount. Conventional wisdom about winter is better represented as:

$$Z_t - Z_{t-1} = \theta_z + u_t \tag{7}$$

where θ_z can be viewed as 'normal' annual snowfall and u_t as the annual surplus or deficit relative to this norm, an example of a *random walk with* (no pun intended) *drift*. This can be rewritten, after repeated substitution, as $Z_t = Z_0 + \Sigma t \theta_z + u_{t+j}$ or even *TREND*$_t$ + *CYCLE*$_t$, where *TREND*$_t$ = Z_0 + $t\theta_z$ and $CYCLE_t = \sum_{j=0}^{t-1} u_{t+j}$. The similarities to the previous decomposition are more cosmetic than real, however. The trend component is not deterministic, but random, since the value of Z_0 must itself be random. And the remainder, $\sum_{j=0}^{t-1} u_{t+j}$, cannot be stationary, since the mean is zero but the variance is neither constant nor, for that matter, even bounded: $\lim_{t\to\infty} E(\sum_{j=0}^{t-1} u_{t+j})^2 = \lim_{t\to\infty} tE(u^2) = \infty$ as $t \to \infty$.

Under these conditions, cumulative snowfall will be *difference stationary*, however: ΔZ_t will be stationary, with mean θ_z and variance $E(u_t^2)$. In broader terms, it is said that a series X_t is *integrated of order d*, written $X_t \sim I(d)$, if its dth difference is stationary: in this case, $Z_t \sim I(1)$. Linear functions of $I(1)$ variables will of course be $I(1)$ and, with an important class of exceptions to be discussed later, a linear combination of $I(1)$ variables will also be $I(1)$. (In fact, if $X_t \sim I(d)$ and $Y_t \sim I(e)$, then $\alpha X_t + \beta Y_t \sim I(f)$, where $f = \max[d, e]$.)

This has two important implications. First, if REC_t is also $I(1)$, the researcher must contend with the modern version of the Yule critique, the problem of *spurious regression*. In what would soon become 'one of the most influential Monte Carlo studies of all time' (Phillips, 1997, p. 273), Granger & Newbold (1974) constructed 100 pairs of independent $I(1)$ variables and found that in simple bivariate regressions, the hypothesis that the slope coefficient was zero was rejected (at the 5% level) almost 80% of the time for conventional critical values of the t statistic. In addition, they found that in most cases, the R^2 was surprisingly high, but the Durbin–Watson statistic, the usual measure of serial correlation, was low, and this combination is still considered an important, if informal, diagnostic. (It should be noted, therefore, that the first results for equation (3) should have sounded the alarm: the R^2 is 0.86 but the DW is about 1.) Granger recalls that when he first presented the results in a seminar at LSE, they were 'met with total disbelief…[t]heir reaction was that we must have gotten the Monte Carlo wrong, [that] we must have done the programming wrong' so that if 'I had been part of the LSE group, they might well have persuaded me not to have done that research at that point' (Phillips, 1997, p. 262).[4]

A little more than a decade later, Phillips (1986), whose later contributions to time series econometrics would rival Granger's, provided the requisite theoretical foundations for these results. In particular, he showed that as sample size increased, so, too, would the value of the t statistic, so that rejection of the null of a zero slope coefficient was, under the usual conventions, inevitable, but that the value of the Durbin–Watson statistic tended to 0.

The second implication is an immediate consequence of the properties of integrated time series: if snowfall is indeed an $I(1)$ process, there is no reason to believe that the measured deviations from an assumed deterministic trend would be stationary, which undermines the conclusions drawn from the modified deviations-from-trend model. In other words, the subsequent rejection of the null that snowfall matters was not as decisive as first seemed and, perhaps worse, if snowfall *did* matter, this transformation could well have obscured its role! From the perspective of most practitioners, then, the classification of individual series as trend or difference stationary had become a critical first step in model specification.

(This is perhaps not the place for a detailed discussion of the various *unit root tests* available to researchers, except to note that the most popular of these – the augmented Dickey–Fuller (1979) and Phillips-Perron (1987) tests, for example – were derived under the null hypothesis of difference stationarity, so that failure to reject is interpreted as evidence in favor of a unit root. The so-called KPSS test proposed in Kwiatkowski *et al.* (1992) is the best known exception. For the series considered here, the augmented Dickey–Fuller test indicates that the null cannot be rejected for *REC, REP* or, consistent with the intuition of Vermonters, *Z*, and the KPSS results are consistent with this: the null of trend stationarity is rejected at the 10% level for *REC, REP* and *Z*. It should be noted, however, that the power of these tests in small samples and against 'local alternatives' is often poor, an issue that will be revisited later.)

If, on this basis, the relationship between recipient rates and cumulative snowfall is estimated in first differences, the results are:

$$\Delta REC = -0.52 - 0.19\Delta Z + \hat{u}_t$$
$$(4.01)\quad(1.61)$$
$$\bar{R}^2 = 0.00 \qquad DW = 2.09 \qquad \rho = -0.14 \tag{8}$$

after correction for serial correlation. The rejection of the pure snowfall model is no less decisive than it was when deviations from some deterministic trend were used. If the first differences in replacement rates and the duration of unemployment are then added to the model, the results become:

$$\Delta REC = -0.41 - 0.18\Delta Z + 4.67\Delta REP + \hat{u}$$
$$(3.62)\quad(1.44)\quad(0.93)$$
$$\bar{R}^2 = 0.33 \qquad DW = 1.89 \qquad \rho = 0.09 \tag{9}$$

Snowfall is still statistically insignificant at any level and the influence of the replacement rate is, in a limited sense, confirmed. (The caveat would lose some of its force if the second result survived the addition of other plausible determinants of UI claim behavior.)

As mentioned earlier, the second problem with models based on transformed data, whether deviations from deterministic trend or first differences, is that information about relationships between *levels* is lost. If the data are trend stationary, the problem is easily solved: it is an implication of the Frisch–Waugh (1933) Theorem, perhaps better known as the *partialling out* result, that the addition of a time trend to a model is equivalent to the transformed model in which each variable is instead detrended.

If the data are difference stationary, the problem is more complicated, and it is Granger's solution, and his appreciation for its broad(er) implications, rather than his other influential contributions to econometrics, that are featured in his Nobel citation. What this solution shares with other recent econometric innovations is that it was both difficult to see but almost 'obvious' once seen. Granger's own description of his epiphany is instructive:

> I do not remember where it took place now, but [David Hendry] was saying that he had a case where he had two $I(1)$ variables, but their difference was $I(0)$, and I said that is not possible, speaking as a theorist... So I went away to prove I was right, and I managed to prove that he was right. Once I realized this was possible, then I immediately saw how it was related to... [the] error correction model and their balancing. So, in a sense, all the main results of cointegration came together in a few minutes. I mean, without any proof, at least not any deep proof, I just sort of saw what was needed... [and] I could see immediately what the main results were going to be... It is one of those things that, once pointed out to people, all kinds of other things made sense, and I think that is why it was accepted so readily.
>
> (Phillips, 1997, pp. 274–275)

Hendry's (2004) own account of this exchange provides some additional context. The members of the 'LSE school' had wrestled with the representation of equilibrium relationships and disequilibrium dynamics in non-stationary data for some time. By the late 1970s, there was a consensus of sorts that *error correction models* – which relied on precise combinations of data in differences and levels, and about which more below – were often adequate. (The intuition for such models, Hendry [2004] believes, can be traced back to Klein's [1953] emphasis on the 'great ratios' of economics: total wages and national income are both trended, for example, but their ratio or, expressed in natural logarithms, their difference, did not *seem* to be.) The problem was that the solution was based on 'ocular econometrics' (Hendry, 2004, p. 198) and the imposition of *a priori* structure.

To cultivate some intuition for this solution, recall that linear combinations of nonstationary $I(1)$ variables are, as a rule, also $I(1)$, so that Granger's suspicions about Hendry's claim were, in some sense, well-founded. This means, for example, that if Y_t and X_t are both $I(1)$, the linear combination $Y_t - \beta X_t = \alpha + u_t$

– that is, the combination embedded in the classical linear model – will also be $I(1)$, as will (therefore) the error term u_t. In the absence of some sort of 'equilibrium relationship' between Y_t and X_t, the two series will therefore tend to drift apart from one another over time. But if there is such a relationship, some sort of mechanism that prevents such drift, there will exist one (and, in this case, no more than one) combination such that $Y_t - \beta X_t$, and therefore u_t, will be stationary or $I(0)$. In this special case, the two variables are said to be *cointegrated*, the term that Granger (1981) coined almost two decades ago. To be more precise, the vector of N random variables $\mathbf{X}_t = (X_t^1, X_t^2, \ldots, X_t^N)$ will be *cointegrated of order d,b*, denoted $\mathbf{X}_t \sim CI(d, b)$, if each $X_t^i \sim I(d)$ and there exists some *cointegrating vector* $\beta = (\beta^1, \beta^2, \ldots, \beta^N)$ such that $Z_t = \sum_{i=1}^{N} \beta^i X_t^i \sim I(d-b)$. There can be at most $N - 1$ such vectors, each of them unique up to a scale factor, but there will often be fewer. The most common procedures to determine this number, and therefore the number of equilibrium relationships, are those described in Johansen (1988), another pre-eminent contributor to the literature. So in the simple bivariate case, if Y_t and X_t are both $I(1)$, then each will be non-stationary in levels but stationary in first differences, but if, in addition, (Y_t, X_t) is $CI(1, 1)$, then some linear combination $Y_t - \beta X_t$ will also be stationary.

Murray's (1994) variation on the *drunkard's walk* metaphor, the standard illustration of the most famous $I(1)$ process, the *random walk*, provides some home-spun intuition. In the parable of the 'drunk and the dog', it is impossible to predict where the next steps of either will take them – in which case the best forecast of where each will be a few hours from now is where each started, which isn't much of a prediction – unless the dog is *hers*, in which case the two never drift far apart. It will still be difficult to predict where the pair will be, but the distance between them will be stationary. Or, in other words, their paths will be cointegrated.

From this intuition comes the almost 'obvious' test for cointegration first proposed in Engle & Granger (1987), perhaps the most cited paper in either laureate's vita. In terms of UI claim behavior, if REC_t and REP_t are $CI(1,1)$, it should be that $REC_t - \alpha - \beta REP_t = u_t$ is not $I(1)$ but $I(0)$ – that is, stationary – for some β. We do not know the 'true' value of β or observe the 'true' errors u_t, but there are natural proxies for both, namely the least squares estimates and the associated residuals. The Engle–Granger test is, in effect, a unit root test of the residuals, where rejection of the null (difference stationarity) is interpreted as (indirect, to be sure) evidence of cointegration. In this case, it is difficult to reject – for some specifications of the test, it can be rejected at the 10% level, but no lower – so that the evidence of an equilibirum relationship between *REC* and *REP* is, at best, mixed. (This should not come as much of a surprise: this is, after all, a 'toy model'.)

The *Granger Representation Theorem*, first articulated in Granger & Weiss (1983), then provides the desired relationship between levels and (first or other) differences of cointegrated time series. As the previous quotation and the subsequent discussion both hinted, the connection can be described in terms of the *error correction models* or ECMs that predated this work. (The most familiar

ECM is perhaps the DHSY model of consumption – Davidson *et al.*, 1978 – but (the other) Phillips' (1957) much earlier work on stabilization is another example.)

To illustrate, consider a dynamic version of the simple bivariate model, $Y_t = \gamma_0 + \gamma_1 X_t + \gamma_2 Y_{t-1} + \gamma_3 X_{t-1} + e_t$, which has the steady state equilibrium $Y = \alpha + \beta X$, where $\alpha = \gamma_0/(1 - \gamma_2)$ and $\beta = (\gamma_1 + \gamma_3)/(1 - \gamma_2)$. It is not difficult to show that the model can be rewritten as:

$$\Delta Y_t = \gamma_1 \Delta X_t + (\gamma_2 - 1)(Y_{t-1} - \alpha - \beta X_{t-1}) + e_t \tag{10}$$

This is the so-called error correction form: period-to-period fluctuations in Y_t depend both on fluctuations in X_t and the extent to which the model was in disequilibrium the previous period, $Y_{t-1} - \alpha - \beta X_{t-1}$. If $(Y_t, X_t) \sim CI(1,1)$, then all of the variables in the ECM are $I(0)$ and its coefficients can be estimated with standard (classical) methods. If Y_t and X_t are not cointegrated, on the other hand, then $Y_{t-1} - \alpha - \beta X_{t-1}$ will not be stationary, and classical methods are inappropriate.

To provide a more formal statement of the theorem, recall that if the N random variables $\mathbf{X}_t \sim CI(d, b)$, there will exist some $r \times N$ matrix $\mathbf{B}$ of rank r such that the r random variables $\mathbf{Z}_t = \mathbf{B}'\mathbf{X}_t \sim I(0)$. (This is just a restatement of the previous definition, where the rows of $\mathbf{B}'$ are the cointegrating vectors.) Now suppose that the evolution of $\mathbf{X}_t$ can be modeled as a vector autoregression of order k, denoted $VAR(k)$, a generalization of the dynamic model in the previous paragraph:

$$\mathbf{X}_t = \alpha + \phi_1 \mathbf{X}_{t-1} + \phi_2 \mathbf{X}_{t-2} + \cdots + \phi_k \mathbf{X}_{t-k} + \epsilon_t \tag{11}$$

where α is a column vector, and $\phi_1, \ldots, \phi_k$ square matrices, of coefficients. The theorem asserts that there will exist an $N \times r$ matrix $\mathbf{A}$ such that:

$$\mathbf{I} - \phi_1 - \phi_2 - \cdots - \phi_k = \mathbf{AB}' \tag{12}$$

and $k - 1$ square matrices $\Psi_1, \Psi_2, \ldots, \Psi_k - 1$ such that:

$$\Delta \mathbf{X}_t = \Psi_1 \Delta \mathbf{X}_{t-1} + \Psi_2 \Delta \mathbf{X}_{t-2} + \cdots + \Psi_{k-2} \Delta \mathbf{X}_{t-k+1} + \alpha - \mathbf{AB}'\mathbf{X}_{t-1} + \epsilon_t \tag{13}$$

which is the multivariate version of the error correction model.[5]

For the UI data, the equation we are most interested in is:

$$\Delta REC_t = \alpha_1 + \lambda_1 (\beta_1 REC_{t-1} + \beta_2 REP_{t-1}) + \sum_{i=1}^{k-1} \gamma_1^i \Delta REC_{t-i}$$

$$+ \sum_{i=1}^{k-1} \gamma_2^i \Delta REP_{t-i} + \epsilon_{1t} \tag{14}$$

where $\beta_1 REC_{t-1} + \beta_2 REP_{t-1}$ or, after normalization, $REC_{t-1} - \beta_2 REP_{t-1}$, is often understood as last period's deviation from equilibrium, and the parameter λ_1 measures the *speed of adjustment*.

Engle & Granger's (1987) two step estimator for equation (14) was the first, and remains the simplest, available to time series econometricians. Building on the work of Stock (1987), who showed that least squares estimates of the cointegrating vector $[\hat{\beta}_1, \hat{\beta}_2]$ were *superconsistent* – that is, converged more rapidly than usual – they demonstrated that if these estimates were substituted into the ECM and the values of the other paramaters $\alpha_1, \lambda_1, \gamma_1^1, \ldots, \gamma_1^{k-1}, \gamma_2^1, \ldots, \gamma_2^{k-1}$ estimated via maximum likelihood, the results would be both consistent and asymptotically normal.

The Johansen (1988) test reveals, however, that the evidence that REC_t and REP_t are cointegrated is at best mixed. Nevertheless, for $k = 4$, the maximum likelihood estimate of the (standardized) cointegrating vector is [1, 5.67], while the estimate of λ_1 is -0.12. So if an equilibrium relationship does exist, the speed of adjustment is quite slow, consistent with the view that, in the short run, fluctuations in the replacement rate can drive claim behavior far from its eventual 'equilibrium'. This said, the fitted values of the estimated ECM track the observed first differences remarkably well, as illustrated in Figure 8.

Three extensions of the CI framework deserve special mention in this context. Hylleberg *et al.* (1990) introduced the notion of *seasonal cointegration*. Granger & Lee (1989) developed *multicointegration* to model stock-flow relationships. In their example, if sales and output are $CI(1, 1)$ then the difference, or investment in inventories, will be stationary, but the stock of inventories will not be. If the stock of inventories and sales are also cointegrated, however, then sales and output will be multicointegrated. And Granger & Swanson (1995) have considered *nonlinear cointegration*.

4 A few words about causality and prediction

Granger (1986) was also the first to notice an important connection between CI models and his own much earlier work (Granger, 1969) on causality. In particular, he perceived that if a pair of economic time series was cointegrated, then one of them must *Granger cause* the other. Most readers will recall that the definition of Granger causality embodies two crucial axioms (Granger, 1987): *uniqueness,* which is the principle that the 'cause' contains unique information about the 'effect', and *strict temporal priority.* In operational terms, this amounts to a condition on prediction variance: in crude terms, if one stationary time series is better predicted with a second series than without it, the latter is said to cause the former. It was not Granger's (1969) paper that launched a thousand cauality test ships, however, but rather Sims' (1972): regressing the logarithm of current nominal GNP on a number of its own lags and lags of the logarithm of either 'broad money' or the monetary base, and then vice versa, he famously concluded that 'money causes income' but that 'income does not cause money'. A little more than three decades later, empirical macroeconomists continue to publish variations on this simple exercise, among them a number of

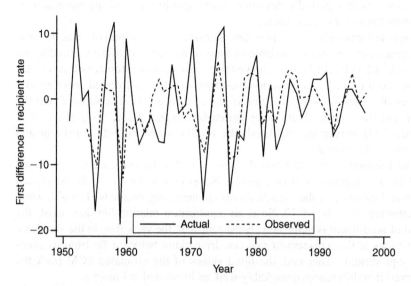

Figure 8 Actual and predicted difference, error correction model

post Keynesians who believe – mistakenly, it seems to me – that the debate with the mainstream about the endogencity of money, or for that matter the internal debate between structuralist and accommodationist explanations of endogeneity, will be resolved on this basis.[6]

Granger himself remains ambivalent about Sims' (1972) paper. Much later, he would observe that 'part of the defense of the people who did not like the conclusion of [this] paper was that this was not real causality, this was only "Granger causality" [and] they kept using the phrase...everywhere in their writings, which I thought was very inefficient, but...made my name very prominent' (Phillips, 1997, p. 272). More important, he believes that the most common form of the test, based on a comparison of *in sample* fits, violates the spirit, and perhaps the letter, of his own definition, which emphasizes the importance of (out of sample) predictability.

If Granger's (1969) causality paper is the most visible of his other contributions to econometric theory, it remains his most controversial. Tobin's (1970) sharp reminder of the perils of *post hoc ergo propter hoc* reasoning in economics was written in response to Friedman & Schwartz (1963), but it can also be read as a critique of the later Sims (1972). It was for this reason that Leamer (1985) would recommend that econometricians substitute 'precedence' for 'causality'. In a similar vein, Zellner (1979) dismisses the notion that causal relations can be defined, or detected, without respect to economic laws.

Granger himself remains unrepentant. He believes that the test – the intuition for which is found outside economics, in the work of the mathematician Norbert Weiner – is 'still the best pragmatic definition [or] operational definition'

(Phillips, 1997, p. 272). And he believes that the philosphers have started to come around:

> The philosophers…initially did not like this definition very much, but in recent years several books on philosophy have discussed it in a much more positive way, not saying that it is right, but also saying that it is not wrong. I view that as supporting my position that it is probably a component of what eventually will be a definition of causation that is sound.
>
> (Phillips, 1997, p. 272)

At the least, Granger's paper remains the point of departure for most 'pragmatic' discussions of causality in economics, a number of which (Hoover [2001] for example) have produced viable extensions or alternatives. It is also embedded in other econometric concepts: it is part, for example, of the definition of strong exogeneity (Engle *et al.*, 1983).

In some sense, Granger's research on causality can be viewed as a particular manifestation of his interest in prediction or forecasting, one that he shares with co-laureate Engle. Published at the same time as the (now, if not then) better known causality paper, for example, Bates & Granger (1969) were the first to prove the once counterintuitive result that pooled forecasts tend to perform better than individual ones. For those familiar with James Surowiecki's (2004) *The Wisdom of Crowds,* the intuition is similar: pooled forecasts allow differential biases to offset one another. And in the last few years, Granger (2001) has returned to the problem of forecast evaluation.

Diebold (2004, p. 169) believes that 'Engle's preference for parametric, parsimonious models [also reflects a] long-standing concern with forecasting… [that] guard against in-sample overfitting or data mining', but adds that he is also responsible for several more specific contributions to the literature. Engle & Yoo (1987), for example, was one of the first papers to explore the properties of forecasts made on the basis of cointegrated systems. From a broader perspective, the whole ARCH framework can be understood as an attempt to produce better forecasts, or at least better estimates of forecast error variances.

5 Trouble in paradise?

It seems reasonable to suppose that with the increased attention that ARCH and CI models have received since the Royal Academy's announcement, more economists outside the mainstream will be tempted to experiment with one or both. There is reason to be cautious, however. The most important operational criticism of the common trends framework, for example, is that testing for unit roots or estimating cointegrating vectors is problematic in small(ish) samples. For the researcher armed with annual, or even quarterly, data, for example, the benefits are uncertain. Miron (1991, p. 212), himself a contributor to the technical literature, believes that 'since we can never know whether the data are trend stationary or difference stationary [in finite samples], any result that relies on the distinction is inherently uninteresting.' The implicit advice, that researchers should fit both sorts of models to time series data, even in those cases where test results *seem* decisive, strikes (at least) me as sound. For the UI claim data, for example, the conclusion that recipient and replacement rates share a common trend, or that short run fluctuations in replacement rates are associated with substantial movements in claims, is a more robust one than it would have been if both alternatives had not been considered.

One of the most persuasive illustrations of this problem is Perron's (1989) paper on unit root tests in a world which, if trend stationary, is trend stationary *with structural breaks*. It is important to appreciate that at the time the paper was published, the conventional wisdom held that almost all macroeconomic time series were either $I(1)$ or $I(2)$: Nelson & Plosser's (1982) often cited article, for example, found that for 13 of 14 series – the one exception was the unemployment rate – the null hypothesis of a unit root could not be rejected. The immediate and widespread success of Engle & Granger (1987), which provided researchers with a tractable framework for the analysis of relationships between such series, owed at least a little to this near consensus. What Perron (1989) showed, however, was that if one allowed for just two structural breaks – what he describes as the 'intercept shift' of the Great Crash of 1929 and the 'slope shift' of the oil price shock of 1973 – around an otherwise stable, trend stationary, process, the unit root hypothesis could now be rejected for 11 of the same 14 series! While later studies have qualified Perron's reversal – Zivot & Andrews (1992), for example, endogenized the selection of breakpoints and found that 6 of the 14 series were not difference stationary – the lesson for empirical researchers, heterodox or otherwise, is clear: there is still much to be learned from old fashioned, if more flexible, decompositions of economic time series.

ARCH models suffer from their own small sample woes, as Engle himself understood from the beginning (Engle *et al.,* 1985). On the basis of their own Monte Carlo studies, for example, Hwang & Periera (2003) find that at least 250 observations are required to offset the bias problem in ARCH(1) models, and more than 500 in GARCH(1,1) models. This is seldom a constraint with daily, or even weekly, financial market data, but it represents a very long time indeed when the data source is annual state UI reports!

(At this point, little is known about the interaction of these small sample problems. Mantalos [2001] finds, however, that $I(1)$ series with *GARCH*(1, 1) errors, the null hypothesis tends to be *overrejected* or, in other words, that cointegration is detected more often than it should be.)

A second practical concern about ARCH/GARCH models is related to their common, and sometimes lucrative, application to financial market data. The most important of these involve the use of conditional variances to improve estimates of *value at risk,* as embodied in J. P. Morgan's influential RiskMetrics paradigm. In this context, it is important to ask how well this class of models captures the stylized facts of asset markets. It has already been observed, for example, that clustered volatility and the *information release effect* can be represented, and it can be shown that another variant, Nelson's (1991) EGARCH, can accommodate a *leverage effect*.[7] But there is some evidence (Brock & Potter, 1993; Brock & de Lima, 1996) that there is otherwise unmodelled *nonlinear* structure in financial data.

The contribution of ARCH/GARCH models to the 'new financial econometrics' raises broader questions, however, about the *existence* of such structure. In a recent critique, Mayer (1999), for example, observes that '[Basle's] abdication of supervisory function followed J. P. Morgan's publication of its RiskMetrics methodology, which supposedly enabled banks to measure the extent of their risks looking forward into the realm where *uncertainty*, not of probability, reigns' (emphasis added).

Concerns about statistical inference in a world where outcomes are uncertain, rather than probabilistic, extend to CI models, too. Davidson (1991) is perhaps the most prominent of the post Keynesians to assert that economic processes are non-ergodic and thus non-stationary, and that this difference cannot be 'undone' with the use of differenced data. If true, the structure uncovered in such models will often be an artifact. Lawrence Klein, the Nobel laureate who for decades embodied the older Cowles Commission approach to macroeconometrics, shares a practical concern about the (over)use of differences, if not the post Keynesian premise:

> I do not think economic data are necessarily stationary or that economic processes are stationary. The technique of cointegration, to keep differencing the data until stationarity is obtained and then relate the stationary series, I think can do damage. It does damage in the sense that it almost always done on a bivariate or maybe trivariate basis. That keeps the analysis simple... but the world is not simple.
>
> [I] would conclude that one should accept the fact that economic data are not stationary, relate the non-stationary data, but include the explicit [deterministic] trends and think about what could cause the trends in the relationship. One then uses that more complicated relationship with trend variables. *Successive differencing, as it is done in cointegration techniques, may introduce new relationships,* some of which we do not want to have in our analysis.
>
> (Klein, 1994, p. 34, emphasis added)

Klein (1994, p. 34) also expresses some unease that the 'youngest... generation of econometricians simply do [this] mechanically... and do not understand the original data series as well as they should.'

The heterodox economist who is still tempted to use the CI framework must also consider its unfortunate – but I believe inessential – link to the 'real business cycle' or RBC paradigm. The near consensus that once existed that almost all macro time series were $I(1)$ or $I(2)$ but that subsets of these formed cointegrated systems was, and to some extent still is, linked to the rise of RBC models. (I am tempted to add that if, as some believe, the term 'heterodox' is too broad to be useful, the widespread rejection of such models could be the exception that proves the rule.) The reason is not difficult to infer: if real output has a 'strong unit root', for example, then one *could* interpret its evolution over time in terms of a series of permanent shocks or, as Shapiro & Watson (1988) concluded, as random increases in potential income, rather than a sequence of transitory shocks around some deterministic trend/potential. Furthermore, as King *et al.* (1991, p. 320) reminded their readers, in the presence of technology shocks, 'balanced growth under uncertainty implies that consumption, investment and output [will be] integrated.'

There are at least two reasons to suppose that the connection is more tenuous than first seems, however. First, as De Long & Summers (1988) have observed, the strength of the unit root in real output is in some measure an artifact, a consequence of macroeconomists' preoccupation with post-Second World War data. (Of course, to the extent that earlier data are either unavailable or unreliable, the preoccupation is an understandable one.) Viewed from this perspective, the diminished importance of 'transitory fluctuations' in this period has less to do with RBCs than with the success of old fashioned Keynesianism at stabilization, a point also made, albeit in a different context, by Tobin (1982).

The second is that whether or not balanced growth is *sufficient* for cointegration, it does not follow that it is also *necessary*. It is not clear that old fashioned Keynesianism, or any other heterodox approach, *requires* that the evolution of critical time series be limited to stationary fluctuations around some deterministic trend. It is not clear to me, for example, that the existence of a stochastic trend is incompatible with some sort of Harrodian, or demand driven, model of economic growth.

There is another, more subtle, explanation for this connection, one that is related to current methodological debates in econometrics. The recent concern over the use of *incredible restrictions* as a means of identification, the fashion for 'unrestricted' vector autoregressions, the interest in cointegrating vectors and ECMs and, to a lesser extent, the use of ARCH models can all be understood as manifestations of the LSE or *general-to-specific* approach to empirical research. Like 'rational' expectations, however, general-to-specific is not always the unalloyed virtue it first seems. For each new variable added to an ECM, for example, there is a substantial increase in the number of new parameters to estimate, a mild version of the *curse of dimensionality*. (To assume *a priori* that some of these coefficients are zero is, of course, to impose the sort of restrictions that 'old fashioned' econometricians have relied on for decades.) As a result, most CI or ECM models tend to be parsimonious and while there are no doubt exceptions to the rule, the models of orthodox economists tend to be 'lower dimensional' than those of their heterodox counterparts (Pandit, 1999). If inflation is 'always and everywhere a monetary phenomenon', for example, then a bivariate VAR is sufficient for many purposes! Pandit (1999) also cites Klein (2004) as a source of examples of cases in which parsimonious models lead to incorrect conclusions.

6 Conclusion

It is not uncommon for some outside the mainstream to remind us that the Bank of Sweden's prize for 'economic science' is newer than, and different from, the other Nobels, or to protest that it resembles a 'beauty contest' that some kinds of contestants will never win. There is some truth to this, of course: the failure to award the prize to Joan Robinson, for example, is still incomprehensible. To dismiss the achievements of those who *have* won, however, because of those who haven't is facile. More than a few laureates have challenged, and sometimes informed, various heterodox traditions. It would be naive to claim, for example, that the influence of Arrow, who shared the 1972 prize, Leontief (in 1973), Myrdal (1974), Lewis (1979), Tobin (1981), Nash (1994), Sen (1998), Akerlof (2001) or Stiglitz (2001) were limited to the mainstream.

Should Engle and/or Granger be added to this illustrious list? However durable their technical accomplishments prove, there is little doubt that each has influenced how we think about and sometimes organize economic data.

Acknowledgments

I thank Carolyn Craven and one of the editors for their comments on an earlier draft. The usual disclaimers hold.

Notes

1 The insured unemployment rate is itself defined to be the ratio of UI *claims* to *covered* employment, but not all workers are covered and not all claims are honored. Inasmuch as both the proportion of covered workers and the disqualification rates have varied over time, fluctuations in the recipient rate must therefore be interpreted with some care.

2 In fact, except for Ramsey's RESET test, it passes all of these tests with flying colors. In the RESET case, the null of no omitted variables can *just* be rejected at the 5% level, but not at the 1% level. Some econometricians would see this as a 'red flag', but most, I suspect, would not.

3 Readers familiar with Hendry's (1980) influential 'Alchemy or science?' paper will have seen this 'trick' before. Stock & Watson's (1988) 'tale of two econometricians' is a more recent variation. To write it off as no more than a rhetorical trick, however, is to underestimate the challenge to applied econometricians.

4 On the other hand, the intuition that some economic relationships were better estimated with differenced data was not novel. Hendry (2004) notes that Fisher (1962) and others had recommended the practice.

5 This is the version of the theorem, or at least part of it, presented in Hamilton's (1994) useful text.

6 The most impressive example of this literature is perhaps Palley (1994), who uses Granger causality tests to evaluate the orthodox, structuralist and accommodationist approaches, concluding that the evidence favors the last of these.

7 EGARCH models were one of the first *asymmetric* conditional variance models, and allow the volatilties of positive and negative shocks to differ.

References

Atesoglu, H. S. (2000) Income, employment, inflation and money in the United States, *Journal of Post Keynesian Economics,* 22, pp. 639–646.

Atesoglu, H. S. (2002) Stock prices and employment, *Journal of Post Keynesian Economics,* 24, pp. 493–498.

Banarjee, A. & Hendry, D. F. (1992) Testing integration and cointegration: an overview, *Oxford Economic Papers,* 54, pp. 225–255.

Bates, J. M. & Granger, C. W. J. (1969) The combination of forecasts, *Operations Research Quarterly,* 20, pp. 451–468.

Blank, R. & Card, D. (1991) Recent trends in insured and uninsured unemployment: is there an explanation? *Quarterly Journal of Economics,* 106, pp. 1157–1189.

Bollerslev, T. (1986) Generalized autoregressive conditional heteroscedasticity, *Journal of Econometrics,* 31, pp. 307–327.

Bollerslev, T., Engle, R. F. & Wooldridge, J. M. (1988) A capital asset pricing model with time-varying covariances, *Journal of Political Economy,* 96, pp. 116–131.

Brock, W. & de Lima, P. (1995) Nonlinear time series, complexity theory and finance, in: G. S. Maddala & C. R. Rao (Eds) *Handbook of Statistics,* 14 (New York: North Holland).

Brock, W. & Potter, S. (1996) Nonlinear time series and macroeconometrics, in: G. S. Maddala, C. R. Rao & H. D. Vinod (Eds) *Handbook of Statistics,* 11, pp. 195–229 (New York: North Holland).

Campbell, J. Y. & Shiller, R. J. (1987) Cointegration and tests of present value models, *Journal of Political Economy,* 95, pp. 1062–1088.

Davidson, P. (1991) Is probability theory relevant for uncertainty: a post Keyensian perspective, *Journal of Economic Perspectives,* 5, pp. 129–143.

Davidson, J. E. H., Hendry, D. F., Srba, F. & Yeo, S. (1978) Econometric modelling of the aggregate time-series relationship between consumers' expenditure and income in the United Kingdom, *Economic Journal,* 88, pp. 661–692.

De Long, J. B. & Summers, L. (1988) On the existence and interpretation of a 'unit root' in US GDP, *NBER Working Paper,* 2716.

Dickey, D. A. & Fuller, W. A. (1979) Distribution of the estimators for autoregressive time series with a unit root, *Journal of the American Statistical Association,* 74, pp. 427–431.

Dickey, D. A., Jansen, D. W. & Thornton, D. L. (1992) A primer on cointegration with an application to money and income, *Federal Reserve Bank of St. Louis Review,* 73, pp. 58–78.

Diebold, F. X. (2003) The ET interview: Professor Robert F. Engle, *Econometric Theory,* 19, pp. 1159–1193.

Diebold, F. X. (2004) The Nobel Memorial Prize for Robert F. Engle, *Scandinavian Journal of Economics,* 106, pp. 165–185.

Ding, Z., Granger, C. W. J. & Engle, R. F. (1993) A long memory property of stock market returns and a new model, *Journal of Empirical Finance,* 1, pp. 83–106.

Engle, R. F. (1973) Band spectrum regression, *International Economic Review,* 15, pp. 1–11.

Engle, R. F. (1974a) Issues in the specification of an econometric model of metropolitan growth, *Journal of Urban Economics,* 1, pp. 250–267.

Engle, R. F. (1974b) A disequilibrium model of regional investment, *Journal of Regional Science,* 14, pp. 367–376.

Engle, R. F. (1976) Policy pills for a metropolitan economy, *Papers and Proceedings of the Regional Science Association,* 35, pp. 191–205.

Engle, R. F. (1982) Autoregressive conditional heteroscedasticity with estimates of the variance of United Kingdom inflation, *Econometrica,* 50, pp. 987–1007.

Engle, R. F. & Granger, C. W. J. (1987) Cointegration and error correction: representation, estimation and testing, *Econometrica,* 55, pp. 251–276.

Engle, R. F. & Kraft, D. (1983) Multiperiod forecast error variances of inflation estimated from ARCH models, in: A. Zellner (Ed) *Applied Time Series Analysis of Economic Data* (Washington: Bureau of the Census).

Engle, R. F. & Liu, T. C. (1972) Effects of aggregation over time on dynamic characteristics of an economic model, in: B. G. Hickman (Ed) *Econometric Models of Cyclical Behavior: Studies in Income and Wealth* (New York: National Bureau of Economic Research).

Engle, R. F. & Manganelli, S. (2001) CAViaR: conditional autoregressive value at risk by regression quantiles, *NBER Working Paper,* W7341.

Engle, R. F. & Rosenberg, J. (1995) GARCH gammas, *Journal of Derivatives,* 2, pp. 47–59.

Engle, R. F. & Yoo, B. S. (1987) Forecasting and testing in co-integrated systems, *Journal of Econometrics,* 35, pp. 143–159.

Engle, R. F., Bradbury, K., Irvine, O. & Rothenberg, J. (1977) Simultaneous estimation of the supply and demand for household location in a multizoned metropolitan area, in: G. K. Ingram (Ed) *Residential Location and Urban Housing Markets* (Cambridge: Ballinger).

Engle, R. F., Hendry, D. F. & Richard, J.-F. (1983) Exogeneity, *Econometrica,* 51, pp. 277–304.

Engle, R. F., Hendry, D. F. & Trumble, D. (1985) Small-sample properties of ARCH estimators are tests, *Canadian Journal of Economics,* 18, pp. 66–93.

Engle, R.F., Granger, C. W. J. & Robins, R. (1986) Wholesale and retail prices: bivariate modeling with forccastable variances, in: D. Belsey and E. Kuh (Eds) *Model Reliability* (Cambridge: MIT Press).

Engle, R. F., Lilien, D. M. & Robins, R. P. (1987) Estimating time varying risk premia in the term structure: the ARCH-M model, *Econometrica,* 55, pp. 391–407.

Frain, J. (1995) Econometrics and truth, *Bank of Ireland Technical Paper,* 2/RT/95.

Fisher, F. M. (1962) *A Priori Information and Time Series Analysis* (Amsterdam: North-Holland).

French, K. R., Schwert, W. G. & Stambaugh, R. F. (1987) Expected stock returns and volatility, *Journal of Finance,* 19, pp. 3–29.

Friedman, M. & Schwartz, A. (1963) *Monetary History of the United States, 1870–1960* (Princeton: Princeton University Press).

Frisch, R. & Waugh, F. V. (1933) Partial time regression as compared with individual trends, *Econometrica,* 1, pp. 221–223.

Granger, C. W. J. (1957) A statistical model for sunspot activity, *Astrophysical Journal,* 126, pp. 152–158.

Granger, C. W. J. (1959) Estimating the probability of flooding on a tidal river, *Journal of the Institution of Water Engineers,* 13, pp. 165–174.

Granger, C. W. J. (1969) Investigating causal relations by econometric models and cross-spectral methods, *Econometrica,* 37, pp. 424–438.

Granger, C. W. J. (1981) Some properties of time series data and their use in econometric model specification, *Journal of Econometrics,* 16, pp. 121–130.

Granger, C. W. J. (1986) Developments in the study of cointegrated economic variables, *Oxford Bulletin of Economics and Statistics,* 48, pp. 213–228.

Granger, C. W. J. (1987) Causal inference, in: J. Eatwell, M. Milgate & P. Newman (Eds) *The New Palgrave: Econometrics* (New York: Norton).

Granger, C. W. J. (2001) Evaluation of forecasts, in: D. F. Hendry & N. R. Ericsson (Eds) *Understanding Economic Forecasts* (Cambridge: MIT Press).

Granger, C. W. J. & Anderson, A. P. (1978) *Introduction to Bilinear Time Series Models* (Gottingen: Vandenhoeck & Ruprecht).

Granger, C. W. J. & Bates, J. (1969) The combination of forecasts, *Operations Research Quarterly,* 20, pp. 451–468.

Granger, C. W. J. & Hatanaka, M. (1964) *Spectral Analysis of Economic Time Series* (Princeton: Princeton University Press).

Granger, C. W. J. & Joyeux, R. (1980) An introduction to long-memory time series models and fractional differencing, *Journal of Time Series Analysis,* 1, pp. 15–30.

Granger, C. W. J. & Lee, T. H. (1989) Investigation of production, sales and inventory relationships using multicointegration and non-symmetric error correction models, *Journal of Applied Econometrics,* 4, pp. 145–159.

Granger, C. W. J. & Newbold, P. (1974) Spurious regression in econometrics, *Journal of Econometrics,* 2, pp. 111–120.

Granger, C. W. J. & Swanson, N. R. (1995) Further developments in the study of cointegrated variables, *Oxford Bulletin of Economics and Statistics,* 58, pp. 537–553.

Granger, C. W. J. & Weiss, A. A. (1983) Time series analysis of error correction models, in: S. Karlin, T. Amemiya & L. A. Goodman (Eds) *Studies in Econometrics, Time Series and Multivariate Statistics in Honor of T. W. Anderson* (San Diego: Academic Press).

Granger, C. W. J., Craft, M. & Stephenson, G. (1964) The relationship between severity of personality disorder and certain adverse childhood influences, *British Journal of Psychiatry,* 110, pp. 392–396.

Hamilton, J. D. (1994) *Time Series Analysis* (Princeton: Princeton University Press).

Hendry, D. F. (1977) On the time series approach to econometric model building, in: C. A. Sims (Ed) *New Methods in Business Cycle Research* (Minneapolis: Federal Reserve Bank).

Hendry, D. F. (2004) The Nobel Memorial Prize for Clive W. J. Granger, *Scandinavian Journal of Economics,* 106, pp. 187–213.

Hooker, R. H. (1901) Correlation of the marriage rate with trade, *Journal of the Royal Statistical Society,* 64, pp. 485–492.

Hoover, K. (2001) *Causality in Macroeconomics* (Cambridge: Cambridge University Press).

Hwang, S. & Periera, P. L. V. (2003) Small sample properties of GARCH estimates and persistence, *Imbec Finance Lab Working Paper.*

Hylleberg, S., Engle, R. F., Granger, C. W. J. & Yoo, B. S. (1990) Seasonal cointegration, *Journal of Econometrics,* 44, pp. 215–238.

Johansen, S. (1988) Statistical analysis of cointegrating vectors, *Journal of Economic Dynamics and Control,* 12, pp. 231–254.

Keynes, J. M. (1940) Comment, *Economics Journal,* 50, pp. 154–156.

King, R. G., Plosser, C. I., Stock, J. H. & Watson, M. W. (1991) Stochastic trends and economic fluctuations, *American Economic Review,* 81, pp. 819–840.

Klein, L. R. (1953) *A Textbook of Econometrics* (Evanston: Row, Peterson & Company).

Klein, L. R. (1994) Problems with modern economics, *Atlantic Economic Journal,* 22, pp. 34–39.

Klein, L.R. (2004) Economic stabilization policy: pitfalls of parsimonious modelling, in: V. Pandit & K. Krishnamurty (Eds) *Economic Policy Modelling for India* (New Delhi: Oxford University Press).

Kwiatkowski, D., Phillips, P. C. B., Schmidt, P. & Shin, T. (1992) Testing the null hypothesis of stationarity against the alternative of a unit root: how sure are we that economic series have a unit root? *Journal of Econometrics,* 54, pp. 159–178.

Leamer, E. E. (1985) Vector autoregressions for causal inference?, *Carnegie Rochester Conference Series on Public Policy,* 22, pp. 255–303.

Lopez, G. J. & Cruz, A. B. (2000) Thirlwall's Law and beyond: the Latin American experience, *Journal of Post Keynesian Economics,* 22, pp. 477–495.

Loranger, J.-G. (2001) Structural form of an accumulation model: an analysis of cointegration of the long term growth of the Canadian economy, *University of Montreal Working Paper.*

Mandelbrot, B. B. (1963) The variation of certain speculative prices, *Journal of Business,* 36, pp. 394–419.

Mantalos, P. (2001) ECM-cointegration tests with GARCH(1,1) errors, *Interstat,* March 2001. Online at http://interstat.stat.vt.edu/InterStat/.

Matthews, P. H., Kandilov, I. T. & Maxwell, B. (2002) Interstate differences in insured unemployment: some recent evidence, *Applied Economics Letters,* 9, pp. 945–948.

Mayer, M. (1999) Somebody turn on the lights, *Derivatives Strategy,* November.

Miron, J. (1991) Comment, *NBER Macroeconomics Annual,* pp. 211–219.

Mizon, G. E. (1995) Progressive modelling of macroeconomic time series, in: K. D. Hoover (Ed) *Macroeconometrics: Developments, Tensions and Prospects* (Boston: Kluwer).

Murray, M. (1994) A drunk and her dog: an illustration of cointegration and error correction, *The American Statistician,* 48, pp. 37–39.

Nelson, C. R. & Plosser, C. I. (1982) Trends and random walks in macroeconomic time series, *Journal of Monetary Economics,* 10, pp. 139–162.

Nelson, D. B. (1991) Conditional heteroscedasticity in asset returns: a new approach, *Econometrica,* 59, pp. 347–390.

Palley, T. (1994) Competing views of the money supply process: theory and evidence, *Metroeconomica,* 45, pp. 67–88.

Pandit, V. (1999) Structural modelling under challenge, *Center for Development Economics / Delhi School of Economics Working Paper,* 98.

Perron, P. (1989) The great crash, the oil price shock, and the unit root hypothesis, *Econometrica,* 57, pp. 1361–1401.

Phelps, E. (1988) Comment on recent developments in macroeconomics, *Journal of Money, Credit and Banking,* 20, pp. 456–458.

Phillips, A. W. (1957) Stabilization policy and the time forms of lagged responses, *Economic Journal,* 67, pp. 265–277.

Phillips, P. C. B. (1986) Understanding spurious regressions in econometrics, *Journal of Econometrics,* 33, pp. 311–340.

Phillips, P. C. B. (1997) The ET interview: Professor Clive Granger, *Econometric Theory,* 13, pp. 253–303.

Phillips, P. C. B. & Perron, P. (1987) Testing for a unit root in a time series regression, *Biometrika,* 75, pp. 335–346.

Rappoport, P. & White, E. N. (1993) Was there a bubble in the 1929 stock market? *Journal of Economic History,* 53, pp. 549–574.

Shapiro, M. D. & Watson, M. W. (1988) Sources of business cycle fluctuations, *NBER Macroeconomics Annual,* pp. 111–148.

Shiller, R. J. (2003) From efficienct markets theory to behavioral finance, *Journal of Economic Perspectives,* 17, pp. 83–104.

Sims, C. A. (1972) Money, income and causality, *American Economic Review,* 62, 540–552.

Stock, J. H. (1987) Asymptotic properties of least squares estimators of cointegrating vectors, *Econometrica,* 55, pp. 1035–1056.

Stock, J. H. & Watson, M. W. (1988) Variable trends in economic time series, *Journal of Economic Perspectives,* 2, pp. 141–174.

Surowiecki, J. (2004) *The Wisdom of Crowds* (New York: Random House).

Taylor, A. (1995) International capital mobility in history: purchasing-power parity in the long run, *NBER Working Paper,* 5742.

Tobin, J. (1970) Money and income: post hoc ergo propter hoc? *Quarterly Journal of Economics,* 94, pp. 301–317.

Tobin, J. (1982) *Asset Accumulation and Economic Activity: Reflections on Contemporary Macroeconomic Theory* (Chicago: University of Chicago Press).

Yule, G. U. (1926) Why do we sometimes get nonsense correlations betweeen time series? A study in the sampling and nature of time series, *Journal of the Royal Statistical Society,* 89, pp. 1–6.

Zacharias, A. (2001) Testing profit rate equalization in the US manufacturing sector: 1947–1998, *Jerome Levy Institute Working Paper.*

Zellner, A. (1979) Causality and econometrics, *Carnegie Rochester Series on Public Policy,* 10, pp. 9–54.

Zivot, E. & Andrews, D. W. K. (1992) Further evidence on the Great Crash, oil price shock and the unit root hypothesis, *Journal of Business and Economic Statistics,* 10, pp. 251–270.

11 The economic contributions of John Kenneth Galbraith

Stephen P. Dunn and Steven Pressman

'The Economic Contributions of John Kenneth Galbraith' by Stephen P. Dunn and Steven Pressman (2005), Volume 17, Issue 2 (Taylor and Francis Ltd, http://www.informaworld.com), reprinted by permission of the publisher.

1 Introduction

The economic contributions of John Kenneth Galbraith can be viewed both negatively and positively. On the negative side Galbraith appears as gadfly, highly critical of traditional approaches to understanding the way the economy works and the economic policies that are pursued. He has criticized economic theory for ignoring and obscuring the economic power accumulated by large corporations. He has criticized politicians who align themselves with the objectives of the large corporation instead of acting in the public interest. And he has censured his fellow economists as *idiot savants*, who perform sophisticated mathematical analysis but who do not seek to understand the real world.

These critical efforts have sought to "emancipate belief" by urging the public to question the prevailing structure of economic knowledge and to challenge the conventional wisdom. In *Economics and the Public Purpose* Galbraith (1973d, Chapter 22) argues that the emancipation of belief is required to challenge the hegemony of accepted beliefs, which exclude the possibility of all contrary thought and prevent a proper understanding of how the economy works. Galbraith argues that the power and prestige of large firms is sustained through the conventional wisdom and that this leads to economic analysis that is neither socially relevant nor useful. Accordingly, he has criticized the various conventional wisdoms that permeate social thought. His goal here has been to increase the receptiveness to other ideas about how the economy operates and the policy agenda that is required once people have a proper understanding of how the economy really works.

More constructively, Galbraith has sought to examine power and its economic relations, and to analyze and understand the actual evolution and workings of economies. An understanding of power is crucial for understanding the firm, for the firm is an institution that seeks to control and supersede the market in order to expand the influence of its bureaucratic apparatus – what Galbraith labels "the technostructure". A proper understanding of the nature of the firm results in an analysis of how power is exercised in society as well the economic consequences that stem from such power. This analysis also yields a rich examination of the factors leading to rising poverty (for those without power) amid more general affluence, the degradation of the environment, and an expansive and imperialistic military-industrial complex with its interest in perpetuating the arms race. Similarly, an understanding of power is necessary for understanding how economic and social policy can counter the power of firms, and work to improve economic performance and the lives of those disenfranchised by the modern mode of production.

Galbraith also highlights the power that ideas have in facilitating social change. He seems to have accepted Keynes's contention that "the ideas of economists and political philosophers ... are more powerful than is commonly understood" (Keynes, 1964, p. 383). But Galbraith also went further than Keynes, arguing that increasingly outmoded economic ideas misinform social policy in a way that supports the corporate power structure, to the detriment of wider society (see Reisman, 1990). In their refusal to yield to the onslaught of circumstance, economic ideas can be socially damaging. Wrong ideas about the firm sustain the prestige of the large corporation and its personnel as well as the increasingly frivolous and unnecessary goods that they produce and promote (Galbraith, 1958a). Wrong ideas about the relationship between the firm and market obfuscate the proper regulatory response (Galbraith, 1967e, 1973d). They make it easier for large firms to resist government regulation, and shields firms pursing practices that may be environmentally unsound and detrimental to national security (Galbraith, 1973d, 2004a). And wrong ideas about how the economy works makes it hard to enact effective policies to support the public interest rather than corporate interests. It is thus necessary to oppose these ideas and point out their flaws.

In what follows, we highlight the role that economic power plays in the economics of John Kenneth Galbraith. We focus on the three main areas where Galbraith has elucidated the ramifications of the concentration of economic power. First, the large firm has acquired economic power emancipating it from the vagaries of the market, and thus giving it increased control over the market. Second, the large firm has acquired power over the consumer, over workers, and over other firms. This has led to pockets of poverty amidst affluence as well as leading to other social problems. Finally, when the goals of society are identified with the industrial system, the interests of the modern corporation dominate the government and public opinion. This results in the pursuit of economic policies that serve the interests of the powerful. To recognize this is to begin to open the door for government policies that will operate in the public interest. For this reason, we need macroeconomic policies that guarantee full employment, wage and price controls in order to stem inflation, redistributive fiscal polices that help reduce the problem of poverty, and all sorts of government policies that provide much needed public goods. We begin, however, by considering Galbraith himself.

2 The life of Galbraith

Since childhood, Galbraith has gone by the name "Ken". He vehemently disliked his given name "John", which came from an Uncle after whom he was named. By the time Galbraith was a teenager, his Uncle John had become a heavy drinker, and the whole family dropped the "John" in favor of "Ken".

Galbraith was born in Iona Station, a small town on the northern shore of Lake Erie, in 1908; and he grew up in Southern Ontario, part of Scottish Canada. This was an area settled by Scottish immigrants in the 1820s and 1830s (Galbraith, 1964g). In his autobiography – *A Life in Our Times* – Galbraith (1981f) regrets that his schooling was interrupted frequently by farm work and that his academic record was rather undistinguished. Parker (1999, p. 154ff.) contends that Galbraith's father, Archie, was a major force in his life, especially after his mother died at the age of 49, when Galbraith was only 14. Archie was both a teacher and the head of a cooperative insurance company that he helped to form. He was also active in local politics and a senior official in the county branch of the Canadian Liberal Party. Galbraith would often travel around the county with his father. "He has often retold the story of his father striding before a crowd gathered in a neighbor's barnyard and mounting a large manure pile. Galbraith says his father called for silence from the surprised onlookers, then with a straight face (but a twinkle in his eye), 'apologized with ill-concealed sincerity for speaking from the Tory platform'" (Parker, 1999, p. 156).

In the fall of 1926, Galbraith enrolled at Ontario Agricultural College (OAC), which is now the University of Guelph, located about 50 miles west of Toronto. His intent was to study agricultural economics. The curriculum at OAC involved mainly practical instruction in the agricultural arts – how to build a good dairy stable and how to raise quality livestock. To earn extra spending money Galbraith wrote a weekly column describing new and useful agricultural practices for his hometown newspaper.

But as the Great Depression began, Galbraith realized it made no sense to improve the quality of livestock if the livestock could not be sold at a decent price. So he switched his field of study to farm economics, which sought to understand the determinants of farm prices. Besides the fact that it let him focus on a practical problem, Galbraith made the switch for pragmatic reasons; he realized that understanding the causes of low farm prices "might help me get a job. As the Depression continued, there would, logically, be a demand for those with a remedy" (Galbraith, 1981f, p. 15).

Galbraith spent five years at OAC, the fifth year due mainly to health problems (tuberculosis) and poor preparation for college (Parker, 2005, p. 33). During his last year there Galbraith noticed a posting for a research assistant position at Berkeley that was sponsored by the Giannini Foundation of Agricultural Economics.[1] It carried a stipend of $60 a month, a good sum of money during the Depression. So he applied for the position, was accepted, and spent his graduate student days at Berkeley (Galbraith, 1971b, p. 259).

Galbraith claims that his years at Berkeley were among the best of his life. In his courses he was introduced to the great economists, both past and contemporaneous – Smith, Ricardo, Marx, Marshall, the German historical school, Veblen, and the early Keynes. He also had competent teachers who encouraged debate rather than squashing it. During his second year his stipend was raised to $70 per month. In his third year, Galbraith was sent to Davis to head up the Departments of Economics, of Agricultural Economics, and of Accounting and Farm Management. He was also required to teach courses in all of these areas, and his annual pay was increased to $1800 (Galbraith, 1971b, p. 269). Apparently, the administrative and teaching demands were not that great, and Galbraith had enough time to write his doctoral dissertation during the year. His PhD thesis, on the expenditures of California counties, "was without distinction.... The purpose was to get the degree" (Galbraith, 1981f, p. 22).

In the spring of 1933, Galbraith received an offer from Harvard for an instructorship position at an annual salary of $2400. Harvard offer in hand and ready to bargain, he went to negotiate with his Dean, for Galbraith heard this was how academics advanced. To his horror, the Dean "congratulated me warmly on my offer, gave me the impression that he thought Harvard was being reckless with its money and said that I should go.... The great love of my life was over" (Galbraith, 1971b, p. 270). And so Galbraith went off to Harvard, where – save an unhappy sojourn to Princeton and a stint as Editor of *Fortune* magazine – he spent the rest of his academic life, albeit with much time off to pursue his political and his writing interests.

Galbraith quickly became involved in policy issues at Harvard and also began to make important political connections. In late 1933, the Brookings Institution decided to study the operations of the Farm Credit Administration, and Galbraith was put in charge of this study. In the autumn of 1935 Galbraith first met Joseph Kennedy, Jr. and two years later John F. Kennedy arrived at Harvard (Galbraith, 1981f, pp. 53–60).

An important early influence on Galbraith was his work for the Agricultural Adjustment Administration (AAA) beginning in 1934. This early experience in Washington taught Galbraith the importance of power, a theme that appears in much of his more mature work in economics. Due to oversupply, the government was paying farmers not to grow crops, but this resulted in many surplus tenant farmers and sharecroppers. One key issue was how to divide government payments between farmers and their employees. The farmers, of course, wanted all the government money, but this created problems as their employees became extremely poor and migrated to northern cities. Liberals, like Galbraith, wanted large fractions of the money to go to the poor farm workers. The eventual compromise was that money would continue to go only to farmers; but farmers agreed not to get rid of their employees and to provide them with some support.

More importantly, at Harvard Galbraith's economic analysis moved beyond agricultural economics (see Bruce, 2000). Several factors were at work in this transformation. In 1935 he began a monograph on the causes of the great depression with the industrialist Henry S. Dennison – essentially focusing on the effects of monopolistic competition in a manner that (less formally) echoes

Kalecki (1935). The work of Berle & Means [1932] demonstrated how power in the firm had been usurped by managers, leaving shareholders as passive recipients of corporate profits. However, the major influence on Galbraith occurred following publication of *The General Theory*, when Keynes "reached Harvard with tidal force" (Galbraith, 1981f, p. 67). Galbraith, along with the younger Harvard faculty, read Keynes avidly. Keynes was an inspiration both for his incisive analysis and because he was able to write in a manner that could grab the attention of his colleagues and the general public. Galbraith also admired Keynes's pragmatic side – his ability to identify a real world problem, analyze it, and develop appropriate and considered policy solutions tailored to it.

The year 1936 also saw Galbraith's political involvement deepen. He volunteered to help out on the Roosevelt re-election campaign and took the message of Keynesiansim to Washington (Galbraith, 1971b, Chapter 3). And at the suggestion of several other Democrats, he decided to apply for American citizenship.

In the autumn of 1937 Galbraith became an American citizen and married Catherine Merriam Atwater – known as "Kitty". The newlyweds took a ship to England and headed to Cambridge, where Galbraith was to serve as a Rockefeller Fellow. Keynes, who was recovering from his first heart attack, did not meet with Galbraith. But Galbraith established close and lifelong friendships with Richard Kahn, Joan Robinson, Piero Sraffa and Michal Kalecki. Once a week he would head to London to attend London School of Economics (LSE) seminars run by Friedrich von Hayek and Lionel Robbins. On weekends and holidays Galbraith and his new wife would tour the English countryside and continental Europe (Galbraith, 1981f, pp. 70–79).

Returning to Harvard in 1938, Galbraith was asked to head up a commission to review the public works programs of the New Deal. This meant frequent travel to Washington, and deeper immersion in the politics of the time. In 1939 Galbraith had his first face-to-face meeting with FDR (Galbraith, 1981f, p. 95). In 1940 Lauchlin Currie recruited Galbraith to serve as the resident economist for the American Farm Bureau Federation, "a government-organized lobby on behalf of government services for agriculture" (Galbraith, 1981f, p. 98). But Galbraith's talents as a writer were quickly discovered, and he spent most of his time writing political speeches and memos after being asked to be part of the White House speechwriting team for the 1940 election.

In 1941 Galbraith became deeply involved in the planning for World War II, working as director of the National Defense Advisory Commission under the Secretary of Agriculture, Chester Davis. Following the attack on Pearl Harbor, Currie called Galbraith to Washington and asked for his help in facilitating economic stabilization and resource mobilization by controlling prices in the War economy. Galbraith became deputy administrator of the Office of Price Administration (OPA), giving him effective control over the prices of most US goods until 1943 when price controls were lifted. Galbraith (1981f, p. 170ff.) argues that his work at the OPA was a great success. National income grew a great deal during the war, shortages were limited to a few items like whiskey and gasoline, and when the controls were removed there was only a small increase in prices, thereby demonstrating that inflationary pressures were actively managed and not just kept temporarily under control. Galbraith's work at the OPA also inspired a novel contribution to the theory of price control. He argued for controls on wages and prices as a way to deal with inflation in the post-war world (Galbraith, 1952b). What is more, this experience cemented his belief that wage and price controls are the most effective solution to the problem of inflation – a view he maintained throughout his life.

As the OPA was disbanded due to mounting political pressure, Galbraith joined the editorial staff of *Fortune* magazine, and worked there from 1943 to 1948. Galbraith credits his experience at *Fortune*, and especially its owner, Henry R. (Harry) Luce, for helping him develop his well-known ability to write with humor and grace (Galbraith, 1981f, p. 264; 1986e, pp. 409–416). Galbraith (1981f, p. 268) also credits his years at *Fortune* with a consolidating his understanding of how the large corporation dominates the American economy, instructing him about how large firms actually operate, underscoring the need to move beyond the myths of the firm perpetuated in neoclassical textbooks, and helping him to understand how decisions were actually made in the large corporation and how these decisions impacted society.

In the fall of 1944, George Ball was asked to provide an independent assessment of the results of the air force bombing of Germany. Ball asked Galbraith to join the efforts and to be in charge of assessing the economic effects of both German mobilization and the air attacks. Working under Galbraith was a virtual who's who of distinguished economists including Nicholas Kaldor, E.F. Schumacher, Paul Baran, Tibor Scitovsky, and Edward Dennison (who went onto become a major luminary in modern statistical analysis). They began their study believing that the air attacks had greatly damaged the German economy. Much to their surprise they found that the German bombing *actually aided the war effort* because it destroyed civilian businesses in the big cities, leaving many people without jobs and in need of employment. But the military factories of Germany were generally located on Greenfield sites outside the big cities that were bombed. So the bombing generated an increased supply of labor for producing military goods (Galbraith, 1981f, pp. 199–205).[2]

Based on this study Galbraith concluded that the German war economy was badly run. He made this case in *Fortune* (Galbraith, 1945), despite misgivings from the editors; indeed, its radical thesis was at odds with the dominant interpretation of the German war machine (Galbraith, 1981f, p. 229). According to Galbraith, Hitler's intrusion into technical areas, where he had no competence, resulted in poor decision-making and created serious problems for the German economy. Another problem, Galbraith argued, was German overconfidence at the beginning of the war. After quickly occupying large parts of Europe, Hitler expected that his easy successes would continue. This led to considerable under-mobilization by Germany. Galbraith (1946a) also produced a ten-point plan that anticipated the Marshall Plan for redeveloping Europe that was set forth by Secretary of State George Marshall in the spring of 1947.

During the fall of 1948 Galbraith returned to Harvard and academic life. His teaching responsibilities included agricultural economics and industrial organization, but his focus was more on writing and politics. Soon came two books on power relationships, *American Capitalism* (Galbraith, 1952a) and *A Theory of Price Control* (Galbraith, 1952b), plus a history of the stock market bubble of the 1920s and its subsequent crash, *The Great Crash* (Galbraith, 1955c).

In the summer of 1955 Galbraith arranged for a year-long sabbatical. He used a Guggenheim Fellowship to go to Switzerland in order to write a book on poverty. This he combined with a good deal of travel, including his first trip to India, where he saw the poverty of less developed countries first hand. Published in 1958, *The Affluent Society*, along with Michael Harrington's (1962) *The Other America*, helped bring the problem of poverty amidst much affluence to the attention of the American public and culminated in President Johnson declaring a "war on poverty" in 1964.

After finishing *The Affluent Society*, Galbraith went on a lecture tour of Poland and Yugoslavia in May of 1958 at the invitation of Oscar Lange. During the trip he spent a lot of time with Michal Kalecki. His diary of this trip (Galbraith, 1958d) focused on the uneven quality of life in Eastern Europe. Galbraith noted both the clean streets and the high educational achievements attained; but he also remarked on the poor quality of workmanship on buildings and roads, and the general drabness of life there.

In the fall of 1959 Harvard appointed Galbraith to the Paul Warburg Chair in Economics, established in honor of one of the architects of the Federal Reserve System and one of its original Governors. At the same time, Harvard gave Galbraith two terms off to begin work on the sequel to *The Affluent Society* – what was to become *The New Industrial State*. Work on the book was interrupted when John Kennedy was elected President in November 1960 and appointed Galbraith Ambassador to India.[3]

Notwithstanding his extensive academic activities, the 1950s and the 1960s were also a period of high political activity. Galbraith was one of the founders of the liberal Americans for Democratic Action. And he was an adviser and speechwriter for Adlai Stevenson in his two Presidential campaigns, and then for John Kennedy in his 1960 Presidential campaign.

In the 1952 Stevenson campaign, Galbraith wrote on farm policy and economics. John Bartlow Martin (1976) describes some rather tense meetings of Stevenson's speech writers during the heat of the campaign. In an obscure Springfield, Illinois saloon where the writers lunched to avoid the press and relax, they sat around a table next to the jukebox. As Martin (1976, p. 636) reports, "Once when somebody started to put a nickel in the jukebox, Galbraith said to him, 'I'll give you a dime if you don't play it'." Between the 1952 and 1956 Presidential campaigns, Galbraith (1981f, p. 296f.) attempted to teach Keynesian economics to Stevenson, who was skeptical of running budget deficits and thought Keynes a subversive.

Over time his relationship with Stevenson cooled, and Galbraith began to actively support John Kennedy. Surprisingly, Galbraith was more actively involved in the Stevenson campaigns than the Kennedy campaign, since he was personally closer to Kennedy than to Stevenson. Nevertheless, his Ambassador appointment was testament to his political standing and access to the corridors of power. Although Galbraith desired to be appointed to Kennedy's old Senate seat in Massachusetts, Kennedy pressed Galbraith to serve as US Ambassador to India. From India, Galbraith sent Kennedy telegrams advising against the growing US involvement in Vietnam, against the planned (and infamous) Bay of Pigs operation in Cuba, and against clandestine CIA operations in India (Galbraith, 1969c, 1998d). In May of 1963, Galbraith resigned as Ambassador to return to Harvard. He continued to provide advice to Kennedy; and after Kennedy was assassinated in November 1963, to Lyndon Johnson. Galbraith had especially strong misgivings about the escalating war in Vietnam and on the question of reducing poverty in the US. In 1964, Johnson appointed Galbraith to the White House Task Force that was responsible for formulating a "war on poverty".

But as Johnson increased US involvement in Vietnam, Galbraith became a leader of the anti-war movement. In November 1967 Galbraith published *How to Get Out of Vietnam* (Galbraith, 1967b), which argued for pulling US troops back to the cities and coastal areas, setting up some sanctuaries that could be defended, and waiting out the opposition. Two years later, *How to Control the Military* (Galbraith, 1969h) explained both how the military, and the firms supplying their needs, had acquired considerable power and influence over US government policy and the articulation of national interests. It forcefully argued that arms control agreements were necessary, as were elected politicians who would stand up to the military-industrial complex. He also wrote about revitalizing the Democratic Party and making it a true alternative to the Republican Party (Galbraith, 1970g).

During the late 1960s, the 1970s and the early 1980s, Galbraith continued to play an active, if somewhat diminished, role in politics. In 1968 he worked in the Presidential campaign of Senator Eugene McCarthy (seconding his nomination at the Chicago Democratic convention), and in 1972 he worked for Senator George McGovern, serving as a delegate for McGovern at the Democratic convention in Miami. He then worked in the Presidential campaigns of Representative Morris Udall in 1976 and Senator Edward Kennedy in 1980.

In the 1970s, Galbraith continued his effort to bring economic ideas to a broad and more general public. He worked on the British Broadcasting Corporations (BBC) television series (which was syndicated in the US on PBS) *The Age of Uncertainty* (Galbraith, 1977a), and his book *Almost Everyone's Guide to Economics* (Galbraith & Salinger, 1978) was geared, as the title proclaimed, to increase general economic literacy.

During the 1970s and 1980s Galbraith also began to receive a great deal of professional recognition. In 1972 he served as President of the American Economic Association (Galbraith, 1973g); and in 1976 he was honored by the Association of Evolutionary Economics – receiving its Veblen-Commons award (Galbraith, 1977b). In 1982 he was elected to the 50 member American

Academy of Arts and Letters, the first economist to be so honored. Two years later, he became President of the Academy.

Galbraith continued to be active professionally during this time period. He provided both the "moral and financial support" to help start the *Journal of Post Keynesian Economics* (King, 2002, p. 135), which began publishing in 1978 under the joint editorship of Paul Davidson and Sidney Weintraub (see Galbraith, 1978l). Following the untimely death of Weintraub in 1984, Davidson (another longstanding friend of Galbraith's) became its sole editor (Galbraith, 1985o). Immediately the journal became the major publication outlet for Post Keynesian economists, with Galbraith serving as the Chairman of the Honorary Board of Editors.

Although retiring from Harvard in 1975, and greatly reducing his active engagement in politics not long after, Galbraith continued to write about economic and policy issues throughout the 1980s and the 1990s. He strongly opposed the conservative trend in the US and the resurgence of greed as a primary motivation for individual behavior. He was especially critical of the Reagan administration policies, but also opposed the Clinton administration reductions in domestic spending and welfare reform as unnecessary and an undesirable accommodation to conservative Republicans in Congress. His writings in the 1980s and 1990s also emphasized the importance of knowing history in order to understand the economy, and the importance of understanding the locus of power in order to understand the real world. The *Anatomy of Power* (Galbraith, 1983a) expounds the nature of power and its relation to the economic and political system. *Economics in Perspective* (Galbraith, 1987d) integrates economic history and the history of economic thought. *The Culture of Contentment* (Galbraith, 1992a) and *The Good Society* (Galbraith, 1996b) examine the reduced concern with addressing the needs of the poor in the late twentieth century. *A Journey in Economic Time* (Galbraith, 1994f) provides an overview and history of economic policy making in the US over the last century. And *Name Dropping* (Galbraith, 1999h) takes us on a trip of the economic policies of Presidents Roosevelt, Truman, Kennedy and Lyndon Johnson.

In what follows we summarize Galbraith's principle economic contributions. Readers can find more details, and the numerous criticisms that have been leveled at Galbraith, in the several excellent overviews of his work (Hession, 1972; Sharpe, 1973; Gambs, 1975; Pratson, 1978; Reisman, 1980; Stanfield, 1996). The two Galbraith (1977, 2001) readers, the three Festschriften (Bowles *et al.*, 1989; Sasson, 1999; Keaney, 2001), as well as the collection of interviews with Galbraith (Stanfield & Stanfield, 2004) also offer an excellent overview and discussion of Galbraith's thought. Finally, Parker's (2005) intellectual biography provides more information on the life of Galbraith and the development of his thought.

3 Power and the firm

In his early work, Galbraith (1936, 1938a, 1943, 1947b, 1949d; Dennison & Galbraith, 1938) explored the ramifications of the rise of the large, modern corporation. But it was not until *American Capitalism* (Galbraith, 1952a) that he began to make a decisive break from the neoclassical model and begin to create an alternative theoretical system that captured the change ushered in by the large firm in advanced economies. *American Capitalism, The Affluent Society* (Galbraith, 1958a) to some degree, and especially *The New Industrial State* (Galbraith, 1967e) analyze the impact of highly concentrated economic power and its nexus to technology. In these works Galbraith argues that the large firm should not be viewed as an historical aberration. The modern corporation is not an exception that proves the competitive rule; rather, it is a consequence of the evolution of a mode of production that has come to dominate the modern economy, differing markedly from the conventional analysis of oligopolies presented in economics textbooks.

In the conventional wisdom, competition ensures that scarce resources with alternative uses are efficiently utilized. The pursuit of self-interest combines with competition to promote the wider social good:

> The efficient and the progressive were rewarded with survival and growth. The inefficient were and unprogressive were penalized by extinction.... Competition was also the instrument of change. As the tastes of the sovereign consumer altered, the demand for some products rose and so did their prices.
>
> (Galbraith, 1958a, p. 40)

In the dominant view firms are (or should be made to be) powerless. They are (or should be) sole conduits for the demands coming from the market. Prices (including the wages of workers) are set by (impersonal) market forces, and the prospect of power and supra-normal profits are checked by competition. This competitive ideal solidifies into the widespread view, held by many economists, that the sole route to maximize social welfare is to make markets more competitive and promote private enterprise.

The view that receives elaboration is one where the individual firm, run by either single owner or small management executive, seeks to maximize firm profits and their resultant income. Firms that do not seek to maximize profits will be driven out of business by other firms that operate more efficiently and grow through profitable accumulation. According to Galbraith, this view – which continues to dominate economic instruction – is outmoded and approximates an earlier period in history that has since been superceded. It is a view that no longer elucidates reality; instead, it serves to obscure it. Today the firms that produce and sell the majority of the goods and services are large bureaucracies, dominated by professional managers. What is more, although markets have ceased to be competitive, Galbraith (1952a, 1952b, 1967e) argues that the standard predictions regarding the consequences of this shift – inefficiency and the ruthless exploitation of economic power – have not been supported by facts. Few customers of large corporations complain of exploitation, anti-trust laws are seldom invoked, and the instances of oligopoly are typically associated with the greatest output and the most robust growth (Galbraith, 1973d).

In sharp contrast to the traditional theories of oligopoly, which depict the large firm as resulting from significant economics of scale in production costs, Galbraith explains the rise of the modern corporation as a means to facilitate technological change by emancipating it from the uncertainties of the market. Echoing Schumpeter (1942), Galbraith supplants the conventional preoccupation with technology or steady state production with an examination of the forces of conscious design that enable large-scale technological change to take place.

Galbraith (1967e, pp. 32–35) identifies several important consequences of technology – it increases the length time to complete tasks, it requires more capital, which is inflexibly committed, it requires specialized manpower (which calls for organization) and it entails planning (which supersedes the market). That is to say, advanced technology requires large specialized investments in capital and labor to be inflexibly committed over long periods of time. As the price of failure is great, it must be avoided at all costs. Of course, "The greatest source of insecurity ... l[ies] in competition" (Galbraith, 1958a, p. 100). Thus, avoiding failure means escaping the tyranny and hazards of the market; the solution to the problem of economic insecurity is to mitigate the factors that conspire to impinge upon the processes of production.

As the firm grows, and as production processes become increasingly complex and technologically more sophisticated, there is an increasing need for a team of dedicated bureaucratic specialists to administer the decisions of the modern business firm. Echoing the notion of bounded rationality (Simon, 1955), Galbraith notes that the complexities of modern technology mean that one person can no longer be familiar with all the aspects of engineering, procurement, quality control, labor relations and marketing, which are necessary for doing business.

As group decision-making and technical expertise become more important, power passes from the individual owner to those people with the requisite knowledge of the production process – the technostructure. The technostructure represents a new class and a new factor of production. It is comprised of the diffuse decision-making structure of the large corporation, and it affects the use and promulgation of modern technology. It encompasses an array of managerial, technical, legal, engineering, accounting, and advertising expertise. The technostructure selects products and chooses production techniques, including the number and type of workers to employ; they develop marketing and pricing policy; and they are responsible for organizing access to finance (internally or externally).

Organization is the manner by which the technostructure achieves co-ordination and makes decisions. Organization exists as a necessary response to the imperatives of complex technology and the diffusion of requisite knowledge that needs to be brought to bear in its realization. Its decision-making conventions and structures permit informed, reliable and coordinated decisions, and it enables the pursuit and alignment of common objectives across a range of specialists. Thus, the decisive factor in economic success is no longer the heroic individual but rather organized intelligence. "It is not to individuals but to organizations that power in the business enterprise and power in society has passed" (Galbraith, 1967e, p. 75).

As power passes to the technostructure, the behavior of the modern corporation will increasingly reflect its aims and objectives. The technostructure will choose those goals and strategies that facilitate its survival and reproduction, such as growth and uncertainty mitigation (what Galbraith refers to as "the protective need"), and those that enhance its status and position, such as the pursuit of technical virtuosity (what Galbraith refers to as "the affirmative need"). Moreover, unlike owners with a vested interest in maximizing profits, professional managers gain little from direct profit maximization. They will not be interested in profit maximization per se, or the maximization of shareholder value, as an end in itself; rather, they seek to maximize their own power, prestige and affluence. Such motivations are more closely aligned with the growth of the firm.

Survival for the technostructure is likely to mean achieving a minimum amount of earnings so that the independence of these decision-makers can be maintained. Low earnings or losses will challenge the autonomy of the technostructure. Once the flow of earnings are above an acceptable level, the preeminence of the technostructure is assured. Firm growth assures this minimum level of profits and prevents the discharge of members of the technostructure as a cost saving measure. Growth also serves the "affirmative" or psychological needs of the technostructure – the prestige that generally comes from working for a large well-known firm. Finally, the pursuit of growth and technical virtuosity means more jobs and promotions for members of the technostructure.

Of course, profits continue to be necessary to the technostructure's economic and material well-being. But, to reiterate, this need not entail profit maximization. The market is no longer enforcing this goal. And the technical complexities of modern technology mean that ascertaining how to maximize profits is no easy matter. As Galbraith (1967e, p. 122) points out:

> profit maximization – the only goal that is consistent with the rule of the market – is no longer necessary. The competitive firm had no choice of goals. The monopoly could take less than the maximum; but this would be inconsistent with its purpose of being a monopoly. But planning is the result not of the desire to exploit market opportunity but the result among other factors, of the unreliability of markets. Subordination to the market, and to the instruction that it conveys, has disappeared. So there is no longer, a priori, reason to believe that profit maximization will be the goal of the technostructure. It could be, but this must be shown.

What is more, focusing on growth and survival also directs attention to the various policies pursued by the technostructure to make the market more reliable and predictable. The market and the forces of competition generate considerable uncertainties for the large firm. To thrive, firms must seek to control the market rather than being subservient to it. For example, investment in new technology is costly; and firms wish to avoid the prospect that, after expensive investment, there will be little or no demand for the goods they produce. Large investments of time and money must be protected if the costs of technological change are to be recovered and its benefits realized:

> Technology, with its companion commitment of time and capital, means that the needs of the consumer must be anticipated – by months or years.... By the same token, while common labor and carbon steel will be forthcoming in response to a promise to pay, the specialized skills and arcane materials required by advanced technology cannot similarly be counted upon. The needed action in both instances is evident: in addition to deciding what the consumer will want and will pay, the firm must take every feasible step to see what it decides to produce is wanted by the consumer at remunerative prices. And it must see that the labor, materials and equipment that it needs will be available at a cost consistent with the price it will receive. It must exercise control over what is sold. It must exercise control over what is supplied. It must replace the market with planning.
>
> (Galbraith, 1967e, p. 41)

To reduce the uncertainties surrounding large commitments of time and money, the firm must either supersede the market or subordinate it to the requirements of planning. Planning is thus a consequence of advanced technology, and planning replaces the market as a means of allocating resources. For Galbraith, planning entails not only co-ordination, as with Coase; it is also about how the firm prepares for, and attempts to control, unforeseen events. Rather than viewing the firm as resulting from a purely *instrumental* choice of economizing on the costs between alternative modes of contracting, for Galbraith the corporation is an institution that copes with, mitigates, or eliminates, uncertainties.[4] The large firm emerges in response to the uncertain nature of markets. This, according to Galbraith, is a primary reason for the observed growth of the large firm and its nexus to the political apparatus. The technostructure, through the modern corporation, must lever its power to ensure its continued reproduction and, by so doing, reduce the risks it is subject to.

The uncertainties of the market are mitigated in a variety of ways (Galbraith, 1967e, pp. 43–45). Through vertical integration it takes over suppliers and outlet sources. By developing many diverse products, the firm can absorb the consequences of a drastic change in consumer tastes or the aversion of consumers to a particular product. By spending money on advertising the firm attempts to manage consumer tastes. Long-term contracts between producers and suppliers attempt to eliminate the uncertainty of short-term market fluctuations.[5] Moreover, the larger the firm, the more likely it can mold the future.

Perhaps the most hotly debated strategy that the modern corporation uses to mitigate uncertainty concerns managing the response of the consumer. In the conventional wisdom the firm is subservient to the given preferences of consumers. According to Galbraith, consumer demand is not exogenous, but is shaped by institutional processes and by particular influences such as advertising (see Anderson & Dunn, 2006 for an examination of Galbraith's thesis in the context of the tobacco industry).[6] It is the need to protect the investment of capital and time that creates a strong incentive to ensure that what is produced gets sold. If large capital outlays on advanced technology are to be recouped, and if the technical virtuosity of the technostructure is to be maintained, then the response of the consumer must be managed (Galbraith, 1967e, p. 208). This explains the not insignificant growth in advertising by the modern firm.

In identifying the process of want management, Galbraith (1958a) first articulated the notion of a *dependence effect*. The dependence effect is a portmanteau concept and embodies passive and active aspects. The passive aspect is the process of emulation whereby social norms and localized cultural comparisons induce consumption patterns, i.e. the social pressure to "keep up with the Jones's". The active aspect refers to the contriving of specific social wants and, equally important, the creation and reproduction of a consumer culture.[7] Nevertheless Galbraith accepts that advertising and other attempts at consumer manipulation may not be perfect, but its power, presence and influence must be acknowledged and analyzed.

One of the principle deficiencies of the dependence effect, however, was that it did not articulate a clear rationale for the management of the consumer. In *The New Industrial State* Galbraith linked the processes of managing the response of the consumer with the need to protect upfront large scale investment in technology and the interests of the technostructure. This management of the consumer by the firm is referred to by Galbraith as "the revised sequence". Rather than firms satisfying the wants and demands of the consumer, the modern firm "accommodates the consumer to the goals of the technostructure and provides a climate of social belief that is favorable to this result" (Galbraith, 1967e, p. 235). Like the dependence effect, the revised sequence is broader than just the management of specific consumer demand by the firm. Consumers must be able to buy goods as well as desire them, so the technostructure has a vested interest in ensuring the state takes general responsibility for this.[8] State "[r]egulation of aggregate demand is necessary to give certainty to this planning and to protect the technostructure" (Galbraith, 1967e, p. 229). This underlines the symbiotic relationship between the modern corporation and the state, while also explaining the early appearance of Keynesian policies before the widespread acceptance of the Keynesian theoretical system and the latent Keynesianism of the Reagan era!

The rise of the modern corporation thus is viewed as undermining Smith's invisible hand and usurping the doctrine of consumer sovereignty (cf. Chandler, 1977). Indeed, an important consequence of the revised sequence is that the goods produced through the planning system are accorded higher privilege and status than other productive and life affirming activities that do not find direct expression through the market. As such, the promotion and elevation of goods produced by private firms results in increasingly meaningless products being accorded higher social virtue than those goods meeting many basic human needs that the private enterprise system has not been able to produce.

The organizations that are able to emancipate themselves from the vagaries of the market comprise, what Galbraith refers to as "the planning system", and account for around half of the total production in a modern industrialized economy. Small firms populate the other half of the economy, what Galbraith refers to as "the market system". These are firms that appear to approximate the neoclassical model. Like the firms that are part of the planning system, they wish to escape the uncertainty of the market. However, their power is restrained by free competition.

Both the market and the planning systems are interdependent structures that form part of Galbraith's (1977b) bimodal view of mature economies. Indeed, the resulting distribution of power, dominance, and control of prices by the planning sector, means that the terms of trade favor the large corporation. The large firm exploits this power for its own ends, providing it with a relatively secure and favorable income. The consequence is that the market sector receives lower and less secure income (Galbraith, 1973d, pp. 65–66).

One implication of this bimodal view is that it allows policy makers to ascertain the nature and extent of the planning system's influence over society. Such knowledge may be marshaled to serve the development of policy, new institutional structures and broader social aims (Galbraith, 1973d, Chapters 21–31). For example, Galbraith argues (in a manner that echoes Williamson's (1975, 1985) transaction cost analysis of firm size) that there is no sense breaking up the large corporation in the hope of restoring the neoclassical competitive ideal. This would entail rejecting the technology that underpins the escape from the tyranny and insecurity of the market. Moreover, to break up large corporations would undermine the technical dynamism that provides for much contemporary wealth (even if such wealth is inequitably distributed).[9] Finally, such trust busting is unnecessary, not least because the development of sources of countervailing power (see below) further mitigates the scope for abuse of such dominance (Galbraith, 1952a).

This more enlightened response entails harnessing the productive capacity of large corporations but mitigating their economic and social power. This requires enlightened policy regarding the planning system. Such a policy "consists in disciplining its purposes – in making these serve, not define the public interest" (Galbraith, 1973d, p. 240). This means developing appropriate regulation to fetter the abuses of corporate power and making the corporate form more democratically accountable. Such a program of reform, which anticipates the recent concern with corporate governance, is necessary to confront the power of the large corporations that dominate the economy. Galbraith's analysis of poverty, and what should be done to alleviate it, is likewise informed by this view of the modern firm.

4 Power and poverty

In the conventional wisdom the existence of poverty is typically explained as a consequence of the actions and choices of individuals, or the result of damaging and erroneous government policies. Individualist explanations have tended to be more prevalent, especially in the US where Social Darwinism (see Hofstadter, 1944) has had a strong hold on the popular imagination. According to this doctrine, the economic and social world is characterized by a power struggle in which the inevitable outcome is a "survival of the fittest". People who pursue education and possess the drive and the desire to be productive will succeed. In contrast, sloth, the failure to take individual initiative and an unwillingness to learn and develop socially useful skills are choices that relegate certain individuals to mediocrity or failure. As a consequence, such individuals are more likely to receive low wages and experience frequent bouts of poverty throughout their life. On the standard view, this outcome is the result of individual choices.

The second dominant explanation of poverty focuses on the unintended consequences of an extensive social welfare safety net. These analyses focus on policies that create perverse economic incentives for people, and promote a reliance on government benefits rather than economically contributing to society (Murray, 1984). Government policies are also identified as failing to encourage the high levels of saving and investment that are thought to be required if the economy and individual incomes are to grow. Governments running large budget deficits are viewed as discouraging private savings and investment, including investment in human capital (Seidman, 1990).

In contrast to this mainstream view, radical economists have identified several dysfunctional institutions that contribute to poverty, and have stressed the need to eliminate them. Radical economists point out that capitalists in developed countries need a large number of compliant workers who are willing to work hard for low wages. This "reserve army of the unemployed" is integral to the capitalist mode of accumulation according to radical economic theory. It functions to discipline workers by holding their economic power in check; but such an army of unemployed individuals consigns a sizable minority to poverty.

Similarly, radical development economists fault colonial systems, which have perpetuated feudal agrarian land systems where most of the land is owned by a very small minority. This excludes a great many people from both land ownership and the income that comes from owning the land. Great numbers of people are therefore forced to work on the land for subsistence wages.

Thus, in the radical view the locus of poverty arises in the endemic class exploitation in developed countries and the history of colonial oppression in less developed countries. By subjugating the masses and denying workers the rewards of their labor, such people are condemned to a life of poverty.

Galbraith acknowledged the relevance of parts of both the neoclassical and the radical analyses of poverty. He recognizes the problems created by institutional structures, and he stresses the need to develop new ones. Similarly, he agrees with the mainstream perspective on the need to improve access to education and to develop human capital as a means of increasing individual capabilities and individual incomes. But Galbraith also rejects large parts of both the neoclassical and radical analyses.

While believing that the radical perspective is correct to focus on institutional problems that contribute to poverty, Galbraith contends that it fails to correctly identify the institutions that contribute to poverty, and thus its solutions are erroneous. In particular, the class analysis of capitalism fails to account for the rise of the technostructure and the associated (albeit uneven) affluence ushered in by the modern corporation. So, too, does the radical institutional analysis. In *The Nature of Mass Poverty* Galbraith (1979f) notes that some capitalist countries (e.g., India) have done worse than some Communist countries (e.g., China) when it comes to reducing poverty. It is thus unwarranted to conclude *a priori* that government intervention will necessarily hinder the workings of the free market and result in lower economic growth, unemployment and poverty. Similarly, in *Economic Development* Galbraith (1964b, p. 16) points out that colonialism is not a recent problem in Latin America, yet most of Latin America is still poor. Moreover, Australia, Canada and the US were all British colonies at one point; however, all now experience general prosperity. So colonialism does not seem to be the institutional culprit responsible for poverty.

While Galbraith stresses the importance of investing in human capital, his analysis of the modern corporation leads him to reject the marginal productivity theory of distribution on which the traditional analysis of poverty rests. In a world of technological advance, where general affluence is possible, the tradition of despair and scarcity in radical and mainstream economics has been made obsolete (see Galbraith, 1958a, Chapters 3–6). Contra the marginal productivity theory of value, the wealth of the technostructure and the affluent is *not* derived from their hard work and their contributions to economic output, but from their possession of economic power. In addition, the emergence of the large corporation and the technostructure has ushered in an epoch where cooperation underpins economic success (as opposed to individualistic competitive struggle). And one consequence of Keynesianism is that it is the state, and not individuals, that must assume responsibility for assuring a sufficient level of aggregate demand and its associated levels of employment.

Thus, it appears that neither dysfunctional institutions nor dysfunctional individual behaviors are the main cause of poverty. Instead, for Galbraith poverty is a problem that stems from the lack of adequate power that manifests itself in several ways. First, poverty is due to a social imbalance that results in a lack of public goods. This is seen most clearly in developed countries which, through the modern corporation, have achieved a large measure of affluence and have a large (potentially redistributable) social surplus available for antipoverty efforts. Similarly, the poverty of less developed nations is also the result of a social imbalance. Many of these countries spend far too much on arms and the military, and fail to provide necessary public services like decent health care, adequate sanitation, and quality education (Galbraith, 1983k, Chapter 4). A second problem is that the poor are trapped in a vicious cycle of cumulative causation that they cannot overcome on their own. The poor lack economic power relative to the technostructure because social processes and a lack of social infrastructure undermines their life chances and social mobility. This analysis applies to both the pockets of poor in developed countries as well as the large number of poor households in less developed countries.

These considerations underpin Galbraith's analysis of poverty. We first outline his (Galbraith, 1958a, p. 246) analysis of "insular poverty" – the pockets of poverty in developed countries. This is the problem of poverty amidst plenty, of a minority of households on the cusp of subsistence in rich, vibrant economies. It is the problems of urban slums as well as rural decline and isolation in areas like Appalachia. We then consider the "mass poverty" of less developed nations. This is the poverty of an entire nation, where most of the population lives on the brink of starvation. It is the poverty of vast areas of Africa, of China and India, and of rural areas and urban slums in Latin and South America.

Galbraith first raised the issue of insular poverty in *American Capitalism* (Galbraith, 1952a, Chapter 8). There he noted that the affluence created by technological advance can cause problems for those who do not benefit from the new technology, and who are relegated to receiving low wages for work that is no longer in demand. *The Affluent Society* extends this analysis considerably. Galbraith (1958a, p. 248) again insists that technology does not in itself help reduce poverty; but now he identifies some of the causes of poverty with technology itself. That is to say, the general affluence created by technology and associated management of the consumer blinds us to the situation of the poor and makes them increasingly powerless and invisible.

A world of affluence also creates political problems for the poor. As a small powerless minority, politicians have little incentive to speak out for the poor and thus are unlikely to use the legislature to help them, as this will not garner votes. In addition, with general affluence, there is a greater tendency to blame the poor for their condition – for if most people can succeed why shouldn't everyone succeed? This explains why individualist explanations of poverty are so popular and prevalent in the affluent society. It also explains why affluent societies often lack the political and economic will to solve problems of insular poverty (Galbraith, 1992a, 1996b).

This argument achieves its clearest theoretical treatment in *Economics and the Public Purpose* (Galbraith, 1973d), which describes how the bimodal economy consisting of the planning and market systems gives rise to poverty in developed capitalist economies. Large firms, which are part of what Galbraith calls the "planning system", have acquired enormous economic power. As noted above, they have power to control prices and the resources that enable them to mold public opinion. Moreover, the climate of consumerism generated through the management of demand equates happiness with those goods produced by the private sector of the economy. And large firms can influence the political process to their advantage in a way that overrides the needs of the poor.

In contrast, small firms are subject to the dictates of the market. They have little economic power and little ability to sway public opinion or the political process. They are thus disadvantaged relative to the planning system. The result is unequal economic development – the planning system produces too many goods and the market system produces an inadequate supply of goods. Likewise, important public goods such as access to high quality health care and education, that might benefit those in the market system, are likely to be underprovided, as the needs of the planning system predominate and skew public expenditure.

Given its lack of economic power, the market system is at a disadvantage relative to the planning system. Firms in the market system must sell its goods at lower prices to the planning system but will be forced to buy goods produced by firms in the planning system at higher prices. And just as there is a dual economy, there is a dual labor market. Not everyone is employed by large corporations. Some people work for the smaller firms that comprise the market system. These people are at a disadvantage compared to planning sector workers and get paid considerably lower wages. So people are more likely to end up poor when they work for smaller firms or when they are unable to land jobs with firms in the planning sector.

Another important cause of insular poverty is the preoccupation with private production and consumption that results from the rise of the modern corporation and its need to plan and advertise. As we have seen, Galbraith recognized the power held by large corporations over consumers, and their need to manufacture consumer demand. Demand, he claims, does *not* originate with the consumer; it is contrived for the consumer by the firm through advertising (see Anderson & Dunn, (2006) for a more detailed discussion). Large firms thus possess a degree of influence over the pattern of consumer spending, which sustains the prestige of the goods that they produce and sell.

The consequence of elevating private production and neglecting the provision of public goods is a situation of private affluence amid public squalor. In a much-quoted passage Galbraith (1958a, pp. 98f.) highlights this contrast:

> The family which takes its mauve and cerise, air-conditioned, power-steered and power-braked automobile out for a tour passes through cities that are badly paved, made hideous by litter, blighted buildings, billboards, and posts for wires that should long since have been put underground.... They picnic on exquisitely packaged food from a portable icebox by a polluted stream and go on to spend the night at a park which is a menace to public health and morals. Just before dozing off on an air mattress, beneath a nylon tent, amid the stench of decaying refuse, they may reflect vaguely on the curious unevenness of their blessings.

Affluence itself causes poverty in yet another way. As firms focus more on producing goods and services for affluent consumers, they will naturally produce fewer goods for low-income households. With less supply, the price of such goods increases, making the lives of the poor and near poor more difficult.

In his analysis of poverty Galbraith (1958a, p. 250) follows Veblen (1898) and Myrdal (1944, 1968). He views poverty as a self-perpetuating cycle of cumulative causation. Those living in a poor community receive a poor education and poor public services. They lack the training and good health necessary to improve their economic condition. The poor are also powerless economically and politically, making it hard for them to obtain the government services that might improve their lives. People living in poor areas also come to accept their poverty and see little means of escape. This reinforces their political powerlessness and contributes to the inadequate provision of public goods that may alleviate their predicament. In this way, poverty reproduces itself in poor areas, and across generations.

Nevertheless, an affluent society need not accept this. The provision of public goods and services could keep pace with the production of private goods (Galbraith, 1958a). The good society diverts public resources away from supporting the technostructure and towards helping the poor (Galbraith, 1967e). Thus, Galbraith has long argued for a strong welfare state providing benefits like job protection and basic income guarantees, as well as an acknowledged and legitimate role for unions. Moreover, at the end of *The Affluent Society*, Galbraith provides a rationale for human capital or education programs, targeting especially the children of the poor. One such program, Head Start, became a key part of Lyndon Johnson's Great Society program.

Of course, all these activities have to be paid for. Funds must be channeled away from supporting the provision of increasingly irrelevant and superfluous private commodities, and instead be used to provide the public goods that address unmet public needs. Towards this end, Galbraith has advocated higher sales taxes in order to finance these important sorts of government spending (e.g., public transportation, education, police protection). He has also advocated greater income taxes on the wealthy, holding that the tax system must be made progressive enough so that the rich protest loudly and vehemently. That is the only way to know that the taxes imposed on the rich are high enough!

The mass poverty of less developed countries is quite different than the insular poverty of developed nations. Poor countries do not have sufficient wealth and income to support the many more poor people in need of assistance. In addition, the psychological propensities leading people to accept their condition are even greater than in developed countries (see Sen, 1999). In a poor country then, a poverty of hope casts its spell on the entire nation as people come to believe that there is no option other than accommodate to the reality of their circumstances.

For such reasons, Galbraith (1979f, Chapter 3) contends that "an equilibrium of poverty" exists in less developed countries. Galbraith goes on to explain how mass poverty perpetuates itself and how attempts to improve things easily get derailed. Living at bare subsistence means there can be no savings and no money for agricultural improvements like irrigation, hybrid seeds, or fertilizer. Likewise, new technologies are always risky, embodying many uncertainties, including the possibilities of starvation and premature death. Thus, even if there are savings, these savings are not likely to be used for improved cultivation methods. If people manage to save out of their subsistence incomes, these savings will be hoarded as a buffer against bad harvests in the future rather than used as a means to employ more advanced and efficient means of production. Subsistence farmers are naturally reluctant to invest in any new technology that might increase output but would also be risky and thus threaten starvation during a bad year. Finally, even if savings are invested and lead to improved agricultural output, or even if landowner revenues are redistributed to the poor, this will not necessarily solve the problem of mass poverty. Greater income will mean the survival of more people, people who would have otherwise died, and so family per capita food consumption would be little changed and poverty will persist. Reinforcing all this is the human tendency to accommodate oneself to one's condition. This means accepting a life on the edge of starvation rather than seeking to better oneself and escaping poverty. It is through this diagnosis of the problems of the poor that Galbraith (1979f, Chapter 3) objects to many of the mainstream policy solutions to the problem of mass poverty.

Galbraith (1979f) argues that historically there have been three ways to break out of the cycle or equilibrium of poverty in less developed countries – trauma, migration, and education. By trauma Galbraith means horrific disasters, things like wars and famines that reduce the population to a point that those who remain are finally able to sustain themselves on the land. These are essentially the negative checks to population growth first noted by Malthus [1798] many years ago. Since this is not a civilized means of reducing poverty, nor a desirable solution to the problem of poverty, it is easy to reject; and so we are left with migration and education as practical solutions.

Migration has been one of Galbraith's favorite policy solutions for dealing with poverty. Among the many successes of migration as a solution to mass poverty, Galbraith (1979f, Chapter 8) points to his ancestors, the Scottish Highlanders, who came to the US and Canada in the nineteenth century, as well as the successful streams of migration from Ireland, Italy, Sweden and Eastern Europe to North America in the nineteenth and early twentieth centuries. More recently there has been migration from Mexico and Latin America to the US. There has also been a great deal of migration from poorer parts of Europe to wealthier areas of Europe. Turks, Italians and Greeks have migrated to Germany. Millions of Portuguese, Italians and Spaniards are living in France, making up around 10 percent of the French labor force. And more recently there has been migration from the transitional economies of Eastern Europe to the wealthier nations of Western Europe. Although migration brings cultural tensions and conflicts, it will always lead to a greater standard of living for those who migrate. The country receiving these immigrants will also benefit. Besides contributing to their new country by augmenting the labor supply and, in many instances, by performing arduous and tedious work that long-term residents seek to avoid, the reduction in population in their native country makes the problem of survival easier for those who remain and do not migrate.

Besides migration, the other principal policy instrument is greater education or the development of human capital. In the context of the less developed world, education means ensuring basic numeracy and literacy (Galbraith, 1979f, pp. 100–103). This requires free and compulsory education. The compulsion is needed because otherwise families will tend to keep their children at home where they can help with home production and with chores. Education also helps poor farmers understand the need for using technical innovations, which will help reduce mass poverty. Education is necessary, too, as a means to control population growth. And education is always a good antidote to the psychology of accommodation, especially when the education instructs children about how much better things are in other parts of the world. Finally, education is necessary in order to underpin an enlightened public administration which further promotes and develops mass education and channels public funds into other related areas that will sustain further growth (e.g., transportation, communication and public health) (Galbraith, 1964b, p. 66).

Migration and education policies both work to empower the poor who are living in mass poverty. Education helps people to recognize the things that they need to do to improve the chances of escaping poverty. Education also lets people know that things can be different and that they can do things to make their lives better. And migration allows those people with ambition and desire to move to places where it is highly likely that their lives will improve.

Finally, in the less developed world, as in the developed world, some social balance must be provided by the state. As early as *Economic Development*, Galbraith (1964b, p. 66) noted that the first stage of development requires the education, communication and transportation that must be provided by the state. In addition, state initiatives to improve health and state support for developing heavy industry are prerequisites for economic development. But these are difficult things for a poor nation to do. So, developed Western nations must help redress this social balance with adequate foreign aid (Galbraith, 1961d, 1964b).

Radical economists tend to dismiss the analysis of insular and mass poverty developed by Galbraith. They regard it as unrealistic and utopian since it requires the state aligning with the needs of the majority of its population rather than with the interests of the powerful business classes. Galbraith, in contrast, argues that in democratic societies the state must be made to reflect the needs of society, and in doing so must counter the power of the large business firm. This brings us to Galbraith's last major contribution, which is a consideration of the requisite emancipatory response to the power structure in society.

5   A vision of political economy: power, the state and society

Galbraith's (1973g) Presidential address to the American Economic Association criticized economists for ignoring power relationships and thereby promulgating irrelevant theories regarding how the real world works. Economic thinking removes power from the realm of discourse by assuming that the market mitigates firm power and by denying its salience. Yet the failure of economists to recognize the historical evolution of the modern business enterprise, and its growing economic power, means that attention is diverted away from questions of great social urgency. In this way, economics serves a political or "instrumental" function (Galbraith, 1971b, Chapter 4). Much economic analysis promotes a view of the business firm as subordinate to the society through the market and the democratic process. In doing so, economics functions less as an explanatory science and more as a belief system that promotes a conservative agenda: "Economics has been not a science but a conservatively useful system of belief defending that belief as a science" (Galbraith, 1971b, p. 59ff.).

By eschewing the study of power and change, economists have failed to address pressing social trends. For Galbraith, "in eliding power – in making economics a nonpolitical subject – neoclassical theory, by the same process, destroys its relation with the real world" (Galbraith, 1973g, p. 2). And it contributes little to contemporary political debates by failing to illuminate many of the serious social concerns of modern society – war, environmental decay and, of course, poverty.

Indeed, Galbraith argues that the conventional wisdom fails to shed light on many contemporary concerns such as the overproduction of private goods and the underproduction of public goods; the superfluous nature of much technical innovation directed at irrelevant commodities; the failure of economic growth to ameliorate enduring social problems; the uneven distribution of government expenditure, reflected in excessive spending on the military and other forms of social infrastructure (e.g., roads) and the relative neglect of other spending (environmental protection, mass transit and public education); the increasingly skewed income distribution between different sectors and personnel; the enduring distinction between the high and low wage industries; the unresponsiveness of the modern corporation and international institutions to public pressure and opinion; the problems of economy-wide coordination; and the continuing fear of inflation as opposed to deflation.

In contrast, Galbraith (1973d, Chapters 20–22) argues that his analysis of the economic power possessed by large firms allows these concerns to be voiced and addressed appropriately. For example, he argues that the evolution of the modern corporation is not wholly malign; it encourages technological development and, by so doing, contributes to (uneven) improvements in our standard of living. For this reason, Galbraith maintains, it is better to limit the power of large firms than to eliminate that power by breaking it up. Governments should seek to encourage the development of countervailing power in the private sector of the economy by, for example, supporting labor unions and smaller competitive businesses.[10] Power between the planning and the market systems can be made more equal according to Galbraith (1973d) by implementing policies including minimum wage legislation, guaranteed minimum incomes, protective tariffs and support for small businesses. Whenever it is difficult or impossible to develop countervailing power, the government must itself counter the power of large corporations by making sure there is an adequate supply of those things that have social value but that are not produced by large corporations – public goods, a clean environment, arms control, full employment, decent incomes to all workers, and relatively low levels of inflation.

In advocating a strong role for the state Galbraith highlights the need to recognize the nexus between big business and the modern state. Galbraith (1973d, p. 188) has remarked, paraphrasing Marx, that the modern state "is not the executive committee of the bourgeoisie, but it is more nearly the executive committee of the technostructure." While wielding considerable power and influence motivates the large firm according to Galbraith, their intentions are less Machiavellian than Marx thought. The modern corporation seeks to secure a response from domestic and foreign governments to mitigate the uncertainties that surround accumulation and production, and to support the affirmative and protective goals of strategic decision-makers.

The nexus between the technostructure and the state means that public spending will tend to follow and favor the interests of the large corporation. Elements of public spending that align themselves with the narrow interests of the technostructure receive the requisite sanction from that authority. "The planning system, it will be evident, exists in the closest association with the state. The obvious core of this relationship is the large expenditure by the government for its products. This pays for the products of those corporations, most notably the large, specialized weapons firms that exist by selling to the state. And it pays also for the technical development that sustains the cycle of innovation and obsolescence and thus the continuity of the demand" (Galbraith, 1973d, pp. 171–172).

This also leads to an analysis of the issues raised in recent debates on globalization (see Dunn, 2005). Although the multinational firm greatly impairs the sovereignty of national governments it "is not because of its transnational character; it is because the impairment of sovereignty – the accommodation of the state to the purposes and needs of the corporate technostructure – is the very essence of the operations of the planning system" (Galbraith, 1973d, p. 188).

What is more, in recognizing the domination of modern economic life by large corporations and the symbiotic nexus between the modern corporation and the state, the resultant skewing of public expenditure is understood. This calls for action to limit the claims of the Military Industrial Complex and of the technostructure on public expenditure. This requires taking action to redress the imbalance of public expenditure by encouraging the provision of more socially desirable goods and services. It also necessitates securing the independence of the state through political reform to ensure that the regulation of corporate power by the state is not subject to industry capture.

A further consequence of the bimodal image of the modern economic system is its inflationary bias. Galbraith argues that it is no coincidence that the emergence and dominance of the modern corporation occurs at the same time that inflation emerges as a major macroeconomic policy issue. The modern corporation has a vested interest in maintaining high levels of effective demand, which heightens inflationary pressures. The inflationary consequences of higher levels of demand have long been recognized. In several works, Keynes (1940, 1971) argued that the way to control inflation was to manage demand in the economy. This could be done either directly through taxation or reduced spending, or indirectly through higher interest rates. For example, in *How to Pay for the War*, Keynes (1940) suggested a policy of forced savings to reduce spending temporarily during World War II. After the war, these savings would get released, and would spark demand when war spending was no longer stimulating the economy. The monetarist counter-revolution, in contrast, argued that inflation is always and everywhere a monetary phenomenon and accordingly control of the money supply is needed to control inflation (Friedman & Schwartz, 1963). With less money, there would be less purchasing power chasing the same amount of goods, and thus would reduce the inflationary pressures in the economy.

Galbraith accepts neither the monetarist solution to the problem of inflation nor the fiscal solution of Keynes – arguing that both fail to assimilate the consequences of institutional change in the industrial structure into the conduct of macroeconomic policy. Galbraith does not think that monetary policy is an effective way to manage aggregate demand and control inflation because the planning system does most of the investing in the economy on the basis of long-term planning decisions. Accordingly, "most investment will be extremely unresponsive to moderate increases in the rate of interest" (Galbraith, 1958a, p. 234) and there will be little decline in spending in response to changes in monetary policy. What is more, monetary policy works by raising interest rates and thereby impacting "the cost or availability of credit for capital" (Galbraith, 1958a, p. 181). Large corporations will be somewhat insulated from such short run changes, because they have recourse to retained profits or internally generated funds. The effect is thus that anti-inflationary monetary policy discriminates against firms in the market system. Smaller firms will be less insulated, and so another case against monetary policy is that it discriminates against the market system.

But Galbraith's main argument against using monetary policy to control inflation is that, to the extent that it does work, it works in socially undesirable ways by reducing demand and increasing unemployment. This last argument also holds against the anti-inflation fiscal policies of Keynes. According to Galbraith, Keynes was right that tight fiscal policy can control inflation, but what he failed to emphasize is that it does so by imposing unacceptably large costs on the economy.

Another anti-inflation policy frequently advocated by economists is greater competition. Those espousing this view argue that the government should weaken monopoly power and restore the efficacy of the market. In contrast to most economists, and again reflecting his bimodal view of the modern economy, Galbraith rejects government policies to promote competition as an ineffective way to reduce inflationary pressures. Somewhat perversely, the pursuit of such policies only serves to consolidate the power of the large firms. Reflecting the power of the large firm, efforts to introduce greater competition are focused on dismantling countervailing power (e.g., trade unions, minimum wage polices) rather than confronting the original power of the large firm. But even if anti-trust policy did help reduce inflationary pressures, there would be a large loss. Policy makers risk losing the dynamism, efficiency and demand creation that comes from large firms that undertake large-scale investment over long time horizons, and drawing on technically sophisticated research and development, which yields more efficient means of production.

Rejecting the standard accounts of inflation, Galbraith (1952a, 1973d, 1977b) presents a cost-push analysis. The development of power blocs makes the economic system more inflationary; and the greater the economic power, the greater the forces in the economy that tend to increase prices. In the market system increases in wages and costs of production will be fought. In contrast, the pursuit of such a policy in the planning system might result in a protracted labor dispute which would taint the prestige of the technostructure and undermine the growth of the firm. And as the consumer is subject to management by the firm, the effect of an increase in prices is likely to be inconsequential. This too contributes to the inflationary bias of the industrial system. Finally, high levels of demand in the economy provide the conduit for higher wages to be passed onto the consumer as higher prices, and for people experiencing higher prices to demand higher wages from their employer. The stage is set for a wage–price spiral.

To counter this, Galbraith (1973d, 1977b) argues for the development of appropriate institutions, such as wage and price controls, to minimize inflation. Controls are required, according to Galbraith, because inflation is caused primarily by the pressures of higher incomes on prices and higher prices on incomes.[11] Inflation results because firms and unions have acquired power over the market. "Wages act on prices and prices on wages as capacity is approached. Controls prevent this interplay. In doing so, they allow the economy to function closer to capacity without price increases" (Galbraith, 1958a, p. 186). Price controls ameliorate inflationary pressures and allow the expansion of aggregate demand problems and let us use traditional macroeconomic policies to deal with the unemployment problem.

The alternative is that a pool of unemployed resources will be needed to discipline wage and price claims and maintain price stability (cf. Kalecki, 1943). But this cure is worse than the disease. For Galbraith, the only reasonable solution to the inflation problem is for the government to prevent the market power of labor unions and large businesses from causing inflation. To achieve the twin goals of full employment as well as price stability, Keynesian macroeconomic policies, which expand effective demand, must be combined with some kind of incomes policy to address the inevitable inflationary pressures that arise when the economy approaches full employment. This radical analysis of inflation echoes Post Keynesian conflict theories of inflation (see Wray, 2001) and is a hybrid of Keynes and Kalecki.

To many, the control of prices is an anathema to the whole structure of economic theory. Controls induce needless rationing and generate an associated bureaucracy to monitor compliance. Similarly government administered pricing or interference in the labor market is viewed as leading to a sub-optimal allocation of resources. Accordingly, it is argued that the most efficient way to allocate scarce resources is to unfetter the market. Galbraith disputes such claims.

First, he reiterates the fact that large firms are not price takers. Rather, firms in the oligopolistic sector of the economy are price makers and thus "it is relatively easy to fix prices that are already fixed" (Galbraith, 1952b, p. 17). In the planning system the dominant convention is to set prices based on some mark-up over the costs of production. Moreover, the mark-up itself is also based on conventions reflecting the interests and objectives of incumbent technostructures. The fact that prices are set by the corporation to reflect the interests of the technostructure means that prices in the industrial system no longer function as indices of scarcity. As Galbraith (1973d, p. 127) notes in the modern economy "the role of prices is greatly diminished. They are much more effectively under the control of the firm". In the planning system prices play other roles than purely allocative ones. In response to changes in general market conditions prices may be held constant or altered. Any constancy of price in the face of demand changes is thus rationalized as reflecting the objectives and decisions of firms and the members of the technostructure running firms. Likewise any price changes will reflect the interests of the firm and not the sovereign wishes of the consumer.

As a result, controls on prices should be viewed as representing an attempt by governments to align pricing conventions so that they have more socially desirable outcomes. Monitoring such controls is made easier, according to Galbraith, by the fact that prices need to be controlled only in the oligopolistic sector of the economy, since market power exists only in this sector. Consequently, only a thousand or so firms need to be monitored. Enforcement is also assisted by the fact that large oligopolistic firms are all in the public eye.

6 Galbraith's place in economic thought

Several key themes stand out in the work of Galbraith. He recognizes the economic power held by large firms, and argues that such power is one of the main reasons for the success of the US economy in the post World War II era. But this power also creates numerous problems that must be addressed by the state taking on a greater role in the economy. The state must counter the power of the large firm and assist in providing goods and services that are not subject to the imperatives of organization and technology, and are thus not produced by the large firm. The state must also use its power to mitigate macroeconomic problems such as unemployment, inflation and poverty.

In analyzing the changing industrial structure, and its consequences and policy implications, Galbraith has also sought to counter the false beliefs of economists as well as the psychological propensity to accept given ideas. He has done this not only by pointing out that received views are erroneous and serve a certain conservative purpose, but also by attempting to offer an alternative theoretical structure. He has done it with writing that has sought to counter accepted beliefs with good, clear prose. And he has done this with wit and humor as his tools, and by going over the heads of the economic profession by getting involved in politics and writing for the educated non-economist. Finally, he has done this by insisting that economics be relevant to what is going on in the real world. For all these reasons, the economic contributions of J.K. Galbraith deserve renewed attention.

What is more, in developing his overarching vision of how the economy works, and in recognizing the changing institutional structure of modern economies, Galbraith has introduced several important notions and modes of analysis that are now widely accepted by many economists.

For example, Galbraith's discussion of the relationship between technology and organization predates and parallels Williamson's (1975, 1985) recognition of the importance of asset specificity for the study of organizations (Dunn, 2001, 2005). According to Williamson, asset specificity is critical in that once an investment has been undertaken the buyer and seller become locked into a trans-action for a considerable period, referred to as '*ex post* bilateral dependence'. In contrast, Galbraith argues that the imperatives of modern technology and the associated commitments of time, capital and specialized labor in an uncertain environment entail that planning supersedes the market. 'Planning exists because this (market) process has ceased to be reliable ... (the firm) must replace the market with planning' (Galbraith, 1967e, p. 41). Galbraith moves beyond the limiting view of "in the beginning there were markets", towards a view that "in the beginning there was an absence of a need for extensive planning as technology was not that sophisticated!"

Similarly, Galbraith's emphasis on the importance of education, and his argu-ment that human capital development is necessary to solve the problem of poverty represents one of the earliest statements of human capital theory. Even before the work of Becker (1962) and Schultz (1993) in the early 1960s, Gal-braith (1958a, Chapter 18) recognized that education was both an investment good and a consumption good. Moreover, he lamented that the investment component of education was not generally recognized arguing that human capital and knowledge was a decisive factor of production in a modern economy (cf. Hodgson, 1999).

Another salient aspect of Galbraith's theoretical structure concerns his analy-sis of savings. Economists have long focused on the sharp drop in savings rates in the US and throughout most of the developed world (Maddison, 1992; Seidman, 1990; Walker, Bloomfield, & Thorning, 1990), and have pointed to rising household debt ratios as a potential problem facing the US economy during the early twenty-first century (Godley, 2000).

Galbraith anticipated such concerns back in the 1950s when he recognized that in order to sustain its production and planning processes, the technostructure requires that consumers be able to buy the goods that are produced. Accordingly, "The process of persuading people to incur debt, and the arrangement for them to do so, are as much a part of modern production as the making of the goods and the nurturing of wants" (Galbraith, 1958a, p. 200). This means lower savings rates and higher levels of indebtedness for the household. Thus it is no surprise, as Stanfield (1983, p. 591) notes, that "Easier credit checks, lower down-payments, longer repayment terms, and other inducements for people to go further and further into debt are permanent and necessary fixtures of the con-sumer society described in *The Affluent Society.*"

Such an analysis can be marshaled to explain the recent precipitous decline in savings rates and the associated rise in consumer debt and bankruptcies. More-over, it helps to identify the role of consumer debt in supporting higher levels of consumption and augmenting demand in the economy. Yet the bimodal view also highlights the increasingly precarious nature of such an explosion of debt which adds to macroeconomic instability (cf. Minsky, 1982; Godley, 2000).

Galbraith was also one of the first economists to argue against using traditional economic measures of growth (such as GDP or industrial production) in order to estimate economic and social well-being. Galbraith argued that many of the goods that get produced and sold do not satisfy important needs; some of them are just frivolous – comic books, narcotics, pornography, switchblade knives and guns. All goods produced by the planning system are counted as part of GDP, but cognizance of the management of the consumer by the large corporation suggests that all need not address basic human needs or improve substantively the quality of life. Galbraith notes the perversity that goods that pollute the environment and manipulate and manage consumer demands, and those goods that threaten civic society, such as nuclear weapons, count towards GDP, whereas some things that many people value, such as leisure time, safe streets, a clean environment, and a world safe from nuclear destruction, do not get counted in GDP. Moreover, such technical considerations regarding measurement are not without consequence. The bias toward consumerism fuels the emulatory processes that characterize the rat race and results in people working harder and harder in order to consume more and more (Schor, 1991).

Another notable aspect of Galbraith's analysis is his identification of the problem of a rising underclass, which received considerable attention in the US beginning in the 1980s (Auletta, 1982; Wilson, 1987). This problem was first anticipated and analyzed by Galbraith (1958a, pp. 97, 327f.) in the 1950s. And *A Theory of Price Control* (Galbraith, 1952b) preceded both Hicks and Okun in recognizing the salience of classifying the economy into fix and flex price sectors (Colander, 1984; cf. Galbraith, 1936).

Notwithstanding such contributions, many mainstream economists reject (and have forgotten!) his system of thought. They typically view Galbraith as more of a social theorist than an economist, or they tend to see him as an ambitious system builder who prefers to substitute generalization for rigorous analysis. On a more personal level, economists tend to regard Galbraith with the same disdain that Galbraith has heaped on them through ridiculing their outdated views of the firm and their inability to explain what is going on in the real world because of an infatuation with unrealistic, formal modeling. The result has been that "Galbraith's work on the modern corporation, and public policy toward it, has been scantily explored in the journals" (Davidson & Weintraub, 1978, p. 5).

More interesting is the relationship between Galbraith and two heterodox schools of thought that have expressed a great deal of appreciation for his work – the Institutionalists and the Post Keynesians. We noted earlier that Galbraith received the Veblens-Commons award from the Association for Evolutionary Economics to honor his contributions to Institutionalist thinking (see Galbraith, 1977b), and that Galbraith was instrumental in the founding and development of the *Journal of Post Keynesian Economics*. But although the *Journal of Post Keynesian Economics* has had a symposium on Galbraith's theory of the firm, and the *Journal of Economic Issues* has had a symposium on the twentieth anniversary of *The New Industrial State*, it would not be unfair to suggest that Galbraith's economic contributions have also been pretty much ignored by both Institutionalists and Post Keynesians.

Such neglect is unwarranted, we would argue, as Galbraith's system of thought has much to add to the development of an alternative to the conventional wisdom – something to which both of these schools of thought aspire. With his focus on the relationships between power, the firm, and the state, the Galbraithian system facilitates the integration of the economics of Keynes, Kalecki, and the Institutionalists into a comprehensive vision of political economy. While Institutionalists have focused on the origins and nature of power and generally espoused a view of macroeconomics that is compatible with Post Keynesianism, they have not sought to integrate them into their analysis. Similarly, while Post Keynesians have acknowledged the presence and role of firm power, they have been reluctant to move beyond their models of imperfect competition and aggregate demand, and to analyze the impact of organizational power on wider social and economic processes (Peterson, 1989). Galbraith's vision offers a starting point to develop a research agenda along these lines. As such, he should be viewed as a foundational figure for integrating Insititutionalist and Post Keynesian economics. Several features of this integration stand out.

First, Galbraith shares many methodological similarities with Institutionalists and with Post Keynesians. For both these schools, economic theory must be realistic and must describe the general features of our real world experience (see Dunn & Mearman, 2006). Both schools employ cumulative causation models, where history and real individual behavior interact, rather than equilibrium models based on optimizing behavior. Finally, both schools reject the idea that economic analysis must begin with individuals who are rational and who know their desires and preferences.

Galbraith, too, rejects much of orthodox analysis because it fails to explain real world phenomena. Instead, he adopts an historicist orientation that recognizes the importance of cumulative causation. We saw earlier the historical embeddedness of his analysis of the firm and its evolutionary implications for society, as well as his incorporation of processes of cumulative causation processes into his analysis of poverty. Galbraith also eschews methodological individualism, and its implication that knowledge of atomistic behavior is sufficient to explain macroeconomic outcomes. Instead, he adopts a Post Keynesian-Institutionalist view that individual actions are socially conditioned and culturally contingent. In this framework, conventions and manufactured habits play an important role in individual behavior and can lead to sub-optimal results. Emulation and conspicuous consumption, developed and reinforced by advertising, result in low savings rates, high consumer indebtedness, and the neglect of public goods; myriad economic institutions contribute to a wage-price spiral; and economic institutions contribute to the psychic accommodation to mass poverty.

Second, Galbraith's analysis of the firm accords with the Post Keynesian analysis of uncertainty. Galbraith considers the impact of uncertainty on firm behavior, and in doing so lays a foundation for further contributions to the development of a Post Keynesian theory of the firm As Dunn (2001, p. 157) notes, Post Keynesians have traditionally focused on uncertainty at the macro-economic level and have largely neglected uncertainty when it comes to think-ing about the firm. However, as we have seen, Galbraith argues that many of the organizational strategies pursued by the firm, including the use of long-term money contracts, helps reduce the uncertainty faced by it. In doing so Galbraith develops a view of modern corporation that is consistent with Post Keynesian monetary theory and thus offers the prospect of further development (cf. David-son, 1972).

Third, Galbraith's bimodal image of the planning and market sectors accords with a Kaleckian view of the modern economy. For both of these thinkers, the economy is principally characterized by an oligopolistic sector, dominated by the major corporations, and a competitive sector which covers agriculture and certain input markets, and is in the service of the more dominant sector. Like Kalecki, Galbraith presents an analysis of capitalism where organization brings power in addition to income and where the decisions of individual workers, con-sumers, and households are of limited significance. And as Ray Canterbury (1984, p. 78) has pointed out, Galbraith's notion of firm power and Kalecki's notion of the degree of monopoly have much in common. Of course, class con-flict for Galbraith is different than class conflict for Kalecki. The reason for this difference stems from Galbraith's analysis of the technostructure. The persua-sive power and respectability of the technostructure means that social conflict has become more diffuse and hidden. Moreover, for Galbraith the division between the planning sector and the market sector has more contemporary rele-vance than the outmoded distinction between the owners of the means of pro-duction and workers who must labor for their income (which has been somewhat usurped by the emergence of the technostructure).

Fourth, Galbraith offers an alternative to the stagnationist theses espoused by some Post Keynesians. Steindl (1945), for example, has integrated Marxist and Kaleckian ideas on the advantages enjoyed by large firms in their competitive struggle with smaller enterprises in order to explain why increasing concentra-tion was a salient feature of advanced capitalist development. Steindl (1952) also argued that the emergence of oligopoly has stifled (price) competition and resulted in higher prices, reduced sales, higher margins and profits, as well as a degree of excess capacity at the level of the firm to smooth variations in demand. But excess capacity and under production also creates a propensity for the economy-wide stagnation. While this thesis offers a convincing explanation of the Great Depression, it proves a less satisfactory explanation of the rise in living standards witnessed over the twentieth century, and especially the post-World War II era. For Galbraith it is this that requires explanation, and he seeks to provide one by by focusing on the large firm and its nexus to the state, technological advance and economic growth.

Fifth, like many Post Keynesians and Institutionalists, Galbraith accepts that in a monetary production economy the level of economic activity is set by the level of effective demand. As such Galbraith (1973d, p. 37) firmly rejects Say's Law. For Galbraith, there is little reason to think that the level of effective demand will automatically be consistent with full employment and the purchase all of the goods that the planning system is able to furnish. Indeed, the Revised Sequence is a planning response to the absence of factors automatically ensuring a high and stable level of demand for the goods produced by the planning system. This also explains why the planning system may seek a protective response from the state – by buying (directly) its goods (e.g., the defense industries) and lobbying for policies to that support the (general) demand for its products (e.g., by pursing Keynesian macroeconomic policies, engaging in road building, etc.). But such institutional responses do not work precisely and do not conspire to reinstitute Say's Law (indeed the conservative retrenchment saw the state weaken the countervailing power of labor market institutions through reductions in levels of aggregate demand).

Sixth, like all Post Keynesians, Galbraith rejects the monetarist inflation story, where increases in the stock of money *cause* inflation. Rather, for Galbraith, inflation arises from the real side of the economy, with increases in the stock of money being caused by income conflict among different groups in society (including the technostructure). As noted above, inflation may be controlled by slowing down the economy and increasing unemployment, but Galbraith advances controls on prices as a better means of dealing with this problem – a perspective shared by many Post Keynesians (for example Cornwall, 1977, 1994).

Seventh, like many institutionalists, Galbraith noted a dichotomy between the workings of the financial system and the workings of technology. At the beginning of the twentieth century, Veblen (1904, 1921) distinguished business activities from the technical processes of production, and thus capitalists from engineers. Capitalists, for Veblen, were predators, only interested in making profits. Engineers, who designed processes, were concerned with productivity and efficiency. Somewhat naively, Veblen thought that machine processes would facilitate a greater planning of production and distribution, would ultimately supersede the need for a price system, and would end the waste of conspicuous consumption. Such concerns are evident in Galbraith, who analyzed technological development and its nexus to the business enterprise, as well as the consequences of a dual economy that resulted from the uneven development of technology. But Galbraith went further than Veblen. He also addressed the important issue of dealing with the unequal power between those parts of the economy dominated by the machine process and those that are not amenable to machine processes.

Eighth, Galbraith acknowledges and analyzes the financial instability endemic to modern capitalism (Galbraith, 1955c, 1990e). *The Great Crash 1929* (Galbraith, 1955c) provides an historical description of the events preceding and accompanying a particular financial crisis, but one with devastating impact. Its analysis represents a study in mass psychology and can be viewed as an embellishment of the animal spirits and irrational psychology of financial institutions. Reminiscent of Keynes (1964) and Minsky (1982), it describes how human proclivities of greed, euphoria, frustrated expectations and panic move financial markets, how changes in the economy provoke heightened expectations of return, and lead to excess, fraud, and eventual collapse.

Finally, Galbraith's system attempted to generalize *The General Theory*, taking into account institutional processes that have changed the structure and nature of economic society and altered the efficacy of simple Keynesian policies. Like Keynes, Galbraith pointed out how certain institutions, such as the stock market and the modern corporation, distort rationality and economic outcomes. But Galbraith recognized the need to move beyond Keynes and consider the ramification of modern economic development and the impact upon analysis:

> [Keynes] was right to the extent that economics is concerned with the production of goods and the prevention of depressions ... [but h]e did not see that, with economic development, power would pass from the consumer to the producer. And, not seeing this, he did not see the increasing divergence between producer or planning purpose and the purpose of the public. And he did not see that – since power to pursue the planning purpose is unequally distributed – development would be unequal. And therewith the distribution of income. Nor did he see that the pursuit of such purpose would threaten the environment and victimize the consumer. And he did not see that the power which allows producer purpose to diverge from public purpose would ensure that inflation would not yield to a simple reversal of the policies that he urged for unemployment and depression. Nor did he foresee the problems of planning co-ordination, national and international.
>
> (Galbraith, 1973d, p. 342)

In sum, the central themes of Post Keynesian economics, which include a concern for history, uncertainty, distributional issues, and the importance of political and economic institutions in determining the level of economic activity, are all central tenets of the Galbraithian system. Likewise, the central themes of the Institutionalists – economic power, how institutions affect individual behavior, and the importance of understanding the real world by actually examining it – are all major aspects of Galbraith's economics. His system thus allows a marriage of Veblen, Keynes and Kalecki in an updated and comprehensive *vision* of the modern economy. It should form the foundation of renewed efforts to develop an alternative to the conventional wisdom.

But more is at issue than theory. Post Keynesian economists have tended to focus on methodology and macroeconomics to the exclusion of the key issues of our time. It is here that Galbraith has provided us with his greatest service. He has used the ideas of Keynes and extended them so that they could be employed in understanding contemporary policy issues and devising policy proposals for our economic and social problems.

For example, he has supported increased immigration as a means of dealing with the problem of mass poverty. Galbraith (1979) has argued that reducing the excess labor supply in less developed countries is the most promising way to improve their living standards and escape from mass poverty. He has also argued that a country accepting immigrants would also benefit. The people who do immigrate are usually those who are very ambitious and industrious individuals, and so countries receive hard workers who would add the most to the economic growth of the country in which they settle. Immigrants also add to the effective demand of the country they move to. Finally, immigrants perform jobs that domestic residents are not willing to do and they perform undesirable jobs at wages well below what domestic workers would accept (Galbraith, 1979, p. 134).

Galbraith (1958) has also supported government redistribution as a solution to the problem of poverty in developed nations. Typically, economists frown on redistributive policies because of their adverse incentive effects. But for Galbraith and Post Keynesians, any adverse incentive or substitution effects should be small, while the income effects of government redistribution are thought to be relatively large. This view has been buttressed by Pressman (2002–2003, 2005, 2006b). Pressman (2007) has also extended these basic principles to the issue of the size of the middle class in developed countries, showing that it is government redistributive tax and spending policies that are a major determinant of the size of the middle class across nations and over time.

We have also both been at the forefront of work following in the tradition of Galbraith – using his Post Keynesian approach and arguing that government policies are necessary to counter the power of large firms in order to provide much needed public goods and to deal with serious social and economic problems. We have both relied on Galbraith in order to make the case for government policies to deal with the sorts of microeconomic issues that have generally been ignored by Post Keynesian economists but are major areas of public concern – the problem of health care (Dunn, 2006), the problem of education (Pressman, 2006a), and the problem of crime (Pressman, forthcoming).

Acknowledgments

We would like to thank Jamie Galbraith and Ron Stanfield for help and advice. Dunn's research has been supported by *The Commonwealth Fund*, a New York City-based private independent foundation. The views presented here are those of the authors and not necessarily those of *The Commonwealth Fund* their directors, officers, or staff.

Notes

1 It resulted in a series of three papers published by the Giannini Foundation (see Voorhies, Galbraith & Todd, 1933a, 1933b; Galbraith, 1934).
2 The economic report was published as *The Effects of Strategic Bombing on the German War Economy* (US Strategic Bombing Survey, 1945). Galbraith also partici-

pated in an assessment of aerial bombing on the Japanese economy. This study concluded that the Japanese economy was damaged by the US bombing raids (US Strategic Bombing Survey, 1946).

3 The story of Galbraith's time in India appears in *Ambassador's Journal* (1969c).

4 A major shortcoming of Galbraith's discussion of the firm is that he does not articulate how the technostructure adapts and changes. For example there is no discussion of why the U-form mode of organization was replaced by the M-form mode of organization. While all the elements of the modern New Institutional Economics appear to be there – complexity, uncertainty, and asset specificity – orthodox theorists are inclined to dismiss Galbraith's thesis suggesting that the absence of an economizing perspective ultimately resists the explandum of change. Indeed, the absence of such a perspective may explain Galbraith's (1988j) admitted failure to foresee the rationalization and downsizing of American industry in the 1980s. Nevertheless, although Galbraith does not specifically evaluate the reasons for the evolution of certain governance structures, his framework does permit such an explanation – organizational changes that enhance the power of the technostructure are pursued, but the absence of conventional market forces means that a complacent technostructure will exhibit sclerotic tendencies and/or may be challenged by other technostructures (such as those originating in Japan). Such considerations warrant more theoretical consideration.

5 That is to say, although Galbraith notes that integration offers the prospect of controlling the price and supply of strategic factors under conditions of uncertainty, he also recognizes the role of long-term, money-denominated contracts. The firm can enter into large long-term contracts as a strategic response to uncertainty. Contracts and their enforceability are a major source of stability and security for the modern corporation. Money-denominated contracts occupy a pivotal role in protecting the prices and costs and safeguarding the sales and supplies at these prices and costs. Galbraith argues that as production takes *time and planning*, money-denominated contracts represent the means by which uncertainties about the future may be mitigated. A large and extensive web of money-denominated contracts, cascaded downward, greatly facilitates the future planning and stability necessitated by advanced technology.

6 Indeed as Hodgson (2001) points out, no author has brought these ideas to the attention of the modern reader more clearly and definitively than Galbraith. Indeed many are inclined to see this as Galbraith's principle conclusion. But as should be clear from this discussion, their nexus to the imperatives of technology and organization are paramount and must not be hidden from view nor treated in isolation.

7 For example Galbraith ties consumer debt directly to the process of want creation: "It would be surprising indeed if a society that is prepared to spend thousands of millions to persuade people of their wants were not to take the further step of financing these wants, and were it not then to go on to persuade people of the ease and desirability of incurring debt to make these wants effective. This has happened ... The Puritan ethic was not abandoned. It was merely overwhelmed by the massive power of modern merchandising" (Galbraith, 1958a, p. 200).

8 That is "Members seek to adapt the goals of the corporation more closely with their own; by extension the corporation seeks to adapt social attitudes and goals to those of the members of its technostructure. So social belief originates at least in part with the producer. Thus the accommodation of the market behavior of the individual, as well as of social attitudes in general, to the needs of producers and the goals of the technostructure is an inherent feature of the system" (Galbraith, 1967e, p. 217).

9 In Galbraith's (1967e, p. 50) own words: "The small firm cannot be restored by breaking the power of the larger ones. It would require, rather, the rejection of the technology which since earliest consciousness we are taught to applaud. It would require that we have simple products made with simple equipment from readily available materials by unspecialized labor. Then the period of production would be short;

the market would reliably provide the labor, equipment and materials required for production; there would be neither possibility nor need for managing the market for the finished product. If the market thus reigned there would be, and could be, no planning."

10 Countervailing power is similar to James Madison's idea of dividing up power in government so that no branch of government, or no particular individual, can gain too much power over everyone else. As an economist, Galbraith focuses mainly on economic power rather than political power, although the two never can be neatly separated. From this perspective, the state must serve as another branch of the economy, and must contain the power of large firms similar to the way the judiciary constrains the power of the executive branch of government.

11 As noted above, Galbraith has been interested in the issue of controlling inflation for most of his professional career. He was effectively the US price czar during World War II, and he has continuously advocated wage and price controls to keep inflation in check. In some of his earliest writings, Galbraith (1941b, 1952a, 1952b, 1955b, 1958b) argued for controlling prices in selected industries. And in testimony before the Joint Economic Committee of Congress on July 20, 1971 he called for permanent wage and price controls in the US.

References

Anderson, S.J. & Dunn, S.P. (2006) Galbraith and the management of specific demand: evidence from the tobacco industry, *Journal of Institutional Economics*, 2, pp. 273–296.

Auletta, K. (1982) *The Underclass* (New York: Random House).

Becker, G. (1964) *Human Capital* (Chicago: University of Chicago Press).

Berle, A. & Means, G. (1991)[1932] *The Modern Corporation and Private Property* (Somerset, NJ: Transaction Publishers).

Bowles, S., Edwards, R. & Shepherd, W.G. (Eds) (1989) *Unconventional Wisdom: Essays in Honor of John Kenneth Galbraith* (Boston: Houghton Mifflin).

Bruce, K. (2000) Conflict and conversion: Henry S. Dennison and the shaping of John Kenneth Galbraith's economic thought, *Journal of Economic Issues*, 36(4), pp. 949–967.

Canterbury, E.R. (1984) Galbraith, Sraffa, Kalecki and supra surplus capitalism, *Journal of Post Keynesian Economics*, 7, pp. 77–90.

Chandler, A.D. (1977) *The Visible Hand: The Managerial Revolution in American Business* (Cambridge, MA: Harvard University Press).

Colander, D. (1984) Galbraith and the theory of price control, *Journal of Post Keynesian Economics*, 7, pp. 30–42.

Cornwall, J. (1977) *Modern Capitalism: Its Growth and Transformation* (New York: St. Martin's Press).

Cornwall, J. (1994) *Economic Breakdown and Recovery* (Armonk, NY: M.E. Sharpe).

Davidson, P. (1972) *Money and the Real World* (London: Macmillan).

Davidson, P. & Weintraub, S. (1978) A statement of purposes, *Journal of Post Keynesian Economics*, 1(1), pp. 3–8.

Dunn, S. (2001) Galbraith, uncertainty and the modern corporation, in: M. Keaney (Ed.) *Economist with a Public Purpose: Essays in Honour of John Kenneth Galbraith* (London & New York: Routledge).

Dunn, S. (2005) John Kenneth Galbraith's neglected contribution to the theory of the multinational corporation, *Challenge*, 48, pp. 80–112.

Dunn, S. (2006) Prolegomena to a Post Keynesian health economics, *Review of Social Economy*, 64(3), pp. 273–299.

Dunn, S. & Mearman, A. (2006) The realist approach of J.K. Galbraith, *Challenge*, 49, pp. 7–30.

Friedman, M. & Schwartz, A. (1963) *A Monetary History of the United States* (Princeton: Princeton University Press).

Gambs, J. (1975) *John Kenneth Galbraith* (Boston: Twayne Publishers).

Godley, W. (2000) Drowning in debt, *Policy Notes*, 2000/6, Jerome Levy Economics Institute.

Harrington, M. (1962) *The Other America* (Baltimore: Penguin Books).

Hession, C. (1972) *John Kenneth Galbraith and His Critics* (New York: New American Library).

Hodgson, G.M. (1999) *Economics and Utopia: Why the Learning Economy is not the End of History* (London: Routledge).

Hodgson, G.M. (2001) From Veblen to Galbraith: what is the essence of institutional economics?, in: M. Keaney (Ed.) *Economist with a Public Purpose: Essays in Honour of John Kenneth Galbraith* (London: Routledge).

Hofstadter, R. (1944) *Social Darwinism in American Thought* (Boston: Beacon).

Kalecki, M. (1935) A macrodynamic theory of business cycles, *Econometrica*, 3(3), pp. 327–344.

Kalecki, M. (1943) Political aspects of full employment, *Political Quarterly*, 12, pp. 322–331.

Keaney, M. (ed.) (2001) *Economist with a Public Purpose: Essays in Honour of John Kenneth Galbraith* (London: Routledge).

Keynes, J.M. (1940) *How to Pay for the War* (London: Macmillan).

Keynes, J.M. [1923](1971) *A Tract on Monetary Reform*, Volume IV, *The Collected Writings of John Maynard Keynes* (London: Macmillan).

Keynes, J.M. [1936](1964) *The General Theory of Employment, Interest and Money* (New York: Harcourt, Brace).

King, J. (2002) *A History of Post Keynesian Economics Since 1936* (Cheltenham, UK: Edward Elgar).

Maddison, A. (1992) A long-run perspective on savings, *Scandanavian Journal of Economics*, 92, pp. 181–196.

Malthus, T. (1959)[1798] *An Essay on the Principle of Population as it Affects the Future Improvement of Society, with Remarks on the Speculations of Mr. Godwin, M. Condorcet, and other Writers* (Ann Arbor: University of Michigan Press).

Martin, J.B. (1976) *Adlai Stevenson of Illinois* (Garden City, New York: Doubleday).

Minsky, H. (1982) *Can "It" Happen Again?* (Armonk, NY: M.E. Sharpe).

Murray, C. (1984) *Losing Ground: American social policy 1950–1980* (New York: Basic Books).

Myrdal, G. (1944) *An American Dilemma* (New York: Harper & Brothers).

Myrdal, G. (1968) *Asian Drama: An Inquiry into the Poverty of Nations* (New York: Pantheon Books).

Parker, R. (1999) Early influences on Galbraith's worldview and economics, in: H. Sasson (Ed.) *Between Friends: Perspectives on John Kenneth Galbraith* (Boston: Houghton Mifflin), pp. 147–159.

Parker, R. (2005) *John Kenneth Galbraith: His Life, His Politics, His Economics* (New York: Farrar, Straus & Giroux).

Peterson. W.C. (1989) Market power: the missing element in Keynesian economics, *Journal of Economic Issues*, 23, pp. 379–391.

Pratson, J. (1978) *Perspectives on Galbraith: Conversations and Opinions* (Boston: CBI Publishing).

Pressman, S. (2002–03) Fiscal policy and work incentives – an international comparison, *Journal of Income Distribution*, 11, pp. 51–69.

Pressman, S. (2005) Income guarantees and the equity – efficiency tradeoff, *Journal of Socio-Economics*, 34, pp. 83–100.

Pressman, S. (2006a) A prolegomena to any future Post Keynesian education policy, *Journal of Post Keynesian Economics*, 29, pp. 455–472.

Pressman, S. (2006b) What can Post Keynesian economics teach us about poverty?, in: R. Holt & S. Pressman (Eds) *Empirical Post Keynesian Economics* (Armonk, NY: M.E. Sharpe), pp. 21–41.

Pressman, S. (forthcoming) Expanding the boundaries of the economics of crime, *International Journal of Political Economy*.

Pressman, S. (2007) The decline of the middle class: an international perspective, *Journal of Economic Issues*, 41, pp. 181–200.

Reisman, D. (1980) *Galbraith and Market Capitalism* (New York: New York University Press).

Reisman, D. (1990) Galbraith on ideas and events, *Journal of Economic Issues*, 24, pp. 733–760.

Robinson, J.V. (1977) What are the questions?, *Journal of Economic Literature*, 15(4), pp. 1318–1339.

Sasson, H. (Ed.) (1999) *Between Friends: Perspectives on John Kenneth Galbraith* (Boston: Houghton Mifflin).

Schor, J. (1991) *The Overworked American: The Unexpected Decline of Leisure* (New York: Basic Books).

Schultz, T. (1993) *The Economics of Being Poor* (Oxford: Blackwell).

Schumpeter, J. (1942) *Capitalism, Socialism and Democracy* (New York: Harper & Row).

Seidman, L. (1990) *Saving for America's Economic Future* (Armonk, NY: M.E. Sharpe).

Sen, A. (1999) *Development as Freedom* (New York: Random House).

Sharpe, M.E. (1973) *John Kenneth Galbraith and the Lower Economics* (White Plains: International Arts and Sciences Press).

Simon, H. (1955) A behavioral model of rational choice, *Journal of Political Economy*, 69, pp. 99–118.

Stanfield, J.R. (1983) *The Affluent Society* after twenty-five years, *Journal of Economic Issues*, 17, pp. 589–607.

Stanfield, J.R. (1996) *John Kenneth Galbraith* (New York: St. Martin's Press).

Stanfield, J.R. & Stanfield, J.B. (Eds) (2004) *Interviews with John Kenneth Galbraith* (Jackson: University Press of Mississippi).

Steindl, J. (1945) *Small and Big Business: Economic Problems of the Size of Firms* (Oxford: Blackwell).

Steindl, J. (1952) *Maturity and Stagnation in American Capitalism* (Oxford: Blackwell).

US Strategic Bombing Survey (USSBS) (1945) *The Effects of Strategic Bombing on the German War Economy*, October 31.

US Strategic Bombing Survey (USSBS) (1946) *The Effects of Strategic Bombing on Japan's War Economy*, December.

Veblen, T. (1898) Why is economics not an evolutionary science? *Quarterly Journal of Economics*, 12(3), pp. 373–397.

Veblen, T. [1904] (1978) *The Theory of Business Enterprise* (New Brunswick: Transaction Publishers).

Veblen, T. [1921] (1983) *The Engineers and the Price System* (New Brunswick: Transaction Publishers).

Walker, C., Bloomfield, M. & Thorning, M. (1990) *The U.S. Savings Challenge* (Boulder: Westview Press).

Williamson, O.E. (1975) *Markets and Hierarchies: Analysis and Anti-trust Implications: A Study in the Economics of Internal Organisation* (New York: Free Press).

Williamson, O.E. (1985) *The Economic Institutions of Capitalism: Firms, Markets, Relational Contracting* (London: Macmillan).

Wilson, W.J. (1987) *The Truly Disadvantaged: The Inner City, the Underclass, and Public Policy* (Chicago: University of Chicago Press).

Wray, L.R. (2001) Money and inflation, in: R. Holt & S. Pressman (ed.) *A New Guide to Post Keynesian Economics* (London & New York: Routledge), pp. 79–81.

Bibliography and references to the work of J.K. Galbraith

Baran, P.A. & Galbraith, J.K. (1947) Professor Despres on "Effects of Strategic Bombing on the German War Economy", *Review of Economic Statistics*, 29(2), pp. 132–134.

Chamberlin, E.H., Wright, D.M., Abramson, V., Harris, A.L. & Galbraith, J.K. (1946) Discussion, *American Economic Review*, 36(2), pp. 139–153.

Clapham, B.I. & Galbraith, J.K. (2000) John Kenneth Galbraith: world of ideas, *Canadian Investment Review*, 13(4), p. 17.

Dean, V.M. & Galbraith, J.K. (1950) *Can Europe Unite?* (New York: Foreign Policy Association).

Dennison, H.S. & Galbraith, J.K. (1938) *Modern Competition and Business Policy* (New York: Oxford University Press).

Dennison, H.S., Filene, L.A., Flanders, R.E., Leeds, M. & Galbraith, J.K. (1938) *Toward Full Employment* [J.K. Galbraith was the ghost writer for this monograph] (New York: Whittlesley House).

Eliot, T.H. & Galbraith, J.K. (1992) *Recollections of the New Deal: When the People Mattered* (Boston: Northeastern University Press).

Flanders, R.E., Galbraith, J.K., Mason, E.S., Neal, A.C., Phillips, C.F. & Wright, W. (1947) *Pricing Problems and the Stabilization of Prosperity* (Washington, DC: Chamber of Commerce of the USA).

Galbraith, J.K. (1934) California County Expenditures, *Giannini Foundation of Agricultural Economics; No. 55; Bulletin; No. 582* (Berkeley, CA: Agricultural Experiment Station).

Galbraith, J.K. (1936) Monopoly power and price rigidities, *Quarterly Journal of Economics*, 50(3), pp. 456–475.

Galbraith, J.K. (1937) The farmers' banking system: four years of F.C.A. operations, *Harvard Business Review*, 15(3), pp. 313–320.

Galbraith, J.K. (1938a) Rational and irrational consumer preference, *Economic Journal*, 48(190), pp. 336–342.

Galbraith, J.K. (1939a) Fiscal policy and the employment–investment controversy, *Harvard Business Review*, 18(1), p. 24.

Galbraith, J.K. (1939b) Hereditary land in the Third Reich, *Quarterly Journal of Economics*, 53(3), pp. 465–476.

Galbraith, J.K. (1941a) Defense financing and inflation: some comments on Professor Hansen's article, *Review of Economic Statistics*, 23(2), pp. 78–93.

Galbraith, J.K. (1941b) The selection and timing of inflation controls, *Review of Economic Statistics*, 23(2), pp. 82–85.

Galbraith, J.K. (1943) Price control: some lessons from the first phase, *American Economic Review*, 33(1), pp. 253–259.

Galbraith, J.K. (1945) Germany was badly run, *Fortune*, 32(6), Dec. 1945, pp. 173–200.

Galbraith, J.K. (1946a) *Recovery in Europe* (Washington, DC: National Planning Association).

Galbraith, J.K. (1946b) Reflections on price control, *Quarterly Journal of Economics*, 60(4), pp. 475–489.

Galbraith, J.K. (1947) The disequilibrium system, *American Economic Review*, 37(3), pp. 287–302.

Galbraith, J.K. (1949a) Appraisal of marketing research, *American Economic Review*, 39(3), pp. 415–416.

Galbraith, J.K. (1949b) *Beyond the Marshall Plan* (Washington: National Planning Association).

Galbraith, J.K. (1949c) Commodity marketing – going where?, *American Economic Review*, 39(3), p. 415.

Galbraith, J.K. (1949d) Monopoly and the concentration of economic power, in: H.E. Ellis (Ed.) *A Survey of Contemporary Economics* (Philadelphia: The Blakiston Company).

Galbraith, J.K. (1950a) *America and Western Europe* (New York: Public Affairs Committee).

Galbraith, J.K. (1953b) Farming an abandoned farm, *New York Times Magazine*. Reprinted in Galbraith (1960d), pp. 144–150.

Galbraith, J.K. (1951) The strategy of direct control in economic mobilization, *Review of Economic Statistics*, 33(1), pp. 12–17.

Galbraith, J.K. (1952a) *American Capitalism: The Concept of Countervailing Power* (Boston: Houghton Mifflin).

Galbraith, J.K. (1952b) *A Theory of Price Control* (Cambridge: Harvard University Press).

Galbraith, J.K. (1953a) Appraisals of New Fabian essays, *Review of Economic and Statistics*, 35(3), pp. 200–210.

Galbraith, J.K. (1953b) The poor countries, *Encounter*, 1, pp. 68–72.

Galbraith, J.K. (1954a) Countervailing power, *American Economic Review*, 44(2), pp. 1–6.

Galbraith, J.K. (1954b) The defense of business: a strategic appraisal, *Harvard Business Review*, 32(2), pp. 37–43.

Galbraith, J.K. (1954c) Economic preconceptions and the farm policy, *American Economic Review*, 44(1), pp. 40–52.

Galbraith, J.K. (1954d) Perils of the big build-up, *New York Times Magazine*, March 7, pp. 12, 39–40.

Galbraith, J.K. (1955a) The businessman as philosopher, *Perspectives USA*, #13, pp. 57–59.

Galbraith, J.K. (1955b) *Economics & the Art of Controversy* (New Brunswick: Rutgers University Press).

Galbraith, J.K. (1955c) *The Great Crash, 1929* (Boston: Houghton Mifflin).

Galbraith, J.K. (1956a) Can we solve the farm problem Mr Benedict?, *Journal of Farm Economics*, 38(3), pp. 878–882.

Galbraith, J.K. (1956b) On the economics of FDR, *Commentary*, 22(2), pp. 172–175.

Galbraith, J.K. (1956c) *Inequality in Agriculture: Problem and Program* (Guelph: University Press, Department of Agricultural Economics. & Ontario Federation of Agriculture).

Galbraith, J.K. (1957a) Are living costs out of control?, *Atlantic Monthly*, 199(2), pp. 37–41.

Galbraith, J.K. (1957b) Gray on caricature, *Journal of Farm Economics*, 39(2), pp. 539–541.

Galbraith, J.K. (1957c) Market structure and stabilization policy, *Review of Economic Statistics*, 39(2), pp. 124–133.

Galbraith, J.K. (1957d) A Note on Wilcox review, *Journal of Farm Economics*, 39(4), p. 1045.

Galbraith, J.K. (1958a) *The Affluent Society* (Boston: Houghton Mifflin).

Galbraith, J.K. (1958b) A comment on market structure and stabilization policy: reply, *Review of Economic Statistics*, 40(4), pp. 415–416.

Galbraith, J.K. (1958c) The days of boom and bust, *American Heritage*. Reprinted in Galbraith (1960d), pp. 82–97.

Galbraith, J.K. (1958d) Galbraith on market-structure and stabilization policy – comment, *Review of Economics and Statistics*, 40(2), p. 168.

Galbraith, J.K. (1958e) *Journey to Poland and Yugoslavia* (Cambridge: Harvard University Press).

Galbraith, J.K. (1958f) The mystery of Henry Ford, *Atlantic Monthly*, 201(3), pp. 41–47.

Galbraith, J.K. (1958g) Rival economic theories in India, *Foreign Affairs*, 36(4), pp. 587–596.

Galbraith, J.K. (1959a) Developed economic attitudes and the underdeveloped economy, *Public Policy*, 9, pp. 73–83.

Galbraith, J.K. (1959b) Heresy revisited, *Encounter*, 12(1), pp. 45–53.

Galbraith, J.K. (1959c) Mr. Hunter on countervailing power: a comment, *Economic Journal*, 69(273), pp. 168–170.

Galbraith, J.K. (1959d) The pleasures and uses of bankruptcy, *The Reporter*. Reprinted in Galbraith (1960d), pp. 138–144.

Galbraith, J.K. (1959e) Royalty on the farm, *The Reporter*. Reprinted in Galbraith (1960d), pp. 151–159.

Galbraith, J.K. (1959f) The social balance, *Educational Record*, 40(3), pp. 183–188.

Galbraith, J.K. (1960a) The age of the wordfact, *Atlantic Monthly*, 206(3), pp. 87–89.

Galbraith, J.K. (1960b) For public and potent building, *New York Times Magazine*, October 9, pp. 34, 64, 68, 70.

Galbraith, J.K. (1960c) Introduction, in: R. Shaplen (Ed.) *Kreuger: Genius and Swindler* (New York: Knopf).

Galbraith, J.K. (1960d) *The Liberal Hour* (Boston: Houghton Mifflin).

Galbraith, J.K. (1960e) Mr. Nixon's remedy for inflation, *Harper's Magazine*, February, pp. 29–34.

Galbraith, J.K. (1961a) Economic power and the survival of capitalism, in: S. Tsuru (Ed.) *Has Capitalism Changed?* (Tokyo: Iwanami Shoten).

Galbraith, J.K. (1961b) Ed O'Connor, *New Yorker*, June 24. Reprinted in Galbraith (1971b), pp. 231–237.

Galbraith, J.K. (1961c) *On Criticism in the Open Society* (New Delhi: United States Information Service).

Galbraith, J.K. (1961d) A positive approach to economic aid, *Foreign Affairs*, 39(3), pp. 445–457.

Galbraith, J.K. (1962a) The approach to poverty, *Department of State Bulletin*, 46(1200), pp. 1024–1027.

Galbraith, J.K. (1962b) Dissent in a free society, *Atlantic Monthly*, 209(2), pp. 44–8.

Galbraith, J.K. (1962c) Economic-development – rival systems and comparative advantage, *Department of State Bulletin*, 47(1201), pp. 13–17.

Galbraith, J.K. (1962d) The language of economics, *Fortune*. Reprinted in Galbraith (1971b), pp. 32–44.

Galbraith, J.K. (1962e) The poverty of nations, *Atlantic Monthly*, 210(4), pp. 47–53.

Galbraith, J.K. (1963a) Introduction, in: G. Steinem (Ed.) *The Beach Book* (New York: Viking Press).

Galbraith, J.K. (1963b) A communication, *Washington Post*, November 25, p. A13.

Galbraith, J.K. (1963c) John Strachey, *Encounter*, 21(3), pp. 53–54.

Galbraith, J.K. (1963d) *The Mclandress Dimension* (Boston: Houghton Mifflin).

Galbraith, J.K. (1963e) On our quarrel with success, *Department of State Bulletin*, 49, pp. 52–56.

Galbraith, J.K. (1964a) The balance of payments: a political and administrative view, *Review of Economic Statistics*, 46(2), pp. 115–122.

Galbraith, J.K. (1964b) *Economic Development* (Boston: Houghton-Mifflin).

Galbraith, J.K. (1964c) Economics and the quality of life, *Science*, 145(3628), pp. 117–123.

Galbraith, J.K. (1964d) Experiment in India, *Saturday Review*, 15 August, pp. 20–23.

Galbraith, J.K. (1964e) Reflection on the Asian scene, *Journal of Asian Studies*, 23(4), pp. 501–504.

Galbraith, J.K. (1964f) *The Scotch* (Boston: Houghton Mifflin).

Galbraith, J.K. (1965a) *Economic Policy Since 1945: The Nature of Success* (New York: Graduate School of Business Administration, New York University).

Galbraith, J.K. (1965b) Economics vs the quality of life, *Encounter*, 24(1), pp. 31–39.

Galbraith, J.K. (1965c) Foreign policy: the stuck whistle, *Atlantic Monthly*, 215(2), pp. 64–68.

Galbraith, J.K. (1965d) Galbraith's reply, *Encounter*, 24(6), p. 92.

Galbraith, J.K. (1965e) U.S. embassy geese, *New York Times*, June 14, p. 32.

Galbraith, J.K. (1966a) Agenda for American liberals, *Commentary*, 41(6), pp. 29–34.

Galbraith, J.K. (1966b) Planning ahead – reply, *Commentary*, 42(3), p. 14.

Galbraith, J.K. (1966c) The starvation of our cities, *The Progressive*, December. Reprinted in Galbraith (1986e), pp. 19–25.

Galbraith, J.K. (1966d) William F. Buckley, Jr, *New York Herald Tribune*, 16 October. Reprinted in Galbraith (1971b), pp. 237–40.

Galbraith, J.K. (1967a) Capitalism, socialism, and the future of the industrial state, *Atlantic Monthly*, 219(6), pp. 61–67.

Galbraith, J.K. (1967b) *How to Get Out of Vietnam: A Workable Solution to the Worst Problem of Our Time* (New York: New American Library).

Galbraith, J.K. (1967c) Interview: the public sector is still starved, *Challenge*, 15(3), pp. 18–21.

Galbraith, J.K. (1967d) Market planning and the role of government, *Atlantic Monthly*, 219(5), pp. 69–79.

Galbraith, J.K. (1967e) *The New Industrial State* (London: Hamilton). Citations are to the 2nd Ed. (Harmondsworth: Penguin Books, 1972).

Galbraith, J.K. (1967f) The new industrial state: planning and the modern corporation, *Atlantic Monthly*, 219(4), pp. 51–57.

Galbraith, J.K. (1967g) *The Non-Potable Scotch: A Memoir on the Clansmen in Canada* (Harmondsworth: Penguin Books).

Galbraith, J.K. (1967h) *Planning, Regulation and Competition: Evidence to the Subcommittees of the Select Committee on Small Business, US Senate, 90th Congress, 1st Session* (Washington, DC: US Government Printing Office).

Galbraith, J.K. (1967i) The polipollutionists, *Atlantic Monthly*, 219(1), pp. 52–54.

Galbraith, J.K. (1967j) Review of a review, *Public Interest*, 9, pp. 109–118.

Galbraith, J.K. (1967k) Vietnam – a way out of Vietnam – thoughts and possibilities for revision of American politics, *Europa Archiv*, 22(23), pp. 851–863.

Galbraith, J.K. (1967l) Vietnam: the moderate solution, *Christianity and Crisis*, 27, pp. 185–190.

Galbraith, J.K. (1968a) The case for constitutional reform at Harvard, *Harvard Alumni Magazine*, December 23. Reprinted in Galbraith (1986e), pp. 109–113.

Galbraith, J.K. (1968b) The future of the industrial system, *McKinsey Quarterly*, 5(1), p. 26.

Galbraith, J.K. (1968c) Introduction, in: J. Mill (Ed.) *The History of British India* (New York: Chelsea House Publishers).

Galbraith, J.K. (1968d) *The Triumph: A Novel of Modern Diplomacy* (Boston: Houghton Mifflin).

Galbraith, J.K. (1969a) 1929 and 1969 – Financial genius is a short memory and a rising market, *Harper's*, 239(1434), pp. 55–62.

Galbraith, J.K. (1969b) *The Affluent Society* after ten years, *Atlantic Monthly*, 223(5), p. 37–44.

Galbraith, J.K. (1969c) *Ambassador's Journal: A Personal Account of the Kennedy Years* (London: Hamilton).

Galbraith, J.K. (1969d) The Amercian ambassador, *Foreign Service Journal*. Reprinted in Galbraith (1971b), pp. 147–159.

Galbraith, J.K. (1969e) Berkeley in the thirties, *Atlantic Monthly*. Reprinted in Galbraith (1971b), pp. 259–270.

Galbraith, J.K. (1969f) The big defense firms are really public firms and should be nationalized, *The New York Times Magazine*, November 16, pp. 50, 162–170.

Galbraith, J.K. (1969g) The consequences of technology, *Journal of Accountancy*, 127, p. 44.

Galbraith, J.K. (1969h) *How to Control the Military* (Garden City, NY: Doubleday).

Galbraith, J.K. (1969i) John Steinbeck, *Atlantic Monthly*, 224(5), p. 65–67.

Galbraith, J.K. (1969j) Professor Gordon on "The Close of the Galbraithian System", *Journal of Political Economy*, 77(4), pp. 494–503.

Galbraith, J.K. (1969k) Remarks on planning and market, *Politicka Ekonomie*, 17(11), pp. 1048–1049.

Galbraith, J.K. (1969l) Reply, *Harvard Alumni Magazine*, February 24. Reprinted in Galbraith (1986e), pp. 113–116.

Galbraith, J.K. (1970a) Dwight D. Eisenhower, General, *Book World, Washington Post*, June 28. Reprinted in Galbraith (1971b), pp. 212–216.

Galbraith, J.K. (1970b) Economics as a system of belief, *American Economic Review*, 60(2), pp. 469–478.

Galbraith, J.K. (1970c) The Nixon Administration and the great socialist revival, *New York*, 21 September. Reprinted in Galbraith (1971b), pp. 86–97.

Galbraith, J.K. (1970d) Odyssey of a friend, W. Chambers letters to W.F. Buckley, Jr, 1954–1961, *New Republic*, 162(13), pp. 17–19.

Galbraith, J.K. (1970e) Plain lessons of a bad decade, *Foreign Policy*, 1, pp. 31–45.

Galbraith, J.K. (1970f) Richard Nixon, *Life*, 27 March. Reprinted in Galbraith (1971b), pp. 216–220.

Galbraith, J.K. (1970f) Wage–price controls – the cure for runaway inflation, *New York Times Magazine*, June 7, pp. 25, 104–105.

Galbraith, J.K. (1970g) *Who Needs the Democrats, and What It Takes to Be Needed* (Garden City, NY: Doubleday).

Galbraith, J.K. (1970h) Why do you go to Gstaad?, *Holiday*, January. Reprinted in Galbraith (1971b), pp. 253–259.

Galbraith, J.K. (1970i) Winning in November is not enough, *New Republic*, 162(24), pp. 13–14.

Galbraith, J.K. (1971a) Albert Speer was the man to see, *New York Times Book Review*, 10 January, pp. 2–3, 30–31.

Galbraith, J.K. (1971b) *A Contemporary Guide to Economics, Peace, and Laughter* (Boston: Houghton Mifflin).

Galbraith, J.K. (1971c) The day Nikita Khrushchev visited the establishment, *Harper's Magazine*, February. Reprinted in Galbraith (1971b), pp. 199–207.

Galbraith, J.K. (1971d) Do you sincerely want to Be rich?, *Washington Post*, August 15. Reprinted in Galbraith (1979a), pp. 311–317.

Galbraith, J.K. (1971e) East Pakistan: we can help – but without arms, *New York Times*, 19 August, p. 35.

Galbraith, J.K. (1971f) Galbraith answers Crosland, *New Statesman*, 22 January, p. 101.

Galbraith, J.K. (1971g) Introduction, in: J.-J. Servan-Schreiber & M. Albert (Eds) *The Radical Alternative* (New York: Norton).

Galbraith, J.K. (1971h) Patterns from a difficult decade in American foreign policy, *Europa Archiv*, 26(5), pp. 159–170.

Galbraith, J.K. (1971i) Preface, in: R.A. Butler (Ed.) *The Art of the Possible* (Boston: Gambit).

Galbraith, J.K. (1971j) The United States, *New York*, November 15. Reprinted in Galbraith (view), pp. 215–229.

Galbraith, J.K. (1971k) Who's minding the store?, in: P. Nobile (ed.) *The Con III Controversy: the critics look at the Greening of America* (New York: Pocket Books).

Galbraith, J.K. (1971l) *The American Left and Some British Comparisons* (London: Fabian Society).

Galbraith, J.K. (1972a) Buckley V. Vidal, *Esquire*, 13 October, pp. 1113–1115.

Galbraith, J.K. (1972b) The Case for George McGovern, *Saturday Review*, 1 July.

Galbraith, J.K. (1972c) Competing with government, *New York Times*, September 17, p. E10.

Galbraith, J.K. (1972d) Contemporary capitalism and the problem of unequal growth, *Acta Oeconomica*, 9(2), pp. 117–126.

Galbraith, J.K. (1972e) Eleanor and Franklin revisited, *New York Times Book Review*, 19 March, p. 2.

Galbraith, J.K. (1972f) The emerging public corporation, *Business & Society Review*, 1, p. 54.

Galbraith, J.K. (1972g) Galbraith has seen China's future and it works, *New York Times Magazine*, 26 November, pp. 38–39, 88–94.

Galbraith, J.K. (1972h) Foreword, *American Economic Review*, 62(2), pp. R7-R8.

Galbraith, J.K. (1972i) Recent economic policy: the deeper perspective, *SAM Advanced Management Journal*, 37(4), pp. 13–21.

Galbraith, J.K. (1973a) *A China Passage* (Boston: Houghton Mifflin).

Galbraith, J.K. (1973b) Controls or competition – what's at issue? comment, *Review of Economics and Statistics*, 55(4), p. 524.

Galbraith, J.K. (1973c) Conversation with an inconvenient economist, *Challenge*, 16(4), pp. 28–37.

Galbraith, J.K. (1973d) *Economics and the Public Purpose* (Boston: Houghton Mifflin).

Galbraith, J.K. (1973e) Economics: unequal development and the theory of social action, *Proceedings of the Royal Society of Medicine*, 66(6), pp. 559–564.

Galbraith, J.K. (1973f) Introduction, in: T. Veblen, *The Theory of the Leisure Class* (Boston: Houghton Mifflin).

Galbraith, J.K. (1973g) Power and the useful economist, *American Economic Review*, 63(1), pp. 1–11.

Galbraith, J.K. (1974a) Across Australia by train, *Travel and Leisure*. Reprinted in Galbraith (Annals), pp. 221–229.

Galbraith, J.K. (1974b) Corporations in the eighties, *Annals of Public & Cooperative Economics*, 45(3/4), p. 267.

Galbraith, J.K. (1974c) Diplomat, *New York*, October 21, pp. 130–131.

Galbraith, J.K. (1974d) The higher economic purpose of women, *MS Magazine*, May. Reprinted in Galbraith (1979a), pp. 36–46.

Galbraith, J.K. (1974e) Hindsight, *New Republic*, 171(8), p. 8.

Galbraith, J.K. (1974f) Neuroses of the rich, *Playboy*, February. Reprinted in Galbraith (1979a), pp. 148–152.

Galbraith, J.K. (1974g) *Of Men and Foreign Policy* (Santa Barbara, CA: Center for the Study of Democratic Institutions).

Galbraith, J.K. (1974h) The paintings of Husain, *Boston Globe*, December 1. Reprinted in Galbraith (1986e), pp. 162–164.

Galbraith, J.K. (1974i) Richard Nixon, *Boston Globe*, August 18. Reprinted in Galbraith (1986e), pp. 393–396.

Galbraith, J.K. (1974j) Scotland's greatest son, *Horizon*, Summer. Reprinted in Galbraith (1979a), pp. 86–102.

Galbraith, J.K. (1974k) Solving unemployment without inflation, *Social Policy*, 5(3), pp. 4–5.

Galbraith, J.K. (1974l) The technostructure, *New York Certified Public Accountant*, 44, p. 75.

Galbraith, J.K. (1974m) Vesco and the joy of swindling, *New York*, November 18. Reprinted in Galbraith (1979a), pp. 317–322.

Galbraith, J.K. (1974n) What comes after General Motors? *New Republic*, 171(18). Reprinted in Galbraith (1979a), pp. 73–85.

Galbraith, J.K. (1975a) Apothegms of avarice, *Harpers*, 251(1503), pp. 64–65.

Galbraith, J.K. (1975b) Capitalism's failures: tasks for the democratic left, *New Republic*, 173(7/8), p. 18.

Galbraith, J.K. (1975c) The coming of J.M. Keynes, *Business & Society Review*, 15, pp. 32–38.

Galbraith, J.K. (1975d) The conservative-majority fallacy, *New York*, December 22. Reprinted in Galbraith (1979a), pp. 47–53.

Galbraith, J.K. (1975e) Diplomats all, *The CPA*, 45, p. 12.

Galbraith, J.K. (1975f) The Downing Street papers, *New Statesman*, December 12, pp. 758–759.

Galbraith, J.K. (1975g) The economics of the current anxiety, *McKinsey Quarterly*, 3, p. 31.

Galbraith, J.K. (1975h) *Money: Whence It Came, Where It Went* (London: Deutsch).

Galbraith, J.K. (1975i) Pros and cons of controls, *Fortune*, 91(5), p. 130.

Galbraith, J.K. (1975j) Recessional, *Harvard Gazette*, June 12. Reprinted in Galbraith (1986e), 129–136.

Galbraith, J.K. (1975k) Seymour Edwin Harris, *Review of Economic and Statistics*, 57(1), pp. vi–vii.

Galbraith, J.K. (1975l) *Socialism in Rich Countries and Poor* (Ahmedabad Bombay: Ajit Bhagat Memorial Trust; distributed by Commerce Publications Division).

Galbraith, J.K. (1975m) Will the answer be controls?, *The Listener*, 30 January, pp. 131–132.

Galbraith, J.K. (1976a) Conservative majority myth, *Dissent*, pp. 123–126.

Galbraith, J.K. (1976b) Economic logic – reply, *New Republic*, 174(17), p. 27.

Galbraith, J.K. (1976c) Preface, in: S. Tsuru (Ed.) *The Collected Works* (Tokyo: Kodansha).

Galbraith, J.K. (1976d) The halls of ivory, *New York Times*, April 30, p. 22.

Galbraith, J.K. (1976e) Political novels past and present, *New York Times Book Review*, September 12. Reprinted in Galbraith (1979a), pp. 279–285.

Galbraith, J.K. (1976f) Tempted to say boob, *Fortune*, 93(4), p. 70.

Galbraith, J.K. (1976g) Wherein a tax cut is termed 'obscene', *New York Times*, December 3, p. 27.

Galbraith, J.K. (1977a) *The Age of Uncertainty* (London: British Broadcasting Corporation).

Galbraith, J.K. (1977b) The bimodal image of the modern economy: remarks upon receipt of the Veblen-Commons Award, *Journal of Economic Issues*, 11(2), pp. 189–200.

Galbraith, J.K. (1977c) Capitalism, socialism and democracy – Schumpeter, J A, *New Society*, 40(758), pp. 74–75.

Galbraith, J.K. (1977d) Crime and no punishment, *Esquire*, December. Reprinted in Galbraith (1979a), pp. 323–330.

Galbraith, J.K. (1977e) Economic choices, *Harpers*, 254(1523), pp. 8–10.

Galbraith, J.K. (1977f) *The Galbraith Reader: From the Works of John Kenneth Galbraith* (Ipswich, MA: Gambit).

Galbraith, J.K. (1977g) Galbraithian guide to economic folkways of Americans, *Fortune*, 96(2), p. 97.

Galbraith, J.K. (1977h) Humble quislings, *New Republic*, 177(1), p. 7.

Galbraith, J.K. (1977i) It started with Adam Smith, *New York Times Magazine*, May 15, pp. 23–24.

Galbraith, J.K. (1977j) My forty years with the F.B.I., *Esquire*, October. Reprinted in Galbraith (1979a), pp. 155–181.

Galbraith, J.K. (1977k) The seven wonders of the modern world, *New York Times*, November 27, pp. 322–323.

Galbraith, J.K. (1977l) A very specific guide to the economic folkways of American business and businessmen, *Fortune*, August. Reprinted in Galbraith (1986e), pp. 230–233.

Galbraith, J.K. (1978a) Advice to Exxon, *Challenge*, 21(4), pp. 58–59.

Galbraith, J.K. (1978b) Alger Hiss and liberal anxiety, *Atlantic Monthly*, May. Reprinted in Galbraith (1979a), pp. 303–310.

Galbraith, J.K. (1978c) All Washington's gone AVOL … voluntarily, *New York Times*, April 4, F3.

Galbraith, J.K. (1978d) Defending the multinational corporation, *The CPA Journal*, 48, p. 64.

Galbraith, J.K. (1978e) Defense of multinational company, *Atlantic Community Quarterly*, 16(2), pp. 193–207.

Galbraith, J.K. (1978f) The defense of the multinational company, *Harvard Business Review*, 56(2), pp. 83–93.

Galbraith, J.K. (1978g) Further on Churchill and the Churchill style, *Esquire*, October 24. Reprinted in Galbraith (1986e), pp. 306–309.

Galbraith, J.K. (1978h) The investment balance, *Modern Office Procedures*, 23(6), p. 12.

Galbraith, J.K. (1978i) Labor, leisure, and the new class, *Modern Office Procedures*, 23(10), p. 10.

Galbraith, J.K. (1978j) The North Dakota plan, *Atlantic Monthly*, 242(2), pp. 24–25.

Galbraith, J.K. (1978k) On Post Keynesian economics, *Journal of Post Keynesian Economics*, 1(1), pp. 8–11.

Galbraith, J.K. (1978l) On security and survival, *Modern Office Procedures*, 23(11), p. 12.

Galbraith, J.K. (1978m) The position of poverty, *Modern Office Procedures*, 23(9), p. 12.

Galbraith, J.K. (1978n) Production and price stability, *Modern Office Procedures*, 23(4), p. 12.

Galbraith, J.K. (1978o) The theory of social balance, *Modern Office Procedures*, 23(5), p. 12.

Galbraith, J.K. (1978p) The transition to new goals, *Modern Office Procedures*, 23(7), p. 12.

Galbraith, J.K. (1978q) The trouble with economists, *New Republic*, 178(2), pp. 15–22.

Galbraith, J.K. (1978r) Writing, typing & economics, *Atlantic Monthly*, 241(3). Reprinted in Galbraith (1979a), pp. 285–294.

Galbraith, J.K. (1979a) *Annals of an Abiding Liberal* (Boston: Houghton Mifflin).

Galbraith, J.K. (1979b) Are public libraries against liberty?, *American Libraries*, 10(8), pp. 482–485.

Galbraith, J.K. (1979c) Being a diagnosis of inflation: causes and cures, *New York Times*, January 12, p. A23.

Galbraith, J.K. (1979d) The great Wall Street crash, *New Republic*, 181(15), pp. 17–25.

Galbraith, J.K. (1979e) How to get ahead, *New York Review of Books*, 26, pp. 4–6.

Galbraith, J.K. (1979f) *The Nature of Mass Poverty* (Cambridge, MA: Harvard University Press).

Galbraith, J.K. (1979g) The origin of the document, *Atlantic Monthly*, 244(1), p. 50.

Galbraith, J.K. (1979h) Socialism for corporations, *Washington Post*, October 3, p. A22.

Galbraith, J.K. (1980a) Foreword, in: C. Worswick (ed.) *Princely India: Photographs by Raja Deen Dayal, 1884–1910* (New York: Knopf).

Galbraith, J.K. (1980b) Henry Robinson Luce – and *Fortune Magazine*, in: *Writing for Fortune* (New York: Time Inc.).

Galbraith, J.K. (1980c) H.L. Mencken: The Baltimore Oracle, *Book World, Washington Post*, September 14, pp. 1–3.

Galbraith, J.K. (1980d) Two pleas at Berkeley, *New York Review of Books*, 27, pp. 25–26.

Galbraith, J.K. (1981a) Barabara Ward: in memory, *The Economist*, June 6. Reprinted in Galbraith (1986e), pp. 95–97.

Galbraith, J.K. (1981b) The conservative onslaught, *New York Review of Books*, 27, pp. 30–35.

Galbraith, J.K. (1981c) The economics of the arms race – and after, *Bulletin of the Atomic Scientists*, 37(6), pp. 13–16.

Galbraith, J.K. (1981d) Galbraith on Galbraith, *Fortune*, 104(4), p. 21.

Galbraith, J.K. (1981e) The language is an alibi, *Washington Post*, September 27, p. C8.

Galbraith, J.K. (1981f) *A Life in Our Times: Memoirs* (Boston: Houghton Mifflin).

Galbraith, J.K. (1981g) The management problem of the 80s, *Management International Review*, 21(1), pp. 4–6.

Galbraith, J.K. (1981h) The market and Mr. Reagan, *New Republic*, 185(12), pp. 15–18.

Galbraith, J.K. (1981i) Marketing's changing economic climate, *Marketing Times*, 28(1), p. 10.

Galbraith, J.K. (1981j) Musings of a (relative) conservative, *New York Times*, May 31, p. F3.

Galbraith, J.K. (1981k) The old left strikes back: what has the new right got right? not much, says its favorite foe, *Canadian Business*, 54(9), p. 133.

Galbraith, J.K. (1981l) A policy divided against itself cannot stand – the market and Reagan, *New Republic*, 185(12), pp. 15–18.

Galbraith, J.K. (1981o) Up from monetarism and other wishful thinking, *New York Review of Books*, 28(3), pp. 27–31.

Galbraith, J.K. (1981p) The uses of excuses for affluence, *New York Times Magazine*, May 31, pp. 10–13.

Galbraith, J.K. (1982a) The budget and the bust, *New Republic*, 186(11), pp. 9–13.

Galbraith, J.K. (1982b) The confident speculators, *Atlantic Monthly*, 249(5), p. 100.

Galbraith, J.K. (1982c) Recession economics, *New York Review of Books*, 29, p. 34.

Galbraith, J.K. (1982d) The second imperial requiem, *International Security*, 7(3), pp. 84–93.

Galbraith, J.K. (1982e) The social consensus and the conservative onslaught, *Millennium Journal of International Studies*, Spring, 11, pp. 1–13.

Galbraith, J.K. (1982f) The way up from Reagan economics, *Harvard Business Review*, 60(4), p. 6–12.

Galbraith, J.K. (1982g) The wonders of Robertson Davies, *New York Times Book Review*, February 14, pp. 7–8.

Galbraith, J.K. (1983a) *The Anatomy of Power* (Boston: Houghton Mifflin).

Galbraith, J.K. (1983b) The anatomy of power: interview, *Challenge*, 26(3), pp. 26–33.

Galbraith, J.K. (1983c) David Niven, *Boston Globe*, August 3. Reprinted in Galbraith (1986e), pp. 406–408.

Galbraith, J.K. (1983d) *Economics and the Arts: The W.E. Williams Memorial Lecture Given at the National Theatre on 18 January 1983* (London: Arts Council of Great Britain).

Galbraith, J.K. (1983e) Eleanor Roosevelt, *Esquire*, December. Reprinted in Galbraith (1986e), pp. 389–392.

Galbraith, J.K. (1983f) *Essays from the Poor to the Rich* (Bombay: Bharatiya Vidya Bhavan).

Galbraith, J.K. (1983g) From drips to digitals, *New Republic*, 189(15), pp. 34–36.

Galbraith, J.K. (1983h) Further on economics and the arts, *Ethos*. Reprinted in Galbraith (1986e), pp. 144–151.

Galbraith, J.K. (1983i) Joan Robinson: A word of appreciation, *Cambridge Journal of Economics*, 7(3/4), p. 211.

Galbraith, J.K. (1983j) Preface, in: A. Trollope *Barchester Towers* (Harmondsworth, UK: Penguin).

Galbraith, J.K. (1983k) *The Voice of the Poor: Essays in Economic and Political Persuasion* (Cambridge, MA: Harvard University Press).

Galbraith, J.K. (1984a) Corporate man, *New York Times Magazine*, January 22, p. 39.

Galbraith, J.K. (1984b) The heartless society, *New York Times Magazine*, September 2, pp. 20–21, 44–45.

Galbraith, J.K. (1984c) Keynes, Roosevelt, and the complementary revolutions, *Challenge*, 26(6), pp. 4–8.

Galbraith, J.K. (1984d) Money in American fiction, *New York Times*, October 21. Reprinted in Galbraith (1986e), pp. 67–74.

Galbraith, J.K. (1984e) Reading about the rich, *New York Times Book Review*, October 21, pp. 1, 54–55.

Galbraith, J.K. (1984f) Reagan vs. the military, *New York Times*, February 5, p. E19.

Galbraith, J.K. (1984g) Russia, *New Yorker*, September 3. Reprinted in Galbraith (1986e), pp. 264–275.

Galbraith, J.K. (1985a) The complete politics of arms control: the American context, *Proceeding of the Groupe de Bellerive*. Reprinted in Galbraith (1986e), pp. 8–18.

Galbraith, J.K. (1985b) The concept of work as a species of fraud, *Parade*, February 10. Reprinted in Galbraith (1986e), pp. 42–45.

Galbraith, J.K. (1985c) Eulogy: a tribute to Weintraub, Sidney, *Journal of Post Keynesian Economics*, 7(4), pp. 508–509.

Galbraith, J.K. (1985d) How to get the poor off our conscience, *Humanist*, 45(5), p. 5.

Galbraith, J.K. (1985e) Humanistic economics, *The Progressive*, 49(8), pp. 41–42.

Galbraith, J.K. (1985f) Let's be plain about politics and money, *New York Times*, November 28, p. A27.

Galbraith, J.K. (1985g) Reagan's 'facts' – artistic license, *New York Times*, September 27, p. A27.

Galbraith, J.K. (1985h) Russia's big problem, *Fortune*, 111(3), p. 15.

Galbraith, J.K. (1985i) Taking the ting out of capitalism, *New York Times*, May 26, p. F1.

Galbraith, J.K. (1986a) A journey to Argentina, *New Yorker*, 62(9), pp. 70–77.

Galbraith, J.K. (1986b) Let the politicians run foreign policy, *Washington Post*, December 24, p. 15.

Galbraith, J.K. (1986c) *Revolutions Reconsidered* (Sackville NB: Mount Allison University).

Galbraith, J.K. (1986d) The Scotch: an excursion backward in time, *Reader's Digest*, February. Reprinted in Galbraith (1986e), pp. 276–284.

Galbraith, J.K. (1986e) *A View from the Stands* (Boston: Houghton Mifflin).

Galbraith, J.K. (1986f) The year of the spy, *New York Times*, January 5, p. E19.

Galbraith, J.K. (1987a) The 1929 parallel, *Atlantic Monthly*, January, 259(1), pp. 62–66.

Galbraith, J.K. (1987b) The American economy now— and when the returns come in, *Business Forum*, 12(3), pp. 8–11.

Galbraith, J.K. (1987c) Economic development: engine of democracy, *New York Times*, August 25, p. A21.

Galbraith, J.K. (1987d) *Economics in Perspective: A Critical History* (Boston: Houghton Mifflin).

Galbraith, J.K. (1987e) *A History of Economics: The Past as the Present* (London: H. Hamilton).

Galbraith, J.K. (1988a) Baseball: socialist as apple pie, *New York Times*, August 7, p. E23.

Galbraith, J.K. (1988b) Coolidge, Carter, Bush, Reagan...: no wonder people don't bother to vote, *New York Times*, December 18, p. A19.

Galbraith, J.K. (1988c) Critical issues of the twenty-first century, *Vital Speeches of the Day*, 54(6), p. 185.

Galbraith, J.K. (1988d) The future of global economic systems, *Asian Finance*, 14(12), p. 22.

Galbraith, J.K. (1988e) How businesses behave, *New Republic*, 198(25), p. 42.

Galbraith, J.K. (1988f) Interest groups by any other name, *New York Times*, May 29, p. E17.

Galbraith, J.K. (1988g) Interview: the political asymmetry of economic policy, *Eastern Economic Journal*, 14(2), pp. 125–128.

Galbraith, J.K. (1988h) Time and the new industrial state, *American Economic Review*, 78(2), pp. 373–376.

Galbraith, J.K. (1988i) Tribute, in: *The Proceedings of the Archibald Macleish Symposium May, 1982* (Landam MD: UP of America).

Galbraith, J.K. (1988j) The world economy in perspective, *Journal of Economic Development*, 13(2), pp. 7–16.

Galbraith, J.K. (1989a) Friendly advice to a shrinking military, *New York Times*, November 22, p. A25.

Galbraith, J.K. (1989b) Ideology and economic reality, *Challenge*, 32(6), pp. 4–9.

Galbraith, J.K. (1989c) A look back: affirmation and error, *Journal of Economic Issues*, 23(2), pp. 413–416.

Galbraith, J.K. (1990a) (Class) war in the Gulf, *New York Times*, November 7, p. A31.

Galbraith, J.K. (1990b) Galbraith defends Galbraith, *Fortune*, 121(3), p. 161.

Galbraith, J.K. (1990c) Interview: John Kenneth Galbraith, *Aurora Online*, http://aurora.icaap.org.

Galbraith, J.K. (1990d) The rush to capitalism, *New York Review of Books*, 37(16), p. 51.

Galbraith, J.K. (1990e) *A Short History of Financial Euphoria* (Knoxville: Whittle Direct Books).

Galbraith, J.K. (1990f) *A Tenured Professor: A Novel* (Boston: Houghton Mifflin).

Galbraith, J.K. (1990g) What's wrong with this picture?, *American Heritage*, 41(8), pp. 57–64.

Galbraith, J.K. (1990h) Which capitalism for Eastern Europe?, *Harper's Magazine*, 280, pp. 19–21.

Galbraith, J.K. (1991a) Economics in the century ahead, *Economic Journal*, 101, pp. 41–46.

Galbraith, J.K. (1991b) In tribute to Del Paine, *Fortune*, 123(4), p. 152.

Galbraith, J.K. (1991c) Let's borrow more money: that's the way to end this recession, *New York Times*, May 16, p. A23.

Galbraith, J.K. (1991d) Reflections – 1960, *Grand Street*, 10(1), p. 26.

Galbraith, J.K. (1991e) The sting of truth, *Scientific American*, 264(5), p. 136.

Galbraith, J.K. (1991f) What sort of capitalism is best for former communist nations?, *Utne Reader*, 43, pp. 106–107.

Galbraith, J.K. (1991g) Writing and typing, *Nieman Reports*, 45(1), pp. 32–34.

Galbraith, J.K. (1992a) *The Culture of Contentment* (Boston: Houghton Mifflin).

Galbraith, J.K. (1992b) Culture of contentment, *New Statesman & Society*, 5(201), pp. 14–16.

Galbraith, J.K. (1992c) The economic hangover from a binge of greed, *Business and Society Review*, 81, pp. 6–7.

Galbraith, J.K. (1992d) The functional underclass, *Proceedings of the American Philosophical Society*, 136(3), pp. 411–415.

Galbraith, J.K. (1992e) Introduction, in: T.H. Eliot (Ed.) *Recollections of the New Deal: When the People Mattered* (Boston: Northeastern University Press).

Galbraith, J.K. (1992f) Toeing the hard line, *New Statesman & Society*, 5(192), p. 14.

Galbraith, J.K. (1992g) The university: reflections over the years, *Academe*, 78(5), pp. 10–12.

Galbraith, J.K. (1992h) What monuments the religious have wrought!, *New Choices for Retirement Living*, 32(8), p. 26.

Galbraith, J.K. (1993a) The autonomous power of organization, in: J. Brauer & M. Chatterji (Eds) *Economic issues of disarmament: Contributions from peace economics and peace science* (New York: New York University Press), pp. 43–46.

Galbraith, J.K. (1993b) Countervailing power: memoir and modern reality, in: C. Kerr & P. Staudohar (Eds) *Labor economics and industrial relations: Markets and institutions* (Cambridge: Harvard University Press), pp. 431–434.

Galbraith, J.K. (1993c) Foreword, in: S. Tsuru (Ed.) *Japan's Capitalism, Creative Defeat and Beyond* (Cambridge: Cambridge University Press).

Galbraith, J.K. (1993d) Foreword, in: A. Gregory (Ed.) *The Gilded Age: The Super-Rich of the Edwardian Era* (London: Cassell).

Galbraith, J.K. (1993e) Introduction to the *American Journal of Agricultural Economics'* 75th anniversary issue, *American Journal of Agricultural Economics*, 75, p. 1.

Galbraith, J.K. (1993f) Raising Keynes, *Washington Monthly*, 25(12), p. 46.

Galbraith, J.K. (1993g) Recession? why worry? *New York Times*, May 12, p. A19.

Galbraith, J.K. (1993h) The return of Keynes, *NPQ: New Perspectives Quarterly*, 10(2), p. 10.

Galbraith, J.K. (1994a) The autonomous military power: an economic view, in M. Chatterji, H. Jager & A. Rima (Eds) *The Economics of International Security: Essays in Honour of Jan Tinbergen* (London: Macmillan Palgrave), pp. 9–13.

Galbraith, J.K. (1994b) Capitalism's dark shadows, *Washington Monthly*, 26(7/8), p. 20.

Galbraith, J.K. (1994c) False economies, *New Statesman & Society*, 7(290), p. 24.

Galbraith, J.K. (1994d) The good life beckons, *New Statesman & Society*, 7(287), pp. 14–16.

Galbraith, J.K. (1994e) The good society considered – the economic dimension, *Journal of Law and Society*, 21(2), pp. 165–170.

Galbraith, J.K. (1994f) *A Journey through Economic Time: A Firsthand View* (Boston: Houghton Mifflin).

Galbraith, J.K. (1994g) The 'living industry' and the environment, *EPA Journal*, 20(3/4), p. 41.

Galbraith, J.K. (1994h) *The World Economy since the Wars: A Personal View* (London: Sinclair-Stevenson).

Galbraith, J.K. (1995a) Blame history, not the liberals, *New York Times*, September 19, p. A21.

Galbraith, J.K. (1995b) Our forked tongue, *New York Times*, February 6, p. A17.

Galbraith, J.K. (1996a) Foreword: the indebted society, in: J. Medoff & A. Harless (Eds) *The Indebted Society: Anatomy of an Ongoing Disaster* (Boston: Little, Brown).

Galbraith, J.K. (1996b) *The Good Society: The Humane Agenda* (Boston: Houghton Mifflin Co.).

Galbraith, J.K. (1996c) The good society: the economic dimension, in: P. Arestis & M. Sawyer (Eds) *Employment, Economic Growth, and the Tyranny of the Market: Essays in Honour of Paul Davidson*, Vol. 2 (Aldershot, UK: Edward Elgar).

Galbraith, J.K. (1996d) Interview: John Kenneth Galbraith, in: D.C. Colander & H. Landreth (Eds) *The Coming of Keynesianism to America: Coversations with the Founders of Keynesian Economics* (Cheltenham, UK: Edward Elgar).

Galbraith, J.K. (1997a) Globalisation and the politics of resistance: preface, *New Political Economy*, 2(1), pp. 5–9.

Galbraith, J.K. (1997b) The imperatives of consumer demand, in: M. Casson (Ed.) *Culture, Social Norms and Economics: International Library of Critical Writings in Economics*, Vol. 83 (Cheltenham, UK: Edward Elgar).

Galbraith, J.K. (1997c) Mr. Galbraith's principle, *Across the Board*, 34(6), p. 14.

Galbraith, J.K. (1997d) The new internationalism: the fact and the response, *UN Chronicle*, 34(3), p. 62.

Galbraith, J.K. (1998a) Evading the obvious, *New York Times*, October 12, p. A19.

Galbraith, J.K. (1998b) John Maynard Keynes: from retrospect to prospect, *Journal of Post Keynesian Economics*, 21(1), pp. 11–13.

Galbraith, J.K. (1998c) *Letters to Kennedy* (Cambridge, MA: Harvard University Press).

Galbraith, J.K. (1998d) More than vague dinner conversation, *New Statesman*, 127, pp. 25–26.

Galbraith, J.K. (1998e) *The Socially Concerned Today* (Toronto & Buffalo: University of Toronto Press).

Galbraith, J.K. (1998f) To a market pollyanna, *Civilization*, 5(6), pp. 61–69.

Galbraith, J.K. (1999a) *The Affluent Society* 40 years on, *Dollars & Sense*, 226, p. 49.

Galbraith, J.K. (1999b) Challenges of the new millennium, *Finance and Development*, 36(4), pp. 2–5.

Galbraith, J.K. (1999c) The commitment to innocent fraud, *Challenge*, 42(5), pp. 16–20.

Galbraith, J.K. (1999d) The epic years, *Washington Monthly*, 31(3), p. 42.

Galbraith, J.K. (1999e) Free market fraud, *Progressive*, 63(1), p. 54.

Galbraith, J.K. (1999f) How Keynes came to America, in: *Keynesianism and the Keynesian Revolution in America: A Memorial Volume in Honour of Lorie Tarshis*, (Ed.) L. Tarshis, O.F. Hamouda & B.B. Price (Cheltenham, UK: Edward Elgar), pp. 8–17.

Galbraith, J.K. (1999g) A liberal's debt to Canadians, *Maclean's*, 112(31), p. 40.

Galbraith, J.K. (1999h) *Name-Dropping: From F.D.R. On* (Boston: Houghton Mifflin).

Galbraith, J.K. (1999i) Peace through patience, not air power, *New York Times*, April 15, section 4, p. 17.

Galbraith, J.K. (1999j) *The Unfinished Business of Our Century* (Bryn Mawr: American College).

Galbraith, J.K. (1999/2000) Why diplomats clam up, *Nieman Reports*, 53/54(4/1), pp. 189–190.

Galbraith, J.K. (2000a) Foreword: the social left and the market system, in: B.K. Gills (Ed.) *Globalization and the Politics of Resistance* (Basingstoke, UK: Macmillan).

Galbraith, J.K. (2000b) Preface, in: B. Kreisky, M.P. Berg, J. Lewis & O. Rathkolb (Eds) *The Struggle for a Democratic Austria: Bruno Kreisky on Peace and Social Justice* (New York: Berghahn Books).

Galbraith, J.K. (2001a) Economic delusion, political disaster, *New York Times*, March 11, section 4, p. 15.

Galbraith, J.K. (2001b) *The Essential Galbraith* (Boston: Houghton Mifflin).

Galbraith, J.K. (2001c) What happened to the good society? interview with John Kenneth Galbraith, *Challenge*, 44(4), pp. 5–13.

Galbraith, J.K. (2002a) The clumsy multinational, *Harvard Business Review*, 80(9), p. 128.

Galbraith, J.K. (2002b) Foreword – globalization: what it is and what to do about it, *Annals of the American Academy of Political and Social Science*, 581, pp. 6–7.

Galbraith, J.K. (2003a) Afterword: A Japanese social initiative – the relevant view, in: J.M. Harris & N.R. Goodwin (Eds) *New Thinking in Macroeconomics: Social, Institutional, and Environmental Perspectives* (Cheltenham, UK: Edward Elgar).

Galbraith, J.K. (2003b) The managers have stolen capitalism, *New Perspectives Quarterly*, 20, pp. 81–83.

Galbraith, J.K. (2003c) What has the new right got right?: not much, says its favorite foe, *Canadian Business*, 76(17).

Galbraith, J.K. (2004a) *The Economics of Innocent Fraud: Truth for Our Time* (Boston: Houghton Mifflin).

Galbraith, J.K. (2004b) Innocent fraud, *Across the Board*, 41(2), p. 10.

Galbraith, J.K. (2006) Liberty, happiness ... and the economy, *The Atlantic Monthly*, 297(3), pp. 46–47.

Galbraith, J.K. & Baker, J.F. (1975) Interview: John Kenneth Galbraith, *Publishers Weekly*, 18 August, pp. 10–12.

Galbraith, J.K. & Basco, S. (2003) On Bush, greed, and God's Minister: John Kenneth Galbraith speaks out, *TomPaine.Com*, 4 April.

Galbraith, J.K. & Black, J.D. (1935) The quantitative position of marketing in the United States, *Quarterly Journal of Economics*, 49(3), pp. 394–413.

Galbraith, J.K. & Black, J.D. (1936) The production credit system of 1933, *American Economic Review*, 26(2), pp. 235–247.

Galbraith, J.K. & Black, J.D. (1938) The maintenance of agricultural production during depression: the explanations reviewed, *Journal of Political Economy*, 46(2), pp. 235–247.

Galbraith, J.K. & Blanton, K. (1996) Interview: a Conversation with John Kenneth Galbraith, *Boston Globe*, 28 April (City Edition), p. A97.

Galbraith, J.K. & Canadian Broadcasting Corporation (1965) *The Underdeveloped Country* (Toronto: Canadian Broadcasting Corporation).

Galbraith, J.K. & Conway, L. (1997) Interview; the Ken Galbraith (and Bill Buckley Show), *Nieman Reports*, 51(4), pp. 53–55.

Galbraith, J.K. & Davis, W.A. (1995) Interview: The Lion in Winter: the Harvard prof's latest lesson: how to age wisely, *Boston Globe*, October 24, p. 55.

Galbraith, J.K. & Dietrich (2003) Interview: J.K. Galbraith: liberal politics and the economics of the modern business firm, *New Political Economy*, 8(3), pp. 385–400.

Galbraith, J.K. & Dunn, S.P. (2002) The origins of the Galbraithian system: Stephen P. Dunn in conversation with J.K. Galbraith, *Journal of Post Keynesian Economics*, 24(3), pp. 347–365.

Galbraith, J.K. & Evans, F. (1987) Interview: a conversation with John Kenneth Galbraith, *Business Forum*, 12(3), pp. 12–17.

Galbraith, J.K., Fergenson, P.E. & Fergenson, L.R. (1989) Galbraith on marketing and the marketplace: an interview, *Review of Business*, 11(3), p. 29.

Galbraith, J.K., Grether, E.T., Mason, E.S., Neal, A.C., Sumner, J.D. & Heflebower, R.B. (1947) Content and research uses of price control and rationing records, *American Economic Review*, 37(2), pp. 651–666.

Galbraith, J.K., Higgins, B.H., Woytinsky, W.S. & Brownlee, O.H. (1948) Discussion, *American Economic Review*, 38(2), pp. 443–451.

Galbraith, J.K. & Holton, R.H. (1955) *Marketing Efficiency in Puerto Rico* (Cambridge: Harvard University Press).

Galbraith, J.K., Jarrett, H. & Future, R.F.T. (1958) *Perspectives on Conservation; Essays on America's Natural Resources* (Baltimore: Johns Hopkins University Press).

Galbraith, J.K. & Karier, T. (1992) Interview: John Kenneth Galbraith looks back at the Reagan-Bush era, *In These Times*, 10–23 June, pp. 18–19.

Galbraith, J.K. & Kaur, H. (1998) Interview: a gentler, kinder approach – the Galbraith way, *Business Times*, 12(51), p. 4.

Galbraith, J.K., Kuh, E. & Thurow, L.C. (1971) The Galbraith plan to promote the minorites, *New York Times Magazine*, August 22, pp. 9, 35, 38–39.

Galbraith, J.K. & Kunimatsu, T. (1999) Interview: Galbraith says capitalism will prevail, *Daily Yomiuri*, 10 January, p. 1.

Galbraith, J.K. & Laurence, M. (1968) The *Playboy* interview: John Kenneth Galbraith, *Playboy*, June, pp. 63–78, 138, 164–174.

Galbraith, J.K. & Lewis, A. (1966) Interview: The world through Galbraith's eyes, *New York Times Magazine*, 18 December, pp. 25, 88–92.

Galbraith, J.K. & MacNeil, R. (1992) Interview: conversation with John Kenneth Galbraith, *MacNeil/Lehrer News Hour*, 1 July (Transcript #4368), pp. 12–16.

Galbraith, J.K. & Mcclaughry, J. (1973) Interview: Galbraith and his critics, *Business & Society Review*, 8, pp. 12–16.

Galbraith, J.K. & McCracken, P.W. (1983) *Reagonomics: Meaning, Means, and Ends* (New York: Free Press).

Galbraith, J.K. & Menshikov, S. (1988) *Capitalism, Communism and Coexistence: From the Bitter Past to a Better Prospect* (London: Hamish Hamilton).

Galbraith, J.K. & Navasky, V.S. (1967) Interview: Galbraith on Galbraith, *New York Times Book Review*, June 25, pp. 2–3.

Galbraith, J.K. & Olsen, W. (1987) Interview: America will feel the crunch of Reagan revolution, *Tribune*, Business, pp. 1–6.

Galbraith, J.K. & Pressman, S. (1989) Interview: conversation, *Review of Political Economy*, 1, pp. 381–386.

Galbraith, J.K. & Salinger, N. (1978) *Almost Everyone's Guide to Economics* (Mount Vernon, NY: Consumers Union).

Galbraith, J.K. & Solo, C.S. (1953) Puerto Rican lessons in economic development, *The Annals of the American Academy of Political and Social Science*, 285, pp. 55–59.

Galbraith, J.K. & University of London. (1967) *A Beginner's Guide to American Studies: ... An Address Given on the Occasion of the Official Opening of the Institute of United States Studies, University of London, on 12th May 1967* (London: University Institute of United States Studies).

Galbraith, J.K., Ulmer, H., Melville, J., Weidenbaum, M. L. (1976f) The case for and against national economic planning, *Challenge*, 19(1), p. 30.

Galbraith, J.K. & Wallace, M. (1978) *A Guide to Today's Economy* (New York: Encyclopedia Americana/CBS News Audio Resource Library,).

Gauhar, A. & Galbraith, J.K. (1983) North–South dialog: an interview with J.K. Galbraith, *Third World Quarterly*, 5(2), pp. 263–269.

Levine, D. & Galbraith, J.K. (1970) *No Known Survivors: David Levine's Political Plank* (Boston: Press).

Moraes, F.R., Galbraith, J.K. & Howe, E. (1974) *John Kenneth Galbraith Introduces India* (London: Deutsch).

Randhawa, M.S. & Galbraith, J.K. (1968) *Indian Painting: the Scene, Themes, and Legends* (Boston: Houghton Mifflin).

Rudenstine, N., Galbraith, J.K. & Thomson, J.C.J. (1995) Rudenstine, Galbraith and Thomson talks, *Nieman Reports*, 49(3), p. 37.

Samuelson, P.A. & Galbraith, J.K. (1975) Economic policy – where is it leading?, *Boston University Journal*, 23(1), pp. 30–36.

Sweezy, P.M., Galbraith, J.K., Tolchin, S.J. & Browne, R.S. (1985) Can socially responsible societies compete economically?, *Business and Society Review*, (52), pp. 11–14.

Voorhies, E.C., Galbraith, J.K. & Todd, F.E. (1933a) *Economic Aspects of the Bee Industry*, Giannini Foundation of Agricultural Economics Paper No. 39; Bulletin No. 555 (Berkeley: Agricultural Experiment Station).

Voorhies, E.C., Galbraith, J.K. & Todd, F.E. (1933b) *Honey Marketing in California*, Giannini Foundation of Agricultural Economics Paper No. 38; Bulletin; No. 554 (Berkeley: Agricultural Experiment Station).

Yadin, Y., Maeda, Y. & Galbraith, J.K. (1962) *Guildhall Lectures* (Manchester: Granada TV Network Limited).

12 Kydland and Prescott's Nobel Prize

The methodology of time consistency and real business cycle models

James E. Hartley

'Kydland and Prescott's Nobel Prize: The Methodology of Time Consistency and Real Business Cycle Models' by James E. Hartley from *Review of Political Economy* (2006), Volume 18, Issue 1 (Taylor and Francis Ltd, http://www.informaworld.com), reprinted by permission of the publisher.

On October 11, 2004, Finn Kydland and Edward Prescott were awarded the Bank of Sweden Prize in Economic Sciences in Memory of Alfred Nobel. The press release stated that the prize was awarded 'for their contributions to dynamic macroeconomics: the time consistency of economic policy and the driving forces behind business cycles' (Royal Swedish Academy of Sciences, 2004b). The Presentation Speech by Jörgen Weibull (2004) further focuses attention on just a pair of papers: Kydland & Prescott (1977), where the time consistency result is found, and Kydland & Prescott (1982), where the importance of technological fluctuations in explaining business cycles is found.

The Royal Swedish Academy explained that Kydland and Prescott showed that the public's expectations of future policy choices can give rise to a time consistency problem unless the policy maker commits to a rule binding future behavior to follow a predetermined course. Lacking such a rule, economies can become trapped in a high inflation equilibrium even if everyone in the economy, including the policy maker, would prefer lower inflation. The practical effect of this research was to focus attention on institutions instead of policy choices, leading to the recent spate of central bank reforms (Royal Swedish Academy of Sciences, 2004b).

Kydland and Prescott also furthered the integration of research on business cycles and economic growth. Just as growth theory had long suggested that technological change drives economic growth, Kydland & Prescott (1982) argued that the same changes drive short-run cyclical fluctuations. The result of this research was a new set of models which showed business cycle behavior arising as the result of the utility maximizing decisions of households and the profit maximizing decisions of firms in the face of changes in technology (Royal Swedish Academy of Sciences, 2004b).

What unites these two seemingly unrelated papers? When asked that question, Prescott replied, 'The methodology' (Snowden & Vane, 1999, p. 264). Thus, it is to the methodology behind this work that we turn our attention. What exactly was it that Kydland and Prescott were trying to accomplish? The answer is a bit surprising. In neither case, did Kydland and Prescott set out to demonstrate the thing for which their work became so influential.

1 Biographical details

Collaboration between Finn Kydland and Edward Prescott was a very natural thing. Both began their college education with the expectation of having careers in engineering and management, but through the influence of particular teachers, migrated out of that field and into economics (Nobel Foundation, 2004). Prescott graduated from Swarthmore in 1962; Kydland from the Norwegian School of Economics and Business Administration in 1968. Both ended up at Carnegie Mellon University for their doctoral work. Prescott arrived first, receiving his PhD in 1967; his first job was at the University of Pennsylvania, but he returned to Carnegie-Mellon in 1971, where he served as Kydland's thesis advisor. After receiving his PhD in 1973, Kydland returned to Norway. In 1975, Prescott took a sabbatical leave and went to the Norwegian School of Business to work with Kydland on the time consistency paper, eventually published in 1977.

Since that collaboration, Kydland and Prescott have maintained a continuous association. In addition to the 1977 paper on time consistency, Kydland & Prescott (1974, 1980a, 1980b) co-authored a few other papers on optimal control theory. Their collaborative work on real business cycle models spanned an even greater period of time. After the 1982 paper, Kydland and Prescott co-authored three other papers on the methodology of these methods (1990, 1991a, 1996), as well as a couple of papers on particular aspects of the models themselves (1988, 1991b).

While the Nobel Committee mentioned only their collaborative work, both Kydland and Prescott have separately written a large amount of influential work on time consistency, real business cycle models and a host of other important topics. A non-comprehensive listing of their separately published work appears at the end of the reference section.

2 Time consistency

The idea of time consistency is explained best in a few examples from Kydland & Prescott (1977). First, suppose there is a flood plain in which it is socially optimal to have no housing. However, if the government will take costly measures to prevent the plain from flooding should houses be built there, then a time consistency problem arises. Even if the government has announced that it will not take flood control measures to protect houses in a flood plain, a rational agent may well know that once the houses are built, the government will, in fact, take such measures and thus the agent may proceed to build such housing. The only way for the government to convince people not to build in a flood plain is to commit to a rule and abandon all discretion in the matter. Only in this manner will people's expectations about future government action be altered.

Similarly, consider patent law. Suppose an inventor approaches the government and offers to work on a technological advance in exchange for some sort of patent protection in the event that the research results in a new invention. The government would optimally offer such patent protection since to deny such protection will mean that the invention will not be made at all and it may be better to give the inventor monopoly rights than not to have the product. However, once the invention has been discovered, then it is optimal for the government to renege on its prior agreement. Given that the product has already been invented, there is no longer any benefit to awarding monopoly rights to the production of the product. The time inconsistency is that what was an optimal policy at one time is no longer an optimal policy at a later time.

A final example, and the one for which Kydland and Prescott's paper is most closely associated, is monetary policy. The question is whether a monetary policy of doing what is best in any given time period produces a better outcome than abandoning period-by-period discretion in order to follow a rule. Suppose that an expectations-adjusted Phillips Curve characterizes the economy, so that unemployment is at the natural rate when actual inflation equals expected inflation, but unemployment is lower if actual inflation is above expected inflation. Also suppose that the central bank dislikes both unemployment and inflation, but that there is some degree to which they are willing to accept higher inflation in exchange for lower unemployment. In this case, if the public has rational expectations and understands both the nature of the Phillips Curve and the central bank's objective function, the economy can get stuck in a high inflation equilibrium despite the fact that there is a Pareto superior equilibrium at a lower inflation rate. A central bank which promised to lower the inflation rate in this case, however, would not be believed by the public; the public would know that if it lowered its expectation of the inflation rate, the central bank would, if it were using optimal control theory, inflate the economy at a rate higher than the expected level in order to lower the unemployment rate. The solution to the model in this case is an equilibrium in which unemployment is at the natural rate, but inflation is higher than zero.

Kydland & Prescott (1977) is described by the Royal Swedish Academy (2004a) as having 'a far reaching impact on reforms carried out in many places (such as New Zealand, Sweden, Great Britain, and in the Euro area), aimed at legislated delegation of monetary policy decisions to independent central bankers with different kinds of pre-specified price-stability objectives.' However, this emphasis on the implication for monetary policy of time inconsistency was *not* the original contribution in Kydland & Prescott (1977). Contemporaneously with Kydland and Prescott's work, Calvo (1978a, 1978b) had been working out the implications of time inconsistency for monetary policy, and Calvo cites Auernheimer (1974) as the first to note the time inconsistency problem in monetary policy. Similarly, the idea that the time inconsistency problem is 'a common explanation for events that, until then, had been interpreted as separate policy failures' (Royal Swedish Academy, 2004b) was also not original to Kydland & Prescott (1977); Buchanan (1975) describes the general problem, including the now familiar two-person game theory version of Kydland and Prescott's result, and shows how a number of problems (though not including the monetary policy problem) are all variants of the general phenomenon.

The original and important contribution of Kydland & Prescott (1977) was the *method* of modeling time inconsistency. In the midst of the 1970s, many macroeconomists believed that the best means of thinking about policy was to use optimal control theory to design the best policy response to a given economic situation. The rational expectations revolution was in its early stages when Kydland and Prescott wrote their paper showing that if agents have rational expectations about the future, and in particular about the policy choices which will be made by future governments, then a government which used optimal control theory to make its policy decisions on a period by period basis will generate economic outcomes which are inferior to those that would result if the government were to simply follow a predetermined rule. The important contribution of Kydland and Prescott's paper was this demonstration that time inconsistency problems can arise as a result of the public's ability to form expectations about the future.

While Kydland and Prescott do give the inflation problem some attention in their paper, the focus of their paper is the theoretical observation that optimal control theory fails to give desirable outcomes in a rational expectations model. The full implications of their model for monetary policy were not worked out in future years by Kydland and Prescott. Instead, the most well-known articulation of the monetary policy model is a pair of papers by Barro & Gordon (1983a, 1983b), and the most widely cited solution to the problem—hire central bankers who are particularly averse to inflation—was worked out in Rogoff (1985).

There is no doubt that time inconsistency has proven to be a fertile ground for theoretical research and that it is mentioned in nearly every discussion of central bank design. It is a larger question, however, whether the idea has any *empirical* relevance. As noted by Blinder (1998) in discussing the current Federal Reserve and Mayer (1995) in looking at the historical record, it is not at all clear that time inconsistency has had any influence on the actual conduct of monetary policy by central bankers.

The implications for monetary policy, however, did not form part of Kydland and Prescott's intention in writing their dynamic inconsistency paper. Instead, Kydland and Prescott were interested in the general theoretical issues. As they noted in a footnote,

> The original objective of this research was to demonstrate the applicability of optimal control methods in a rational-expectations world. We recognized the nonoptimality of the consistent solution obtained by using control-theory techniques, but initially considered this a minor problem. Further thought, in large part motivated by C. A. Sims's criticism of our initial analysis, led us to the radical conclusions of this essay.
>
> (Kydland & Prescott, 1977, p. 621)

In other words, it was the methodological feature of their paper that originally interested them. Thinking about their paper in that way, it is not as surprising that Kydland and Prescott did not spend more time subsequently working out the theory of time consistency and its implications for monetary policy. Instead, they turned their attention to another set of dynamic models, developing the real business cycle model that would be a focus of their work for the next two decades.

3 Real business cycles

In the introduction to his edited volume, *Macroeconometrics: Developments, Tensions, and Prospects,* Kevin Hoover relates the following anecdote:

> This chapter [a reprint of Kydland & Prescott, 1991a] is the only one that reprints previously published work. The strategy in compiling this volume was to include new and up-to-date statements of the various points of view. To my surprise, however, I could not persuade any of at least twenty prominent practitioners of the calibration methodology to contribute a new account of calibration to the volume.
>
> (Hoover, 1995b, p. 9n)

This was a rather odd state of affairs for a method that had been in existence for over a decade, and one that had, in many ways, become one of the most prominent methods in macroeconomics. As King & Rebelo (1999, p. 930) note in their essay in the *Handbook of Macroeconomics,* 'Real business cycle analysis now occupies a major position in the core curriculum of nearly every graduate program. At a recent NBER conference, a prominent Cambridge economist of the New Keynesian school described the RBC approach as the new orthodoxy of macroeconomics, without raising a challenge from the audience.'

The reason Hoover was unable to find anyone willing to write a new essay on the real business cycle method could be that it has already been so well explicated that the people whom Hoover approached believed that writing another explication was unnecessary and redundant. If asked, most real business cycle researchers would presumably assert that Kydland and Prescott have already provided ample justification for the methods they pioneered. Indeed, while many economists have worked on the real business cycle program, it is, at its heart, Kydland and Prescott's program. In a discussion of whether there was a better name for real business cycle theory, Randall White observed, 'I sort of like 'the [dynamic general equilibrium] model.' Although 'the Kydland–Prescott Model' (KPM) is even better—it's accurate and fair.'[1]

What we will see is this: in five different programmatic manifestos over a span of 15 years, Kydland and Prescott have offered five different—and in many ways mutually incompatible—justifications for the models they were advocating.

3.1 *What is a real business cycle model?*

It is helpful at the outset to review the basic structure of a real business cycle model. At its most basic level, a real business cycle model is simply a representative agent choosing consumption and leisure to maximize utility.[2] The intertemporal utility function has the form:

$$\sum_{t=0}^{\infty} \beta^t u[c_t, (1 - h_t)]$$

where β the discount rate and c is the consumption level. We normalize a time period to be 1, so h is the amount of time spent working, and $1 - h$ is thus the amount of time spent in leisure. Utility is assumed to increase at a decreasing rate with both consumption and leisure. We can specify the following functional form for the utility function:

$$u[c_t, 1 - h_t] = \ln c_t + A \ln (1 - h_t)$$

where A measures the relative preference for leisure and consumption (i.e., the larger A, the greater the representative agent's relative preference for leisure).

The agent faces three constraints. The first is the production function, which is assumed to be Cobb–Douglas:

$$y_t = e^{zt} k_t^{1-\theta} h_t^\theta$$

where y is total output, k is the capital stock, z is the level of technology, and θ is the labor share. Additionally, output is divided into consumption, c, and investment, i. The second constraint is the rule for capital formation:

$$k_{t+1} = (1 - \delta)k_t + i_t$$

where δ is the depreciation rate. Finally, technology evolves according to the following rule:

$$z_{t+1} = \rho z_t + \varepsilon_{t+1}$$

where ε is normally distributed with a mean of 0 and a standard deviation of σ_ε.

Combining all of the above yields the social planning problem which constitutes a real business cycle model:

$$\text{Max } E_0 \sum_{t=0}^{\infty} \beta^t (\ln c_t + A \ln (1 - h_t))$$

subject to

$$c_t + i_t = e^{zt} k_t^{1-\theta} h_t^\theta$$

$$k_{t+1} = (1 - \delta)k_t + i_t$$

$$z_{t+1} = \rho z_t + \varepsilon_{t+1}$$

While strikingly simple in structure, the model captures a number of interesting tradeoffs. There is, for example, the intratemporal tradeoff of leisure today versus consumption today, but there is also the intertemporal tradeoff of leisure today versus consumption tomorrow via the production of investment goods. In the absence of the technology shock process, the model would move to a steady-state. The technology shock, however, introduces another interesting dynamic. With a positive technology shock, current work effort is unusually productive, and thus the agent will substitute leisure today for leisure tomorrow, i.e., the agent will 'make hay while the sun shines.'

The agent chooses c_t, h_t, and i_t (or, equivalently, k_{t+1}) given the state variables, k_t and z_t. To solve the model, the parameters, β, A, δ, θ, ρ and σ_ε must be set, and, as is discussed below, this is normally done by looking at microeconomic empirical evidence. It is a straightforward matter to modify the simple model above in any number of directions, and the development of the real business cycle literature has contained innumerable such extensions. Moreover, there have been several methods developed to solve the mathematics of the problem above. Hartley *et al.* (1998) contains a selection of those extensions as well as a user's guide to solving the model (Chapter 2). Similarly, Cooley (1995) contains several extensions and papers devoted to explaining solution routines.

The real business cycle literature is quite large and a full discussion of it exceeds the scope of the present paper. Interested readers can consult Hartley *et al.* (1998) for a collection of the relevant research and a discussion of the overall research program. The question we will consider here is limited to the work of Kydland and Prescott. What exactly did Kydland and Prescott set out to accomplish, how did they articulate what they were doing and to what extent do they provide a defense of the method used?

3.2 *Kydland & Prescott (1982)*

The real business cycle literature got started almost by accident. Consider the opening paragraph of the paper that spawned the whole literature, Kydland & Prescott's, 'Time to Build and Aggregate Fluctuations':

> That wine is not made in a day has long been recognized by economists (e.g., Böhm-Bawerk (1891)). But, neither are ships nor factories built in a day. A thesis of this essay is that the assumption of multiple-period construction is crucial for explaining aggregate fluctuations. A general equilibrium model is developed and fitted to U.S. quarterly data for the post-war period. The co-movements of the fluctuations for the fitted model are quantitatively consistent with the corresponding co-movements for U.S. data. In addition, the serial correlations of cyclical output for the model match well with those observed.
>
> (Kydland & Prescott, 1982, p. 1345)

It is not difficult to determine what it is about the model in this paper that Kydland and Prescott argue is important. Both the title and the opening paragraph declare the importance of time-to-build, and this emphasis is carried throughout; the paper concludes with, 'A crucial element of the model that contributed to the persistence of output movements was the time-to-build requirement' (Kydland & Prescott, 1982, p. 1368). Moreover, the model favored by Kydland and Prescott is not compared to a model with a different shock process, but rather to a model with a different process for building capital. Now there would be nothing extraordinary about this paper's focus on time-to-build, if it were not for the history of Kydland and Prescott's models after this paper. After the time-to-build feature is declared to be 'crucial' for explaining fluctuations in this paper, it never shows up again. None of the subsequent canonical real business cycle models have time-to-build in them at all.

Instead, it is the role of the shock process that comes to the fore. In particular, Kydland and Prescott subsequently highlight the importance of the technology shocks in explaining aggregate fluctuations. In the 1982 paper, however, the technology shock is seemingly unimportant. Neither the abstract nor the conclusion of the paper even mention the technology shock process. The total of what Kydland and Prescott say about technology shocks in the introduction to their paper is this: 'The exogenous stochastic components in the model are shocks to technology and imperfect indicators of productivity. The two technology shocks differ in their persistence' (p. 1345). In fact, the most extensive discussion of the technology shock process in the paper is to note that part of the reason the model does not fit the data perfectly well could be due to the simplicity of having technology shocks be nothing other than 'pure productivity shocks' (Kydland & Prescott, 1982, pp. 1365–1366).

How is the model evaluated? Kydland and Prescott declare: 'The test of the theory is whether there is a set of parameters for which the model's co-movements for *both* the smoothed series and the deviations from the smoothed series are *quantitatively* consistent with the observed behavior of the corresponding series for the US post-war economy' (Kydland & Prescott, 1982, p. 1359). But then, in the next paragraph, they note that they 'rig' the model to yield the right co-movements for the smoothed series, and two paragraphs down, the test of the theory has suddenly changed to simply 'quantitatively explaining the co-movements of the deviations' (Kydland & Prescott, 1982, p. 1360). Nowhere do Kydland and Prescott explain why evaluating whether the model can also explain the smoothed series is dropped as a test of the model.

Kydland and Prescott proceed to compare the co-movements of the deviations to similar statistics from the US economy. Nowhere do they provide an explanation for how they chose which statistics to compare, and nowhere do they provide any explanation of how close the numbers need to be to pass 'the test.' In fact, the only way we know that it is possible to fail the test is that Kydland and Prescott declare that the properties of a model which uses adjustment costs rather than time-to-build are 'grossly inconsistent with the US data' (Kydland & Prescott, 1982, p. 1367). They do not provide a table with the results from such a model, but they do describe several of what they consider the largest inconsistencies. Particularly noteworthy is that they explicitly consider the case in which the adjustment cost is zero, which is equivalent to a model with no adjustment cost and no time-to-build. They declare that this model is also 'inconsistent with the observations' (Kydland & Prescott, 1982, p. 1368), thereby rejecting the model they subsequently use as an exemplar in their future work.

Two elements of the discussion are, in light of what comes after, surprisingly absent. First, there is virtually no mention of growth theory. The extent of the discussion of growth theory in general is comments like 'Our approach integrates growth and business cycle theory. Like standard growth theory, a representative infinitely-lived household is assumed' (Kydland & Prescott, 1982, p. 1345). Growth theory merely sits in the background throughout the paper, never being highlighted in any way. The Solow–Swan growth model is never mentioned.[3] This is not to say that Kydland and Prescott do not have a growth model in the back of their minds when writing this paper, but rather that from reading this paper there is no doubt that it is time-to-build, and not the general growth model, that is the important thing in the model.[4]

Also noteworthy by its absence is any discussion or defense of the calibration procedure used to evaluate the model. Kydland and Prescott simply use the calibration procedure without comment. Rather, they explain why they do not use more conventional methods: 'We chose not to test our model versus the less restrictive vector autoregressive model. This most likely would have resulted in the model being rejected, given the measurement problems and the abstract nature of the model' (Kydland & Prescott, 1982, p. 1360). Why their preferred test of the model is superior to or at least as good as other methods is not explained.

The first real business cycle model is thus justified on rather interesting grounds. The important feature of the model is that it shows us the importance of time-to-build, and we should take it seriously because it passes the test designed by Kydland and Prescott. As we shall see, both of these matters fall by the wayside: time-to-build disappears, and the idea that such models need be or even can be tested is dismissed.

3.3 Prescott (1986a)

The history of the technology shock used in real business cycle work is easy to detail. In 1982, Kydland and Prescott simply calibrated the process. The process was selected 'to be such that the estimate of the variance of cyclical output for the model equaled that of the cyclical output for the US economy during the sample period' (Kydland & Prescott, 1982, p. 1362).

This selection process left an uneasy feeling. It seemed somewhat improper to pick the driving process for the model in a manner designed to insure that at least one of the desired results (appropriate variance of output) was achieved. The 'test' of the model was too similar to the model selection criterion. Prescott, himself, recognized the problems with this procedure.

In our 1982 paper, Kydland and I searched over processes for the technological change process. We did sensitivity analysis with the other parameters, but found the conclusions relatively insensitive to their assumed
values (except for the distributed lag of leisure parameters just discussed).
The parameters of the technological change process did affect our predictions of the aggregate implications of uncertainty in the technology parameter. In fact, Lucas [1987] criticized us for searching for the best fit.

(Prescott, 1986b, p. 31)

So, in 1986, Prescott proposed an alternative: the Solow residual (Prescott,
1986a). At first glance this seems to be a perfect choice. The process of building
a real business cycle model involves using other studies to get specific parameter
values. Thus, it seems logical to use the same process here; use Solow residual
studies to fix the technology shock parameters.

However, with the introduction of the Solow residual came the introduction
of a revisionist history of the development of real business cycle models. In
1986, Prescott redefines the entire enterprise of studying business cycles. While
earlier economists found business cycles to be puzzling phenomenon needing
some explanation, Prescott (1986a, p. 9) argues that Kydland & Prescott (1982)
demonstrated that far from being a puzzle, business cycle phenomena are actually predicted by 'standard' economic theory.

What is this 'standard economic theory'? It turns out to be the growth model
developed by Solow (1956) and Swan (1956). According to Prescott in 1986,
what he and Kydland were doing in 1982 was simply applying growth models to
short run fluctuations to see what would happen. Prescott declares that even he
was surprised that the technological fluctuations used in growth theory were sufficient to explain short run phenomena.

Now, as we noted above, Kydland & Prescott (1982) actually gives scant
attention to technological shocks and growth theory. The 'surprise' that technological fluctuations alone explain so much is not mentioned in the 1982 paper.
Indeed, while the 1982 paper focuses almost entirely on the propagation
mechanism (time-to-build), the 1986 paper focuses almost exclusively on the
impulse mechanism (the Solow residual). 'Time-to-build' which Kydland and
Prescott declared was 'crucial' for explaining business cycles in 1982 is not
even mentioned in Prescott (1986a).

Also gone in 1986 is any mention of the 'test' of the model used in 1982. In
fact, there is no test of the model at all. While Prescott does not mention any
tests which he thinks his model needs to pass in order to be taken seriously, he
does preemptively dismiss two other forms of testing. First, he declares that 'statistical hypothesis testing' will reject his model because his model is 'highly
abstract' and thus 'necessarily false.' This echoes the claim made in the 1982
paper. Similarly, in 1986, he rejects comparison of paths:

An alternative approach is to compare the paths of the growth model if the
technological parameters $\{z_t\}$ were those experienced by the U.S. economy.

We did not attempt this because theory's predictions of paths, unlike its predictions of the statistical properties, are sensitive to what Leamer (1983, p. 43) calls 'whimsical' modeling assumptions. Another nontrivial problem is that the errors in measuring the innovations in the z_t process are as large as the innovations themselves.

(Prescott, 1986a, p. 16)

Having ruled out the tests that might be used by other economists, and having completely dropped any mentioned of testing the model by the process he and Kydland used in 1982, Prescott leaves us with no explanation of why he believes his model is of interest other than the simple declaration that he is using 'standard' theory. Moreover, Prescott's reasons for rejecting the comparison of paths as a test of the model were ultimately rejected by even Prescott, himself. Hansen & Prescott (1993) perform exactly such a comparison, but nowhere in that later paper is there any explanation of why Prescott changed his mind.

So, instead of 'testing' the model as in 1982, Prescott now advocates simply 'comparing' the statistical properties of the model to the corresponding statistics from the US economy. In essence, the model 'test' of 1982 has now become a 'comparison,' with no possibility of finding the model to be inaccurate. At one level, this change can be seen as merely semantic. When examining the preferred model, the 'test' and the 'comparison' are equivalent. However, the change in words does have substantive implications when considering alternative models. In the 1982 paper, alternatives to the preferred model are tested and found to be 'grossly inconsistent with the US data for the post-war period,' 'the opposite of what the US data show,' a 'failure,' and 'inconsistent with the observations' (Kydland & Prescott, 1982, pp. 79, 80). Recall that every one of these alternative models was in the same general class as the model being used in Prescott (1986a). However, the argument of the 1986 paper reverses the role of the model and the evidence. When, for example, Prescott finds that the predicted labor elasticity of output is too high, he does not argue that this is a 'failure' of the model, but rather that it shows that we do not have good measures of labor elasticity, that if we could measure labor elasticity better, then we would find the value predicted by the model. Indeed, Prescott entitles the paper 'Theory Ahead of Business Cycle Measurement' for exactly this reason.

The semantic change from 'test' to 'comparison' between 1982 and 1986 signals a change in method. In 1982, Kydland and Prescott are sounding a very Marshallian note, in which when a theory and evidence are in conflict, it is the theory that is assumed to be in error. Thus, it is perfectly in line with Marshallian method to conclude that the models without time-to-build are 'failures' because they are 'grossly inconsistent' with the data. However, the 1986 paper switches instruments and sounds a very Walrasian note, in which the theory is assumed to be true and the comparison with the world is used not to verify the theory, but to see where the world is defective.[5] Walras (1926 [1954], p. 71) draws the comparison between economic theory and geometry; when we find in the real world that circles do not have equal radii, we do not fault the theory, but rather the data. Prescott's argument that the difference between the theory and the data is that we are not 'measuring' very well is remarkably Walrasian. In 1986, Prescott is arguing that we 'know' the model being presented is correct since it is the Solow growth model, and the comparison to the data is not meant to verify this fact (why verify what we know to be true?), but rather to see where we are not measuring things very well.

If we already know the theory to be true, why is a comparison of the model to US data interesting? Prescott declares that he and Kydland were simply following in the footsteps of Slutzky (1927) and Lucas (1977) in seeing how we can generate processes that resemble business cycle phenomena. However, there is no evidence of this link in the 1982 paper. Slutzky (1927) is not referenced at all in the 1982 paper and Lucas (1977) is not referenced in this context. Moreover, as a defense of real business cycle modeling techniques, Prescott is on shaky ground. Slutzky (1927) had no model; rather, he simply showed that random shocks can produce a series that looks cyclical. Lucas (1977) does indeed call for the study of business cycle phenomena and not just the path of an economy. But, Lucas mentions a broad set of statistics that are of interest.

> Those regularities which are observed are in the *co-movements* among different aggregative time series.
> The principal among these are the following. (i) Output movements across broadly defined sectors move together. (In Mitchell's terminology, they exhibit high *conformity;* in modern time series language, they have high *coherence.*) (ii) Production of producer and consumer durables exhibits much greater amplitude than does the production of nondurables. (iii) Production and prices of agricultural goods and natural resources have lower than average conformity. (iv) Business profits show high conformity and much greater amplitude than other series. (v) Prices generally are procyclical. (vi) Short-term interest rates are procyclical; long-term rates slightly so. (vii) Monetary aggregates and velocity measures are procyclical.
> (Lucas, 1977, p. 9)

Prescott rather selectively chooses from that list; indeed, despite claiming that he is following Lucas 'in defining the business cycle phenomena as the recurrent fluctuations of output about trend and the co-movements among other aggregate time series' (Prescott, 1986a, p. 10), he proceeds to build a model in which *none* of Lucas' seven regularities can appear. The closest Prescott's model can come to any of Lucas' seven regularities is that the relative volatility of consumption and investment can be compared; since consumption is less durable than investment in the model, this is *similar,* but not identical, to Lucas' second regularity. Prescott offers no reason for changing the set of regularities to be considered. In fact, since Prescott has not followed Lucas in defining the set of interesting statistics a business cycle model should replicate, there is absolutely no explanation in this paper for why Prescott has chosen the statistics he has as the interesting ones to consider.

Thus, in 1986, the real business cycle model is defended on the grounds that it is simply the application of the standard long-run growth model to the short run. There is no defense of the use of growth theory; there is no defense of the practice of calibration; there is no defense of the lack of a 'test' of the model. Instead, real business cycle models are justified on the grounds that they are nothing exceptional, that the theory is so manifestly true that 'if the economy did not display the business cycle phenomena, there would be a puzzle' (Prescott, 1986a, p. 21).

3.4 *Kydland & Prescott (1990)*

The 1986 justification of real business cycle models was not persuasive to many economists. Mankiw, in a 1989 *Journal of Economic Perspectives* article, provided a prominent summary statement of the criticisms of real business cycle models. First, Mankiw argued that there were two criteria on which one could judge a model: internal consistency (does the model cohere as a model?) and external consistency (does the model fit the facts of the real world?). He argued that most economists wanted a model with at least some external consistency, and that real business cycle models aimed only for internal consistency. If one wants a model that fits the facts, Mankiw argued, then the real business cycle model was not terribly interesting.

Moreover, Mankiw demolished Prescott's 1986 argument that it was reasonable and indeed benign to simply see how far you could go using the long-run growth model to explore short-run fluctuations. Mankiw noted that most economists believe that the classical dichotomy holds in the long-run, but not in the short run. The real business cycle use of a long-run model with the classical dichotomy built in to study a time frame which many do not think the classical dichotomy holds 'pushes the Walrasian model farther than it has been pushed before' (Mankiw, 1989, p. 81). Prescott's 1986 justification suddenly looked a lot less innocuous.

Faced with criticisms of this sort, Kydland and Prescott revamped the justification for the real business cycle model in their 1990 paper 'Business Cycles: Real Facts and a Monetary Myth.' The new justification reversed the roles of theory and evidence. In 1986, it was clearly theory that was foremost; Prescott argued that they were using a well tested theory and simply seeing what came out of it. In 1990, it is empirical evidence that is foremost; Kydland and Prescott argue that there was a set of facts that needed to be explained and a model was built to explain them. This new justification is in essence arguing that Mankiw could not be more wrong, that not only are real business cycle models externally consistent, but that the models were actually built for the sole purpose of being externally consistent.

Kydland & Prescott (1990) present a series of statistics they define as the 'business cycle facts.' Seemingly a dispassionate display of the facts of business cycle behavior, there is little doubt about what theory is being supported by the statistics reported; the content of the paper functions as a brief for real business cycle models. Kydland and Prescott report a series of facts, all of which are the sort of facts one would find if real business cycle models are correct. The clear implication of the paper is that real business cycle models were built specifically to explain this set of facts.

To get a set of business cycle facts, Kydland and Prescott must first determine the trend growth rate predicted by theory. From the 1986 paper, one might expect that the Solow–Swan growth model would be used to establish the trend. However, neither the growth model as described in Prescott's 1986 paper, nor the Solow–Swan growth model in general, is used at all. Instead the discussion of growth theory is a discussion of the merits of the Hodrick–Prescott filter (Hodrick & Prescott, 1997).[6] Does the Hodrick–Prescott filter yield the sort of growth path that would be predicted by the Solow–Swan growth model? Is the filter simply a quick statistical method of using that model, or 'steady state growth theory' more generally, to take out the trend? Kydland and Prescott do not address questions like that. Instead, they defend the use of the filter by noting, 'the implied trend path for the logarithm of real GNP is close to the one that students of business cycles and growth would draw through a time plot of this series' (Kydland & Prescott, 1990, p. 9).

The only further defense of this procedure offered up by Kydland and Prescott is seemingly innocuous:

> We have learned that this procedure for constructing a smooth curve through the data has a long history in both the actuarial and natural sciences. [Stephen] Stigler (1978) reports that actuarial scientists used this method in the 1920s. He also notes that John von Neumann, who undoubtedly reinvented it, used it in the ballistics literature in the early 1940s. That others facing similar problems developed this simple scheme attests to its reasonableness. What is surprising is that economists took so long to exploit this scheme and that so many of them were so hostile to the idea when it was finally introduced into economics.
>
> (Kydland & Prescott, 1990, p. 9)

This is a curious defense of using the Hodrick–Prescott filter to proxy for the long-run growth model. That one can draw a 'smooth curve through the data' is not particularly shocking, nor is it particularly relevant that in other fields, people draw smooth curves. The real issue is whether the curve so drawn means anything, whether the deviations of the line from the curve mean anything.

Kydland and Prescott have come a long way from Prescott (1986a). The whole notion that it is the well-tested growth theory that is being used in real business cycle models has vanished. Neither the trend nor the path of economic growth is derived by using anything resembling the Solow growth model at all. Solow's work is still important however, but in a different way altogether. Kydland & Prescott (1990, p. 4) highlight the procedure used by Solow: '[N]o one can deny that the reporting of growth facts has scientific value: Why else would Kuznets have received a Nobel Prize for this work? Or Solow, as well, for developing a parsimonious theory that rationalizes these facts—namely, his neoclassical growth model?' Kydland and Prescott thus argue that they first followed (Nobel meriting) Kuznets by establishing the facts and then they moved on to following (Nobel meriting) Solow by building a theory to fit those facts.

Kydland and Prescott are thereby arguing that real business cycle theory was developed to fit pre-established empirical regularities. Instead of discussing the history of the real business cycle theory, they focus on development of atheoretical techniques used to try to mimic the empirical regularities of the business cycle. Mitchell, Frisch and Slutzky are all discussed as first having seen some empirical regularities and then having tried to build a model to capture those regularities.

This intellectual history leaves a question which is begging to be answered. How is it that real business cycle models existed for eight years before the publication of the paper outlining the facts which they were allegedly built to explain? The obvious retort would be that researchers knew these facts as the model was being developed, but nobody had bothered to write a paper outlining all of them until 1990. But, this answer runs into the curious case of the cyclicality of the real wage.

Is the real wage procyclical? Summers (1986) had criticized real business cycle models for predicting procyclical real wages, when real wages are actually acyclical. Kydland & Prescott (1990, pp. 13–14) report the facts: 'This finding that the real wage behaves in a reasonably strong procyclical manner is counter to a widely held belief in the literature. [For a fairly recent expression of this belief, see the article by Lawrence Summers (1986, p. 25), which states that there is "no apparent procyclicality of real wages."]' Reading this, it appears that Kydland and Prescott were right to try and build models explaining a procyclical real wage and that critics like Summers were simply ignoring the facts.

But, Kydland & Prescott (1990) is not the first response to Summers (1986). Prescott (1986b) is a direct response to Summers' article, and in that paper, Prescott does not chide Summers for believing in acyclical real wages. Instead, Prescott (1986b, p. 28) wrote, 'As stated in the introduction of "Theory Ahead of Business Cycle Measurement"...the business cycle puzzle is, Why are there large movements in time allocated to market activities and little associated movements in the real wage, the price of people's time?...The behavior of these prices in our models conforms with that observed.' (This claim—that the model explains acyclical real wages—is made, however, with no presentation of the relevant values in either the 1986 or the 1982 paper.) And so, we have the following oddity: in 1986 Prescott argues real wages are acyclical and that that real business cycle models explain that fact; in 1990, Kydland and Prescott argue that real wages are *strongly* procyclical and chide people who think otherwise. How is it then that real business cycle models were built to explain previously known facts when those facts seem to have been unknown even to the people building the models?

Indeed this whole justification of real business cycle models as models that were built to explain the facts is quickly dropped. There is no further attempt in the literature to refine or verify the 'facts.' Indeed, by changing the method of taking out a trend, it turns out to be fairly simple to find a different set of 'facts' (see Pagan, 1997; Canova, 1998; and Hartley, 1999, for examples). The 1990 justification of real business cycle models was clearly incomplete, and thus it was not long before Kydland and Prescott offered another one.

3.5 Kydland & Prescott (1991a)

In 1991, Kydland and Prescott published 'The Econometrics of the General Equilibrium Approach to Business Cycles,' which was the first full articulation of the real business cycle program, tracing the intellectual heritage of these models. However, the heritage traced here is completely different from that suggested in Kydland and Prescott's three earlier papers. Here, they offer two new histories: (1) the real business cycle program is a natural extension of the Econometric Society's 1930s' work, particularly that of Frisch, and (2) the program is simply the application of computable general equilibrium models to business cycles.

The invocation of Frisch comes first. Right at the outset of the paper, Kydland and Prescott argue that both the substance (real shocks cause business cycles) and the method (calibration exercises) are outgrowths of what Frisch was doing in 1933 before the systems of equations people came along and took over macroeconomics. Now, with the death of the systems equations program, economists are returning to the methods developed by Frisch. In short, there is nothing particularly novel in the real business cycle program; it is merely the fulfillment of the Econometric Society dream, possible because of the development of mathematical techniques unavailable in the 1930s.

This justification of the real business cycle program is notable in two ways. First, the elevation of Frisch is striking. In their 1990 paper, Frisch is just one of four progenitors. Moreover, in 1990, Frisch's sole contribution is the introduction of the impulse-propagation language. Now, a year later, Frisch's importance has been increased manifold. It is no longer simply some terminology that he provided to the program, but the whole substance of the program as well. Similarly, comparing the 1982 real business cycle justification with the 1991 paper dramatically illustrates the change in emphasis that has been occurring. In 1982, the focus was on the propagation mechanism; the impulse was clearly of secondary importance. In 1991, the impulse mechanism has become the important part of the model; the propagation mechanism is clearly secondary.

This invocation of Frisch gives the real business cycle program a level of respectability and history it had heretofore lacked. The chief problem with the use of Frisch in this way is that it is a misreading of Frisch. Hoover (1995a) dissects Kydland and Prescott's claims of following in Frisch's footsteps and finds that real business cycle models bear little resemblance to Frisch's business cycle models. Specifically, the models Frisch was building were macroeconomic models, not microfoundational stochastic dynamic optimal growth models in which agents maximize subject to constraints, nor did Frisch advocate calibration-style methods as the sole preferred technique, but rather he used them simply for illustrative purposes (Hoover, 1995a, pp. 31–32).

But Kydland and Prescott do not stop at using Frisch to provide some heritage for their method; they also tag onto the developing computable general equilibrium program. Kydland and Prescott outline a quite scientific looking five-step method for doing economics: (1) Define a Question; (2) Specify a Model Economy; (3) Calibrate the Model; (4) Conduct Computational Experiments; and (5) Report the Findings. This outline is similar to the steps listed in papers that outline how to construct computable general equilibrium models (e.g., see Shoven & Whalley, 1984). Indeed, Kydland and Prescott clearly announce that they are trying to build on the computable general equilibrium work of Johansen (1960), Harberger (1962), Shoven & Whalley (1972) and Scarf (1973).

However, it is hard to believe that real business cycle models were developed as an explicit attempt to incorporate business cycles into computable general equilibrium models (CGEM). The 1982, 1986 and 1990 papers do not mention any of the four computable general equilibrium developers upon which Kydland and Prescott now argue they are building. Indeed, it is only now, a decade after Kydland and Prescott's first real business cycle paper, that this connection is mentioned and that this mechanical-sounding five step procedure is described. Indeed, as one of Prescott's colleagues at the University of Minnesota has noted in a discussion of the development of computable general equilibrium models, 'Parallel developments have taken place in macroeconomics, but apparently in complete isolation from those in the CGEM field. Kydland & Prescott (1982) introduced a method of 'calibration' for a macroeconomic model (though it is, and is described as, a general-equilibrium model, in the dynamic sense)...' (Chipman, 1996, p. 48).

Nevertheless, since Kydland and Prescott are now claiming that their model is in the computable general equilibrium family, it is worth making the comparison explicit. Hoover (1995a, pp. 27–28) makes exactly this comparison, concluding that Kydland and Prescott have not entirely adopted the computable general equilibrium method. Kydland and Prescott have much more casual parameter selection procedures, perfunctory robustness tests, and aggregation than the allowed standards accepted by computable general equilibrium researchers (e.g., Mansur & Whalley, 1994).

There is a deeper problem with this justification of real business cycle models than that they are simply not particularly good examples of CGE models. Even after we acknowledge the resemblance of Kydland and Prescott's method to that used by CGE researchers, we are still left with the question of whether the particular model being used by Kydland and Prescott is useful for answering the question they want to use it to answer. For example, the use of growth theory, and the Solow growth model in particular, is nowhere defended. Assuming everything Kydland and Prescott say about how to develop good models is true, there still needs to be some justification of why a model developed for use in explaining long run growth can be used to study short-run fluctuations.

Similarly, the question of selecting parameters for the calibration exercise is glossed over. In the debate between Prescott (1986a) and Summers (1986), the question of whether Prescott was using the right parameter values looms large. Yet Kydland & Prescott (1991, p. 170) simply declare that the necessary information can 'sometimes' be found in individual level data, 'in many other cases' from aggregate information, and 'in some cases' from 'dramatic price experiments' in history. They provide examples of how the parameters they need for calibration 'easily can be obtained' from the aggregate information and determined 'with a great deal of confidence' from historical episodes. But, as Shoven & Whalley (1992, p. 105) note, 'It is rather surprising how sparse (and sometimes contradictory) the literature is on some key elasticity values. And although this procedure might sound straightforward, it is often exceedingly difficult because each study is different from every other.'

So, how do Kydland and Prescott solve these problems? How do they choose which numbers to use when there is not a single, precise estimate of exactly the value they need? How do they know when the model is calibrated correctly; indeed, how do they know that the answer they get is reliable without knowing if the numbers used to calibrate it are correct? Kydland and Prescott give no answers to questions like these. It cannot be the case that Kydland and Prescott are simply relying on the case made for calibration in the computable general equilibrium literature. Shoven & Whalley (1984, p. 1020; 1992, pp. 105–106) list two reasons for the use of calibration in developing models: (1) in some computable general equilibrium models there are 'many thousands of parameters,' so estimation is infeasible; (2) much of the data used is only in value terms, and the need to separate out price and quantity measures makes it difficult to construct time series with consistent units. Neither of these two reasons applies to the sorts of parameters calibrated in real business cycle models; thus Kydland and Prescott need an additional justification.

As it is examined, this claim to a link between real business cycle models and computable general equilibrium models looks increasing tenuous. References to the real business cycle model are scarce in the computable general equilibrium literature. Ginsburgh & Keyzer (1997) have a short section on real business cycle models, but its tone is less than enthusiastic. They note that the original real business cycle models had no market imperfections, nor government intervention, concluding that the success of these models was 'modest' (Ginsburgh & Keyzer, 1997, p. 290). However, as they note, such things are being incorporated into models intended to explain the business cycle. But, they offer this conclusion:

> [T]axes and other distortions may undermine the single-agent construct that uses dynamic programming. One then has to cope with the Euler equations of every consumer separately and link these through capital accumulation and commodity balance equations. For this procedure one can use a grid or an approximation. Recall also that such imperfections can lead to indeterminacy of solutions, though this problem is neglected in the RBC literature.
>
> (Ginsburgh & Keyzer, 1997, p. 291)

In other words, real business cycle models might prove worthwhile if they start using the procedures commonly used by computable general equilibrium theorists and addressing the problems commonly addressed in that literature.

Kydland and Prescott's 1991 paper moved away from justifying real business cycle models as an interesting set of models and on to justifying them by the procedure used to develop them. But this first attempt to justify the procedure is far from complete, resembling something akin to computable general equilibrium on the cheap, and thereby raising more questions than it answered. Five years later, Kydland and Prescott wrote a similar paper, trying to fill in all these missing details.[7]

3.6 *Kydland & Prescott (1996)*

On a cursory reading, Kydland and Prescott's 1996 paper, 'The Computational Experiment: An Econometric Tool' is just a recapitulation of their 1991 paper. Both are intended to explain the procedure used in real business cycle work; both have a five-step procedure for doing economic research; both use business cycle research as an example of following the five-step procedure. However, on closer inspection, the papers are different in several, rather illuminating ways.

The first noticeable change from 1991 to 1996 comes in the five-step procedure advocated by Kydland and Prescott. While the number of steps stays the same, the actual steps change. The vacuous 'report the results' step from 1991 is dropped and a new step, 'Use a well-tested theory' is added between 'Pose the Question' and 'Construct a Model Economy.' This new step is a welcome addition. As we noted above, the 1991 paper gave absolutely no explanation for how one was to decide on what model economy to create; it gave no rationale for using growth theory as a basis for business cycle research. Indeed, by completely omitting any rationale for using growth theory, the 1991 paper seems logically disconnected from the 1986 and 1990 papers, both of which put growth theory at the centerpiece of the justification.

Thus, the 1996 paper can be read as bringing the 1991 paper back into line with Kydland and Prescott's earlier justifications. But does it provide a compelling rationale for using growth theory to study business cycles? The way the matter is raised is at first glance rather problematical. We are instructed to 'use a well-tested theory' to study economic questions, but there is absolutely no discussion of how to get a well-tested theory in the first place. Kydland & Prescott (1996, p. 72) argue: 'a researcher needs a theory that has been tested through use and found to provide reliable answers to a class of questions.' They go on to argue that the neoclassical growth model is such a 'well-tested theory' and thus is useful for studying business cycles.

But, what sort of tests does a theory have to pass to become 'well-tested'? How do we know the answers are 'reliable'? What is the standard? And why can we not just use those same standards and tests to study business cycles? The answers to questions like those are not hinted at in Kydland and Prescott's exposition. Indeed, as Kydland and Prescott expound upon this step, the whole procedure becomes more and more puzzling:

We recognize, of course, that although the economist should choose a well-tested theory, every theory has some issues and questions that it does not address well. In the case of neoclassical growth theory, for example, it fails spectacularly when used to address economic development issues. Differences in stocks of reproducible capital cannot account for international differences in per capita incomes. This does not preclude its usefulness in evaluating tax policies and in business cycle research.

(Kydland & Prescott, 1996, p. 72)

In short, it is hard to see what makes a theory 'well-tested' and it is even harder to see how Kydland and Prescott so confidently know which sort of questions the theory can be used to answer. In particular, since Kydland and Prescott readily admit that the Solow growth model 'fails' to explain development, it is not at all clear why they are certain it can be successful at explaining business cycles. After all, issues of development are rather closely linked to issues of economic growth, and the model's failure to explain development might give one pause before using it to examine other issues.

Moreover, we still do not have any explanation of the use of the Hodrick–Prescott filter as a proxy for a growth model in detrending data. Faced with criticisms such as those by Harvey & Jaegar (1993) and Cogley & Nason (1995) that, rather than mimicking the trend implied by growth theory, the Hodrick–Prescott filter actually generates business cycle dynamics regardless of whether or not they are in the data, Kydland and Prescott seemingly give up the attempt to defend their preferred filter:

> Given the finding that business cycle fluctuations are quantitatively just what neoclassical growth theory predicts, the resulting deviations from trend are nothing more than well-defined statistics. We emphasize that given the way the theory has developed, these statistics measure nothing. Business cycle theory treats growth and cycles as being integrated, not as the sum of two components driven by different factors. For that reason, talking about the resulting statistics as imposing spurious cycles makes no sense. The Hodrick–Prescott filter is simply a statistical decomposition that summarizes in a reasonable way what happens at business cycle frequencies.

(Kydland & Prescott, 1996, pp. 76–77a)

Now it is not obvious what Kydland and Prescott mean with this argument. But, whatever it means, it is very clear that Kydland and Prescott have radically altered their rationale for using the Hodrick–Prescott filter. In 1990, Kydland and Prescott argued for the need to use the Hodrick–Prescott filter on these grounds:

> Because economic activity in industrial market economies is characterized by sustained growth, Lucas defines business cycles as deviations of real gross national product (GNP) from trend rather than from some constant or

average value. But Lucas does not define *trend*, so his definition of business cycle deviations is incomplete. What guides our, and we think his, concept of trend is steady state growth theory.

(Kydland & Prescott, 1990, p. 8)

So, in 1990, it is clear that Kydland and Prescott think the Hodrick–Prescott filter is a proxy for the trend implied by steady-state growth theory. When pressed on the matter, however, Kydland and Prescott in 1996 retreat to saying that the Hodrick–Prescott filter is simply a statistical decomposition.

Another noticeable change between the 1991 and 1996 papers shows up in the discussion of calibration. While both papers have a calibration step, the rationale and method of calibration is rather different. In 1991, calibration involves obtaining information on selected parameters from individual data or studies in other areas of applied economics. As we noted above, this sort of procedure is fraught with problems because in many cases the requisite data do not exist and, in other cases, there are conflicting estimates. It is not clear in the 1991 paper how we know when a model has been calibrated properly. In 1996, however, Kydland & Prescott (1996, p. 74) offer up an explanation for how we know when the model is calibrated correctly: 'Thus, data are used to calibrate the model economy so that it mimics the world as closely as possible along a limited, but clearly specified, number of dimensions.'

While this is more detail than was offered in 1991, it is still insufficient to know what exactly this prescription means. How do we know what dimensions should be used for calibration? How do we know when we are close enough? How many dimensions should be used? Which dimensions should be used? When Kydland & Prescott (1996, p. 80) state, 'In calibration, we sometimes make the model economy inconsistent with the data on one dimension so it will be consistent on another,' how do we know how to implement this correctly; what is the weighting criterion by which the important dimensions can be determined? How do we determine if we are using the appropriate dimensions? In short, what exactly does a well-calibrated model look like and, once we have found it, how do we know what sorts of questions such a model can be usefully used to answer?

The weakness of Kydland and Prescott's defense of calibration is particularly striking. It is not the case that calibration is simply an indefensible procedure. Hoover (1995a) offers up a justification for the procedure that is vastly more complete than anything Kydland and Prescott offer. It is not surprising that Kydland and Prescott do not simply latch onto Hoover's defense; Hoover (1995a, p. 40) concludes by noting 'Although calibration is consistent with appealing accounts of the nature and role of models in science and economics, of their quanfication [*sic*] and idealization, its practical implementation in the service of real-business-cycle models with representative agents is less than compelling.' What is surprising is that Kydland and Prescott have never answered such charges, nor have they provided any other defense of the procedure they advocate.

While Kydland and Prescott's paper can be used to provide an explanation for what they have been doing, it does not justify the procedure at all. In the end, this paper turns out to be so much preaching to the choir. Kydland and Prescott seem to be aware of this fact. In a footnote (1996, p. 73n) they simply state: 'We will not debate the legitimacy of these methods, since such debates serve to define schools rather than to produce agreement.'

3.7 Confidence?

There has thus been a remarkable change over the years in the proffered justifications for real business cycle models and the real business cycle method. None of the interesting questions raised by the successive justifications were ever explored in more detail in Kydland and Prescott's programmatic manifestos. If time-to-build is crucial, why does it vanish? If the models are good because they build on established growth theory, why was there no move to use new growth theory? If the models were developed to explain business cycle facts, why is there no extensive search for the facts? If the models are simply meant to follow in Frisch's footsteps, why was there not a move toward macroeconomic models more like those used by Frisch? If the models are meant to be following the practice of computable general equilibrium theorists, why do the models retain the representative agent assumption instead of moving toward models with more complicated structures? If the trend is assumed to be explained by the Solow–Swan growth model, why is it removed with the atheoretical Hodrick–Prescott filter? And so on, and so on. While many of these issues were explored by others in the broader real business cycle literature, those explorations were never mentioned by Kydland and Prescott as advances in our understanding of the models; instead, Kydland and Prescott changed the agenda, generating a new set of rationales for the literature as a whole.

In the end, the rationales, the justifications, the methodology, are seemingly tacked on to the literature as so many afterthoughts—not really meant to be convincing in themselves, but rather to provide some respectability to those already convinced. Kydland & Prescott (1991, p. 171) argue, 'The issue of how confident we are in the econometric answer is a subtle one which cannot be resolved by computing some measure of how well the model economy mimics historical data. The degree of confidence in the answer depends on the confidence that is placed in the economic theory being used.' It seems that they could have added: the degree of confidence placed in the economic theory being used does not depend on whether the reasons we have offered for such confidence will hold up under scrutiny. All of which prompts the question: if one is not genetically disposed to placing confidence in real business cycle theory, what should convince one of its usefulness?

4 Conclusion

The story here may be nothing more than an example of the law of unintended consequences. In the mid-1970s, Kydland and Prescott set out to use optimal control theory in a rational expectations model, and ended up being credited with a sea change in the manner in which economists think about central banking. In the early 1980s, Kydland and Prescott set out to look at the effect of time-to-build and ended up being credited with a monumental change in the manner in which economists study the macroeconomy. The process by which this happened was described by that greatest of all economists, William Shakespeare:

> Our wills and fates do so contrary run,
> That our devices still are overthrown
> Our thoughts are ours, their ends none of our own.
>
> (*Hamlet*, Act 3, Scene 2)

Acknowledgment

I would like to thank Kevin Hoover, Thomas Mayer, and Stephen Perez for helpful comments and Batool Zaidi for assistance with the research.

Notes

1 The discussion is on Christian Zimmerman's Quantitative Macroeconomics and Real Business Cycle Home Page (http://ideas.uqam.ca/QMRBC/vote.html). For those interested, the proposed name DGE (dynamic general equilibrium) received the most votes. Nevertheless, that 'Kydland Prescott Model' was one of the seven choices reveals the close association of the program with Kydland and Prescott.
2 A discussion of the rationale for using representative agent models to study the macroeconomy is found in Hartley (1997) and a more general discussion of the methods used in the New Classical research program is found in Hoover (1988, 2001).
3 Similarly, Kydland and Prescott do not argue that their model is an outgrowth of any other particular growth model. Lucas (1975), for example, is mentioned only in a footnote in which they note that capital also plays an important role in Lucas' model but that Lucas' model has a crucial role for 'gradual diffusion of information,' which is not necessary in Kydland and Prescott's model.
4 The relative lack of importance of growth theory can also be implicitly seen in the above mentioned comparison of the time-to-build model to a model with no time-to-build. Both models have the same structure, and thus if the model with time-to-build is to be considered a growth model, then the model without time-to-build must also be considered a growth model, yet Kydland and Prescott argue that the model without time-to-build is 'inconsistent with the observations.'
5 Walras, for example, writes, 'Pure theory is the guiding light for applied theory.... When we have traced out the plan of a normal organization of production and distribution, we shall see clearly where the actual organization is satisfactory and where is it defective and must be modified' (quoted in Hutchison, 1953, p. 211).
6 The filter works as follows: a series y is broken into two parts, the trend component, g, and the cyclical component, c; so, $y_t = g_t + c_t$. The trend component is chosen to solve the following problem:

$$\underset{\{gt\}t=-1}{\text{Min}} \left\{ \sum_{t=1}^{T} c_t^2 + \lambda \sum_{t=1}^{T} [(g_t - g_{t-1}) - (g_{t-1} - g_{t-2})]^2 \right\}$$

The value of λ affects the smoothness of the trend; the larger the value of λ, the smoother the trend.

7 Some readers may wonder about the absence of an explicit discussion of Cooley & Prescott (1995) in this timeline. While that paper is an overview of the details of the real business cycle program, including a discussion of the canonical simplified model and an overview of the methods by which such models are solved and simulated, it is not a methodological defense of the research program, nor does it offer any insight into the reasoning behind the program that is not present in the papers discussed more fully in the methodological timeline presented here.

References

Auernheimer, L. (1974) The honest government's guide to the revenue from the creation of money, *Journal of Political Economy,* 82(3), pp. 598–606.

Barro, R. J. & Gordon, D. B. (1983a) A positive theory of monetary policy in a natural rate model, *Journal of Political Economy,* 91, pp. 589–610.

Barro, R. J. & Gordon, D. B. (1983b) Rules, discretion and reputation in a model of monetary policy, *Journal of Monetary Economics,* 12, pp. 101–121.

Böhm-Bawerk, E. von (1891) *Positive Theory of Capital,* trans. by W. Smart (London: Macmillan).

Blinder, A. S. (1998) *Central Banking in Theory and Practice* (Cambridge, Massachusetts: MIT Press).

Buchanan, J. M. (1975) The Samaritan's dilemma, in: E. Phelps (Ed.) *Altruism, Morality, and Economic Theory,* pp. 71–85 (New York: Russell Sage Foundation).

Calvo, G. (1978a) On the time consistency of optimal policy in a monetary economy, *Econometrica,* 46(6), pp. 1411–1428.

Calvo, G. (1978b) Optimal seigniorage from money creation: an analysis in terms of the optimum balance of payments deficit problem, *Journal of Monetary Economics,* 4(3), pp. 503–517.

Canova, F. (1998) Detrending and business cycle facts, *Journal of Monetary Economics,* 41, pp. 475–512.

Chipman, J. S. (1996) Empirical methods in computable-general-equilibrium modelling, in: E. S. de Dios & R. V. Fabella (Eds) *Choice, Growth and Development: Emerging and Enduring Issues: Essays in Honor of José Encarnación,* pp. 37–54 (Quezon City: University of the Philippines Press).

Cogley, T. & Nason, J. M. (1995) Effects of the Hodrick–Prescott filter on trend and difference stationary time series: implications for business cycle research, *Journal of Economic Dynamics and Control,* 19(1–2), pp. 253–278.

Cooley, T. F., (Ed.) (1995) *Frontiers of Business Cycle Research* (Princeton, New Jersey: Princeton University Press).

Cooley, T. F. & Prescott, E. C. (1995) Economic growth and business cycles, in: T. Cooley (Ed.), *Frontiers of Business Cycle Research* (Princeton, New Jersey: Princeton University Press), pp. 1–38.

Frisch, R. (1933) Propagation problems and impulse response problems in dynamic economics, in: *Economic Essays in Honour of Gustav Cassel: October 20th, 1933,* pp. 171–205 (London: George Allen and Unwin).

Ginsburgh, V. & Keyzer, M. (1997) *The Structure of Applied General Equilibrium Models* (Cambridge, Massachusetts: MIT Press).

Hansen, G. D. & Prescott, E. C. (1993) Did technology shocks cause the 1990–1991 recession? *American Economic Review,* 83(2), pp. 280–286.

Harberger, A. C. (1962) The incidence of the corporation income tax, *Journal of Political Economy,* 70(3), pp. 215–240.

Hartley, J. E. (1997) *The Representative Agent in Macroeconomics* (London: Routledge).

Hartley, J. E. (1999) Real myths and a monetary fact, *Applied Economics,* 31, pp. 1325–1329.

Hartley, J. E., Hoover, K. D. & Salyer, K. D. (Eds) (1998) *Real Business Cycles: A Reader* (London: Routledge).

Harvey, A. C. & Jaeger, A. (1993) Detrending, stylized facts and the business cycle, *Journal of Applied Econometrics,* 8, pp. 231–247.

Hodrick, R. J. & Prescott, E. C. (1997) Postwar U.S. business cycles: an empirical investigation, *Journal of Money, Credit, and Banking,* 29(1), pp. 1–16.

Hoover, K. D. (1988) *The New Classical Macroeconomics* (Oxford: Blackwell).

Hoover, K. D. (1995a) Facts and artifacts: calibration and the empirical assessment of real-business-cycle models, *Oxford Economic Papers,* 47(1), pp. 24–44.

Hoover, K. D. (Ed.), (1995b) *Macroeconometrics: Developments, Tensions, and Prospects* (Boston: Kluwer Academic Publishers).

Hoover, K. D. (2001) *The Methodology of Empirical Macroeconomics* (Cambridge: Cambridge University Press).

Hutchison, T. W. (1953) *A Review of Economic Doctrines, 1870–1929* (Oxford: Clarendon Press).

Johansen, L. (1960) *A Multi-Sectoral Study of Economic Growth* (Amsterdam: North-Holland).

King, R. G. & Rebelo, S. T. (1999) Resuscitating real business cycles, *Handbook of Macroeconomics,* volume 1, pp. 927–1007 (Amsterdam: Elsevier).

Kydland, F. E. & Prescott, E. C. (1974) Optimal stabilization: a new approach, *Proceedings of the Fifth Annual Conference on Modeling and Simulation,* Pittsburgh.

Kydland, F. E. & Prescott, E. C. (1977) Rules rather than discretion: the inconsistency of optimal plans, *Journal of Political Economy,* 83(3), pp. 473–493.

Kydland, F. E. & Prescott, E. C. (1980a) A competitive theory of fluctuations and the feasibility and desirability of stabilization policy, in: S. Fischer (Ed.) *Rational Expectations and Economic Policy,* pp. 169–187 (Chicago: University of Chicago Press).

Kydland, F. E. & Prescott, E. C. (1980b) Dynamic optimal taxation, rational expectations, and optimal control, *Journal of Economic Dynamics and Control,* 2(1), pp. 79–91.

Kydland, F. E. & Prescott, E. C. (1982) Time to build and aggregate fluctuations, *Econometrica,* 50(6), pp. 1345–1369.

Kydland, F. E. & Prescott, E. C. (1988) The workweek of capital and its cyclical implications, *Journal of Monetary Economics,* 21(2/3), pp. 343–360.

Kydland, F. E. & Prescott, E. C. (1990) Business cycles: real facts and a monetary myth, *Federal Reserve Bank of Minneapolis Quarterly Review,* 14(2), pp. 3–18.

Kydland, F. E. & Prescott, E. C. (1991a) The econometrics of the general equilibrium approach to business cycles, *Scandinavian Journal of Economics,* 93(2), pp. 161–178.

Kydland, F. E. & Prescott, E. C. (1991b) Hours and employment variation in business cycle theory, *Economic Theory,* 1(1), pp. 63–81.

Kydland, F. E. & Prescott, E. C. (1996) The computational experiment: an econometric tool, *Journal of Economic Perspectives,* 10(1), pp. 69–86.

Leamer, E. E. (1983) Let's take the con out of econometrics, *American Economic Review,* 91, pp. 31–43.

Lucas, R. E., Jr. (1975) An equilibrium model of the business cycle, *Journal of Political Economy,* 83, pp. 1113–1144.

Lucas, R. E., Jr. (1977) Understanding business cycles, in: K. Brunner & A. H. Meltzer (Eds), *Stabilization of the Domestic and International Economy,* pp. 7–29, Carnegie-Rochester Conference Series in Public Policy (Amsterdam: North Holland).

Lucas, R. E., Jr. (1987) *Models of Business Cycles* (Oxford: Basil Blackwell).

Mankiw, N. G. (1989) Real business cycles: a new Keynesian perspective, *Journal of Economic Perspectives,* 3(3), pp. 79–90.

Mansur, A. & Whalley, J. (1984) Numerical specification of applied general-equilibrium models: estimation, calibration, and data, in: H. E. Scarf & J. B. Shoven (Eds) *Applied General Equilibrium Analysis* (Cambridge: Cambridge University Press).

Mayer, T. (1995) The monetarist debate and the new methodology, *Doing Economic Research: Essays on the Applied Methodology of Economics,* pp. 73–91 (Aldershot, England: Edward Elgar).

Nobel Foundation (2004) Interview with Finn E. Kydland and Edward C. Prescott, http://nobel prize.org/economics/laureates/2004/kydland-interview.html.

Pagan, A. (1997) Policy, theory and the cycle, *Oxford Review of Economic Policy,* 13(3), pp. 19–33.

Prescott, E. C. (1986a) Theory ahead of business cycle measurement, *Federal Reserve Bank of Minneapolis Quarterly Review,* 10(4), pp. 9–22.

Prescott, E. C. (1986b) Response to a skeptic, *Federal Reserve Bank of Minneapolis Quarterly Review,* 10(4), pp. 28–33.

Rogoff, K. (1985) The optimal degree of commitment to an intermediate monetary target, *Quarterly Journal of Economics,* 100, pp. 1169–1189.

Royal Swedish Academy of Sciences (2004a) The Bank of Sweden Prize in Economic Sciences in Memory of Alfred Nobel 2004—Information for the Public, http://nobel-prize.org/economics/laureates/2004/public.html.

Royal Swedish Academy of Sciences (2004b) Press Release: The Bank of Sweden Prize in Economic Sciences in Memory of Alfred Nobel 2004, http://nobelprize.org/economics/laureates/2004/press.html.

Scarf, H. (with the collaboration of Hansen, T.) (1973) *Computation of Economic Equilibrium* (New Haven: Yale University Press).

Shoven, J. B. & Whalley, J. (1972) A general equilibrium calculation of the effects of differential taxation of income from capital in the U.S., *Journal of Public Economics,* 1(3/4), pp. 281–321.

Shoven, J. B. & Whalley, J. (1984) Applied general equilibrium models of taxation and international trade: an introduction and survey, *Journal of Economic Literature,* 22, pp. 1007–1051.

Shoven, J. B. & Whalley, J. (1992) *Applying General Equilibrium* (New York: Cambridge University Press).

Slutzky, E. (1927) The summation of random causes as the source of cyclic processes, in: *Problems of Economic Conditions,* Conjuncture Institute, Muskrat (Moscow), vol. 3, no. 1. Revised English version, 1937, in *Econometrica,* 5, pp. 105–146.

Solow, R. M. (1956) A contribution to the theory of economic growth, *Quarterly Journal of Economics,* 70(1), pp. 65–94.

Snowden, B. & Vane, H. (1999) *Conversations with Leading Economists* (Cheltenham, UK: Edward Elgar).

Stigler, S. M. (1978) Mathematical statistics in the early states, *Annals of Statistics,* 6, pp. 239–265.

Summers, L. H. (1986) Some skeptical observations on real business cycle theory, *Federal Reserve Bank of Minneapolis Quarterly Review,* 10(4), pp. 23–27.

Swan, T. W. (1956) Economic growth and capital accumulation, *Economic Record,* 32, pp. 334–361.

Walras, L. (1926 [1954] *Elements of Pure Economics,* trans, by W. Jaffe (London: George Allen & Unwin).

Weibull, J. (2004) The Bank of Sweden Prize in Economic Sciences in Memory of Alfred Nobel 2004, http://nobelprize.org/economics/laureates/2004/presentation-speech.html.

Principal work by Kydland & Prescott not referenced above

Finn E. Kydland

Backus, D. K., Kehoe, P. J. & Kydland, F. E. (1992) International real business cycles, *Journal of Political Economy,* 100(4), pp. 14–29.

Backus, D. K., Kehoe, P. J. & Kydland, F. E. (1994) Dynamics of the trade balance and the terms of trade: the J-curve? *American Economic Review,* 84(1), pp. 84–103.

Backus, D. K., Kehoe, P. J. & Kydland, F. E. (1995) International business cycles: theory and evidence, in: T. Cooley (Ed.) *Frontiers of Business Cycle Research,* pp. 331–356 (Princeton: Princeton University Press).

Bordo, M. D. & Kydland, F. E. (1995) The Gold Standard as a rule, *Explorations in Economic History,* 32(4), pp. 423–464.

Bordo, M.D. & Kydland, F. E. (1996) The Gold Standard as a commitment mechanism, in: T. Bayoumi, B. Eichengreen & M. P. Taylor (Eds) *Modern Perspectives on the Gold Standard,* pp. 55–100 (Cambridge: Cambridge University Press).

Dittmar, R. D., Gavin, W. T. & Kydland, F. E. (1999a) The inflation-output variability tradeoff and price-level targets, *Federal Reserve Bank of St. Louis Review,* 81(1), pp. 23–31.

Dittmar, R. D., Gavin, W. T. & Kydland, F. E. (1999b) Price-level uncertainty and inflation targeting, *Federal Reserve Bank of St. Louis Review,* 81(4), pp. 23–33.

Dittmar, R. D., Gavin, W. T. & Kydland, F. E. (2005) Inflation persistence and flexible prices, *International Economic Review,* 46(1), pp. 245–261.

Freeman, S. & Kydland, F. E. (2000) Monetary aggregates and output, *American Economic Review,* 90(5), pp. 1125–1135.

Hotz, V. J., Kydland, F. E. & Sedlacek, G. L. (1988) Intertemporal preferences and labor supply, *Econometrica,* 56(2), pp. 335–360.

Gavin, W. T. & Kydland, F. E. (1999) Endogenous money supply and the business cycle, *Review of Economic Dynamics,* 2(2), pp. 347–369.

Gavin, W. T. & Kydland, F. E. (2000) The nominal facts and the October 1979 policy change, *Federal Reserve Bank of St. Louis Review,* 82(6), pp. 39–61.

Gomme, P., Kydland, F. E. & Rupert, P. (2001) Home production meets time to build, *Journal of Political Economy,* 109(5), pp. 1115–1131.

Kydland, F. E. (1975) Noncooperative and dominant player solutions in discrete dynamic games, *International Economic Review,* 16(2), pp. 321–335.

Kydland, F. E. (1976) Decentralized stabilization policies: optimization and the assignment problem, *Annals of Economic and Social Measurement,* 5(2), pp. 249–261.

Kydland, F. E. (1977) Equilibrium solutions in dynamic dominant-player models, *Journal of Economic Theory,* 15(2), pp. 307–324.

Kydland, F. E. (1979) A dynamic dominant firm model of industry structure, *Scandinavian Journal of Economics,* 81(3), pp. 355–66.

Kydland, F. E. (1982) Predicting the price level in a world that changes all the time: a comment, *Carnegie-Rochester Conference Series on Public Policy,* 17, pp. 57–65.

Kydland, F. E. (1983) Implications of dynamic optimal taxation for the evolution of tax structures: a comment, *Public Choice,* 41(1), pp. 229–235.

Kydland, F. E. (1984) Labor-force heterogeneity and the business cycle, *Carnegie-Rochester Conference Series on Public Policy,* 21, pp. 173–208.

Kydland, F. E. (1989) Monetary policy in models with capital, in: F. van der Ploeg & A. de Zeeuw (Eds) *Dynamic Policy Games in Economics: Essays in Honour of Piet Verheyen* (Amsterdam: Elsevier), pp. 267–288.

Kydland, F. E. (1991a) Inflation, personal taxes, and real output: a dynamic analysis, *Journal of Money, Credit, and Banking,* 23(3), pp. 575–579.

Kydland, F. E. (1991b) Macroeconomic implications, in: R. W. Eberts & E. L. Groshen (Eds) *Structural Changes in US Labor Markets: Causes and Consequences* (Armonk, NY: Sharpe), pp. 207–213.

Kydland, F. E. (1992) On the econometrics of world business cycles, *European Economic Review,* 36(2–3), pp. 476–482.

Kydland, F. E. (1994) Heterogeneous agents in quantitative aggregate economic theory, *Journal of Economic Dynamics and Control,* 18(3–4), pp. 849–864.

Kydland, F. E. (1995a) Business cycles and aggregate labor market fluctuations, in: T. Cooley (Ed.) *Frontiers of Business Cycle Research* (Princeton: Princeton University Press), pp. 126–156.

Kydland, F. E. (1995b) Liquidity effects and transactions technologies: comment, *Journal of Money, Credit, and Banking,* 27(4), pp. 1458–1461.

Kydland, F. E. & Peterson, D. M. (1997) Does being different matter? *Federal Reserve Bank of Dallas Economic Review,* Third Quarter, pp. 2–11.

Kydland, F. E. & Wynne, M. A. (2002) Alternative monetary constitutions and the quest for price stability, *Federal Reserve Bank of Dallas Economic and Financial Policy Review,* 1(1).

Kydland, F. E. & Zarazaga, C. E. J. M. (1997) Is the business cycle of Argentina 'different'? *Federal Reserve Bank of Dallas Economic Review,* Fourth Quarter, pp. 21–36.

Kydland, F. E. & Zarazaga, C. E. J. M. (2002a) Argentina's lost decade, *Review of Economic Dynamics,* 5(1), pp. 152–165.

Kydland, F. E. & Zarazaga, C. E. J. M. (2002b) Argentina's recovery and excess capital shallowing of the 1990s, *Estudios de Economia,* 29(1), pp. 35–45.

Edward C. Prescott

Boyd, J. H. & Prescott, E. C. (1986) Financial intermediary-coalitions, *Journal of Economic Theory,* 38(2), pp. 211–232.

Boyd, J. H., Prescott, E. C. & Smith, B. D. (1988) Organizations in economic analysis, *Canadian Journal of Economics,* 21(3), pp. 477–491.

Chari, V. V., Kehoe, P. J. & Prescott, E. C. (1989) Time consistency and policy, in: Barro, R. J. (Ed.) *Modern Business Cycle Theory,* pp. 265–305 (Cambridge, MA: Harvard University Press).

Cole, H. L. & Prescott, E. C. (1997) Valuation equilibrium with clubs, *Journal of Economic Theory,* 74(1), pp. 19–39.

Cooley, T. F., Hansen, G. D. & Prescott, E. C. (1995) Equilibrium business cycles with idle resources and variable capacity utilization, *Economic Theory,* 6(1), pp. 35–49.

Cooley, T. F. & Prescott, E. C. (1973a) An adaptive regression model, *International Economic Review,* 14(2), pp. 364–371.

Cooley, T. F. & Prescott, E. C. (1973b) Tests of an adaptive regression model, *Review of Economics and Statistics,* 55(2), pp. 248–256.

Cooley, T. F. & Prescott, E. C. (1976) Estimation in the presence of stochastic parameter variation, *Econometrica,* 44(1), pp. 167–184.

Díaz-Giménez, J. & Prescott, E. C. (1997) Real returns on government debt: a general equilibrium quantitative exploration, *European Economic Review,* 41(1), pp. 115–137.

Díaz-Giménez, J., Prescott, E. C., Fitzgerald, T. & Alvarez, F. (1992) Banking in computable general equilibrium economies, *Journal of Economic Dynamics and Control,* 16(3/4), pp. 533–560.

Hansen, G. D. & Prescott, E. C. (1995) Recursive methods for computing equilibria of business cycle models, in: T. Cooley (Ed.) *Frontiers of Business Cycle Research* (Princeton: Princeton University Press), pp. 39–97.

Hansen, G. D. & Prescott, E. C. (2002) Malthus to Solow, *American Economic Review,* 92(4), pp. 1205–1217.

Hayashi, F. & Prescott, E. C. (2002) The 1990s in Japan: a lost decade, *Review of Economic Dynamics,* 5(1), pp. 206–235.

Hopenhayn, H. A. & Prescott, E. C. (1992) Stochastic monotonicity and stationary distributions for dynamic economies, *Econometrica,* 60(6), pp. 1387–1406.

Hornstein, A. & Prescott, E. C. (1991) Insurance contracts as commodities: a note, *Review of Economic Studies,* 58(5) pp. 917–928.

Hornstein, A. & Prescott, E. C. (1993) The firm and the plant in general equilibrium theory, in: R. Becker, M. Boldrin, R. Jones & W. Thomson (Eds) *General Equilibrium, Growth, and Trade. Volume 2. The Legacy of Lionel McKenzie,* pp. 393–410 (San Diego: Academic Press).

Imrohoroglu, A. & Prescott, E. C. (1991a) Evaluating the welfare effects of alternative monetary arrangements, (revised version of Imrohoroglu & Prescott (1991b)), *Federal Reserve Bank of Minneapolis Quarterly Review,* 15(3), pp. 3–10.

Imrohoroglu, A. & Prescott, E. C. (1991b) Seigniorage as a tax: a quantitative evaluation, *Journal of Money, Credit and Banking,* 23(3), pp. 462–475.

Kehoe, T. J., Levine, D. K. & Prescott, E. C. (2002) Lotteries, sunspots and incentive constraints, *Journal of Economic Theory,* 107(1), pp. 39–69.

Kehoe, T. J. & Prescott, E. C. (1995) The discipline of applied general equilibrium, *Economic Theory,* 6(1), pp. 1–11.

Kehoe, T. J. & Prescott, E. C. (2002) Great depressions of the 20th century, *Review of Economic Dynamics,* 5(1), pp. 1–18.

Lim, S. S., Prescott, E. C. & Sunder, S. (1994) Stationary solution to the overlapping generations model of fiat money: experimental evidence, *Empirical Economics,* 19(2), pp. 255–277.

Lucas, R. E., Jr. & Prescott, E. C. (1971) Investment under uncertainty, *Econometrica,* 39(5), pp. 659–681.

Lucas, R. E., Jr. & Prescott, E. C. (1974) Equilibrium search and unemployment, *Journal of Economic Theory,* 7(2), pp. 188–209.

Lucas, R. E., Jr. & Stokey, N. L. (with Prescott, E. C.) (1989) *Recursive Methods in Economic Dynamics* (Cambridge, MA: Harvard University Press).

Mehra, R. & Prescott, E. C. (1985) The equity premium: a puzzle, *Journal of Monetary Economics,* 15(2), pp. 145–161.

Mehra, R. & Prescott, E. C. (1988) The equity risk premium: a solution?, *Journal of Monetary Economics,* 22(1), pp. 133–136.

McGratten, E. R. & Prescott, E. C. (2000) Is the stock market overvalued?, *Federal Reserve Bank of Minneapolis Quarterly Review,* 24(4), pp. 20–40.

McGratten, E. R. & Prescott, E. C. (2003) Average debt and equity returns: puzzling? *American Economic Review,* 93(2), pp. 392–397.

McGratten, E. R. & Prescott, E. C. (2004) The 1929 stock market: Irving Fisher was right, *International Economic Review,* 45(4), pp. 991–1009.

Parente, S. L. & Prescott, E. C. (1992) Technology adoption and the mechanics of economic development, in: A. Cukierman, Z. Hercowitz & L. Leiderman (Eds) *Political Economy, Growth, and Business Cycles,* pp. 197–224 (Cambridge, Massachusetts: MIT Press).

Parente, S. L. & Prescott, E. C. (1993) Changes in the wealth of nations, *Federal Reserve Bank of Minneapolis Quarterly Review,* 17(2), pp. 3–16.

Parente, S. L. & Prescott, E. C. (1994) Barriers to technology adoption and development, *Journal of Political Economy,* 102(2), pp. 298–321.

Parente, S. L. & Prescott, E. C. (1999) Monopoly rights: a barrier to riches, *American Economic Review,* 89(5), pp. 1216–1233.

Parente, S. L. & Prescott, E. C. (2000) *Barriers to Riches* (Cambridge, MA: MIT Press).

Prescott, E. C. (1972) The multi-period control problem under uncertainty, *Econometrica,* 40(6), pp. 1043–1058.

Prescott, E. C. (1973) Market structure and monopoly profits: a dynamic theory, *Journal of Economic Theory,* 6, pp. 546–557.

Prescott, E. C. (1975) The efficiency of the natural rate, *Journal of Political Economy,* 83(6), pp. 1229–1236.

Prescott, E. C. (1977a) Should control theory be used for economic stabilization?, *Journal of Monetary Economics, Supplementary Series,* 7, pp. 12–38.

Prescott, E. C. (1977b) Should control theory be used for economic stabilization? a rejoinder, *Journal of Monetary Economics, Supplementary Series,* 7, pp. 101–102.

Prescott, E. C. (1987) A multiple means-of-payment model, in: W. A. Barnett & K. J. Singleton (Eds) *New Approaches to Monetary Economics,* pp. 42–51 (New York: Cambridge University Press).

Prescott, E. C. (1988) Robert M. Solow's neoclassical growth model: an influential contribution to economics, *Scandinavian Journal of Economics,* 90(1), pp. 7–12.

Prescott, E. C. (1997) On defining real consumption, *Federal Reserve Bank of St. Louis Review,* 79(3), pp. 47–53.

Prescott, E. C. (1998) Needed: a theory of total factor productivity, *International Economic Review,* 39, pp. 525–52.

Prescott, E. C. (1999) Some observations on the great depression, *Federal Reserve Bank of Minneapolis Quarterly Review,* 23(1), pp. 25–31.

Prescott, E. C. (2001) Business cycle research: methods and problems, in: Punzo, L. P. (Ed.) *Cycles, Growth and Structural Change: Theories and Empirical Evidence,* pp. 283–300 (London: Routledge).

Prescott, E. C. (2002) Richard T. Ely Lecture: prosperity and depression, *American Economic Review,* 92(2), pp. 1–15.

Prescott, E. C. (2004) Why do Americans work so much more than Europeans?, *Federal Reserve Bank of Minneapolis Quarterly Review,* 28(1), pp. 2–13.

Prescott, E. C. & Boyd, J. H. (1987a) Dynamic coalitions: engines of growth, *American Economic Review,* 77(2), pp. 63–67.

Prescott, E. C. & Boyd. J. H. (1987b) Dynamic coalitions, growth and the firm, in: E. C. Prescott & N. Wallace (Eds) *Contractual Arrangements for Intertemporal Trade,* pp. 146–160 (Minneapolis: University of Minnesota Press).

Prescott, E. C. & Lucas, R. E., Jr. (1972) A note on price systems in infinite dimensional space, *International Economic Review,* 13(2), pp. 416–422.

Prescott, E. C. & Mehra, R. (1980) Recursive competitive equilibrium: the case of homogenous households, *Econometrica,* 48(6), pp. 1365–1379.

Prescott, E. C. & Ríos-Rull, J.-V. (1992) Classical competitive analysis of economies with islands, *Journal of Economic Theory,* 57(1), pp. 73–98.

Prescott, E. C. & Shell, K. (2002) Introduction to sunspots and lotteries, *Journal of Economic Theory,* 107(1), pp. 1–10.

Prescott, E. C. & Townsend, R. M. (1984a) General competitive analysis in an economy with private information, *International Economic Review,* 25(1), pp. 1–20.

Prescott, E. C. & Townsend, R. M. (1984b) Pareto optima and competitive equilibria with adverse selection and moral hazard, *Econometrica,* 52(1), pp. 21–45.

Prescott, E. C. & Visscher, M. (1980a) Organization capital, *Journal of Political Economy,* 88(3), pp. 446–461.

Prescott, E. C. & Visscher, M. (1980b) Sequential location among firms with foresight, *Bell Journal of Economics,* 8(2), pp. 378–93.

13 Aumann and Schelling

Two approaches to game theory

S. Abu Turab Rizvi

'Aumann's and Schelling's Game Theory: The Nobel Prize in Economic Science, 2005' by S. Abu Turab Rizvi from *Review of Political Economy* (2007), Volume 19, Issue 3 (Taylor and Francis Ltd, http://www.informaworld.com), reprinted by permission of the publisher.

1 Introduction

The 2005 Nobel Prize in Economic Sciences was awarded to Robert Aumann and Thomas Schelling for contributions to 'our understanding of conflict and cooperation' by 'extending and applying game theory' (Royal Swedish Academy of Sciences, 2005a, p. 1(4)).[1] The citation pointed out the importance of Schelling's work on strategic aspects of negotiations, much of which was written against the backdrop of the Cold War. It also referred to Schelling's analysis of the aggregate patterns that can arise from individual behavior as in his model of residential segregation. Aumann's contribution is seen to rest with the explanation of cooperation in the long run, along with his explorations of common knowledge and correlated equilibrium. Both authors are cited for showing the logic behind seemingly irrational behavior.[2]

The awarding of the Nobel to Aumann and Schelling provides an occasion to explore their contributions to game theory.[3] Their work shows starkly contrasting styles about how to approach the study of strategic interaction. A discussion of their contributions therefore invites reflections on how best to proceed with game theory. Their work helps us answer the question – if you are going to do game theory, how should you do it? I begin with the issue of contrasting styles, to which I return following a discussion of the contributions of the two laureates.

2 Two contrasting styles

The usual paper in economics begins with the statement of a problem, followed by a review of the relevant literature. Then the economist develops a model (mathematical, econometric, or both) followed by its results. The economist then gives some applications and concludes with directions for further research. Schelling's method contrasts with this standard approach. He begins with illustrations and applications and never strays too far from everyday and policy topics, rarely using quantitative machinery.

> I always try to find something that I can put in the first paragraph to make the article sound interesting...that has been part of my style. I wrote a textbook in international economics that had about a dozen policy chapters. I tried to have the first page of every chapter present an interesting puzzle or phenomenon that would get the interest of the readers.
>
> (Steelman, 2005, p. 2)

This style reflects Schelling's priorities in keeping the analysis simple, accessible, and relevant. He would sooner be an economist who knows some game theory than a game theorist who happens also to be an economist; in his words, someone who is 'more interested in the mathematics aspect of the discipline than the social sciences aspect' (Steelman, 2005, p. 3). He advised his dissertation student Michael Spence, later a Nobel Prize winner, to keep his theoretical development (on excess competitive expenditure) brief, and to greatly multiply the number of examples in his articles and book (Steelman, 2005, p. 3).

One result of this style and focus has been Schelling's great influence outside of economics and, within economics, in encouraging a particular style of research.[4] As of late 2004, his work had garnered 6,767 citations, well ahead of the work of John Harsanyi, George Akerlof, Reinhard Selten, and Michael Spence, all of whom were awarded the Nobel before him (Klein *et al.*, 2005, pp. 160–161). Economists though were slow to appreciate his work. Indeed,

> In the normal pattern of intellectual development, information-based and game theory applications in economics, principally developments of the 1970s and 1980s, would have percolated slowly into neighboring disciplines...Schelling's work simply preempted the process by a few decades, contributing fundamental game theory insights to political science, psychology, and sociology long before economists found that conjectural equilibria and commitment difficulties were central to our science. Perhaps because he stayed away from the *Journal of Advanced Economic Gobbledygook,* Schelling's pathbreaking conceptual work received less attention from his home discipline than it deserved.
>
> (Zeckhauser, 1989, p. 154)[5]

Nor has Schelling's influence among his students proceeded in the way we might expect of a high-powered academic economist. While he has trained some well-known individuals (Michael Spence, Richard Nelson, and, less in the academic mold, Daniel Ellsberg), his main impact on students has been through his 'survey undergraduate course in "Conflict and Strategy," now approaching its 30th birthday, and his decade-old graduate course at the Kennedy School on the economic underpinnings of public policy formulation' (Zeckhauser, 1989, p. 154).[6] This is consistent with Schelling's accessibility and policy focus. Given

Harvard's central role in educating leaders in the academic, policy, legal, and financial fields, the influence of Schelling is widespread. Zeckhauser, speaking more personally, says that a 'semester with Thomas Schelling changed the way many of us thought about the world. At my 25th college reunion, the course was still the subject of discussion' (Zeckhauser, 1989, p. 155).

Robert Aumann's approach provides a deep contrast to Schelling's. Aumann was trained as a mathematician, receiving a PhD in algebraic topology from MIT. He had met John Nash there and they discussed the strategy of dueling. Aumann went next to Princeton for a post-doctoral fellowship to study operations research. He was presented a problem by Bell Labs on how to defend a city against a squadron of bombers, most of which were decoys, but some of which were armed with nuclear weapons. He remembered his conversation with Nash and began to study game theory, although for some time his main interest was in knot theory. After taking a job at Hebrew University, he was invited back to Princeton to take part in Oskar Morgenstern's research group, the Econometric Research Program (1960–1961). There he recalls meeting Clive Granger, Sidney Afriat, and Reinhard Selten, all of whom Morgenstern also brought to Princeton. At the end of this year, Princeton hosted the conference on 'Recent Developments in Game Theory,' for which Aumann served as an 'office boy.'[7] This explains how Aumann, a mathematician, became involved in game theory and economics.

Aumann has had 13 doctoral students, nearly all of whom have stayed in Israel. He describes his approach to selecting them:

> I always had a policy of taking only those students who seemed very, very good...capable as scientists and specifically as mathematicians. All of my students came from mathematics.
>
> (Hart, 2005, p. 41)

Aumann's favoring of mathematicians and the mathematical approach comes despite his feeling that game theory is the discipline that allows one to formalize the interactively rational part of a wide variety of fields – biology, chemistry, statistics, economics, law, computer science, political science, psychology, and mathematics, among them. It provides a global method rather than an approach to specific problems and constructs. Consequently, while it leaves many problems and issues in these fields untouched, it links the fields together through the development of interactive rationality:

> Unlike other approaches to disciplines like economics or political science, game theory does not use different, ad-hoc constructs to deal with various specific issues, such as perfect competition, monopoly, oligopoly, international trade, taxation, voting, deterrence, animal behavior, and so on. Rather, it develops methodologies that apply in principle to all interactive situations, then sees where these methodologies lead in each specific application.
>
> (Hart, 2005, p. 37)

For disciplines that have an interactively rational part, game theory provides a universal method. Because of this, in Aumann's view, game theory is best seen as being based on axioms in which rationality plays an important part. His method is to deduce conclusions from initial axioms and then apply these conclusions to particular situations. He does *not* seek to learn from specific situations and build a theory based on observation. In contrast to Schelling, the telling anecdote or application is not essential for Aumann. What matters for him is the rational, the interactive, and the formal core.

Whereas Schelling sees himself as an outsider to the main trends in modern game theory, Aumann is very much a part of it. He is the first and founding president of the Game Theory Society (established in 1999), a society he feels is important because 'Game theory has become a big discipline, or rather a big *inter-discipline*. It is time to have a tool for gathering game theorists in all kinds of senses. Conferences, journals, the Web' (Hart, 2005, p. 38). As such, Aumann has become a champion of the modern flowering of game theory, helping to organize conferences, reflect on the state of the discipline in positive terms, and to make large claims about the relevance of the field. The approach he takes is technical, mathematical, and deductive. Given that he argues that rationality is primary, interactive rationality is widespread, and so game theory finds very wide application. This approach differs markedly from the more literary and technically modest approach of Schelling.

3 Schelling's contributions

In writing about Schelling, Klein *et al.* (2005), and Dixit & Zeckhauser (1996), tend to highlight several of his books: *The Strategy of Conflict, Arms and Influence, Micromotives and Macrobehavior,* and *Choice and Consequence* (respectively 1960b, 1966, 1978, 1984a). The last two books are collections of essays from a diversity of sources. This supports the view that the nature of Schelling's influence might best be gauged by the broad array of topics he has addressed (Latzko, 1998, pp. 7–8).

There are three overlapping, organizing themes in Schelling's work (Latzko, 1998, pp. 7–8): strategy, choice, and policy. The strategic issues analyzed include arms control and other problems of the Cold War and nuclear age (Schelling, 1960a, 1960b, 1966, 1984 g, 1985/1986, 1987, 1989a, 1989b; Schelling & Halperin, 1961). The policy issues that Schelling addresses include organized crime (Schelling, 1967, 1984f), global warming (Schelling, 1990, 1992), energy (Schelling, 1979), environment (Schelling, 1983), foreign aid (Schelling, 1955), the valuation of human life (Schelling, 1968), residential segregation (Schelling, 1971a, 1971b, 1972), and the role of economics (Schelling, 1984b). The context of choice is explored in articles on self-command and addiction (Schelling, 1980, 1984c, 1984d) and consumption as a mental process (Schelling, 1984e). I consider only Schelling's work on self-command and on game theory below.

4 Schelling on self-command

Schelling's work on self-command shows how his approach diverges from standard consumer theory (Latzko, 1998, pp. 8–9). He sees an analogy between interactions among people and among different motives within a single person (Rizvi, 2001). In this sense, this work relates to the better-known concern with strategic interaction and game theory. Yet, the Nobel Prize citation does not mention Schelling's articles on intrapsychic phenomena, such as struggles over addiction and weakness of will.

Schelling's exploration of this topic flags an important theme in his work – that constraining one's options can be reasonable and even welfare enhancing. For example, a professor worries that he will spend too much money during the school year and has his university deduct current pay to be returned during the summer months, forgoing the interest on the deferred funds in the process. Schelling gives us a way to understand a wide range of phenomena, including ones as mundane as placing alarm clocks across the room from one's bed, to those as serious as addiction to cigarettes or overeating. He recognizes that it is rational to want, in one's present state of mind, to constrain future options, so that who we are in a future state of mind will not succeed in impeding our current goals. We do things now to frustrate ourselves in the future. This contrasts with the standard microeconomic analysis, where reduction of options is never welfare enhancing. In that view, if a choice set is smaller, achievable utility is constrained. However, for Schelling.

> This phenomenon of strategic interaction among alternating preferences is a significant part of most people's decisions and welfare [that] cannot be left out of our account of the consumer. We ignore too many important purposive behaviors if we insist on treating the consumer as having only values and preferences that are uniform over time, even short periods of time.
>
> (Schelling, 1984d, p. 5)

As Latzko (1998, p. 10) and Rizvi (2001) point out, Schelling's view opposes the idea that explanations based on changing preferences should be abjured by economists, as has been argued by Stigler & Becker (1977).

For Schelling, a unitary individual with an obvious objective function to maximize may not exist:

> I suggest that the ordinary human being is sometimes...not a single rational individual. Some of us...are more like a small collectivity than like the textbook consumer...'rational choice' has to be replaced with something like collective choice.
>
> (Schelling, 1984b, p. 93)

If humans are not *single* rational individuals, it is problematic to infer their welfare positions from their choice behavior (as in the revealed preference approach). Under the heading of the 'ethics of policy', Schelling discusses the vexed problem of whose welfare it is that policy should seek to advance – the smoker who is trying to quit or the smoker craving a cigarette? In this and more subtle cases, the presence in one individual of numerous motives vitiates the attempt to have a simple maximand for economic policy to address. The problems of social choice are reproduced even at the level of the individual.

5 Schelling on game theory

While the Nobel Committee did not single out his work on self-command, it did refer to Schelling's most influential book, *The Strategy of Conflict,* which analyzed strategic conflicts among nations at the height of the Cold War. A typical situation analyzed by Schelling involves a negotiation (Schelling, 1956; reprinted in Schelling, 1960b) in which the players want to press their advantages but also want to avoid a breakdown. This is what has been called 'a cooperative conflict'.

It was in this framework that Schelling originally came to the conclusion that restricting your options can be good for you. 'In bargaining, weakness is often strength, freedom may be freedom to capitulate, and to burn bridges behind may suffice to undo an opponent' (Schelling, 1960b, p. 22). If my adversary is convinced that I will not make a further concession, she will settle for what I am willing to accept, unhappy with the prospect of a breakdown in talks. Much depends on my ability to convince her that I cannot make further concessions.

Schelling (1960b, p. 81) observes, 'what one player *can* do to avert mutual damage will affect what another player *will* do to avert it.' He describes three ways to convince your opponent what you will do, each of which might involve restricting your options: making commitments, issuing threats, and making promises. Threatening a reprisal if a desired outcome does not materialize, or promising a concession if it does, can be effective ways of responding. Schelling emphasized that all of these actions must be *credible* and not subject to revision as might become expedient as events unfold. Contrary to the expectation that skilful negotiation requires concealment, commitments need to be made clearly and observation by the other side is important for them to be believed. If the US trade negotiator is bound by what Congress will approve, this strengthens her bargaining position. Or, if she is known for carrying out her threats, even ones that seem costly to her, her opponents are more likely to back down in the face of them.

Another contribution by Schelling concerns focal points. Strategic and other interactions notoriously have too many possible solutions. No player may have the ability to make one particular result come to be realized. Yet, it might be commonly known that a particular outcomes are focal – that is, they possess 'prominence, uniqueness, simplicity, or some rationale that makes them qualitatively differentiable' from the alternatives (Schelling, 1960b, p. 70), even if other outcomes are more efficient or advantageous. In the ultimatum bargaining game, an equal split can acquire focal status even though the two parties are not in equal positions. Here, players reject theoretically rationally preferable divisions, to the detriment of their financial interests. In discussing focal points, Schelling says

> My argument was that in overt negotiations something is required to get people to arrive at a common expectation of an outcome. And the ability to reach such a conclusion without communication suggested to me that there was a psychological phenomenon, even in explicit negotiations, which may work to focus bargainers eventually on that commonly expected outcome.
>
> (Steelman, 2005, p. 1)

In establishing the focal point concept, Schelling was an early proponent of conducting experiments in economics. In experiments involving his students, he was able to confirm a number of focusing mechanisms that allowed subjects to coordinate their expectations. The well-known example is that, in a certain milieu (prior to the use of mobile phones), if two people had not agreed where to meet in New York City, the focal outcome was to go the information desk at Grand Central Station.

Dixit & Zeckhauser (1996, pp. 267–269), in reviewing these contributions, point out that Schelling developed these concepts with the minimum of mathematical apparatus even though 'in modern game theory, few get far without displaying mathematical rigor.' Some of his concepts, though plausible and useful, rely on induction from a variety of circumstances, and are 'usually ignored or poorly treated in formal models.' Psychological phenomena and influences based on cultural factors are difficult to formalize.

At the same time, some of Schelling's ideas, for example credibility in its relation to subgame perfection, which requires that a player find no incentive to deviate from an equilibrium strategy, have been formalized (in this case by Reinhard Selten, another Nobel Prize winner). Dixit & Zeckhauser (1996, p. 269) conclude that Schelling 'can work intuitively, yet develop concepts that have broad generality, and that are ultimately addressed in mathematically rigorous form by others.'

Schelling's work raises the issue of whether and in what way mathematical formalization is necessary in economics for insight and relevance, even in a field as technical as game theory. His own approach has been decidedly 'low tech.' He does not keep up with modern game theory, sees himself as a social scientist rather than as a technical economist, saying that 'game theory is intellectually useful, but at the most elementary level' (Schelling, 1984a, p. 214). His library has only 12 books on game theory, of which he only finds a few useful, including Luce & Raiffa (1957), which is 'about the most useful book' he has read. Most of the other authors, Schelling says, 'are entranced by very sophisticated concepts, but it is hard for them to find any applications' (Aydinonot, 2005, p. 2).

While he does find some contemporary game theoretic work interesting, Schelling acknowledges that he simply may not understand much of it, and resists being made part of the modern revival of game theory, saying that 'people keep saying that game theory revolutionized economics in the last fifteen or twenty years. I really do not see that.' He prefers to point to work nearly 50 years old (Aydinonot, 2005, p. 2).

6 Aumann on repeated games

Aumann's Nobel Prize was awarded for his work on repeated games, in particular the use of mathematical technique to illuminate game theory, so as 'to develop concepts and hypotheses.' His work is credited with showing that 'peaceful cooperation is often an equilibrium solution in a repeated game, even between parties with strong short-run conflicts of interest,' and in demonstrating, in his work with Michael Maschler, that the analysis of repeated games may continue even with asymmetric (generally, incomplete) information where one party knows more than another about certain aspects of the repeated game. With his work on common knowledge, he has also helped to build the cognitive foundations of game theory; i.e., the implications of the parties' knowledge about aspects of the game including 'knowledge about each others' knowledge' (Royal Swedish Academy of Sciences, 2005a, p. 3(4)). 'Aumann's formalization of the concept of common knowledge allowed for the systematic analysis of the relation between the knowledge of the parties and the outcome of the game' (Royal Swedish Academy of Sciences, 2005a, p. 3(4)). Finally, the Nobel award statement refers to Aumann's concept of 'correlated equilibrium', of which Nash equilibrium is a special case. Interestingly, the statement makes no mention of Aumann's most heavily cited work, which is in general equilibrium theory rather than game theory and which characterizes the continuum of perfect competition and establishes equilibrium in this setting.[8] Aumann (1964, 1966) showed that the core of an economy is the same as the set of its competitive equilibria as long as agents in the economy are seen as being negligible. This led to a long program of research, associated with the name of Werner Hildenbrand, in general equilibrium theory on approximations to this ideal in what came to be known as large economies (see Rizvi, 2004).

Aumann's work in game theory has explored the underpinnings of work that has had great impact – the study of long-run cooperation (Aumann, 1981). Firms, individuals, and countries engage in repeated interactions, often of indefinite length. Threats, promises, retaliation, and contracts can all be understood as making sense when interaction is ongoing. The most common way to study ongoing interaction is through the repeated games framework in which the same players meet to play the same game over and over again. An example involves the well-known Prisoners' Dilemma game. In it, two players can play two pure strategies, indicating cooperation (C) or defection (D), which they choose simultaneously. Table 1 gives players' outcomes (in units), with the first payoff being that for the row player, with a < b < c < d.

The dominant strategy – the choice that yields a higher outcome no matter what the other player does – is D for each player. Yet both players are better off if they both play C. If the game is played once, the only Nash equilibrium is for both players to defect.

Yet cooperation may be sustained in every period if the game is repeated. Suppose the same two players meet to play the game repeatedly over an infinite future. They try to maximize the average payoff per game played over this future and they may discount future payoffs, so that more a distant payoff means less. In this setting, players may repay defection with lack of cooperation in future periods. The gain from defecting in a given round of play (i.e., d – b) may be outweighed by the loss of cooperation in the future. It will be easier to construct such a strategy if players care enough about future outcomes; that is, as long as they do not discount the future too much.

Aumann (1959) not only showed this was possible, he also proved a more encompassing result (Royal Swedish Academy of Sciences, 2005b). Call G* the supergame obtained by repeating the stage game, G. He showed that any average payoff that is feasible in G*, and that does not violate individual rationality (no player is assigned a payoff that is less than the lowest payoff which the player can receive in G), can be sustained as a Nash equilibrium in G*. He proved this in a setting in which there are many players and there can be deviations by groups of players. When the deviating group has just one member, the result is the Folk Theorem for repeated games, according to which the set of Nash equilibria of G* coincides with the set of individually rational and feasible payoffs. Feasibility means that the payoffs, one for each player, can be obtained as the convex combination of the pure strategies in G. Individual rationality means that no player receives a payoff that is lower than the lowest payoff the player could be held to in the stage game. While the Folk Theorem may seem surprising, it is important to remember that an infinite repetition of G allows for the discovery of responses to deviations from a given payoff vector that would sustain the payoff vector in question.

The Folk Theorem was a conjecture that was 'in the air' – part of the folk wisdom – among game theorists in the 1950s such as Schelling (1956) and Luce & Raiffa (1957). Luce & Raiffa felt that cooperation was possible if the game could be repeated enough times. Schelling (1956, p. 301) provided the intuition for such a result based on threats resulting from deviations: 'What makes many agreements enforceable is only the recognition of future opportunities for agreement that will be eliminated if mutual trust is not created and maintained, and whose value outweighs the momentary gain from cheating.' However, Aumann was able to state the result precisely and in a general way, and his statement allowed the development of mathematical approaches to repeated games (for example, Friedman, 1971).

Table 1 Prisoners' dilemma

	C	D
C	c,c	a,d
D	d,a	b,b

With Shapley, Aumann made another contribution to the analysis of repeated games containing complete information (Aumann & Shapley, 1976). Rubinstein (1976, 1979) came up a similar result. These works show that all feasible and individually-rational outcomes can be sustained, not just as Nash equilibria, but also as subgame perfect Nash equilibria. Subgame perfection makes the connection between the folk theorem and punishing deviations from a given line of play. In a subgame perfect equilibrium in this context, no player will find it profitable to deviate from punishing a player who deviates, or from punishing a player who deviates from punishing a player, and so on. Subgame perfection is a refinement of Nash equilibrium, and many Nash equilibria are not subgame perfect. Aumann & Shapley showed that if players discount future payoffs and maximize the expected present value of their payoff streams, the set of subgame perfect equilibria shrinks (Royal Swedish Academy of Sciences, 2005b). Even so, the Folk Theorem may be demonstrated in this setting.

We can assess the importance of the Folk Theorem. It asserts that if players are sufficiently patient, then any feasible and individually-rational payoffs can be supported by equilibrium. This shows that cooperation is indeed possible. Intuitively, players can make it not worthwhile for any player to deviate from cooperative play, given the infinite repetition of the stage game and the relevance of future stages. But this also establishes too much. Nearly any set of payoffs (with discount factors high enough) is an equilibrium outcome.

> The various folk theorems show that standard equilibrium concepts do very little to pin down play by patient players. In applying repeated games, economists typically focus on one of the efficient equilibria, usually a symmetric one. This is due in part to a general belief that players may coordinate on efficient equilibria, and in part to the belief that cooperation is particularly likely in repeated games. It is a troubling fact that at this point there is no accepted theoretical justification for assuming efficiency in this setting.
> (Fudenberg & Tirole, 1991, p. 160)

In other words, the theory of repeated games has shown the possibility but not the likelihood of cooperative play. The mathematization of an intuitive idea from 50 years ago has yielded very little definiteness. In Fudenberg and Tirole's view, the cooperative solution tends to be focused on because of the analyst's beliefs, beliefs that this is likely, and not on a deduction from axioms. It is nonetheless possible that even if behavior may not be deduced in this way, individuals may in fact cooperate, despite what game theory says. In experiments, individuals tend to cooperate even when they are told that there will be a finite number of repetitions of the stage game, although in this situation game theory predicts that defection will result. How might game theory be made consistent with this observation, which was accepted by Schelling, on the basis of common sense and observation rather than on deduction from axioms? One idea is to posit that players receive some satisfaction from cooperation that is not captured in the stated payoffs. While this 'does not seem implausible,' it 'is a bit too convenient, and seemingly much too powerful; once we admit the possibility that payoffs are known to be mis-specified, it is hard to see how any restrictions on the predicted outcome of the experiment could be obtained' (Fudenberg & Tirole, 1991, pp. 167–168). The method of proceeding inductively from experimental results and observation, while suggestive for those who would mathematize game theory, differs fundamentally from the mathematical solution. It is hard to see what basis there is for accepting or rejecting any number of observations and experimental results in an otherwise deductive framework, unless the reason is convenience or establishing a theoretically favored outcome.

It needs to be remembered that much of the work on game theory during the 1950s onwards was spurred by the Cold War.[9] Aumann, Michael Maschler, and Richard Stearns wrote a series of reports for government agencies and contractors in the 1960s on arms control negotiations. This work, though not collected and published until 1995 (Aumann & Maschler, 1995), was hard to obtain earlier. Aumann and his collaborators (Aumann & Maschler, 1966, 1967, 1968; Stearns, 1967; Aumann et al., 1968) explored repeated games with incomplete information – that is, when some or all of the players did not have knowledge of aspects of the underlying game. For example, the US might not know how many nuclear weapons the USSR had or how it viewed different proposals for arms control. Having such private information opens up the study of gains to be made by either hiding or revealing this information. Here, Aumann built on the work of Harsanyi, augmenting his other work on repeated games with complete information.

7 Aumann on common knowledge

Aumann (1976) is often credited with introducing the first formalization of the concept 'common knowledge' into economics. However, as Aumann acknowledges, the idea was earlier developed by the philosopher David Lewis (1969), who attributed it to Schelling (1960b).[10] Common knowledge differs from mutual knowledge. A fact is commonly known if every player knows it, every player knows that everyone knows it, and so on ad infinitum. An event is mutually known if every player knows it, with no further assumption that every player knows that everyone knows it, etc. Common knowledge is important in game theory for a number of reasons.

The main reason is that something like common knowledge seems to be involved in the reasoning that goes into figuring out how to play a game, particularly in figuring out how to play Nash equilibrium, the most popular equilibrium concept in game theory. (This section is based on Rizvi, 2004, pp. 31–36.) A player plays his part of a Nash equilibrium because he thinks the other player will play hers, which he believes since he thinks she thinks he is playing his part, and so on (Brandenburger, 1992, p. 90). Since this sounds like the definition of common knowledge, game theorists thought that common knowledge of strategies underpins Nash equilibrium (e.g., Kreps & Wilson, 1982, p. 885; Brandenburger & Dekel, 1989; Milgrom & Roberts, 1991, p. 82).

Not only did Aumann's (1976) paper lead game theorists to explore the relationships between knowledge assumptions and game solutions, Aumann himself contributed to this literature. The work of Aumann & Brandenburger (1995; a paper available since 1991) and Polak (1999) taught us that Nash equilibrium is tied to common knowledge in a less straightforward manner than was thought for much of the 1980s.

Nash equilibrium is a set of strategies, one for each player, such that each player's strategy is the best response for the player, given the strategies of the other players. Aumann & Brandenburger (1995, p. 1161) suppose that players are rational, know their own payoffs, and know the choices made by others. Then the players' choices of strategies will constitute a pure strategy Nash equilibrium, if one exists. Only the fact of rationality and mutual, not common, knowledge of choices needs to be assumed. Since Nash equilibrium in pure strategies need not exist in finite games, we need to turn our attention to mixed strategies, for which the existence of Nash equilibrium is guaranteed. In this more general setting, the requirement of common knowledge reappears. Mixed strategies are not straightforward. Their most compelling interpretation, since players do not seem to randomize, and they gain nothing by choosing a mixed strategy over a pure strategy, was proposed by Harsanyi (1973). In this view, the probabilities in the mixed strategy equilibrium are the conjectures players make about the actions of other players, the actions not being chosen by randomization. The equilibrium then involves knowledge of conjectures. When there are more than two players, the knowledge requirements increase significantly, and involve common knowledge. For a player's actions to be part of equilibrium, other players must have the same assessment of what that player will do. What guarantees this is the common prior assumption (CPA) and common knowledge of conjectures (Aumann & Brandenburger, 1995). Thus, common knowledge reappears in the justification of Nash equilibrium. Games cannot be limited to two people or to pure strategies. In the general case, common knowledge will be needed, along with mutual knowledge of the structure of the game and of the rationality of the players.

Aumann's formulation of common knowledge and its use in specifying the epistemic conditions needed for various solution concepts to be well founded raise several issues. All of these arise from the steep requirements imposed by the formalization of common knowledge. Thus, as Aumann & Brandenburger (1995) have shown, if common knowledge of conjectures is required for Nash equilibrium to be well founded, this seems too be too much knowledge for players to have. They must all know, know that each knows, know that each knows that each knows (and so on) what each conjectures each other's play to be. Not only is requiring this amount of knowledge implausible, the very implausibility suggests that this is, in fact, not how players proceed in interactive situations. Their own thinking cannot possibly be based on implausibly steep knowledge requirements. In this situation, the approach followed by Aumann and other game theorists may be less than useful. They have succeeded in showing that highly formal and mathematical game theory is not relevant for the study of actual choices of players. Instead, a more inductive approach, based on experiments and a more modest approach to the capabilities of players may be appropriate.[11] But, as Fudenberg & Tirole's (1991) comment suggests, it is hard to meld that more inductive approach with the deductive approach based on axioms.

Similar difficulties can be seen in Aumann's reliance on the CPA. It, too, shows the unpalatable choices faced by theorists concerned with formalizing knowledge. The CPA asserts that players have the same beliefs prior to receiving any information. Before Aumann used it, the CPA was employed by Harsanyi (1967, 1968a, 1968b), who relied on the work of Savage (1954). Given the CPA, differences in beliefs can be attributed to differences in information. (The following discussion is based on Rizvi, 2004, pp. 40–42). Gul (1998) has been critical of the CPA as an actual description of players' beliefs formation (see also Morris, 1995). Since players receive information throughout their lives, he finds it improbable that there is some common starting point for any group of players when they are blank slates waiting to be written on by information. Aumann (1998) concedes that this is a thought experiment, but holds that game theory is full of thought experiments used to underpin its procedures. This is true in economics more broadly. He points to the assumption of given preferences in microeconomics as an example of an implausible but useful assumption. That brings us to the second reason – beyond the claim that the CPA describes actual belief formation – for the use of the CPA. That is, the CPA is eminently useful; it is convenient for modeling purposes, as the large volume of work building on Harsanyi has shown (see the survey of Aumann & Heifetz, 2002). While consistent belief formation without the CPA is possible (Gul, 1998), such models are few and not tractable, so they are generally not used. Here, too, we find that a key construct used and defended by Aumann has led game theorists into an awkward corner.

Aumann's (1976) formalization of common knowledge was a means to an end. He wanted to demonstrate that it was impossible to 'agree to disagree.' Two agents beginning with a common prior may come across different information. We may then expect differences in their assessments of the probability of an event. For example, one agent might have private information about the prospects for a particular firm. On this basis, we intuitively expect the agent to have a different posterior probability for the firm's stock price going up. Aumann showed that if agents have a common prior and the posterior probabilities they assign to an event are common knowledge, the probabilities couldn't be different. Intuitively, what accounts for this result is that by acting on the basis of different information, the agents reveal it, leading others to revise their beliefs. This process results in posterior beliefs being the same.

Aumann's result has led to impasses in important areas of economic theory.[12] Directly influenced by the agreement result, Milgrom & Stokey (1982) published the first 'no-trade' theorem, which asserts that new information cannot spark trade among rational agents even if this information is asymmetrically held. It even turns out that the no-trade results arise in settings without the common prior assumption (Bacharach, 1985; McKelvey & Page, 1986; Dow *et al.*, 1990). The no-trade theorems are important because they run counter to the expectation that it is precisely heterogeneous beliefs about the value of an asset that leads to trade. If there were common posteriors about this value, there would be no trade on this account. Rather than providing an underpinning to an important empirical phenomenon, the no-trade theorems show that the formalization is incapable of capturing it. The theory fails to illuminate an important set of practices in the economy – it holds that they are impossible. Aumann's result is based on assumptions, of course, and it is possible to try to weaken the assumptions in order to avoid the result (Moscati, 2006, p. 8). The problem is that once the assumptions are weakened enough, tractability is often lost. For more on this issue, consult Samuelson (2004, pp. 379–381).

Moscati (2005) points out some other aspects of Aumann's work on knowledge that have received less attention. First, because Aumann's model of common knowledge was stated in set-theoretic terms, the implications of his assumptions for players' knowledge are not obvious (Milgrom, 1981, p. 220). Milgrom (1981) and Bacharach (1985) develop more intuitively clear models of common knowledge that are equivalent to Aumann's, but in which the implications for the reasoning abilities of agents are more evident. For example, Moscati (2005, pp. 12, 14) refers to Milgrom's model, in which it is shown that if one event is common knowledge and a second event logically follows from it, then the second event is also common knowledge. Thus, Aumann's players must have 'strong reasoning abilities.' Similarly, in Bacharach's model, agents must know the logical implications of everything they know. Moreover, agents are aware of all logical truths, that is, all propositions that are true in the world the modeler supposes. Thus, they are omniscient and not unaware of anything.[13] Bacharach (1985, p. 171) concludes that epistemic assumptions that are obscured by Aumann's formulation of common knowledge are 'unrealistically strong' and 'clearly describe hyper-rational persons' (Bacharach, 1985, pp. 189, 171) even while it is not clear how to proceed without losing the results that have been obtained in this setting (Moscati, 2005, p. 16).

We can see a clear pattern in the implications of Aumann's contributions on common knowledge. Agents have too much knowledge in a mixed strategy equilibrium, and differential information will not lead to exchanges, even while requiring that players begin with common information and assuming hyper-rationality on the part of the players. That is, the contributions not only ask for heroic assumptions, they also result in conclusions that are hard to make consistent with what we see in the world around us.

It should be pointed out that Aumann does not claim that actual agents possess common knowledge of, for example, rationality. He says, 'So CKR [common knowledge of rationality] is not 'justified.' It does not happen' (Van Damme, 1998, p. 207). But he holds it is important to study it, just as studying perfect gases and perfect competition is important, even if they do not exist, just to see what holds in an ideal state (Van Damme, 1998, p. 208). This would be a reasonable position if, when these ideal situations were approximately satisfied, the conclusions derived in these ideal states were approximately true. That is, if the ideal situations did not mislead you when you dealt with approximations to them. But Aumann (1992) himself shows that:

> departures from CKR can lead to behavior that is very different from that of CKR, for example in the centipede game. The departures from CKR are small both in the sense of being tiny probabilities and also in that the failure is at a high level of CKR. In other words, you get mutual knowledge of rationality to a high level, and after that level CKR fails only by a very small probability; and nevertheless, the results are very different from those under CKR.
>
> (Van Damme, 1998, p. 207)

Thus, Aumann's position is unsatisfactory. Similarly, Aumann (1992) has developed a model in which an agent has a non-zero chance of behaving irrationally. Other agents then find it rational to deviate from what otherwise would have been rational play. In this sense, in a particular case, Aumann is able to consider irrational play with the goal of addressing some paradoxes in backward induction (see Rizvi, 2004). But what this example does not resolve is the issue of how much irrationality may be introduced in an optimizing game theory framework before the framework loses its usefulness. This is a special concern since Aumann defines game theory as the interactively rational part of knowledge (Hart, 2005). Thus, while Aumann has made an interesting foray into the study of irrational behavior, he sticks more generally to models requiring rationality.

Finally, Aumann has been concerned with evaluating the state of game theory (Aumann, 2003). In a paper in which he answers the question 'What is game theory trying to accomplish?,' Aumann (1985, 1997) argues that game theory should be judged by how well it performs in applications. Thus, Nash equilibrium is to be judged highly because it is extensively used. Von Neumann and Morgenstern's stable sets are not as successful since they are difficult to calculate, cumbersome, and so are little used. He is not interested in refining game theory so that it more closely represents reality. He is interested in concepts that are more fecund in generating further research. This is a difficult position to accept for those who believe that economic theory should illuminate reality (see Rizvi, 1994a). More recently, Aumann has again refused to discriminate among competing concepts, arguing that as long as they are useful, they should be pursued. Asked if he should be interested in equilibrium concepts that select among multiple equilibria or in concepts, such as correlated equilibrium (Aumann, 1987), which 'coarsen' the set of equilibria (perhaps to include Nash equilibrium as a subcase), he replies:

> I love correlated equilibria and I also love subgame perfect equilibria; I have written papers, which I hope the world will enjoy, on both subjects…

So I do both, and I think that one 'should' not do this or that exclusively, but one should develop both concepts and see where they lead. There are important things to say about correlated equilibria and there are important things to say about subgame perfect equilibria. This idea that correlated equilibria represent the truth, or that subgame perfect equilibria represent the truth, is an idea that I reject.

(Van Damme, 1998, pp. 202–203)

8 Conclusion

Schelling and Aumann show two ways of approaching game theory: the inductive approach of Schelling, based on examples, experiments, and the embeddedness of agents in their surroundings and culture; and the deductive approach of Aumann, in which agent behavior is universal, based on the postulate of rationality, and can be deduced from a set of axioms.[14] I have tried to show that Aumann's approach has led to some notable dead ends in game theory and economics: while his general approach is successful in creating and sustaining a large research program, its progress in illuminating economic reality seems limited. The common knowledge formalization assumes hyper-rational agents. It leads to the impossibility of trade based on different information. It relies on an unrealistic assumption of common priors. And, when it is used to underpin the concept of Nash equilibrium, agents are supposed to have much more knowledge than is plausible. Yet agents, in experiments and in more natural settings, do seem to be able to find their ways in interactive situations. Thus, the deductive approach is unable to illuminate actual behaviors that call out for explanation. When we turn to the theory of repeated games, the Folk Theorem does show that cooperation is possible. But it shows much more than that. Since any individually rational and feasible pattern of payoffs is possible, there are too many equilibria, not just the ones with desirable theoretical rationales. The failure of the project of 'refining' these equilibria so that acceptable ones remain shows that this approach has not worked, either.[15] Aumann's work helps to show some of the many impasses that are faced by rational choice game theory.

But one might argue that Schelling's work can also be mathematized, and is not essentially different from Aumann's deductive approach. In fact, one might continue, Schelling's work complements Aumann's as follows. Innocenti (2007, pp. 5–6) traces this possible line of descent, showing how one might see Schelling's own work on common knowledge and tacit coordination as providing the intuitive background that was later formalized by others (Janssen, 2001; Sugden, 2001). Moreover, Schelling never seemed to discard the postulate of rationality, arguing for instance, 'The premise of 'rational behavior' is a potent one for the production of theory' and is helpful in many other ways (Schelling, 1960b, p. 4). In this way of viewing Schelling's work, the empirical and experimental flourishes are not essential to his way of proceeding, but merely show the broader application to which his work can be put.

Nevertheless, this interpretation seems to put some of Schelling's most sympathetic admirers ill at ease. Zeckhauser argues that:

> Schelling, in essence, plays his games in a world that is richer than most game theory analyses. He acknowledges that players may choose 'dominated' strategies not only to create reputations, but to adhere to ethics, build self-respect, or reflect generosity. To say that Schelling is merely exploring metagames, while perhaps technically correct, seems to miss the richness.
>
> (Zeckhauser, 1989, pp. 158–159)

Innocenti (2007) puts forward a convincing argument that is a variant of Zeckhauser's, to the extent that he also sees a 'richness' in Schelling's work that is difficult to formalize. He argues that Schelling's empiricism assumes that players are heterogeneous and so do not follow the same rules of inference in formulating strategies. They are instead embedded in real environments and the game solution is determined inductively from this situation. This way of looking at Schelling distinguishes his procedure from that of Aumann's deductive approach to game theory.

Notes

1 Schelling, now at the University of Maryland, taught at Harvard for most of his long career. Aumann teaches at Hebrew University of Jerusalem.

2 Aumann, however, seems quite hostile to explanations based on behavioral economics, holding that experimental settings are too artificial and that departures from rationality do not show up in empirical work (Hart, 2005, pp. 31–35). He has discussed irrationality in game theory, however, and I consider this work below.

3 Their other contributions that do not have a strategic (theoretic) component are not explored here for reasons of space. For a discussion of Schelling's relation to the Cold and Vietnam wars, see Sent (2007). Aydinonat (2007) investigates Schelling's model of residential segregation.

4 This style can also be confusing for those used to another way of writing. Innocenti (2007, p. 2) points out, 'Indeed, his books are so full of real people and case studies that one often gets the impression that the vast amount of telling anecdotes makes the reader miss the key point.'

5 I have argued for a distinct but compatible thesis, that game theory was ignored by economists while general equilibrium theory was dominant, but when the latter was seen to become stalled in the early and mid 1970s, game theory (and other aspects of economics) came to be embraced by the economics profession (Rizvi, 1994a).

6 Zeckhauser was writing at a time when Schelling was still at Harvard pursuing his long career there.

7 All of these biographical details are taken from Aumann's account in an interview with Hart (2005).

8 The lack of mention seems to be an indication of the increasingly bad odor in which general equilibrium theory has been held over the past 20 years, in an era in which game theory and other approaches are favored to it. The high level of citations reflects, however, the dominance of general equilibrium theory at a time when game theory was quiescent (see Rizvi, 1994b, for more on this argument).

9 Aumann says, 'It is difficult to imagine now how serious the Cold War was. People were really afraid that the world was coming to an end.' Harold Kuhn and Oskar

Morgenstern had started a consulting firm, Mathematica, in the early 1960s, and in 1964, it started to work for the US Arms Control and Disarmament Agency. Aumann and Mike Maschler were involved with Mathematica and saw repeated negotiations as repeated games. This thought inspired the work referred to in this paragraph (Hart, 2005, p. 9).

10 Surprisingly, Lewis and Aumann gave the concept 'common knowledge' the same name (Hart, 2005, p. 17).

11 This has been the view of Reinhard Selten for some time, in contrast to Aumann's (Selten, 1985). Selten's first publication was an experimental study of oligopoly, he was an early admirer of Herbert Simon, and he wrote in his autobiographical comments upon winning the Nobel Prize that 'At the University of Bonn my work [for the past 10 years] and that of most of my assistants is concentrated on experimental economics. It is our goal to help to build up a descriptive branch of decision and game theory which takes the limited rationality of human behavior seriously' (Selten, 1994).

12 Aumann recalls that the agreement theorem came out of conversations with Frank Hahn and Kenneth Arrow. When he showed the result to Arrow, however, Arrow would not believe, initially, that it was true. This shows the extent to which the agreement theorem is unsettling to economic theory (Hart, 2005, p. 17)

13 The study of models in which agents may be unaware of something is in its infancy.

14 It has been argued, however, that Schelling's involvement with the Vietnam War did not show this embeddedness and that his approach was too abstract to understand the true costs of the strategies he proposed. See Sent (2007).

15 Norde *et al.* (1996). For more on this, see Rizvi (2005).

References

Aumann, R. (1959) Acceptable points in general cooperative n–person games, in: A. W. Tucker & R. D. Luce (Eds) *Contributions to the Theory of Games IV,* pp. 287–324 (Princeton: Princeton University Press).

Aumann, R. (1964) Markets with a continuum of traders, *Econometrica,* 32, pp. 39–50.

Aumann, R. (1966) Existence of competitive equilibria in markets with a continuum of traders, *Econometrica,* 34, pp. 1–17.

Aumann, R. (1976) Agreeing to disagree, *Annals of Statistics,* 4, pp. 1236–1239.

Aumann, R. (1981) Survey of repeated games, in: V. Böhm (Ed.) *Essays in Game Theory and Mathematical Economics in Honor of Oskar Morgenstern, Vol. 4* (Mannheim: Bibliographisches Institut).

Aumann, R. (1985) What is game theory trying to accomplish?, in: K. Arrow & S. Honkapohja (Eds) *Frontiers of Economics,* pp. 28–76 (Oxford: Basil Blackwell).

Aumann, R. (1987) Correlated equilibrium as an expression of Bayesian rationality, *Econometrica,* 55, pp. 1–18.

Aumann, R. (1992) Irrationality in game theory, in: P. Dasgupta, D. Gale, O. Hart & E. Maskin (Eds) *Economic Analysis of Markets and Games: Essays in Honor of Frank Hahn,* pp. 214–227 (Cambridge & London: MIT Press).

Aumann, R. (1997) On the state of the art in game theory, an interview, in: W. Albers, W. Güth, P. Hammerstein, B. Moldovanu & E. van Damme (Eds) *Understanding Strategic Interaction: Essays in Honor of Reinhard Selten,* pp. 8–34 (Berlin: Springer). Reprinted in *Games and Economic Behavior,* 24 (1998), pp. 181–210.

Aumann, R. (1998) Common priors: a reply to Gul, *Econometrica,* 66, pp. 929–938.

Aumann, R. (2003) Presidential address, *Games and Economic Behavior,* 45, pp. 2–14.

Aumann, R. & Brandenburger, A. (1995) Epistemic conditions for Nash equilibrium, *Econometrica,* 63, pp. 1161–1180.

Aumann, R. & Hart, S. (Eds) (1992, 1994, 2002) *Handbook of Game Theory with Economic Applications,* 3 Vols (Amsterdam: Elsevier).

Aumann, R. & Heifetz, A. (2002) Incomplete information, in: R. Aumann & S. Hart (Eds) *Handbook of Game Theory with Economic Applications, Vol. 3* (Amsterdam: Elsevier).

Aumann R. & Maschler, M. (1966) Game theoretic aspects of gradual disarmament, Report ST-80 (Princeton, NJ: Mathematica Inc).

Aumann R. & Maschler, M. (1967) Repeated games with incomplete information: a survey of recent results, Report 116 (Princeton, NJ: Mathematica Inc).

Aumann R. & Maschler, M. (1968) Repeated games of incomplete information, the zero–sum extensive case, Report 143 (Princeton, NJ: Mathematica Inc).

Aumann R. & Maschler, M. (1995) *Repeated Games with Incomplete Information* (Cambridge, MA: MIT Press).

Aumann R., M. Maschler, M. & Stearns, R. (1968) Repeated games of incomplete information: an approach to the non-zero sum case, in: *Report of the U.S. Arms Control and Disarmament Agency ST-143,* pp. 117–216.

Aumann R. & Shapley, L. (1976) Long-term competition: a game theoretic analysis, Hebrew University mimeo. Reprinted in N. Megiddo (Ed.) (1994) *Essays in Game Theory in Honor of Michael Maschler* (Berlin: Springer Verlag).

Aydinonat, N. (2005) An interview with T.C. Schelling: interpretation of game theory and the checkerboard model, *Economic Bulletin,* 2, pp. 1–7.

Aydinonat, N. (2007) Models, conjectures and exploration: an analysis of Schelling's checker board model of residential segregation, *Journal of Economic Methodology,* 14, pp. 429–454.

Bacharach, M. (1985) Some extensions to a claim of Aumann in an axiomatic model of knowledge, *Journal of Economic Theory,* 37, pp. 167–190.

Brandenburger, A. (1992) Knowledge and equilibrium in games, *Journal of Economic Perspectives.* 6, pp. 83–101.

Brandenburger, A. & Dekel, E. (1989) The role of common knowledge assumptions in game theory, in: F. Hahn (Ed.) *The Economics of Missing Markets, Information, and Games* (New York: Oxford University Press).

Dow, J., Madrigal, V. & Werlang, S.R. (1990) Preferences, common knowledge, and speculative trade, Working paper, Fundaçao Getulio Vargas, Rio de Janeiro.

Dixit, A. & Zeckhauser, R. (1996) Thomas Schelling, in: W. J. Samuels (Ed.) *American Economists of the Late Twentieth Century* (Brookfield, VT: Edward Elgar).

Friedman J. (1971) A non-cooperative equilibrium for supergames, *Review of Economic Studies,* 38, pp. 1–12.

Fudenberg D. & Tirole, J. (1991) *Game Theory* (Cambridge, MA: MIT Press).

Gul, F. (1998) A comment on Aumann's Bayesian view, *Econometrica,* 66, pp. 923–928.

Harsanyi, J. (1967) Games with incomplete information played by 'Bayesian' players, I: the basic model, *Management Science,* 14, pp. 159–182.

Harsanyi, J. (1968a) Games with incomplete information played by 'Bayesian' players, II: Bayesian equilibrium points, *Management Science,* 14, pp. 320–324.

Harsanyi, J. (1968b) Games with incomplete information played by 'Bayesian' players, III: the basic probability distribution of the game, *Management Science,* 14, pp. 486–502.

Harsanyi, J. (1973) Games with randomly disturbed payoffs: a new rationale for mixed-strategy equilibrium points, *International Journal of Game Theory,* 2, pp. 1–23.

Hart, S. (2005) An interview with Robert Aumann. http://www.ma.huji.ac.il/~hart/papers/md–aumann.pdf

Innocenti, A. (2007) Player heterogeneity and empiricism in Schelling, *Journal of Economic Methodology* (forthcoming).

Janssen, M. (2001) Rationalizing focal points, *Theory and Decision,* 50, pp. 119–148.

Klein, D.B., Cowen, T. & Kuran, T. (2005) Salute to Schelling, keeping it human, *Econ Journal Watch,* 2, pp. 159–164.

Kreps, D. & Wilson, R. (1982) Sequential equilibria, *Econometrica,* 50, pp. 863–894.

Latzko, D. (1998) Thomas Schelling's dissent from the narrow scope of economics, in: R. Holt & S. Pressman (Eds) *Economics and it Discontents: Twentieth Century Dissenting Economists* (Cheltenham, UK: Edward Elgar).

Lewis, D. (1969) *Convention: A Philosophical Study* (Cambridge, MA: Harvard University Press).

Luce, R. & Raiffa, D. (1957) *Games and Decisions: Introduction and Critical Survey* (New York: Wiley).

McKelvey, R.D. & Page, R.T. (1986) Common knowledge, consensus, and aggregate information, *Econometrica,* 54, pp. 109–127.

Milgrom, P. (1981) An axiomatic characterization of common knowledge, *Econometrica,* 49, pp. 215–218.

Milgrom, P. & Roberts, J. (1991) Adaptive and sophisticated learning in normal form games, *Games and Economic Behavior,* 3, pp. 82–100.

Milgrom, P. & Stokey, N. (1982) Information trade and common knowledge, *Journal of Economic Theory,* 26, pp. 17–27.

Morris, S. (1995) The common prior assumption in economic theory, *Economics and Philosophy,* 11, pp. 227–253.

Moscati, I. (2005) Models for common knowledge. Working Paper, Bocconi University, Milan.

Nash, J. (1950) The Bargaining Problem, *Econometrica,* 18, pp. 155–162.

Nash, J. (1953) Two-person cooperative games, *Econometrica,* 21, pp. 128–140.

Norde, H., Potters, J., Reynierse, H. & Vermeulen, D. (1996) Equilibrium selection and consistency, *Games and Economic Behavior,* 12, pp. 219–225.

Polak, B. (1999) Epistemic conditions for Nash equilibrium, and common knowledge of rationality, *Econometrica,* 66, pp. 673–676.

Rizvi, S.A.T. (1994a) Game theory to the rescue?, *Contributions to Political Economy,* 13, pp. 1–28.

Rizvi, S.A.T. (1994b) The microfoundations project in general equilibrium theory, *Cambridge Journal of Economics,* 18, pp. 357–377.

Rizvi, S.A.T. (2001) Preference formation and the axioms of choice, *Review of Political Economy,* 13, pp. 141–159.

Rizvi, S.A.T. (2004) Deception and game theory, in: C. Gerschlager (Ed.) *Deception in Markets: An Economic Analysis* (London: Palgrave).

Rizvi, S.A.T. (2005) Experimentation, general equilibrium and games, in: P. Fontaine & R. Leonard (Eds) *The Experiment in the History of Economics* (London: Routledge).

Royal Swedish Academy of Sciences (2005a) The Prize in Economic Sciences 2005. www.kva.se.

Royal Swedish Academy of Sciences (2005b) Robert Aumann's and Thomas Schelling's Contributions to Game Theory: Analyses of Conflict and Cooperation. www.kva.se.

Rubinstein A. (1976) Equilibrium in supergames, Center for Mathematical Economics and Game Theory, Hebrew University. First part reprinted in N Megiddo (Ed.) (1994) *Essays in Game Theory in Honor of Michael Maschler* (Berlin: Springer Verlag).

Rubinstein A. (1979) Equilibrium in supergames with the overtaking criterion, *Journal of Economic Theory*, 21, pp. 1–9.

Samuelson, L. (2004) Modeling knowledge in economic analysis, *Journal of Economic Literature*, 42, pp. 367–403.

Savage, L. (1954) *The Foundations of Statistics* (New York: Wiley).

Schelling, T. (1955) American foreign assistance, *World Politics*, 7, pp. 606–626.

Schelling, T. (1956) An essay on bargaining, *American Economic Review*, 46, pp. 281–306.

Schelling, T. (1960a) Arms control: proposal for a special surveillance force, *World Politics*, 13, pp. 1–18.

Schelling, T. (1960b) *The Strategy of Conflict* (Cambridge, MA: Harvard University Press).

Schelling, T. (1966) *Arms and Influence* (New Haven, CT: Yale University Press).

Schelling, T. (1967) Economics and criminal enterprise, *Public Interest*, #7, Spring, pp. 61–78.

Schelling, T. (1968) The life you save may be your own, in: S. Chase, Jr. (Ed.) *Problems in Public Expenditure Analysis* (Washington, DC: Brookings Institution).

Schelling, T. (1971a) Dynamic models of segregation, *Journal of Mathematical Sociology*, 1, pp. 143–186.

Schelling, T. (1971b) On the ecology of micromotives, *Public Interest*, #25, pp. 61–98.

Schelling, T. (1972) A process of residential segregation: neighborhood tipping, in: A. Pascal (Ed.) *Racial Discrimination in Economic Life*, pp. 157–184 (Lexington, MA: D.C. Heath).

Schelling, T. (1978) *Micromotives and Macrobehavior* (New York: W.W. Norton).

Schelling, T. (1979) *Thinking through the Energy Problem* (New York: Committee for Economic Development).

Schelling, T. (1980) The intimate contest for self-command, *Public Interest*, #60, Summer, pp. 94–118.

Schelling, T. (1983) Prices as Regulatory Instruments, in: T. Schelling (Ed.), *Incentives for Environmental Regulation* (Cambridge, MA: MIT Press).

Schelling, T. (1984a) *Choice and Consequence* (Cambridge, MA & London: Harvard University Press).

Schelling, T. (1984b) Economic reasoning and the ethics of policy, in: *Choice and Consequence* (Cambridge, MA: Harvard University Press).

Schelling, T. (1984c) Ethics, law, and the exercise of self-command, in: *Choice and Consequence* (Cambridge, MA: Harvard University Press).

Schelling, T. (1984d) Self-command in practice, in policy, and in a theory of rational choice, *American Economic Review*, 74(2), pp. 1–11. Reprinted in Schelling (2006).

Schelling, T. (1984e) The mind as a consuming organ, in: *Choice and Consequence* (Cambridge, MA: Harvard University Press).

Schelling, T. (1984f) What is the business of organized crime? In: *Choice and Consequence* (Cambridge, MA: Harvard University Press).

Schelling, T. (1984g) Who will have the bomb? In: *Choice and Consequence* (Cambridge, MA: Harvard University Press).

Schelling, T. (1985/86) What went wrong with arms control?, *Foreign Affairs*, 64, pp. 219–233.

Schelling, T. (1987) Abolition of ballistic missiles, *International Security*, 12, pp. 179–183.

Schelling, T. (1989a) Are the superpowers moving toward new strategic policies and a new strategic relationship?, in: A. Clesse & T. Schelling (Eds) *The Western Community and the Gorbachev Challenge* (Baden-Baden: Nomos).

Schelling, T. (1989b) From an airport bench, *Bulletin of the Atomic Scientists,* 45, pp. 29–31.

Schelling, T. (1990) Global environmental forces, *Technological Forecasting and Social Change,* 38, pp. 257–264.

Schelling, T. (1992) Some economics of global warming, *American Economic Review,* 82(1), pp. 1–14.

Schelling, T. & Halperin, M. (1961) *Strategy and Arms Control* (New York: Twentieth Century Fund).

Selten, R. (1985) Comment to R.J. Aumann: what is game theory trying to accomplish?, in: K. Arrow & S. Honkapohja (Eds) *Frontiers of Economics* (Oxford & New York: Basil Blackwell).

Selten, R. (1994) Autobiography. http://nobelprize.org/nobel_prizes/economics/laurcates/1994/selten–autobio.html

Sent, E.-M. (2007) Some like it cold: Thomas Schelling as a cold warrior, *Journal of Economic Methodology,* 14, pp. 455–471.

Stearns R. (1967) A formal information concept for games with incomplete information. Report of the U.S. Arms Control and Disarmament Agency ST-116, Chapter IV, pp. 405–433.

Steelman, A. (2005) Interview: Thomas Schelling, Federal Reserve Bank of Richmond. www.richmondfed.org/publications/economic_research/region_focus/spring_2005/interview.cfm.

Stigler, G. & Becker, G. (1977) *De Gustibus Non Est Disputandum, American Economic Review,* 67, pp. 76–90.

Sugden, R. (2001) The evolutionary turn in game theory, *Journal of Economic Methodology,* 8, pp. 113–30.

Van Damme, E. (1998) On the state of the art in game theory: an interview with Robert Aumann, *Games and Economic Behavior,* 24, pp. 181–210.

Zeckhauser, R. (1989) Distinguished fellow: reflections on Thomas Schelling, *Journal of Economic Perspectives,* 3, pp. 153–164.

14 On the contributions of Barbara Bergmann to economics

Paulette I. Olson

'On the Economic Contributions of Barbara Bergmann to Economics' by Paulette Olson from *Review of Political Economy* (2007), Volume 19, Issue 4 (Taylor and Francis Ltd, http://www.informaworld.com), reprinted by permission of the publisher.

1 Introduction

Many in the economics profession would argue that Barbara Bergmann deserves the Nobel Prize for her extensive contributions to economics. Yet in its almost 40-year history, no woman has ever won the Prize, including Joan Robinson, one of the most prominent economists of the 20th century. Moreover, Dr Bergmann does not belong to the school of economic thought from which the majority of Nobel laureates have been selected; namely, the Chicago School.[1] She is not only an outspoken critic of the latter, she proudly claims the title of feminist economist—a research area that is rarely understood within the profession and often dismissed as political. In addition, she has questioned the reasons for the Nobel Prize in economics in the first place. She believes that it is disingenuous to award a Prize in Economic Science, because economics as currently practiced fails as a field of scientific inquiry. Rarely, she argues, does the Bank of Sweden award the honor to those who are the most deserving; namely, economists engaged in systematic observation of economic behavior such as Amartya Sen, Herbert Simon, and Gunnar Myrdal. According to Bergmann, the Nobel award:

> frequently occasions embarrassment, since we have to explain to the public what the achievement of the newest laureate is. That achievement is usually not the discovery of something previously unknown, like the form of DNA molecule or the genetic code. Rather, it is a totally made-up simplified representation of some process we all know takes place.
>
> (Bergmann, 1999b, pp. 52–53).

This quote and other such displays of irreverence in her work endears her to many in the profession who agree that the 'emperor wears no clothes' (Folbre,

1998, pp. 159–160). Yet it also dramatically reduces her chances of receiving the Nobel Prize.

Nevertheless, it is an important exercise to document Bergmann's life and work in the hope that someday the economics profession will eventually recognize her many important contributions to the Economic Science. To this end, an outline of her major contributions is presented below. We begin by presenting personal background information to provide the historical and social context for understanding Bergmann's subsequent research interests and priorities. Then we present a brief sketch of her theoretical framework and philosophical perspective. Section 4 details her critique of economic methodology together with an overview of her major contributions to economic methodology. Central to her work on methodology is a strong desire to make economics more policy-relevant by collecting meaningful data about economic actors as they conduct their affairs. The final section provides an outline of her major contributions in the development of a feminist analysis of labor markets and the family. The common thread that runs through Bergmann's work is a steadfast commitment to solving the problems of real people. For this reason, her work has inspired a generation of feminist economists dedicated to the pursuit of an emancipatory economic science.

2 Personal background[2]

Bergmann was born in the Bronx on July 20, 1927. Her father was born in the United States to immigrant parents from the Russian region of Poland while her mother was born in Romania and came to the United States around 1903 with her mother and four siblings. They settled in the lower East Side of Manhattan. Both sets of grandparents fled anti-Semitism in Eastern Europe. As children of immigrants, her parents were expected to earn their keep. In contrast, Barbara's generation—both boys and girls—were expected to succeed scholastically and financially. The boys were expected to become doctors and lawyers; the girls were expected to marry such professionals. Because New York City at the time provided tuition-free public colleges, this was not an unrealistic goal.

Both of her parents worked. Her father was a typographer. Throughout the Great Depression, he continued to earn a union wage of $50 a week. Nevertheless, she witnessed the humiliation and demoralizing effect of joblessness all around her. This experience inspired her later work on unemployment and poverty and convinced her that the government had an important role to play in assisting people under certain circumstances; when faced with problems beyond their control, or have legitimate needs that exceed their available resources.

Bergmann's later work on lone motherhood was influenced by another early experience. During World War II, her father became a merchant seaman and died from a heart attack aged 45. Her mother became a single mother while Barbara was still in high school. She would work her entire life.

Although Bergmann acknowledges that the market system often fails to meet the needs of everyone, she is mostly satisfied with the capitalist system, and argues for the limited role of government in the form of regulation and social safety nets. Accordingly, Bergmann considers herself a liberal or 'left of center.' But she has not always had liberal tendencies. She recalls at age 17 a more conservative mindset. From the vantage point of scholastic achievement and good career prospects, she began to fret about the government taxing away her riches and giving it to the undeserving poor. In retrospect, she refers to this period in her life as '...a brief spasm of immaturity and selfishness.'

Her contempt for Marxism is rooted in another childhood experience. Her sixth grade teacher, an avowed communist and '...a fanatical admirer of Stalin's Russia,' devoted much class time to Soviet accomplishments. When Bergmann's class was taken to World's Fair, they were forced to spend much of the day in the Russian pavilion. As a result of this experience, Bergmann equates Marxism with fanaticism and is suspect of anyone sympathetic with communism or communist regimes.

Bergmann's junior high school experience in Queens had a different learning outcome. It was here that her interest in mathematics was sparked. Although her mother wanted her to become a professional pianist for which she had the requisite talent, Barbara had other plans. After she graduated from Forest Hills High School, she applied to the engineering college at MIT much to the chagrin of the interviewer who reportedly denied her admittance. Luckily she had applied to Cornell University as well and was accepted on full scholarship, majoring in mathematics. At Cornell she also became interested in economics. She recalls reading Gunnar Myrdal's book, *An American Dilemma,* which explores race relations in the United States, influencing her later analysis of race-based discrimination. She graduated with a BA in mathematics and economics in 1948.

Bergmann's propensity for feminism was honed soon after graduation. Not only derided by her mother for not finding a husband at Cornell, she had the misfortune to graduate in the midst of a recession and had difficulty finding a job. She recalls having both sexism and anti-Semitism working against her. This influenced her later work on gender-based discrimination and occupational segregation. Jobs were segregated by sex and she was over-qualified for the traditionally female jobs being offered. Rather than settle, she continued to apply for male-defined jobs. When nothing materialized, she briefly worked as a typist and as a result of her mother's prodding attended the Teaching College at Columbia University. After a year, the federal government rescued her from its 'useless curriculum' and offered her a position at New York's Regional Office of the Bureau of Labor Statistics (BLS). She began her career in economics answering phones and addressing public inquiries about the Consumer Price Index. She was hired on the lowest rung of the professional career ladder, but was promoted several times and within two years became head of her unit.

At the BLS, Bergmann gained an appreciation for collecting and using data rather than relying solely on abstract modeling to explain economic phenomena. Her later work on racial discrimination was also informed by what she witnessed there. Although she promoted the only black employee in her unit, he was not allowed to sit in public view, and was soon replaced by someone else. When she visited the wage-survey division in Washington DC in 1962, in the midst of the civil rights movement, attitudes had not changed, and race-based job segregation was still common practice. Nevertheless, Bergmann heralds the capabilities and serious dedication of her colleagues at the BLS and challenges the claim that government workers are overpaid, inefficient, and unproductive.

It was also at the BLS that Bergmann was encouraged by a research economist to apply for graduate school. Accordingly, she applied to Harvard-Radcliff and was admitted on fellowship despite the disingenuous recommendation from her boss who failed to mention her intellectual acumen, but felt compelled to note that she was 'a young lady of culture and refinement.' Bergmann excelled at Harvard where she served as a teaching assistant for statistician and sociologist, Fred Mosteller, and for economists, Wassily Leontief and Franco Modigliani. Like most women in male-dominated fields, she lacked a mentor. However, she recalls being intellectually challenged by several professors in the graduate program. She credits Alvin Hansen for providing her with a firm grounding in Keynesian macroeconomics and Gottfried Haberler for influencing her highly accessible writing style. But the professors who had the greatest impact on her economic thinking were Edward Chamberlin and Guy Orcutt. Chamberlain was a pioneer in experimental economics and Orcutt was a pioneer in computer simulation of the macroeconomy.

At the dissertation stage, Bergmann worked with Edgar Hoover to produce an input–output model of the New York Metropolitan Area. She was awarded a PhD in 1959, and from 1958 to 1961 she worked at Harvard as an econ-math instructor. Between 1960 and 1961, she served as a senior research associate for the Harvard Economic Research Project. She eventually left Harvard to take a position as a senior staff economist for the Council of Economic Advisors in Washington DC during the Kennedy Administration. In 1962, she accepted an associate professor position at Brandeis University without tenure, and in 1963, she joined The Brookings Institution as a senior staff member, traveling to Peru and Bolivia as part of a research team studying the impact of highway investment on development. It was also during this time that she met her husband, Fred Heinz Bergmann, a genetic scientist at the National Institutes of Health. They were married in 1965.

By this time Barbara had accepted an associate professor position at the University of Maryland where she taught graduate courses in macro, micro, econometrics and other standard fare. During President Johnson's 'war on poverty,' Bergmann secured research funding to set up and direct the Project on the Economics of Discrimination at the University of Maryland and developed a course on poverty and discrimination; one of the first of its kind in the nation. In this pre-personal-computer era, she also introduced a course on computer methods in economics, sharing her passion for computer simulation with her students.

During an academic leave (1966–1967) to work at the Agency for International Development as a senior economic advisor, her child, Sarah, was born. David was adopted later. Like all working mothers, Bergmann faced the double burden of work and family. Because there were few childcare centers in the late

1960s, she hired a full-time housekeeper and childcare provider. This life-changing experience clearly influenced her later work on childcare issues.

As an academic, Bergmann always kept one foot in the policy-making arena. From 1977 to 1988, she served on the Congressional Budget Office Panel of Economic Advisors, and periodically testified before Congress on race and gender issues throughout the 1970s and 1980s. She also served on the board of directors for the Public Interest Economics Center (1975–1976), the American Economic Association Advisory Committee to the Census Bureau (1977–1982) and the Price Advisory Committee for the US Council on Wage and Price Stability (1979–1980). During the early 1980s, she became a regular contributor to the Sunday business section of the *New York Times,* writing on a variety of economic topics such as the Reagan recession, unemployment, social security, affirmative action, poverty and welfare reform. Her critique of economic methodology was also shared in these pages.

In addition to her government and academic work, she devoted enormous time and effort providing leadership and working with organizations on behalf of women. She served as a member of the Advisory Board to the Women's Law Project (1974–1980); as a Senior Research Associate at the Council on Contemporary Families (2003), as Vice President of the American Economic Association (1976); as Chair of the Committee for the Status of Women in the Economics Profession, as President of the Eastern Economic Association (1974), the American Association of University Professors (1990–1992), the Society for the Advancement of Socio-Economics (1994–1995), and the International Association for Feminist Economics (1998). She also served on numerous editorial boards and received many professional awards—most recently, the 2004 CSWEP Carolyn Shaw Bell Award. As testament to the interdisciplinary nature of her contributions to women's issues, in 2006 she was installed as a Charlotte Perkins Gilman Fellow by the American Academy of Political and Social Sciences.

In 1988, she left the University of Maryland as Professor Emerita to become a Distinguished Professor at American University. Today, she is a professor Emerita at both universities. She lives with her husband in Washington DC where she continues to publish and champion policies designed to help working women.

3 Theoretical underpinnings

Central to Bergmann's theoretical framework is the principle of equality; in particular, racial and gender equality. For Bergmann, the key to attaining equality is rooted in the job market. Everyone, regardless of race or gender, should be guaranteed access to decent paying jobs that support a family with dignity.

Bergmann's emphasis on labor market equality is consistent with the liberal feminist tradition in economics; in particular, the 19th century writings of Harriet Taylor and John Stuart Mill. Taylor and Mill employed utilitarian arguments in favor of equal rights for women under the law and linked women's roles as wife and mother and their resulting lack of occupational choice and low wages to their economic dependence on men (Pujol, 1992, pp. 23–37). Bergmann builds on this tradition by arguing in favor of state action in pursuing policies that ensure equal opportunity for all in the labor market.

The effect of racial inequality on black workers and urban communities figures prominently in Bergmann's early work. The main body of her work, however, focuses on the impact of gender inequality on women—as workers, wives and mothers. Gender inequality, for Bergmann, is located in an 'ancient system' of socially-sanctioned gender relationships based on male privilege and female subordination—what she calls a 'sex-role caste system' (Bergmann, 1986a, 2005b). Under this system, women were assigned familial roles and confined to the private sphere of the home. Men were assigned public roles in the 'male world' of work and politics. This meant that men and women had radically different lives and functions. While women were confined to a single occupation —that of housewife—men enjoyed a wide choice of lifestyles and occupations. According to Bergmann, although women have 'emerged' and felt freer to enter the 'male world' since World War II, the disappearance of the sex-role caste system is far from complete. Gender inequality in the labor market remains firmly entrenched as a result of lingering sexist attitudes about women's domestic roles and productive capabilities. Bergmann contends that those who benefit by keeping women occupationally segregated from men have little incentive to change their behavior (Bergmann, 1974e). Thus, she advocates for stronger enforcement of existing employment laws such as affirmative action and pay equity.[3]

Gender relations within the family also penalize women in the labor market. According to Bergmann, because of the tradition that men have little or no domestic responsibilities, wives and/or mothers who work face a double-burden that negatively impacts their labor market opportunities. The penalty for single working mothers is even greater. Lacking another adult person in the household to assume domestic tasks, the single mother bears the full double-burden of paid and unpaid work. Bergmann, therefore, sees an important role for government in giving working mothers the resources necessary to compete in the 'male world' on an equal footing with men, such as subsidized high-quality childcare and reliable child-support payments. Bergmann argues against initiatives designed to compensate housewives and paid parental leave because these initiatives reinforce the sex-role caste system. The housewife role is considered so disadvantageous to women that any effort that leads to its demise is more than welcome (Bergmann, 1982a, p. 230). Thus, she favors the outsourcing of housework and childcare, shifting these activities from the private to the public sphere (Bergmann, 1998a).

Bergmann's theory of a sex-role caste system is not limited to a feminist analysis of the labor market and the family. It is also used to analyze the economics profession. For Bergmann, the failure of 'non-feminist' economists to take seriously feminist claims of discrimination and unfairness in the labor market demonstrates their allegiance to the old regime. This allegiance is embedded in their theories; in particular, in their assumptions of rationality and perfect competition. Rational beings, such as employers, are posited as free from sexist baggage; if not, it is assumed they will be driven from the competitive marketplace by non-discriminating firms who hire cheaper but equally productive substitutes for white males. If an occupation is devoid of females, then it is assumed that either they are excluded by employers because of evidence of women's low productivity in that occupation or they have shunned the occupation as incompatible with their family responsibilities. As Bergmann points out, these assumptions are contradicted by the facts. Many successful firms have been convicted of long-standing discrimination in the courts (Bergmann, 1986a, 1996a, 2005b). For Bergmann, the secret of continued business success among discriminators is that their competitors discriminate too and that this behavior may result in increased profits (Bergmann, 1974e).

Bergmann also questions the emphasis on the role of 'choice' by mainstream economists. In mainstream accounts, women's choices are seen as powerfully conditioned by their household roles as wives and mothers. This leads to a view that women's inferior position in the labor market is biologically and socially determined and in no way connected to the discriminatory practices of employers or co-workers. Bergmann has a less benign view of women's 'choices.' She sees 'choice' as a process with feedback effects operating within an institutional framework of economic constraints. For instance, the higher turnover rates of women relative to men are interpreted by most economists as a sign that women have 'chosen' to devote more time to housewifery. For Bergmann, turnover rates are part of a vicious cycle whereby women are relegated to low-paying dead-end jobs with no penalty for high turnover and 'choose' to quit only to be re-employed in similar work (Bergmann & Adelman, 1983, p. 511). The combination of entry-level discrimination, irrelevant hiring criteria, sexual harassment and internal labor markets that govern promotions within firms likewise constrain the 'choice' of women workers. In addition, she sees the 'choice' for single working mothers between expensive childcare centers and unlicensed neighborhood providers as no choice at all. In her framework, the only economic actors enjoying the discretion of 'choice' are employers.

4 Methodological perspective

Throughout her professional career, Bergmann has repeatedly argued for a radical overhaul of economic methodology. What is particularly troubling to her is that virtually all economic 'knowledge' is the product of introspection. That is, economists construct their theories by sitting and mulling over a few factual tidbits they have gathered casually in the course of their everyday lives rather than seeking first-hand knowledge about their subject matter (Bergmann, 1987h, 1999b).

Bergmann's skepticism about economic theorizing began at Harvard in a course taught by Edward Chamberlain. His student-run market experiments challenged the 'holy grail' of economic thinking; namely, equilibrium under conditions of perfect competition. The experiments typically generated an average price different from the predicted equilibrium price. Bergmann learned the lesson that theory, no matter how logically tight, could misrepresent the actual functioning of the market. The following year she took statistics from Guy Orcutt who introduced her to computer simulation as a method for investigating the effects of public policy on household behavior. In both cases, the hook for Bergmann was the ability to explore complex explanations of real world phenomena (Olson & Emami, 2002, pp. 59–60).

Her skepticism grew when she was asked to testify as an expert witness in a lawsuit. Her task was to explain to the judge how an unfettered, competitive labor market was supposed to work. In the process of preparing for her court appearance, the attorney interrupted and asked how she knew the 'facts' she espoused. When Bergmann explained that it was 'agreed-upon theory,' the attorney was unsatisfied. Bergmann was told to testify in court that she had conducted many studies because the judge needed to be convinced that the methodology of economics was on par with that of other expert witnesses whose methodology is based on direct observation of their subject matter (Bergmann, 1987h, pp. 192–193). This experience made her realize that everything she knew about the labor market came from the private musings of economists, not from a systematic, first-hand study of workers or their employers.

Bergmann concluded that the failure of economics to advance like other sciences is rooted in the resistance by economists to adopt methods of direct observation of economic phenomena. She agrees that economic theories are often clever. But, for her, they are no substitute for direct empirical research (Bergmann, 1987h, p. 196). For one thing, theorizing is based on imagined scenarios and a standard set of assumptions about human rationality and avarice that often conflict with reality. For another, it is impossible to separate the low-quality musings from the high-quality musings in a way that would gain universal agreement within the profession. Despite these flaws, she argues, economists proceed to 'investigate' their factual tidbits by running regressions. In addition, they use mathematical notation to obscure the weak link between available data and the actual behavior the data are suppose to represent. The results of a regression are then used to bolster one theoretical argument over another. But truth is never revealed because it is often the case that empirical support provided by results is weak, inconclusive and easily countered by other regressions. Indeed, thousands of regressions are run as a technical exercise rather than as a sincere search for new knowledge. As Bergmann observes, regression running on sexy topics may boost the career prospects of individual economists who can show the existence of logical possibilities, but it fails to advance the 'science' of economics because it does little to increase the store of economic knowledge.

Bergmann has recently interpreted the resistance to adopt direct empirical methodology, especially in macroeconomics, as a political move (Bergmann, 2005d). She notes that data on important macroeconomics issues such as unemployment, inflation and international trade are scarce, indirect, and difficult to interpret. Thus, appeals to 'the evidence' will seldom yield decisive outcomes in settling controversies. This encourages macro theorists to champion far-fetched claims of knowledge and predictions. Politicians eager to find a theoretical justification for their policy positions are thus 'free to choose' among economists with a similar ideological bent. This process may advance the careers of those involved, but it does little to improve policy making or the workings of the economy.

Bergmann recognizes that the musings/regression methodology will be difficult, if not impossible, to eliminate unless something better is substituted. To this end, she has spent the better part of her research life exploring ways to improve economic methodology in an effort to make it more policy-relevant. Unlike other economists, her theoretical musings are consistently based on a wealth of primary data that she (and sometimes her students) have collected and analyzed. Particularly compelling is the data she derives from discrimination complaints filed with the Equal Employment Opportunity Commission to highlight the subtle and overt discriminatory practices that limit women's access to jobs and restrict their promotional opportunities within firms (Bergmann, 1986a, 1996a, 2005b). In addition, she applauds the use of 'situation tests' to identify systematic discrimination in housing and labor markets. This experimental method sends two people of different race/gender and claiming identical qualifications to apply for the same house or job (Bergmann, 1974c, 1996a, 2005d). She believes that the methods of economists should become more like those of anthropologists and other behavioral scientists who likewise study human behavior. She repeatedly notes the lack of information about the behavior of business people, but sees hope in the work of Alan Blinder who used survey methodology to investigate pricing decisions (Bergmann, 2005d, p. 12). Her view of behavioral and experimental economics is guarded because there is little if any direct observation involved. Instead, experiments are conducted in a laboratory using students as substitutes for real economic actors. Thus, she remains somewhat skeptical of this methodology (Bergmann, 2005d, pp. 11–12).

Bergmann has always approached economic problems using policy-relevant methodology. For example, in her 1969 examination of the 'urban crisis,' she developed an accounting system of complex relationships between the characteristics of an urban economy and its unique problems. These relationships were folded into an input–output model, highlighting the effects of economic activities by firms, households and government on the well-being of black residents, air quality and the fiscal sufficiency of the urban core. The accounting system offered a blueprint for reducing urban unemployment by making explicit employment patterns by industry. The significance of the accounting system, she notes, is not its use as a predictive system, but its use as a policy tool to show 'those interested in urban problems, including businessmen themselves, the way in which business behavior affects these problems' (Bergmann, 1969b, p. 645).

Perhaps Bergmann's least appreciated contribution is her pioneering work in computer simulation. A recent book about 'cutting edge' economists discusses current simulation models under development (Colander *et al.,* 2004). However, Bergmann's work dating back to the early 1970s is completely ignored. Free computer usage at the University of Maryland allowed her to set up a micro simulation of the labor market which she used in her graduate course and led to a host of articles explaining the usefulness of simulated markets in evaluating and formulating public policy (Bergmann, 1973b, 1973c, 1974a, 1974b, 1975c, 1977, 1980b, 1980c, 1982m, 1984c, 1987h, 1988b, 1990a, 1990b, 2005d, Eliasson *et al.*, 1977). For example, in *Econometrica,* Bergmann promotes the benefits of using small-scale micro-simulation as a tool for integrating theory with regressions (Bergmann, 1973c). While the subtext of the article is an examination of how unemployment rates, wage rates and turnover interact to contribute to the poverty rate among the working poor, the aim of the paper is to showcase the merits of 'prepared' over 'raw' regressions in improving predictability. According to Bergmann, the benefits of simulation over conventional methods are several: it 'prepares' the data for regressions by exploring for nonlinearities and variable interactions that are inherent in the phenomena under study; it may include the effects of additional explanatory variables when the number of observations is small; it is relatively easy to incorporate monthly, quarterly and/or annual data in the same simulation; and, more importantly, it can be designed to describe the complex processes of the economy in a more realistic way. The ease of adding complexity to a basic simulation framework not only provides a better understanding of the workings of the economy, thereby improving predictive accuracy, it also allows an economist to build on the work of others, a standard practice in other sciences.

Much of Bergmann's work with computer simulation techniques reflects her 12-year collaboration with Robert Bennett at the University of Maryland. Their book, *A Microsimulated Transactions Model of the United States Economy* (Bennett & Bergmann, 1986) extends microsimulation methodology by modeling the micro behavior of businesses, banks, a monetary authority, and government agencies in addition to household behavior, the focus of Orcutt's work (Orcutt *et al.*, 1976). Their aim is to develop a highly-useful, policy-relevant model of the macroeconomy based on microfoundations. The model is microsimulated in the sense that decision-making rules are specified for each economic actor, permitting the incorporation of rational as well as non-rational behavior discovered through direct observation. The model also keeps track and reports on the interactions among the various actors, reflecting the dynamic nature of real transactions and monetary flows. Individual transactions are then added up to get the macroeconomic totals for the hypothetical economy. These totals are then 'blown up' to the scale of the US economy. Bergmann notes that both the transaction and conventional macro models are limited as policy tools by the serious lack of micro data on business firms. The difference in how this limitation is treated by the two models, however, is instructive. In Bergmann's transactions model, it is transparent. In standard models, it is conveniently concealed in theories, macro equations and regression running (Bergmann & Bennett, 1984c, pp. 93–94).

Another example of Bergmann's policy-relevant methodology is her 'basic needs budget' approach (BNB) which she developed with Trudi Renwick to measure poverty in the US (Renwick & Bergmann, 1993). Unlike the official method, which calculates the poverty-line solely based on food expenditures, the BNB approach requires that the analyst specify and justify an adequacy standard for seven budget categories, including food, housing, health care, transportation, clothing, childcare, and personal care/miscellaneous. The BNB approach also adjusts for differences in family size, the employment status of parent(s), ages of the children, and geographic differences in the cost of living. Besides the family's budget expenses and tax obligations, the BNB method also accounts for the family's non-cash benefits available from public and private sources in response to conservative concerns that the official rate ignored food stamps and Medicaid benefits. The results of this approach led to a conclusion that the poverty line should be higher for families without a full-time caretaker and that the surest way to reduce poverty in the United States without reducing work or marriage incentives is to subsidize health insurance for all low-income families and childcare for their children under six.

5 Main contributions

The debates over the definition of structural unemployment, the urban crisis and the racial wage gap appears to have galvanized Bergmann's work on racial inequality (Bergmann, 1965a, 1967, 1969a, 1971a, 1971b, 1972, 1973f). Unlike her contemporaries, she offered a demand-side explanation of racial differences in unemployment and income. The main explanatory variable for Bergmann was racial discrimination. In the debate over wage determination, for example, she agreed that blacks possessed less education, training and experience than whites and that this may, in part, account for the black–white wage differential. But rather than blame the victim, she highlighted the impact of institutionalized racism in the US on the employment status of black men. Specifically, she calculated that the nation invested roughly $50 billion less on the human capital of adult black males relative to their white counterparts. This underinvestment was traced to school segregation and employment discrimination (Bergmann, 1969a). In another article, she showed that raced-based occupational segregation was greater in industries insulated from the open market, and in metropolitan areas in which fair employment laws had failed to pass. In other words, the lack of competitive pressure to lower labor costs and the prevalence of racist attitudes both helped to explain the discriminatory hiring practices of employers, and thus the low earnings of blacks. She also found evidence that efforts to curb the discriminatory behavior of employers had a greater payoff than efforts to improve black education, challenging human capital theory (Bergmann & Lyle, 1971b).

Bergmann first gained prominence by formalizing the 'crowding' hypothesis in a path-breaking article in the *Journal of Political Economy* (Bergmann, 1971a).[4] It posits that employers discriminate against blacks by excluding them from occupations reserved for whites. Because the demand for blacks in 'white jobs' is restricted, blacks are crowded into a comparable few jobs reserved for them. The overcrowding in these occupations drives down wages. For simplification, blacks and whites are assumed to have equal education and abilities.

Thus, without the existence of discrimination they would be paid equally. Bergmann then shows that blacks were indeed confined to a limited number of occupations and that occupational integration would have little effect on 'white' earnings. In a subsequent path-breaking article, she explored the effects of crowding on both blacks and women and found that discrimination is profitable if it is standard employment practice (Bergmann, 1974e). This finding challenges the conclusions of Becker's 'taste for discrimination' theory (Becker, 1957) that predicts market forces will eventually eliminate both hiring and pay discrimination because it is assumed unprofitable.[5] For Bergmann, discrimination is both rational and profitable.

The crowding theory of wage determination entered labor textbooks in its market-based form, featuring separate supply and demand curves by race and gender. But as a theory of wages, it never rivaled the 'taste for discrimination' theory in the mainstream literature for several reasons. First, discrimination is impossible to quantify, and second, a test of the hypothesis requires direct observation. Both are considered beyond the purview of economics. Consequently, economic journals continue to showcase regressions that solve for discrimination as an unexplained residual, after accounting for more 'legitimate' reasons for women's lower wages such as education, training and work experience. The 'crowding' hypothesis did, however, gain ground among feminist economists and other social scientists that recognized the radical implications of Bergmann's model. By making 'discrimination' explicit, Bergmann pointed the way towards a feminist understanding of how gender- and race-based labor markets are socially constructed. Thereafter, the discriminatory process and its effects became the focus of studying women's disadvantaged position in the labor market. For this reason, Bergmann is often considered a pioneer in the development of feminist analysis of the labor market. Feminist scholars in various disciplines, armed with large data sets, have extended her analysis of race- and gender-based wage differentials and have often used the results to advocate for pay equity (Ferber & Lowry, 1976; Treiman & Hartmann, 1981; Reskin, 1984; Reskin & Hartmann, 1986; Jacobs & Steinberg, 1990; England, 1992; Sorenson, 1994; Figart & Lapidus, 1995; Lapidus & Figart, 1998; Gibson *et al.,* 1998).

Bergmann's most important contribution to economics is her comprehensive treatise, *The Economic Emergence of Women* (Bergmann, 1986a, 2005b). It was one of the first books of its kind, examining the evolution of women's dual careers as homemakers and labor-force participants. It also contains Bergmann's policy recommendations for achieving an equitable future such as pay equity, affirmative action and childcare assistance. The recent publication of the second edition attests to its continued popularity among a variety of disciplines.

According to Bergmann, women's economic emergence into the workforce is the result of economic forces set in motion by the industrial revolution; namely, technological change and capital accumulation. These forces, in turn, led to a long-term rise in the real wage. This meant that, from a family perspective, women's time became too valuable to be spent entirely in the home. The important role played by social and demographic factors in women's emergence is also emphasized such as lower birthrates, higher educational attainment, higher divorce rates, older age at marriage and other changes in social norms. The result of the interplay of all these factors is that working women rather than housewives are now the social norm. A reversal of this trend is, for Bergmann, highly unlikely.

The book also provides a historical and social context for further discussion of the 'crowding' hypothesis. For Bergmann, job segregation by gender is not a neutral or benign process. Rather it is rooted in history, tradition and misogyny. Historically, women entered the labor market when almost all jobs, except domestic servant, were reserved for men. Through tradition, paid work was defined as a 'male' arena unfit for respectable women. In addition, misogynous behavior within the labor market operates to exclude women from jobs that would make them equal or superior to men. Together these processes explain the overcrowding of women into a limited number of jobs defined as female. Crowding does more than lower the wages in occupations traditionally held by women. In addition, it lowers women's pay in jobs that are mixed-sex and mostly male; it prevents women from accumulating human capital and experience which allow them to earn better wages; and since overcrowding reduces the productivity of women's labor, overall efficiency is lower than would exist in a single sex-blind labor market (Bergmann, 2005b, pp. 89, 98). Occupational segregation also sets up a vicious cycle by reinforcing misinformed beliefs about differences in women's capabilities, preferences, and social roles. For Bergmann, government action is required to ensure occupational integration to mitigate these effects such as affirmative action policies.

Indeed, Bergmann is not shy about tackling controversial policy issues like affirmative action. Her book, *In Defense of Affirmative Action,* has been widely reviewed and discussed in both scholarly and popular outlets such as *The New Yorker* (Wolfe, 1996) and *The New York Times Book Review* (Berman, 1996). In this provocative book, she confronts the conservative opponents of affirmative action head on (Bergmann, 1996a). As the title suggests, her main thesis is that affirmative action is necessary and justified as a policy tool to prevent current discrimination and to eradicate inequality based on race and gender. As always, she uses ample documentation and supportive materials to challenge the claim that affirmative action is unnecessary because discrimination no longer exists. She examines and responds to various opposing arguments with deftness and calm logic. For example, she questions the logic behind the opposition to affirmative action that sees 'merit' as the single most important criteria for deciding employment, promotions and college admissions by pointing to examples of long-standing preferences to which almost no one objects, including, among others, veteran benefits, bosses hiring friends and relatives, colleges admitting the children of alumni, and students with athletic abilities. She admits that affirmative action is about quotas, and argues that without quotas little progress toward eliminating discrimination will be made. She notes that numerical goals are pervasive in all aspects of management because they have proven to be effective. A number of large corporations favor affirmative action in part because they wish to expand the talent pool. Finally, she concedes that affirmative action policies will impose costs on some members of privileged groups. The alternative to affirmative action, however, is the continuation of the status quo.

Bergmann argues that affirmative action has done little to eliminate the gender pay gap, especially for the majority of women working in traditionally female jobs. The problem is gender-based occupational segregation. As long as the latter is allowed to persist, wages will be determined in separate gendered markets. Employers who maintain segregated jobs, she emphasizes, are violating the Civil Rights Act and should, in addition to dismantling their segregationist methods of hiring, training and promoting, be forced to adopt a wage structure that equally values the human capital of their workers regardless of sex. Thus, she advocates pay equity or comparable worth policies that are designed to realign and improve wages in jobs still dominated by women. As with all of her work, she offers a practical solution by presenting job evaluation schemes that have been used within firms and could be used to determine wages based on job characteristics rather than the sex of the worker. Her advocacy for pay equity is rooted in her desire to force discriminatory employers to pay in the present period what the future market wage would be in a world where men and women had equal access to all jobs. Ultimately, gender equity in the labor market, she contends, requires a combination of affirmative action policies and pay equity (Bergmann, 1984a, 1985a, 1985c, 1985e, 1986a, 1987f, 1989a, 2005b).

Bergmann claimed another first in economics when she analyzed the occupation of the housewife, emphasizing the inherent economic risks to women in this 'peculiar occupation' (Bergmann, 1981d, 1986a, 2005b). The longer the housewife's tenure, Bergmann argues, the greater the risk—both physical and financial. The greatest risk facing housewives within 'the job' is sexual or physical abuse from their more powerful partners. A housewife's 'job mobility' also entails high financial risk which, in part, explains why women often stay in abusive marriages. Unlike other employee–employer relations, marriages are costly and difficult to dissolve. Moreover, the work experience attained as a housewife is not valued by employers. Even with the assistance of court-ordered child support and/or alimony payments, it may be difficult to financially support herself and her children. These and other arguments about the unique 'live-in' features of housewifery are used to compare the job of housewife to other less-risky occupations and to demonstrate how the comfort and interest of men are served by homemakers with impoverished alternatives in a monetary economy.

Bergmann's analysis of the family contrasts sharply with the 'new home economics' which invokes the theory of comparative advantage to explain why women 'specialize' in housework (Becker, 1981). The latter assumes that the household division of labor is a rational response by spouses to their exogenously given sex-role differences, and thus in no need for reform. For Bergmann, this is 'preposterous' because it ignores the fact that men's market advantage is derived from employment discrimination and men's traditional refusal to assume their fair share of domestic responsibilities when women work outside the home (Bergmann, 1995f, 1996d).

Bergmann has also prescribed a number of policy initiatives aimed at assisting the growing number of single mothers. Her main objective is to design policies that channel economic resources to poor families, allowing them to maintain a minimally decent living standard. For instance, she advocates rigorous enforcement of parental child-support payments (Bergmann, 1981e, 1981f, 1982g, 1983a, 1983b, 1983c, 1986a, 1995e, 2005b). Although the latter has received widespread political support in recent years, resulting in federal and state-level involvement and sometimes criminal convictions for violators, these measures have not resulted in the reliable delivery of child support. Poor enforcement, Bergmann argues, has made the custody of children a financially difficult experience for women. Rigorous enforcement of child support obligations shifts the financial burden to the father. This may have the effect, Bergmann argues, of increasing fathers' requesting custody of their children (Bergmann, 2005b, p. 163). Nevertheless, she concludes, a better child support system by itself will do little to eradicate poverty among single mothers. In addition, they require access to high paying jobs and government subsidized health care, childcare and housing (Bergmann, 2005, p. 164).

Declining federal support for 'welfare' during the 1980s and early 1990s provides the historical context for Bergmann's subsequent book, *Saving Our Children from Poverty: What the United States Can Learn from France* (Bergmann, 1996b). By focusing on child poverty, Bergmann shifted the welfare debate away from vitriolic diatribes against poor mothers to the real needs of poor children. She compares US family and childcare policy with the French system and argues that the latter is far superior because it has produced much lower child poverty rates. Bergmann advocates a modified version of the French system, selectively adopting those features of the French welfare system that have been successful and adaptable to the US system. In particular, she proposes a 'help for working parents' program (HWP) that includes, among others, vouchers for high-quality childcare, health insurance for all families with children, free childcare for preschoolers, expansion of existing programs such as earned-income tax credits and food stamps and housing assistance in high rent areas. To gain political support, she advocates extending childcare and healthcare benefits to middle income families. For Bergmann, government provisioning of high-quality childcare is essential for two main reasons. First, it allows single working mothers in minimum-wage jobs to maintain their families above the poverty line. Second, it provides a work incentive by making most benefits available to poor working families, thereby encouraging labor force participation and increasing workforce attachment. She notes that the largest roadblock to the proposal is the misleading claim that the United States cannot afford it. With some political will, she argues, the HWP plan could be financed by a modest rearrangement of budget priorities (Bergmann, 1987d, 1987e, 1988a, 1993, 1994a, 1994b, 1995b, 1995c, 1995d, 1996b, 1996c, 1996e, 1996f, 1997a, 1997b; Hartmann & Bergmann, 1995).

For Bergmann, childcare is an indispensable ingredient of any policy aimed at eliminating child poverty. This is the focus of a co-authored book, *America's Child Care Problem: The Way Out* (Heilbrun & Bergmann, 2002) in which the current system of childcare financing and delivery is reviewed and found wanting. The main problem is that good quality childcare is not affordable for the majority of families who need it. The 'way out' consists of three main proposals: federal financing with state and local government administration of services primarily provided by private-sector childcare facilities; the expansion of licensure requirements and higher qualifications for childcare workers, thereby improving the quality and safety of childcare provisioning; and finally, increased and better information about childcare to parents who routinely overestimate its quality. Bergmann starts from the premise that childcare is a 'merit good' (Bergmann, 1994a). That is, the high cost of quality childcare excludes most women from the market. In general, mothers who want to work are forced to stay home. Single mothers are forced to use low-quality childcare because they have to work. Thus, the public provisioning of affordable high quality childcare is required to help women obtain a decent life for their families. Bergmann notes that employers will also benefit from subsidized childcare in the form of lower absenteeism and turnover among employees who are less distracted by childcare problems (Bergmann, 2001). In addition, children will benefit by spending their days in a safe, non-violent environment, in which cognitive skills are developed, nourishing meals are provided, and health and psychological problems are addressed, producing better learners and workers (Bergmann, 1994a, p. 1084).

From time to time, when Republican administrations attempted to dismantle the social security system, Bergmann was there to defend it (Bergmann, 1981b, 1982a, 1982l). Her most recent foray into this debate is a primer on social security entitled, *Is Social Security Broke: A Cartoon Guide* (Bergmann, 2005a). The book offers a succinct critique of the arguments favoring privatization and arguments in favor of keeping social security 'as is' with a touch of Bergmannesque humor in the form of cartoons. Less than humorous are the implications of privatization for elderly women. As Bergmann points out, one of the main sources of income for elderly women without husbands is Social Security. Thus, privatization may adversely affect women by increasing their risk of financial loss, thereby increasing the number of elderly women living in poverty. Bergmann traces the precarious financial position of elderly women to the gender biases in the design of the social security system established during the 1930s when men were the primary breadwinners and women spent most of their married lives at home. Like the income tax system, social security is more generous to one-earner couples than two-earner couples with the same income; a result known as the 'housewife bonus.' For instance, divorced women who work their entire lives in the low-wage job market and contribute to social security receive lower benefits than housewives who remain married. In essence, divorced women receive a zero rate of return on their labor force contributions. And as the number of housewives dwindles, fewer elderly women are able to reap the reduced benefits associated with the sex-role caste system (Bergmann, 2005b, pp. 149–151).

6 Conclusion

Bergmann's contributions to economics are both numerous and varied. Thus, it is difficult to provide a fair treatment of the breath and depth of her thinking. What the foregoing essay has attempted to capture is her unique ability to blend theoretical, empirical and advocacy work. Unlike most economists, she is not content to engage in introspection or regression running. Her objective is not to seek individual glory or win the Nobel Prize by misusing mathematics in an attempt to prove questionable hypothesis. Her primary goal is to make economics policy-relevant in the pursuit of social change. By grounding her theoretical arguments in empirical evidence about real people she has indeed furthered that goal.

She does not dismiss the research findings of other disciplines. Rather, she incorporates relevant information from many disciplines in her work to bolster her arguments. By writing for a host of scholarly journals outside the field of economics, she engages in interdisciplinary dialogue in an effort to gain widespread support for her policy initiatives.

She does not pretend value neutrality with respect to social and economic issues. Rather, she believes that economists have a moral obligation to develop policy initiatives that lead to a more equitable and just future. Consequently, her work focuses less on theory development and more on addressing feminist issues—asking questions and finding answers—in an attempt to move the policy discussion forward.

She acknowledges that her policy proposals will involve both winners and losers. Indeed, she estimates the costs and presents it without apology. She does not deny, for instance, that it will cost billions of dollars to begin subsidizing child-care and healthcare for those who need it and that it will cost more rather than less to eliminate child poverty. She admits that affirmative action programs are about quotas and that some members of previously advantaged groups will lose. She agrees that profit-maximizing employers will shift the cost of pay equity raises for women workers onto men in the form of slower wage increases. This honesty reveals her deep and unwavering commitment to make the world a better place for everyone, especially single working mothers and their children.

As a public intellectual she has indeed made her mark. By testifying before Congress, providing organizational leadership, writing for major newspaper and magazine articles, participating on radio and television shows, and writing highly accessible books, Bergmann has brought an economic point of view on women's issues to a broader public. But her impact on the profession beyond feminist economics has been tempered in large part by the nature of her subject matter—women, children and other marginalized groups. Indeed, it is difficult to imagine the significance given to the work of Milton Friedman or the more recent Nobel laureate, Edmund Phelps, by the Bank of Sweden had their work focused on issues of concern to working women. Perhaps, however, it would be more appropriate that Bergmann receive the Peace Prize like the recent recipient, economist Muhammad Ynus, who helped to improve the lives of millions of poor people. After all, Bergmann, like Ynus, deserves a real Nobel Prize!

Notes

1 Since 1969, nine Nobel Prizes have been awarded to University of Chicago laureates. By comparison, Harvard, Berkeley and Columbia Universities each received four awards; MIT received three; and Princeton and Stanford each received two (source: http://nobelprize.org/nobel_prizes/economics/laureates).
2 The information contained in this section comes from two main sources (Olson & Emami, 2002; Bergmann, 2005e) and from an extensive interview with Bergmann on February 24, 1998.
3 Pay equity is the term used in the United States for a policy that requires jobs with equivalent demands and working conditions to be paid equally. Pay equity policy is often understood to mean 'comparable worth' policy which is '...designed to raise the wages of jobs held predominantly by women until they equal the wages of comparable jobs held predominately by men (Hartmann & Figart, 1999, p. 70).
4 Bergmann credits Edgeworth's 1922 article for the 'crowding' idea. However, the 'overcrowding' theory of women's wages was first developed by Barbara Bodichon and Millicent Garrett Fawcett, which Edgeworth failed to cite (Pujol, 1992, p. 97).
5 In less recognized papers, she examined the large racial disparity in the incidence of employment (Bergmann, 1980a) and, based on her findings, argues that the upgrading of blacks relative to whites in pay and occupational status would occur faster with a lower overall unemployment rate (Atkinson & Bergmann, 1972).

References

Becker, G.S. (1957) *The Economics of Discrimination* (Chicago: University of Chicago Press).
Becker, G.S. (1981) *A Treatise on the Family* (Cambridge, MA: Harvard University Press).
Becker, G.S. (1985) Human capital, effort and the sexual division of labor, *Journal of Labor Economics,* 3(1), part 2, pp. S33–S58.
Berman, P. (1996) Redefining fairness, *The New York Times Book Review,* 14 April, pp. 32–38.
Colander, D., Holt, R.P.F. & Rosser, J.B. (2004) *The Changing Face of Economics: Conversations with Cutting-edge Economists* (Ann Arbor: University of Michigan Press).
England, P. (1992) *Comparable Worth: Theories and Evidence* (New York: Aldine deGruyter).
Ferber, M.A. & Lowry, H.M. (1976) The sex differential in earnings: a reappraisal, *Industrial and Labor Relations Review,* 29, pp. 377–387.
Figart, D.M. & Lapidus, J. (1995) A gender analysis of labor market policies for the working poor in the US, *Feminist Economics,* 1(3), pp. 60–81.
Folbre, N. (1998) Barbara, the market, and the state, *Feminist Economics,* 4(3), pp. 159–168.
Gibson, K.J., Darity, W.A. & Myers, S.L. (1998) Revisiting occupational crowding in the United States: a preliminary study, *Feminist Economics,* 4(3), pp. 73–96.
Hartmann, H.I. & Figart, D. (1999) Comparable worth/pay equity, in: J. Petersen & M. Lewis (Eds) *The Elgar Companion to Feminist Economics* (Cheltenham, UK: Edward Elgar), p. 70.
Jacobs, J.A. & Steinberg, R.J. (1990) Compensating differentials and the male-female wage gap: evidence from the New York comparable worth study, *Social Forces,* 69(2), pp. 439–468.

Lapidus, J. & Figart, D.M. (1998) Remedying 'unfair acts': US pay equity by race and gender, *Feminist Economics,* 4(3), pp. 7–28.

Mincer, J. & Polachek, S. (1974) Family investment in human capital: earnings of women, *Journal of Political Economy,* 82(2), part 2, pp. S76–S108.

Myrdal, G. (1944) *An American Dilemma* (New York: Harper & Brothers).

Olson, P.I. & Emami, Z. (2002) *Engendering Economics: Conversations with Women Economists in the United States* (London: Routledge).

Orcutt, G., Caldwell, S. & Wertheimer, R. (1976) *Policy Exploration through Microanalytic Simulation* (Washington, DC: The Urban Institute).

Polachek, S. (1981) Occupational self-selection: a human capital approach to sex differences in occupational structure, *Review of Economics and Statistics,* 63(1), pp. 60–69.

Pujol, M.A. (1992) *Feminism and Anti-feminism in Early Economic Thought* (Aldershot, UK: Edward Elgar).

Reskin, B.F. (Ed) (1984) *Sex Segregation in the Workplace: Trends, Explanations, Remedies* (Washington, DC: National Academy Press).

Reskin, B.F. & Hartmann, H.I. (Eds) (1986) *Women's Work, Men's Work: Sex Segregation on the Job* (Washington, DC: National Academy Press).

Sorensen, E. (1989) Measuring the effect of occupational sex and race composition on earnings, in: R.T. Michel, H.I. Hartmann & B. O'Farrell (Eds) *Pay Equity: Empirical Inquiries,* pp. 49–60 (Washington, DC: National Academy Press).

Treiman, D.J. & Hartmann, H.I. (Eds) (1981) *Women, Work, and Wages: Equal Pay for Jobs of Equal Value* (Washington, DC: National Academy Press).

Wolfe, A. (1996) Affirmative Action, Inc. *The New Yorker,* 72, pp. 106–115.

The works of Barbara R. Bergmann

Atkinson, L.C. & Bergmann, B.R. (1972) The prospect of equality of incomes between white and black families under varying rates of unemployment: a comment, *Journal of Human Resources,* 7(4), pp. 545–547.

Bennett, R. & Bergmann, B.R. (1986) *A Microsimulated Transactions Model of the United States Economy* (Baltimore: John Hopkins University Press).

Bergmann, B.R. (1965a) An approach to an absolute measure of structural unemployment, in: A.M. Ross (Ed.) *Employment Policy and the Labor Market,* pp. 256–268 (Berkeley, CA: University of California Press).

Bergmann, B.R. (1965b) Debt servicing in sanction-free situations: a comment, *National Banking Review,* 2(4), pp. 569–570.

Bergmann, B.R. (1966) The Cochabamba–Santa Cruz Highway in Bolivia, in: G.W. Wilson, L.V. Hirsch & M. Klein (Eds) *The Impact of Highway Investment on Development,* pp. 17–54 (Washington, DC: The Brookings Institution Transportation Research Program).

Bergmann, B.R. & Kaun, D. (1967) *Structural Unemployment in the United States* (Washington, DC: U.S. Department of Commerce).

Bergmann, B.R. (1969a) Investment in the human resources of negroes, in: J.F. Kain (Ed) *Race and Poverty: the Economics of Discrimination,* pp. 52–57 (Englewood Cliffs, NJ: Prentice Hall).

Bergmann, B.R. (1969b) The urban economy and the 'urban crisis,' *American Economic Review,* 59(4), pp. 639–645.

Bergmann, B.R. (1971a) Effect on white incomes of discrimination in employment, *Journal of Political Economy,* 79(2), pp. 294–313.

Bergmann, B.R. & Lyle, J.R. (1971b) Occupational standing of negroes by areas and industries, *Journal of Human Resources,* 6(4), pp. 411–433.

Bergmann, B.R. & Krause, W.R. (1972) Evaluating and forecasting progress in racial integration and employment, *Industrial and Labor Relations Review,* 25(3), pp. 399–409.

Bergmann, B.R. (1973a) Assessing the impact of alternative economic outcomes on social objectives, in: A. Brody & A.P. Carter (Eds) *Input Output Techniques,* pp. 31–43 (Amsterdam: North-Holland).

Bergmann, B.R. (1973b) Labor turnover, segmentation and rates of unemployment: a simulation-theoretic approach (College Park: Project on the Economics of Discrimination, University of Maryland).

Bergmann, B.R. (1973c) Combining microsimulation and regression: a 'preferred' regression of poverty incidence on unemployment and growth, *Econometrica,* 41(5), pp. 955–963.

Bergmann, B.R. (1973d) The economics of women's liberation, *Annals of the New York Academy of Sciences,* 208, pp. 154–160.

Bergmann, B.R. (1973e) Sex discrimination in wages: comment, in: O. Ashenfelter & A. Rees (Eds) *Discrimination in Labor Markets,* pp. 152–154 (Princeton, NJ: Princeton University Press).

Bergmann, B.R. (1973f) Can we end racial discrimination under capitalism? In, J.H. Weaver (Ed) *Modern Political Economy: Radical and Orthodox Views on Crucial Issues,* pp. 312–318 (Boston: Allyn & Bacon).

Bergmann, B.R. (1974a) A microsimulation of the macroeconomy with explicitly represented money flows, *Annals of Economic and Social Measurement,* 3(3), pp. 475–489.

Bergmann, B.R. (1974b) Studying black-white differences in the context of a simulation of the labor market, in: G.M. Furstenberg, B. Harrison & A.R. Horowitz (Eds) *Patterns of Discrimination,* pp. 5–26, Volume 2 (Lexington, MA: Lexington Books).

Bergmann, B.R. (1974c) Towards more useful modes of research on discrimination in employment and pay, *Sloan Management Review,* 15(3), pp. 43–45.

Bergmann, B.R. (1974d) Unfairness of how to analyze fairness of women's salaries on your own campus: reply, *AAUP Bulletin,* 62(1), pp. 126–128.

Bergmann, B.R. (1974e) Occupational segregation, wages and profits when employers discriminate by race and sex, *Eastern Economic Journal,* 1(2/3), pp. 103–110.

Bergmann, B.R. (1975a) Equality in retirement benefits: the need for pension reform, *Civil Rights Digest,* 8, pp. 25–27.

Bergmann, B.R. (1975b) Combining microsimulation and regression: reply, *Econometrica,* 43(3), pp. 529–531.

Bergmann, B.R. (1975c) Empirical work on the labor market: is there any alternative to regression running? Have economists failed?, *Eastern Economic Journal,* 2(3), pp. 16–24.

Bergmann, B.R. & Maxfield, M. Jr. (1975d) How to analyze the fairness of faculty women's salaries on your own campus, *AAUP Bulletin,* 61(3), pp. 262–265.

Bergmann, B.R. (1976) Reducing the pervasiveness of discrimination, in: E. Ginzberg (Ed) *Jobs for Americans,* pp. 120–141 (Englewood Cliffs, NJ: Prentice Hall).

Bergmann, B.R. & Bennett, R.L. (1977) Macroeconomic effects of a Humphrey-Hawkins type program, *American Economic Review,* 67(1), pp. 265–270.

Bergmann, B.R. (1980a) Discrimination and unemployment, in: E. Malinvaud & J.S. Fitoussi (Eds) *Unemployment in Western Countries,* pp. 420–442 (London: Macmillan).

Bergmann, B.R. & Bennett, R. (1980b) Policy explorations with the transactions model of the United States, in: R.H. Haveman & K. Hollenback (Eds) *Microeconomic Simulation Models for Public Policy Analysis,* Volume II, pp. 22–38 (New York: Academic Press).

Bergmann, B.R., Devine, J.R., Gordon, P. Reedy, D., Sage, L., & Wise, C. (1980c) The effect of wives' labor force participation on inequality in the distribution of family income, *Journal of Human Resources,* 15(3), pp. 452–455.

Bergmann, B.R. & Darity, W. (1980d) Social relations, productivity and employer discrimination, *Monthly Labor Review,* 104(4), pp. 47–49.

Bergmann, B.R. (1981a) The economics of expectation, *The New York Times,* September 20, p. 3.

Bergmann, B.R. (1981b) Relax, social security is doing its job, *The New York Times,* November 15, p. 3.

Bergmann, B.R. (1981c) Charity needs coercion, *The New York Times,* December 13, p. 3.

Bergmann, B.R. (1981d) The economic risks of being a housewife, *American Economic Review,* 71(2), pp. 81–86.

Bergmann, B.R. (1981e) The economic support of 'fatherless' children, in: P.G. Brown, C. Johnson & P. Vernier (Eds) *Income Support: Conceptual and Policy Issues,* pp. 195–211 (Maryland: Rowman & Littlefield).

Bergmann, B.R. (1981f) The share of women and men in the economic support of children, *Human Rights Quarterly,* 3(2), pp. 103–112.

Bergmann, B.R. (1982a) The housewife and social security reform: a feminist perspective, in: R.V. Burkhauser & K.C. Holden (Eds) *A Challenge to Social Security: The Changing Roles of Women and Men in American Society,* pp. 229–233 (New York: Academic Press).

Bergmann, B.R. (1982b) An affirmative look at hiring quotas, *The New York Times,* January 10, p. 3.

Bergmann, B.R. (1982c) Here is why you lost your job, *The New York Times,* February 7, p. 3.

Bergmann, B.R. (1982d) Investment is the business of business, *The New York Times,* March 7, p. 3.

Bergmann, B.R. (1982e) Lobbying: shakedown on Capitol Hill, *The New York Times,* April 4, p. 3.

Bergmann, B.R. (1982f) A threat ahead from word processors, *The New York Times,* May 30, p. 3.

Bergmann, B.R. (1982g) It's single parents who need help, *The New York Times,* May 2, p. 3.

Bergmann, B.R. (1982h) A vicious cycle of high rates, *The New York Times,* June 27, p. 3.

Bergmann, B.R. (1982i) The sound and fury over poverty, *The New York Times,* August 22, p. 3.

Bergmann, B.R. (1982j) Why the football union can hit hard, *The New York Times,* September 19, p. 3.

Bergmann, B.R. (1982k) Who's to blame for the economy, *The New York Times,* October 17, p. 3.

Bergmann, B.R. (1982l) Social security's overblown problem, *The New York Times,* November 14, p. 3.

Bergmann, B.R. (1982m) The failures of a chair-bound science, *The New York Times,* December 12, p. 3.

Bergmann, B.R. (1983a) Setting appropriate levels of child support payments, in: J. Cassetty (Ed) *The Parental Child Support Obligation: Research, Practice, and Public Policy,* pp. 115–118 (Lexington, MA: Lexington Books).

Bergmann, B.R. (1983b) Women's plight: bad and getting worse, *Challenge,* 26(1), pp. 22–26.

Bergmann, B.R. & Adelman, I. (1983c) The economic report of the President's Council of Economic Advisors: the economic role of women, *American Economic Review,* 73(4), pp. 509–514.

Bergmann, B.R. (1983d) Feminism and economics, *Academe,* 69(5), pp. 22–25.

Bergmann, B.R. & Gray, M. (1984a) The economics of compensation claims under Title VII, in: H. Remick (Ed) *Comparable Worth and Wage Discrimination: Technical Possibilities and Political Realities,* pp. 155–172 (Philadelphia: Temple University Press).

Bergmann, B.R. (1984b) Report of the committee on the status of women in the economics profession, *American Economic Review,* 74(2), pp. 457–462.

Bergmann, B.R. & Bennett, R.L. (1984c) Macroeconomic models on microfoundations—data requirements, *Review of Public Data Use,* 12(2), pp. 91–96.

Bergmann, B.R. (1985a) The economic case for comparable worth, in: H.I. Hartmann (Ed) *Comparable Worth: New Directions for Research,* pp. 71–85 (Washington, DC: National Academy Press).

Bergmann, B.R. (1985b) Is there a conflict between racial justice and women's liberation?, *Rutgers Law Review,* 37(4), pp. 805–817.

Bergmann, B.R. (1985c) Pay equity—how to argue back, *Ms,* 14, p. 112.

Bergmann, B.R. (1985d) Report of the Committee on the Status of Women in the Economics Profession, *American Economic Review,* 75(2), pp. 448–453.

Bergmann, B.R. (1985e) Comparable worth for professors, *Academe,* 71(4), pp. 8–10.

Bergmann, B.R. (1986a) *The Economic Emergence of Women* (New York: Basic Books).

Bergmann, B.R. (1986b) The economic well-being of women: comment, *Science,* 233, p. 510.

Bergmann, B.R. (1987c) The task of a feminist economics: a more equitable future, in: C. Farnham (Ed) *The Impact of Feminist Research in the Academy,* pp. 131–147 (Bloomington, IN: Indiana University Press).

Bergmann, B.R. (1987d) A fresh start on welfare reform, *Challenge,* 30(5), pp. 44–50.

Bergmann, B.R. & Roberts, M. (1987e) Income for the single parent: child support, work, and welfare, in: C. Brown & J. Peckman (Eds) *Gender in the Workplace,* pp. 247–270 (Washington, D.C.: Brookings Institution).

Bergmann, B.R. (1987f) Pay equity—surprising answers to hard questions, *Challenge,* 30(2), pp. 45–51.

Bergmann, B.R. (1987g) Women's roles in the economy: teaching the issues, *Journal of Economic Education,* 18(4), 393–408.

Bergmann, B.R. (1987h) Measurement, or finding things in economics, *Journal of Economic Education,* 18(2), pp. 191–201.

Bergmann, B.R. (1987i) Comment on Higgins' 'Women in the Islamic Republic of Iran: legal, social and ideological changes', *Signs: Journal of Women in Culture and Society,* 12(3), pp. 606–607.

Bergmann, B.R. (1988a) A workable family policy, *Dissent,* 35(1), pp. 88–93.

Bergmann, B.R. (1988b) An experiment on the formation of expectations, *Journal of Economic Psychology,* 9(2), pp. 137–151.

Bergmann, B.R. (1989a) What the common economic arguments against comparable worth are worth, *Journal of Social Issues,* 45(4), pp. 67–80.

Bergmann, B.R. (1989b) Why do most economists know so little about the economy?, in:

S. Bowles, R.C. Edwards, & W.G. Shepherd (Eds) *Unconventional Wisdom: Essays in Honor of John Kenneth Galbraith,* pp. 29–37 (Boston: Houghton Mifflin).

Bergmann, B.R. (1989c) Does the market for women's labor need fixing? *Journal of Economic Perspectives,* 3(1), pp. 43–60.

Bergmann, B.R. (1990a) Micro-to-macro simulation: a primer with a labor market example, *Journal of Economic Perspectives,* 4(1), pp. 99–116.

Bergmann, B.R. (1990b) A microsimulated model of inventories in interfirm competition, *Journal of Economic Behavior and Organization,* 14(1), pp. 65–77.

Bergmann, B.R. (1990c) Feminism and economics, *Women's Studies Quarterly,* 18(3/4), pp. 68–74.

Bergmann, B.R. (1991a) Do sports really make money for the university?, *Academe,* 77(1), pp. 28–32.

Bergmann, B.R. (1991b) Professors should back national health insurance, *Academe,* 77(3), p. 62.

Bergmann, B.R. (1991c) Bloated administrations, blighted campuses, *Academe,* 77(6), pp. 12–16.

Bergmann, B.R. (1993) The French child welfare system: an excellent system we could adapt and afford, in: W.J. Wilson (Ed) *Sociology and the Public Agenda,* pp. 341–350 (Newbury Park, CA: Sage Publications).

Bergmann, B.R. (1994a) Economic issues in child-care policy, *Pediatrics,* 94(6), pp. 1083–1084.

Bergmann, B.R. (1994b) Curing child poverty in the united states, *American Economic Review,* 71(2), pp. 76–80.

Bergmann, B.R. (1995a) Probing the opposition to affirmative action, *Gender, Work and Organization,* 2(2), pp. 89–94.

Bergmann, B.R. (1995b) Welfare that works, *The Nation,* 260, p. 114.

Bergmann, B.R. & Hartmann, H.I. (1995c) Instead of 'cut 'em off': a program to help working parents, *The Nation,* 260(17), pp. 592–595.

Bergmann, B.R. & Hartmann, H.I. (1995d) A welfare reform based on help for working parents, *Feminist Economics,* 1(2), pp. 85–89.

Bergmann, B.R. & Wetchler, S. (1995e) Child support awards—state guidelines vs. public opinion, *Family Law Quarterly,* 29(3), pp. 483–493.

Bergmann, B.R. (1995f) Becker's theory of the family: preposterous conclusions, *Feminist Economics,* 1(1), pp. 141–150.

Bergmann, B.R. (1996a) *In Defense of Affirmative Action* (New York: Basic Books).

Bergmann, B.R. (1996b) *Saving Our Children from Poverty: What the United States can Learn from France* (New York: Russell Sage Foundation).

Bergmann, B.R. (1996c) Real welfare reform: help for working parents, *Challenge,* 39(5), pp. 34–37.

Bergmann, B.R. (1996d) Becker's theory of the family: preposterous conclusions, *Challenge,* 39(6), pp. 9–12.

Bergmann, B.R. & Hartmann, H.I. (1996e) A welfare reform program based on help for working parents, in: R. Albelda, N. Folbre & the Center for Popular Economics (Eds) *The War on the Poor,* pp. 123–124 (New York: The New Press).

Bergmann, B.R. (1996f) Child care: the key to ending child poverty, in: I. Garfinkel, J.L. Hochschild & S. McLanahan (Eds) *Social Policies for Children,* pp. 112–135 (Washington, D.C.: Brookings Institution).

Bergmann, B.R. (1997a) Government support for families with children in the United States and France, *Feminist Economics,* 3(1), pp. 85–94.

Bergmann, B.R. (1997b) Work–family policies and equality between women and men, in: F.D. Blau & R.G. Ehrenberg (Eds) *Gender and Family Issues in the Workplace*, pp. 277–279 (New York: Russell Sage Foundation).

Bergmann, B.R. (1998a) The only ticket to equality: total androgyny, male style, *Journal of Contemporary Legal Issues*, pp. 75–86.

Bergmann, B.R. (1998b) Watch out for family friendly policies, *Dollars and Sense: The Magazine of Economic Justice*, 215, pp. 10–11.

Bergmann, B.R. (1999a) Making child care 'affordable' in the United States, *Annals of the American Academy of Political and Social Science*, 563(May), pp. 208–219.

Bergmann, B.R. (1999b) Abolish the Nobel Prize for economics, *Challenge*, March–April, pp. 52–57.

Bergmann, B.R. (2000) Subsidizing child care by mothers at home, *Feminist Economics*, 6(1), pp. 77–88.

Bergmann, B.R. (2001) Decent child care at decent wages, *The American Prospect*, 12(1), pp. 8–9.

Bergmann, B.R. (2004) What policies toward lone mothers should we aim for? *Feminist Economics*, 10(2), pp. 240–246.

Bergmann, B.R. (cartoons by J. Bush) (2005a) *Is Social Security Broke? A Cartoon Guide to the Issues* (Ann Arbor: University of Michigan Press).

Bergmann, B.R. (2005b) *The Economic Emergence of Women*, 2nd edn (New York: Palgrave/St. Martin's Press).

Bergmann, B.R. (2005c) A Swedish-style welfare state or basic income: which should have priority? *Politics and Society*, 32(1), pp. 107–118.

Bergmann, B.R. (2005d) The current state of economics: needs lots of work, *The Annals of the American Academy*, pp. 1–16.

Bergmann, B.R. (2005e) Pushing for a more humane society, *Newsletter of the Committee on the Status of Women in the Economics Profession*, Fall, pp. 1, 9–10.

Bergmann, B.R. (2006a) Reducing inequality: merit goods vs. income grants, *Dissent*, 53(1), pp. 67–72.

Bergmann, B.R. (2006b) Curing the nursing shortage–the role of compensation, *New England Journal of Medicine*, 354(15), pp. 1648–1649.

Brown, C.V., Bergmann, B.R. & Swartz, K. (1978) Unemployment rate targets and anti-inflation policy as more women enter the workforce, *American Economic Review*, 68(2), pp. 90–94.

Eliasson, G., Orcutt, G. & Bergmann, B. (Eds) (1977) *Micro-simulation—Models, Methods and Applications* (Stockholm: Almqvist & Wiksell International).

Folbre, N., Bergmann, B.R., Agarwal, B. & Floro, M. (Eds) (1993) *Women's Work in the World Economy* (New York: New York University Press).

Gray, M. & Bergmann, B.R. (2003) Student teaching evaluations, *Academe*, 89(5), pp. 44–46.

Hartmann, H.I. & Bergmann, B.R.(1995) Get real—look to the future, not the past, *Feminist Economics*, 1(2), pp. 109–119.

Heilbrun, S.W. & Bergmann, B.R. (2002) *America's Child Care Problem: The Way Out* (New York: Palgrave/St. Martin's Press).

Renwick, T.J. & Bergmann, B.R. (1993) A budget-based definition of poverty: with an application to single-parent families, *Journal of Human Resources*, 28(1), pp. 1–24.

15 Edmund Phelps and modern macroeconomics

Robert W. Dimand

'The Economic Contributions of Ed Phelps' by Robert Dimand from *Review of Political Economy* (2008), Volume 20, Issue 1 (Taylor and Francis Ltd, http://www.informaworld.com), reprinted by permission of the publisher.

On October 9, 2006, Edmund S. (Ned) Phelps, McVickar Professor of Political Economy at Columbia University, was awarded the Royal Bank of Sweden (Sveriges Riksbank) Prize in Economic Science in Memory of Alfred Nobel. Announcing the prize, the Swedish Academy of Sciences emphasized that 'Mr. Phelps showed how the possibilities of stabilization policy in the future depend on today's policy decisions: Low inflation today leads to expectations of low inflation also in the future, thereby facilitating future policy.' The Academy's announcement focuses on the introduction of the natural rate hypothesis and the expectations-augmented Phillips curve by Phelps (1967) and by Milton Friedman (1968), who was the Nobel laureate in economics 30 years before Phelps.

Phelps and Friedman extended the Phillip curve trade-off between inflation and unemployment by postulating that the rate of change of money wages depends on the expected rate of inflation (just as nominal interest depends on expected inflation in the Fisher equation of Fisher, 1896). They argued that expected inflation is endogenous, responding adaptively to errors in expectations so that expected inflation is a distributed lag of past inflation rates (cf. Fisher, 1926/1973, in which Irving Fisher correlated US unemployment with a distributed lag of price level changes). Expansionary monetary policy could not produce a lasting reduction in unemployment at the cost of increasing inflation, because the higher inflation would come to be expected, and the rate of unemployment would gravitate back towards its natural rate (the non-accelerating inflation rate of unemployment, or NAIRU). The Phillips curve is thus not a menu for policy choice: any attempt to deliberately move along it will change expectations of inflation, and cause the trade-off to shift. (A.W.H. Phillips did not think that the interesting historical correlation he had found in British data offered a menu for policy choice, and may even have suggested to Friedman that adaptive expectations would be useful in analyzing the inflation-unemployment trade-off – see Leeson, 2000).

Friedman's (1968) presidential address to the American Economic Association, was widely influential,[1] especially among policy-makers, even though Phelps (1967) appeared in print first (Friedman, 1966, had previously, in a comment in a conference volume, denied any stable relationship between unemployment and different rates of steady inflation). However, working economists, looking for more formal and technical analysis, were led into the microeconomic foundations of employment, unemployment, inflation, and money wage dynamics by Phelps (1967, 1968, 1969, 1972a, 1979) and above all by 'the Phelps volume' (Phelps *et al.*, 1970). This body of work reoriented the methodology of modern macroeconomics, focusing attention on the choice-theoretic underpinnings of aggregate variables, particularly with regard to how labor markets work. New Classical economists such as Robert Lucas (1981) introduced the hypothesis of rational expectations (agents make no systematic errors in their predictions), an approach that Phelps evaluated sympathetically but by no means uncritically (Frydman & Phelps, 1983). But the New Classical economists were not responsible for the modern emphasis on the choice-theoretic microeconomic foundations of the macroeconomic analysis of employment, inflation, and fluctuations. That had already been achieved by Phelps and his associates in a series of path-breaking publications from 1967 to 1972. As Axel Leijonhufvud remarked, 'A case can be made that modern macroeconomics stems more from the natural rate doctrine than from rational expectations' (Leijonhufvud, 2004, p. 811).

But there is much more to Phelps's contribution to economics than just that one great breakthrough associated with the natural rate hypothesis, the expectations-augmented Phillips curve, and choice-theoretic microeconomics foundations. The 'islands model' of imperfectly communicating markets was introduced by Phelps (1969), and hysteresis by Phelps (1972a). While Lucas (1981) looked at how monetary misperceptions cause fluctuations around the natural rate (Lucas, together with Leonard Rapping, had contributed to Phelps *et al.*, 1970), Phelps (1994) developed a structuralist macroeconomics that analyzed structural booms and slumps as changes in the natural rate of unemployment (see also Fitoussi & Phelps, 1986, 1988; Phelps & Zoega, 1997, 1998, 2001; Hoon & Phelps, 1992, 1997, 2007; Hoon *et al.*, 2005).

Phelps also stands out from other macroeconomic theorists in having a serious, longstanding, scholarly and personal concern with economic justice (see Phelps, 1973b, 1975). This concern motivated the second body of research cited by the Swedish Academy of Sciences, Phelps's analysis of the trade-off between consumption by current generations and consumption by future generations, starting with his early work on 'golden rules' of capital accumulation and economic growth (Phelps, 1961b, 1965c, 1966a, 1966b; see also Phelps & Shell, 1969). This concern with the justice and morality of economic processes motivated his influential study of statistical theory of racial and gender discrimination in labor markets (Phelps, 1972a, 1972b). It also motivates what may well turn out to rank among his most important contributions, his books on *Rewarding Work: How to Restore Participation and Self-Support to Free Enterprise*

(Phelps, 1997), *Enterprise and Inclusion in Italy* (Phelps, 2002a), and *Designing Inclusion: Tools to Raise Low-End Pay and Employment in Private Enterprise* (Phelps, 2003b). Stimulated by spending 1969–70 at Stanford's Center for Advanced Study in the Behavioral Sciences while John Rawls (1971) was there finishing *A Theory of Justice,* Phelps (1987, 1995a, pp. 98–99) gave serious attention to what would constitute justice in society's design of the reward structure motivating production and exchange. As director since 2001 of the Center on Capitalism and Society at Columbia University's Earth Institute, Phelps is highly unusual among the elite of top-level theorists capable of publishing in the inaugural volume of *Journal of Economic Theory* (Phelps & Shell, 1969) in choosing to devote his talents and energy to bringing economic theory to bear on how to make capitalism inclusive and rewarding for all, not just the fortunate.

Phelps (2007, pp. 554–558) devoted the concluding section of his Nobel Lecture to consideration of what constitutes 'The Good Economy: Innovative and Inclusive', a serious philosophical inquiry beyond what might typically be expected of a macroeconomic theorist. He proposes, citing precedents from Aristotle to John Rawls's concept of self-realization, that the essence of the good life is a career of challenge and personal development, which need not be correlated with reported happiness: 'a morally acceptable economy must have enough dynamism to make work amply engaging and rewarding; and have enough justice, if dynamism alone cannot do the job, to secure ample inclusion' (Phelps, 2007, p. 558). These philosophical reflections about the nature of justice, the good life, and the good economy that promotes the good life have a direct, practical significance for economics: Phelps sees 'a debate in the making between, on the one hand, those *neoclassicals* who would put the emphasis on *pushing* more resources into the economy (more technology or more human capital) as a way of raising output and employment; and, on the other hand, those *modernizers* who favor a strategy of *pulling* existing resources into innovative activity and general business activity through reforms of labor law, company law, and the financial sector' (Phelps, 2007, pp. 557–558).

1 Beginnings

Edmund Phelps was born in Evanston, Illinois, on July 26, 1933, to parents who lost their jobs in the Great Depression (Henderson, 2006). He graduated from Amherst College in Massachusetts in 1955. He would have majored in philosophy at Amherst, but his father cajoled him into trying an economics course in his second year: 'I was hugely impressed to see that it was possible to subject the events in those newspapers I had read about to a formal sort of analysis [but] I had a vague sense that the microeconomics taught in one set of courses was not communicating with the macroeconomics in the other courses' (Phelps, 1995a, p. 91). He did his postgraduate studies at Yale University, where he was influenced by macroeconomists James Tobin, William Fellner, Henry Wallich, and Arthur Okun (all at some point members of the President's Council of Economic Advisers), and, among microeconomists, Thomas Schelling (like Tobin, a future

Nobel laureate). He received his PhD in economics in 1959. After working as an economist at the RAND Corporation (1959–60), Phelps returned to teach at Yale from 1960 to 1966 (with a year as a visiting associate professor at MIT, 1962–63), taking charge of the principles of economic course and editing Norton's Problems of the Modern Economy series of policy-oriented books of readings for undergraduate economics courses (e.g. Phelps, 1962b). Phelps's long-time concern with making state-of-the-art modern economics accessible to beginning undergraduates was reflected much later in his innovative *Political Economy, An Introductory Text* (Phelps, 1985), described by Michael Weinstein (1987, p. 179) as 'a modernist (his word) vision of asymmetric and imperfect information, incentive compatibilities, and a host of other problems of coordination and reward that plague real economies.' At the time Phelps was there, Yale published the *Yale Economic Essays,* a journal primarily devoted to articles based on Yale doctoral dissertations in economics. Phelps (1961a) published there, was part of the then-burgeoning empirical literature on whether US inflation in the 1950s (running at rates that seem enviably low in retrospect) was due to cost-push or demand-pull factors. Phelps's choice of topic coincided with the research interests, at that time, of one of his teachers, Fellner (1959), although Phelps (1995a) credits another of his teachers, James Tobin, with suggesting the topic. Phelps (1990a, p. 98) remarked that contemporary analysis of struggles over the mark-up 'is quite reminiscent of the formulation by William Fellner of thirty years ago.'

Phelps (1962a) contributed to the neoclassical theory of investment decisions by profit-maximizing firms, following Robert Solow (1956, 1957), Trevor Swan (1956), and James Tobin (1955) in developing a growth model with substitution between capital and labor instead of the Harrod–Domar assumption of strict complementarity between the two factors of production.[2] The novel feature of Phelps (1962a), and of a simplified exposition in Phelps (1962b), relative to the articles of Solow, Swan, and Tobin six or seven years before, was Phelps's emphasis that while investment serves to modernize as well as to increase the capital stock (hence, his was an exercise in modeling vintage capital), once the economy has reached a steady state, the average age of machines would be independent of the propensity to save. In a comment, Robin Matthews showed that such independence depends on unitary elasticity of substitution between capital and labor (a Cobb–Douglas production function). Phelps first achieved recognition among economists for his work on optimal capital accumulation (Phelps, 1961b, 1965c, 1966a, 1966b) and on how tax policy affects capital accumulation (Phelps, 1965a; Phelps & Shell, 1969). 'The Golden Rule of Accumulation' holds that a constant returns to scale economy achieves its highest attainable consumption path when the profit rate is equal to the rate of accumulation of capital (the share of profits in output equal to the share of net investment in output). The golden rule, like Paul Samuelson's overlapping generations model and the Baumol–Tobin square root rule for transactions demand for money, was subsequently discerned in the mathematical appendix to Maurice Allais (1947), unknown to Anglophone economists (see also Allais,

1962), but Phelps's formulation was independent and his exploration of the issue fuller.

Certain life-long characteristics of Phelps as an economist are already evident in his early publications, beyond his remarkable technical skills (and the influence of his Yale teachers, e.g. Tobin, 1955 and Fellner, 1959). His interests lay with technically-rigorous research that was relevant to crucial issues of public policy, as in *Fiscal Neutrality toward Economic Growth* (Phelps, 1965a), his first book (apart from edited volumes). Most of all, presaging his later work on economic justice and on designing structural reforms to make capitalism more inclusive, Phelps was concerned with using theory and policy to make people better off: 'golden rules' of economic growth (Phelps, 1961b, 1965c, 1966a, 1966b) consider which growth path maximizes welfare, while Phelps (1965b) analyzed how even inflation that is correctly expected by economic agents affects economic welfare (as people engage in costly transactions to economize on holding real money balances whose purchasing power is shrinking). He did not pursue theoretical brilliance primarily for its own sake, but for the sake of understanding and, where feasible, improving the real world. (It is, of course, easier for a young assistant professor to take such an interest in the real world when his peers and elders are already aware of his technical virtuosity.) Sorting out the classes of vintage capital models in which the average age of machines in independent of the propensity to save in steady state growth is interesting as an abstract exercise in pure theorizing, but even more so in shedding light on the appropriate policy encouraging or discouraging saving to achieve the most desirable steady state growth path.

His early work won Phelps election as a Fellow of the Econometric Society in 1966. 'Yet,' recalls Phelps (1995a, p. 93), 'I came to feel that I was simply winning (or losing) footraces by a few steps. I saw that if I was to do anything of unusual depth and distinctiveness I would have to think much harder than I had generally done – to raise the level of my game. There is, as I was to appreciate better, a big difference between scanning existing models for their unnoticed implications, on the one hand, and, on the other, acquiring an independent empirical sense of how in some overlooked or misunderstood way the economy works.' Phelps's publications at Yale (1960–66) won him recognition as a rising star in the profession, but those published while he was at the University of Pennsylvania (1966–71) changed how economists do macroeconomics.

'One might have thought that this success at playing the game would be rewarded with promotion to tenure. However, Yale had squandered one tenure slot after another in those years, building up what must have been the largest Economics Department in the country, until the President was finally resistant to creating yet another' (Phelps, 1995a, p. 93). Mark Blaug and Gerard Debreu were among other young economists of distinction who had left Yale earlier in the 1960s when it was made clear that there would be no tenure for them. Northwestern and Pennsylvania offered Phelps full professorships. As Phelps (1995a, p. 93) himself put it, his departure from Yale to Penn in January 1966 'marked a kind of passage into my years of high creativity, which were nearly continuous for a decade.'

2 The natural rate hypothesis and the Phelps volume

In his March 1969 preface to 'the Phelps volume' (Phelps *et al.*, 1970, p. vii), Phelps wrote that, 'Last year several of us were excited to learn that we were not alone. Similar life existed on other campuses. Evidence was found of nearly a dozen drafts and fragments, all on the subjects of wage, price, job, and production decisions under incomplete information. An economics of disequilibrium seemed to be forming. A meeting was suggested to see whether we spoke the same language and thought the same theorems.' It was held on January 25–26, 1969, at the University of Pennsylvania, where Phelps then taught. The ten papers from this gathering (plus two more commissioned to cover gaps) became 'the Phelps volume,' *Microeconomic Foundations of Employment and Inflation Theory* by 15 authors (Phelps *et al.*, 1970). No editor was named, but Phelps wrote the introduction and was listed first among the authors, with the others listed on the cover in the order in which their papers appeared in the book. In addition to the introduction, Phelps contributed a revised version of his 1968 *Journal of Political Economy* article (which had inspired many of the contributions by other authors) and a joint paper with Sidney G. Winter, Jr, on 'Optimal Price Policy under Atomistic Competition.' The conference and the subsequent conference volume gave a decisive impetus to formal research on the microeconomic foundations of macroeconomics, changing not the specific models and theories that macroeconomists propounded or the policies they advocated, but the methodology through which they conducted macroeconomics, whether New Classical, Real Business Cycle, or New Keynesian (see Phelps, 1990a, for an overview of these schools of macroeconomic thought). Phelps (1995b, p. 13) acknowledged Lerner (1949) and Fellner (1959) as having had the concept of a natural rate: The postulate that inflation was neutral for the equilibrium path of output, employment and some other 'real' variables was introduced by Abba Lerner in the 1940s and by William Fellner (a great teacher of mine) in the 1950s. Perhaps my 1967 paper and Friedman's were more emphatic and explicit about homing in to the natural rate (on which I was more cautious in my 1968 paper)." But while Lerner (1949), Fellner (1959), and Friedman (1968) had the idea of the natural rate, Phelps *et al.* (1970) showed economists how to use the concept in modeling macroeconomic dynamics with explicit choice-theoretic foundations. Phelps (1995a, p. 103) refers to 'Milton Friedman's critique of the Phillips curve, in which nothing useful was put in its place.' The 1970 'Phelps volume' put something in its place, a methodological approach that macroeconomists could use.

Phelps (1967, 1968; Phelps *et al.* 1970) and Friedman (1968) saw what Phelps (1967) termed 'equilibrium unemployment' as voluntary investment in search and consumption of leisure, plus structural unemployment (mismatching of workers and jobs due to unforeseen changes in the mix of skills and locations demanded by employers). Equilibrium unemployment, what Friedman called the natural rate of unemployment (by analogy to Knut Wicksell's natural rate of interest), is not quite the same as optimal unemployment: if income taxes distort the consumption/leisure trade-off or payroll taxes depress labor demand, then equilibrium employment will be less (and unemployment greater) than what is socially optimal. Also, Phelps (1973a) noted, inflation is a form of taxation (also a theme of Keynes, 1923), so that if government revenue is needed to pay for public goods and the possible sources of tax revenues are all distorting, the optimal level of the inflation tax must be chosen jointly with the optimal levels of other distorting taxes. But deviations from equilibrium unemployment are the fault of incomplete information: if actual inflation equals expected inflation, however high or low that inflation rate may be, unemployment will be at its natural rate, implicitly assumed to be unique. Unemployment less than the natural rate requires, according to the natural rate hypothesis, that some workers are fooled into giving up valuable leisure in exchange for a smaller real wage than they think they are getting. In contrast, John Maynard Keynes (1936) saw unemployment as an excess supply of labor, a failure of market-clearing that keeps some workers involuntarily unemployed even though they would accept jobs at the prevailing real wage or a lower real wage.

In his introduction to Phelps *et al.* (1970, p. 20n), Phelps reported, "My too-brief search of the literature for the scholarly purposes of this study turned up few writers before Keynes (or after) who ever asked why quantity effects should be expected to accompany the price effects of monetary and other macroeconomic disturbances. To my surprise, one of the few, D.H. Robertson [1929], put his finger on the above behavior of markups: 'The stimulus of rising prices is partly founded in illusion...[the business leader] is spurred on...by imaginary gains at the expense of his fellow business men. It is so hard to believe at first that other people will really have the effrontery or the good fortune to raise their charges as much as he has raised his own.'" Fisher's *The Money Illusion* (1928) shared that insight: price changes cause quantity changes because agents, whether workers (households) or firms, have only imperfect information about whether a change in their nominal receipts represents a change in their real income due to a relative price shift (see also Stigler, 1961 on the economics of information). Although Lucas (in the articles collected in Lucas, 1981) is now generally associated with it, Phelps (1969) introduced the 'islands model' of imperfectly communicating markets (see also introduction to Phelps *et al.,* 1970, pp. 6–7, and Phelps, 1990a, p. 12), to which Lucas added rational expectations while preserving Phelps's result about quantity effects due to agents adjusting their estimate of the general price level by only a fraction of any observed change in their own prices. Phelps 'found it instructive to picture the economy as a group of islands between which information flows are costly' with an auction on each island every morning determining that island's market-clearing money wage and employment (Phelps *et al.,* 1970, p. 6). While workers could observe the money wage offered to them on their own island, they would not incur the cost of continuously monitoring prices and money wages on other islands. If the workers on an island observed an increase in their money wage, they had to evaluate the likelihood that this represented an increase in their real wage due to a change in technology or the composition of demand (in which case they would wish to supply more labor), as opposed to a nominal shock raising prices and money wages across all islands (in which they would not wish to change the amount of labor they supplied). The more often past changes in money wages had turned out to be real wage changes (relative price shocks), the more employment would respond to any alteration in the money wage. Phelps (1969) used this framework to explain why, with costly information flows, nominal shocks have short-run real effects. In place of the adaptive expectations (learning from errors) assumed by Phelps, Lucas (1972) incorporated rational expectations (no systematic mistakes in forecasting) into Phelps's islands model to explain why there would still be an observed correlation between employment and price level changes (because of unpredictable random shocks to prices) even if any systematic monetary policy would be correctly forecast and neutral. Phelps (1995b, p. 21) refers to 'Robert Lucas' (1972) model, based on my parable of imperfectly communicating "islands".' Phelps's role in developing this approach is downplayed in the textbooks: the section in David Romer's *Advanced Macroeconomics* on 'The Lucas Imperfect-Information Model' (Romer, 1996, pp. 241–255) refers just once to the model as 'the Lucas–Phelps model', with a reference to Phelps's introduction to Phelps *et al.* (1970).

Phelps (1965b) had considered whether anticipated inflation affects employment. Phelps (1967, 1968), like Friedman (1966, 1968), held that only unanticipated inflation matters for output and employment. In the Friedman–Phelps expectations-augmented Phillips curve, the rate of increase of money wages and of prices depends on expected inflation and the gap between unemployment (u^*) and the natural rate of unemployment (u^*), with u equal to u^* when actual inflation π equals expected inflation π^e:

$$\pi = f(u - u^*) + \pi^e$$

with a coefficient of one on expected inflation, as in Fisher's equation relating nominal and real interest. If expectations are adaptive (error-correcting), expected inflation will gravitate towards any steady rate of inflation. To keep u below u^* by continuing to fool workers, the rate of inflation would have to keep accelerating (even that possibility for systematically stimulated employment and real output would be ruled out by the rational expectations hypothesis). However, Friedman presented this intuition only verbally, whereas Phelps wrote out the equations for the labor market dynamics and drew the famous diagram for the expectations-augmented Phillips curve, showing a vertical long-run Phillips curve (for expected inflation equal to actual inflation) and a family of downward-sloping short-run Phillips curves, each drawn for a particular expected rate of inflation (see Phelps *et al.,* 1970, p. 148). As with Alfred Marshall's 'scissors' diagram of supply and demand, Irving Fisher's two-period consumption-smoothing diagram, and J.R. Hicks's IS/LM diagram, a simple diagram served to capture the trained intuition of the discipline.

The policy implication of the Friedman–Phelps natural rate hypothesis was that attempts to reduce unemployment below its natural rate by expanding aggregate demand would be fruitless in the long run – and would not even be desirable if feasible in the short run, because it would be a policy of tricking workers into surrendering valuable leisure (or truncating useful search that would produce the best matching of workers to jobs). Typically, macroeconomists using natural rate models tended to treat the natural rate of unemployment as unique and as more or loss constant over time, attempting to estimate the natural rate econometrically and deploying natural rate arguments to depict proposals for government action to reduce unemployment and poverty as futile and counter-productive. The monetary misperceptions version of New Classical economics (Lucas, 1981) attributed fluctuations around the natural rate to unpredictable, random nominal shocks, while Real Business Cycle theory (the non-monetary version of New Classical economics) emphasized the impact of technology shocks on potential output and labor demand, with less attention to unemployment. Natural rate models with a constant or slowly changing natural rate of unemployment are by no means as generally accepted (see Stiglitz *et al.,* 1997) as the methodological message of Phelps *et al.* (1970) about the need for explicit choice-theoretic microeconomic foundations of macroeconomics recognizing imperfect information and market frictions. Prolonged US expansions in the past decade and a half have held unemployment well below what NAIRU was believed to be, without rekindling inflation. British and, more recently, Canadian experience has been similar.

But Phelps did not think of the natural rate of unemployment as constant over time. Instead, he has devoted himself to structuralist theorizing about fluctuations in the natural rate (e.g. Phelps, 1994). Nor is he opposed to governmental policies to reduce unemployment and poverty: rather, he opposes misguided, fruitless policies that attempt to achieve those goals without changing the natural rate. He is passionately committed to the quest for constructive measures that will lower the natural rate of unemployment and secure the inclusion of currently marginalized and impoverished workers in the general prosperity. Neither of these aspects of Phelps is brought out in the 33-page summary by the Royal Swedish Academy of Sciences (2006) of 'Edmund Phelps's Contributions to Macroeconomics.' Apart from Phelps's paper on 'The Trouble with Rational Expectations and the Problem of Inflation Stabilization' (in Frydman & Phelps, 1983), the only reference that the Swedish Academy makes to anything that Phelps has published in the three decades since 1978 is a paragraph about Phelps (1994), plus a passing remark that, like Phelps (1968), Phelps (1994) considers the relationship between a firm's relative wage and its labor turnover (Royal Swedish Academy, 2006, pp. 10, 14–15). Nor, among Phelps's earlier writings, does the Royal Swedish Academy (2006) cite the books he edited on *Economic Justice* and on *Altruism, Morality and Economic Theory* (Phelps, 1973b, 1975), although the concerns central to those books can be seen as motivating his macroeconomic research.

3 Structuralist macroeconomics

The Royal Swedish Academy of Sciences (2006, p. 14) noted that "A lasting contribution from this book [Phelps, *Inflation Policy and Unemployment Theory,* 1972a] is the idea of *hysteresis* in the unemployment rate: an increase in unemployment may turn out to be (partially) irreversible, as a result of workers' loss of skill and morale.... Phelps's idea remained largely ignored for more than a decade, but came to life again in the mid-1980s when economists struggled to understand the seemingly permanent rise in European unemployment" with a footnote reference to "the influential study of European unemployment by Layard *et al.* (1991)." The Swedish Academy added that the persistent European unemployment also led Phelps to study the structural causes determining equilibrium unemployment in *Structural Slumps* (Phelps, 1994) and 'in a number of journal articles' (no dates or other details given): 'This work forms part of a comprehensive research literature that has developed over the last twenty years, to a large extent inspired by the work of Layard, Nickell and Jackman (1991).'

This brief account by the Royal Swedish Academy of Sciences underplays Phelps's role in the revival of a structural changes of an endogenous equilibrium unemployment rate based on his 1972 analysis of hysteresis. The Swedish Academy did trace the concept of hysteresis to Phelps (1972a), whereas the widely-read textbook by David Romer (1996, pp. 469–473) starts from Blanchard & Summers (1986) without mention of Phelps. However, Fitoussi & Phelps (1986, 1988), Phelps (1988), and Calvo & Phelps (1983) were not inspired by Layard *et al.* (1991), which they predated, but instead built directly upon Phelps (1972a, 1978a). The names of Richard Layard, Stephen Nickell, and Richard Jackman do not appear in the references or index of Fitoussi & Phelps (1988), Phelps (1990a, p. 98) has one passing mention of Layard and Nickell in a list of authors on the wage curve, and Phelps's interest in 'unemployment considered as an *equilibrium phenomenon* springing from *endogenous job rationing,* hence involuntary' (Phelps, 1992a, p. 1476) predating their important and valuable book. Possibly the author or authors of the Swedish Academy study misread a footnote in Phelps's review article on Layard *et al.* (1991), stating 'my feelings that what I refer to as the *structuralist,* or sometimes the *modern-equilibrium,* paradigm is the seminal development of the past decade and, in any case, the development from which the work under review stems' (Phelps, 1992a, p. 1477n) – that is, Layard *et al.* (1991) stemmed from a body of work in which Fitoussi & Phelps (1986, 1988) figured prominently, not that his work on structuralist macroeconomics stemmed from Layard *et al.* (1991). Phelps (1992a, p. 1489) concluded,

> The authors have taken a huge risk in throwing out nearly the whole corpus of general equilibrium theory in favor of a focus on some social and political parameters. When they do throw in a macro variable, such as the trade balance, no open-economy variable is provided to underpin it. Since there is no apparent effort to analyze the influence of their explanatory variables

alongside that of standard economic variables we cannot have much confidence in their findings. There are not many findings in this volume that I am persuaded by, so far. Maybe for that very reason I have also felt challenged by this work. It would not surprise me that a great many economists will want to see whether they can do better.

Phelps's structuralist macroeconomics (which is distinct from the Post Keynesian usage of the same term by Lance Taylor, 1983) emphasizes the dependence of the equilibrium unemployment rate (the natural rate) on past rates of unemployment (hysteresis), payroll taxes and labor market legislation, and on real exchange and interest rates. That payroll taxes, unemployment benefits, and restrictions on the hiring and firing of workers matter for employment, and in particular for the high European unemployment of the 1980s and 1990s, is generally accepted, and many if not most macroeconomists use the concept of hysteresis introduced by Phelps (1972a). The role of the real interest rate and real exchange rate in determining equilibrium unemployment in an open economy is more distinctively connected with Phelps and his associates Jean-Paul Fitoussi, Hian Teck Hoon and Gylfi Zoega (Fitoussi & Phelps, 1986, 1988; Phelps, 1994; Phelps & Zoega 2001; Hoon & Phelps, 2007). This sets their approach apart from supply-side economics, which focuses more narrowly on the impact of tax incentives on factor supplies, and from real business cycle theory, which emphasizes random shocks to productivity growth (see the chapters on supply-side economics and real business cycles in Phelps, 1990a). One notably thought-provoking application of this structuralist approach is the claim that the fiscal policies of the Reagan Administration were expansionary for the US but contributed strongly to high European unemployment in the 1980s. The Reagan Administration's tax cuts, increased defense spending, and record budget deficits (together with the tight money policy of the Volcker Federal Reserve) sharply raised real interest rates throughout the world, reducing investment in physical and human capital. In Europe, the contraction of investment was not offset by the US fiscal expansion that had pushed up real interest (which raises questions, however, about the impact on European exports of the appreciation of the US real exchange rate in the 1980s, another result of US monetary and fiscal policy).

Frydman & Phelps (1983) expressed reservations about rational expectations as an inherent property of economies. Phelps (1995a, p. 102) remarks that,

> An agent cannot use the analyst's model to form his expectations since he has little or no idea of how, quantitatively, the other agents are using that model or even if they have not switched to some quite different model... the expectations-of-expectations problem may prevent agents from converging to the rational-expectations equilibrium. The scepticism and hostility that research so admirably basic as this met in the profession was sad to see, even for a near 50-year-old veteran such as myself who had seen the tactics of 'scorn and derision', in Harry Johnson's memorable phrase, used before.

In his Nobel Lecture, Phelps (2007, pp. 544–545) criticizes neoclassical economic theory (as exemplified by Samuelson, 1947) for having

> *abstracted* from the *distinctive character* of the modern economy – the endemic uncertainty, ambiguity, diversity of beliefs, specialization of knowledge, and problem solving. As a result it could not capture, or endogenize, the *observable phenomena* that are endemic to the modern economy – innovation, waves of rapid growth, big swings in business activity, disequilibria, intense employee engagement, and workers' intellectual development... At Yale and at RAND, in part through my teachers William Fellner and Thomas Schelling, I gained some familiarity with the modernist concepts of Knightian uncertainty, Keynesian probabilities, Hayek's private know-how and M. Polanyi's personal knowledge. Having to a degree assimilated this modernist perspective, I could view the economy at angles different from neoclassical theory.

This approach to incomplete knowledge contrasts with the rational expectations hypothesis (see also Phelps, 1990a, Ch. 3). As with Phelps's structural modeling of a changing equilibrium rate of unemployment, his view of uncertain knowledge is not stressed by those, such as the Royal Swedish Academy of Sciences (2006) or Henderson (2006), who prefer to celebrate the Phelps–Friedman natural rate hypothesis simply as setting the stage for New Classical economics.

4 Conclusion

Friedman (1966, 1968) and Phelps (1967, 1968) each independently introduced the natural rate hypothesis and the expectations-augmented Phillips curve, advancing the concept of equilibrium unemployment in place of Keynes's excess supply of labor, but only Phelps did so in the context of a formal model. The 'Phelps volume' (Phelps *et al.*, 1970) marked a major advance in choice-theoretic micro-economic foundations of macroeconomics subject to imperfect information and market frictions, such as the 'islands model' of Phelps (1969). That much is well recognized, notably by the Royal Swedish Academy of Sciences (2006), as are Phelps's reservations in Frydman & Phelps (1983) about the informational requirements of rational expectations, buttressed by empirical evidence that expectations are at least in part backward-looking. But the Royal Swedish Academy (2006) gives a quite misleading picture of Phelps as someone who contributed little to macroeconomics in the last three decades, giving Phelps (1994) only a passing paragraph, stressing the supposed inspiration by Layard *et al.* (1991). On the contrary, Phelps's work on structural booms and slumps, looking at non-monetary determinants of changes in the equilibrium unemployment rate, is a continuous development, a substantial and important body of work stretching from Phelps (1972a) on hysteresis through Calvo & Phelps (1983) on non-Walrasian equilibria and Fitoussi & Phelps (1986, 1988) on Europe's structural slump in the 1980s to Phelps (1988, 1994), Phelps &

Zoega (2001) on structural booms, and on to the present (Hoon & Phelps, 2007, forthcoming). Much of this work (e.g., Phelps, 1994a; Phelps & Zoega, 1998) stresses empirical testing of structuralist macroeconomics against competing Keynesian, supply-side, and New Classical approaches.

Leijonhufvud (2004, pp. 814–815, reviewing Aghion *et al.*, 2004) gives an insightful account of where Phelps stands in macroeconomics:

> Although Phelps distinguishes himself as a 'structuralist' rather than a 'New Keynesian' (cf., Phelps, 1990a), he has played an important role in the development of New Keynesianism and remains close to this school. What he has in common with the New Keynesians above all is the view that labor markets will settle down to equilibria where jobs are rationed at equilibrium wage rates. To New Keynesians, and to Phelps, therefore, the natural rate of unemployment is not an efficient state but one that might potentially be improved by policy, albeit not by just inflating nominal aggregate demand.

The last remark draws attention to another central characteristic of Phelps overlooked in Royal Swedish Academy (2006). He cares passionately about the justice and morality of economic processes and outcomes (Phelps, 1973b, 1975, 1987, influenced by Rawls 1971), and is no mere high-brow, abstract theorist, but someone who devotes his expertise as an economic theorist to devising macroeconomic policies, labor market reforms, and tax incentives to make capitalism more inclusive and to raise the incomes and facilitate the self-sufficiency of the poorest and marginalized in society (Phelps, 1997, 1999a, 2002a, 2003b). Phelps does not just describe the equilibrium unemployment rate – he proposes to change it.

Acknowledgments

I am grateful for helpful comments from Roger Backhouse, David Colander, Edmund Phelps, Steven Pressman, and participants in the 2007 annual meetings of the History of Economics Society and the European Society for the History of Economic Thought.

Notes

1 In a six-paper symposium on NAIRU (Stiglitz *et al.*, 1997), all six papers refer to Friedman (1968), three cite Phelps (1968), but none mention Phelps (1967). James Galbraith (in Stiglitz *et al.*, 1997, p. 93) writes of 'Milton Friedman's remarkable 1968 presidential lecture to the American Economics Association, as close as economists get to delivery from Olympus', that 'Perhaps no other presidential address has ever been so influential.'

2 Phelps taught a course on capital theory with Robert Solow while visiting MIT in 1962–63.

Principal Works of Edmund S. Phelps and other references

Aghion, P., Frydman, R., Stiglitz, J. & Woodford, M. (Eds) (2004) *Knowledge, Information, and Expectations in Modern Macroeconomics: In Honor of Edmund S. Phelps* (Princeton, NJ: Princeton University Press).

Allais, M. (1947) *Économie et Intérêt* (Paris: Imprimerie National).

Allais, M. (1962) The influence of the capital-output ratio on real national income, *Econometrica*, 30(4), pp. 700–728.

Blanchard, O.J. & Summers, L. (1986) Hysteresis and the European unemployment problem, *Brookings Papers on Economic Activity*, 1986(1), pp. 15–78.

Calvo, G.A. & Phelps, E.S. (1983) A model of non-Walrasian general equilibrium: its Pareto inoptimality and Pareto improvement, in: J. Tobin (Ed.) *Macroeconomics, Prices and Quantities: Essays in Memory of Arthur M. Okun*, pp. 135–157 (Washington, DC: Brookings Institution).

Fellner, W.J. (1959) Demand inflation, cost inflation, and collective bargaining, in: P.D. Bradley (Ed.) *The Public Stake in Union Power* (Charlottesville: University of Virginia Press).

Fisher, I. (1896) *Appreciation and Interest* (New York: Macmillan).

Fisher, I. (1926/1973) A statistical relation between unemployment and price changes, *International Labour Review*, 13(6), pp. 785–792. Reprinted as Lost and found: I discovered the Phillips curve – Irving Fisher, *Journal of Political Economy*, 81(2), pp. 496–502.

Fisher, I. (1928) *The Money Illusion* (New York: Adelphi).

Fitoussi, J.-P., Jestaz, D., Phelps, E.S. & Zoega, G. (2000) Roots of the recent recoveries: labor market reforms or private sector forces?, *Brookings Papers on Economic Activity*, 2000(1), pp. 237–311.

Fitoussi, J.-P. & Phelps, E.S. (1986) Causes of the 1980s slump in Europe, *Brookings Papers on Economic Activity*, 1986(2), pp. 487–513.

Fitoussi, J.-P. & Phelps, E.S. (1988) *The Slump in Europe: Reconstructing Open Economy Theory* (Oxford & New York: Basil Blackwell).

Friedman, M. (1966) Comments, in: G.P. Schultz & R.Z. Aliber (Eds) *Guidelines, Inflation Controls, and the Market Place* (Chicago: University of Chicago Press).

Friedman, M. (1968) The role of monetary policy, *American Economic Review*, 58(1), pp. 1–17.

Frydman, R. & Phelps, E.S. (Eds) (1983) *Individual Forecasting and Aggregate Outcomes: 'Rational Expectations' Examined* (Cambridge, UK & New York: Cambridge University Press).

Henderson, N. (2006) You might have him to thank for your job: Professor who solved stagflation wins Nobel, *Washington Post*, October 10, p. D1.

Hoon, H.T. & Phelps, E.S. (1992) Macroeconomic shocks in a dynamized model of the natural rate of unemployment, *American Economic Review*, 82(4), pp. 889–900.

Hoon, H.T. & Phelps, E.S. (1996) Payroll taxes and VAT in a labor-turnover model of the 'natural rate', *International Tax and Public Finance*, 3(3), pp. 369–383.

Hoon, H.T. & Phelps, E.S. (1997) Growth, wealth and the natural rate: is the jobs crisis a growth crisis?, *European Economic Review*, 41(3–5), pp. 549–557.

Hoon, H.T. & Phelps, E.S. (2007) A structuralist model of the small open economy in the short, medium and long run, *Journal of Macroeconomics*, 29(2), pp. 227–254.

Hoon, H.T. & Phelps, E.S. (Forthcoming) Future fiscal and budgetary shocks, *Journal of Economic Theory*.

Hoon, H.T., Phelps, E.S. & Zoega, G. (2005) The structuralist perspective on real exchange rate, share price level and employment path: what room is left for money?, in: W. Semmler (Ed.) *Monetary Policy and Unemployment: In Honour of James Tobin,* pp. 107–132 (London & New York: Routledge).

Keynes, J.M. (1923) *A Tract on Monetary Reform* (London: Macmillan).

Keynes, J.M. (1936) *The General Theory of Employment, Interest and Money* (London: Macmillan).

Layard, R., Nickell, S. & Jackman, R. (1991) *Unemployment: Macroeconomic Performance and the Labour Market* (Oxford: Oxford University Press).

Leeson, R. (Ed.) (2000) *A.W.H. Phillips: Collected Works in Contemporary Perspective* (Cambridge, UK: Cambridge University Press).

Leijonhufvud, A. (2004) Celebrating Ned, *Journal of Economic Literature,* 42(3), pp. 811–821.

Lerner, A.P. (1949) The inflationary process – some theoretical aspects, *Review of Economics and Statistics,* 31, pp. 193–200.

Lucas, R.E. (1972) Expectations and the neutrality of money, *Journal of Economic Theory,* 4(2), pp. 103–124.

Lucas, R.E. (1981) *Studies in Business Cycle Theory* (Cambridge, MA: MIT Press).

Ordover, J.A. & Phelps, E.S. (1979) On the concept of optimal taxation in the overlapping-generations model of economic growth, *Journal of Public Economics,* 12(1), pp. 1–26.

Petrucci, A. & Phelps, E.S. (2005) Capital subsidies versus labor subsidies: a trade-off between capital and employment?, *Journal of Money, Credit and Banking,* 37(5), pp. 907–922.

Phelps, E.S. (1961a) A test for the presence of cost inflation in the United States 1955–57, *Yale Economic Essays,* 1, pp. 28–69.

Phelps, E.S. (1961b) The golden rule of accumulation: a fable for growthmen, *American Economic Review,* 51(4), pp. 638–643.

Phelps, E.S. (1962a) The new view of investment: a neoclassical analysis, *Quarterly Journal of Economics,* 76(2), pp. 548–567. Reprinted (with comment by R.C.O. Matthews, 78(1), pp. 164–172, and reply by E.S. Phelps & M.E. Yaari, 78(1), pp. 172–176) in J. E. Stiglitz & H. Uzawa (Eds) *Readings in the Modern Theory of Economic Growth* (Cambridge, MA: MIT Press, 1969).

Phelps, E.S. (Ed.) (1962b) *The Goal of Economic Growth* (New York: W.W. Norton).

Phelps, E.S. (1965a) *Fiscal Neutrality toward Economic Growth: Analysis of a Taxation Principle* (New York: McGraw–Hill).

Phelps, E.S. (1965b) Anticipated inflation and economic welfare, *Journal of Political Economy,* 73(1), pp. 1–17.

Phelps, E.S. (1965c) Second essay on the golden rule of accumulation, *American Economic Review,* 55(4), pp. 783–814.

Phelps, E.S. (1966a) *Golden Rules of Economic Growth* (New York: W.W. Norton).

Phelps, E.S. (1966b) Models of technical progress and the golden rule of research, *Review of Economic Studies,* 33(2), pp. 133–145.

Phelps, E.S. (1967) Phillips curves, expectations of inflation and optimal unemployment over time, *Economica,* new series, 34(3), pp. 254–281.

Phelps, E.S. (1968) Money wage dynamics and labor market equilibrium, *Journal of Political Economy,* 76(4, Part 2), pp. 678–711 (revised, with appendix, in Phelps *et al.,* 1970).

Phelps, E.S. (1969) The new microeconomics in inflation and employment theory, *American Economic Review: Papers and Proceedings,* 59(2), pp. 147–160.

Phelps, E.S. *et al.* (1970) *Microeconomic Foundations of Employment and Inflation Theory* (New York: W.W. Norton).

Phelps, E.S. (1972a) *Inflation Policy and Unemployment Theory: The Cost-Benefit Approach to Monetary Planning* (New York: W.W. Norton).

Phelps, E.S. (1972b) The statistical theory of racism and sexism, *American Economic Review,* 62, pp. 659–661. Reprinted in A. Amsden (Ed.) *The Economics of Women and Work* (Harmonds-worth, UK: Penguin, 1980).

Phelps, E.S. (1972c) Money, public expenditure, and the labor supply, *Journal of Economic Theory,* 5(1) pp. 69–78.

Phelps, E.S. (1973a) Inflation in the theory of public finance, *Swedish Journal of Economics,* 75(1), pp. 67–82.

Phelps, E.S. (Ed.) (1973b) *Economic Justice: Selected Readings* (Hardmondsworth, UK: Penguin).

Phelps, E.S. (Ed.) (1975) *Altruism, Morality, and Economic Theory* (New York: Russell Sage Foundation).

Phelps, E.S. (1977) Rational taxation, *Social Research,* 44(4), pp. 657–667.

Phelps, E.S. (1978a) Commodity-supply shock and full-employment monetary policy, *Journal of Money, Credit and Banking,* 10(2), pp. 206–221.

Phelps, E.S. (1978b) Inflation planning reconsidered, *Economica,* new series 45(178), pp. 109–123.

Phelps, E.S. (1978c) Transnational effects of fiscal shocks in a two-country model of dynamic equilibrium, *Journal of Monetary Economics,* 9(Supplement), pp. 145–179

Phelps, E.S. (1978d) Disinflation without recession: adaptive guideposts and monetary policy, *Weltwirtschaftsliches Archiv,* 100(2), as reprinted in Phelps (1979).

Phelps, E.S. (1979) *Studies in Macroeconomic Theory,* Vol. 1: *Employment and Inflation* (New York: Academic Press).

Phelps, E.S. (1980) *Studies in Macroeconomic Theory,* Vol. 2: *Redistribution and Growth* (New York: Academic Press).

Phelps, E.S. (1982) Cracks on the demand side: a year of crisis in theoretical macroeconomics, *American Economic Review Papers and Proceedings,* 72(2), pp. 378–381.

Phelps, E.S. (1983) The trouble with 'rational expectations' and the problem of inflation stabilization, in: Frydman & Phelps (Eds) 1983, pp. 31–41.

Phelps, E.S. (1985) *Political Economy: An Introductory Text* (New York: W.W. Norton).

Phelps, E.S. (1987) Distributive justice, in: J. Eatwell, M. Milgate, & P. Newman (Eds), *The New Palgrave: A Dictionary of Economics* (London: Stockton Press).

Phelps, E.S. (1988) A working model of slump and recovery from disturbances to capital-good demand, *American Economic Review: Papers and Proceedings,* 78(2), pp. 346–350.

Phelps, E.S. (1990a) *Seven Schools of Macroeconomic Thought: The Arne Ryde Lectures* (Oxford: Clarendon Press & New York: Oxford University Press).

Phelps, E.S. (1990b) The effects of productivity, total GDP demand, and 'incentive wages' on unemployment in a non-monetary customer-market model of the small open economy, *Scandinavian Journal of Economics,* 92(2), pp. 353–367.

Phelps, E.S. (1991) The effectiveness of macropolicies in a small open-economy dynamic aggregative model, in: W.C. Brainard, W.D. Nordhaus & H.W. Watts (Eds) *Money, Macroeconomics, and Economic Policy: Essays in Honor of James Tobin* (Cambridge, MA: MIT Press).

Phelps, E.S. (Ed.) (1991) *Recent Developments in Macroeconomics,* 3 vols. (Cheltenham, UK: Edward Elgar).

Phelps, E.S. (1992a) A review of *Unemployment, Journal of Economic Literature*, 30(3), pp. 1476–1490.

Phelps, E.S. (1992b) Consumer demand and equilibrium unemployment in a customer-market incentive-wage economy, *Quarterly Journal of Economics*, 107(3), pp. 1003–1032.

Phelps, E.S., in collaboration with H.T. Hoon, G. Kanaginis, & G. Zoega (1994) *Structural Slumps: The Modern Equilibrium Theory of Unemployment, Interest, and Assets* (Cambridge, MA: Harvard University Press).

Phelps, E.S. (1995a) A life in economics, in: A. Heertje (Ed.) *The Makers of Modern Economics*, Vol. II, pp. 90–113 (Aldershot, UK, & Brookfield, VT: Edward Elgar).

Phelps, E.S. (1995b) The origins and further development of the natural rate of unemployment, in: R. Cross (Ed.) *The Natural Rate of Unemployment, Reflections on 25 Years of the Hypothesis*, pp. 15–31 (Cambridge, UK: Cambridge University Press).

Phelps, E.S. (1997) *Rewarding Work: How to Restore Participation and Self-Support to Free Enterprise* (Cambridge, MA: Harvard University Press).

Phelps, E.S. (1999a) Moral hazard and independent income in a modern intertemporal-equilibrium model of involuntary unemployment and mandatory retirement, in: G. Chichilnisky (Ed.) *Markets, Information and Uncertainty* (Cambridge, UK: Cambridge University Press).

Phelps, E.S. (1999b) Behind the structural boom: the role of asset valuations, *American Economic Review: Papers and Proceedings*, 89(2), pp. 63–68.

Phelps, E.S. (2002a) *Enterprise and Inclusion in Italy* (Boston: Kluwer Academic).

Phelps, E.S. (2002b) Income tax cuts without spending cuts: hazards to efficiency, equity, employment, and growth, *Journal of Policy Modeling*, 24(4), pp. 391–399.

Phelps, E.S. (2003a) Reflections on Parts I and II, Reflections on Parts III and IV, in: P. Aghion, R. Frydman, J. Stiglitz & M. Woodford (Eds) *Knowledge, Information, and Expectations: Essays in Honor of Edmund Phelps*, pp. 271–281, 550–563 (Princeton, NJ: Princeton University Press).

Phelps, E.S. (Ed.) (2003b) *Designing Inclusion: Tools to Raise Low-End Pay and Employment in Private Enterprise* (Cambridge, UK: Cambridge University Press).

Phelps, E.S. (2004a) The boom and the slump: a causal account of the 1990s/2000s and the 1920s/1930s, *Journal of Policy Reform*, 7(1), pp. 3–19.

Phelps, E.S. (2004b) Effects of China's recent development on the rest of the world, *Journal of Policy Modeling*, 26(8–9), pp. 903–910.

Phelps, E.S. (2007) Macroeconomics for a modern economy, *American Economic Review*, 97(3), pp. 543–561.

Phelps, E.S. & Riley, J.G. (1978) Rawlsian growth: Dynamic programming of capital wealth for intergenerational 'maximin' justice, *Review of Economic Studies*, 45(1), pp. 103–120.

Phelps, E.S. & Shell, K. (1969) Public debt, taxation, and capital intensiveness, *Journal of Economic Theory*, 1(3), pp. 330–346.

Phelps, E.S. & Taylor, J.B. (1977) Stabilizing powers of monetary policy under rational expectations, *Journal of Political Economy*, 85(1), pp. 163–190.

Phelps, E.S. & Velupillai, K. (1988) Optimum fiscal policy when monetary policy is bound by a rule, in: K. Arrow & M. Boskin (Eds) *The Economics of Public Debt: Proceedings of a Conference held by the International Economic Association*, pp. 116–130 (London: Macmillan).

Phelps, E.S. & Zoega, G. (1997) The rise and downward trend of the natural rate, *American Economic Review: Papers and Proceedings*, 87(2), pp. 283–289.

Phelps, E.S. & Zoega, G. (1998) Natural-rate theory and OECD unemployment, *Economic Journal,* 108(448), pp. 782–801.

Phelps, E.S. & Zoega, G. (2001) Structural booms: productivity expectations and asset valuations, *Economic Policy: A European Forum,* 32, pp. 85–126.

Rawls, J. (1971) *A Theory of Justice* (Cambridge, MA: Harvard University Press).

Robertson, D.H. (1929) *Money* (New York: Cambridge University Press).

Romer, D. (1996) *Advanced Macroeconomics* (New York: McGraw Hill).

Royal Swedish Academy of Sciences (2006) Edmund Phelps's contributions to macroeconomics, www.kva.se, October 9, 33 pp.

Samuelson, P.A. (1947) *The Foundations of Economic Analysis* (Cambridge, MA: Harvard University Press).

Solow, R.M. (1956) A contribution to the theory of economic growth, *Quarterly Journal of Economics,* 70, pp. 65–94.

Solow, R.M. (1957) Technical change and the aggregate production function, *Review of Economic Statistics,* 39, pp. 312–320.

Stigler, G.J. (1961) The economics of information, *Journal of Political Economy,* 69, pp. 213–225.

Stiglitz, J., Gordon, R.J., Staiger, D., Stock, J.H. & Watson, M.W., Blanchard, O. & Katz, L., Rogerson, R. & Galbraith, J. (1997) Symposium: The natural rate of unemployment, *Journal of Economic Perspectives,* 11(1), pp. 3–108.

Swan, T. (1956) Economic growth and capital accumulation, *Economic Record,* 32(63), pp. 334–361.

Taylor, L. (1983) *Structuralist Macroeconomics* (New York: Basic Books).

Tobin, J. (1955) A dynamic aggregative model, *Journal of Political Economy,* 63(2), pp. 103–115.

Weinstein, M.M. (1987) Review of *Political Economy: An Introductory Text,* by Edmund S. Phelps, *Journal of Economic Perspectives,* 1(2), pp. 179–182.

Index

accumulation 413, 415
Adams, P. 137
Adelman, I. 394
affirmative action 392, 393, 399, 400–1,
404; *see also* Bergmann, Barbara; race;
women's issues
Agarwal, B. 76
Aghion, P. 424
Akerlof, George 6–7, 144–9, 150–1,
153–6, 157, 275, 367; adverse selection
151–3; asymmetric information 144,
145, 146, 149–52, 153–6, 157; Clinton
administration 146; economic
development 155–6; efficiency wage
hypothesis 153–4; Ely Lecture 146, 154,
156; information economics 144–5;
labor market models 157; lemon model
151; near rationality theory 154–5; New
Classical school 145, 153, 156–7; New
Keynesian macroeconomics 145, 153–5,
156; rational expectations: real world
problems 144–5, 151; sticky wages 153;
unemployment 145, 153–5, 156, 157;
unemployment, involuntary versus
voluntary 146; unemployment models,
psychological and sociological 146,
154; used car market (lemon model) 151
Alkire, S. 75
Allais, Maurice 415
Altman, Morris 176, 186, 187
Anderson, Martin 110, 111
Anderson, S.J. 294, 299
Andrews, D.W.K. 272
Arestis, P. 103, 108, 109
Arms and Influence 369
Arrow, Kenneth 38, 43, 68, 149–50, 154,
275; *Social Choice and Individual
Values* 68
Arrow impossibility theorem 73
Arthur, B. 109
Aslanbeigui, N. 76
asymmetric information 144, 145, 146,

149–52, 153–6, 157; near rationality
theory 154–5; signaling 6, 144, 146,
151–3; signaling equilibrium 151;
signals 152
Atesoglu, H.S. 259
Auernheimer, L. 337
Auletta, K. 309
Aumann, Robert J. 10, 366, 368–9,
373–82; agreement theorem 374,
378–9, n383; Bacharach, M. 379;
Bacharach's model 379; background
368–9, n382; Cold War and 376, n382;
common knowledge (CKR) 366, 373,
376–81; common knowledge of
rationality (CKR) 366, 373, 376–81;
common prior assumption (CPA) 377,
378–9; complete information 375;
correlated equilibrium 366, 373,
380–1; deductive approach to game
theory based on axioms 369, 376, 378,
381–2; Econometric Research Program
368; equilibrium theory 373; game
theory 373–81; game theory and
cooperation 366, 373–6, 381; game
theory and inductive approach 377–8;
game theory and nuclear deterrence
368, 376; game theory and rational
choice 366, 368–9, 374–5, 377–80,
381; Game Theory Society 369;
Hildenbrand, Werner 373; irrationality
model 380; long-run cooperation 373;
Maschler, Michael and 373, 376; math
background of 368; mathematical
approach to game theory 373;
Milgrom, P. 376, 378–9; Milgrom's
model 378–9; Nash, John 368; Nash
equilibrium 373–5, 376–7, 380, 381;
no-trade theorem 378–9; Prisoners'
Dilemma 373–4; Recent Developments
in Game Theory conference 368;
repeated games 373–6, 381; Shapley,
L. and 375; strategy 368, 373, 374,

For Product Safety Concerns and Information please contact our
EU representative GPSR@taylorandfrancis.com Taylor & Francis
Verlag GmbH, Kaufingerstraße 24, 80331 München, Germany